Developmental Psychobiology

George F. Michel and Celia L. Moore

Developmental Psychobiology

An Interdisciplinary Science

A Bradford Book
The MIT Press
Cambridge, Massachusetts
London, England

Second printing, 1999

This book was set in Times Roman by Asco Trade Typesetting Ltd., Hong Kong
and was printed and bound in the United States of America. This book was printed
on recycled paper.

Library of Congress Cataloging-in-Publication Data

Michel, George F., 1944–
  Developmental psychobiology: an interdisciplinary science /
George F. Michel, Celia L. Moore.
     p.   cm.
  "A Bradford book."
  Includes bibliographical references (p.   ) and index.
  ISBN 0-262-13312-1
  1. Developmental psychobiology. I. Moore, Celia L., 1942–
II. Title.
QP363.5.M53   1995
599′.0188—dc20   94-47023
                                                          CIP

To the memory of our teachers, Dorothy Dinnerstein and Daniel S. Lehrman

Contents in Brief

Contents in Detail

Preface

The title of this book incorporates two concepts that are rather difficult to define. After several decades of investigation, the concept of development still lacks a generally accepted intrinsic definition (cf., Collins, 1982; Harris, 1957; van Geert, 1991). Consequently, in the pragmatics of conducting research, "development" is often applied to any investigation that examines some psychological phenomena over the course of more than a few weeks in "adult" subjects, or more than a few hours in "neonatal" subjects. Sometimes the concept of development is used simply to denote that the human subjects in the research were not 20 to 50 years of age.

It is generally agreed that development refers to the psychological changes that are associated with the passage of time in an individual's life. Of course, psychological development must of logical necessity occur over time. However, that does not mean that time is the most relevant dimension of development. Moreover, the time boundary distinguishing a developmental from a nondevelopmental change is usually defined implicitly. Consequently, for any particular psychological characteristic, there are time periods commonly used by researchers who investigate the development of that characteristic. These time periods then become the implicit definition of a developmental change.

Although a general consensus may exist among investigators about what is considered to be developmental change for some particular psychological characteristic (e.g., facial expression of emotion), the processes of its development usually cannot be compared with those of another characteristic (e.g., motor coordination), because the implicit definition of what constitutes a developmental change may be different. Without explicit definitions of developmental change and the processes governing development, investigations will remain fragmented among different research domains.

In this book we provide an explicit definition of development, although that definition is not reducible to one or even a few sentences (see chapters 1 and 3). This definition is used in certain subfields of psychobiology. We believe that it has the advantage of explicitness, which means that developmental research in different realms of inquiry can be integrated more successfully.

The concept of psychobiology, as we use it, also requires special consideration. There is a long list of fields of interdisciplinary research that combine biology and psychology (e.g., physiological psychology, psychopharmacology), and new interdisciplinary fields continue to emerge (e.g., neuropsychology, health psychology, gerontology). However, defining psychobiology by research that simply combines a biological and a psychological focus fails to achieve the level of coherence expected of an intellectual discipline (see chapters 1 and 2). Thus, such a simple combination will not result in a balanced productive synthesis of psychology and biology. In this book, we attempt to create such a synthesis.

Two specific criteria are sometimes used to define psychobiology. The primary criterion is that any psychological phenomenon, trait, or ability must be identified and described according to how it is expressed in the specific situations in which it typically occurs. This criterion encourages a natural history orientation in the description of psychological phenomena. Such an orientation means that the psychological characteristic must not be described by some indirect assessment technique or convenient laboratory method.

For example, emotional state cannot be described by performance on a paper and pencil task, or operationally defined by activity in a running wheel. The operational definitions must be derived instead from the situation in which the emotional state becomes an important component of the description of the individual's performance. Thus, for rodents, it may be justified to infer emotional state from the number of grids crossed in an open-field situation, because this is a common situation encountered by rodents in which the concept of emotional state appears to be apt.

Of course, this primary criterion presents a special problem for human psychobiological research because so much about human psychology is inferred from performance on questionnaires or specially devised tasks contrived for age-normative assessment. Thus, a psychobiological approach to human psychology requires extensive alteration in the manner of conducting research.

The second criterion for establishing a synthetic discipline of psychobiology is that the entire spectrum of biology must be brought to bear on the psychological phenomenon. This means that the evolutionary perspectives of phylogenetic history and adaptive significance must be integrated with developmental study. It also means that causal analyses of the mechanisms and processes constituting development must consider the whole organism—not just its nervous system or its genes. All aspects of the individual, from social and ecological milieu to cellular physiology of all organ systems, must be incorporated into the developmental analysis.

To meet the second criterion, we use Tinbergen's (1963a) account of how the spectrum of biology can be employed in the investigation of behavior.

He proposed that each of the four biological questions of phylogeny, ontogeny, proximate causation, and evolutionary function requires distinct answers that are not derivable from the answers to any of the other questions. Nevertheless, the answers to these four questions do relate to one another, and together they provide a coherent psychobiological account of behavior.

This book expands on the description of the discipline of developmental psychobiology that we provided in an earlier book (Michel & Moore, 1978). In the time since publication of that book, the discipline has grown substantially in both extent and sophistication. We have used some of this new work to exemplify our points, but we have not attempted to summarize the wealth of new and exciting findings in the field. Instead, we focus on the process of doing developmental psychobiology. We intend to provide the reader with the basic framework needed to adopt a developmental psychobiological perspective on behavior. Specific research information is presented to highlight the problems of synthesizing biology and psychology and the scientific value of using the two criteria described above for achieving this synthesis.

We often use historical information to describe some aspect of developmental psychobiology because we believe that many modern concepts can be best understood within the framework of their development. "Although history cannot tell us what is true, it can help us more readily see what assumptions we are making today and what alternatives might be available" (Smith, 1992, p. 261). Too many students are convinced that research and theories older than 20 years have little to contribute to modern understanding. We want to correct that impression. Much of what is typically considered to be historical progression toward some ideal end state is really contingent expression of earlier conditions. That is, history (like developmental phenomena) is often emergent from contingent events occurring earlier in time and is seldom progression toward some goal.

Chapter 1 begins with a brief historical account that reveals some of the contingent events occurring in biology that led to the emergence of the disciplines of developmental and comparative psychology. This chapter also provides a description of the characteristics of development. Chapter 2 examines the problems associated with four common attempts to integrate psychology and biology, and chapter 3 provides one means by which their integration may be accomplished without disrupting the integrity of each discipline.

Chapter 4 reveals the history of the nature of the relationships among genetics, evolution, and development that led to several misconceptions about the relation of biology to psychology. Chapters 4 and 5 together demonstrate how modern notions of developmental, molecular, and evolutionary biology can be incorporated into a developmental psychobiological perspective that avoids these misconceptions.

In chapter 6 we examine embryological development, particularly as it relates to the development of the nervous system. Throughout this chapter, the bidirectional influences of structure and function are emphasized. Chapter 7 provides an account of modern information about the behavioral development of the embryo and the relation between embryonic and post-embryonic behavioral systems. Chapter 8 describes modern notions about cognitive development, particularly as it relates to the sensorimotor, intellectual, and language development of human infants, and examines these notions from the perspective of developmental psychobiology. Chapter 9 demonstrates the important role that the study of animal behavior from a natural history orientation can play in the comprehension of human psychological development. Chapter 10 provides an argument for the role of developmental psychobiology in uniting both the two major styles of explanation in science and the cellular-molecular and population branches of biology.

We intend this book to be a guide for both students and professionals who wish to extend their knowledge into a neighboring discipline. Each chapter is designed in part to challenge the conventional wisdom and the traditional "official" views of many subdisciplines in both biology and psychology. Such challenge is not motivated by some perverse desire to play gadfly, but by the realization that every science is a dynamic process involving continuous re-examination and replacement, if necessary, of its basic constructs. Science is a dialectical process; it is not a system of received truth. If science is to provide an understanding of reality that is an effective alternative to common sense and folk wisdom, then we must become comfortable with dynamic conceptions of reality. We have tried to incorporate that dynamic into a synthetic account of developmental psychobiology that retains the intellectual integrity of both biology and psychology. We hope that reading this book will create the kind of intellectually exciting educational experience that we had in writing it.

We thank five reviewers who read an earlier version of most chapters. Their careful, detailed, and very useful comments were much appreciated. Peter H. Wolff also read drafts of many chapters, and we thank him for his cogent comments. Several of our students provided useful feedback as the book went through its many stages. Of these, Kathleen Kotwica, Linda Lambrecht, and Stacia Finch merit special thanks. We also thank our colleague Marliese Kimmerle for thoughtful discussion of the manuscript in progress. Any remaining errors and misconceptions are entirely our own.

Creating a book is a large undertaking, and we have been fortunate to have the help of several assistants and the magnificent staff at the MIT Press. Our student assistants, André Gibeau, Linda Hendry, Ojingwa Leclair, Erika Pelzer, and Beth Zagorski, made frequent trips to the library and xerox machine, checked references, and helped with permissions. A special thanks goes to Michael Pollard, who drew many of the illustrations and gave excellent technical advice. We particularly thank Fiona Stevens, whose enthusiastic encouragement, gentle prodding, and intelligent editorial advice got this book moving in the first place. Our prose has been much improved by the careful work of Katherine Arnoldi. Any confusing constructions that remain are the result of our own intransigence. Finally, we thank Jennifer Michel for being there and cheering us on.

Developmental Psychobiology

1 Biological Roots of Developmental Psychology

How does the individual organism manage to adjust itself better and better to its environment? How is it that we, or the amoeba, can learn to do anything? This latter problem is the most urgent, difficult and neglected question of the new genetic psychology.
—James Mark Baldwin (1895, p. 185)

James Mark Baldwin was a major contributor to the history of both psychology and biology (Boakes, 1984). He contributed to both developmental psychology and evolutionary theory. The psychological contributions include views of cognitive development that are direct ancestors of Jean Piaget's theory, and notions of social learning that anticipated modern concepts of personality and social development.

Baldwin's major contribution to evolutionary theory was to link habit formation with natural selection; that is, animals have general adaptive capacities that allow them to solve environmental problems by trial and error. He reasoned that this process led to the formation of habits that fit as solutions to problems typically encountered by the animals in their environments. If the same problems recur generation after generation and if their solution is of major importance for survival, then natural selection will favor animals that solve the problems more quickly. This evolutionary hypothesis became known as the **Baldwin effect**.

The Baldwin effect is an important precursor to Waddington's (1956) theory of genetic assimilation whereby, over generations, genes eventually come to underlie the adjustments that individuals make to those environmental conditions that remain constant across generations. Waddington proposed that the metabolic adjustments that individuals make to an increase in ambient temperature become easier over generations. That is, random variations across generations in genes involved in metabolism will result in retention of those variations that are more conducive to individual adjustment to the invariant higher temperature.

With his extensive knowledge of biology (from physiology to evolution) and psychology (from cognitive development to social skill), and his ability to integrate these two disciplines in an attempt to understand the development of behavior, Baldwin was the first developmental psychobiologist.

Developmental psychobiology has developed as a discipline that integrates information drawn from evolutionary and developmental biology, physiology, and other areas of biology, with the various subdisciplines of psychology to address developmental questions about behavior.

Biology and Psychology

Biology and psychology have a long history of mutual interaction, and the growth of each discipline often depended on individuals who were expert in both (Boakes, 1984). Although all current subdisciplines of psychology draw on modern biological information to some degree, developmental psychology shares with comparative psychology extensive reliance on the biological disciplines. Perhaps this is because developmental psychology involves examination of all of the topical phenomena of psychology (motivation, social relations, cognition, emotion, etc.) across all ages. Therefore, developmental psychologists have had to consider the role of biology not only in topical phenomena but also in the age characteristics associated with any phenomenon, whether the phenomenon was stable or changed across the individual's life.

Although the influence of biology is widespread in developmental psychology, it is not easy to specify exactly how its disciplines should contribute to developmental psychology. There are at least two reasons why this is so. One is that biology is an extraordinarily broad and diverse field, encompassing both the biochemistry of cell activity and the processes that integrate species in ecosystems, and it is held together loosely by a complex and multilevel framework. A second is that developmental psychology, which itself encompasses a diverse and heterogeneous set of research domains, has borrowed from different parts of biology at different times in history to meet a variety of unrelated needs. For example, information about the postnatal developmental changes in the nervous system was employed to account for the universal sequence of development of motor abilities (Gesell, 1946; McGraw, 1946), the developmental changes in sensory and perceptual abilities (Peiper, 1963), and the acquisition of language (Chomsky, 1965; Lenneberg, 1967). Information from genetics was used to account for individual differences in development and for the notion of behavioral maturation (Scarr & Kidd, 1983). Information from neural biochemistry, endocrinology, and the functioning of the autonomic nervous system has been used to account for motivational, emotional, and temperamental characteristics of the developing individual (Nash, 1978).

Thus, biology, a heterogeneous scientific discipline, has had only bits of its corpus of knowledge and techniques appropriated, unsystematically, to address only certain restricted issues and phenomena in developmental psychology. The diversity and complexity of the two disciplines, combined with a history of sometimes haphazard borrowing of one from the other make unification difficult. Many developmental psychologists often have too little understanding of the scope and limits of biological knowledge, and many biologists are often unfamiliar with anything other than the common sense or folk psychological aspects of developmental psychology.

Because **behavior** is a function of whole, living organisms, it is as much an aspect of biology as psychology. Therefore, understanding it requires the synthesis of psychology and biology, and as such, the study of behavioral development may present the greatest of all scientific challenges. It is hardly surprising that the study of behavior has often led researchers in both fields to raid each other's territory. It is hard to overstate the value of this interdisciplinary effort but, unless undertaken with care, it will result only in confusion.

In this chapter we briefly sketch the history of two subdivisions of psychology—developmental and comparative psychology—showing their common origin in Darwin's theory of evolution and their influence on each other's development. We maintain that psychology should be considered an aspect of biology rather than a separate discipline. However, we do not advocate that psychological phenomena should be explained by biological theories. Ecological phenomena are not explained by biochemical theories of cellular function (cytology), nor are cellular phenomena explained by ecological theories; yet both ecology and cytology are aspects of biology.

Psychology and biology have been separated by traditions of training that provide students with different methods, techniques, interests, and aims. These differences led inevitably to problems for people attempting interdisciplinary study. The problems are not insurmountable, but they must be faced squarely before a psychobiological approach to the study of development can be fashioned. We discuss two difficulties, distortion of meaning and confusion of description with explanation, that can occur when concepts are borrowed from one field to be used in another. The concept of imprinting illustrates these problems.

The Darwinian Legacy

The publication of Darwin's theory of evolution played a key role in the formation of developmental psychology as a discipline (Boakes, 1984). Darwin's theory on the origin of species greatly influenced Haeckel's notion that individual ontogeny reduplicates species phylogeny (Gould, 1977), which, in turn, influenced many developmental psychologists (e.g., Werner, 1948). Also, Darwin's publication of the biography of his infant child contributed to the growing status of the importance of descriptive information about human development.

Darwin's theory also was highly instrumental in the formation of a sister discipline—comparative psychology (Boakes, 1984). His books *The descent of man and selection in relation to sex* (1871) and *The expression of emotions in man and animals* (1872) deliberately required comparison of the behavior of animals with that of humans for the explicit purpose of identifying the evolution of human psychological characteristics.

Thus, Darwin is the common trunk from which the branches of comparative and developmental psychology derive. The two continue to have much in common, and we contend that they have much to contribute to each other. We believe that both fields require us to think carefully about organisms that differ from human adults in important ways, and to think about the relationships connecting these different organisms to us.

Both of these psychological disciplines borrowed much from biology. The most important loan was the recognition of the continuity between human beings and other animals. This recognition brought a shift in perspective regarding the traditional subject matter of psychology: the adult human. It also brought a shift in psychology's realm of interest to include children and other animals. If the human being is an animal that has undergone evolution, then two quite different things follow. First, the evolutionary processes that shaped the characteristics of all species must be the same that shaped human characteristics. Humans, like all the other animals, must be subject to natural selection and must have evolved through a system of adaptation to their environment. Second, the fact of evolution implies that humans, like the other animals, have a phylogenetic past that relates them to all other living creatures. In other words, scientists can establish the evolutionary relationship of human beings to other living species by tracing the lines of descent back to common ancestors. These two ideas are, respectively, the adaptive and historical theories of evolution. How Darwin came to develop these revolutionary ideas will be discussed in chapter 4.

When first confronted with Darwin's theory, many biologists and psychologists had already begun to reject the idea that a human being can be divided into a psychological mind or soul and a biological body. It was consequently a short step from their existing way of thinking to the recognition that, if the flesh of human beings evolved, then so did their psychological capacities. It followed that if that was true, the use of these capacities must have important consequences in terms of the survival and reproduction of the individual. Human psychological capacities must have specific functions.

An evolutionary outlook brought about a major reorientation in the subject matter of psychology. The traditional concerns of psychology—to describe and analyze of the structure of the psyche, or mind—were no longer important in this new mode of thought. Rather, questions based on the intriguing notion of functional, or adaptive, evolution were asked. Psychologists, no longer content simply with analyzing mental structure, began to question the function of various mental processes. How does the possession of the different capacities of mind aid in the survival of the individual?

It is not too surprising that this functional psychology soon led to concern with the individual's observable behavior. Studies of the adaptiveness of animals revealed that behavior is an important means by which an organism regulates its relationship to its environment. At the same time, physiologists, who recognized that behavior was not really so different in kind from other functional or regulatory processes of the body, began to adapt, for the study of behavior, concepts and methods that originally were designed for studying organ functioning. A focus on behavior not only brought the content of psychology within reach of physiology's tools, but also led to the introduction of animals as tools for understanding human psychology.

Behavior, unlike mental structures, can be observed in the simplest as well as in the most complex of animals. This fact suggested to psychologists that they could conveniently ascertain general rules of behavior in the same way that physiologists were already ascertaining general rules of organ functioning—by working with animals. The consequence of the functional reorientation in biological and psychological thought that originated in Darwin's theory was that physiologists, experienced in the study of animals, began to extrapolate to humans, and psychologists, once confined to the vagaries of the human mind as revealed by introspection, began to add the behavior of animals to their subject matter. In this early period (1880–1920) it was sometimes difficult to distinguish a psychologist interested in behavior from a physiologist interested in behavior. They both aimed at understanding the mechanisms of behavior, and both conceived of behavior as a regulatory, adaptive, or functional process.

It was evolutionary theory, however, that captured the most attention of psychologists as well as of people in general. The idea of human kinship with other living beings was scandalous and exciting, discussed at the turn of the century not only in academia but also in pulpits and courtrooms. It held the promise that the study of contemporary animals would yield insights into the characteristics of the phylogenetic ancestors of human beings and hence into basic human nature. For psychologists, the historical aspect of evolutionary theory implied that the characteristics of the human mind have phylogenetic precursors that must be observable in present-day animals. Darwin himself came to this conclusion and began the task of examining precursors of human mentality with the publication of *The descent of man and selection in relation to sex* (1871) and *The expression of the emotions in man and animals* (1872). He was prompted to engage in this task in part because many people refused to consider that humans are involved in the evolutionary process. Darwin's presumed purpose was to demonstrate that all those characteristics considered specific to humans (e.g., intelligence, emotional feeling), and used to support arguments against human participation in evolution, can be found in simpler form in most animals.

The Anecdotalists and the Origin of Comparative Psychology

In the wake of Darwin's publications (1859–1872), a group of natural historians emerged, most of whom were intent on demonstrating the continuity between the human mind and the mind of animals. Their method for demonstrating this continuity was simply to collect stories or anecdotes about animals and their behavior from breeders, pet owners, and other such animal enthusiasts. The most notable of the **anecdotalists**, as they are called, was George Romanes (1848–1894), a thoroughly convinced Darwinian and an important figure in the establishment of mental evolution as a field of study. Romanes and others of the anecdotalist school emphasized naturalistic and descriptive studies. However, their attempts to establish a commonality between humans and animals resulted in an anthropomorphic distortion in most of their observations, reports, and interpretations.

Anthropomorphism, the attribution of human characteristics to other animals, is still very difficult to avoid and can be found even in some modern literature (Kennedy, 1992; Michel, 1991a). Why is anthropomorphism so seductive, and what is wrong with it, anyway? Animals can do many marvelous things. Consider for a moment the intricate web of a spider, the worldwide migration of birds, the complex social organization of ants, the communicative abilities of honeybees, or the behavior of your own pet. In all of these examples it can be observed that animals are able to execute highly complex tasks that serve definite purposes. The spider's web is not only a marvel of architecture; it is also designed in such a way that it will catch small insects that provide the spider's food. Honeybees have a means of communicating that not only is intricately structured but also allows them to transmit information about the location and type of food to other bees in the hive (figure 1.1). Should the behaviors of the spider and the bee be considered purposeful? Is the honeybee guided by altruistic motives? Is its communication a symbolic language? (box 1.1).

When humans engage in comparably complex behavior, they are capable of perceiving and being guided by their goals. In other words, their behavior is purposeful in the ordinary sense of "intended." People can describe their behavior in terms of its aims and purposes, and their descriptions are obviously well understood by others. In the early stages of animal behavior studies, especially among anecdotalists, it was a common mistake to assume that a complex behavioral outcome implies equally complex causes, and that the causes underlying complex behavior in animals are of the same order of complexity as the causes underlying complex behavior in humans.

For example, it was assumed that the processes a spider goes through when building its web are similar to those humans would go through were they to build a similar web. These processes include having a clear conception of the relationship between the behavior and the goal, bringing to bear architectural knowledge sufficient for web construction. Thus, the spider's

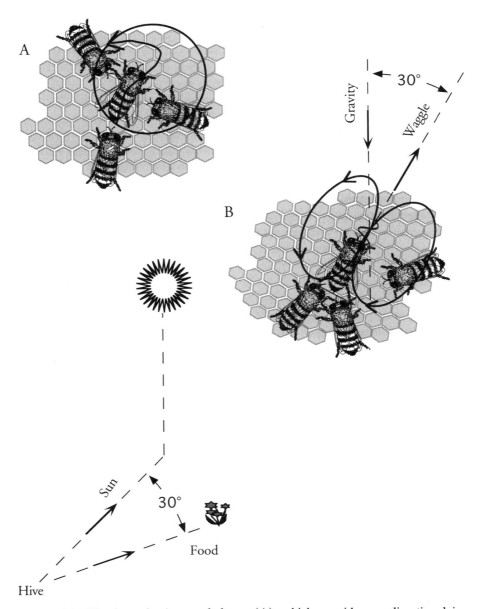

Figure 1.1 The honeybee's round dance (A), which provides no directional information, is performed when the food source is within 80 meters of the hive. The waggle dance (B) is presumed to provide information about the distance in the frequency, intensity, and duration of the waggle component; and direction, in the angle of orientation of the waggle component relative to gravity, to the food source from the hive relative to the sun (after von Frisch, 1964).

Box 1.1   Bee Communication

Do problems of anthropomorphism occur in modern research? The study of honey bee communication reveals some of the subtlety with which human conceptual processes can color the observation and interpretation of animal behavior (Kak, 1991).

A honeybee colony consists of 10 to 40 thousand female worker bees, most of which retrieve pollen and nectar to the hive from flowers spread over 60 or more square miles. After decades of research, the Austrian biologist Karl von Frisch (1964) was convinced that the special "dances" that the bees perform on the vertical surfaces of the honeycombs in their hives contain symbolic information about the distance and direction to food sources that other bees in the hive use to locate flower patches (figure 1.1). The dance of bees has been called a language and has served as an influential basis on which to investigate the ability of animals to communicate symbolically (Beer, 1991; Griffin, 1984). But what is the evidence for these conclusions?

When a forager bee finds a food source, she returns to the hive and performs a "dance." If she has collected within about 30 to 80 meters (90 yards) of the hive, this will be a round dance. It is dark inside a hive, so the other bees "know" about the dance either by following the dancer or sensing the vibrations it produces. Followers (recruits) may then fly out of the hive and search for the food source. Their search pattern is determined by their having tasted nectar provided by the dancer or smelled her floral scent. These tastes and odors identify the flowers that the dancer has visited. Because experienced bees have learned the location of specific patches of flowers, they fly directly to the food source.

If a forager bee returns from a food source more than 80 meters from the hive, she performs a waggle dance. It is thought to convey symbolic information about distance and direction of food relative to the hive. Distance information in the range of 80 to 600 meters may be coded in three ways: by the number of times that the bee runs through a complete dance circuit for a given unit of time, by the number of abdominal waggles given during the straight run portion of the dance, and by the frequency with which sound bursts are produced while dancing. The less energy expended in flying to a food source (or the more energy expended in returning to the hive), the more waggles, the more revolutions per time unit, and the higher the frequency of sound bursts.

The waggle dance is also thought to indicate the direction of the food source from the hive. On the way to a food source, the forager apparently notes the angle between the food and the sun. She later transposes this information onto the vertical surface of the comb when she performs the straight-run portion of the waggle dance. If she waggle-walks straight up the comb, the nectar will be found by flying directly toward the sun. If she waggle-walks 30 degrees to the right, the nectar source is 30 degrees to the right of a line drawn between the hive and the sun, and so on. Thus, the sun-compass information is converted into a symbolic code based on gravity. Von Frisch concluded that the recruited bees can use the information gained by following a dancer to narrow their field of search to the correct distance and direction from the hive.

However, some researchers raised questions about the von Frisch evidence (Wenner, 1967; Wells & Wenner, 1973). The aspects of behavior that go into the dance are not uncommon in insects. Moths often shake their abdomen after landing, and the duration of shaking increases linearly with the energy expended in the flight. Dung beetles and many species of ants translate sun angle into gravity angles in their locomotor behavior. Blow flies fed sugar solution will run in circles (round dance?) when the sugar solution is withheld, and the richer the sugar solution the more rapid the circling. They will also run in circles even when taken to a different location. The circling is oriented with respect to both light and gravity, although it does not indicate direction. Many species of insect regurgitate food when they meet a conspecific, and this often induces foraging-like activity in the conspecific. Thus, the forager's behavior is a common characteristic of many species of insects that have fed and expended energy in flying. It need not represent intentions to communicate on the part of the forager bee.

However, the waggle dance is interpreted to be a symbolic representation of direction and distance information. If the recruited bees use this information to find food, then they can be said to communicate on a symbolic level previously thought to be restricted to humans. Indeed, in a series of experiments that altered the dance pattern, James Gould (1975) showed that the recruited bees could be fooled into foraging in a direction and distance unrelated to the original food source. But Gould was not able to misdirect the recruited bees to the middle of a lake. He concluded that bees are not only capable of communicating symbolically but they are also intelligent enough to detect deceptive information.

Wenner and Wells (1990) offered an alternative interpretation. They observed that experienced bees use the odors on the dancing bee to identify the type of flower source. Since experienced bees have some equivalent of an olfactory map of their foraging area (the ability to create olfactory maps is common in insect species), the returning forager's activities simply provide the hive bees with the olfactory cue to the appropriate places to visit on the map. This interpretation fits all of the data concerning the abilities of insects in general, and honeybees in particular, without requiring symbolic communication. Moreover, the results of Gould's deception experiment may be explained without attributing to the bee an intellectual ability to recognize deceptive communication. That is, bees would not go to the middle of the lake because it is an empty spot in their olfactory map, much like the blind spot in the human eye.

Thus, two interpretations of honeybee communication: one requires symbolic communication and a rather sophisticated intelligence whereas the other does not. Some (Gould & Towne, 1987; Gould, 1992) concluded that the bee typically communicates as Wenner and Wells suggest, but that she can communicate as described by von Frisch. However, the evidence in favor of von Frisch's notion is weak at best (cf. Michelsen, 1993). Michelsen (1993) used a mechanical model of a dancing bee and apparently managed to recruit a small number of bees over the course of several hours to an olfactorily marked pseudofood source. However, since the recruited bees could have included those that had established an olfactory map containing the pseudofood source, even the results of this study do not eliminate the explanation of Wenner and Wells. Therefore, if Morgan's canon were to be invoked, we would have to conclude that the honeybee's dance is not a language.

behavior was considered purposeful: the web is built to catch insects, and insects are caught to provide nourishment. Web spinning was also considered thoughtful behavior, because it involves some of the basic principles of architectural and physical design.

Indeed, until recently, researchers (e.g., Fabré, 1913/1956) often accounted for the peculiarities of insect behavior with descriptions of the insect's thoughts. For example, to witness the digger wasp's paralyzing sting, Fabré removed a paralyzed cricket from the clutches of a wasp that was dragging her victim to the burrow containing her eggs, and immediately provided the wasp with an unparalyzed substitute. Fabré writes, "She comes face to face with the prey substituted for her own. She examines it, walks around it gingerly, then stops, moistens her foot with saliva and begins to wash her eyes. In this attitude of meditation, can some such thought as the following pass through her mind: 'Come now! Am I awake or am I asleep? Do I know what I am about or do I not? That thing's not mine. Who or what is trying to humbug me?' " (Fabré, 1956, p. 59).

Psychologists recognized that the anecdotal, anthropomorphic method was fallacious, that projections of introspectively known motives and capabilities onto animals can be in error. For example, it was shown that the form of a cecropia silkworm's cocoon is not decided by the silkworm's purpose or knowledge but by the structure of its spinning apparatus and the properties of the local environment it chooses as a spinning site. It is possible to structure the environment of this caterpillar so that it will spin, but fail to spin a cocoon (Van der Kloot & William, 1953a, 1953b).

As a means of protecting themselves against the seductive fallacy of anthropomorphism, psychologists took to heart a dictum proposed by C. Lloyd Morgan (1852–1936). Known as *Morgan's canon*, it advised that, if there are two or more possible explanations of some behavior, one should always choose the one presupposing the simplest of mental processes, even if it is not the most appealing. This simplest explanation assumes the least complex functioning on the part of the behaving organism. Attribution of human emotions and purposes to animals is effectively precluded if this dictum is followed, because some other, simpler explanation can always be sought and can usually be found.

With some important exceptions, psychologists turned their backs on natural history, perhaps because of the association with anecdotalism. However, natural historians continued to flourish in biology and to develop some powerful conceptual and methodological tools primarily for studying natural selection. They continued to be interested in behavior, particularly as it is involved in sexual selection, and, as we will show later, natural history reentered psychology in the midtwentieth century through the discipline of ethology.

Although the natural history method was dropped by the mainstream of psychology in favor of the experimental method, a legacy of the early post-

Darwinian era was retained: fervent belief in the basic similarity of humans and animals. In the behaviorist movement, especially as it was embodied by John B. Watson (1878–1958), the anecdotalists' contention that they could find human characteristics in animals was completely inverted. Watson insisted that psychology must stick to observables, and observable behavior is movement of muscles and secretions of glands. His attempt to follow Morgan's canon resulted in complex functionings in both humans and animals being either ignored or explained in terms of processes so simplistic that they seriously distorted the phenomena studied. Explanation of all behavior in terms of simple Pavlovian conditioning was the goal. By this reasoning, the mechanism of behavior is the same in all species; differences among organisms and among species lie merely in the content or quantity of conditioned responses.

Watson, a psychologist, thought he had achieved the physiologists' goal of formulating general laws of behavior. To be fair, we must note that the young Watson was often cautious and restrained in his explanations of behavior. Although he is often portrayed as a simplistic radical environmentalist and psychological reductionist, careful examination of his work reveals contributions, such as naturalistic studies of animals, that extend beyond this narrow framework (Boakes, 1984).

Some Early Conceptions of Psychological Development

Before the behaviorist movement, the systematic study of babies and small children was not possible in psychology. No methods were available to evaluate these nonverbal creatures other than anecdotal descriptions of their innocence or depravity. Once behavior was admitted as a fitting subject, however, it became as possible to study preverbal humans as it was to study animals or adult humans. Watson found that the concepts and methods that he had championed for the study of animal behavior were also quite applicable to infants and toddlers. After his early work with animals, therefore, he turned his attention to children and began a new trend in developmental psychology.

The history of developmental psychology did not begin with the behaviorists and their revolutionary methodology, however; several earlier theoretical approaches to child development can be found in the history of Western civilization (Ausubel, 1957). The oldest conception of development—**preformationism**—is that there is no development in the sense of qualitative change; everything is formed from the beginning. Those people whom we now automatically think of as children were, in this conception, considered to be simply small versions of adult humans. This reflected general thought at the time: adults and children played the same games, did similar work, and wore similar clothes. The only difference was that children, not having experienced as much, did not know as much. In paintings typical of this period, children look like miniature adults (Aries, 1962). Were the features that strike us so immediately as characteristic of children, rather than of adults, perceived at all?

According to Ausubel (1957), preformationism is conceptually in the tradition of instantaneous creation and original sin. The ultimate moment for this doctrine occurred when someone looked at a human sperm under the newly invented microscope and saw inside the sperm a tiny but perfectly featured human being (a homunculus). This vision was drawn, reproduced in textbooks, and dutifully seen by others (except by those who argued that the homunculus was in the ovum) who looked at sperm through microscopes—at least for a while.

The methodology of preformationist theories consisted of casual armchair observations and philosophical reflections, much like the anecdotal method of the early students of animal behavior. Similarly, the armchair developmentalists were committed to a projective mode of thinking. They had no precise observational and experimental methods available, and their recourse was to project explanations devised for a privately known existence (thoughts, feelings, purposes, etc.) onto others, including children.

Because people's views of themselves change, the projections they make also change. With a change in the intellectual climate, preformationism was replaced by another way of conceiving of development: **predeterminism** (Ausubel, 1957). The predeterminist movement began to grow in strength during the nineteenth century, gaining support from popular demands for sociopolitical reform and from the new intellectual climate fostered by general acceptance of Darwin's theory of evolution. Largely through the works of Rousseau, people became aware of development in the sense of qualitative change during the life span. Children were perceived as smiling, fat-cheeked cherubs. The idea of original sin fell into disfavor. "Savages," supposedly free from the obstacles of civilization, were seen as noble and pure—the perfect products of a cherubic beginning.

In the predeterminist scheme, development is an orderly and preordained progression through a series of distinct stages. The goal of this progression is a good and perfect person, and, as this end is predetermined, it can best be achieved in a supportive, nurturant, and permissive environment, not an interactive one. Hence, whereas "savages" may be noble, "civilized" people —those who live under a system of social and political restrictions— cannot be.

Because Darwin's theory was designed to account for diversity and continuity among the various life forms, and because development within a single life span also includes change and continuity, some of those who attempted to understand the changes revealed by the predeterminist approach looked to the notion of evolution for useful explanations of individual development. Some embryologists, notably Haeckel (1834–1919), arrived at the idea that the series of highly orderly and predictable qualitative changes observable in the form and functioning of an embryo were reflections of progressive changes in the phylogenetic past of that embryo. That is, they hypothesized that an embryo retraces in abbreviated form during its development all of the evolutionary changes that its ancestors have gone through (see chapters 5 and 6). This is Haeckel's law: **ontogeny** (an individual's development) recapitulates phylogeny (the evolutionary history of a species).

G. Stanley Hall (1846–1924) borrowed the recapitulation concept from embryology and applied it to the postembryonic psychological functioning of the developing person. Psychological development consisted of a recapitulation of the then prevalent notions about the historical course of western civilization. The predeterminist's conception of development as a series of qualitatively different stages occurring in a preestablished and invariant sequence, and having a predetermined end point was thereby both explained and supported by the theory of evolution.

The predeterministic view of children and of development was based on the same flawed methodology employed by the preformationists. Anecdotal descriptions were used, usually derived from casual observation or from an adult's memory of his or her childhood. One of the more advanced, and certainly the most popular, means of gathering developmental information was the baby biography, a narrative account of the progressive achievements of a baby, usually kept by a parent. Unfortunately, this source of information was either openly derived from, or subtly influenced by, the projections of the parent.

The behaviorist movement established a methodology that for the first time allowed psychologists actually to investigate the developing organism experimentally. Together with introducing animals into their laboratories at the beginning of this century, psychologists began to look, as scientists, at babies and children. This was certainly an essential first step toward understanding human development. Unfortunately, however, the behaviorist movement brought to psychology an extreme environmentalist viewpoint. The commitment to this outlook had the effect of preventing psychologists from understanding the phenomenon of qualitative change articulated by such predeterminists as Hall. This extreme **environmentalism** constituted, in effect, a denial of the existence of development, although a denial quite different from that of the preformationists.

If the only real difference between one species and another is in the number and content of conditioned responses (Watson, 1924) or Stimulus-Response (S-R) bonds (Thorndike, 1932), then the differences in the same organism at different points in the life span can be accounted for in the same way. A young child could thus be said to possess all the same psychological capacities as an adult, because all these capacities can be reduced to the formation of simple S-R units. Development, then, is merely a quantitative affair; the only stages necessary to describe development are immaturity (the learning stage) and maturity (the learned stage) (Bijou & Baer, 1961).

To many people—often those committed to the environmentalist position—developmental psychology is the same as child psychology; however, it involves more than an examination of the child. Development is a lifelong process, and understanding it requires empirical knowledge of the specific factors responsible for each particular transition or trend. The environmentalists tend not to search for these factors. They assume instead that the factors are the same, for any stage or for any organism, as those governing the changes in behavior that are observed in specific learning experiments conducted with adult rats, pigeons, or humans. Whether working with children, adults, or senior citizens, environmentalists seem interested mainly in demonstrating that the same contrived situation will modify all these subjects' behavior in much the same way. Any of the more complex phenomena of developmental transitions are assumed to be mere extensions of the factors effecting these simple changes. Evidence from other researchers, however, brought into question this simplistic position, even for its most firmly established phenomena (Hinde & Stevenson-Hinde, 1973; Schneirla, 1966; Seligman, 1970).

As shown in this brief historical sketch, developmental and comparative psychology converged in the early twentieth century. They became accepted and even popular parts of mainstream psychology. Although developmental psychologists occupied themselves primarily with establishing age norms in children, and comparative psychologists studied learning primarily in white rats, exciting undercurrents were kept alive in both disciplines. In developmental psychology, the work of Heinz Werner (1948, 1957) and his students (e.g., Werner & Kaplan, 1963; Wapner & Werner, 1957) examined developmental phenomena as a special kind of process, independent of time, that could be observed to underlie a wide variety of phenomena from the formation of a percept (microgenesis), the emergence of abstract reasoning in the individual, the pattern of recovery of function after brain damage, and the dissolution of functioning in psychopathology, to the historical progression of culture.

In comparative psychology, Schneirla and his students retained a natural history orientation to the study of animal behavior (Maier & Schneirla, 1935) (figure 1.2). In Europe, Piaget (e.g., 1952) and Freud (Wolff, 1960) were constructing theories of human psychological development that combined features of psychology and biology, and the ethologists (Schiller, 1957) were constructing theories of animal behavior that were consistent with a natural history approach. These European efforts eventually had a major impact on American psychology, but at the time were relatively unknown in the United States.

In contrast to conceptions then popular in the United States, Werner (1957) proposed that development can be distinguished from other modes of change by its process. This process exhibited a distinct pattern of progression from a beginning state of undifferentiated, global responsiveness to

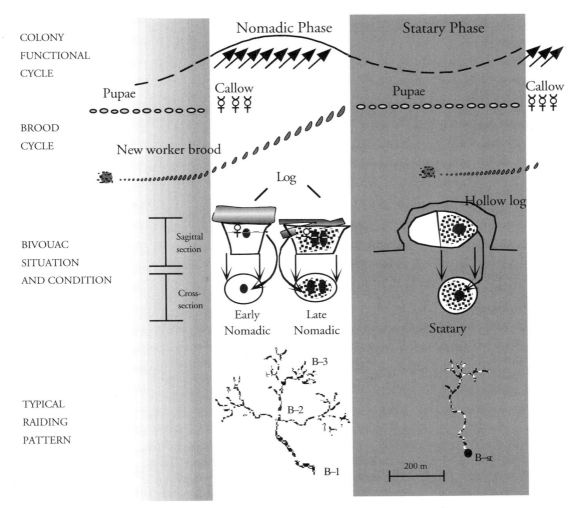

Figure 1.2 The dynamic properties of developing systems are illustrated by the regular cycles in army ant behavior and physiology. The cyclical production of broods that develop from eggs to larvae to pupae to callow workers is coupled with cyclical changes in type of bivouac and raiding pattern. B1–B3: successive bivouac sites in the nomadic phase; B-st: statary bivouac site (redrawn from Schneirla, 1971).

external events. Development entails progressively greater differentiation, or the formation of subsystems within the whole (modularization, in modern terms), and is completed with an hierarchical integration of the subsystems. Although drawn from certain embryological theories, this characterization of developmental change meant that development was potentially possible in any temporally extended event, however brief. Consequently, Werner and his students conducted research designed to reveal the developmental process in events as brief as forming a percept and as long as the historical formation of civilization.

Schneirla considered the study of animal behavior to be an integral aspect of biology. Thus, he found it essential to understand how the animal's behavior fit its environmental circumstances. Schneirla was impressed with the power of studying individual animal development as a means of achieving this understanding, and he therefore incorporated the **epigenetic** concepts that were then prevalent in embryology into his explanations of animal behavior. These concepts were considered alternatives to those of pre-formationism, predeterminism, and environmentalism.

Unlike many of his contemporaries who turned to the study of animals only as a convenient model for some aspect of human behavior, Schneirla championed the idea that it was interesting and important in its own right. With his broadly biological, developmental orientation, his conception of comparative psychology was at odds with the conception then popular in the United States. Schneirla and Werner both worked outside the mainstream of ideas shared by most of their contempories, but the ideas of both these men are consistent with modern formulations of the principles of developmental science.

We describe these developmental principles in the next section. They serve throughout the book as the framework for identifying and describing contemporary developmental psychobiology and for evaluating the appropriateness of interdisciplinary activities in this field.

Principles of Developmental Science

Not all events that take place over the age of an individual are developmental (Baltes, 1983; Werner, 1957). Developmental phenomena are marked by certain general requirements and characteristics. As long ago as 1957, Anderson defined these requirements and characteristics in a manner that is not only still relevant, but also consistent with modern formulations of dynamic systems theories (Lintern & Kugler, 1991). Development requires an open system in which *irreversible* changes in organization can occur as a result of relations among elements within the system, and as a result of transactions between the system and its surrounding environment.

Machines can be constructed that will engage in events that change over time, but development cannot be said to have occurred unless the input to the machine results in irreversible changes in the organization of the machine (cf. Werner, 1957). Of course, computers may be programmed to simulate developmental phenomena by changing their operations as a function of particular contingencies. These simulations can provide valuable insight into actual developmental events (Plunkett & Sinha, 1992; Siegler & Munakata, 1993), even though the machine has not changed in any fundamental way and will engage in the same sequence of changes as often as it is instructed to do so by the programmer (box 1.2).

In addition to the property of irreversible progression, developing systems are *active*, as Anderson (1957) noted. Their activity is dynamic in the sense of attaining and maintaining a coherence of organization in relation to their environment. The activity is not merely reactive to the environment. Instead, developing systems seek input and transform it with their organizing properties. Thus, environmental input becomes incorporated into the developing system. Moreover, the activity of the system produces changes in the surrounding environment. Thus, there are reciprocal contributions between developing systems and their environments as each becomes constructed. Systems establish patterns of dynamic equilibria both within themselves, and between themselves and their environments. These patterns resist reactive change but enable rapid adjustment to environmental variation.

The characteristic of system activity is familiar to developmental psychologists such as when infants manipulate the objects of their environment. The manual skills they demonstrate provide tactile-haptic experiences that contribute to the development of more sophisticated manual skills (Michel, 1994) and haptic and visual perceptual abilities (Bushnell & Boudreau, 1993). Also, the patterns of social interactions (e.g., between parent and child or among peers) reveal similar types of activities. For example, Vandell (1979a, 1979b) demonstrated that social skills that toddlers establish with their mothers are those employed during initial peer interactions. Since mothers provide much of the support for their toddlers' skills, and this support cannot be supplied by other toddlers, initial social interactions among toddlers fail to materialize. Nevertheless, the opportunity for frequent contact among toddlers gradually leads to the establishment of social skills that outstrip those manifested with mothers, and promote changes in the mother-toddler social patterns. Thus, toddlers change their environment, that is, the specific social experiences provided by the mother.

Developing systems also exhibit the characteristic of *growth*, or changes in complexity with time. Since developing systems are coherent with their environment, they adjust to environmental variation. As the adjustments of the system to the variation inherent in the environment become more complicated, coherence is threatened. This leads to a different, more complex level of organization that reduces the complicated nature of the array

Box 1.2   The Emergence of Social Organization in Honeybees

In box 1.1 we described the controversy surrounding the question of whether the dance of the foraging honeybee is a form of symbolic communication. The controversy illustrated the problem of anthropomorphism. Here again we use honeybees to illustrate an important problem in the study of development. Formal computer modeling of the social structure of the honeybee hive provides insight into how complex behavioral characteristics can emerge as self-organized patterns derived from rather simple initial properties.

A typical bee colony consists of 10 to 40 thousand female workers, zero to several thousand male drones, and 1 egg-laying queen. The female workers do all of the necessary work of the colony, with each one changing the set of tasks she performs as she ages. After metamorphosis from the larval form, the workers clean the cells of the hive for two days. From 2 to 11 days of age, they care for immature bees and tend to the queen. Workers then switch to the task of processing and storing food that is brought to the hive. When they reach 20 days of age, workers become foragers, spending 1 to 3 weeks collecting pollen and nectar. Then they die. At any instant, the colony exists in an organized state, reflecting the number of workers engaged in the four different tasks. This state of organization and the division of labor of adult bees has often been explained as an energy-efficient outcome of natural selection.

Kauffman's (1987) artificial network model reflects his theory that it need not be natural selection that produces specific adaptive traits. Instead, these traits may emerge as self-organized consequences of the basic structure of complex systems. Page and Mitchell (1991; Mitchell, 1992) used Kauffman's model to simulate the honeybee colony. Their computer model incorporated three assumptions: the individual "bees" in the simulated colony had to exhibit the behavioral properties known to be possessed by solitary species; there had to be genetic variations among individuals; each "bee" had minimally to tolerate the presence of other individuals. Given these three simple properties, Page and Mitchell allowed "bees" to interact in the model and found that the division of labor and task specialization emerged automatically from the complexity of social interaction among them.

This modeling study tells us that it is not necessary to invoke the selective value of efficient use of energy to explain the origin of the particular organizational scheme used to divide labor within a honeybee colony. Of course, if the emergent social organization was sufficiently at variance with environmental pressures, the bees would fail to reproduce themselves and eventually disappear from the natural world. Therefore, some secondary fit between the organization and environmental pressure must exist. However, the hive social structure need not have been created by natural selective pressures to achieve this fit.

Artificial neural network models provide some remarkable demonstrations of how complex patterns of organization can emerge spontaneously when experience affects a large number of interconnected units that possess rather simple properties. As we indicate below, such computer simulations provide useful models for exploring how coordinated behavior can emerge from the spontaneous interactions among large numbers of unstable elements. These models and the formal theories that accompany them (e.g., Yates, 1987) provide an important perspective in conceptualizing development.

of previous adjustments. This defines growth (Anderson, 1957; see also chapter 3).

Changes in coherence represented in the different levels of organization are represented in the notion of *stages* in development, and stage theories have played a major role in developmental psychology. For example, the monolithic stage theory of Piaget dominated the field for over two decades. Piaget proposed that the individual's cognitive development goes through three distinct stages of organization—sensorimotor, concrete operational, and formal operational. Since he considered cognition to permeate other aspects of the individual's psychological abilities (moral judgments, attitudes, values, etc.), these abilities also would have the three-stage developmental pattern.

During the 1980s, general stage theories that apply across all or many domains of ability fell into disfavor in developmental psychology (Lautrey, 1993). Although children are no longer thought of as progressing through general stages, developmental progression is still recognized by many. Siegler and Manakuta (1993), for example, suggest that children produce a variety of ways of adjusting to conditions at any particular age, and that this variety provides the raw material for change. They state that developmental change is alteration in the relative frequency of reliance on different ways of adjusting. However, the components of existing abilities are organized and, with change, may be reorganized into entirely new configurations of relationship. The organization at each new level is dynamic, which means that even after children have acquired more sophisticated modes of adjusting, they may continue to use less sophisticated ones, depending on circumstances. Of course, it becomes an empirical question, then, whether the levels of organization within individual domains (e.g., political attitudes, moral judgment, reasoning about the physical world) contribute to or reflect transdomain levels of organization (i.e., stages).

Anderson (1957) proposed that the increased complexity established by the progressive reorganization of developing systems results in a more capable, adaptive system because the previous adjustments have been organized into units—they have become achievements or skills. These achievements require less resources (time and energy) than the initial adjustments. They also may be incorporated into the construction of more complex units of organization. Because of their progressive nature, however, achievements can have cumulative effects in that they restrict the options (direction) for subsequent organization. Thus, at any time, the abilities and options available to the individual are a consequence of that individual's particular history of adjustments and the way in which they have been organized into coherent units.

However, growing systems lose potential as they gain realized achievement. Changes accumulate that both reduce the range of options available and simultaneously increase the number of achievements that can be used for future growth and adaptive function (Anderson, 1957). For example, each human language system has its own restricted set of sounds for the construction of speech, from the 15 sounds in certain Polynesian dialects to the approximately 45 in English to the 75 in certain European and Asian language groups (Bornstein & Lamb, 1992). Adults have great difficulty discriminating and producing the sound distinctions of other language groups (e.g., Japanese with English [l] and [r] distinction, or English speakers with the Welch [l] and [ll]). Nevertheless, all human infants initially are capable of both discriminating and producing nearly all the sounds that occur in any human language. Differences in the vocal tracts, anatomy of the oral cavity, and respiratory patterns between infants and adults act as constraints that promote a particular universal developmental scheme for speech sound production (Kent 1984; Lester & Boukydis, 1991). Consequently, toddlers in four language communities (English, French, Swedish, Japanese) have a very high degree of commonality for speech-sound use (Vihman, 1991).

During their first year, infants come to restrict both production and discrimination to the sounds of the native language of their milieu. This change is dependent on the toddlers hearing their own speech and the speech of others (Oller & Eilers, 1988; Snow, 1987). Thus, they achieve a greater level of ability with their native language but at the expense of reducing their facility with other languages.

The cumulative property of development means that the developmental origins of any achievement can extend far back into an individual's life history. Any developmental achievement will have both events that precipitated its occurrence and a complex of historically derived causal relations that enable the events to be precipitating. Thus, developmental phenomena necessitate adoption of the historical style of science (Gould, 1989b; chapter 10).

The fact that developing systems are organized, having both internal coherence and coherence in relation to the environment, also sets requirements for how the developmental scientist comprehends development. Perhaps the most important requirement is to expect that there will *not* be a linear relation between the input from the environment and the adjustment to that input. Too often it is assumed that a large environmental perturbation or variation will have a major impact on development, whereas a small variation will have little or no impact. However, the repertoire of achievements may emerge either gradually (even if the environmental input is massive or of short duration) or rapidly (even if the environmental input is minor or of long duration). Furthermore, adjustments to some input may be affected by aspects of the individual's organization that derive from events and relations that share neither time nor function in common with the adjustment. Thus, developmental causality will not be identified necessarily by an immediate temporal relationship between some event and the adjustment it precipitates; nor will it be identified by an obvious functional similarity between an event and the adjustment. For example, the development of reading ability may not require practice with books; rather it may depend on the development of certain forms of neural processing derived from motor skills acquired quite a long time before reading begins.

Consider the rules of conduct characteristic of social interactions among people. They bear little functional similarity to the syntactic rules characteristic of the structure of linguistic expression. However, Shatz (1981) discovered that the structural organization of young children's gestures, as constrained, constructed, and prompted by social interaction with adults, reflects a formal similarity to certain basic syntactic rules that will be seen subsequently in children's language. She proposed that the pattern of social interaction between adult and child provides the experience whereby the child may acquire and consolidate a set of procedures and rules that may be applied to other domains, such as language. Others (e.g., Greenfield, 1991) also argue that rules acquired in the developmental organization of manual actions provide the basis for the development of syntactic rules in language (see chapter 8), even though the two different rule systems exhibit no functional or phenomenal similarity.

Development emerges *from* earlier conditions; it is not directed *toward* later conditions. This sets a challenge for the researcher, because it requires one to examine the developmental consequences of specific environmental inputs or aspects of organization that have no intuitive relation to the pattern under study. This challenge is a recurrent theme throughout this book, and is perhaps best appreciated with examples of how it may be met that are described in later chapters.

Attending to development as an emergent phenomenon has profound consequences for both research and theory. Bryant (1990) posited that the discovery of causal explanations for developmental phenomena is hindered because developmental phenomena are so often described in terms of what an adult can do compared with what a child cannot. For example, because children cannot judge what is or is not an appropriate construction for any utterance, the grammar of children's language is identifiable only by what it shares and does not share with adult grammar (see chapter 8). To state the problem in this way leads to explanatory attempts using concepts of final causation in which development is directed toward some adult character. This manner of description prevents consideration of how the abilities that are present in a child at any one time emerged from the antecedent causal events in the child's life.

Since final causation is difficult to examine empirically, developmental research rarely tests causal hypotheses (Bryant, 1990). Instead, it simply describes changing forms of ability at different ages (Aristotle's formal causes) without reference to antecedent-consequent relations (Aristotle's efficient causes). Consequently, as Bryant noted, most developmental research, particularly that on human development, demonstrates what develops rather than what prompts the development. The efficient causation is too often assigned to vague abstractions such as learning, maturation, heredity, sociocultural environment, or some interaction among these categories. Ascribing efficient causation to such abstractions preserves the value of simply describing the changing forms of ability at different ages. Of course, the differences in ethical and moral considerations that apply for human versus animal research mean that efficient causes will be more readily demonstrated experimentally for animal than human development.

When attention is directed toward the particular adult characteristic that will eventually be achieved, the causal connections that are proposed may be based on formal similarity between earlier-appearing phenomena and the adult characteristic (e.g., the speech of adults, the babbling of toddlers). However, without direct assessment of the antecedent-consequent relation, the only connection between the old and new is that the new replaces the old (Bryant, 1990). We have to examine the child's early behavior for experiences that lead to developmental changes. Obviously, the child's early skills likely provide the basis for later development. However, they must be examined for what they provide for subsequent abilities, and not for how similar or disparate they are from an adult's abilities. For example, a priority of developmental research must be to specify exactly how the toddler's social and manual skills provide for the acquisition of subsequent social, motor, and *cognitive* abilities (Lockman & Thelen, 1993). Identification of similarities between infant and adult skills is not developmental research.

A further consideration is that causation in development is coactional. It always results from the *relationship* of at least two and often more components within the system or between the system and its context (Gottlieb, 1992). Causation does not reside in individual components themselves or in the context of the system. Therefore, the relationship among the components of the developing system must be specified to identify causality. Moreover, living systems consist of components that represent different levels of organization. Thus, developmental phenomena can exist *simultaneously* at different levels (e.g., cells, tissue, organ systems, individual, family). A complete explanation of any phenomenon would require description of events at all levels without giving primacy to any one, and a set of rules that would allow translations of descriptions across levels. However, this is currently impractical. Nevertheless, we can and should construct causal explanations of developmental phenomena within the framework of this ideal.

Since certain levels of organization provide functions that are components in other levels of organization, the functional character of any level depends on the proper functioning of the components from other levels (see chapter 3). This highlights the value of *holistic reductionism*. Holistic accounts of psychological phenomena operate with a notion that causation of behavioral events arises from the influence of more complex levels of organization on the more simple levels that make up its components. Thus, the behavior of the individual is caused by the social milieu in a kind of *downward causation*. Reductionistic accounts, in contrast, operate with *upward causation*: the behavior of an individual is caused by the operation of the brain. Holistic reductionism operates with the idea that the different levels of organization are complementary; they can be neither antithetical nor alternative. Nor can causation operate between levels. Rather, comprehension of psychological phenomena is improved by the description and analysis of the temporal events that occur simultaneously at all levels of organization. It is a necessary method to examine the various levels of organization involved in the manifestation of any psychological ability. However, this does not mean that the ability should be explained only by examining the levels of organization it incorporates (see chapter 2).

The function of any component will be influenced by the overall functioning of the level in which it operates by a *partially coupled* feedback relationship (figure 1.3). This type of feedback allows each level of organization to be semiindependent yet interactive (Gottlieb, 1992). For example, the individual is a component in a family system. His or her actions are constrained by the particular pattern of relationships among the family members, and this pattern defines the family system. Nevertheless, the individual's actions are not completely constrained by the family organization, since family members are only partially coupled. Thus, the individual can both alter the family level of organization and, in certain cases, operate relatively independent of it.

The family level of organization does not cause individual behavior, nor does the individual's level of organization cause the family's functions. Yet, knowledge of both levels may be necessary to understand either a family's or an individual's actions. In a similar manner, knowledge of neural cells may be required to understand an individual's behavior, without assigning causal primacy to that knowledge.

Since components of a system are only semiindependent (partially coupled), the number of potential influences on development is both very large and nonlinear. Each component may have its own developmental history with consequent variations in both rate of development and causal factors

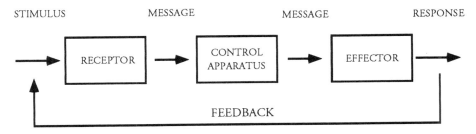

Figure 1.3   The concept of feedback was essential to the construction of early systems theories (redrawn from von Bertalanffy, 1968). Compare with figure 5.4A.

among components. Therefore, production of any consistent pattern of organization or achievement is a complicated "developmental choreography" in which the ontogenies of the separate components are spatially and temporally coordinated (Atchley & Hall, 1991). This means that development takes on the characteristics of a dynamic system.

The characteristics of development, as described above, are much more sophisticated than those represented in many of the modern interactionist approaches. In these latter approaches, development occurs simply because a "genetic envelope sets the limits on the modifiability of the structure of the organism: plasticity explains the modifiability within those limits" (Rosser, 1994, pp. 6–7). Nevertheless, decades ago, the complex dynamic nature of development was well recognized by Anderson, Schneirla, Werner, and some other intellectual forebears of contemporary developmental psychobiology. However, rigorous description of dynamic properties had been difficult to achieve.

In recent years, **dynamic systems theories** have experienced significant advances in methodology and descriptive rigor. These advances hold promise as useful tools for dealing with the properties of developing systems. A vocabulary of concepts now exists by which dynamic systems are analyzed, including nonlinear causality, attractors, and perturbation (Kugler, 1986). In the next section we provide a brief introduction to these ideas.

Dynamic Systems and Development

Most investigators would agree that there are many influences on the development and expression of behavior. This would make behavior the function of a complex system. Labeling the system responsible for behavior as complex involves more than merely acknowledging that explanations for behavior are complicated. Rather, it places the investigation of behavior within the domain of the study of complex systems. Recently, the properties of complex systems have been the topic of intensive examination, and the rules governing understanding of these properties have been applied toward explanations of the development of behavior (Thelen, 1993).

Patten and Auble (1981), defining a system as "a partially interconnected set of components" (p. 897), note that complexity derives from the pattern of relations among the components of a system. Complexity increases according to the number of other components that one component (the focal component) can affect, including those that affect the focal component. Complexity also increases according to the number of other components that can affect the focal component, including those that the focal component affects. Thus, one measure of degree of complexity is the number of components and some estimate of the number of influences (both those affecting a component and those the component affects) associated with each one.

This definition of complexity applies easily within a level of organization, and it allows computational scientists to construct computer programs that simulate systems that differ in complexity so that the consequences of providing different kinds of input to, and perturbing, these systems can be discovered. As yet, its applicability to analyses involving more than one level of organization has not been determined.

The results of simulation studies reveal that although a system can be regarded as a network of interconnected components, not every component is connected to every other component; nor are all connections equally strong. This provides a kind of structure to the system that constrains its range of functioning (the things that the system can do). This structure will allow **emergent** principles or properties (i.e., principles or properties that are not directly derivable from some piecemeal assessment of the components and their connections). Thus, some principles may be discernable only in the operation of the total system. These simulation studies then are consistent with the idea that psychological development is an emergent property rather than an outcome directed by some blueprint or code.

Because components may be members of more than one subsystem of a system, complex systems cannot be characterized by unidirectional causality. They also require contextual interpretations of causality. The consequences of change in one component of a complex system depends on the preceding, current, and succeeding states of the other components. The importance of a change in state of any component depends to greater or lesser extent on the states of the other components. For example, sleep in young infants represents the confluent organization of a large number of components (coherence patterns of central nervous system activity, autonomic nervous system activity, core body temperature, blood sugar levels, condition of the digestive and excretory systems, etc.). Environmental perturbations (e.g., noise, vibration) will change the state of certain aspects of some of the components of the sleeping infant. However, depending on the current state of each of these components, which, in turn, represents the history of their preceding states, the perturbations may or may not result in a change in the infant's state. Thus, a complex system is a dynamic system in which stability is a consequence of dynamic processes.

Lintern and Kugler (1991) compared two approaches to the computational study of dynamic systems: the theory of parallel distributed processing (PDP) (Rumelhart & McClelland, 1986a), sometimes called **connectionist modeling**, and dissipative systems theory (DST) (Prigogine & Stengers, 1984). These approaches have much in common. Both are concerned with identifying the processes of self-organization, distinguishing the macrostates and microstates of a system, and mapping the relation between the states. To understand better the similarities and differences between these two approaches, we have to clarify exactly what is meant by micro and macrostates.

These are relative terms. Any organized system exhibits two aspects: the processes manifested by the operation of the system (**macro**) and the components or subsystems whose relationship to one another represent the structural organization of the system. Each of these subsystems can manifest processes that, relative to the system as a whole, are the **microstates**. Thus, a neural cell is a subsystem of the nervous system. Each cell in the nervous system can exhibit processes (microstates), and the nervous system as a whole can exhibit processes (macrostates). However, the cell's states can be macrostates to the microstates of the cell's components (e.g., nucleus, mitochondria).

The microstates of the individual cells contribute to the macrostate of the nervous system, but they do not determine it (in the sense of cause it). Rather, the nervous system cannot exhibit any processes that are prohibited because they require microstates that are beyond the possible range of microstates of the neurons. Thus, the interactions of neurons constrain the potential range of macrostates of the nervous system. In turn, the microstates of neurons are constrained by the macrostates of the nervous system that derive, in part, from the structural organization of its components. The state of the nervous system, as a whole tends to restrict the states of the neurons to those few that permit coherent functioning. Any approach toward understanding dynamic systems must address the relation between microstates and macrostates.

Both the PDP and the DST approaches to dynamic systems incorporate notions from the second law of thermodynamics. However, they differ with respect to how the emergence of macrostates from the actions of microstates is handled. As described by Lintern and Kugler, PDP uses a "cooling" model to account for the emergence of macrostates, whereas DST uses a "heating" model.

In a cooling model, the structure and order of a macrostate emerge by the careful relaxation of a system into a minimum energy, or attractor, state. This **attractor state** reduces the variation in the activity of the microstate. Achievement of the attractor state results in the emergence of the macrostate with its various properties. Because the system "relaxes" into an attractor state, its dynamics will be progressive and end in a single state. This can be likened to the issue of finality of development; that is, how nearly all humans can develop language skills (some of which appear to be universal) despite quite different developmental circumstances.

The phenomenon of emergence in the achievement of an attractor state means that features of organization in the macrostate (e.g., behavior) are not represented in some program code in the microstate. There is no "intelligence" in the single elements of the system, or in groups of elements, or in feature-processing subsystems. The system has no codes, programs, schemas, symbolic representations, or other elements that govern the emergence of the behavior of the macrostates. This is an important consequence, because until the advent of dynamic system theory, most developmental theories required the assumption of codes, programs, and such to account for how the patterns of organization could occur in a similar manner across individuals.

Lintern and Kugler observed a limitation of PDP systems for explaining behavior. They must be appropriately tuned to generate interesting behavior. That is, the pattern of relations among the components on the microlevel (the system's architecture) has to be selected by the programmer, and the parameters that constrain the use, type, and relations among the system's microstates have to be established by the programmer. In a sense, the programmer is the "code" for the way the system develops. To be sure, the programmer provides a very simple code. However, at present, there is no principled basis for this tuning within PDP theory; it must be supplied by the programmer. Therefore, Lintern and Kugler propose that PDP incorporates in its setup some of the details that it should explain. This restricts its usefulness as a conceptual model of development.

Dissipative systems theory has all of the positive characteristics of the PDP theory but avoids the problem of setup assumptions. This is achieved by treating the laws of thermodynamics, particularly the second law, as a description of universal and natural regularities that have causal potency. Any rules necessary to "tune" the architecture and parameters on the microlevel of a system must be derived from the second law of thermodynamics. In this manner, DST does not incorporate into its setup any of the details it is designed to explain. This is of particular importance to developmental theory, if the intent is to explain how a behavior develops without assuming that development begins with some form of the behavior, or some code or program designed to specify its creation.

As Lintern and Kugler note, thermodynamics studies the structure of systems composed of large numbers of components in which it is impossible to characterize the state of each component. By using aggregate measures, three types of system structures can be described that vary according to the way in which they interact with the environment. **Isolated systems** are those that do not interact with the environment. **Closed systems** allow environmental energy to enter and endogenous energy to escape, but there is no exchange of matter. **Open systems** exchange both matter and energy with the environment.

According to the first law of thermodynamics, the total amount of energy in a system remains the same (conservation of energy). According to the second law, every system moves toward a state of complete disorder in which energy is distributed evenly throughout the system. Such equilibrium coincides with the disappearance of all structural differentiation (positive entropy). There is no organization. However, open systems can exhibit negative entropy (negentropy) by incorporating into their own system the dissipation of energy and matter of other systems in their environment.

They "feed" on the dissolution of other systems. Thus, periodically, open systems can achieve increased levels of internal complexity; they can move away from equilibrium and remain for some time in a state of disequilibrium. And, as Anderson (1957) asserted, development requires an open system.

Similar to thermodynamic theory, Prigogine and Stengers (1984) proposed that all systems may be classified into three different patterns of organization: equilibrated, near-to-equilibrium, and far-from-equilibrium. Equilibrated systems, like isolated systems, are stable, with their energy frozen into structure. The structure can be destroyed, but otherwise they do not change. According to Prigogine, they can be decomposed and treated as though they were the sum of their elementary parts.

Near-to-equilibrium systems can assume a limited number of organizational states without losing their structural identity. Their range of states allows dampening of certain perturbations that might otherwise destroy their basic structure. Like sponge rubber, they are able to adjust to certain perturbations (e.g., compression) so that they can return to their original organization (shape) at the end of the perturbation. Although they cannot be treated as though they were the sum of their parts, they do not exhibit growth.

In contrast, far-from-equilibrium systems can be transformed by perturbation. They can increase in complexity. Moreover, their internal configurations are in fluctuation. Such fluctuation typically does not alter the state of the system. However, in combination with the energy in the environment, the system's organization can be radically destabilized, and a cascading series of structural changes can be set in motion that end only when the system is again in a state of dynamic stability. Thus, changes in systems depend on the relation of the internal state of fluctuation and the pattern of environmental perturbations.

Unlike near-to-equilibrium systems, changes in organization of far-from-equilibrium systems are irreversible and contingent. They are sensitive to the timing and character of three things: initial conditions, specific perturbations, and particular fluctuations of their own internal processes. The transitions between periods of stability are sensitive to random fluctuations of internal processes and environmental processes that "choose" the next pattern of stability. These patterns of stability are represented in the organization of new states of matter—dissipative structures. These structures can be destroyed, but they cannot return to their previous state. They grow.

According to Lintern and Kugler, the second law of thermodynamics justifies the stochastic (probabilistic) fluctuation of the states of elements on the microlevel and the threshold effects in the transitions among ordered states. Thus, in an open system, changes in matter and/or energy create the nonlinear breaks in organization. Such breaks are called points of bifurcation. Each break will be initiated by stochastic fluctuations at the microlevel as energy changes. However, the fluctuations will have limited influence on the macrolevel until the energy change induces fluctuations that overcome the resistance on the macrolevel (threshold). Such energy change may be boosted by environmental input. Once threshold is reached, the macro pattern again constrains activity at the microlevel.

The new macro organization ensures (only stochastically) that one of the previously equiprobable patterns now dominates system behavior. Consequently, the newly dominant behavior of the system alters the range of equiprobable patterns that become available. Unlike closed systems and PDP models (Lintern & Kugler, 1991), cessation of energy or change in matter does not result in a return to previous states or a homogeneous state. Progressive change is assured. In biological systems, the direction of change is governed in part by the constraints inherent in the organism-environment system.

Peter Wolff (1987) used metaphors derived from DST models of dynamic systems to describe the transitions in behavioral states of human infants. He notes that large numbers of components of the infant contribute to each of its macrostates (awake, asleep, etc.) and that random fluctuations will occur in the microstates of these components throughout the day. In addition, variations in environmental factors will occur that can perturb the state of the infant. At certain macrostates of sleep, the microstates of the components are so entrapped (or synchronized) by the macrostates that most environmental perturbations (noise, shaking, light) will have little effect on the infant's state (it remains asleep).

The entrapment or synchronization of the microstates cannot last because of random fluctuations of these states. The co-occurrence of an appropriate set of random fluctuations means that certain environmental perturbations have an increased probability of disrupting the organization, leading to the transition to another state (waking). Of course, waking will occur without obvious perturbation because the random fluctuations of the states of the components will provide for the potential disruption of the coherence achieved in sleep (e.g., decreases in blood sugar levels). Wolff's analysis demonstrates the metaphoric strength of DST models for describing stability and transitions between stable states of the human infant.

Thelen (1992), among others, used dynamic systems theory to challenge traditional motor theory's reliance on an executive controller (programs or schemas encoded in the central nervous system) to explain how motor acts are coordinated into functional actions. Dynamic motor theory proposes that the body is a system that generates patterns from the actions of its components. The nervous system is an important component but not the controlling component; it must act in concert with the physical constraints on the components of the body's parts. There is no hierarchy of control but rather "a heterarchy of cooperativity among diverse elements" (Thelen, 1992, p. 93). Thus, independent walking in human infants emerges relatively late in development compared with other species and other forms of infant locomotion, because the relatively heavy heads and short heavy legs of infants make balance and the coordination of leg movements relative to gravity somewhat more difficult. The development of independent walking is not programmed.

Thelen (1992) also used dynamic systems theory to show that developmental invariance in the appearance of various sorts of behavioral abilities does not derive from some central nervous system "clock" but rather is a "property emerging from the confluences of constraints arising from the nature of the task, the neural and mechanical linkages of the body, and the particular flow of energy through the body" (p. 94). Thus, the temporal sequence in development of walking in which newborn "stepping" disappears in the second or third month and then reappears during the achievement of independent walking is an emergent property of complex systems; it is not controlled by genes or maturation. The newborn's spontaneous supine kicking activity appears to be the pattern from which walking will develop. Changes in the patterns of interlimb coordination during kicking are essential for achieving independent walking. Genes enable development but not more than any other component in the system (Nijhout, 1990).

Although dynamic systems theories were not devised to account for developmental phenomena, they appear to be good models of such phenomena (see also van der Mass & Molenaar, 1992). They provide a formal language (Yates, 1987) for describing processes of self-organization and for determining how novel behavioral forms can emerge from antecedent conditions that do not contain such forms or programs for their construction. They also provide the means for predicting the conditions within which a system will undergo a discontinuous change from one stable state to another. They enable identification of the control parameters that can affect such discontinuous changes in state, and they allow for the prediction of limited novel patterns that are likely to emerge after a transition. They offer the developmental researcher the conceptual and analytic means for examining developmental events (Wolff, 1992).

However, Aslin (1993) raised several questions about the usefulness of dynamic systems theories for the study of development. Although possible in principle, it is difficult to apply the methods generated by the theories to the nonperiodic events that characterize most developmental phenomena. Further, the theories have not eliminated the executive function (program, motivation, intention, etc.) because they have not yet been able to specify how behavioral goals are initiated or to account for why a system falls into a certain attractor state or leaves one attractor for another. Neither have they accounted for why different control parameters become effective at different phases of development. Despite these shortcomings, Aslin praises dynamic systems theories for reinforcing the recognition that detailed descriptions are necessary for both macro- and microstates of developmental phenomena and for providing the conceptual and methodological tools for describing the complexity of development.

In addition to the difficulties raised by Aslin, it is also not evident how dynamic systems theories can help to identify the basic units of behavioral development. To understand the dynamics of any system, information about the behavior of, and interactions among, the system's basic units is required. Unfortunately, developmental investigations of behavior often lack clear-cut notions about what constitutes the basic units of developmental change. Resolving this problem can be difficult because, as indicated above, development involves complicated hierarchical processes in which qualitatively new units arise, and the properties of basic units change when new hierarchical levels of organization of the basic units arise. Moreover, although basic units may be described, located, and measured independent of each other (in that sense that they are primary), their developmental effects can be understood only in relation to their interdependency, which may be either linear or nonlinear (Hopkins & Butterworth, 1990).

Despite this problem and several others common to all developmental theories (Aslin, 1993), we consider the dynamic systems theories to be good models on which to construct the developmental psychobiological approach. They offer a way of describing developmental change that is consistent with the meaning of development as applied in this discipline. They do not, however, assist in defining the concept of psychobiology. For this, we turn to a consideration of how the parental disciplines of biology and psychology are integrated for the developmental study of behavior.

Psychobiology

For many psychologists and biologists, psychobiology is defined primarily by specific kinds of research activities that combine some biological and psychological techniques and concepts. Thus, the psychological subdiscipline "physiological psychology" would be considered psychobiology. Traditionally, physiological psychologists examined the relation between standard psychological topics (learning, motivation, memory, perception, attention, aggression, sleep, psychopathology) and the structural organization and physiological functioning of the nervous system. It is this combination of certain aspects of psychology (topic areas) and biology (techniques) that prompts the label "psychobiology."

Psychopharmacology would be labeled psychobiology for similar reasons. Psychopharmacologists examine the relations between the traditional topics of psychology and the presence in the body of natural, synthetic, and refined drugs commonly taken for medicinal, ritual, or recreational purposes. In our society, psychopharmacologists also address issues of drug addiction and abuse, the use of drugs to resolve psychological problems (sleep disturbances, phobias and panic attacks, childhood behavioral problems such as attention deficit disorder and hyperactivity, etc.), and the impact of specific dietary preferences (coffee–caffeine, candy–sugar, snacks–salt/fats, etc.) on psychological performance.

Human behavior-genetics research could also be labeled psychobiological because statistical techniques from population genetics (a part of biology) are applied to various psychological constructs (intelligence, personality, emotion) to identify their heritability. Moreover, various chromosomal abnormalities (Kleinefelter's syndrome, Turner's syndrome, trisomy 21, fragile X syndrome) are examined for their relation to psychological performance (measures of intellectual achievement, personality, aggressive attitudes, etc.). Lately, modern biochemical techniques derived from molecular genetics have been used to chart the transmission of psychological disorders (e.g., depression, schizophrenia) through families and to identify abnormalities in the genes. Such research contributes to an atmosphere in which biology is considered relevant to understanding and explaining psychological phenomena, and promotes the acceptance of psychobiology.

Because psychophysiologists relate common measures of psychological performance to measures of electrical and magnetic changes that are associated with brain activity and to measures of activity of the autonomic nervous system, psychophysiology may be labeled psychobiological as well. Indeed, these four subdisciplines represent only a part of the range of activities that are considered to fall under that rubric.

However, the study of behavioral development requires a multilevel approach to an organism that has an adaptive relation to its environment. Thus, the meaning of psychobiology in developmental psychobiology implies integration at the conceptual level, and not merely a simple combination whereby psychological topics and concepts are examined using biological techniques. The goal of developmental psychology is to integrate the two disciplines by some principled means that preserve the breadth and internal coherence of each.

How Can Biology and Psychology Be Integrated?

The Two Disciplines

Before the two scientific disciplines can be integrated, the basic features of each must be understood. Scientific disciplines have fuzzy boundaries. There is no way to define either biology or psychology so as to draw a hard and fast line between them. Biology is often defined as the study of life. However, the subject matter of psychology is clearly an aspect of the study of life. It follows, therefore, that the various psychological disciplines could readily be considered subdivisions of biology (Millikan, 1984).

Another approach to defining biology and psychology by separate subject matter is to be more specific in listing those aspects of life that belong in each discipline. Thus, biology could be defined as the study of animals and plants, and the functions of their tissues and organs, whereas psychology could be defined as the study of the mind, emotions, motives, personality, and social interactions. Although lists such as these do characterize biology and psychology differently, they do not completely define either field. An attempt to generate complete lists would inevitably run up against subject matter with ambiguous status. What does one do, for example, about human neuropsychology or animal behavior, neither of which can be placed only in one field or the other? It is not possible to divide the subject of life between biologists and psychologists without either creating numerous anastomoses between the two parts, or excluding from both some of the most interesting phenomena that life has to offer. It is often more helpful to define scientific disciplines by the questions they ask rather than by the phenomena they examine. As we will show later, it is not important whether behavior is studied as biology or as psychology. What is important is the types of questions asked about the behavior and how the answers may be interrelated.

Although it has an overarching unity, biology is such a large and diverse field that no one can master it all. For practical reasons, it has been subdivided both horizontally and vertically. The major horizontal division is between plant and animal life, a reasonably unambiguous and theoretically unremarkable cleavage. The vertical subdivisions, however, are defined by different levels of analysis of the same phenomenon and have important theoretical implications.

Consider, for example, two different approaches to the mammalian kidney, which is capable of producing concentrated urine. A cellular biologist might be drawn toward investigating mechanisms for ion transport in the loop of Henle, a structure in the kidney, by methods and ideas similar to those used to study similar processes in the functioning of neurons. At the other end of the vertical spectrum, an ecologist would attend to the facts that such desert mammals as hopping mice can produce urine that is up to 25 times as concentrated as their blood plasma, whereas beavers, like other mammals that live near fresh water, can concentrate urine to only twice the level of plasma (Schmidt-Nielsen, 1990). The ecologist would seek to explain these facts through the use of evolutionary concepts identical to those used to explain the pattern of similarities and differences among animals in all manner of attributes having nothing to do with kidneys.

The cellular biologist and the ecologist are not in conflict: they are merely doing different things. The two levels of inquiry, and the many others in between, reflect pronounced differences in the kinds of questions that are asked, the methods that are used to answer them, and the constructs, concepts, and theories that are applied to arrive at satisfactory explanations. This is a theme to which we will return often.

Biologists are quite diverse in what they study and how they study it. They frequently appear to be far apart on many issues, but they are unified in at least three important ways. The first is by their common subject matter —life. Second, they are unified by their shared acceptance of the modern theory of evolution. The third way is best characterized by the notion of tradition.

Traditions in science arise from common features and historical continuity in professional training. When science was relatively new and relatively small, all scientists shared the same traditions (in the second half of the nineteenth century, many of them made contributions to physics, chemistry, biology, and psychology). Growth brought increased information and diversity in the techniques for acquiring more information. This resulted in increased specialization in science. Since the late nineteenth century, divergence in the professional training of biologists and psychologists has led to increasingly separate traditions.

As the two disciplines gained members, widened their knowledge, and developed new techniques of investigation, their students began to focus on separate sets of course materials and to feel connected with different historical antecedents. Psychologists traced their interests back to philosophical concerns about how people acquire and use knowledge—how they come to know, regulate, and cope with their existence. In contrast, biologists traced their interests to philosophical concerns with the order of living entities and the functioning of their parts. As a result, successive generations of students in the two fields were trained by different mentors, exposed to separate course materials, and provided with different kinds of research skills.

The biological and behavioral sciences have grown explosively for the past several decades. The number of theories, phenomena, and techniques within the province of each discipline has mushroomed, making it very difficult for students of one discipline to obtain more than a smattering of exposure to the content and conceptual frameworks of the other. The information overload places strains on students within disciplines as well, but it is in the nature of training to ensure that some common ground will be maintained.

The majority of biologists and psychologists have little or no formal training in the other discipline; what little there is is likely to be patchy and idiosyncratic. Thus, today, when biologists and psychologists share an interest in the same phenomenon, they are less likely to be as familiar with each other's theories, concepts, and methods than are scientists from the various subdivisions within either field. Because this lack of familiarity with each other's traditions allows the examination of phenomena from fresh perspectives, it can have the positive effect of stimulating further development. Unfortunately, it often results in some animosity, a good deal of confusion, and the creation of pseudoproblems. A pseudoproblem is one that has no means of solution or that can be solved only by clarifying concepts or the way in which the question is stated, not through further examination of the phenomenon in question.

By asking what unifies the traditional biological disciplines into a common science, we have arrived at a historical reason for the fact that psychology is not frequently thought of as a part of biology. Psychological phenomena are indeed a part of life, and many psychologists, like biologists, endorse the theory of evolution as a foundation for their science. Nothing inherent in their subject matter or theoretical persuasions divides them. The division is a matter of disciplinary tradition that defines the set of important questions, specifies acceptable research techniques and explanatory patterns, and identifies the criteria for analyzing error.

Current Disciplinary Trends

Traditions have a way of changing. The vertical divisions in biology are not stable strata: the two poles are moving apart, creating stress lines if not outright fissures in the structure of the field. If, as seems likely, the current trend continues, a formal disciplinary separation may be made between molecular and ecological biology. This poses a crisis for whole-organism biology. With its focus on the physiology and behavior of whole organisms, it is necessarily tied to each pole.

In 1975 Wilson took note of these trends in his treatise, *Sociobiology*. He predicted that the study of behavior at the level of the whole organism would disappear, pulled apart and swallowed into the two biological poles as they complete their division. This has not yet happened, nor do we think it likely (see chapter 10). To understand why, it helps to consider disciplinary changes within psychology as well.

Psychology's claim to unity is based on common interest in explaining the behavior and mental processes of humans. As a discipline, however, it may be even more loosely federated than biology. In part, this is because it straddles two of the great divisions in human knowledge: the natural and the social sciences. Individual psychologists usually identify with one or the other of these divisions, but rarely with both. In universities, disciplines are embodied as departments, and departments are grouped into divisions. Psychology is typically, but not always, in the social science division. This may be true even when the majority (or all) of the psychologists on a faculty identify themselves as natural scientists.

The diversity within psychology's purview is handled by the formation of subdisciplines or programs to guide the advanced training of students. One line of cleavage between these programs is, again, that between the social and natural sciences—the soft and the hard, according to departmental slang. Perhaps a more modern descriptive account would distinguish between a psychology built on folk psychological theory versus one that challenges the commonsense notions of folk psychology (Stich, 1983). This latter distinction cuts across both social and natural science endeavors.

According to Stich, we are all "professional" psychologists because we must exist in a social world in which interpreting and predicting the psychological states of others are essential for adequate functioning. As a consequence of participating in our social worlds, we have accumulated a body of psychological information and several informal theories that work fairly well part of the time. Many psychologists are interested in finding ways to regulate social and personal activities more efficiently and effectively than is possible with folk psychology. Therefore, they made folk theories more explicit and logically consistent, and they chose to use rigorous methods of accumulating the information necessary to improve the folk theories.

However, these activities led them to discover psychological phenomena unnoted in folk theory and also to construct theories that directly contradict folk theory. For example, although there is a folk theory of forgetting, there is none for memory, especially one that incorporates constructive processes and the distinction between explicit and implicit memory. These latter aspects of the phenomena of memory led, in turn, to the creation of theories that contradict folk theory. As a result, some research psychologists rejected the value of folk psychological theory.

Just as folk physics and folk biology are inappropriate foundations for the scientific versions of physics and biology, folk psychology is an inadequate basis for a scientific psychology. Moreover, just as the physical and biological sciences improved our understanding of the physical and biological world, scientific psychology will improve our understanding of social and psychological processes. Thus, psychology is dividing between those who seek to improve folk psychology and those who seek to replace folk psychology with a nonintuitive scientific psychology.

Unlike biology, however, psychology as a discipline has no well-established tradition for providing its undergraduate or graduate students with either a common core of knowledge or a foundation in other natural sciences. Instead, students are more likely to choose from an undergraduate "Chinese restaurant menu" of coequal alternatives and to confine their advanced training to their chosen subdiscipline. One result is a fair amount of heterogeneity in the knowledge, conceptual vocabularies, and methodological approaches of psychologists. Of interest, this diversity provided psychologists with the freedom to define their separate educational programs in different ways. This in turn led increasingly to the formation of interdisciplinary programs for the advanced training of students.

These various social movements, the polarization of biology away from the organismal level, the division between folk and scientific psychology, and the growth of both animal behavior and behavioral neuroscience as interdisciplinary fields of study, allowed biologists interested in organismic biology to join with psychologists oriented toward natural science to create a large number of new programs in the biological study of behavior. There is a surprising degree of concordance across different institutions in what many of these programs include, whether the programs are free-standing or housed in either the biology or psychology department. The programs may have ambiguity as administrative units and may lack a common name, but they do constitute a recognizable field of study. In the most important sense of the word, they reflect a new, emerging discipline that synthesizes organismal biology and psychology as a natural science.

We contend that the integration of the two fields has been mutually beneficial, and that these benefits are increased as the integration becomes more complete. The synthetic integration points to significant new phenomena and problems, and helps to clarify the appropriate uses of explanatory concepts so that recurring, seemingly insoluble problems and pseudoproblems can be solved. When the synthesis is broadened to include more than the nervous system and the use of animals solely as models of human characteristics, it also leads to the discovery that behavioral development is influenced by factors hitherto regarded either as unlikely or as theoretically uninteresting (see chapters 3 and 9).

The Hazards of the Interdisciplinary Endeavor

Scientists are likely to turn to another discipline's store of facts, concepts, and theories when they exhaust those within their own discipline without arriving at a satisfactory explanation of the phenomenon they are studying. In multidisciplinary work, scientists from two or more fields bring their separate insights and technical skills to bear on a common phenomenon. Generally speaking, the disciplines are not themselves changed in any significant way by this activity, although the phenomenon, like the elephant described by several blind men touching its separate parts, may be comprehended more completely. **Interdisciplinary** work, on the other hand, involves transactions between two or more disciplines that lead to changes in the concepts and rule systems of at least one of the disciplines.

Despite its benefits, interdisciplinary work entails hazards. For some time now it has been quite fashionable for psychologists and psychiatrists in the field of child development to direct their attention to the role of biology in psychological development. The focus of this attention has occasionally come to rest on scientists involved in the study of animal behavior, particularly in the field of ethology. The ethologist is concerned with understanding the behavior of animals as completely as possible. Acquiring this understanding means not only systematically describing an animal's behavior and identifying the social and environmental features that affect its occurrence, but also describing the evolutionary and developmental history of the behavior and exploring the physiological mechanisms involved in its organization. Given this broad domain of concern, ethology appears to be an area in which biology and psychology can be integrated.

With such attention directed toward their work, ethologists are often faced with the question of what it is that psychologists would like to know about or would find helpful. As Lehrman (1974) observed, this question embodies the most pernicious problem of the cross-disciplinary exchange of information—the distortion of meaning.

Scientific disciplines are distinguishable not only by their content but also by the way in which they view nature. In other words, a context of methods, techniques, interests, and aims uniquely associated with any particular scientific discipline contributes to the meaning of the concepts and terms it uses and to the meaning of the phenomena and data it derives. Thus extracting some phenomenon or concept from the context of its discipline for the purpose of applying it in another discipline robs it of some of the essential aspects of its meaning. People frequently experience this distortion when they try to relate an amusing incident. Lacking the enrichment provided by the narrator's knowledge and of the circumstances, the listener never fully appreciates the humor of the incident. The narrator usually saves face by remarking, "I guess you had to be there." So, too, may the biologist or psychologist not fully appreciate the meanings of concepts and phenomena drawn from the other discipline.

Consider, for example, the concept of **imprinting**. It was originally used by ethologists to describe the process by which certain types of newly hatched birds, such as chicks and ducklings, direct their social responses toward a particular class of objects in preference to others. In the natural course of events, a parent is a prominent feature of the early environment. This early exposure to the parent is the basis for establishing a preference for following the parent and choosing it as a social companion. In the absence of a mother hen, newly hatched chicks will approach a wide range of bright or moving objects. After a period of exposure, they form a selective social attachment to an object: when close to it, they will emit contentment calls; if it moves away, they will follow it; if subsequently exposed to a new object, they run away from it and emit distress calls. This phenomenon is called filial imprinting (Bateson, 1987a).

The fact that a young bird behaved socially toward a parent or some substitute was not considered a sufficient basis for concluding that imprinting was responsible for the attraction. This conclusion required a specific set of experimental operations. First, the young bird had to be shown to have no preference for some particular stimulus—a moving box or flashing light, for example—as an object of its social responses unless it had been exposed to that stimulus for a period of time. Second, it had to be demonstrated that exposure to the stimulus would induce a social preference. Therefore, the researcher exposed some animals to a stimulus and then assessed their social preference by comparing their behavior toward the previously experienced stimulus with their behavior toward an unfamiliar one. If the birds preferred to follow or stay in the vicinity of the stimulus to which they were previously exposed rather than to respond in these ways to the new stimulus, it was concluded that imprinting had occurred, provided, of course, that naive birds or ones with different experiences did not make the same choice.

Lorenz (1937/57) made several claims about the processes underlying imprinting that he believed, distinguished it from any other kind of learning. Two of the features be postulated were that imprinting is confined to a short, well-defined *critical period* in the life cycle and that it is *irreversible*. According to the former idea, exposure to an object must occur within the critical period or filial attachment would not be acquired. The beginning and end of this critical period were thought to be determined by maturational factors uninfluenced by the environment. In its strongest interpretation (Jaynes, 1956), irreversibility meant that once imprinted, a bird would never again address filial behaviors to dissimilar stimuli.

Modern research does not support Lorenz's claims about the learning, critical periods, or irreversibility during imprinting. These early ideas were altered, refined, and extended in a number of ways to explain more completely the process by which young precocial birds form filial preferences. Thus, most ethologists thought about imprinting as a descriptive label for a class of phenomena having certain characteristics. They then sought explanations for these characteristics in terms of ontogenetic changes, internal and external proximate mechanisms, evolutionary function, and phylogeny, and they allowed new information to change their explanatory ideas (e.g., Bolhuis, 1991).

In contrast, imprinting was extracted from the field of ethology and applied to human development as an explanatory concept. In its new context, it was used to explain, among other things, the formation and maintenance of mother-infant emotional and social relations (Bowlby, 1969; but see also 1988 for a more modern interpretation), early infantile autism (Moore & Shiek, 1971), adult infant-carrying positions (Salk, 1973), the soothing effects of certain sounds (Salk, 1962), and adult psychosexual fetishes (Sutherland, 1963).

Employing concepts that function as descriptive labels in one field as explanatory concepts in a second field is inappropriate. It can create the illusion of understanding when really only superficial resemblances exist between the phenomena of the two fields. The surface similarity between imprinting in domestic chicks and the attachment of a human infant to its mother led some to postulate that the two processes are the same. However, it is rare that the operations defining imprinting in birds have been applied to humans. The stimuli to which the infant is exposed are seldom manipulated, and preferences are often inadequately assessed. When a preference is noted, imprinting often serves as a mere nominal explanation for it.

In the statement "human infants prefer their own mothers because they have been imprinted to them," the word "because" is meaningless; imprinting is simply a term that restates the observed preference. By accepting a word as the explanation, that is, by accepting a nominal explanation, the researcher becomes less likely to search for the factors responsible for the formation of social preferences. Or worse still, the researcher may presume that the factors responsible for the preference in ducks are similar to those responsible for the preference in humans. Even if it were to be found that filial attachment in humans, like imprinting in chicks, involves learning to prefer one kind of social companion through exposure, it would not follow that the explanations of the process would be the same in the two species.

Because imprinting was originally associated with the concepts of critical period and irreversibility in ethology, these subsidiary notions were often assimilated into human studies. Yet there has been little recognition in the human studies of the changes in use and meaning of these terms within ethology (see Bateson, 1979, 1981).

The concept of critical period, for example, was replaced by that of sensitive period by ethologists (Bateson 1979). This is because research showed that the time period during which exposure to a stimulus will lead to imprinting can be altered by appropriate environmental changes (Moltz & Stettner, 1961; Bateson, 1987b). That is, whereas it is possible to determine the time period during which exposure to certain stimuli is most likely to result in imprinting, it is also possible for imprinting to occur during other time periods, provided that the stimuli are appropriate and the exposure long enough (Bateson, 1966, 1973).

The sensitive period results from a number of different developmental processes, each of which is subject to some alteration. The onset of the sensitive period is timed by the development of visual and auditory systems, and the termination occurs when imprinting has taken place—imprinting is a self-delimiting process. Thus, the sensitive period for imprinting to a visual stimulus can be extended by rearing chicks in the dark (Moltz & Stettner, 1961), and it will be ended whenever imprinting has occurred, whether more rapidly to an effective stimulus or more slowly to a suboptimal one such as the walls of a cage (Bateson, 1966; 1987b). This is a very different idea from that of critical period, which was thought to be a window of receptivity to stimulation that opened and shut in time to a fixed clock.

Jaynes (1956) noted that Lorenz's claim of irreversibility could be interpreted to mean that chicks could never alter the object of filial responses once imprinted, or that chicks could address filial behavior to a dissimilar stimulus while retaining information about the originally imprinted stimulus. Research evidence supports the second interpretation. Although the learning that takes place during imprinting is relatively enduring, it is not irreversibly fixed and immutable to further experience. A chick can imprint to more than one stimulus and can change its filial preference. Furthermore, new filial attachments can be formed outside the time boundaries of the sensitive period and may be based on processes that are different from those underlying the earlier imprinting. Unlike the metaphor suggested by its name, imprinting is not a rapidly formed, unchanging impression; that is, it is not like an imprint in wax that is soft only briefly (Bateson, 1987b) (figure 1.4).

Recently, Lickliter, Dyer, and McBride (1993) criticized the majority of imprinting studies for using rearing conditions that are distinctly different from the typical context within which imprinting occurs in the natural setting. In the natural setting, the newly hatched bird would be confronted with a continuous array of visual, auditory, and social stimuli from its mother and siblings. Yet, in the typical imprinting study, the hatchling is reared in social and often visual isolation. Lickliter et al. (1993) reviewed a series of elegant studies that demonstrated the importance of the hatchling's species-typical social environment for establishing and maintaining imprinting.

For example, Johnston and Gottlieb (1981) showed that despite even 24 hours of exposure to a natural stuffed hen, most mallard ducklings did not exhibit a preference for the familiar model (e.g., mallard hen) when it was paired with unfamiliar stuffed hens of other species of duck (e.g., pintail or redhead). However, if the mallard ducklings were allowed social experience with siblings after initial exposure to the stuffed hen, they did demonstrate a preference for associating with it during the imprinting test (Johnston & Gottlieb, 1985). Lickliter and Gottlieb (1987) showed that this social interaction with siblings must occur after exposure to the imprinting model. Moreover, the sibling social interaction must be with ducklings of the same species (Lickliter & Gottlieb, 1988); social experience with ducklings from a different species was ineffective.

Continued social experience with siblings appears to interfere with the maintenance of maternal imprinting if the young birds are not provided with more continuous exposure to the maternal model. Of course, in the natural setting, young ducklings are normally in continuous interaction with the mother. Thus, as Lickliter et al. (1993) note, "under conditions in which the formation of the maternal bond normally occurs, social contact with siblings (and the resulting peer imprinting) may serve to impede the development of the maternal preference. Consequently, active and ongoing maternal involvement may be necessary to both establish and maintain the social attraction to the hen on the part of precocial avian hatchlings. This presumptive requirement of repeated and relatively continuous exposure to the mother hen stands in contrast to most conventional interpretations of imprinting, which have posited that a brief exposure to the mother is sufficient to form a strong and enduring maternal preference" (pp. 193–194).

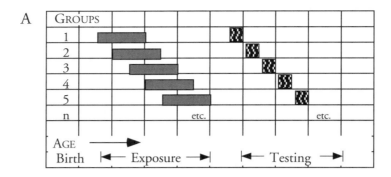

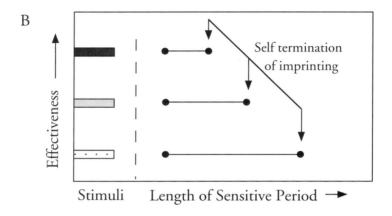

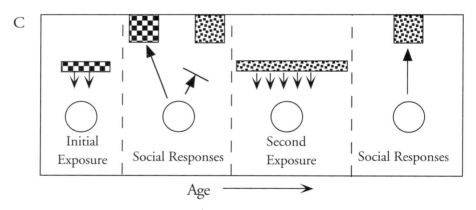

Figure 1.4 (A) Many groups are necessary to control for the length of exposure to the imprinting stimulus, age at onset of exposure, and age at testing (redrawn from Bateson, 1987b). (B) The duration of a sensitive period for initial imprinting varies as a function of the quality of the imprinting stimulus. (C) A change in social preference will occur after initial imprinting, given sufficient exposure to an effective stimulus.

These essential and far-reaching changes in the understanding of imprinting were lost when the concept was extracted from the animal literature and injected into the study of human development. A closer connection between the two fields would have retained the stimulating and provocative effect that the concept of imprinting has had, and simultaneously, it would have allowed developmental psychologists to take advantage of refinements and changes in the concept to a greater extent and with greater speed than has been the case (see Bernal & Richards, 1973).

The imprinting example also illustrates a further problem in cross-disciplinary transfer of concepts. That is, concepts developed in the pursuit of the answer to a question intrinsic to one discipline frequently become attached to a question intrinsic to a second discipline, merely because of some resemblance between the two questions; for example, "Why does the duckling prefer its parent?" and "Why does the infant prefer its parent?" As the concept moves from its original context to a new one, it is necessarily adjusted (distorted) to fit. For example, imprinting, redefined as attachment, has been assimilated into psychoanalytic conceptions of object relations and entangled with conceptions of dependency. Distortion of this nature is an unavoidable consequence of cross-disciplinary endeavors. It should not be taken lightly, however; nor should the problem of changed meaning of transplanted facts and concepts be left unstated. To avoid the issue is to be both misleading and confusing, both of which are contrary to the fundamental tenets of science.

Of course, the best protection scientists can have against being misled by the cross-disciplinary distortion of meaning is to become as familiar with allied disciplines as they are with their own. Obviously, it is often not possible to develop this familiarity, and so this solution is, at the least, impractical. However, researchers can gain some protection from the conceptual problems inherent in cross-disciplinary work by reading widely in the literature of fields bordering on their own. This will increase their appreciation of phenomena and concepts that are not directly related to their own interests, as well as their sensitivity to the context in which borrowed concepts that are relevant to their own discipline derive their meaning. Another way to protect from distortion is to adopt an attitude or a conceptual framework that is flexible enough to incorporate relatively unchanged, concepts from many disciplines (see chapter 3).

The Lure of Biological Explanations

Another factor affecting the synthesis of biology and psychology is the special allure biological explanations have in human society. Throughout Western history, differences in physical and psychological characteristics among people were explained in terms of biological differences (Alper & Natowicz, 1992; Chorover, 1979). Biological theories, supported by research, were proposed to explain differences between the sexes and among ethnic and racial groups. Social movements for racial and sexual equality, as well as the discovery of conceptual and methodological flaws in the research supporting biological explanations, occasionally placed such explanations in disfavor. However, interest continues in determining biological explanations for individual differences in intelligence, aggression, psychoses, criminality, marital fidelity, and the like (Koshland, 1990).

Now as in the past, biological explanations for social and personality differences that mark societal problems are often consistent with the attitudes and values associated with the more politically and monetarily powerful groups in society. As observed by Alper and Natowicz (1992), however, the contemporary interest in biological explanations for psychological characteristics exhibits a surprising twist. That is, members or advocates of less powerful groups (racial and ethnic minorities, homosexuals) are often turning to these explanations to advance their cause.

Alper and Natowicz (1992) offer three reasons for the contemporary appeal of biological explanations of individual differences. First, they appear to provide concrete and easily understood explanations for complex psychological phenomena (development of intellectual ability, morality, social conduct) that have long withstood comprehension. Second, they allow what some believe to be troublesome psychological characteristics (e.g., homosexuality, drug abuse) to be considered the equivalent of diseases. Because many diseases can be successfully treated by modern biological medicine, this holds out the hope for similar management. Third, they are thought to demonstrate that the difference is not a consequence of conscious choice. It is hoped, perhaps naively, that this third reason, in turn, will have the positive social consequence of removing blame and discrimination against individuals having the difference in question.

Unfortunately, none of these three reasons withstands scrutiny. As we hope to convince the reader, biological explanations are not simple; neither are they necessarily more concrete than psychological explanations. Furthermore, using a disease metaphor to examine troublesome psychological phenomena may delay rather than speed the discovery and application of appropriate techniques to eliminate them from society. For example, considering homosexuality a disease could direct efforts toward seeking its "cure" rather than toward changing the legal and social institutions that discriminate against homosexuals.

Political objectives should be justified on their own terms, and not by appeals to biological explanations. Little historical evidence supports the idea that society would not discriminate against psychological differences cast as biologically inevitable. Indeed, societies have frequently discriminated against physical differences associated with genetic defects (Billings et al., 1992). Providing biological explanations for psychological differences is not likely to change societal laws and rules, and it is unlikely that such explanations will automatically foster social tolerance.

When biology and psychology are integrated in a mutually supportive manner, however, complex psychological phenomena can be comprehended more fully, thereby providing a foundation for effective changes. The social and political implications of current and future psychobiological research are profound and require discussion among scientists, clinicians, and the public. We hope that this book will demonstrate to the reader the value of integrating biology and psychology for addressing societal problems.

In this book we examine some of the problems associated with the integration of psychology and biology. We provide a conceptual framework for the study of developmental psychobiology that should remove much of the confusion and misapprehension that can otherwise accompany interdisciplinary study. Also, we introduce sufficient information to guide the acquisition of basic understanding of those concepts from the biological domains of evolution, genetics, embryology, and developmental biology that are relevant to developmental psychobiology. We then address specific issues in neurobehavioral development in relation to the discipline of developmental psychobiology. Finally, we examine the relation between the study of animal behavior and the study of human development.

Most of the examples are drawn from animal research. The developing human is as legitimate a subject for developmental psychobiological analysis as any other species, and to many a more interesting one. However, in contrast to human research that requires more methodological compromises, animal research provides the least equivocal evidence. More often than animal research, research on humans may be interpreted in several, occasionally contradictory, ways. In choosing examples, we focus on those that highlight the important features of the developmental psychobiological approach that are especially relevant to understanding human development. We do want to emphasize, however, that animal research has not been used as a model of any specifically human concern. Examination of animal behavior for its own sake and on its own terms can provide powerful information for understanding (see chapter 9).

Summary

In this chapter we introduced the concept of development within its historical context in biology and psychology. We described development as a dynamic, progressive process that results in hierarchically ordered complexity that increases with growth. It involves self-organizing processes that achieve coherence both within the individual organism and between the individual and its environmental surround.

We demonstrated how traditions have separated psychology from biology and splintered both disciplines into many subfields. Nevertheless, there is both historical and conceptual justification for the integration of biology and psychology. We urged interdisciplinary integration rather than multidisciplinary research activity. Multidisciplinary work can lead to the borrowing of concepts across disciplines. Although such borrowing helps forge links between disciplines, it can be a major problem in the early stages of unification and must be done with care. Borrowed concepts that are descriptive labels in their own discipline may become explanatory concepts in the new discipline. Moreover, much of the meaning of a concept, derived from the intellectual context of the original discipline, will be missing in the new discipline. This results in a distortion in the meaning of the borrowed concept that often goes unrecognized. In the next chapter we describe four specific philosophical problems that also plague the integration of biology and psychology.

2 Biology and Psychology: Problems for a Synthesis

Western thought is replete with psychophysical dualism.... Psychophysical dualism began about 2100 years ago in the West, three centuries after Hellenic Greeks had developed a naturalistic and systematic psychology.... From the 17th through the 19th centuries various philosophers wrestled with the dilemma of how to have a nonphysical mind acting on a physical body.... Psychology today is replete with computer-brain analogies, double world, brain-produced mind or consciousness, reductionism, and organocentrism—all legacies from the Hellenistic retreat from nature. The debates about whether psychological events have internal or external causation, or both,... descend from this mentalism.
—N. W. Smith (1992, pp. 261–270)

In this chapter we introduce and define four philosophical positions that have prevented the union of biology and psychology. We discuss how various reversals of the traditional hierarchy in the sciences have improved understanding of psychobiology, and point the way toward a mutually respectful merger of the fields. We present some of the conceptual, methodological, and empirical problems that arise when culture and biology are considered to be separate influences. We also examine some of the fallacies inherent in theories of biological imperatives in the social construction of behavior.

Psychology and biology have converged at many different points in their histories, and both have grown as a result. However, a few persistent problems emerge, in one guise or another, whenever one tries to synthesize an interdisciplinary approach from the two. The problems stem from some of the positions that have been taken on the issue of the relationship of biology to psychology. Four interrelated but separable positions have been most common: a hierarchical conception of science, reductionism, culture-biology dualism, and the biological imperative. We believe that these four widely endorsed positions create serious problems for a psychobiology of development.

The Hierarchy of Science

The Hierarchy

"[T]he material universe is organized into structures that are capable of analysis at many different levels ... Conventional scientific languages are quite successful when they are confined to descriptions and theories entirely within levels" (Lewontin, Rose, & Kamin, 1984, p. 277). This success has contributed to the pervasive conception that some natural hierarchical ordering among scientific disciplines corresponds to these different levels of analysis. In this scheme, each discipline is dependent on the achievements of the discipline below it. Physics is the most basic science, followed in order by chemistry, biology, psychology, sociology, and so on. This order appears so natural that, for example, people often talk of the biological basis of psychology, but do not speak seriously of the psychological basis of biology.

Acceptance of hierarchical **levels**, whether implicit or explicit, can lead psychologists to conceive of the relationship between psychology and biology—especially between psychology and the fields of physiology and molecular biology—as one in which biological knowledge forms the basis for psychological knowledge, but never the reverse. That is, concepts, laws, and theories of physiology are considered important sources for the formation of the concepts, laws, and theories of psychology. Psychology, however, is thought to play no formative role in physiology, and at best, it can provide new problems to be solved by physiologists. "The biological basis of behavior," or some similar phrase, appearing in virtually every introductory psychology textbook, indicates the extent of acceptance of this belief. Ayala (1974, 1985) named this belief epistemological reductionism.

A hierarchical conception also has implications for the way in which scientists think about themselves and about their colleagues. The more fundamental a science, the more powerful its explanations, and thus the better it is, or so the thinking goes. This reasoning leads to a state of affairs in which certain biologists, chemists, or physicists who are relatively naive with respect to psychology can write on the subject of psychology and have their work accorded the status of an expert's, even by psychologists (e.g., Crick, 1966; Lorenz, 1966; Wilson, 1978). The reverse is rare or nonexistent.

The same social dynamics frequently lead psychologists to adopt the trappings of their colleagues in physiology and biochemistry. Psychology laboratories abound in the latest physiological and biochemical equipment, and psychology journals are filled with the jargon of physiology. To be sure, much of this activity is in the service of furthering the understanding of behavior, but one suspects that at least some of the motivation has more to do with promoting the feeling of status in the psychologist than with answering psychological questions. Of course, many individuals, psychologists by training, are quite sophisticated in the biological literature, and vice versa. We do not wish to imply that one ought to stay within the bounds of one's own discipline; only that such trespassing should be done with enough knowledge of the terrain to avoid serious disturbance of the cultivated landscape.

One unfortunate consequence of the view that biology and psychology are hierarchically related is that progress can be hindered. The discovery that some piece of behavior is heritable, or correlated with the activity of a particular area of the brain, or dependent on the presence of some particular chemical, often has the effect of ending psychological inquiry. The behavior is presumed to be as understood as psychologists can make it. Further elucidation of the phenomenon is then left to the experts at a more basic level of the scientific pyramid. Yet many significant advances in the understanding of behavior have come from such inversions in this hierarchy of science.

Please note that the term "inversion" has meaning only if one begins with the scientific pyramid. We use it ironically to make the contribution of psychology to biology more salient. We do not wish to imply that causality has only a top-down arrow. This would merely invert the bottom-up direction of causality associated with the hierarchy of science notion. As will be evident throughout this book, we prefer to think of the relations among levels of causal organization in terms of mutuality, reciprocity, and coaction (cf. Gottlieb, 1992).

Some Inversions in the Hierarchy of Biology and Psychology

In many instances, research at the psychological level has advanced beyond the limits of fields closer to the base of the scientific pyramid. These advances then point the way to new discoveries in the more basic science. Some striking examples of these inversions are provided by behavior genetics, hormones and behavior, and psychoneuroimmunology.

Genes and Behavior

A good illustration of the importance of psychological investigation for furthering the understanding of biologically based phenomena is the relationship between genetic and developmental analyses of behavior. The behavior geneticist is interested primarily in characterizing the relationship between individual genetic differences and differences in behavior among the members of some population. The developmentalist is interested primarily in ascertaining the conditions of ontogeny necessary for the occurrence of some behavior or behavioral change in the individual. Given these differences, it would be inappropriate to assume that a genetic analysis of behavior can substitute for a developmental analysis. Two studies of the behavior of mice nicely illustrate the importance of distinguishing between the two approaches.

A common mode of demonstrating genetic influences on behavior involves rearing two or more inbred strains of mice in virtually identical environments. An inbred strain is a population of animals all of which have the same genes, and is the result of many generations of brother-sister matings. Differences between strains on some behavioral measure, such as fighting or visual exploration, are presumed to result from the genetic differences.

In an elegant series of experiments, Ressler (1963) investigated the development of the differences in adult weight and visual exploration between two strains of mice—one with white fur (BALB/c) and the other with black fur (C57BL/10). He began his developmental studies with the knowledge that even when the two strains are reared in the same highly controlled laboratory conditions and given access to the same amount of food, the white mice are significantly heavier and more exploratory as adults than the black mice.

Ressler **cross-fostered** the young of both strains immediately after birth. Thus, the BALB/c (white) foster parents raised C57BL/10 (black) young, and vice versa. Other parents raised foster young from within their own strain. When tested as adults, the mice of either strain that had been raised by the white foster parents were significantly heavier and more exploratory than mice of the same strain raised by black foster parents. In other words, similar adult behavioral and weight characteristics were observed in genetically different mice—those from both the white- and black-furred strains—provided that the mice were raised for the first 21 days after birth by foster parents from the same strain.

Ressler suggested that the inherited differences in behavior between the two genetic strains are mediated in part by differences in parental care. The foster parents from the white strain lick, handle, and carry the young more than foster parents from the black strain (Ressler, 1962, 1963). Many studies have now demonstrated important mediating roles played by parental stimulation in a wide range of physiological and behavioral processes in mammals, including those that underlie growth and exploration (Smotherman & Bell, 1980; Hofer, 1983; Moore, 1992; also see chapters 5 and 7). The quality of milk and other aspects of the postnatal maternal environment may also play roles in offspring development, as Ressler noted.

Both maternal and offspring characteristics affect the expression of maternal behavior. In the cross-fostering experiments (Ressler, 1962, 1963), the strain of the young also influenced the amount of handling and stimulation provided by either strain of foster parent. Pups from the white genetic strain elicited more handling behavior from both white and black foster parents than pups from the black strain. Thus, in animals that typically exhibit some sort of parental care, the gene-behavior relationship must be clarified by detailed study of the developmental course and of the consequences of these social behavioral experiences. Indeed, even differences in the prenatal environment of the mother's uterus can significantly affect the adult behavioral characteristics exhibited by two strains of mice.

DeFries, Weir, and Hegmann (1967) observed that daily physical stress (swimming, noise) throughout the latter half of pregnancy in two strains of mice produced offspring whose level of activity in an open field was a function of both fetal and maternal genotypes. That is, mothers of one strain responded to the physical stress differently from mothers of the other strain, and their reactions interacted with the genotype of the fetuses to produce adults that differed in exploratory tendencies and fearfulness. The experiences of the mother affect her uterine environment, which in turn contributes to fetal development (DeFries, Thomas, Hegmann, & Weir, 1967). Therefore, conditions of pregnancy, as well as maternal and fetal genotypes, must be considered when evaluating mammalian behavior-genetic studies.

The developmental effects of the maternal environment can even be transmitted across more than one generation (Dennenberg & Whimby, 1963). For example, second-generation offspring of mice were more responsive in a visual exploration task if their foster *grandmothers* had been from the more stimulating white strain (Ressler, 1966). Thus, the differences in parental environment provided by the black and white foster parents so affected the development of the young they reared that, when they became mothers, they provided different environments for their own offspring than would have been the case if their mother had come from the same strain. When members of the new generation in turn became adults, characteristics of their visual exploration were more like those of their foster grandparents' strain than like those of their own genetic strain! The observation that the social environment can have effects across generations through its effect on the developmental psychobiology of the organism has interesting ramifications for understanding heredity (chapter 5).

Postweaning experiences and context must also be considered when interpreting the relation between genetic and behavioral factors. The C57BL/10 strain of mice has been reported to be highly aggressive and easily trained to fight strangers. However, Cairns (1972b) was not able to train them to fight in his laboratory. Careful comparison of the rearing conditions in his laboratory with those in which fighting was observed revealed the source of the difference in behavior. Apparently, this strain can be trained to fight strangers only if its members are reared in individual isolation cages for at least three to four weeks before testing. The procedure used by Cairns did not include isolation housing, which turned out to be the essential element of training. His procedure of rearing several mice in each cage right up until the time of testing produced mice that were unlikely to fight in the situation that was used.

Subsequent observation revealed that these group-reared mice spent little time being aggressive and a lot of time clumped together in small heaps.

Clumping together apparently allowed them to become accustomed to the stimulation provided by other mice, even strangers. Indeed, detailed behavioral analysis of the mice in the fighting arena showed that isolation-reared mice are more likely than group-reared mice to investigate vigorously and to explore their partner, and are more intensely reactive to the stimulation provided by their partner's exploratory investigation of them. These two factors ensure that the isolation-reared animals will "become entrapped in an escalating relationship" (Cairns, 1972b, p. 397). That is, as their exploration elicits responses from their partner, the mice become even more vigorous in their exploration of the partner, until the interaction escalates into a fight.

Genes do influence behavior, but in complex animals the pathway by which they do so includes the important developmental consequences of an individual's interaction with social and physical environments. Moreover, developmental and genetic analyses provide different, possibly complementary, perspectives on the organization of behavior. Most often genetic analysis of behavior sets up intriguing problems to be resolved by developmental investigations (see chapter 5 for more information on this topic). Therefore, the discovery that a behavioral pattern can be influenced by genetic manipulations should be viewed more as a beginning of psychological inquiry than as the end.

In a purely ideal sense, the notion of a hierarchy of science may have some validity. However, given the rather immature state of biology and psychology as scientific disciplines (cf. Hull, 1972), the only supportable position concerning their relationship is that advancement in either one will be instrumental in the development of the other. Neither the language of biology nor the language of psychology is so rigorously developed that the statements of one can be basic to the statements of the other. Therefore, just as new developments in biology can modify purely psychological conceptions, so too can new developments in psychology modify purely biological conceptions.

Hormones and Behavior

Perhaps the most important advance in modern endocrinology has been the understanding of the relationship between the functioning of the *pituitary gland* and the functioning of the nervous system. The pituitary, sometimes called the master gland because its secretions control the functioning of so many other important glands, is located just beneath the brain. It is a small structure with two major, functionally separate lobes—anterior and posterior. The posterior lobe of the pituitary is connected to the brain by a stalk containing the axons of neurosecretory nerve cells that originate in the brain and terminate within the gland. Hormones secreted by the posterior lobe are involved in regulating constriction of blood vessels, smooth muscle contraction, and milk letdown, all of which can be stimulated by tactile, olfactory, visual, and auditory experience. Hormones secreted by the anterior lobe are involved in the regulation of growth, metabolism, and sexual physiology, among other processes. Although there is a rich network of blood vessels between the brain and the anterior pituitary, there is no neural connection between them. Consequently, endocrinologists long considered the **anterior pituitary** to be an endogenously regulated structure, with its hormonal secretions unaffected by the neurological functioning of the organism.

Harris (1955), in a series of important and beautifully designed experiments, demonstrated that the brain exerts control over the functioning of the anterior pituitary. By interrupting and reestablishing the blood connection between brain and anterior pituitary, he and his colleagues showed that substances essential for pituitary regulation are secreted within the brain. These neurosecretory substances, called releasing hormones, travel by way of blood vessels to the anterior pituitary, where they regulate the secretory activity of the cells. The secretions of the cells of the anterior pituitary are emptied into the general systemic circulation and quickly reach their target organs. Other endocrine glands, such as the thyroid, gonads, and adrenals, depend on the hormones produced by the anterior pituitary for their normal functioning (figure 2.1).

Long before Harris demonstrated the mechanism by which the brain exerts its control over the pituitary, behavioral evidence indicated that the nervous system is involved in the control of the endocrine system. The work of Rowan (1931) and Marshall (1936), for example, showed that the annual cycles of gonadal hormonal secretion in birds are controlled by changes in day length and other external stimuli.

This and other behavioral evidence strongly implied that the nervous system must provide the link between endocrine system functioning and changes in the environment. However, it was several decades before endocrinologists arrived at the understanding of endocrine system regulation achieved earlier by scientists focusing on the behavior of animals.

The notion that hormones can affect behavior has been subscribed to by scientists since antiquity. It was observed repeatedly that castration of domestic animals, for example, frequently led to behavioral changes. As Gilbert White (1789/1981) put it, "Castration has a strange effect: it emasculates both man, beast, and bird, and brings them to a near resemblance to the other sex.... Capons have small combs and gills, and look pallid about the head, like pullets; they also walk without any parade, and hover chickens like hens" (p. 178).

During the 1930s and 1940s scientists began systematic study of the relationship between hormones and behavior by applying such standard endocrinological techniques as gland removal and injection of glandular extracts. It was found that hormones do indeed affect many behavioral patterns, ranging from sexual performance to care of the young, aggression, social

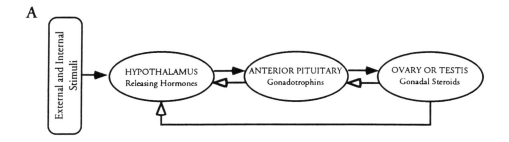

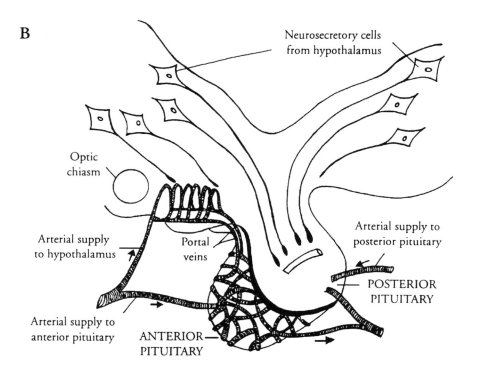

Figure 2.1 (A) The anterior pituitary, the gonads, and the brain constitute an integrated neuroendocrine system that is regulated by feedback and open to stimulation from the external environment. (B) The human pituitary gland.

relations, and even various learning abilities (Beach, 1948; Becker, Breedlove, & Crews, 1992).

The fact that nervous system involvement in behavior is so pervasive led researchers interested in the relationship between hormones and behavior to hypothesize that hormones operate by affecting neural functioning. Evidence directly supporting this hypothesis was obtained by means of a synthesis of the methodologies of neurology and endocrinology, disciplines within physiology heretofore quite separate from each other. Instead of injecting hormones into the general blood supply, researchers implanted tiny amounts of crystalline hormones in circumscribed areas of the brain. As a result, two important discoveries were made: first, hormones can affect behavior centrally by altering the activity of brain cells involved in the performance of the behavior, and second, certain brain cells monitor the level of hormones in the blood, thus serving as an essential link in the feedback control of the endocrine system.

As a result of this synthesis of endocrinology and neurology, we can understand why hormones such as androgen are maintained at relatively constant levels. In many male vertebrates the brain produces gonadotropin-releasing hormones when androgen drops below a certain level, and stops producing them when circulating androgen rises above a certain level. Thus, the nervous system is a target organ for many hormones, with particular populations of cells having receptors for particular hormones.

The endocrine system and the nervous system are mutually dependent, and understanding of either of them is aided by a neuroendocrinological approach. Although many factors were involved in the development of neuroendocrinology as a science, a convincing argument can be made that this advance in physiology owes much to antecedent advances in the study of behavior; in particular, to developments in the study of hormones and behavior. Indeed, work on hormone-behavior relationships has continued to develop, with researchers using psychological terms and concepts for which there are no available physiological translations.

Consider, for example, the reproductive cycle of the ring dove, which consists of a series of both behavioral and hormonal changes (Lehrman, 1965). The ring dove reproductive cycle can be divided usefully into five phases—courtship, nest building, egg laying, incubation, brooding young—with changes in the types of behaviors and environmental stimuli that predominate. The causal interconnections among behavior, hormones, and environmental stimuli that underlie these phases were analyzed in a series of studies (reviewed by Cheng, 1979; Lehrman, 1965, 1971; Michel, 1986).

The male's bow-cooing behavior, the female's receptive preening and crouching, and the male and female behaviors of kah calling, courtship preening, and nest-site solicitation (wing flipping, nest cooing) predominate during the courtship phase. The expression of these behaviors depends on the presence of *testosterone* in the male dove and *estrogen* in the female dove. However, before testosterone can affect the male's behavior, it must be aromatized into estrogen in the neurons. The testosterone levels are dependent on the long days associated with spring. This dependence involves a neural pathway from the eyes to the hypothalamic areas regulating the secretion of gonadotropin from the pituitary. Gonadotropin stimulates the growth of the male's testes and the secretion of testosterone. The presence of a companion dove also increases secretion of testosterone. The female's secretion of estrogen from her ovary is increased by gonadotropin secretion from her pituitary as a result of seeing and hearing a male bow-coo to her. Also as a result of gonadotropin secretion, her ovary begins to develop an egg.

Thus, the courtship phase emerges from the joint influences of social and environmental stimuli and the actions of certain hormones on particular parts of the nervous system. Moreover, in reproductively experienced doves the effects of the previous experience contribute to the emergence of courtship. The previous experience makes the female's secretions of estrogen from her ovary much more tightly associated with the specific character of the courtship stimuli directed toward her by a male. In the male, previous experience makes his behavior less dependent on the specifics of his hormonal state, and therefore, he can rapidly adjust his behavior to the specific characteristics of the female he is courting. Experienced males are better able to stimulate an unreceptive female into a receptive state than inexperienced ones. Perhaps the combination of these experiential effects with familiarity between mates is responsible for the observation that previously mated doves will likely remate in subsequent reproductive seasons.

Of further interest, experienced males exhibit more courtship than reproductively naive males despite equivalent levels of circulating testosterone. Injections of estrogen remove the courtship differences between them. Since courtship depends on the change of testosterone into estrogen within neurons, experience must facilitate the ability of neural cells to change testosterone into estrogen (Cheng, Klint, & Johnson, 1986). Thus, experience can affect the biochemical processes within neural cells.

The nest-building phase involves much nest cooing and wing flipping in the nesting area, bringing material to the area, and constructing the nest. These behaviors are dependent on the presence of testosterone in the male and estrogen in the female. The male's behavior seems to depend on decreasing levels of testosterone, brought about in part by the nest site solicitation and nesting behavior of the female. In contrast, the female's nesting behavior is associated with increases in estrogen secretion.

The high levels of testosterone secreted during the courtship phase result in an increase in progesterone receptors on neurons in the male's hypothalamus. This means that the male's nervous system becomes more sensitive to the low levels of secretion of progesterone from his adrenal glands. This increased sensitivity to progesterone contributes to the transition to the incubation phase of the cycle. The female's transition to incubation is also influenced by progesterone. However, her progesterone levels increase as a consequence of the processes associated with releasing an egg from the ovary.

After a series of progesterone injections, reproductively experienced male and female doves will establish incubation within two hours after being placed in the presence of a nest and eggs. Reproductively experienced doves injected with any other hormone will not establish incubation until they have participated in the courtship and nest-building phases of a cycle.

Reproductively naive doves will not establish incubation after a series of progesterone injections until they have gone through a truncated courtship and nest-building phase lasting two to three days. Therefore, when going through their first reproductive cycle, participation in courtship and nest building prepares their nervous system for progesterone to have a facilitating effect on the transition to incubation. In reproductively experienced doves, progesterone can have its impact relatively independent of whether the dove has begun a cycle of courtship and nest building.

Shortly after incubation begins, prolactin, the hormone responsible for the development of cropmilk, begins to be secreted from the dove's anterior pituitary. The secretion of prolactin is controlled by a neuropeptide, vasoactive intestinal polypeptide (VIP), produced in hypothalamic neurons located near the third ventricle. These neurons double in size during the course of incubation and remain enlarged until the young feed independently (Cloues, Ramas, & Silver, 1990). Cropmilk is the protein-rich substance formed from the cells lining the inner surface of the dove's crop, a part of its digestive system. The parent doves feed this substance to their young during the first few days after the squabs have hatched.

Although prolactin is ineffective in initiating incubation, once incubation has started, it is responsible for maintaining incubation and for the rapid transition to the care of the young after they have hatched. It is interesting that prolactin is secreted in response to the tactile stimulation received from the nest and eggs during incubation and to the visual stimulation of observing an incubating mate! However prolactin secretion in response to observing an incubating mate can occur only in doves that have had the opportunity to initiate incubation before being separated from the nest and eggs.

Prolactin is important for the transition to the brooding (care of young) phase. However, stimuli from the newly hatched young induce the increased secretion necessary for the parents' attention to the young. The secretion of prolactin by reproductively experienced doves is more sensitive than that of naive doves to the stimuli provided by both incubation and the presence of newly hatched young. This may account for the greater success that doves have in rearing young from subsequent cycles compared with their first reproductive cycle (figure 2.2).

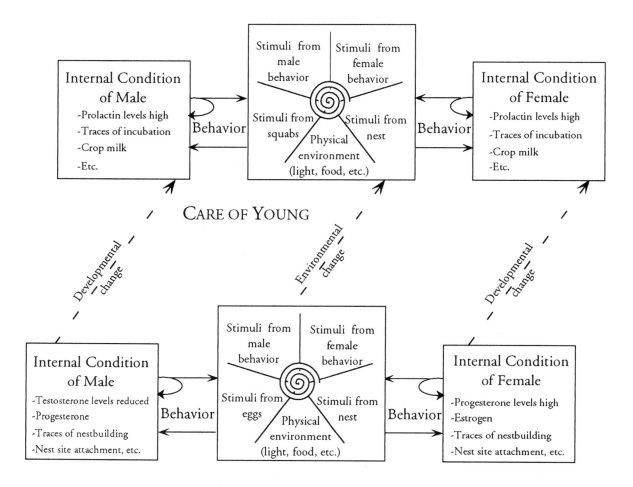

Figure 2.2 The reproductive cycle of the ring dove is regulated by interwoven relationships among the internal milieu, behavioral patterns, and the external environments of both members of the mated pair (after Lehrman, 1965).

It is relatively easy to translate into neuroendocrinological terms the fact that a ring dove will secrete prolactin in response to stimulation from its eggs, mate, and young, and the fact that progesterone injected into doves will induce them to incubate eggs. However, it is not so easy to translate the equally evident fact that ring doves must have had particular social and environmental experiences before they secrete prolactin in response to stimulation from the nest, eggs, and mate, or before they will incubate in response to progesterone. Indeed, understanding this experiential aspect of the neuroendocrine system is far more advanced on a psychological level of investigation than on the physiological level. For this reason, Lehrman

(1964) emphasized the psychological dimension in his description of the psychobiological organization of the ring dove reproductive cycle.

The regulation of the reproductive cycle of the ring dove appears to depend, at least in part, on a double set of reciprocal interrelations. First, there is an interaction of the effects of hormones on behavior and the effects of external stimuli—including those that arise from the behavior of the animal and its mate—on the secretion of hormones. Second, there is a complicated reciprocal relation between the effects of the presence and behavior of one mate on the endocrine system of the other and the effects of the presence and behavior of the second bird (including those aspects of its behavior induced by these endocrine effects) back on the endocrine system of the first. The occurrence in each member of the pair of a cycle found in neither bird in isolation, and the synchronization of the cycles in the two mates, can now readily be understood as consequences of this interaction of the inner and outer environments.   (p. 54)

Besides demonstrating an inversion of the hierarchy of science, the ring dove research demonstrates several features of psychobiology that are important for constructing a truly interdisciplinary field:

1. Hypothalamic, pituitary, and gonadal functions, essential for the regulation and organization of the reproductive behaviors exhibited by the doves, are determined in good part by the social and environmental stimuli characteristic of the reproductive cycle.

2. Environmental and social stimuli operate directly through neural connections from visual, auditory, and tactile sensory systems to the hypothalamic structures controlling pituitary function, or indirectly by altering the dove's own behavior, which, through neural mechanisms involving internal feedback, stimulate the hypothalamic-pituitary complex.

3. Changes in the levels of circulating hormones affect the relative frequency of expression (increasing in some cases, decreasing in others) of specific behavior patterns *and* the dove's sensitivity to specific types of social and environmental stimuli.

4. Experience alters the pattern of regulation of behavioral expression by its influence on the sensitivity of the nervous system to specific hormones and social and physical stimuli. Experience (a psychological concept) is as much an aspect of the dove's biology as its hormonal condition.

Psychoneuroimmunology

The science of immunology provides another good example of a fertile interdisciplinary field that inverts the hierarchy of science. Although the field of immunology grew rapidly in the early part of this century, it was a rather insular science during the first six decades (Lloyd, 1987). The *immune system* was originally thought to operate as an entirely autonomous, self-contained system, with immune reactions regarded as specific or nonspecific physiological responses to pathogens or tissue damage. This scientific stance contrasted with folk wisdom about the origins of illness, which maintained that emotionally distressing events can literally make one sick. The scientific evidence for such influences was highly controversial, and there seemed to be no plausible mechanism to support them. It was therefore easy to dismiss the possibility of an impact of psychological processes on the activities of the immunological system.

Eventually, however, the weight of evidence demonstrating a causal effect of negative social conditions and other sources of psychological distress on the ability of the immune system adequately to contain infections became too great to brush aside (Kennedy, Glaser, & Kiecolt-Glaser, 1990). As a result, the immune system was reconceptualized as integrated with other regulatory systems (Kaplan, 1991; Lloyd, 1987). A strong argument can be made that advances gained by psychological research changed the field of immunology. This change has reverberated in recent years, with immunological research informing conceptions of neural (Edelman, 1987) and neurobehavioral (Dennenberg et al., 1992) development (figure 2.3).

Modern immunology incorporates the interrelationships among the nervous system, endocrine system, and immune system as essential features of immunological functioning (Plotnikoff, 1987). A direct anatomical connection between the **autonomic nervous system** and immune system allows autonomic neural functioning to modulate the functioning of the immune system. Because the functioning of the autonomic nervous system is in part a consequence of specific kinds of experiences, the functioning of the immune system is related to an individual's experiences.

Hormones also have both direct and indirect effects on the immune system. Hormones from the pituitary, gonads, and adrenal glands affect the organs (thymus, spleen, lymph nodes) involved in producing and maintaining lymphocytes, cells that are active in the immune response. These hormones also have a direct effect on the lymphocytes themselves, thus providing clear mechanisms whereby hormonal condition can affect immunological functioning. Neurotransmitter substances produced in the central nervous system (enkephalins, endorphins) also directly and indirectly affect the immune system. Thus, the central nervous system, endocrine system, and immune system are integrated and can function interdependently.

The central nervous system regulates the types and amounts of hormones secreted by the endocrine system, the activity of the autonomic nervous system, and the state of the immune system. Moreover, the activity of the autonomic nervous system, the secretions of the endocrine system, and the secretions of the cells of the immune system affect the central nervous system, resulting in a complex of feedback pathways. This complex easily supports theories that psychological states can be related to biological states of health (see figure 2.3). Thus, the psychological evidence forced a change in immunology and fostered conceptions of the interrelations among the

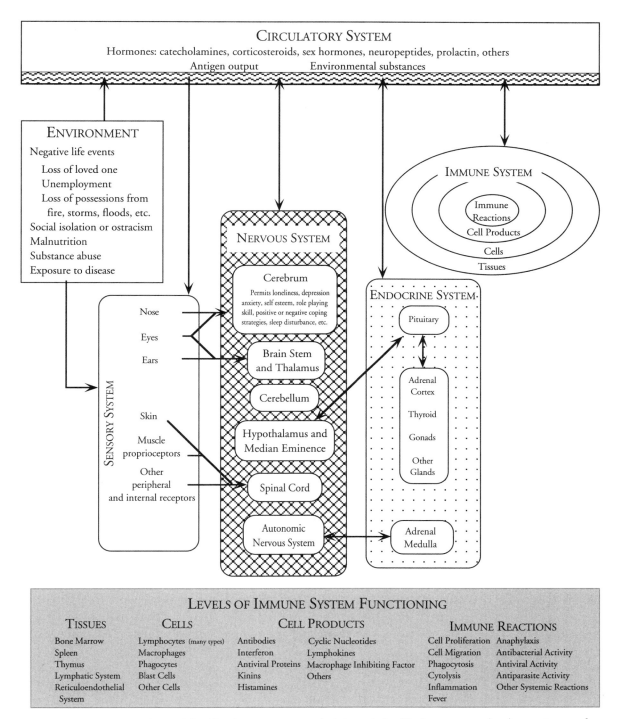

Figure 2.3 The immune system is integrated with the neuroendocrine system and consequently is open to influences from the social and physical environments (after Plotnikoff, 1987).

nervous, endocrine, and immune systems in which psychology and biology could be understood not as independent entities but rather as different aspects of the same discipline—psychoneuroimmunology.

These examples of psychology's importance in the development of biological disciplines are significant because they illustrate the mutuality of the relationship between psychology and biology, and they are directly relevant to the construction of a developmental psychobiology. Each of these examples focuses on psychobiological principles important in the behavioral development of humans and other animals. Human behavior, as well as that of animals, involves a complex of reciprocal interactions between the individual's endocrine and neurological conditions and its experiences with the social and physical environment. It is the changing nature of these relationships during ontogeny that attracts the interest of the developmental psychobiologist.

Reductionism

The concept of a hierarchy of science is closely allied to the notion of **reductionism**. Reductionism assumes different levels of analysis and a hierarchy of scientific disciplines, at least with respect to explanatory scope. Methodological reductionism is the idea that the postulates, laws, and hypotheses of one discipline can be derived completely from the postulates, laws, and hypotheses of another discipline (Ayala, 1974, 1985). Furthermore, it is assumed that derivations result in simpler, more fundamental explanations of events. This sense of reductionism rests on the widely shared belief that nature is all of one piece (Ayala's ontological reductionism). If, as implied by the hierarchical view of science, any discipline can be reduced to the next lower one, it follows that all scientific disciplines can ultimately be reduced to one basic science.

Thus, a methodological reductionist might argue that, since psychological processes are relatively high-order phenomena, the proper way to understand them is to translate them into progressively more elemental processes. However, it is "not so easy to provide the translation rules for moving from one language to another. This is because as one moves up a level the properties of each larger whole are given not merely by the units of which it is composed but of the organizing relations between them" (Lewontin et al., 1984, p. 278). Moreover, Hull (1972) suggested that the successful reduction of one scientific discipline to another depends on each discipline incorporating the concepts, laws, and phenomena of the other. This means that both disciplines are altered, and the translation becomes bidirectional.

Although the ultimate aim of methodological reductionism in psychology may be to achieve a physicochemical explanation, reductionistic psychologists usually move only to the level of a physiological or anatomical analysis in practice. Traditionally, this resulted in explanations of psychological phenomena in terms of the structure and functioning of the nervous system and, more recently, in neurobiochemical terms. Explication of the physiological or biochemical mechanism that is characteristic of some psychological event is considered the explanation of that event. To a reductionist, the best explanation is the one that spells out the mechanism in the greatest detail or that achieves the greatest reduction toward the most elemental laws of science.

In developmental psychology, methodological reductionism is represented by the view that the psychological changes during development are driven entirely by the accompanying physical changes in anatomy, physiology, and biochemistry. There are, however, viable alternatives. It is possible that some causal effects occur within the same level of organization. For example, behavioral change can result from past or current behavior (Chalmers, 1987). Of course, the past or current behavior would be represented in events in the nervous system. Therefore, even when behavioral phenomena affect other behavioral phenomena, there is necessarily simultaneous involvement of anatomy, physiology, and biochemistry. A satisfactory explanation of behavioral change may be achieved without including information about this involvement, but it is also possible to advance a nonreductionistic explanation that includes extensive information about changes at the physiological level (Churchland & Churchland, 1990).

We discussed the value of such holistic reductionism in chapter 1 and described several examples in the previous section. Another example is provided by social effects on reproductive condition. These effects are mediated by changes in the individual's hormonal status. It has been known for some time that stimuli from social companions affect the timing of reproduction among birds. This phenomenon underlies the synchronized reproduction observed in some birds that nest in colonies as well as the synchrony between the male and female of a reproducing pair. These effects are mediated by the neuroendocrine system, and the hormonal changes set in motion by stimuli from social companions have rather profound effects on morphology and physiology, as well as on behavior. For example, after just a week of courtship for as little as 15 minutes each day, the oviduct of a female ring dove increases in weight from less than 1 gram to over 5 grams (Lehrman, Wortis, & Brody, 1961; Barfield, 1971).

It is apparent that the reproductive status of many mammals also depends crucially on the social environment. Some social stimuli have a positive effect on reproduction by stimulating the production of gonadotropins; others actively inhibit these neuroendocrine events. One consequence of social influences on the brain-pituitary-gonad system is reproductive synchrony, as in some colonial birds and some mammals that live in groups. For example, several of the females in a pride of lions typically give birth at the same time. The cubs are then nursed communally, with the mothers alternating between maternal care and hunting (Bertram, 1976). In other instances, social stimuli determine whether an animal will achieve gonadal maturity and be able to reproduce. The effect on the timing of gonadal maturity may result from either excitatory or inhibitory effects of socially provided stimuli on gonadotropin secretion. Inhibitory effects may result in a phenomenon called reproductive suppression (box 2.1).

Reproductive suppression and related phenomena can be used to illustrate two differences between holistic reductionism and Ayala's methodological and ontological reductionism. First, an individual's reproductive status (a behavioral characteristic) cannot be understood by examining only its reproductive physiology, as would be required from the adoption of a methodological or ontological reductionism stance. The understanding also requires information about the individual's social milieu. Second, although the characteristics of the social milieu can account for that individual's reproductive status, understanding is expanded by incorporating information about how social experiences contribute to reproductive physiology. In this way holistic reductionism demonstrates that the individual is simultaneously (not separately) a social and a physiological being, and that the causes of behavior occur simultaneously at several levels of organization. Neither the physiological nor the social level of organization is ontologically prior or primary to the other.

With the methodological reductionists, we can agree that there is unity in nature and that there is unity in science. Moreover, living systems are not endowed with some vital essence that nonliving systems lack. We can also agree that it may be possible, at least in theory, to translate all phenomena into terms of physics and chemistry, and that such translations may constitute explanations. However, a physicochemical description of the dynamics of psychological phenomena is not a sufficient explanation of the phenomena. Biology may be important or even necessary to understand psychology, but it is not sufficient. Indeed, for some purposes biology has little or no explanatory value or may be totally beside the point. Nevertheless, attending to biological processes when investigating psychological phenomena is likely to alter or eliminate many folk psychological ideas, such as beliefs and the will (Churchland & Churchland, 1990).

Causal structures emerge at each level of analysis that cannot be predicted by analysis of lower levels (Fodor & Pylyshyn, 1988). In certain cases, reductionism is more an intellectual exercise than a scientific technique. "There are phenomena that may be explicable in terms of events at a microlevel of analysis but that are more easily studied and more fully comprehended by reference to broader and multiple levels of analysis" (Cacioppo & Berntson, 1992, p. 1019).

The reductionist hypothesis does not imply a constructionist one (P. W. Anderson, 1972). Anderson suggests that even if the phenomena, concepts, and laws of one science (e.g., psychology) could be reduced to the more

Box 2.1   The Phenomena of Reproductive Suppression

Naked mole rats provide a dramatic example of reproductive suppression (Jarvis, 1981). These colonial rodents spend their entire lives underground in an elaborate burrow system, feeding on roots and tubers. Most individuals in a colony (which can number over 200) live out their lives in a state of reproductive immaturity, doing such work as digging and tending the young, but not reproducing. Each colony has one large female with a fully developed reproductive tract. Stimuli originating from her inhibit the production of gonadotropins in the remaining females, but if she is removed or dies, another female will grow into reproductive condition and inhibit the hormonal functioning of her colony mates.

Other less dramatic examples are based on similar neuroendocrine mechanisms. Tamarins and marmosets are small New World monkeys that live in family groups consisting of a reproductive pair and their nonreproductive offspring. As primates, they are unusual in many respects, including the fact that they typically give birth to twins and begin a new pregnancy shortly after giving birth. The older offspring assist the parents in caring for new infants. In response to olfactory stimuli from the parents, these offspring fail to secrete gonadotropins and therefore remain reproductively inactive during the time that they live in the family group, even when this period extends well beyond the age at which they would otherwise reproduce (Snowdon, 1990).

Humans do not experience neuroendocrine reproductive suppression from adult companions, but ovulation is inhibited in women who nurse their infant intensively. Stern (1986) measured blood levels of prolactin and the duration of postpartum amenorrhea in a group of American nursing mothers. Prolactin levels were high in mothers who engaged in high levels of nursing, comparable to those in a group of !Kung women, who are known for very frequent and prolonged nursing (Konner & Worthman, 1980). The prolactin levels of the high-nursing women followed by Stern did not decline to that of nonlactating women until two years postpartum. Furthermore, the women reported an average duration of amenorrhea of 15.2 months. This delayed return of ovulatory functioning can be explained by the enhanced prolactin and reduced gonadotropin secretion as a result of stimulation received during nursing.

The effects of suckling stimulation on lactating women has the consequence of spacing births several years apart, even in the absence of deliberate contraception. The typical interbirth interval is three to five years in the !Kung (Konner & Worthman, 1980). Part of the increased spacing may have a behavioral cause. In two modern Western samples of lactating women, the rate of sexual intercourse was reported at an average of 1.25 times per week for up to nine months after parturition, in comparison to 2.5 times per week before conception (Stern, 1986). Whether this behavioral change is due to hormonal condition or other factors is unknown.

fundamental concepts and laws of physics or chemistry, one would not necessarily be able to construct the phenomena, concepts, and laws of psychology from those of physics or chemistry. Presumably, as phenomena and events become more complex, involving more components, entirely new properties appear, and one cannot understand them by means of a reductionist perspective.

Of course this argument depends in part on which of the various sorts of phenomena, concepts, or laws of physics and chemistry are considered (Yates, 1987). As we noted in chapter 1, dynamic systems theories derive from physics and chemistry, but they appear to allow the sort of phenomena associated with human psychological functioning to be incorporated. However, Anderson might maintain that the interpretation of psychology within a dynamic systems framework is not a methodological reduction.

The value of any explanation is determined in part by its appropriateness to the question being asked. As we will posit in the next chapter, a variety of qualitatively different questions may be asked about behavior, each with a different use and each answerable in a qualitatively different way. The important distinctions among questions can be lost through naive reductionism. Moreover, when an explanation constructed at one level of complexity is reduced to more elemental terms, some sources for understanding may be lost. This is particularly true either when the phenomena to be reduced are not clearly defined or identified, or when the level to which they will be reduced is relatively unexplored. As we indicated earlier, biology and psychology may not yet be rigorous enough disciplines for a proper translation of psychology into the terms of biology.

The Distinction Between Necessary and Sufficient Conditions

Methodological reductionists sometimes argue that, unless a psychological construct can be related to a physiological event, it has no validity. Once related to some biological event, the psychological construct is considered to have been explained. This reasoning ignores the useful distinction between necessary and sufficient conditions. A **necessary condition** is one that must be present if a phenomenon or event is to occur. A **sufficient condition** is one the presence of which always initiates the phenomenon or event. This distinction is particularly relevant to understanding the relationship between the anatomical and physiological characteristics of the nervous system and behavioral development.

Like the study of biochemistry, the study of the anatomy and physiology of the nervous system can be thoroughly fascinating. With modern techniques, the different structural components of the nervous system can be teased apart and their physiological characteristics identified. Ever more sophisticated techniques can be used to examine the ultrastructure and functioning of individual cells. There are billions of cells, with myriad interconnections, to arouse our admiration. Besides this diversity of components, the nervous system has a precise regularity in its structural organization. This structural organization has attracted a great deal of attention from physiologically oriented psychologists. Their work revealed systematic correlations between the presence and activity of certain components of the nervous system and the presence of specific behaviors.

The discovery of correlations between neuroanatomy and behavior particularly interested developmental psychologists who study humans. Given that the human nervous system shows signs of continued development for at least 10 to 18 years after birth, might not developmental changes in behavior during this period be the consequence of such endogenously generated maturational changes? This question provoked a good deal of discussion, especially among psychologists interested in the development of cognitive skills (thinking, reasoning, memory, language, etc.). However, the discussion often fails to consider the distinction between necessary and sufficient conditions. Undoubtedly, certain aspects of neural development are necessary conditions for certain aspects of psychological development, but the sufficient conditions for the psychological change may require information about social and individual experiences. To be sure, these experiences will have neural correlates and consequences that simultaneously underlie the psychological changes. These neural events are necessary but not sufficient conditions for the psychological change.

Consider the cognitive skill, which develops during infancy, of our ability to operate as though the objects of the world have properties and an existence that are independent of our active involvement with them. Piaget (1952) called this skill **object permanence**, and noted that it develops in steps during infancy. According to Piaget, at a very young age, objects cease to exist for the infant when they are not immediately perceivable; when they are covered by a napkin, for example. At a later age, the infant will remove the napkin in search for the recently covered toy. Furthermore, if there are two napkins (A and B) in front of the infant and the adult hides the toy under the napkin on the left (A), the infant will readily retrieve the toy from under that napkin. However, an infant at this stage has more difficulty with a sequence in which the researcher hides a toy under the left napkin (A) but prevents the infant from retrieving the toy; then, in full view of the infant, retrieves the toy from under the left napkin (A) and places it under the right napkin (B). When allowed to retrieve the toy after this sequence of movements, the infant searches for the toy under the left napkin (A). The infant's mistaken performance is called the A-not-B error and it is one of the steps in the development of object permanence. Of course, at later ages the infant correctly retrieves the toy from the B napkin.

Many psychological explanations for the disappearance of this error have been put forth, but none is very satisfactory. In part, the problem stems from the difficulty of always observing the A-not-B error, because it is apparently rather transitory in the infant's development. However, Diamond (1985) developed a technique for testing A-not-B performance that is fairly robust. The infant watches as the researcher hides the toy under one of two cups. After a delay of a few seconds the infant is allowed to reach for a cup to obtain a toy. Infants from about 8 months on will have no problem reaching toward the correct A cup. The researcher continues to hide the toy under the same A cup for several trials. Then, in full view, the researcher hides the toy under the B cup. Infants under 10 months will continue to reach toward the original A cup; older infants will reach for the B cup.

Combining information from developmental neuroanatomy, neuropsychology, and brain lesion work on monkeys, Diamond and Goldman-Rakic (1989) proposed that the disappearance of A-not-B error involved the developmental maturation of the prefrontal area of the cerebral cortex. Humans with brain damage involving the prefrontal lobes and monkeys with lesions of the prefrontal lobes often fail to select the B cup, particularly after some delay between when the item is placed under the B cup and when they are allowed to retrieve it. In the maturational formulation, endogenously generated development on the neural level yields developmental changes in cognitive processes. If this formulation is followed reductionistically, the study of the causes of the development of object permanence can be reduced to an understanding of the development of the brain. Such an assumption confuses necessary and sufficient conditions, however. We have no evidence to demonstrate that the simple development of the prefrontal cortex initiates the change in cognitive development.

In attempting to understand the relation between neural and cognitive development, it is important to start with a clear idea of what is changing in the infant's cognition. Diamond operationalized the A-not-B error to an error on a very particular task to systematize its study. Despite its experimental usefulness, this may have created a difference between what she studied and what Piaget had in mind. In Piaget's original work, the infant was thought to be confused by a perceptual pattern involving an object's disappearance, reappearance, and subsequent disappearance under a different napkin. In the Diamond procedure, infants were trained to respond to the A cup and then to shift their response to the B cup after they were prevented from retrieving the object for a short period of time. Both the Piagetian and the Diamond procedures involved a delay and a new hiding place, but the similarity stops there. For the infant, success or failure on the Diamond task may depend on the ability to break a response set (habitual response to a particular condition), or it may depend on the level of understanding or confusion about the permanent existence of objects. Either explanation would account for the facts, but the implications for cognitive structure are rather different. It is not clear how Diamond's procedure relates to Piaget's theory of the development of object permanence.

It is not even clear how important the A-not-B error is for Piaget's theory. Piaget used the error to describe how an infant might exhibit object permanence for a single hiding condition, but not for two; in other words, for only one of many steps through which the infant was thought to proceed in the developmental course. No one has yet systematically tested whether an infant who displays object permanence in a two-step hiding sequence will do so in sequences of three or more steps.

Furthermore, Lécuyer (1994, personal communication) conducted an experiment in which normal, healthy adults exhibited the A-not-B error. Subjects were shown several "logical doors" (allowing yes, no, and or operations) on a computer screen. In four phases of the study, adults freely explored the operations of each door by "opening" and "closing" them. In two phases, the computer provided two screens "behind" which a door could be hidden. For one phase, a door could be hidden behind one of the screens, and this would be revealed by changes in the output of a door. The subject was required to deduce the hidden location of a door (behind screen A or B) by the changes in the output of that door. After only two trials with the door located behind the A screen, the door was located behind the B screen and its output changed accordingly. Nevertheless, "50% of the subjects still answered on the A side."

Lécuyer's observation calls into question the relationship between the error and object permanence. The adults in his study surely had a firm grasp of object permanence, and it is unlikely that they suffered from some dysfunction of the prefrontal cortex. Clearly, certain task properties can be a sufficient condition for the manifestation of the error. Thus, the A-not-B error may occur for reasons other than failure of object permanence or immaturity of prefrontal cortex.

In the Diamond and Goldman-Rakic account, the infant's cognitive proficiency is assessed by the time delay required before an error is made. The amount of delay the infant can tolerate without making an error steadily increases between ages 7 and 12 months, and this steady increase is thought to represent the slow development of the prefrontal cortex. But is there a sound reason for associating a gradual change in the cognitive skill with a similar change in neural anatomy? Johnson and Morton (1991) raise doubts, pointing out two problematic assumptions in the reasoning: "... first, that the structure matures in a gradual manner and second, that the physiological basis of this maturation must allow information to be retained for a gradually increasing length of time under the conditions of the test ..." (p. 14).

A certain level of development of the prefrontal lobes may be necessary for the manifestation of certain aspects of object permanence. Furthermore, changes in the length of delay that the infant will tolerate before making the error necessarily must be reflected in some neural processes. However, there is no evidence that the gradual development of any neural structure would be reflected directly in a gradual increase in the amount of time that experiential information could be retained for use in performing certain skills. Moreover, evidence that the development of the prefrontal lobes might be necessary for the manifestation of any behavior would not warrant the conclusion that the development of the prefrontal lobes is a sufficient condition of the development of that behavior. It can be concluded that the development of the prefrontal lobes is not a sufficient condition (and indeed it even may not be a necessary condition) for the developmental disappearance of the A-not-B error in the test of object permanence.

When faced with the consistent, careful evidence collected by Diamond and Goldman-Rakic, it is tempting to reach the conclusion that the cognitive changes exhibited by infants during the last few months of their first year reflect the fact that their prefrontal cortex has matured. Examined closely, however, the evidence may suggest something about the necessary neural conditions for cognitive development, but it leaves unasked and unanswered the questions of whether there are other necessary conditions (specific experiential conditions during earlier phases of development, task characteristics, etc.), and whether other aspects of neural development can achieve the same cognitive end. These possibilities remain viable even in the most seductive reductionist account of psychological development.

The Usefulness of Reductionism

Neither reductionism nor the conception of a hierarchy of science logically precludes the development, at each level of science, of concepts specific to that level. Moreover, holistic reductionism can be an effective technique for resolving questions raised by alternative positions within a given level of science that do not appear to be resolvable on that level (Kitcher, 1984). A good case in point concerns the alternative positions about the development of sex roles and sexual identity in humans. No amount of psychological study seems exclusively to support the psychoanalytic, the cognitive, or the social-learning position. Psychobiological examinations of the development of sex-related behavior in animals suggest that components of all three positions are relevant to understanding the human condition (Moore, 1985; chapter 6).

"[A]nalyses of a phenomenon at one level of organization can inform, refine, or constrain inferences based on observations at another level of analysis" (Cacioppo & Berntson, 1992, p. 1021). Reductionistic study can stimulate more molar research. It also can demonstrate the sufficiency of a more microlevel (e.g., neurophysiological) mechanism as a cause of some psychological phenomenon, and thereby guide the construction of psychological theories. Consider the hypothesis that excessive dopaminergic activity or sensitivity is the mechanism responsible for schizophrenia. At present, the evidence can support three alternative concepts: several physiological mechanisms are capable of generating schizophrenia, and the dopaminergic system is one of them; a large set of biochemical factors from which various subsets can be drawn are capable of producing schizophrenia, and dopamine may be part of one or more of these subsets; and increased dopaminergic activity may result as a consequence of the factors that underlie schizophrenia, but does not contribute to schizophrenia. Despite current uncertainty, physiological analyses improve the behavioral analyses by constraining their direction and refining their questions. It is clear that social and environmental events trigger schizophrenia, but exactly how do they do so? Attention to neurochemical events may help answer that question.

Although simple reductionism may sometimes be inappropriate at the current stage of the scientific development of biology and psychology, a joint psychology-biology language may be useful and appropriate. Indeed, such a language might facilitate an integrated, multilevel analysis of psychological phenomena. After all, "the brain does not exist in isolation but rather is a fundamental but interacting component of a developing or aging individual who is a mere actor in the larger theater of life. This theater is undeniably social, beginning with prenatal care, mother-infant attachment, and early childhood experiences and ending with loneliness or social support and with familial or societal decisions about care for the elderly" (Cacioppo & Berntson, 1992, p. 1020).

There is a coevolution between areas of biology that address psychological issues (e.g., neuroscience, ethology) and areas of psychology that address bodily characteristics associated with psychological abilities (Hardcastle, 1992). Each turns to the other either for evidence to help with problematic issues or for more detailed information to embellish and support its ideas, concepts, and hypotheses. Thus, each discipline sheds light in the areas where the other has provided only spotty illumination, and they are mutually supportive without explanatory dependence. Neither one is autonomous from nor derivative of the other. Perhaps the biggest difference is that the two fields traditionally address different sorts of questions. Any interdisciplinary endeavor must be especially cognizant of the differences in questions between the fields and must provide a means for incorporating the full range of these questions while retaining their differences.

Culture-Biology Dualism

The contemporary belief in the dual nature of culture and biology is a curious combination of reductionism, a hierarchical conception of science, and the ancient belief that the mind and body are two separate kinds of stuff (Oyama, 1985, 1991). Unlike reductionism, **culture-biology dualism** is not a philosophical position that has been explicitly stated and then defended by scientists. It is rather an attitude, an approach, a "logic-in-use" (Kaplan,

1964) that characterizes the work of a large number of scientists engaged in examining the relationship between culture and biology. Some of the flavor of this attitude is captured by such popular phrases as "basic biological nature," "what we are really like," and "cultural veneer." A biological core overlaid with culture is the image that most frequently comes to mind. In addition, the biological is given the special status of defining the real goals underlying everyday motives (Oyama, 1991).

Assumptions Underlying Culture-Biology Dualism

The dualistic position we wish to examine is not found in a set of stated postulates. Rather, it is found in the manner in which research is conducted and interpreted. It is necessary, therefore, to examine some of the implicit assumptions behind such research, and some of the methodological limitations of the research procedures that have been used.

Culture and Biology Are Separable

The primary assumption is that individuals have biological and cultural components that are both conceptually and empirically separable. The components are different in kind, and develop through different means and by different scientific principles. Biological components develop through means traditionally studied by biology, perhaps through an **unfolding** or a readout of DNA-coded information, as claimed by predeterminists, whereas cultural components develop through a process of education or socialization. Of course, what is learned or instilled through socialization will vary with the cultural milieu within which an individual develops. Therefore, cultural aspects are considered to be plastic and variable. In contrast, biology is taken to reveal timeless truths underlying the shifting appearances of culture. Each individual has only one true (invariant) set of biological components, although it is recognized that these may be distorted, repressed, or otherwise hidden by aberrant and destructive developmental events.

The implications of **dualism** for developmental psychology are manifold. Because culture and biology are presumed to develop independently, it is logically possible for them to be in harmony, irrelevant to each other, or in conflict (as they are, for example, in Freud's theory of personality development). Some behavioral scientists claim that understanding biology is unimportant for understanding human behavior, whereas others argue that much of what is important to human psychology is biologically determined.

Of those who advocate biology's importance, some, focusing on undesirable human characteristics, maintain that culture should be designed in such a way as to overcome undesirable biological properties. Thus, through restraints, by making available harmless outlets such as catharsis or redirection, or through selective breeding, biologically determined propensities (e.g., aggressive behavior) may be controlled. Others, taking the view that biology knows best, assert that cultures should be designed so as to establish a harmony with biology. This view is reflected in the concept of the "good" or "permissive" environment. It should be clear that the kind of culture that is labeled desirable will depend on whether biological human nature is considered good or bad, desirable or undesirable.

Whether he or she considers human nature good or bad, the dualist conceives of a developmental psychobiologist as one whose primary task is to distinguish between aspects of behavior that are biologically determined and aspects that are culturally or psychologically determined. Or, as it is sometimes put, the developmental psychobiologist should determine how much a particular behavioral pattern or characteristic is influenced by biology and how much by culture. It is here, in the definition of their task and in the methodology adopted by some developmentalists, that the logic-in-use of culture-biology dualism is most evident.

Several Meanings of the Word Biology

Whenever a term has several nonoverlapping meanings, the danger exists that it will be misunderstood. Biology is such a word, especially when it is used in an explanatory fashion in such phrases as "biologically based" and "biologically determined." Biology is only a loosely unified science; it encompasses several totally distinct questions and totally distinct methodologies. By distinct, we mean that an answer to one question has no bearing on the answers to others, and that a methodology appropriate for answering one question cannot yield answers to a second. Therefore, when a scientist asserts that a behavioral pattern is biologically based, one has no way of knowing in what sense the word biological is used, without further information. This is confusing. Cultural determinants of behavior have been contrasted with biological determinants in many different senses of the term, but these different senses have not always been kept separate. In fact, the different meanings of biological have frequently been treated as equivalent, at least when contrasted with cultural aspects of individuals.

If some of the more widely cited examples of biologically based human behaviors are examined, it will be found that they are supported by such different arguments as the behavior serves a biological function; the behavior has phylogenetic precursors; genes are involved; and neurobiochemical mechanisms have been related to the behavior. Considering these different arguments, two points need emphasizing:

1. Our conception of the dualistic nature of culture and biology takes on quite different meanings depending on the sense in which the term biology is intended.

2. The assertion that behavior is biologically based will raise radically different questions about the nature of development, depending, again, on the meaning attached to biological.

For example, Bowlby (1969) concluded that the attachment behavior that babies exhibit toward their caretakers has the evolutionary function of reducing loss of the infants to predators (see Bowlby, 1988, for a much revised version of his argument). In other words, babies who show these behaviors are more likely to survive the attacks of predators and eventually reproduce than those who do not. At least, such predation was likely to occur during the time period in which these behaviors initially evolved. If Bowlby's argument is correct, this would mean that attachment is biologically based in the sense that it evolved to serve a particular purpose.

In this example, to contrast biological and cultural functions, or assign ultimate causation to one or to the other, would be meaningful only if it were possible to predict different outcomes from cultural and biological analyses. Indeed, it is not. Furthermore, knowing whether the behavior functions for biological or for cultural purposes, or both, would be totally irrelevant to our understanding of the development of the behavior. It would not tell us, for example, whether the behavior develops through id gratification, through a process of secondary reinforcement, through perceptual learning, or through any other explanation that might be advanced. Functional analyses certainly contribute to our understanding of behavior and may aid developmental psychologists by identifying important problems for study, but for answers to developmental questions, quite different sorts of analyses are required.

Notions of Developmental Inevitability

Lorenz (1966) contended that human aggression is biologically based. By this he meant that the occurrence of aggression is developmentally inevitable because it represents an evolutionarily produced maturational program, or design. Evidence for this assertion comes primarily from observations that intraspecific aggression is widespread in the animal kingdom and that it is found in diverse human cultures. From a purely evolutionary perspective, this assertion creates problems that have yet to be solved.

A major difficulty is the old one of distinguishing between **homology** and **analogy**. This difficulty is very great for a characteristic as ill-defined as aggression (Hinde, 1974; Klopfer, 1973). If the aggression exhibited by various species of primates is similar by analogy, then human aggression has no evolutionary history, no explanatory genealogy. If primate aggression is similar by homology, then human aggression has an evolutionary history. However, even if it could be unequivocally established that human aggression is homologous with aggression in other, evolutionarily related primates (that it has phylogenetic precursors), this would tell us absolutely nothing about the *development* of human aggression.

Homology means simply that the observed similarities in aggressive behavior among the species of primates can be traced historically to a trait of a species ancestral to all the contemporary species in question. The concept of homology deals only with developmental outcomes. Therefore, it is not necessarily the case that homologous characteristics have the same underlying genes or that the characteristics have similar developmental histories (Atz, 1970; de Beer, 1958). Neither genetic nor developmental analyses are involved in the establishment of homologies. Of course, the developmental bases of a stable and widespread characteristic such as aggression may pose difficult questions; however, answers to these questions will not be found by establishing phylogenies based on homologies.

The discovery that estimates of genetic differences among individuals can be related to differences in their scores on so-called intelligence tests has long been assumed to identify the biological as opposed to the cultural components of intelligence (Kamin, 1974). This dualist conception prevails despite evidence showing that:

1. No intelligence test could ever identify a noncultural aspect of intelligence (Ryan, 1972);

2. The estimates of genetic differences are both inaccurate (Kamin, 1974) and inappropriate (Hirsch, 1970); and

3. These concepts of genetics have little bearing on the factors affecting the development of intelligence (Hambley, 1972).

Although evidence of this sort should lead scientists and others to reject the dualistic view of intelligence, it has been either overlooked or ignored. To be sure, some of the failure to acknowledge this evidence is a consequence of the racist attitudes among some investigators. Yet even those who reject the racist position find it hard to reject the belief in a biological core to intelligence, although they may also argue for political restraint against using this fact to establish social policy.

As we indicated earlier, a genetic analysis of a behavior can never be a substitute for a developmental analysis. Moreover, any plasticity of problem-solving ability can be a biological phenomenon (chapter 8), and any presumed fixity of this ability can be a cultural phenomenon. The fixity-plasticity dimension of psychological abilities is poorly related to the theory of culture-biology dualism. Problems in education will not be resolved by being covered with smokescreens consisting of arguments about the biological nature of intelligence. Unless handicapped by severe neurological damage, all persons can develop reading, writing, and thinking skills sufficient for dealing with the complexities of modern society. That this has not *yet* been achieved should not be considered a sign that it cannot.

Methodological Consequences of Dualist Assumptions

The Separation of Culture and Biology

The two main assumptions associated with dualism are that biological and cultural components are separable, and that biological components are characterized by developmental inevitability. If these assumptions are accepted, the first logical step in a developmental investigation is to attempt to separate the two factors. Many (e.g., Hutt, 1972) argued that human sex differences are biologically based because animal research shows that they are associated with neuroanatomical and neuroendocrine mechanisms. Therefore, human sex differences, to the extent that they are associated with similar mechanisms, cannot be culturally based. Others (Hampson & Hampson, 1961) propose that these differences are culturally based, or learned from the social environment, and therefore, biological factors are irrelevant to their development. However, these conflicting statements are based on dualistic assumptions, and once the assumptions are rejected, the basis for the conflict may disappear.

It is not necessary—in fact, it may not be possible—to begin a psychobiological analysis by separating biological from psychological components. It can be shown that the very nature of the neurobiological mechanisms underlying sex differences depends, at least in part, on input from the social environment (see chapter 7). Furthermore, it can be shown that the nature of the social influences encountered by a developing individual is affected by the person's neurobiologically based characteristics (Money & Ehrhardt, 1972; Moore, 1985).

The logic-in-use, or the methods of inquiry and the assumptions that are used to draw conclusions from data, of contemporary investigators who seek to separate the cultural from the genetic and physiological determinants of behavior is indistinguishable from that of instinct theorists. It is based on the same dichotomous reasoning that was shown to be untenable when made explicit in instinct theory (Lehrman, 1953, 1970).

Reification

Of interest, the belief in the duality of culture and biology did not arise as a result of research on behavior; it preceded modern behavior study. It stems from two major sources. The first source is the reification, as separate entities, of our two separate ways of knowing about ourselves: introspection and observation. **Reification** is a potentially fallacious thought process whereby a distinction that actually characterizes our *methods of knowing about* something is treated as a real property of, or *distinction belonging to*, the object of study. Historically, people frequently thought of a person—in fact, one single organism—as a composite of two separate things. The mind came to be that which one knows about through introspection (thinking about oneself) and the body that which one knows about through the senses. The mind-body reification was carried to its greatest extremes in religion and mythology, and even had a firm place in science. In more recent intellectual history, some scientists sought to remove its influence (Edelman, 1992; Johnson, 1987; Klein, 1970).

The second and more modern source of culture-biology dichotomy is the reification of various scientific activities. People talk not of the *activities* of chemists, biologists, and psychologists but of the chemical, biological, or psychological *nature* of things. A split that belongs in fact to our disciplinary conception of science has been visited on the organism. Clearly, distinctions must be made if science is to progress, but scientists must always bear in mind the referents of their categories.

Some discoveries in behavioral biology established an interesting paradox for those who would distinguish cultural from biological aspects of behavior by reifying the activities of scientists. One of the best examples is the research done on the Japanese monkey. An ingenious juvenile monkey learned one day that sweet potatoes are better if they are washed in the ocean; she transmitted this discovery throughout the resident troop. Later, she discovered that she could wash grains of wheat, thrown on the beach by researchers, by dropping them into small pools or streams and waiting for them to rise to the surface. This information was also passed along to others. Both of these novel behavior patterns became part of the folklore of this monkey troop; under the watchful eyes of a research team, mothers passed their new habits on to their offspring, and culture was made (Miyadi, 1964).

Japanese monkey culture is by no means independent of Japanese monkey biology. If the monkeys had not been capable of carrying and manipulating objects with their hands, learning the relation between the washing act and the state of the potato, forming and maintaining close, attentive relations with others, and a host of other activities, potato washing would never have occurred or spread. Furthermore, the methods of incorporating the new pattern into the culture and transmitting it to succeeding generations are highly dependent on the species-typical social relations among this group of monkeys. Thus, young monkeys were the first to learn the new pattern. It was transmitted from them to their mothers, and from mothers to new infants born after the behavioral pattern was invented.

Finally, the changes wrought in the life of the Japanese monkeys as a result of incorporating a new behavior pattern into the life of the entire troop may have far-reaching effects on the biology of these members of the species. For instance, food washing led members of the troop to become more familiar with water. Juveniles now spend a great deal of time swimming and playing in the water, thereby developing new sensorimotor skills. Swimming may lead them to inhabit islands previously inaccessible to them, and swimming and diving have already led them to incorporate marine products into their diet (Kummer, 1971).

Because culture may both affect and be affected by the evolutionary process, it is an appropriate area of study for biologists. From this point of view, the dichotomy between culture and biology is clearly nonsensical. Furthermore, if one's interest is in the *development* of behavior, it may be both artificial and misleading to try to separate effects stemming from cultural and biological sources.

We believe that the reification of culture and biology as separate phenomena has many problems associated with it, not the least of which is that it leads to rejection of biology as irrelevant by those who are interested in the "cultural half" of humans, and to a belief in biological imperatives on the part of those who are interested in the "biological half." We believe with Gould (1991) that, "It would be the most extraordinary happening in all intellectual history if the cardinal theory for understanding the biological origin and construction of our brains and bodies had no insights to offer disciplines that study the social organizations arising from such evolved mental power" (p. 51). A genuine partnership between the social and biological sciences will depend on the ability of psychobiology to build conceptual models of development that avoid the assumptions of culture-biology dualism and promote understanding of the coaction of various levels of organization on the development of psychological abilities.

The Biological Imperative

The fourth problem facing the synthesis of biology and psychology involves a belief about the relationship of biological knowledge to the moral-political sphere of human concerns—a belief in what is known as the **biological imperative**. The biological imperative is firmly rooted in the culture-biology dualism and is based on the belief that biology affects behavior by determining it. That is, the effects of biology are inevitable and unchangeable; they must be taken into account by society and either fostered or removed, but they cannot be made to develop differently.

The realization that humans can be selfish, greedy, dishonest, manipulative, or ruthless did not originate with sociobiology or any other biological theory; nor did the realization that it is very difficult to remove these traits from human social conduct. These human problems are only too apparent. Efforts to deal with them are not helped by the argument that socially negative traits must be accepted as the biological facts of human nature. The tendency to equate negative traits with biological nature has led some to argue that what we ordinarily think of as good behavior must not be: individuals who behave well are really acting according to "selfish" evolutionary motives (see Kitcher, 1985, for a cogent critique).

Biological theory will not resolve social problems. However, biologists can provide additional sources of information to consider when seeking solutions or resolutions to social problems. Although we have asserted that biological information is unhelpful when treated as imperatives, it can be extremely useful as a means of understanding behavioral problems.

Biologists are now in a position to explore the behavior of organisms with a thoroughness never before attempted. As their interest in behavior continues and their technical sophistication grows, there is every reason to believe that the range of behaviors recognized as having biological aspects to their causation will continue to grow. All behavior is biologically based, but only in the sense that it is in principle understandable by biologists. In fact, some biologists are now studying culture; consequently, it makes perfectly good sense to maintain that culture is a biological phenomenon. But to hold that all behavior is biologically based is not to hold that all behavior—or even that any behavior—is inevitable and unchangeable by cultural or psychological techniques, or that it is not dependent on psychological or cultural circumstances for its development.

The biological imperative is used to maintain not only that biology determines behavior but that it determines what is best. Biologically caused behavior is natural, and in the present climate of opinion natural means good, presumably for the individual, the society, and the future of the human species. In contrast, culture is thought to distort the natural and to create unnatural behavior. Of course, culture can artificially accelerate changes in the environment so that biologically based behavior, good at an earlier time, is no longer good. However, if we grant that all behavior, culture included, is biologically based, the biological imperative argument loses much of its impact.

Biological imperatives are usually invoked in discussions of issues about which there are many different opinions and that are emotionally charged. Some issues receiving attention recently are sex differences, preferred sex partners, child abuse, and aggression. We would like to point out two obvious fallacies in the biological imperative argument: that of value-based scientific arguments and the naturalistic fallacy.

The Fallacy of Value-Based Scientific Arguments

Value-based arguments are frequently mixed up in scientific ones. The chain of thought that runs from biologically caused to natural to good can, of course, proceed in the opposite direction, especially given the extensive diversity of biological phenomena. If, for example, one favors an arrangement wherein a mother cares for her child for the first few years of life, one has only to look to find biological causes for this arrangement. To use these biological causes to argue against any alternative arrangement is to avoid the debate about the kind of children we wish to raise or about the roles of men and women in society.

Consider the study of mother-infant behavior in monkeys. A rhesus macaque is seriously disturbed by being separated from its mother, and this disturbance continues to affect its development for a long time after they are reunited (Spencer-Booth & Hinde, 1967). Bowlby (1969) reported that when human infants in England and the United States are separated from their mothers, they display disturbances in ways that seem similar to those of the rhesus monkey. This disturbance in infancy may also affect adult social relations. By integrating information from comparative ethology (the naturalistic study of animal behavior), evolutionary theory, and research on the immaturity and dependency of the human infant, Bowlby proposed an evolutionary theory of human caregiving and development that became widely accepted (Goldberg, 1991). The essence of Bowlby's theory was as follows:

1. The human infant requires continuous care and contact with an adult that can be satisfied by only one caregiver—the mother.

2. The infant forms her or his first primary social relationship with the caregiver, and this relationship is the foundation for all subsequent social relationships.

3. The infant's behaviors have been shaped by evolution to elicit care from the appropriate caregiver.

4. The mother is especially adapted to respond appropriately to the care-eliciting behaviors of the infant.

5. During the period from birth to at least two years (possibly four to five years) of age, it is especially important for the infant's social and emotional development to remain in close physical contact with the mother.

The work of Konner (1977) with the !Kung, an African culture of savannah-dwelling hunter-gathers, revealed infant-care practices similar to those supposed to have been characteristic of the human species and our evolutionary ancestors before the advent of agriculture. The !Kung infant is in contact with the mother more than 70% of the time during the first year and in contact with someone else for the remaining time. The infant is also nursed frequently, in short sessions, often four times an hour. Maternal caregiving is affectionate, and the infant easily progresses from a primary maternal relationship to wider social relationships in the troop.

It is often concluded from Bowlby's theory, the observations of the !Kung, and studies of monkeys that the human infant should be provided with continuous maternal care from birth through the second year. It is believed to be a biological necessity for a human mother to spend her time taking care of her infant. It is thus believed that cultural practices should not be allowed to interfere with this pattern of caregiving.

However, consider the observation that different species of macaque monkeys display striking differences in the ease with which a baby can make contact with an adult other than its mother (Kaufman, 1974). For example, when its mother is removed from the troop, the infant pigtail macaque is not able to make contact with another adult and remains squealing and rocking alone in a corner. Bonnet macaque young, in contrast, are able to make contact with other adults when separated from their mothers. Indeed, they receive continuous comfort from all members of the troop. Thus, the harmful effects of mother-infant separation are not present in bonnet macaque monkeys.

Mother-infant separation in England or the United States often occurs when there is no extended family and when it does not seem self-evident that the father ought to stay home from work to care for the child. Early in the twentieth century, Margaret Mead (1928) reported that on one of the islands of Samoa the family is extended such that children move readily from one set of adults to another in a network of warm interpersonal relationships wider than that included in the Western nuclear family. Tronick, Winn, and Morelli (1985) reported a similar pattern in the Efé, a pygmy population of African forest-dwelling hunter-gatherers.

Efé infants "during the first 6 months of life and to a lesser extent throughout the following year and a half experience multiple caretaking, including nursing by women other than the mother" (Tronick et al., 1985, p. 305). Of related interest, the Efé are in contact for part of their yearly migratory moves with a nonmigratory slash-and-burn agricultural population called Walese. The Walese also employ a pattern of several caregivers during the infant's first few months. Tronick et al. identified the benefits that the infant and population obtained from this pattern. The biological character of human caregiving contains a broad range of options with flexibility of selection within that range. "For humans, what we must come to see is that the environment, particularly the social-cultural environment, is the selective force within that range" (p. 318).

In light of the differences in social organization among monkey species and among human cultures, the separation data for the rhesus monkey and the widely accepted notions about the biological nature of human caregiving take on a different appearance. Familiarity with the differences and similarities among the social organizations of monkeys and of human cultures makes it possible to conclude that "separation from a parent-figure is extremely distressing, and has important after-effects, in the absence of a social setting that makes amelioration possible" (Lehrman, 1974, p. 194). Any other conclusions about the biological nature of the mother-infant relationship in humans would reflect social prejudice rather than scientific consideration.

According to Tronick et al. (1985), "child-care practices are really decisions about cultural values: about what we want our children to become"
(p. 294). "Our current views of the early mother-child and father-child
relationships have been couched in a limited viewpoint rather than in a
broadly based biological perspective that includes culture as the most important human adaptation. When we want fathers at the birth of infants, it
has nothing to do with physiological constraints or primate evolution ...
their presence is a question of cultural choices about the kind of people we
want fathers to become ..." (p. 318).

The Naturalistic Fallacy

That human mother-infant relationships as they are found in the Western
nuclear family may have biological causes is beside the point, for one can
just as readily find biological causes for alternative relationships. For example, several nursing caregivers may serve the biological functions of ensuring
adequate milk and enhanced immune support for the Efé infants (Tronick
et al., 1985). A biological imperative argument that is used to support existing arrangements commits the **naturalistic fallacy**: it asserts that what
exists and is familiar is natural, and what is new and different is unnatural.

Social pluralism is not just an invention of human culture. As field studies
of animal societies have increased, so has our appreciation of the variability
in social arrangements that occurs within species (Lott, 1984). This variability is marked among some of the primate species (Rowell, 1972; Fedigan,
1982), but it is also present in such distantly related species as 13-line ground
squirrels (Schwagmeyer, 1990) and hyenas (Kruuk, 1972). Rowell (1972)
described dramatic differences between the social organization of common
baboons living on the open savannah and those living in forests. The dominance relationships and aggressive interactions among males are sufficiently
striking and frequent to have convinced observers of savannah-dwelling
baboons that they are the cornerstone of baboon society, yet these same
interactions are virtually nonexistent among forest-dwelling members of
the same species.

Cotton-top tamarins, a small New World monkey, live in an extended
family unit in which both parents and their older, nonreproducing offspring
cooperatively care for infants, typically born as twins. In many reports, mo-
nogamous pair bonds are formed between the reproducing adults in a family
group, but polyandrous relationships of a female with more than one male
have also been recorded (Snowdon, 1990). Observations such as these create difficulties for those who would argue from knowledge of the natural to
imperatives about the appropriate. There is no basis, other than prior con-
victions, to decide which variant produced in nature is truly natural and
which are distortions. The pluralism in what "is" undercuts the argument
from is to ought that lies at the heart of the naturalistic fallacy (see box 2.2).

Box 2.2   How Aggressive Are Primates?

In the older popular and scientific literature, nonhuman primates were characterized as rather bloodthirsty brutes. This reputation grew out of preconceptions buttressed by observations of fighting, even killing, among captive groups. A different picture emerged from the past three decades of field studies. Cooperation and cohesion are major features of daily group life among natural groups of monkeys and apes. Many concluded that the high level of aggression reported in earlier zoo studies was an aberration caused by placing strangers together in confined quarters (Southwick, 1972), but others maintained that aggression, even if rarely expressed, is a product of natural selection and an integral part of the fabric of primate societies.

The debate centers on two major issues: adult dominance interactions (Rowell, 1972) and infanticide (Hrdy, 1977; Curtin & Dolhinow, 1978). Some observed that dominance relationships formed through winning and losing aggressive encounters have the consequence of maintaining a reasonably peaceful society by inhibiting aggressive tendencies among subordinates. Once the social order is in place, threats and other signals replace overt fights, which become infrequent and truncated in expression. This idea fit with initial studies of common baboons living on the open savannah of Africa. These troops had a clear, dominance-based hierarchy among the adult males, with frequent exchanges of threats and subordinate responses. But later studies of the same species living in more forested regions found no evidence of aggressive dominance hierarchies, even though the baboons were organized into coherent troops. Are baboons inherently aggressive, with contextual factors (forest living) suppressing aggressive expression, or is aggression a characteristic that emerges when the animals interact in particular contexts?

Similar questions can be asked of Hanuman langurs, Asian monkeys that live peacefully in troops of several adult males and females and their immature offspring in some regions. In other regions, each troop has only one adult male, with extra adult males forming groups that live on the outskirts. When these males invade an established troop, high levels of fighting ensue, and the resident male may be defeated and replaced by one of the invaders. Is the violent aggressiveness of the invading males an inherent characteristic, shaped by natural selection, or has it emerged from the stresses and strains of recent changes in habitat caused by human agriculture?

Hanuman langur aggression takes on an added dimension because infants are sometimes killed by canine bites inflicted by males during takeovers. Hrdy noted that a male who successfully takes over a troop and kills resident infants will increase his reproductive success, because the mothers that lose infants will resume estrous cycling more rapidly and become available to mate with him. Infanticide, she stated, is an adaptive strategy of these males. Critics countered that infanticide is a random side effect of the general battleground mayhem that is itself a result of recent peculiarities of the living conditions, not a product of natural selection.

The biological imperative view of biological causation also fails to take into account the fact that biologists themselves engage in qualitatively different activities; the phrase biological cause may refer to several radically different things. This view prevents the understanding of the development of behavior as it asserts that any biological cause of behavior has the same implications for development: the development is inevitable, with only one appropriate outcome!

Summary

In this chapter we identified some of the conceptual positions that have hindered the synthesis of the psychological and biological perspectives. We showed that a hierarchical conception of science and reductionist endeavors do not necessarily preclude an integration of biology and psychology that retains the basic integrity of each. However, the conceptual positions characterized by culture-biology dualism and the biological imperative lead to modes of approaching phenomena that increase confusion and foster the pursuit of answers to pseudoproblems. In the next chapter we present an orientation to the study of behavior and its development that minimizes these difficulties.

3 The Beginnings of a Resolution: A Modern Synthesis

I am convinced there is another way to think, and that this other way, though it requires reworking not only our ideas about genes and environment but quite a bit besides, gives us more and less than the old way. It gives more clarity, more coherence, more consistency and a different way to interpret data; in addition it offers the means for synthesizing the concepts and methods of evolutionary biologists and developmentalists. . . . It gives less, however, in the way of metaphysical guidance on fundamental truth, fewer conclusions about what is inherently desirable, healthy, natural, or inevitable, and this accounts for a good deal of the resistance it has met.
—S. Oyama (1985, p. 9)

In this chapter we address the semantic and conceptual confusions inherent in the concept "innate." We identify and distinguish the different kinds of questions that may be posed concerning any behavioral or psychological event. Then we examine an approach to the study of development that provides for the union of psychology and biology while maintaining the intellectual integrity of both.

One problem that lies at the root of all four of the philosophical positions described in chapter 2 (hierarchy of science, reductionism, culture-biology dualism, biological imperative) is the confusion between scientific activity and nature itself. It is good to remember that all products of scientific activity are symbolic abstractions from nature, based on categories that may be formed differently at different times and by different investigators. However, this does not mean that science is either simply a subjective account or a type of game. The independent replicability of scientific investigation ensures that "reality" constrains the character of the symbolic abstractions that may be applied to nature.

Nevertheless, a multitude of different questions can be asked, and a multitude of different answers can be devised, about the same event. Whether or not a particular answer is acceptable will depend not on some absolute truth or falsity but primarily on whether it is addressed to the interests and aims of the questioner. For example, if you were to ask "Why did you write this book?" and we were to answer in terms of the neuromuscular apparatus that allows coordination among hand, eye, and brain, you would undoubtedly feel that your question had been avoided. On the other hand, an answer in terms of our purposes and intentions would be appropriate, even if not complete or accurate enough to be entirely satisfactory to everyone. There are, of course, further criteria by which an answer is judged, such as the completeness with which it accounts for a phenomenon and its consistency with other knowledge (see Kaplan, 1964).

As we stated earlier, disciplines are distinguishable from each other by virtue of the fact that they look at nature differently—they have specific interests, aims, methods, and techniques. To a lesser degree, any two individual scientists are also distinguishable in this way. Even a single scientist can hold to different interests and aims at different times or when using different research techniques. This diversity provides the excitement of scientific investigation. It also entails some dangers, and these become especially apparent when scientists from different disciplines become interested in the same or similar phenomena. Frequently, the questions posed in the different disciplines are not phrased clearly enough to allow one to know whether or not the answers provided are appropriate. Under these circumstances, arguments—sometimes very extended and divisive ones—may be waged over the correctness of what seem to be two alternative answers to the same question. If these two "answers" really belong to two quite distinct questions, clearly, the argument will not be resolved until the questions themselves are separated, examined, and clarified.

As you might imagine, many such misdirected arguments have marred the interface of biology and psychology. Perhaps the most dramatic and prevalent is the prolonged conflict regarding whether behavioral development is innately or environmentally determined. The "official view" (as it was labeled by Johnston, 1987) is that the controversy is resolved. However, many (Gollin, Stahl, & Morgan, 1989; Johnston, 1985, 1987; Oyama, 1991) conclude that the conceptual inadequacies inherent in the nature-nurture controversy are still prevalent, even among those with an official commitment to their rejection.

The Concept of Innateness

Lehrman (1970) argued that the controversy over innate versus acquired reflects both a *semantic* confusion concerning the word **innate** and a *conceptual* confusion about the relative importance of different kinds of behavioral investigation. These confusions continue to threaten the clarity of interdisciplinary work (Oyama, 1985, 1991) and deserve our attention.

The Semantic Confusion

The word innate has often been used in theorizing about behavioral development in humans and other species. In this sense, it refers to concepts of *developmental fixity.* Innate behavioral patterns are presumed to develop in the absence of any significant influence from the environment. Thus, environmental variation is thought to be irrelevant to the organization of innate behavior, which has a fixed developmental course and terminus. Support for this idea is usually sought in genetic studies. However, when geneticists say that a behavior pattern is innate, they mean simply that they can make a prediction about the distribution of the pattern among members of an offspring population if given knowledge about the distribution of the behavior in the parental population and about who mates with whom. In the geneticists' use of the word, nothing is implied about the role of the environment during the development of the pattern or about the consequences of changing environmental circumstances for the distribution of the pattern in the offspring population (see chapter 5 for a more complete discussion).

In the study of human psychological development, the notion of innate is usually based on a distinction between learned and unlearned behavior and is supported by "argument from precocity" (Fischer & Bidell, 1992). That is, if a behavior that is linked to a specific psychological character or ability is found at a very early age, then the character must be innate. The concept seems especially relevant if the age of appearance is earlier than would be expected if teaching or training were involved in the acquisition of the ability.

Fischer and Bidell note that modern research techniques reveal a wide variety of cognitive, social, and emotional abilities in very young humans. Using ingenious methods, behavioral indicators were identified in very young infants and children. These indicators are believed to represent such complex psychological characteristics as **intentionality**, self-other distinction, emotional sophistication (e.g., empathy, sympathy, deception), and intellectual skill (e.g., ontological concepts of objects, number, natural categories), among others. According to these authors, young infants and children may be capable of fairly complex behavior only under limited circumstances. When the behavior is considered together with other observations in other contexts, the limitations of the initial capacity become evident. They propose that both task complexity and contextual support powerfully affect the age of emergence of any particular ability. Therefore, it is misleading to find a precocious behavior using clever methods and then treat it as though it were a stable capacity independent of the special context used to make it occur.

The ingenuity required to promote the expression of the behavior through appropriately selected task characteristics and contextual support conditions shows that the capacity represents an early step in a developmental pathway for the young child. Developmental progress means that the expression of the ability eventually will not be so dependent on a particular ingenious context. The capacities revealed at young ages only provide starting points that constrain and channel what is possible in development.

Fisher and Bidell (1992) propose that psychological characteristics develop through a sequence involving increasingly organized forms and decreasingly supportive contexts. Thus, any psychological characteristic must be specified by information about where it came from, what it is leading to, and what concurrent skills are connected with it. Neither precocity nor inheritance is an argument for using a notion of innate to explain the behavior of humans or any other species (box 3.1).

The Conceptual Confusion

A multitude of possible variables might be investigated to arrive at an explanation of behavior. Scientists approach these possibilities with interests that lead them to select some variables as worthy of study and to ignore the remainder. There is nothing "wrong" with scientists allowing their interests to affect what they choose to evaluate. It is a necessary step. Not all variables are appropriate to all questions, and it is impossible for an individual to study everything. However, a problem arises when a variable that is judged, perhaps rightly, to be unimportant in one context is assumed to be unimportant in others. This heuristic is an essential aspect of most human functioning, and it is exceedingly cumbersome to have to reconsider and reevaluate each previously unimportant variable for each new situation. However, this common heuristic can result in a conceptual confusion when investigators having one kind of guiding interest devise explanations for phenomena that belong to a different realm of interest.

Conceptual confusions of this nature are particularly apparent when scientists with interests in the functions of behavior devise explanations of developmental phenomena. If an investigator is interested mainly in the functional question of how a pattern of behavior enables an organism to achieve something important for its survival or reproduction, then previous developmental events will be perceived as leading to the occurrence of the behavior. After all, performance of that behavior is vital.

Looking backward from this functional end point, it is easy to view development as a predetermined event, involving the influence of a very limited number of factors operating in a fairly direct developmental pathway. Developmental precursors of the behavior may be recognized only if they have a clear formal or functional resemblance to the fully functional behavior of interest. Because environmental factors have the potential to vary and hence seem unreliable, they may be dismissed as unlikely contributors to the development of behavioral patterns that have great functional significance to the organism. Therefore, the contributions of environmental variables to the development of functionally significant behavioral characteristics are often unstudied.

If, on the other hand, an investigator is interested primarily in ascertaining the ontogenetic causes of some behavior, the behavior will be perceived

Box 3.1   Intentionality in Human Newborn Infants

Intentionality, although difficult to define (Vedeler, 1991), is inferred when someone engages reliably in notable behavioral adjustments *in anticipation of the consequence of some other behavioral action.* That is, if you opened your mouth *before* a juice glass touched your lips, we might infer that you intended to bring the glass to your mouth to drink the juice.

Butterworth (1986) reported that infants were capable of bringing their hands to their mouths just a few hours after birth. Moreover, hand-in-mouth is a common pattern of fetal behavior (Birnholz, 1988; Hepper, Shahidullah, & White, 1991). Much older infants appear to use the action as a means of self-comforting. Finding no simple, reflex explanation, Butterworth raised the question of whether this newborn behavior was intentional, like the anticipatory mouth opening for drinking juice.

Most newborn arm movements fail to contact the body or face, and when they do contact the face, they usually do not contact the mouth. Nevertheless, Butterworth observed instances in which the hand moved "immediately in the direction of the mouth" (1986, p. 28). He also noted that the mouth is more likely to be open immediately before and during an arm movement that ends with the hand in the mouth than when it does not. The apparent directionality and anticipatory quality of some movements led Butterworth to conclude that the newborn's hand-to-mouth movements are often intentional. He also concluded that intentionality has to be an innate aspect of human behavior because it is present at birth.

Other studies (Hopkins, Lems, Janssen, & Butterworth, 1987; Schwartz & Michel, 1992) found little evidence of intentionality in the actions. The hand of a newborn is more likely to enter an open than a closed mouth, but just as likely to contact a closed mouth as an open one. Hand-to-mouth action is very much dependent on posture, occurring more often when newborns lie on their backs than when they sit in someone's lap. Head orientation is also important. If the head is turned to one side, the hand on that side is likely to enter the mouth; if the head is in midline, the hand seldom enters the mouth. Therefore, the likelihood of newborn hand movements coalescing into hand-to-mouth actions seems to depend on the contextual constraints created by posture (supine), orientation of the head (turned to one side), and flexion patterns of the arms (the arm on the side to which the face is turned tends to be more active).

These observations do not negate either the possibility that older infants have intentional hand-to-mouth movements, or the possibility that newborn hand-to-mouth actions are affected by prenatal hand-in-mouth experience. Rather, they suggest that for the newborn, these acts are steps in the development of hand-to-mouth actions that become increasingly more complex while requiring less contextual support. At each developmental step, it is useful to identify prerequisites (conditions necessary for its occurrence), precursors (preceding indicators or predecessors), and simpler versions of intentionality.

Intentionality is likely to refer initially to aspects of specific actions and skills. Later in development, it is likely to be used in reference to abilities with a higher level of behavioral complexity and greater independence of contextual support. Eventually, intentionality refers to patterns that cross or link a wide range of skills. Only at this point does it appropriately characterize a "mental representation of a state of affairs which is yet to be realized"

> (Vedeler, 1991, p. 432). If we are to understand intentionality, systematic developmental research must be used to identify prerequisites, precursors, and simpler manifestations of the construct. The "innate" label is unhelpful, because it usually directs attention only to genes, short-circuiting inquiry into other prerequisites as well as the important precursors and simpler forms.

as arising from the preceding developmental events. The ontogenetic perspective inclines one to look forward from a stage when the behavior is not present. With this perspective, one is led to take stock of the raw materials for further development—what is available within the organism as well as the range of environmental stimuli that surround it. Once this attitude is adopted, precursors may be recognized that have neither formal nor functional resemblance to behavioral patterns that appear later in development.

From the ontogenetic perspective, the range of factors hypothesized and investigated as potential contributors to further development is likely to be rather large and heterogeneous. Moreover, a behavioral characteristic may develop through numerous, and possibly circuitous, pathways. Any regularities in the pattern of environmental conditions of stimulation may be identified as reliable resources for development even of the species-typical behavior that is necessary for survival.

Consider, for example, the observation that newly hatched laughing gull chicks will approach and peck the parent's beak in response to the sound of the parent's croon call. The investigator interested in the functional consequences of behavior knows that if the chicks do not respond appropriately to the croon call, their chances of survival will be reduced. The parent uses this call to attract the chicks, so that they will approach and peck the parent's bill, thereby stimulating the regurgitation of the food on which they feed. Because of the vital importance of this response to the croon call, it might be said that laughing gull chicks are designed with the ability to make the response. Indeed, even embryos apparently can discriminate the croon call from other adult calls two days before hatching. This early expression of differential responsiveness may be cited as evidence of an adapted design, ensuring that appropriate approach behavior will be present and functional the first time that a parent croons before feeding its chicks.

By taking a more causal ontogenetic perspective, Impekoven and Gold (1973) showed that the ability to respond appropriately to the croon call is developmentally dependent on the chicks having heard the call before they hatch. The parent gull frequently makes croonlike calls while resettling on its eggs during incubation. Resettling involves shifting the position and orientation of the eggs, thereby providing vestibular stimulation to accompany the auditory stimulation. Several days before the eggs hatch, the parent's croonlike calls tend to increase the activity of the embryo, and, once the ability to vocalize develops, they increase its peeping. The activity and peeping inside the eggs in turn stimulate the parent to make more resettling movements and, hence, more calls. Chicks hatched in incubators do not show the typical responses to crooning but rather crouch or try to hide. Therefore, prehatching exposure to parental calls is a prerequisite for later filial responses vital for the survival of the young.

Those interested in functional questions would be inclined to investigate the ability of gull chicks to approach croon calls at the time when this ability is first required. If they did so, they would find that the ability is in place, functioning properly. It takes an interest in development to motivate one to study the interaction of parents and their embryos during resettling episodes, because such interaction has no direct and obvious relation to feeding or even to the major function of incubation, thermoregulation.

An egg-bound embryo cannot, of course, perform approach behavior, but any differential responses observed from them might be categorized by those with functional interests as incipient approaches to a feeding parent. The learning that enters into the developmental process might be seen as specially designed or adapted to support the specific survival-related behavior of the hatchling. Those with ontogenetic interests, in contrast, are more likely to see the similarity between the behavior of the embryonic gull and that of other young organisms in like circumstances. That is, the formation of attractions to environmental stimuli that happen to be paired with neurobehavioral activation may be widespread among older embryos and young neonates in birds and mammals (Johanson & Terry, 1988). Newborn rats, for example, become attracted to odors that they initially found aversive, when the odors are paired with vigorous tactile stimulation, such as might be encountered during maternal licking and handling (Pedersen, Williams, & Blass, 1982).

The gull chick example illustrates the importance of recognizing how research interests can shape attitudes toward developmental phenomena. It is a conceptual confusion to assume that, because of the beautiful, functional fit between the croon calls of a feeding parent and the approach and begging of its chicks, this specificity results from a developmental design that is equally specific. However, such confusion does not necessarily follow from adopting a functional perspective. The pursuit of functional questions is important for identifying those features of behavior that have important consequences in the lives of animals. It identifies what development can accomplish. One must, however, switch to a causal perspective to find out how it has been accomplished.

Keeping Questions Distinct

The precise specification of questions is a crucial preliminary step in the scientific process, and the consequences can be very disruptive when this step is overlooked. With respect to behavior, Tinbergen (1963a) noted that four general kinds of questions may be asked: "that of *causation*, that of *survival value*, ... that of *evolution* ... [and] that of *ontogeny*" (p. 411; original emphasis). He suggested that many of the controversies in the study of animal behavior have their roots in confusing one type of question with a qualitatively different one. To help eliminate this confusion, he proposed that each of the four questions should be examined separately from the others and that they should receive equal attention. Then, the answers provided for each question could be integrated without threatening the integrity of each. This proposal was widely adopted by both ethologists (e.g., Hinde, 1982) and comparative psychologists (e.g., Dewsbury, 1990). It has proved useful both as a means of achieving explanatory clarity by starting with clear questions, and as a framework for generating richer explanations of behavior by interrelating ideas drawn from four different perspectives.

Tinbergen's four questions can be grouped into two broad categories: those of function and those of causation. Functional questions require answers in terms of the effects of behavior. Causative questions require answers in terms of the antecedent conditions of the behavior. Because each question is distinct, an answer to any one of them will not be an answer to any of the others. As you will see, this rather subtle point has sometimes not been grasped by even the best of investigators. However, growing numbers of investigators routinely use two or more of the questions in their research programs, and do so appropriately and felicitously.

Functional Questions

Functions, or the effects of behavior, can often be observed in individuals behaving in the here and now. Soon after its eggs hatch, a black-headed gull will get up from the nest, pick up the broken eggshells in its beak, fly or walk some distance from the nest, and drop the shells (figure 3.1). This behavior serves the function for the individual gull of getting eggshells out of the nest. We usually acknowledge this functional aspect of behavior by the manner in which we label it. Instead of using a label describing the entire sequence of movement patterns involved, we select one that describes the end result; in this case, we speak of eggshell removal regardless of whether the gull walks, runs, flies, or hires a van.

Functional questions can be divided into two distinct types (Beer, 1973). Function in the sense of the end accomplished by an individual's act—**biological function**—does not mean the same thing as function in terms of contribution to survival and perpetuation in future generations. This second

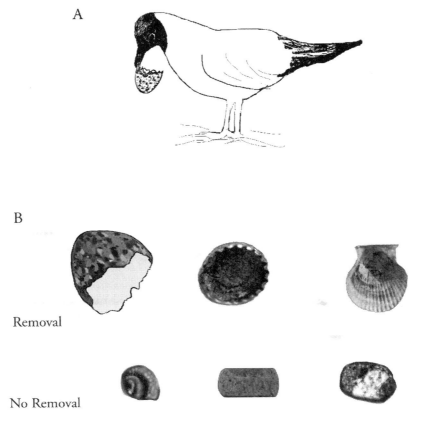

Figure 3.1   The proximate causation of eggshell removal by the black-headed gull includes the physical stimuli from the broken shell and the responsiveness of the parent gull to the stimuli. (A) A black-headed gull carrying an egg shell. (B) Some stimuli that elicit or fail to elicit removal (redrawn from Tinbergen et al., 1962).

type of function refers to evolutionary **fitness**, measured in terms of its contribution to individual survival and successful reproduction. This distinction is an important one, because it is only through differential survival and reproduction that natural selection can act on behavior. The term **adaptation** has been used to refer to both types of functions.

Biologists must describe and manipulate quite different things when answering the two types of functional questions, despite the fact that the terms function and adaptation may be used to designate the subject of interest in both types of investigation. To determine that the biological function of the black-headed gull's behavior is eggshell removal, one has only to observe systematically the relationship between the behavior and the immediate end it achieves; that is, the removal of the eggshell from the nest. However, to determine the contribution of eggshell removal to fitness, Tinbergen and associates had to investigate the relationships among the presence of eggshells, their removal, and survival of viable offspring (Tinbergen et al, 1962).

They found that the presence of a broken eggshell, with its conspicuous white interior, helps predators locate otherwise camouflaged nests. Thus, removing the eggshells makes it more difficult for predators to find black-headed gull nests.

Hence, eggshell removal increases fitness of birds that perform the behavior because it reduces the probability that their newly hatched chicks will be eaten by aerial predators (Tinbergen, 1965). Or, to put it another way, gulls that did not remove eggshells left fewer offspring in each generation than those that did, and became progressively rarer in the population. Of course, fitness would have been the same for birds that buried or ate shells, or produced eggs with camouflaged interiors. Natural selection concerns only the outcome of the behavior, not the behavior itself.

It is the organism that determines the actual object of natural selection. For example, from a very large population of fruit flies, several unrelated lines may be bred for large wings (Lewontin, 1982). As a result of such artificial selection, wing size will increase. However, the wing size will be larger in flies in some lines because of an increase in cell size, in other lines because of an increase in cell number, and in still other lines because of an increase in both size and number of cells. It is the organism that interprets selection, converting selection for wing size into selection for cell size and/ or number. Thus, the same function may be achieved by quite different mechanisms.

As Lewontin (1982) remarks, natural selection may be for cold resistance, "but different species have, in the course of their evolution, converted this pressure into selection for fur (the polar bear), selection for body fat (the seal), or selection for enough brains and skill to wear the bear's fur and eat the seal's fat (the Eskimo)" (p. 159). And, of course, a single mechanism can subserve more than one function.

Careful correlational and experimental methods for investigating the evolutionary function (fitness) of behavior were developed within the zoological tradition of ethology, particularly by Tinbergen and his students. These methods were expanded recently by behavioral ecologists and sociobiologists to include empirical tests of predictions from models. Quantitative models, which were drawn primarily from game theory and microeconomics, are employed to predict how an individual that is adapted to maximize its evolutionary fitness in a particular context might behave (Maynard Smith, 1982). Observational research is then conducted to determine the degree to which real animals match predictions. Nevertheless, identification of evolutionary fitness will ultimately depend on clever and careful experimental investigation.

In an illuminating anecdote, Tinbergen (1965) reported that a distinguished physiologist commented privately that he thought the study of evolutionary fitness was somewhat irrelevant since "no biologist had any doubts about the correctness of selection theory" (p. 538). However, failure to investigate evolutionary processes would be "comparable to resting content with the general statement that life processes are ultimately based on molecular processes, and refraining from concrete biochemical and biophysical analysis" (p. 538). Often we are mistaken in our assumptions about evolutionary fitness. Only systematic investigation can elucidate the precise action of natural selection and identify its relation to other processes governing the development and expression of the characteristics of different species of animals.

Evolutionary function is inherently difficult to study. Despite their usefulness, all of the methods that have been developed to that end are subject to sharp limitations (Hailman, 1982; Kitcher, 1985). Even when done with circumspection, such investigations into the fitness of behavior do not address causal concerns. They direct attention toward the transgenerational consequences of an action, not to its causes. Furthermore, they require one to study distributions of traits in groups and changes in groups over generational time, and not the mechanisms that underlie the expression of these traits in individuals.

Psychologists, like physiologists, however, are interested in individuals and events that are confined to an individual's lifetime. The phenomenon that so intrigued the early functionalists and behaviorists (traceable to the influence of physiologists such as Loeb and Jennings) was the fact that behavior is regulatory. That is, behavior can change or be modified to fit the exigencies of an environment in flux, thus allowing individuals to adjust as circumstances require. When psychologists use such terms as function and adaptive, they usually have in mind biological function, or the end accomplished for an individual by its own individual action.

Frequently, fitness is assumed simply on the basis of information about biological function of the behavior. It is reasoned that an animal would not have behaved as it did unless its behavior were relevant to its fitness (survival and reproduction) in the evolutionary sense. Although this inference may often be correct, it is not necessarily so. Some behaviors are neutral with regard to natural selection, and many reflect developmental compromises. In the latter, the behavior may not be the "best" solution to a problem of selection; rather it represents a form consistent with other developmental characteristics of the individual (chapter 4). Thus, rigorous empirical support is required before the conclusion is drawn that some behavioral pattern has evolved because of its contribution to fitness.

Unfortunately, failure to distinguish between these two kinds of functional questions prevails and is particularly noticeable in many of the popular discussions of the role of evolution in human behavior (e.g., Konner, 1982; Lumsden & Wilson, 1981; Wilson, 1978). Consider, for example, the proposal that men are typically better than women on spatial tasks because spatial skills are important for hunting. Anthropological evidence suggests that men were more likely than women to be hunters during the course of human evolution. Greater success in hunting does indeed follow from greater proficiency in such spatial tasks as maneuvering with respect to prey and accurate throwing of weapons. Thus, hunting is a biological function of spatial ability, and this function is observed more often in men than in women.

This is a descriptive statement based on observing how men and women used their time, the consequences of poorly or accurately aimed rocks, and so forth. It is quite another matter to argue that spatial ability evolved in men as a result of natural selection for better hunters. Each part of this two-fold statement—that spatial ability evolved through selection acting on hunting, and that sex differences in spatial ability resulted from differential selection on the two sexes—requires empirical support gathered through elimination of alternative explanations. One can hypothesize other selection pressures that might have led to improved spatial skills, and one can hypothesize alternatives to natural selection (see chapter 4) to account either for the improvement in spatial skills or for sex differences in manifested spatial ability. It is poor science to rely on the persuasiveness of an intuitively appealing argument rather than to perform careful empirical test of alternative hypotheses.

Function as Separate from Causation

Perhaps even more damaging than the confusion of the two meanings of function is the confusion of causation with function. For example, the black-headed gull does not appreciate the fact that broken shells aid predators in finding their eggs and young. A gull may, on occasion, pick up an eggshell, fly about with it, and then drop it near its own or a neighbor's nest, thereby weakening the antipredator consequence of the behavior. Although eggshell removal may have a goal and a purpose, it is not intentional in the common meaning of that term (figure 3.2).

The early interest in the functional consequences of behavior for the individual led to the recognition that an animal, when prevented from achieving the usual immediate goal or function of a behavior, will change its behavior such that the original goal or function is achieved. A gull confronted with a conspicuous but unmovable small object in its nest will, for example, resort to covering the object with nesting material when attempts at removal fail.

Moreover, any behavior that results in a rapid and efficient attainment of a goal will be exhibited whenever the circumstances appropriate to that function are present. Thus, an animal will exhibit a change in behavior when that change results in the attainment of some necessary commodity, such as food. Behavior frequently has effects that make functional sense to the person observing the behavior. Therefore, in many instances within psychology researchers have looked to function for causative explanations. A familiar example is the suggestion that an animal that learns to perform a task to get food is impelled to do so by a hunger drive.

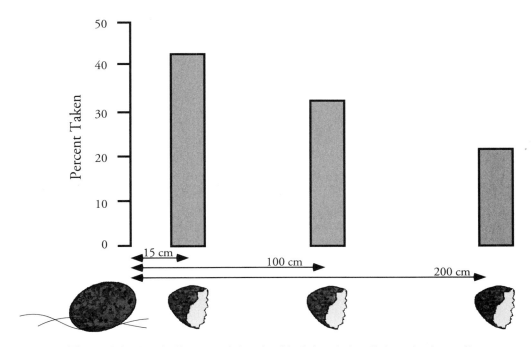

Figure 3.2 Eggshell removal by the black-headed gull has the immediate consequence of removing the broken shell from the nest, which in turn has several biological functions, including preserving the camouflage of the remaining eggs and newly hatched chicks. Tinbergen's experiments show that preserving camouflage contributes to evolutionary fitness, because the danger from aerial predators is greater the closer eggshells are placed to intact, camouflaged eggs (redrawn from Tinbergen, 1963b).

Whether immediate biological function or evolutionary fitness is used to generate a causal explanation, one runs the risk of confusing functional and causal questions. This confusion often takes the form of purposive or **teleological** thought. The instinct theory once espoused by McDougall (1926/1973) is a clear example of the problem with this approach, because it is explicitly teleological. According to this doctrine, an animal's behavior looks sensible and purposive because the ends of the acts are somehow "in" the organism from the outset: the behavior is *caused* by its purpose. Although McDougall's blatant teleology was attacked and discarded on the grounds that it was pseudoexplanatory, other more subtle forms of the argument, such as various drive theories, have survived.

Animals are not driven, organized, energized, or directed by their motivations. When an animal changes its behavior according to a change in external circumstances, we acknowledge that the external change caused the behavioral change. However, the external change initiates processes within the animal that are part of the causal network. Of course, animals also change their behavior when there is no change in the external situation. In such events, the cause of change must obviously be within the animal. However, the relevant internal processes may themselves have been initiated originally by external stimuli. Nevertheless, motivation may be described as a class of reversible processes internal to the individual that are responsible for changes in behavior when there is no concurrent change in circumstances. Defined in this manner, the functional aspect of motivation does not assume causal efficacy.

Causal Questions

Tinbergen's (1963a) causal questions can be divided into three types: proximate causation, phylogenetic (historical) causation, and ontogenetic causation. All three types of **causation** concern events and elements that are antecedent to the behavior under study. One of the major dimensions separating them is the length of time taken into account.

Proximate Causation

At the level of the individual and on a short time scale there is causation equivalent to what we usually mean when we speak of causes—immediate or proximate causation. The immediate causes of behavior are those antecedent events that contribute to the performance and organization of a behavioral pattern. Some of these events are external and some internal to the organism. For example, the black-headed gull removes eggshells because the shells possess certain stimulative properties, a broken contour and contrasting interior, and because the gull is in a particular reproductive condition that is potentially describable in terms of hormone levels and neural processes. The study of immediate causation is the familiar activity of most of psychology and physiology.

Phylogenetic Causation

This type of causative question covers a much longer time span. Historical or phylogenetic causation may be traced back over several generations. From the biologist's point of view, the questions are about evolution. What were the phylogenetic precursors of this behavior? What was the original characteristic that was changed, perhaps over a great many generations, into the present form?

   Because behavior leaves few clues in fossils, phylogenetic questions are some of the most difficult to answer. Contemporary species must be studied and compared so as to reconstruct a probable picture of their most recent and progressively more remote common ancestors (e.g. Lorenz 1971a). Several methods have been suggested as providing plausible answers to phylogenetic questions about behavior, but all of them have severe conceptual weaknesses (Atz, 1970). Nevertheless, plausible arguments that have been formed provide some intriguing notions about the evolution of behavior.

For example, it is believed that many courtship and other communication patterns evolved through a process called *ritualization* out of patterns more closely tied to individual survival. Part of the courtship behavior of a male mallard duck consists of his pointing his bill in a highly stereotyped fashion at a conspicuous feather on his wing. Examination of the behavior patterns of mallards and other duck species suggest that this behavior evolved out of the phylogenetically older behavior of preening—cleaning and repairing feathers. Thus, a part of the answer to the phylogenetic question regarding the mallard's courtship is that he inherited preening behavior and feathers to preen from his ancestors. Duck courtship differs from that of other animals, lizards, for example, because they do not share an ancestor that preened feathers.

Phylogeny describes the historical course of evolution. Thus phylogenetic questions are often related to questions of evolutionary function. It is a widely accepted hypothesis of evolutionary theory that natural selection is the major force behind phylogenetic change (chapter 4). In the example of ritualized mallard courtship, it is presumably the case that ancestral mallard feathers changed to their present conspicuous form, and elements of ancestral preening changed to their present stereotyped pointing, because the emergence of these features in some individuals led to more successful reproduction than was true for competitors having earlier versions of these characters. This is the functional explanation. However, no inherent connection can be inferred between natural selection and either feathers or pointing. It was their phylogeny, not natural selection, that gave ancestral mallards the raw materials for their particular evolutionary changes. Given a different ancestry, mallards might have improved their courting by shaping their neck into a different posture, or by incorporating a distinctive call instead of a feather, or any of a number of other possibilities.

Ontogenetic Causation

The third type of causal question distinguished by Tinbergen concerns developmental or ontogenetic causation. The time span covered by this type of question is the lifetime of the individual. The search for ontogenetic causes may be thought of as simply a backward extension of the study of immediate causes, provided one remembers that there may be important differences between the way scientists think about events having immediate effects and the way they think about events having effects removed in time. Unlike the long, historical time frame of phylogenetic causes, both immediate and developmental causes operate within the life span of an individual.

Both biologists, such as Lorenz, and psychologists, such as Hall (chapter 1), postulated categories of developmental causes from knowledge and ideas generated to answer phylogenetic questions. This led to some major confusions. Lorenz (1965) distinguished between phylogenetic and ontogenetic sources of information for developmental processes. Despite differences in the concepts and procedures used to identify information from each of these realms, and despite differences in the routes by which information from each of these sources enters the developing organism, he concluded that both phylogenetic and ontogenetic information can shape developmental outcome. Therefore, according to Lorenz, phylogenetic inquiry can explain not only phylogeny; it can also explain development. The practice of explaining ontogeny by phylogeny can be traced to the theories of Ernst Haeckel in the late 1800s. It is interesting to note that the modern discipline of evolutionary ontogenesis directly contradicts Lorenz's proposal (see chapter 4).

Lorenz's formulation had two parts. First, information derived from phylogenetic sources shapes development through readouts from the genetic **blueprint**. Second, information derived from ontogenetic sources shapes development through individual learning from the physical and sociocultural environments. It is implied by this distinction that one could dichotomize different behavioral patterns, or even a single behavioral pattern, into a learned component and a genetic, or phylogenetic, component. The two types of information are qualitatively different only because of their source—one comes from heredity and therefore is unchangeable; the other comes from individual experience and therefore is labile. In Lorenz's view, they contribute to development in an otherwise parallel manner, with contributions that are mutually exclusive and complementary.

Lorenz's formulation influenced the thinking of many developmental psychologists, and it is important to sort out the confusion it invites when the distinction between evolutionary and developmental questions is blurred. To understand the phylogenetic history of a behavioral pattern or to understand the functional dynamics behind the history is not to understand the developmental causes that must operate if the behavior is to be expressed.

Of course, understanding the phylogeny of a particular organism can provide a useful context for exploring its development (Schneirla, 1949). It is equally true that developmental processes are a useful context for exploring phylogeny (Gould, 1977). These statements are very different from the proposition that phylogeny can explain ontogeny, or vice versa, or that phylogeny and ontogeny interact to explain development, as proposed from their different vantage points by both Lorenz (1965) and Skinner (1966).

Developmental questions require developmental inquiry. Understanding the developmental cause of any behavioral pattern involves investigating

the development of new structures and activity patterns from the resolution of the interaction of existing structures and patterns, within the organism and its internal environment, and between the organism and its outer environment. At any stage of

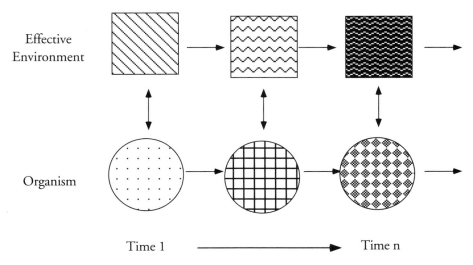

Figure 3.3 Behavioral development results from the interaction of an organism with its environment, both of which change as a consequence of the interaction.

development, the new features emerge from the interactions within the current *stage and between the* current *stage and the environment. The interaction out of which the organism develops is* not *one, as is so often said, between heredity and environment. It is between* organism *and environment! And the organism is different at each different stage of its development.*   (Lehrman, 1953, p. 345; emphasis in original)

Moreover, the environment may differ at different developmental stages of the organism, in part because of earlier activities of the organism itself (figure 3.3).

The organism and its environment are in a reciprocal relationship. The environment shapes the organism and its behavior, while simultaneously, the organism and its behavior are shaping the environment. The task of the developmental psychologist is to detail precisely the individual ontogenetic nature of this reciprocal relationship as it pertains to the occurrence of any particular behavior pattern. Carrying out this task involves understanding the physiological and biochemical processes of the organism as they affect behavior, as well as knowing how the experiences of the environmental events and conditions encountered by the organism affect its physiology, biochemistry, and behavior. Lorenz's distinction between ontogenetic and phylogenetic sources of information, although perhaps useful in thinking about heredity, cannot be applied to analyze development (see box 3.2).

Why Do Birds Sing?

As Tinbergen (1963a) taught us, the question of why birds sing really conceals four separate kinds of questions about the function, the phylogenetic

Box 3.2   The Deprivation Study

At one time **deprivation studies** were conducted to identify the innate aspects of an animal's behavior. A deprivation study isolates the animal from those aspects of the environment thought to be important for it to develop some behavioral characteristic. For social behavior, it was typical to isolate an animal from other members of its species. Later, if the deprived animal performed the species-typical social behavior, it was concluded that the behavior was innate.

Lehrman (1953, 1970) identified several methodological and logical problems with the deprivation study. First, it does not specify the experiences that have been eliminated from the individual's developmental history. Even when a massive deprivation is imposed, not all experiences have been removed. Therefore, failure to observe an effect on development may mean only that the experimenter failed to identify and manipulate the effective experience. Lehrman maintained that such failure cannot be used to conclude that a behavioral pattern does not require experience. Deprivation can be used either to identify an effective experience or to rule out certain experiences as unimportant. It is always necessary to ask *of what was the animal deprived?*

Of course, deprivation experiments are conducted when the role of experience in development is unknown. The objective is to determine whether some hypothesized experience has an effect. The likelihood that such studies will reveal something about development depends greatly on the ingenuity of the experimenter.

For example, certain species of fish school, traveling in groups and adjusting their swimming direction and speed to remain in a group (Shaw, 1970). This may provide some advantage for obtaining food and avoiding predation. Fish reared in isolation readily school on being placed in groups. Clearly, the development of schooling does not depend on the experience of growing in the company of companions. But is it innate, requiring no experience for its development?

What nonsocial experience might be relevant for the development of schooling? A fish that could not sense the presence of companions could not school. Therefore, imposing a deprivation that would disrupt the development of abilities to sense the movements of other fish should affect schooling. However, the fish might also be unable to do a variety of other things. The developmental change might be so general that it could be argued that the manipulation led to such an abnormal fish that schooling could not be expressed.

Consider Lehrman's question: of what was the fish deprived in the isolation study? Experience with other fish that move around it! Were all aspects of that experience effectively removed? The surface tension of the water-air boundary creates a reflection of the isolated fish as it approaches the surface. The boundary between a glass side of a tank and the water also creates mirror conditions. As an isolated fish approaches these boundaries, it undergoes an experience in which a fishlike visual stimulus coordinates its movements in relation to the real fish's movements. This experience becomes common and expected. Using specially designed tanks that eliminated such reflection, Evelyn Shaw (1970) demonstrated that fish isolated from this visual stimulus do not school. Indeed, in many species, schooling is gradually developed as the fry grow in company with one another, and it depends on the perceived contingency of correlated behavior among them.

The deprivation study does not allow identification of innate psychological abilities. However, more refined experiments in which specific experiences are withdrawn and replaced in a controlled manner help determine experiential effects on development.

history, the immediate causation, and the ontogenetic causation of song. These questions are best teased apart and answered separately, but their simultaneous consideration provides a far richer answer to each than would be gained by attending to only one.

It is important to start with a clear idea of what we mean by birdsong. Song is a form of vocalization, but not all vocalizations are considered to be songs. In fact, most bird species do not sing, even though vocalization is an important part of their behavioral repertoire. Vocalizations that are not songs are referred to as calls. The boundary between the two categories is a fuzzy one, but songs are usually distinguished by their relative complexity, repetitiveness, patterned quality, and sustained delivery. There is a great deal of variability in the duration of songs, the number of songs in an individual's repertoire, the number of qualitatively different syllables in a repertoire, and the versatility with which songs are produced (Read & Weary, 1992). Calls are relatively short and simple in form, and may be either loud or soft. Some are seasonal and sex specific, but others are not. Songs are loud and readily detected, and tend to be delivered seasonally, usually, but not always, only by males, and in a localized area (the breeding or courting territory). The variable nature of the vocalizations, both across and within species, makes a clean distinction between them impossible in all instances. This adds to the challenge of answering questions about birdsong.

Singing has a number of immediate consequences or biological functions that have been identified. Some of these consequences may affect the bird's fitness or reproductive success. Singing repels rivals, attracts potential mates, identifies the species and sex of the singer, induces others to reveal their sex, enables identification of familiar neighbors and strangers, and stimulates and synchronizes the reproductive physiology and behavior of pairs and, in certain colony-breeding birds, neighboring birds. Of course, not all of these consequences are observed in all species, nor is the list exhaustive.

Singing is a trait that can be altered by breeding studies, and it is hypothesized to affect reproductive success in a number of different ways. It may prevent hybridization among closely related species. Its role in maintaining a territory may ensure sufficient food and other resources to rear a brood of young. Failure to sing, or to sing an appropriate variant of the species-typical song, may result in failure to find a mate. At a more subtle level, song quality may be used by the female to select a mate, perhaps because it indicates something about the quality of the singer. Song repertoire size and versatility are greater in species in which help from the male in rearing the young is greater (Read & Weary, 1992). Of course, in species in which males provide little or no help in rearing young, females may also select mates with larger song repertoires.

Singing exacts some costs of the singer in terms of energy expended and exposure to predation, and it is therefore assumed to have benefits. Cross-species comparisons found correlations between the complexity of song and both resting metabolic rate and fecundity (Read & Weary, 1992). Therefore, species differences in repertoire size and other measures of complexity may be affected by differences in the costs of singing. The variety of ways in which song, or attributes of song, might contribute to the reproductive success of singers requires careful research to test each hypothesis. Furthermore, there is no a priori reason to assume that a function identified in one species will apply in another.

Little is known about the phylogenetic history of singing. Birds evolved from reptiles, and some reptiles use sounds in their social communication. Although many reptilian sounds are produced by drumming on the substrate, others are produced vocally. Vocal communication is a general avian character, and was probably in place at the time when birds first evolved. It is also probable that the use of calls for territorial defense and mate attraction has a very long history, extending back to the reptilian ancestry. The drumming and calling of contemporary reptiles that use sound to communicate serve these functions. Singing may have evolved from general calls; indeed, some songs seem to be repetitive calls.

The phylogeny of birdsong remains open for investigation. In general, it can be said that birds that sing are more related to one another than to birds that call but do not sing, but this generalization does not shed great light on the evolutionary history of song. It is likely that its study will be helped by breaking this complex behavioral pattern into some of its constituent mechanisms. Thus, as we learn more about the causation and ontogeny of song, sharper questions about phylogeny may be posed.

Much more is known about the immediate causes of singing. A number of environmental factors stimulate singing. Singing is usually confined to a particular season because it is dependent on seasonal changes in environmental stimuli—increasing day length in temperate zones, and changes in rainfall or foliage in equatorial regions. It also varies with the time of day (often most frequent at dawn and/or dusk) and stage of the breeding cycle (often least frequent when nestlings are young). Singing can be stimulated by seeing the approach of a potential rival or mate, or hearing the song of a conspecific, especially an unfamiliar song.

Singing is also dependent on several factors that are internal to the bird (Arnold, 1992; Bottjer & Johnson, 1992; Nottebohm, 1991). Secretion of hormones from the bird's gonads, most typically testosterone from the male's testes, is essential for song. Indeed, in some species, females that normally do not sing will do so if injected with testosterone. The motor systems used to sing are numerous and varied. They include muscles and associated effectors that control respiration and movements of the syrinx, trachea, larynx, beak, and tongue. These systems must be coordinated appropriately. Furthermore, the two sides of the body must be coordinated. This is particularly an issue for the left and right sides of the syrinx, where precise coordination is required. The syrinx is an organ in the throat of a bird located either one each in the two bronchi that extend from each lung and join to form the trachea, or in the trachea itself, depending on the species (Nowicki, Westneat, & Hoese, 1992). It is associated with a paired set of muscles that, when the syrinx is located more in the two bronchi, can be used independently on the left and right sides to produce two different melodies at the same time.

A great deal of attention has been devoted to the neurobiology of song production, and the major neural pathways that are involved have been identified (figure 3.4). When a bird is about to sing, electrical activity is first detected in a group of cells called the nucleus interface (NIf). These cells project to the high vocal center (HVC). The activity of the HVC also changes immediately before the onset of song. Bilateral destruction of the HVC interferes with the use of the syrinx in learned song, but it does not stop movements associated with singing. An operated bird will assume the singing posture and exhibit throat and bill movements normally seen during song. The HVC projects to the robust nucleus of archistriatum (RA). From there, activity travels to two major neuronal groups: the pars dorsalis medialis of nucleus intercollicularis (DM) and the pars tracheosyringealis of the hypoglossal nucleus (nXIIts), the motor neurons that control the muscles used in singing. There is also a pathway from the DM to nXIIts. Axons from the nXIIts form the tracheosyringeal branch of the hypoglossal nerve that directly activates the syrinx. An unusual feature of the motor control of song is that the neural pathway from HVC to syrinx is completely ipsilateral, with the left and right syringeal muscles controlled only by the ipsilateral pathway (Nottebohm, 1991).

The ipsilateral neural arrangement raises questions about left-right coordination. The problem is somewhat different for different species. Chaffinches, white-crowned sparrows, canaries, catbirds, and brown thrashers all produce different sets of sounds with the left and right syringeal muscles. In the first three species, the left side dominates, whereas the two sides are fairly equal in catbirds and brown thrashers. Some mechanism must permit coordinated integration of the two sources of sound into the same song.

One possible mechanism that would allow simultaneous activation of both sets of syringeal muscles was traced to a group of neurons in the thalamus,

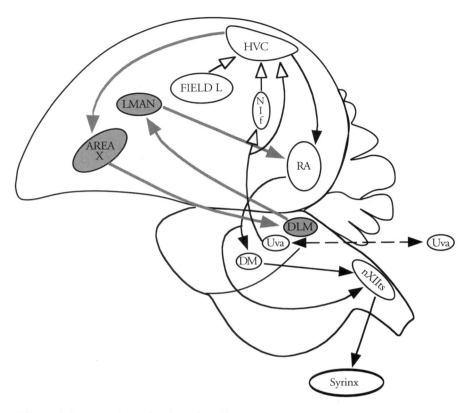

Figure 3.4 Neural mechanisms involved in the development and production of birdsong. Structures and pathways that play specific roles in development are shaded. Open arrows indicate input to the HVC and filled arrows indicate pathways involved in vocal output. The neural control of song is confined to one hemisphere with the exception of connections between the left and right Uva, indicated by the dashed arrow. See text for anatomical details (redrawn from Nottebohm, 1991).

the nucleus uvaformis (Uva). Although this nucleus has only ipsilateral projections to NIf and HVC, the left and right Uva have contralateral projections to one another. Another mechanism is provided by the auditory pathway, which is known to be important during song learning. Each HVC receives ipsilateral auditory input from field L, and a bird might coordinate its vocal output by listening to its own song (Nottebohm, 1991).

Several of these neural structures (particularly HVC) differ in size according to the song repertoire of the species (DeVoogd, Krebs, Healy, & Purvis, 1993), the male's hormonal condition as affected by seasonal cues (Brown & Bottjer, 1993), and hormonal conditions early in development (Burek, Nordeen, & Nordeen, 1994). In many species sex differences in both singing and the size of the neural structures are involved in song production. Often these differences simply depend on sex differences in circulating hormones. Thus, such sex differences in the canary are a consequence of differences in testosterone production. Treatment of adult female canaries with testosterone promotes song production and increases the size of certain brain areas (e.g., HVC) involved in song production (Brown & Bottjer, 1993).

Testosterone treatment does not promote song production in adult female zebra finches; however, this species has no anatomical connections between the HVC and the RA (Brown & Bottjer, 1993). Grisham, Mathews, and Arnold (1994) showed that implants of estrogen in the brain areas close to HVC of nestling (10–15 days after hatching) female zebra finches resulted in adults with male-size neural structures and singing behavior. Brown and Bottjer demonstrated that the formation of neural connections from the HVC to the RA and area X early in development may be necessary for testosterone's influence on adult song production.

Nestlings and young fledglings call, but they do not sing. Song develops over time. Songlike vocal behavior begins during the juvenile period with a subsong. Subsong is more variable in both syllable structure and temporal pattern than is adult song. It appears as a rambling string of notes. When young birds grow up together, they often countersing, and this social interaction can play a role in song acquisition. Subsong gradually takes on the species-typical quality of adult song (Marler, 1991).

Species vary widely with respect to how song develops. This is particularly apparent in the roles of learning and auditory experience. Some (e.g., cowbirds) do not have to hear a song to develop their song. Social interactions are important, however, including input from other modalities. Male cowbirds produce a variety of songs as they enter their first breeding season (West & King, 1988). When housed with adult females, they quickly learned to focus on a particular song. Most songs received no response from the female, but some elicited a wing-stroke behavior from her. This behavior, which is a very rapidly executed visual display, had a remarkable effect on the singing juvenile. Once a song elicited a wing stroke, it occupied an average 63% of further singing, whereas only 19% of songs were of this type beforehand. Songs that elicit wing strokes are also particularly effective in eliciting copulatory postures during the breeding season.

Other birds (e.g., white-crown sparrow, chaffinch, zebra finch, meadowlark) have to hear the song of their father (or in some cases any conspecific) during the nestling and fledgling phases. Only for some species does this involve imitation; indeed, adult zebra finches will sing the song of a Bengalese finch if that was their foster father. Others (e.g., Arizona juncos) have to hear and/or sing subsong with age mates during the adolescent period. Some have to hear themselves performing subsong to develop normal adult song (e.g., canary), whereas others (e.g., robin) must hear themselves as adults in order to sing. Some (e.g., cardinal, catbird, mockingbird) add the songs from other species to their song. Others acquire songs in concert with a singing mate (duetting). Some (Longuemare's hermit hummingbird) acquire songs in singing assemblies (chorales) of as many as 20 birds. The males congregate in the same places year after year and have stable song themes that vary among different assembly groups. Thus, social and auditory experience with age mates, parents, tutors, potential mates, and even oneself can contribute to the ontogeny of birdsong (Eales, 1985; Petrinovich, 1988). Of interest, very little research has been done on whether females respond to songs that are similar to those they heard as nestlings.

It is clear that the neural mechanisms that control mature singing must develop if singing is to occur. As described above, the left hypoglossal nerve is dominant in canaries and chaffinches, and controls the syrinx during song. If that nerve is cut in adults, the birds permanently lose song production. Normal song production will develop, however, if the nerve cut is made in young birds. If the cut is made early enough (17–19 days of age), the nerve will grow back, and both left and right hypoglossi will control the syrinx with no apparent degradation of song. If the surgery is done somewhat later so that the left nerve fails to regenerate, the right hypoglossus will control the syrinx (Nottebohm, 1991). The nerve cut studies demonstrate an interesting difference in plasticity between adult and young birds.

Another interesting difference between the developing and mature bird is that neural mechanisms necessary for the development of song are dispensible once song has been established (Bottjer & Arnold, 1986; Nottebohm, 1991). In addition to the short pathway from HVC to RA, Nottebohm described in canaries a second, recursive loop that connects these two structures (see figure 3.4). This second pathway, which includes area X of lobus parolfactorius, the medial portion of the dorsolateral thalamic nucleus (DLM), and the lateral magnocellular nucleus of anterior neostriatum (lMAN), plays an essential role in development, but not in adult song. Bilateral lesions that destroy lMAN and area X interfere with song learning during development. However, lesions placed in these regions have no effect on the production of learned song.

A similar effect is found in zebra finches. Lesions of the lMAN of the birds between 20 and 40 days after hatching resulted in the loss of over 40% of the neurons of the RA (Johnson & Bottjer, 1994). Similar lesions after 40 days had no effect on RA neuron number. The HVC establishes connections with RA beginning at about 35 days and this may prevent RA neural death. Ontogenetic studies found major changes in the size and connectivity of both lMAN and area X that is coincident with the sensitive period for song acquisition in zebra finches, estimated to occur between 20 and 65 days of age (Nottebohm, 1991).

The pathways involved in song production respond to sound. Therefore, the distinction between what is an auditory and what is a motor circuit is blurred. This raises some interesting developmental possibilities. If areas involved in the control of motor activity also respond to auditory input, then auditory input could affect the ontogeny of neural circuits that are used for producing learned vocalizations. In this way, hearing another singer could shape the development of song control regions in the brain.

As this brief account demonstrates, to answer the question of why birds sing requires investigation of four separate questions. The answers to each of these questions contribute toward the framing of each of the other questions. However, an answer to one question is never an answer to any of the other questions. That was Tinbergen's point.

A Holistic and Epigenetic Approach to Developmental and Comparative Psychology

The orientation to the study of development proposed by Schneirla (1966) and elaborated by others (Lehrman, 1953, 1962, 1970; Moltz, 1965; Rosenblatt, 1970) nicely complements Tinbergen's four questions. Taken together, the orienting ideas provided by Schneirla and Tinbergen are an effective conceptual framework for developmental psychobiology because they avoid many of the problems (described in chapter 2) that plague the integration of biology and psychology. Schneirla's orientation is also valuable because it is consistent with the dynamic systems theories (described in chapter 1). It focuses attention on the emergence of new properties at different levels of organization, processes of self-organization, and the nonlinear and dynamic relation of the individual with its social and physical environmental contexts.

The Schneirla-Tinbergen conceptual framework is **holistic** in the sense that the object of interest is *the entire living and active organism as it exists in its species-typical environment*. The organism has a unity, which is the phenomenon to be understood even though it may often have to be divided into analytical categories (hormonal aspects, neural aspects, social aspects, etc.). Analytical investigations undertaken in this framework are always in the service of a synthesis, namely, understanding the organism as a whole.

The Schneirla-Tinbergen framework is epigenetic because the development of the organism's characteristics emerge from the interpenetrating interaction of the activities of its constituent parts and its environment. Insofar as organisms are alive, they *interact with a stimulative environment*. Consequently, development is defined as the progressive change wrought in an individual through a lifetime of these interactions.

Finally, and perhaps primarily, the framework is *comparative*. Its fundamental objective is to understand the *similarities and differences* in the organization of behavior of all living species. Moreover, it assumes that behavioral organization is best understood through the study of development. The combination of these features yields a conceptual framework that is psychobiological without implying a duality in the organism, comparative without ignoring the important behavioral differences among species, and developmental in its focus.

Schneirla's Perspective on Development

Development, as conceived by Schneirla, is the progressive change in an organism from its beginning to its death; progressive change comes about as a result of an interpenetration of the organism with its environment. An animal's environment is sometimes spoken of as a milieu or context, perhaps as a reminder that environments must be defined from the point of view of the organism's capabilities. The same physical energies may have an effect on one organism but not another, or on an organism at one point in development, but not at a different point. Von Uexküll (1957) spoke of this personal quality of environments as the **Umwelt**, or perceptual-reactive world, of the organism (figure 3.5). Appreciation of the Umwelt is important for understanding the differing effects of the same environmental conditions on development.

Lewontin (1982) expanded on the concept of Umwelt and proposed that the relation between an individual and its environment, which he described as an *interpenetration*, takes at least four forms. First, individuals *assemble* their environments. Thus, some bird species use grass to make a nest and avoid using dirt. For other species, grass is unacceptable and dirt is used to make mud nests. Still other species ignore both dirt and grass, but seek out holes in trees or crevices in stone. The morphology, physiology, and behavior of the individual combine to determine those aspects of "reality" that may be assembled into the individual's environment. For developing individuals, those factors (morphology, behavior, etc.) that determine

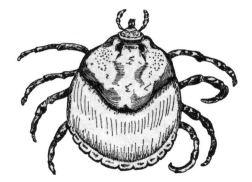

Figure 3.5 A female tick will remain motionless and unresponsive to other physical agents for an indefinite period until she detects the odor of butyric acid, a stimulus that initiates a behavioral sequence leading to a blood meal from a mammal. Von Uexküll used the tick to illustrate his concept of Umwelt (reproduced with permission from von Uexküll, 1957).

which aspects of the world are included in their environment will change as a consequence of previous transactions with their previously assembled environment.

Second, individuals *alter* their environments. This physical alteration comes about by consuming food, depositing waste, constructing artifacts (burrows, dams, nests, etc.), and other activities. Thus, individuals create the conditions that are necessary for their life but, paradoxically, their activities eventually have destructive consequences for themselves or their offspring. Lewontin used the example of a tall white pine creating shade sufficiently dense to prevent survival of its own seedings. The alteration in environments by living organisms is the basis of ecological succession. "[F]ields yield to weeds, weeds to shrubs, shrubs to trees, and trees to other trees as a consequence of the alteration of soil texture, chemistry, moisture, and light created by assemblages of plant species to their own detriment" (Lewontin, 1982, p. 161). For developing individuals, especially those from social species, creation of artifacts or of social routines and expectancies in companions during early phases have consequences for the social and physical environment available in later phases.

Third, individuals *transduce* the environment. Changes in the physical environment are not necessarily represented as the same quality by the individual. Environmental variation is transduced into physiological processes. For developing individuals the transducers themselves will change in part as a consequence of earlier transductions of previous environments. To return to an example from chapter 2, an incubating ring dove transduces stimuli from nest and eggs into a variety of physiological changes, including secretion of prolactin. The same physical stimulus (the nest plus eggs) will have quite different effects on a courting ring dove, an immature ring dove, or a hawk because of differences in their sensory-perceptual systems.

Fourth, individuals *modulate* the pattern of environmental variations. The physical environment is a flux of variations in frequency and amplitude of energies. The pattern of this flux signals the states of the environment. Since environmental variations are transduced by the individual, individuals can damp or amplify the fluctuations. Therefore, environmental signals do not have a linear effect on the individual. For example, fluctuations in the availability of food can be modulated by food-storage strategies.

Individuals readily adapt to the intensity of energies. This enables them to detect quickly the rate of change in intensity rather than level of change. We would immediately avoid entering a bath with 130-degree temperature because it would be too hot given the body's significantly lower skin temperature. However, a slow incremental change in bath water temperature might go unnoticed even to 130 degrees.

Both amplitude and frequency of energy fluctuation can be modulated. The physical environment consists of diurnal, lunar, seasonal, and climatological periodicities as well as cycles and rhythms of individual and social behavioral action. These cycles can be ignored, transduced, combined, and modulated in various ways to increase individual variability.

These forms of individual-environment interpenetration demonstrate that organisms "are not simply *objects* of the laws of nature, altering themselves to bend to the inevitable, but active *subjects* transforming nature according to its laws" (Lewontin, 1982, p. 163). The Umwelt is both a product and a process of development. "[D]evelopmental changes occur as a consequence of reciprocal (bidirectional) relations between the active organism and the active context. Just as the context changes the individual, the individual changes the context. As such, by acting to change sources of their own development, by being both a product and a producer of their contexts, individuals affect their own development" (Lerner, 1983, p. 15).

When we speak of an organism, we are speaking of a creature that has a past; it has already been through a series of interactions with its environment, and it is interacting with its environment as it is being examined by us. Some of the organism's own activities contribute to the construction of its

Figure 3.6 The enormous mounds built by termites in Australia provide clear evidence that animals construct their environments.

environment, which in turn is the milieu for subsequent activity and further developmental change (figure 3.6). Schneirla noted that we may separate an organism from its environment for analytical purposes, but for the organism, there is no separation. There can be no organism without an environmental context; such an eventuality is, quite simply, impossible.

From this perspective it is as reasonable to consider the developmental consequences of self-stimulation as it is to consider the effects of stimulation arising from the external environment. These two categories of stimulation reflect a division that is totally arbitrary when it comes to specifying their effects on the developmental process. Stimulation can indeed affect development in a variety of different ways, but the same range is occupied by self-generated and externally generated stimuli.

A particularly instructive example of self-stimulative effects on development is provided by the behavior of young mallard ducklings, which approach and follow their mother primarily when she utters a special "assembly call." The behavior of the ducklings is not dependent on prior exposure to this maternal call; incubator-hatched ducklings will also approach the source of this call. Indeed, even the duck embryo shows signs of being responsive to the call.

In a series of ingenious experiments, Gottlieb (1971, 1991b) demonstrated that the duckling's responsiveness depends on prior exposure to either the prehatching peeps of its nest mates or *its own peeping*! These birds begin to vocalize some three to four days before hatching. When deprived of the sound of their own peeping and that of their siblings during these three or four days, they show no selective approach to the maternal assembly call after hatching. Indeed, they are susceptible to developing a preference for the calls of another species (chicken) even in the presence of its own species call. Although the complete maternal call does not sound at all like the peeping the embryo makes before hatching, Gottlieb found that the part of the maternal call to which the duckling is initially responsive is similar to the prehatching peep. Thus, the duckling's self-produced stimulation has an important influence on the development of social behaviors vital for its survival.

The Fusion of Maturation and Experience

A distinction between maturation and experience is frequently made in theories of development. It is often the case that maturation is contrasted with experience. For many, this distinction implies a causal dichotomy, which has prompted critics of such dichotomies to conclude that maturation be used exclusively to *describe* growth processes and not to *explain* developmental change (Connolly, 1981; chapter 8). The distinction between maturation and experience had a special meaning for Schneirla (1957), who saw them as convenient for analytic purposes and not an intrinsic division in the developing system. He avoided a causal dichotomy by taking the passage of time into account.

Maturation was used to refer to changes that can be described in terms of anatomy and physiology and other organismic properties, but these changes were brought about in part by experiences encountered during earlier times. Schneirla subdivided maturation into the processes of growth, differentiation, and morphogenesis. *Growth* refers to additive accumulation—of cells, vocabulary words, and so on. **Differentiation** and **morphogenesis** refer to the processes by which the growing organism forms qualitatively different and specialized parts and processes—eyes, legs, nest-building abilities, language, concepts, and so on. Compare Anderson's (1957; chapter 1) explicit recognition that additive growth processes can contribute to qualitative changes, as in the formation of folds in developing nervous systems. This has a modern ring (see chapter 6).

Finally, Schneirla used *experience* to refer to the effect of an organism's environment, or milieu, on the maturational processes. He viewed maturation and experience as inextricably fused processes governing developmental change. However, he did not portray maturation as an intrinsic developmental factor that directs immature organisms to their adult states. In this, he was consistent with modern dynamic systems theories.

Hatching presents an interesting challenge for developing bobwhite quail. These birds are precocial, and their mother leads them from the nest shortly after hatching. The eight or so eggs typically laid by a bobwhite hen are laid one at a time at 24-hour intervals, but all of the eggs hatch within an hour's time. An eight-day spread from the laying of the first egg to the laying of the last egg somehow becomes telescoped into a one-hour spread from the hatching of the first egg to the hatching of the last. Synchronized hatching, which is vital if the young are to survive, results from the embryos' stimulating each other before hatching (Vince, 1974). The loud clicking associated with embryonic respiration appears to be partly responsible for the synchronization, and, because the eggs must be in contact with one another for synchronization to occur, it can be assumed that the effective stimulus probably involves vibrations transmitted from one egg to another.

As a result of interegg social stimulation, developmentally advanced embryos are held back and hatch later than they would if kept in isolation; interegg stimulation advances the hatching time of developmentally younger embryos. Because hatching requires not only postural and behavioral changes in the embryo but also metabolic, anatomical, and physiological changes appropriate for posthatching existence, this elegant study is an excellent illustration of the fusion of maturation and experience in normal development.

The Concept of Experience

The range of events that should be considered as possible experiences contributing to the maturation of an organism is very broad in the epigenetic view of development. Because of this breadth and heterogeneity, it is not possible to define all possible categories of experience a priori. What is and what is not experience is an empirical question that must be investigated for each organism and for each developmental process in which one is interested. It follows, therefore, that experience is not synonymous with learning through conditioning, practice, or observation, although learning, as it is customarily defined can certainly be a part of experience. Whether or not it is an important aspect for the development of a specific behavior pattern is an interesting and important question, but not the only interesting and important experiential question that may be asked about the development of the pattern.

For example, when male guinea pigs that have been raised in isolation from other guinea pigs become adults, they respond to receptive females with less sexual behavior than normally reared males (Valenstein, Riss, & Young, 1955). If they are reared in individual wire mesh cages so that they can smell and see other guinea pigs but have no contact with them, their sexual behavior as adults will be equivalent to that of normal guinea pigs (Gerall, 1963). Male rats raised from birth by mothers that have been experimentally treated to reduce their sense of smell will receive less maternal licking than rat pups usually receive. As adults, the males will engage in less complete masculine sexual behavior (Moore, 1984), a phenomenon that may reflect an effect of maternal stimulation on the maturation of neural mechanisms used during copulation (Moore, Dou, & Juraska, 1992; chapter 6). The infants do not practice sexual behavior, but their experiences during the first few days after birth contribute to their ability to engage in this behavior some months later. In both of these examples, experience with socially provided stimuli during development, even when these stimuli are totally divorced from any sexual behavior, will influence adult sexual behavior. The developmental organization of sexual behavior is not fully understood, but clearly, experience can have an influence unpredictable from any of the conventional theories of learning.

Although it is helpful to distinguish maturation from experience, this should by no means be construed as suggesting two separate processes in the organism, one dependent on the environment and one not. Both growth and differentiation depend on the environment in a very involved and crucial way. Evidence shows that this dependency is characteristic of physiological and anatomical as well as behavioral aspects of organisms.

Dramatic examples of this point can be found in the processes underlying sex determination and reproductive development of some animals. For instance, male and female turtles have no genetic differences, but adult males and females show substantial morphological, physiological, and behavioral differences. Sex is determined in these reptiles by the temperature at which the eggs are maintained during embryonic development (Bull, 1983). In some species, males develop when the eggs are laid in warm areas, such as unshaded sand, and females develop when the eggs are laid in the shade of vegetation. This environmental difference initiates two different sequences of events with developmental repercussions for both anatomy (males are only a fraction of the size of females) and reproductive physiology. They also have ecological and evolutionary implications, as the developmental process limits the geographical range in which two sexes can be formed. Changing ecological conditions, such as the loss of beach vegetation, create severe selection pressures that threaten to distort the sex ratio to the point of eliminating reproduction in some species of these animals.

Some species maintain the ability to change their sex as adults, which entails substantial morphological as well as behavioral and physiological changes. This plasticity is common among fish. Some social species such as coral reef fish use the social behavior of their companions as cues for switching from the more numerous female form to the relatively rarer male form (Demski, 1987; Shapiro, 1983).

Experiential contributions to anatomical development are not limited to such exotic phenomena. As described in detail in chapter 6, they are an integral part of vertebrate neural development. For example, the normal development of the olfactory bulb requires olfactory input. When chemical stimuli are kept from contacting the olfactory mucosa by blocking one of the nares of an infant rat, the ipsilateral olfactory bulb develops to a substantially smaller size than the contralateral stimulated bulb (Meisami, 1976; Brunjes & Frazier, 1986). Furthermore, early exposure to specific odors results in enhanced development of the parts of the olfactory bulb that are active during the processing of those particular stimuli.

These active areas can be visualized and mapped on autoradiographs of olfactory bulbs taken from animals that had been injected with labeled 2-deoxyglucose (a tracer that is taken up into active neurons because of its similarity to glucose) and then exposed to an odor. Axons from olfactory receptors terminate in a layer of the olfactory bulb that is organized into glomeruli, or clusters of dendrites of second-order neurons, relay neurons, and interneurons. The glomeruli exhibit regional specificity in activity for different chemical stimuli. Of related interest, neural activity in the glomerular layer is greater in rats exposed to some particular odor, such as peppermint, if the rats had been repeatedly exposed to that odor as infants. Furthermore, the glomeruli that are active in the processing of that odor are larger in size in the experienced rats (Coopersmith & Leon, 1988).

Evidence shows experiential contributions to the development of all sensory systems, but perhaps the most extensive comes from the well-studied visual system (Hirsch, 1986). One interesting feature of the visual cortex is the orientation selectivity of neurons in area 17, with each cell responding best to line stimuli having a particular orientation in the visual field, but

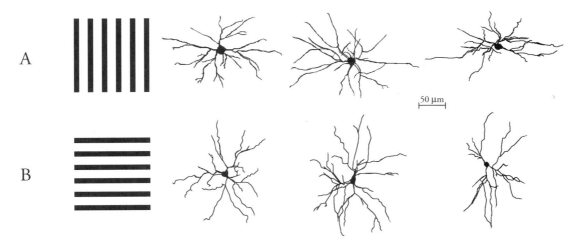

Figure 3.7 Dendritic fields of layer III cells in the visual cortex exhibit morphological differences consistent with visual experience of an environment consisting of vertical (A) or horizontal (B) stripes modified from Tieman & Hirsch, 1982.

with the population of cells as a whole having no particular bias (Hubel & Wiesel, 1962). The preferred orientation is acquired through the visual experience of developing individuals (Hirsch, 1986), as demonstrated by controlled rearing studies (Blakemore, 1974; Blakemore & Cooper, 1970; Hirsch & Spinelli, 1970).

When kittens are reared in biased visual environments having only horizontal stripes on the walls, the preponderance of neurons in area 17 respond best to lines of this orientation. In parallel fashion, a bias for vertical stimuli is found among area 17 neurons if kittens are reared in a vertically striped visual environment. The bias can be detected both by electrophysiological recordings of individual cells and by observing the cats' visually guided behavior. The cats respond well to visual stimuli that correspond to the orientation of stripes in the rearing environment, but have difficulty with stimuli oriented at right angles to these stripes. Furthermore, the dendritic fields of pyramidal cells in layer III of area 17 assume a particular orientation that reflects the rearing environment (Tieman & Hirsch, 1982; figure 3.7).

The environment is not only a good provider, giving sustenance for growth, as the predeterminists would have us believe; it is also a source of structure for the developing organism. Trace effects of experience are woven into all aspects of the developing organism. Gottlieb (1976) classified the experiential involvement in development into three distinct categories. **Maintenance** experiences sustain achieved states of anatomical, physiological, and behavioral development. In this functional category, experience may not be necessary to achieve the development of some feature, but it is necessary for its remaining a feature of the individual. **Facilitative** experience can regulate when a feature appears during development by promoting or inhibiting the rate of development of some specific feature of the individual. However, the feature would appear at some time during development, regardless of the presence of the experiential event. An **inductive** experience could be necessary to bring about the developmental occurrence of some feature. That is, the feature will not develop without the experience.

Experience is notoriously difficult to categorize, and Gottlieb's categories have been a useful first step. Nevertheless, problems remain. Perhaps the biggest difficulty is that the scheme lends itself to an inappropriate dismissal of all but inductive experiences by those who want to retain genetic determinism as an explanation of development. A facilitating experience can be dismissed as mere fine-tuning of a genetically programmed process, and a maintenance experience may be dismissed as irrelevant for understanding development. But these are erroneous conclusions that have more to do with the words used to name the categories than with the developmental processes that they name.

Both facilitating and maintaining experiential influences can have major consequences for development, equal in importance to those categorized as inductive (see Gottlieb, 1992, for a recent discussion of his categories). If a feature (hormone level, vocabulary, muscle, etc.) is maintained, it can participate with other features in the developmental emergence of some new feature. As such, a maintaining experience can be a necessary condition for the development of many other features. Similarly, a facilitative experience may seem merely to alter the rate of development of some feature that would develop anyway, but such rate alteration can have profound effects.

Differential change in the rate of development among features (heterochrony) is a fundamental source of the production of new patterns of organization, and is a major means of the evolution of new species (Gould, 1977). Distinctly different individuals emerge from alterations in the rate of development of specific features. Delaying or accelerating the development of grammatical skills in humans will create differences in intelligence, social skills, emotional range, and other aspects of personality. The individual is an organized system. Alteration of any feature can ramify to affect other features. Facilitative and maintenance experiences can cascade throughout development to produce profound effects on the organism. For example, an experience that facilitates the production of growth hormone or testosterone will result in numerous changes, some of which will appear inductive.

Indeed, whether an experience is categorized as maintaining, facilitating, or inducing a developmental feature may depend on the type of measure that is used. For example, if some end point of development is used to compare a brain nucleus in two animals, and differences in the size and shape of the nucleus are found that depend on an experiential difference between the two animals, then the experience would likely be categorized as inductive. However, measures of the rate of cell division or cell loss in the nucleus might lead to a categorization of the experience as a facilitative one that affects rate of division or loss, even though the final differences in size and shape depend solely on the rate difference.

The individual does not unfold from some preformed blueprint but rather derives its organization, as it progressively changes, from what it is at present and from the stimulative context within which it behaves. What an individual is like at point $X + Y$ in time will depend on what it was like at point X and what its experiences were during the period of transition from X to $X + Y$. To understand individual development, we have to determine exactly how the experience interpenetrates with the individual's characteristics to produce the characteristics expressed in the subsequent phases of development.

From this viewpoint it is possible to envision a multiplicity of alternative developmental outcomes (*multifinality*) and to see that one outcome might be reachable by different pathways (*equifinality*). This view is to be contrasted with the one that asserts that there is one path and one outcome, dictated by an unfolding of previously encoded instructions; from this latter perspective, any deviation from "proper outcome" would have to be viewed as an abnormality brought about by an unsupportive environment. One interesting consequence of discarding the concept of a determined and fixed developmental end is the conclusion that abnormality, if it is to have meaning, must be defined by criteria other than deviation from a proper outcome (Gollin et al., 1989; chapter 9).

The Temporal Characteristics of Development

Development is a historical phenomenon in that previous events affect the manifestation of current and subsequent events. Thus, development is identifiable across time, but is not defined by time. Development does not refer only to the time before reproductive capacity, or to some internal clock controlling the pattern of change in the manifestation of psychological characteristics.

The distinction between sensitive and critical periods can illustrate why an internal clock is a poor metaphor for development. It is a common observation that certain experiential influences seem to be delimited to a particular period of life. Occasionally, exposure to some of these conditions either before or after the particular period of life does not result in the same (or any) developmental changes as arise when the exposure occurs during the "correct" period. For example, song learning and imprinting in birds occur readily after exposure to certain stimuli at a specific period early in life but not ordinarily at other times. Some conclude that the birds have to obtain their experiences during a critical period in their development if they are to have normal song and social relations.

Somewhat similar notions are applied to the social and intellectual development of children. Educational events are restricted to certain age periods considered to represent the time when children are ready for the events to have their developmental influence. Certain aspects of language, cognitive, and social development (Bornstein, 1989) are also thought to depend on a critical period for experiential influence.

Are the onset and the end of the critical period the consequences of some internal clock (the physiological state at different ages) that keeps time independent of the processes that develop during the window of time? In the zebra finch, for example, it was suggested that the end of the critical period for the development of song is specified by physiological changes that accumulate by 65 days after hatching that make further learning impossible. However, we now have ample evidence that the timing of the developmental period is not independent of the processes under development. Song learning (Eales, 1985) in zebra finches and imprinting in various species of birds (Bateson, 1987b; ten Cate, 1989) are self-terminating processes. That is, *"the progress of the learning process itself may influence the ending of the sensitive phase"* (ten Cate, 1989, p. 256; emphasis in original). Preventing zebra finches from learning a song during the first 65 days extends the critical period for learning indefinitely. The undertutored birds sing an abnormal song but when exposed to singing adults, even six months later, they can acquire their normal song. The notion of some internal clock governing the developmental process is unsupported.

Of course, at some periods during development exposure to certain conditions more easily affects development than at others. However, the clock metaphor, suggesting as it does an independent time keeper, is not appropriate for comprehending the historical contingency of developmental phenomena (Bateson, 1979, 1981). Within developmental psychobiology, this notion is captured by the concept "sensitive period" rather than critical period to address the sequential character of experiential influences.

Time (age) does not define a developmental phenomenon. Development may occur in microseconds, or it may occur in decades (Werner, 1957). Development is defined by the ability of the system to reorganize and change as well as to resist change despite changes in the environment.

The Relationship Between Evolution and Development

Phyletic Levels

Schneirla (1949, 1962) advanced the idea that the study of evolution could be informed by developmental analysis, and vice versa. Before one can understand how he conceived of the relationship between evolution and development, one must have a firm idea of his concept of *phyletic levels*. Schneirla repeatedly asserted that we ought not to take our concepts or methods fully formed from other disciplines. If psychologists are interested in ordering the relations among various species, they must set themselves a task of behavioral analysis of all living forms and base their ordering on their analyses. Because psychologists have only living species to work with, their ordering cannot turn out to be a reconstruction of the temporal order of evolution (the phylogenetic tree of genealogy). However, it can contribute to the understanding of evolutionary relationships.

Schneirla suggested that we begin to understand the differences among species by noting gross differences in behavioral complexity. Species that display similarities of behavioral complexity would thus be said to operate at the same phyletic level. An ordering of phyletic levels is very similar to an ordering based on major evolutionary changes that presumably occurred over geologic time. There are exceptions, however. Evolutionarily more advanced creatures may occupy a lower phyletic level as determined by analyses of their behavioral complexity (Maier & Schneirla, 1935; Schneirla, 1949, 1962).

The difference separating phyletic levels is one of complexity, or behavioral plasticity, and one way to characterize the complexity of behavior is in terms of the relationship between structures and function, or between the apparatus with which one behaves and behavior itself. For example, the number of things that an insect can possibly do with its appendages is highly limited. But, because of the structure of human appendages, people can do a larger variety of things with theirs. It is thus important to study the role that structure plays in behavior. The more freedom there is between structure and function, the more complex and plastic the behavioral organization. If a structure can be used only in one or two ways, we may have understood the development of the behavior associated with the structure simply by understanding the development of that structure.

The concept of phyletic levels as related to the structure-function relationship is particularly important to bear in mind when making analogies between the behaviors of different organisms. For instance, some linguists have likened the innate knowledge of linguistic rules that is presumed to be a part of the human nervous system to the innate knowledge of the physical rules of web construction possessed by the spider's nervous system. Nobody teaches the spider how to build a web, nor does anyone instruct the child in the basic rules of language. Both seem to know the rules simply by being a normal spider or child with a normal nervous system. A linguist might argue that, if we can accept the spider's knowledge of web construction as innate, we should also be able to accept the child's knowledge of basic linguistic rules as innate.

Examined from the perspective of phyletic levels, the analogy is superficial, faulty, and of no use for understanding language development. The
spider is a land invertebrate with no internal skeleton of bones, and therefore requires an exoskeleton of hardened waxy chitin for support and
locomotion. There is a sharp physical limit to the mass an animal can
achieve if it possesses an exoskeleton. This limit in mass obviously limits the
number of cells of the animal and consequently the number of cells devoted
to each tissue, organ, and system. Because of these limitations, one invertebrate neuron does the work of many vertebrate neurons in controlling
muscular movements. The vertebrate nervous system, therefore, can achieve a greater refinement of muscular movement and has more plasticity of
movement than the invertebrate system (Vowles, 1961). Moreover, the
neurons of the invertebrate central nervous system are many fewer in number, are more highly specific and delimited in their connections with other
neurons, and are relatively refractory to the consequences of experience
compared with vertebrate central nervous system neurons (Cohen, 1970). In
other words, the spider's nervous system is organized with fewer alternative
pathways and fewer opportunities for interconnections among pathways
than the human's nervous system. This results in a greater correspondence,
for the theorist, between knowledge of neural structure and the explanation
of the behavior for the spider than for the human.

Furthemore, Witt, Reed, and Peakall (1969) demonstrated that part of the
"knowledge of physical rules" necessary for web construction resides in the
length and number of joints of the spider's legs and the physical characteristics of the environment in which the web is spun. Saying that the spider
spins webs according to some innate knowledge does not indicate the means
by which it achieves web construction (which in this case includes the specific
anatomical characteristics of the spider's legs in relation to the physical
conditions of the place where the web is spun). Whatever the means used to
accomplish some behavior of an animal, whether it be web construction or
language construction, the notion of phyletic levels cautions against in-
ferring that those same means are responsible for the accomplishment of
similar behaviors of other animals.

Functional Order

Schneirla used the concept of functional order to describe behaviors of different complexity within each phyletic level. "The highest functional orders
characterizing any psychological level are those utilizing its maximal possible gains through ontogeny" (Schneirla, 1957, p. 85). Random escape from a
frightening stimulus is a behavior with a low functional order; the coordinated hunting pattern of a carnivore, and the orderly movements to food,
water, and shelter of the leaders of a monkey troop are behaviors with a
high functional order.

Even superficially similar behavioral patterns may be organized at different levels of complexity in different species, or in the same species at different ontogenetic stages. For example, differences in the sexual behavior of rats and monkeys can be characterized as differences in functional order, as can differences in the sexual behavior of monkeys and humans (Moore, 1985, 1990). The human species may be more complex than others in the sense of having a larger repertoire of behaviors with a high functional order.

It is necessary to study the ontogeny of each species in which one is interested, because species may differ not only in their adult forms but throughout their ontogeny. It is impossible to extrapolate directly from one species to another, because a capacity that develops in a particular way in one species may develop in quite another way in a second species. Both precocial birds, such as chicks and ducklings, and human babies learn the perceptual attributes of their parents (voice qualities, color and shape, etc.), but the rapid learning process in precocial birds bears only a superficial resemblance to the human learning process. Ants and rats are both good at finding their way about in mazes, but the processes through which they accomplish this task differ markedly (Schneirla, 1957). This makes developmental psychobiological research an essential feature for establishing any animal as a model for human psychology.

The concept of functional orders is relevant also for the distinction between developmental and evolutionary questions. Natural selection may operate on behavioral capacities throughout ontogeny. However, the processes of natural selection are opportunistic; they make use of whatever characteristics the organism already possesses. Therefore, the fact that two behavioral patterns have similar evolutionary functions tells us nothing about how similar their development might be. Neither does the fact that many behaviors share the designation species-typical (i.e., exhibited by all members of a species and not usually by members of other species). Species-typical behavior need not share a similar development; there is no reason to assume, as some do, that to be species typical is to develop through some sort of endogenously controlled maturational organization of the nervous system. The ontogeny of each species and each behavioral pattern must be studied separately before statements can be made about the course of their development. Statements about the similarity of evolutionary function of a behavioral pattern in two different species can conceal important differences between them in the processes by which the behavior is manifested. The concept of functional order prompts us to consider differences in developmental processes and the organization of the behavioral repertoire among different species. As a result, we will be less likely, for example, to consider the processes involved in the social organization of other primates to be equivalent to those involved in the social organization of humans, even when many commonalities have been established (chapter 9).

The Relationship Between the Organism and Its Behavior

The concept of levels is important to understanding the development of the individual and to understanding of the role of behavior in that individual's development (Birch, 1971). As we indicated in chapter 1, individuals are organized into structures that are capable of being analyzed at many different levels (see also Lewontin et al., 1984). Any organism can be considered as consisting of many levels of organization, or systems, ranging from those characteristic of single cells to those involving the relationship of the whole organism to its environment. The simpler systems at each level become important components of the higher-level systems. Each system has emergent properties specific to its level of organization in addition to having the properties of its lower-level components. The emergent properties are dependent on the particular pattern of relationships among the lower-level components. The pattern of organization of the components restricts or constrains the range of properties that each component, if it operated alone, would normally have available. In this sense, emergent properties have a kind of causal capacity.

For example, the water molecule H_2O has emergent properties that are specific to it as well as the properties characteristic of the hydrogen (H) and oxygen (O) atoms. Of course, knowledge of the properties of hydrogen and oxygen atoms is important for understanding the properties of H_2O, but this knowledge alone will not allow one to predict all the properties of water. For example, in high concentrations, both hydrogen and oxygen are highly combustible, but high concentrations of water can douse the flames. The structural organization of the hydrogen and oxygen atoms in the water molecule constrain the properties of these atoms, emphasizing some properties, inhibiting others. Knowing the properties of these atoms alone does not define or predict the properties of the water molecule unless the spatiotemporal organization of their relationship within the molecule is specified. In addition, the emergent properties of the water molecule can now affect other molecules and systems of which water is a component.

The system created by the individual as a whole and its relation to an organized social and physical milieu constitute a new level of organization. It is this new level of organization that is the source of the emergence of behavior. The emergence of patterns of behavior involves the coordinated action of sensory, neuromuscular, skeletomuscular, hormonal, and central nervous systems, which in part depends on specifics of the social and physical milieu. The behavior, in turn, contributes to the condition or state of every one of the systems of the individual by sensory, or experiential, feedback provided by both its performance and the consequences of its performance on the world. This means that, although behavior is dependent on certain lower-level physiological events, it is also a constraint on such events (Sperry, 1965). Behavior also influences the character of the individual's social and physical milieu. Thus, behavior is not another level of organization; it is an emergent property of a new level of organization: the individual as a whole in relation to the social and physical milieu. As Kennedy (1992) proposes, behavior is the physiology of the individual.

One task of the developmental psychobiologist is to define and describe the pattern of events operating simultaneously among the different levels of organization within the organism as the behavior is manifested. Another task is to define and describe the pattern of events operating simultaneously among the different levels of organization within which the individual is a component as the behavior is manifested. Finally, the developmental psychobiologist must examine the history of these various levels of organization during the individual's development. In this way, an epigenetic approach can be psychobiological without being reductionistic and without implying a duality in the organism. The approach therefore is a useful conceptual framework not only for integrating of biological disciplines into developmental psychology but also for investigating and resolving many specifically human developmental problems.

The developmental concepts outlined in this chapter are not foreign to researchers and theorists interested in human development. Because of the necessary limitations on human experimental research, however, human evidence in support of these theories can never be incontrovertibly presented. Therefore, animal research often provides the best evidence for constructing the basic concepts of human developmental psychobiology.

Summary

We presented a conceptual framework that permits the integration of psychological and biological perspectives while avoiding many of the problems that interdisciplinary integration often entails. The framework keeps developmental questions distinct from functional and phylogenetic questions, and by preserving this distinction, helps developmental psychologists avoid pseudoanswers. It also obligates them to pursue truly developmental investigations of developmental questions.

The next two chapters discuss the many perspectives of contemporary genetics and the modern theory of evolution. A comprehensive understanding of these perspectives is necessary to appreciate fully the important distinctions among developmental, behavior-genetic, and evolutionary pursuits and to use genetic and evolutionary information appropriately.

4   **Evolution and Development**

The dominant view of organisms is that they are complex self-reproducing systems whose specific properties have evolved by natural selection acting on spontaneous variation arising from gene mutation and genome rearrangement. In this description there are essentially two sets of forces acting on organisms: internal ones coming from the genome, causing variations in organismic properties (including form); and external ones coming from the environment, determining which of the variants survive and so are adapted.
—B. Goodwin (1990, pp. 52–53)

In the dominant view of organisms, as Goodwin (1990) recognized, internal entities have been reduced to the genome, and external entities have been limited to natural selection. The two are separate, but capable of interacting: the genome produces variants, and natural selection chooses among them. The role of an individual organism is to serve as the arena in which this interaction is played. A cornerstone assumption of the dominant view is that an individual's characteristics are determined by its genes (internal entity). This assumption is captured by the metaphor of a program whereby a set of genetic instructions directs the ontogenetic construction of the organism and much of its behavior. This is done by specifying which molecules are produced, as well as when, where, and in what amounts. The environment (external entity) represents conditions that an individual's phenotype must match if it is to survive and reproduce. Thus, the environment selects naturally (i.e., by neither divine nor human means) the genetic programs that promote the fitness of the individual to the environment.

This dominant view is called the synthetic theory of evolution, and it is an amalgam of evolutionary and genetic theories. It assumes that genes are the only form of inheritance relevant to evolution, and that environmental conditions are the only factors capable of directing the course of change in the genetic pool of a population. All other factors operate randomly and therefore are considered to be incapable of directing evolution. Random factors include genetic drift (fluctuations in the relative frequencies of genes) and gene mutation, and their very randomness is presumed to preclude their playing a significant role in the transmutation of species or the adaptation of organisms to their environment.

The individuals most responsible for forging the synthesis were evolutionists Theodosius Dobzhansky (1951), Ernst Mayr (1963, 1970), and George Gaylord Simpson (1953), and geneticists J. B. S. Haldane (1932), Ronald Fisher (1930), and Sewall Wright (1932). Agreement among these individuals allows them all to be identified as synthetic theorists. But there are also important theoretical differences, including some deep divisions, for example, between Wright and Fisher (see Wright, 1980).

Sociobiology (Wilson, 1975) is a contemporary extension of the synthetic theory of evolution, particularly as it was interpreted by Fisher (1930), who emphasized the gene as the unit on which natural selection acts. Sociobiology extends the theory by providing a link between genetic evolution and sociocultural evolution, with explicit attention to human cultural evolution and social characteristics. The primary goal of sociobiology is to explain societies and cultures in terms of the natural selection of heritable genes. Psychological and sociocultural characteristics of humans, it is argued, evolved in response to specific adaptive problems encountered during the Pleistocene (Buss, 1991). Therefore, cultural traits are understood as adaptations that are determined ultimately by genes that were selected during evolution (Lumsden & Wilson, 1981).

Social and cultural behaviors of interest to sociobiologists include mating rituals, family relationships, patterns of parental caregiving, agonistic encounters, altruistic actions, and even the creation of cultural institutions. The objective of the theory is to explain these social characteristics as evolutionary adaptations in the sense that they are (or were at some earlier stage of evolution) associated with an increase in fitness. Fitness refers to the capacity of different individuals to contribute to the gene pool. Each individual is under natural selective pressure to engage in activities that increase the likelihood that his or her genes will be reproduced. The more fit an individual, by definition, the more likely his or her genes will be represented in the next and subsequent generations.

A key aspect of sociobiological theory is the assumption that the naturally selected genes that underlie fitness determine the development of those traits in individuals. Therefore, the theory has had a profound impact on the study of psychological development. To evaluate that impact, we first must understand the basic principles of the synthetic theory of evolution, the extension of these principles developed by sociobiologists, and some of the phenomena that sociobiology purports to explain.

In this chapter we examine the origins of the synthetic theory of evolution and its contemporary manifestation in sociobiology, identify some of its weaknesses, and describe some alternative evolutionary views. We also examine the relation of evolutionary theories to developmental psychobiology.

The Influence of Darwin and Mendel

Both Mendel and Darwin sought to account for variation and change. This is a significant aspect of the thinking of both men, because the earlier, predominant mode of thinking in biology was typological (Mayr, 1963, 1968). Typologists approach variation by asserting that only those aspects or characters that individuals have in common (their "essence") are relevant for biology; in the Platonic tradition, individual differences are "mere shadows on the wall."

Adaptation, or the close fit between the traits of organisms and the environment they inhabit; is a fact of nature that was recognized long before evolutionary theory arose to explain it. Before Darwin, however, it was commonly believed by the scientific community that each different **species** of plant and animal was separately and instantaneously created by an intelligent, planful creator—by God—and that each species represented the best design for living within its environment. This concept is called the fixity of species. All species, human beings excepted, were thought to be in harmony with nature. Anatomy and **taxonomy** were the most prestigious and popular areas of scientific investigation at the time. Both involved static structures and thus offered researchers little incentive to think in terms of concepts such as process, evolution, and development.

The availability of fossil evidence, providing proof of the existence of species that lived in the past but not in the present, was incorporated into the pre-Darwinian idea of separate and instantaneous creation by many leading scientists. They postulated that the earth's history consisted of a series of geological and biological catastrophes. Like the biblical flood, each catastrophe wiped out most of the life on earth. New species were then created, some of which may have replaced the old. Each species was considered to be immutable, and separate species were thought to be unrelated to each other. It was also believed that the individual members of a species could not vary from one another by much, or else the harmony of life would be disrupted. Thus, individual differences were thought of as uninteresting artifacts of idiosyncratic life histories, or the effects of procedures used to capture or preserve specimens.

Sir Charles Lyell completed his *Principles of geology* in 1833, a book that was later to have a major impact on Charles Darwin (Irvine, 1956). This monumental work played a singularly important role in replacing the early ideas of successive, instantaneous creations with the idea of gradual change. Lyell's geological investigations found no evidence for worldwide geological catastrophes in the earth's history. Instead, he compiled a great deal of convincing evidence for continuous, gradual transformation during this history. Furthermore, he advanced the idea that the same forces that shaped geological change in the past continued to operate in the present. Thus, Lyell provided a dynamic perspective on geology.

Darwin's contributions to biology were many and varied, but one of the most significant was to reorient it away from static conceptions of its phenomena toward more dynamic ones (Mayr, 1984). His theory, picking up Lyell's theme, cleared the way for the growth of subdisciplines concerned with processes of change—developmental biology, physiology, evolution, genetics, and ecology. Even anatomy and taxonomy, fields traditionally at home with static concepts, took on a more dynamic flavor as a result of Darwin's influence.

Darwin, Wallace, and the Growth of Evolutionary Thought

It is difficult to overestimate the importance of Darwin's theory of evolution as a reorganizing force in biology—indeed, in all of science. His ideas were not developed in isolation, however. Both the intellectual milieu in which he lived and idiosyncratic life events were significant in the development of his thought (Bronowski, 1973; Irvine, 1956; Gruber & Barrett, 1974; Desmond & Moore, 1992).

Charles Darwin was from a wealthy, well-established family with a tradition of interest in natural history and medicine. His father was a successful physician, and his grandfather, Erasmus Darwin, was a noted natural historian, poet, and physician. Like many of his class, Darwin was not obliged to work, as he had an independent income that came from investments and land. Nevertheless, in keeping with his British Victorian culture, he was committed to the productive use of time and to physical and intellectual exploration. This, in combination with his father's wishes, led him to begin a medical education at the University of Edinburgh. He found, however, that the study of medicine did not suit him, so he moved to Cambridge University to prepare for the clergy.

During his time at Edinburgh Darwin was exposed to the ideas prevalent among the university intelligentsia, which included **materialism** and the transmutation of species. He was attracted to these radical scientific and medical ideas. After moving to Cambridge he was exposed to another major influence, I. S. Henslow, professor of botany and orthodox Anglican minister. It was Henslow who recommended that Darwin read Lyell's *Principles of geology*. He was also responsible for getting Darwin the position of captain's companion aboard the *HMS Beagle*, which was bound on a five-year voyage to explore the coast of South America. Darwin's position was essentially that of a naturalist, and his task was to describe and collect samples of plants, animals, fossils, and rocks during the trip.

Henslow recommended Lyell's book as a geological guide, not as a source of radical ideas. He had even cautioned Darwin not to believe these ideas.

Irvine (1956) states that, despite this friendly warning, the book taught Darwin a lot more than geological facts. "From [Lyell], Charles learned observation in the highest sense of a thoughtful activity which suggests and tests hypotheses,... he learned how to construct hypotheses,... [and] he came to see nature as logical, regular, and self-explanatory" (p. 37). Because geology is the most historical of sciences, many of the ingredients of the theory of evolution by natural selection were to be found in Lyell's book. Moreover, every place that was visited along the South American coast provided Darwin with evidence that Lyell's theory of geology was right.

Although raw material for Darwin's theory was drawn from all the places they visited, the Galapagos, reached late in the voyage, was particularly instrumental. The Galapagos archipelago is a series of volcanic islands in the eastern Pacific, far off the coast of Ecuador. At no time have they ever been attached to the main continent. Therefore, any species of plant or animal on the islands had to have traveled over 600 miles of ocean to get there from South America. Darwin was struck by many of the **flora** and **fauna**, but a group of Galapagos finches (*Geospiza*) has come to symbolize Darwinian evolution.

Thirteen different species of this group of birds, morphologically and behaviorally different from one another and adapted to different ways of life, were living on the islands. They were similar to finches on the American mainland and had an underlying similarity to one another (Lack, 1947). They often displayed striking differences in morphology, however, such as bill shape and size, and behavior, such as feeding. Could it be that a few pairs of finches from South America had been blown to the islands and, over the course of several generations, changed into these 13 separate species? If so, then how did they come to have the bill shapes, food preferences, eating habits, and other characteristics of birds other than finches? The answer that was eventually reached is that of **adaptive radiation** from a single founding population—transmutation of species.

It took some time for Darwin to recognize the full significance of the finches, as well as similar evidence from other plant and animals species on the Galapagos islands (Sulloway, 1984). Indeed, he did not have many of the necessary facts at the time of his trip. It was only after meeting with a noted ornithologist, John Gould, five months after returning to England that Darwin learned that the 13 species of birds he had collected were appropriately classified in the same finch group. Darwin himself had only identified six of the species as finches, and had not kept the records of the island location for each of his specimens. On realizing its importance, Darwin attempted to reconstruct locality information for the *Beagle* finch specimens from his memory and the notes of his shipmates. Detailed information about this intriguing group of birds came later from other scientists who followed

Darwin to this extraordinary archipelago. Despite the incomplete record at his disposal, the finches were clearly on Darwin's mind when he arrived at his theory of evolution in the spring of 1837 (Sulloway, 1984).

Of interest, another naturalist of the time, Alfred Russel Wallace, was asking similar questions about the diversity he found in nature. Wallace not only asked the same questions as Darwin; he arrived at the same answers. Thus, the theory of evolution by natural selection was published independently by both men.

Despite differences in their backgrounds, the men shared certain experiences that might help to explain why they happened to arrive at the same theory (Bronowski, 1973). Wallace was a product of the same British Victorian milieu as Darwin, except that he was from the working class. He left school at 14, and his early experience with plants and animals was gained in the English countryside, primarily in the context of his work as a land surveyor for the railway. Like Darwin, Wallace had a passion for natural history, and was attracted to the diversity, complexity, and beauty of plants and animals. When he was 25, he began a new career of collecting foreign specimens to sell to collectors and museums in England.

Wallace also visited South America on a collecting trip. He too was struck by the great diversity of plant and animal species and by the big question of how neighboring species had become different from one another. Although Wallace suffered the bad luck of losing his South American specimens and was unable to bring them back to England, he did return convinced that species were related and had diverged from a common stock.

Both Darwin and Wallace had read Malthus's *Essay on population*. Eventually, both realized that, if populations grow faster than their food supplies, animals must compete to survive. This led to the idea that nature acts as a selective force through differential survival. This has the net effect of shaping species so that they fit their environments.

There is evidence that Darwin arrived at the idea of evolution through natural selection much earlier than Wallace. Although he had not published the idea, Darwin discussed it with some of his friends, and wrote a short paper on it that he wanted his wife to have published after his death. Darwin was sensitive to the social controversy that would surround his theory, having observed while at Edinburgh that espousal of such radical ideas as materialism and transmutation of species led to ostracism within the medical community.

It is also quite possible that Wallace's insight was not completely independent. Both men maintained a heavy correspondence with other naturalists of the time, and also wrote each other. It is possible that Wallace was influenced in subtle ways by Darwin's ideas, as written to Wallace and other naturalists with whom Wallace corresponded. Whether his informal knowledge of Darwin's work stimulated Wallace to hit on the idea of natural selection can never be known. However, the record does show that he arrived at his insight in February of 1858, while ill with fever on one of the islands in the Malay archipelago. Wallace remembered what he had previously read in Malthus's book and realized that it held the key to explaining why species differ. He immediately recorded his ideas in a paper, which he sent to Darwin with a request to show it to Lyell, should he find it worthy (Bronowski, 1973).

The receipt of Wallace's paper, together with the urging of his friends, provoked Darwin to publish his own ideas on the subject. The two papers were presented simultaneously in July of 1858 to the Linnean Society of London, a distinguished society of biologists and naturalists that was open to materialist ideas. Contrary to expectations, the papers did not generate immediate public interest. Shortly thereafter (1859), Darwin published *On the origin of species*, an outline of his theory that was to change the course of biology. Although Wallace continued to make substantial contributions to biology and to the theory of evolution after the appearance of Darwin's book, he never became fully integrated into the rather class-conscious society of British naturalists.

Darwin's ideas had begun to germinate on the *Beagle* expedition (1831–1836). Yet, the first publication occurred more than 20 years after Darwin's return to England. This delay has occupied the attention of Darwinian scholars. Clearly, the idea of evolution driven by natural selection required a materialistic philosophy that was at variance with the larger culture of the day. Desmond and Moore (1992) suggest two personal influences that encouraged Darwin to think against the dominant current of his times. One influence was his brother Erasmus, with whom he lived in London. Erasmus and his friends were political and religious radicals who encouraged Darwin's materialistic philosophy. In fact, Darwin wrote the notebooks that recorded additional evidence in support of the transmutation of species while living with his brother. Another influence was the death of his oldest daughter, Annie, of a mysterious illness in 1851. Although Darwin had always believed in the value of competition for both society and nature, he had previously seen it as the basis of a just society and a harmonious nature. However, the death of his daughter, which undoubtedly seemed senseless to him, may have encouraged him to see nature's competition in a new light, as irrational and relentless rather than orderly and harmonious.

Another reason for the delay in publication may have had more to do with the theory itself than with its social context. Darwinian evolution includes two great new ideas: natural selection to explain both adaptation and speciation, and a phyletic tree to describe relatedness among species. These ideas required a radically new way of thinking, and may simply have required a long time to mature (Gruber, 1981; Gruber & Barrett, 1974; Sulloway, 1984).

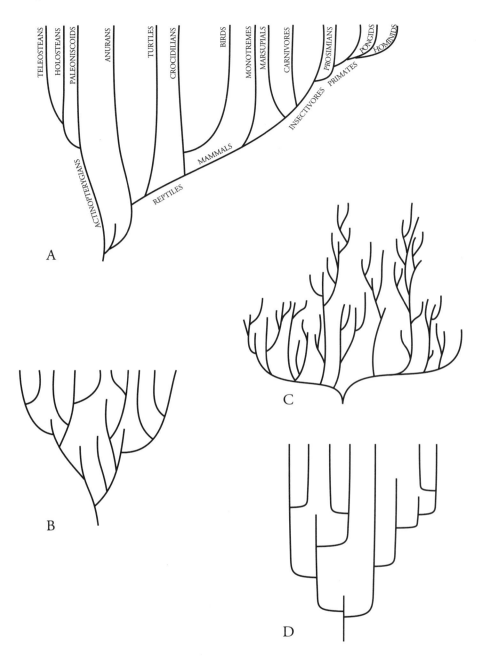

Figure 4.1 A tree is a three-dimensional, branching structure that has been used since Darwin as a metaphor for evolution. But a tree can be drawn in a variety of ways, and how it is drawn reflects certain assumptions, intended or not (Gould, 1989b). (A) Hodos and Campbell (1969) point out that the depiction of contemporary representatives of major animal groups on the tips of branches arranged from left to right on a page may correctly reflect the general sequence in which these groups arose in evolution. However, it is erroneous to think of alligators or cats as

Darwinian Evolution

Because many of the ideas making up Darwin's theory of evolution are so apparently simple and readily understood, it is sometimes a surprise to today's student that they had to wait so long for acceptance. Indeed, many of Darwin's contemporaries ridiculed him for only restating the ideas of others, including some ancient Greek philosophers. However, these critics mistakenly confused the philosophical idea of the chain of life (Lovejoy, 1936) with Darwin's evolutionary theory. This confusion, we might add, is still prevalent in the fields of both psychology (Hodos & Campbell, 1969) and biology (Nelson, 1970; Gould, 1989b).

However, a great conceptual difference exists between the chain of life and the Darwinian tree of life as metaphors of phylogeny. Previous evolutionists sought to arrange all the living species along a single line, which meant that the nonextinct species of birds evolved from one of the nonextinct species of reptiles. Human beings were believed to have evolved from chimpanzees. Darwin's contribution was to show that all living species are related through descent from a common ancestor. Human and chimpanzee are evolutionarily related not because the one evolved from the other, but because they evolved separately from a now extinct common ancestor.

The evolutionary relationships among living species could best be represented, according to Darwinian ideas, by a tree, with the tips of the branches representing the living species (figure 4.1). The connections of the branches with one another, and eventually with the main trunk, represent the descent from common ancestors. In this model, no living species can be considered better adapted (more fit) than any other living species, because they all represent the currently most successful point of their particular branch. Moreover, the model brought meaning and organization to a host of previously unrelated facts from the fields of embryology, taxonomy, physiology, and other biological disciplines.

ancestral to humans, for no currently living species is ancestral to another (redrawn from Hodos, 1970). (B, C) Gould (1989b) notes that evolutionary trees are usually depicted as "cones of increasing diversity," but evidence suggests that evolution involves proliferation of species followed by massive extinction of many variants. Thus a tree might be drawn more aptly as one of "diversification and decimation" (redrawn from Gould, 1989b). (D) The branches of evolutionary trees are usually depicted as gradually sloping from trunks or more major branches, suggesting that evolution is a process of gradual change. However, changes may be abrupt, occurring rapidly at branch points (speciation). This is the concept of punctuated evolution (Eldredge & Gould, 1972). If evolution occurs in this manner, evolutionary trees would be more accurately drawn with branches at right angles (redrawn from Futuyma, 1986).

Darwin's theory, as outlined in *On the origin of species*, accounted for the adaptive fit between species and their environments and for the origin of new species from ancestral species—descent with modification. The theory put together five main points, including both observations of nature and logical deductions.

1. The number of offspring produced always exceeds the number of parents; however, the total number of individuals in a species tends to remain more or less stable from one generation to the next. Thus, offspring die. This is the insight obtained from Malthus's essay on human population.

2. Morphology, physiology, and behavior vary among members of a species. This is the principle of **variation**.

3. Given the conditions of the environment (competition from other individuals for limited resources or stressful conditions), certain variants will be more likely to survive and leave more offspring than others. This is the principle of **natural selection**.

4. Offspring tend to resemble their parents; that is, they somehow inherit the characteristics of their parents. This is the principle of **heredity**. The principles of heredity and natural selection together ensure preservation of those characters that fit the conditions of the environment.

5. As populations spread into new environments and as the conditions of the environment changed during the history of the earth, species changed to fit the new circumstances. Therefore, all living species are linked through their history and can be traced through a series of common ancestors back to the origin of life.

The picture that emerged from the synthesis of these observations and deductions was one of gradual change in which heritable variation was produced through one set of processes and selected by another—natural selection. In the broadness of its scope, the theory of evolution has to rank as one of the greatest achievements of human intellect. It is no wonder, then, that many decades of scientific development (Irvine, 1956) and many years of cognitive growth (Gruber, 1966; Gruber & Barrett, 1974) had to take place before Darwin arrived at a satisfactory presentation of his theory.

As Darwin was well aware, his argument had at least two major weaknesses. Although he hypothesized that variations among individuals were the essential basis for the evolutionary process (natural selection favoring some variants over others), he had no satisfactory way of accounting for their origin. He could not answer the question, "Why is it that individuals are individually different?" Nor could he adequately account for the transmission of traits from one generation to the next—**inheritance**. Unknown to Darwin, Mendel had answers to these key questions.

Mendel and Differentiating Characters

The idea prevailing during Darwin's era was that hereditary material is like a fluid. This meant that every time mating occurred between animals with contrasting characters or traits (e.g., white and black fur), the hereditary material would blend, much like different colors of paint, to produce offspring whose characters were intermediate between those of the parents (gray fur). Generations of such blending would result in loss of variability and a completely homogeneous population. Indeed, many of the complex characters that Darwin and others studied did appear to blend in the offspring populations. Fortunately, Gregor Mendel, an Augustinian monk, chose to examine characters of his pea plants (size, flower color, seed color, texture, etc.) that were dichotomous, or differentiating (e.g., pea seeds are either yellow or green but no color in between) and that could easily be counted.

Working with these *differentiating characters* and using a series of breeding experiments, Mendel deduced the nature of the hereditary material and formulated the basic laws of inheritance. The ingenuity in the design of his experiments suggests that Mendel may have known what results he would obtain before he actually did his experiments (Bronowski, 1973). He grew up in a poor farming family in eastern Europe, and could well have observed these effects of breeding during his boyhood. He later matriculated at the University of Vienna, but was unable to complete the teachers' qualifying examinations. Thus, he may have been motivated to conduct his experiments to prove to himself and to his abbot that he could succeed at something. Although this is only conjecture, it is supported by the fact that he left serious science after eight years of studying inheritance in peas, and turned his energies instead to radical political activities (Bronowski, 1973).

Mendel observed that when plants that were dissimilar in one of the differentiating characters (e.g., tall and short plants) were bred with one another, the offspring uniformly showed only one form of the character (e.g., all were tall). There was an apparent **dominance** of one form of the character over another. The disappearance of the other form of the character was not real, however. Cross-breeding among the offspring plants resulted in a second offspring population, three-fourths of which exhibited the dominant form and one-fourth of which showed the previously missing, or **recessive**, form. This meant that the two forms of the differentiating character retained their purity and did not blend. They were transmitted in the germ cells, or gametes, as two different *formative elements*, or hereditary factors. Thus, Mendel deduced that every individual has two formative elements for each inherited character or trait, one donated by each parent. If they are not alike, one usually dominates over the other. Furthermore, the individual hereditary factors remain unchanged during transmission from one generation to the next.

Mendel also found that each pair of differentiating characters that he observed in his experiments (height in plants, color in flowers and seeds) was transmitted independent of the other pairs of characters. In other words, individuals varied in the combination of hereditary factors that they possessed. All these phenomena, Mendel recognized, could be accounted for by the explanation that the hereditary material is particulate, rather than fluid. Also, the two particles, or formative elements, for a particular differentiating character do not alter each other.

One might have supposed that Mendel's laws of inheritance, accounting as they did for the source and means of transmission of character variability, would have been seen as an ideal solution to Darwin's problems. Instead, the climate of scientific opinion at the time of the rediscovery of genetics (the turn of this century) actually led to a decline in the investigation of evolution. Darwin had proposed a theory of heredity in which characters would always be continuous (i.e., differences within a population would be small and graded) rather than discontinuous or dichotomous. His supporters had devised a statistical system, called biometrical analysis, for investigating heredity that was antithetical to Mendel's basic assumptions. Thus, the growing use and success of Mendelian analyses led to rejection of Darwin's notion of heredity—the biometrical approach—and, strangely enough, to rejection of the concept of natural selection, as well.

The Mendelian laws of inheritance, combined with the concept of gene mutations, appeared to be all that was necessary to account for the variety and evolution of species. Some mutations or combinations of hereditary factors resulted in new species; some did not. Everything could be explained by mutation or recombination of Mendelian factors. Environment (natural selection) caused nothing; genes caused everything. It was as simple as that. It is, of course, well known that this position was held only temporarily. Eventually, it was seen that Mendelian genetics and Darwinian evolution could be integrated.

The Synthetic Theory

The modern synthetic theory of evolution involved a new definition of species and new concepts of the process of natural selection, but in essence it is Darwin's original theory combined with Mendelian genetics. Darwin's theory proposed that natural selection was the causal process underlying the evolutionary phenomena of **phylogeny**, the historical relationships among species; **speciation**, the origin of diversity among populations; and **adaptation**, the fit between an organism's characteristics and its environment. These key ideas are retained in the synthetic theory, but are considered to result from the action of natural selection on variations among **genes** within populations. Thus, in the synthetic theory, a direct, determining relation between genes and traits is posited, and only genetic inheritance is recognized (Mayr, 1982).

The integration of Mendelian and Darwinian concepts into the synthetic theory uses three simplifying assumptions: all heritable traits are determined by genes, with variation in these traits originating from random genetic events; natural selection is the only nonrandom agency that can select among heritable traits; and natural selection arises only from the environment (Odling-Smee, 1988). As we will see, each of these assumptions is currently in dispute.

To relate genes to evolution within the conceptions of the synthetic theory, populations are characterized as genetic collectives that can be described by the relative percentages of various kinds and combinations of genes. The presence of these genes is not known directly, but inferred from observed phenotypic differences and, under artificial conditions, from breeding experiments. The genetic variation available in a population is ultimately due to mutations, which are then weeded out or allowed to multiply by natural selection. In this way, evolution is conceived of as changes in the hereditary makeup of a population, or its **gene pool**, the aggregate of genes and the number and relative frequencies of their alleles.

If a sexually reproducing population is sufficiently large and mating is random, there can be no evolution without mutation of genes within the population or gene flow (input of new alleles) from a different population. The mathematical demonstration of this is known as the Hardy-Weinberg law. Furthermore, Mayr (1963) convincingly showed that mutations alone cannot account for the formation of new species, at least not in sexually reproducing populations. Mayr's search for nonrandom processes that can lead to speciation led him to focus on two phenomena: the physical isolation of one part of a population from another, and nonrandom aspects of sexual reproduction. In certain instances that maximize sampling error, such as the geographical isolation of a few members from the rest of the population, the random fluctuations in gene frequency (**genetic drift**) may be sufficient to carve one parental population into two species. These chance happenings are thought to be rare and to have little significance for speciation when considered alone. Nevertheless, Mayr (1963) proposed that genetic drift in combination with the geographical isolation of relatively small populations could change gene pools sufficiently to accelerate any differential natural selection acting on the isolated population, thereby increasing both the speed and the probability of speciation. He called this the *founder effect*.

Most genetic processes are inherently random, but reproduction is an important exception that can have nonrandom components. Therefore, reproductive processes have central explanatory roles in the synthetic theory, to explain both evolution within a population and the formation of new species. The centrality of reproduction allows natural selection to be redefined as any factor that contributes to differential reproduction of particular alleles or particular combinations of alleles in a population. In the synthetic theory, natural selection leads to the creation of a new adaptive relationship between a population and its environment through a process of differential reproduction of individuals in the population, which has the effect of altering the composition of the gene pool of the population over the course of generations.

A species is an exceedingly important biological concept, but it is difficult to arrive at a single definition suited to all its uses (Cracraft, 1989; Mayr, 1942/1964; Templeton, 1989). Nevertheless, all current definitions recognize that reproductive cohesion is central to the concept. Thus, a species can be defined as a population of individuals that have the potential of mating with one another during the natural course of their lives and producing reproductively viable offspring (box 4.1). The synthetic theory maintains that species will change in their genetic makeup whenever natural selection favors the reproduction of different gene combinations; and a new species will be formed whenever a parental species is physically divided and subjected to differential selection pressures.

Earlier Darwinian theories of natural selection focused on a process of differential survival of individuals. "The cliches of struggle and survival, even for the professional biologist, have focused attention on secondary aspects of the historical process whereby genetic information accumulates. They have focused it on individuals—and it should be on populations; they have focused it on the avoidance of death (perpetuation of the individual)— and it should be on reproduction (perpetuation of the genotype)" (Pittendrigh, 1958, p. 397). Of course, Darwin had proposed that natural selection works on *individuals* engaged in a struggle for reproductive success (Gould, 1992). "Good organic design" and "harmonious ecosystems" are only side consequences of "... the selfish propagation of individuals—that is, organisms struggling for personal reproductive success and nothing else" (Gould, 1992, p. 17). But what did Darwin mean by "individuals"?

To be an entity that can be the object of natural selection, an individual must have five properties (Gould, 1992): a clear beginning in time (birth); a clear ending in time (death); enough stability between birth and death to be recognized as the same entity; ability to reproduce; and ability to produce offspring that resemble the parental entity. Using these five criteria, Eldredge (1985) made the case that at least 16 different biological entities, including base pairs of DNA, genes, cell lines, populations, species, communities, and monophyletic groups, have the requisite properties of individuals. From this, it can be argued that natural selection can operate on genes, organisms, and species, and a variety of other entities. Nevertheless, the synthetic theory adopted the position that genes are the sole focus of natural selection. This shift in emphasis meant that individual organisms, once the focus of Darwinian thought, were relegated to the secondary role of mere vehicles for genes (Dawkins, 1976).

Box 4.1   Mayr's Biological Species Concept

Mayr (1942/1964) proposed a definition of species that has become a widely accepted, integral part of the synthetic theory of evolution: "Species are groups of actually or potentially interbreeding natural populations, which are reproductively isolated from other such groups" (p. 120). This dynamic concept improved on earlier, more static definitions that required similarity of form among members of a species. It allows morphologically similar groups of individuals to be classified as separate species if the criterion of reproductive isolation is met so that genes do not flow from one group to another; it also allows populations that are morphologically distinct to be classified as the same species if interbreeding results in the intermingling of genes across populations. The two populations are on different evolutionary paths in the first instance, and on the same path in the second.

As Mayr acknowledged, his concept has limited applicability. For organisms that reproduce asexually, every clone becomes a species; thus far too many species are generated for the concept to be a useful classification tool. The opposite problem of too few species occurs in groups (many plants) that regularly reproduce by forming fertile hybrids. It is also difficult to decide what "potentially interbreeding" means, particularly with respect to populations that are completely isolated by time or space. Nevertheless, Mayr's theory of biological species remains popular because it works fairly well for classifying most animals into species, and because it fits with the prevailing idea that genes are the target of natural selection, with individual organisms serving as mere vehicles for carrying genes from one generation to the next (Searle, 1992). However, frequent hybridization among natural populations of animals, observed even in the historically important Darwin's finches, is a troublesome fact for Mayr's concept.

Grant and Grant (1992) found that about 9% of the individual finches hatched in one study year were hybrids of the three different species of finches that inhabit one of the tiny Galapagos islands. The hybrids were fertile, breeding successfully with one another and with the parental species. This means that a significant level of gene flow occurred among the three species: the species are not reproductively isolated, and any genetic mutation that arises in one species can spread to another. Finches are not the only example (Grant & Grant, 1992; Searle, 1992).

About 10% of bird species are estimated to form often fertile hybrids with other species. And the eastern and western European forms of house mice are so genetically and morphologically different that many consider them separate species; yet they readily hybridize in some parts of Europe and Japan. Despite the failure of reproductive isolation, useful distinctions can be made among the finches and other hybridizing populations, and a different definition of species is necessary to capture them. One that focuses attention on the organism as a cohesive entity (Templeton, 1989) is more useful to developmentalists than Mayr's biological species concept.

The synthetic theory of evolution by natural selection is a deterministic theory. That is, evolutionary outcomes are thought to be predictable from a complete understanding of the environment and population genetics. But this raises an important assumption about environments—it must be possible to characterize environments in advance in ways that are appropriate to evolutionary prediction. This is done through the concept of a niche, which is an aggregate of selective pressures. The environment is seen from this perspective as a set of definable niches that can be carved apart. Stated in this way, the evolutionary problem for organisms is the generation of characters that match the environmental features comprised by its niche. It is a problem with high stakes, because failure to arrive at a good match will threaten survival and reproduction.

In the synthetic theory, organisms are thought to generate changes in their characters through spontaneously occurring, random genetic processes. These processes are slow to occur and result in small changes at each step. They produce the raw material from which species gradually adapt to the requirements of the niche by differential selection across generations but, because they are random, they do not provide direction to evolutionary change. Thus, it is natural selection that provides the directing and driving force for evolution.

As Goodwin (1990) puts it, natural selection is seen as the "formative or creative agent in the evolutionary process, providing organisms with specific forms and behaviors appropriate to currently prevailing environmental conditions of life" (pp. 54–55). Because all characteristics are viewed as subject to continuous, incremental modification by this process, essentially all of those that any organism possesses are viewed as products of natural selection creating an adaptive fit to a particular niche and leading to increased fitness (survival and reproductive success). This is the adaptationist view.

Sociobiology

Sociobiology is an adaptationist theory. In addition to the basic principles of the synthetic theory of evolution, the fundamental principle underlying all sociobiological work is that social behavior is a product of genes that have been selected for their fitness. Social phenomena are understood as the consequences of natural selection, which works to eliminate characters that fail to meet the constraints of the selective environment and retain those with an adaptive fit. The three typical parts to a sociobiological program of research are to measure the costs and benefits of each social trait in terms that can be related to genetic propagation (i.e., fitness); to identify selective pressures that operated in the past to account for the evolution of social and cultural traits; and to identify current selective pressures that contribute to these traits in their present form.

Societies as Adaptations

One of the major achievements of sociobiology, defined most broadly, is the recognition that animal societies are ecological adaptations. In this respect, sociobiology is an aspect of the broader study of **behavioral ecology** (Krebs & Davies, 1981), which is concerned with both social and nonsocial behaviors as ecological adaptations. Unlike sociobiology in its more circumscribed sense of a particular theory of behavioral adaptation (Wilson, 1975), behavioral ecology is not defined by a particular set of theoretical assumptions. Research in both traditions led to the insight that the **social structure** of any animal species is often a solution to a specific set of problems posed by its environment; distribution of food and predator pressure are two important examples. This insight grew out of an impressive amount of field research documenting social diversity across the animal kingdom (Crook, 1970a; Lott, 1984). This diversity could not be explained by phylogeny but did make sense when considered as adaptations.

One aspect that struck field researchers was the diversity in the **social organization** of natural animal groups. Some species have organizations consisting of large numbers of animals with well defined roles. Others have similar organizations, but only at certain times of the year or in certain environmental circumstances. Many species exhibit organizations of large numbers of individuals, but only a few social roles, if any. In some, individuals are solitary, at times even to the point of not coming together during sexual reproduction—the gametes are merely dispersed on the ground or in water. In others, members select mates for life and then either remain continuously with them or seek them out during each breeding season. Some species have social organizations consisting of a single male, a group of adult females, and offspring. Others have large numbers of females and their offspring, with males venturing to enter the group only during the breeding season and then only at great risk. The list continues.

The diversity of animal social organizations sets intriguing problems for evolutionary theory, because often the social organizations of closely related species can differ to a remarkable degree, whereas those of unrelated species can be quite similar. For example, they are complex among species of crustacea, insects, fish, birds, and mammals, including some primates. These societies have interesting similarities despite the great gaps in phylogenetic relatedness. Comparative studies of social organizations in various groups of animals uncovered correlations with such ecological variables as the distribution of food and predators. It is possible to conclude, therefore, as socioecologists and sociobiologists have done, that social organization is an adaptation to environmental conditions.

The intensive field studies of primates that began in the 1960s yielded many wonderful facts, including the surprising variety in primate societies. In an influential paper, Crook and Gartlan (1966) noted that such diversity

made better sense when species were grouped by shared ecological variables rather than by **genealogy**. For example, the size of a monkey troop is
larger when the food supply is distributed in large clumps, and smaller when
food is distributed in widely separated, small clumps. The adaptation in this
case is that many individuals can feed at the same time only when a relatively large amount of food is available at the same location.

Two closely related monkeys, the common baboon and the hamadryas
baboon, provide an often-cited example. Common baboons live on the open
savannah or in light forest, and in large groups that include many adult
males and females, infants, and adolescents, a pattern that is typical of most
monkey species. The animals travel together and feed on a varied diet that
is relatively abundant and clumped. The hamadryas species, on the other
hand, lives in an arid environment and feeds on acacia trees that grow in
small, widely scattered clumps. These monkeys travel and forage in groups
that include a single adult male, a few adult females, and their dependent
young. Males that do not belong to these mixed-sex groups form small all-
male groups. A similar social organization is found among gelada baboons,
an Ethiopian species that also inhabits a dry environment with sparse, scattered food. Thus, adaptation to the distribution of food has implications for
the group structure, which encompasses the age and sex distribution of it
members, the degree and type of competition among males for reproductive
access, sex differences in roles and behavior, and a host of other variables.

Resources other than food, such as water and sleeping sites, as well as
environmental dangers, such as predators, are also taken into account when
correlating selective pressures with social structure. These environmental
variables are correlated with one another to varying degrees. For example,
the predator density is low in the more arid primate habitats. It is possible
that primates, like birds (Crook, 1965), can be grouped into adaptive grades,
based on clusters of these selective pressures and the adaptively correlated
social organization.

Although subsequent work moved in the direction of quantifying the
relations between specific social and ecological variables, refining and cor-
recting some of Crook and Gartlan's conclusions (Crook, 1970b; Clutton-
Brock & Harvey, 1977), their general point remains and has been extended
to many other animal groups (Krebs & Davies, 1981). It is indeed possible
to study social structure as an adaptation. Perhaps the most persistently
examined aspect is the **mating system**.

Most species of birds form pair bonds, and both male and female parents
take part in caring for young at a single nest. In some species, however,
males may be polygynous, mating with more than one female, with each female maintaining her own brood in a separate nest. This pattern can occur
in redwing blackbirds, a species that forms breeding territories defended by
the male. The functional question that has been asked is why such a pattern
would arise. Although the functional answer for the successful male is clear

enough, is it adaptive for females to mate with a polygynous male? The evidence supports an ecological answer: even if a male has another mate and does not help feed the young, more food can be collected and more offspring fledged on his territory, provided it is sufficiently rich in food, than on the poorer territory of a helping male who has no other mate (Orions, 1969).

The converse question can be asked for mammals that do not frequently have long-term pair bonds and the males of which do not typically care for the young. Nevertheless, some mammalian species do form long-term pair bonds, and in some the males engage in extensive parental care. Why do they do so? Again, an adaptive answer is possible. When conditions are sufficiently demanding and the female is unable to provide adequate care on her own, paternal care may be necessary. Two examples are marmosets and tamarins, small, arboreal primates that form enduring pair bonds and defend territories. These animals are unusual in that they typically give birth to twins, thus setting a challenge for the mother. Fathers carry the young, which has the adaptive consequences of allowing the mother to forage without encumbrance and gain adequate food to support pregnancy and lactation (Snowdon, 1990).

The necessity of providing resources for developing young can also explain parental care in invertebrates, animals among which such care is typical of neither male nor female. In addition to the well-known complex societies of some ants, bees, and wasps, parental care can be observed in scattered instances among insects (Tallamy, 1984). Apart from the rather common parental task of guarding, more extensive care is associated with either extremely harsh environments, where parents provide food, oxygen, or otherwise condition the environment to make it compatible with offspring survival, or with extremely favorable, but rare, conditions that require defense.

For example, several species of burying beetles locate a small, dead vertebrate, such as a mouse or bird, transport the body to an appropriate site, bury it, shape it into a ball cleaned of fur or feathers, and lay eggs on the prepared ball of flesh. The male and female participate in transporting, burying, and preparing the carrion. Carrion is a source of food that is both rich and relatively rare, which makes it adaptive to defend against conspecifics seeking the same resource. Both parents guard the developing eggs and larvae and feed them the carrion as a regurgitated liquid (Milne & Milne, 1976).

Countless other examples could be added from across the animal kingdom. It is indeed impressive that the social organization of a species can be interpreted and even partly predicted from information about a rather limited set of ecological conditions. The conditions most often identified as important include the type of food, including its stability and predictability in the environment; the dispersal pattern, in time and space, of food, shelter, and other resources; the type and number of predators and parasites; and the rate and degree of change in the environment, including climatic factors as well as the resources and dangers noted above. These and other ecological conditions restrict the range of social organizations that would be adaptive in any given environment.

Of course, social organization (and its adaptedness) is also affected by organismic factors, including such simple features as body size, which can in turn alter other organismic characters. Body weight is positively correlated with sexual **dimorphism** in primates (Clutton-Brock & Harvey, 1977), and the degree of sexual dimorphism in a group can affect its organization. The size of an animal is also related to its ability to deal with thermal changes, a fact that has social implications for species in which parents and other companions serve thermoregulatory functions (Alberts & Cramer, 1988). It should be emphasized that similar social organizations can be arrived at through very different mechanisms. These mechanisms are likely to vary across species in ways that make phylogenetic sense (see chapter 3).

The Genetic Measure of Fitness

Another major achievement of sociobiology stems from the (problematical) assumption that natural selection operates at the level of the genome (Maynard Smith, 1964; Hamilton, 1964; Wilson, 1975). Indeed, it is assumed that only the gene can be the unit of selection (Williams, 1966). Social behavior and related characters are explained as techniques for promoting the perpetuation of genes in offspring populations.

By assuming the gene to be the unit of selection, the sociobiologist provides an account for how behavior that aids another individual can arise through natural selection, even though the behavior incurs costs to the helper. This **altruistic behavior** was a major, unresolved problem in selectionist theory. If the individual is the unit of selection and if natural selection is responsible for all adaptive behaviors, then acts that risk an individual's reproductive success, including altruistic acts, should be eliminated. It would be predicted that such individuals would leave fewer offspring than the recipients of the altruistic act, and the number of individuals engaging in heritable altruistic acts would therefore decline over generations. However, if the gene is the unit of selection, then fitness is increased or decreased by social behaviors that affect the reproductive success of others, *provided that they possess the same genes*. This is the concept of **inclusive fitness** (Hamilton, 1964).

Inclusive fitness is increased if relatives help one another. The decreased reproductive success of the individual who helps does not mean decreased reproductive success of the genes, because relatives share genes. **Kin selection** refers to selection acting through social interactions among relatives (Maynard Smith, 1964). Thus, the genes in common between the helping individual and the recipient of the help allow for the maintenance of that behavior, even though it is risky to the helper. Knowledge of the risk to the individual's reproductive success and the degree of genetic relationship between the helper and the one that is helped, allows calculation of the costs and benefits of the behavior. Such calculation can then serve as an estimate of the natural selective pressures operating on that behavior. Sociobiologists use such calculations to characterize the evolution of patterns of social behavior.

Consider child care. The first question posed by the sociobiologist would be, "Why do parents care for their offspring?" Given the conditions of the environment and the abilities of the offspring of certain species, it is easily recognized that parental care is necessary for the survival of the offspring. Therefore, strong natural selection favors parental caregiving. The sociobiologist may assume further that the basic characteristics of the care are genetically heritable.

But why is it often the biological parent who provides the care, and not just any adult? Sociobiologists assume that each individual attempts to maximize the representation of his or her particular genes in the gene pool of the population. This is achieved by reproduction: the more of one's offspring in a population, the more representation of one's genes in the gene pool. Parental care ensures the survival of the offspring and therefore their occurrence in the population; however, it involves some investment of energy and time on the part of the caregiver.

Sociobiologists assume further that there is both a level of care necessary to ensure the survival of the young and a limit to the amount of care that can be provided before it becomes destructive to the caregiver. The central prediction of the theory is that the degree to which an individual will invest resources in caregiving will be related to the degree of genetic similarity between the caregiver and the recipient (kin selection). Therefore, because the biological parent is likely to have more genes in common with its offspring than any other individual in the population, that is the one that will provide the care. Genes of individuals that invest energy in the care of genetically unrelated offspring will quickly disappear from the gene pool after several generations.

Trivers (1971) described another way that helping behavior could arise through natural selection—**reciprocal altruism**. Reciprocal altruism involves helping among genetically unrelated individuals. For it to evolve, the benefits to the recipient must be high, the cost to the helper relatively low, and the likelihood of their positions being reversed in the future high. It is also important that those who do not reciprocate be identified. Computer simulation programs reveal that deceptive behavior can be tolerated only at very low levels in the population. As deception increases, reciprocal altruism decreases and the pressures for deception decrease, which leads to a decrease in deception.

In some instances the fitness interests of individuals coincide. In others, *conflicts of fitness interest* arise between individuals. Parents and offspring, siblings, and mated pairs differ in terms of which outcome of their social interactions will give them the greatest fitness. Again consider the phenomenon of parental caregiving. If parental care is so important for fitness, why does weaning occur? The sociobiological answer lies in the fact that offspring of sexually reproducing animals have only part of their genes in common with a parent. The more parental care the offspring receive, the better their chances of survival. This is the social pattern that would maximize their contribution to the gene pool. However, the more care a parent provides, the less his or her chance of survival and/or of producing more offspring. Therefore, beyond a certain point, providing care to the young reduces the parent's fitness. It is predicted that the interactions between parent and offspring will reflect this conflict of genetic interest, with the traits of offspring having the effect of maintaining or increasing parental care, and the traits of the parent reducing it at the appropriate time. Weaning begins when continued parental investment in one offspring or litter would reduce the parent's total contribution by interfering with subsequent reproduction. Processes of natural selection would ensure the development of mechanisms that allow recognition of when during the course of caregiving that crucial point has been reached. Thus, the sociobiologist might argue that, because of the inherent conflict of fitness interest between parent and offspring, weaning can never be trauma free (Trivers, 1972).

Differences in fitness interests can also occur between males and females, often involving conflict. The conflict centers on sex differences in reproductive mechanisms, which afford different reproductive opportunities and exact different energetic costs. For most sexually reproducing species, there are initial asymmetries in nonbehavioral aspects of reproduction, such as unequal size of sperm and egg, pregnancy, and lactation.

Parental care illustrates the argument that links these initial asymmetries to differences in behavior. Male mammals do not incur gestation or initial feeding costs; therefore they have little investment to lose by engaging in further courtship and copulation. Female mammals, in contrast, have invested heavily in pregnancy and lactation, and have much to lose by neglecting the young so as to court and copulate anew. Because males have invested less initially, they are more likely to desert offspring, which sets conditions that require even more care from the mothers to ensure survival of young. Indeed, under many conditions, males can increase their overall fitness by deserting one mate and their young and pursuing other females. This is not the case for females. They are under selective pressure to keep males from deserting and to increase this parental care, so as to reduce their own costs. Thus, females will attempt to keep males from deserting.

Several general conclusions can be made from this line of reasoning. The parent of whichever sex that at any time has contributed most to the development of offspring is likely to continue contributing, because that parent has the most to lose. Because of sexual asymmetries, optimum reproductive strategies are not the same for males and females. A conflict of fitness interest often exists between members of a pair, with the two sexes required to engage in a variety of behaviors, some of them deceptions, to pursue their most optimum reproductive strategy.

Several complications have to be considered before the sociobiological theory of sexual conflict over parental care is applied to real cases. The asymmetry in initial, nonbehavioral reproductive costs, such as more nutrients in cytoplasm of eggs than of sperm or internal gestation, may have to be balanced by other considerations. For example, males would not be expected to desert in species with a 1:1 sex ratio and a synchronized breeding season. Synchronized breeding requires males to invest a very large amount of energy in competing with other males during courtship and copulation, under conditions in which second chances to mate are sharply limited. In such a context, selective pressure should lead a male to be choosy about a mate, because the female he courts may be the only one he mates, and to help with the care of his relatively few offspring. Desertion is adaptive in males only when the number of his surviving offspring and their eventual reproductive success are equal to or greater than would be the case if he provided parental care. Thus, desertion can be a primary strategy when the male's parental care adds little to the survival or subsequent breeding success of the young, and when he can find other fertile females (Maynard Smith, 1977).

Human Sociality

The sociobiological concepts of natural and sexual selection, parental investment, inclusive fitness, and kin selection have been widely applied to issues of human behavior. For example, they were used to explain the selection of mates (Buss, 1987, 1989b), sex differences in close relationships (Buss, 1989a), the character of masculine and feminine behavior (Crawford, 1989; Daly & Wilson, 1978), rape (Thornhill & Thornhill, 1992), the differential training of boys and girls (Low, 1989), homicide, and the abuse of adopted children (Daly & Wilson, 1988).

Forced copulations, infanticide, intraspecies killing, and cannibalism do sometimes occur among animals. When they do, sociobiologists interpret them as consequences of natural selection operating within the arena of reproductive competition. It is argued by extension that the occurrence of these behaviors among humans may represent the consequences of natural selection, as well. Consider Thornhill and Thornhill's (1992, p. 363) statement that "adaptation underlies all human behavior. Thus, sexual coercion

evolution of rape

by men could either arise from a rape-specific psychological adaptation or it could be a side-effect of a more general psychological adaptation not directly related to rape. Determining the specific environmental cues that men's brains have been designed by selection to process may help us decide which of these rival explanations is correct." This quotation reveals a remarkable degree of faith in the universality of adaptation, which is understood as "designed by selection," as an explanation for behavior.

Although the adaptationist formulation proposed by the Thornhills allows for the fact that not all men rape, it does assert that a genetically based *tendency* to rape when at a reproductive disadvantage is a general characteristic of men. Specifically, the authors hypothesize a genetically programmed connection, shaped by natural selection, between a tendency to rape and particular situations (Thornhill & Thornhill, 1987, 1992). It is important to note that the hypothesized link is between tendency and situation, rather than between behavior and situation; thus, the theory is made to accommodate the fact that men do not always rape even when conditions are "appropriate." A serious limitation in the theory is obvious, because it is difficult to imagine how the hypothesis could be falsified. Careful, critical attention should be given to adaptationist arguments such as this. They have profound implications for how we understand the causation and development of personality characteristics and how we establish public policies to deal with human problems.

Transcultural sex differences in mate selection have also been explained by sociobiological principles. Men tend to choose mates on the basis of physical attractiveness, whereas women tend to do so on the basis of the resources that can be gained from them (Buss, 1989b). Since female fertility is age dependent and since certain physical characteristics (smooth skin, good muscle tone, etc.) are associated with age, physical features can be an indicator of fertility in women. In contrast, male fertility is not as age dependent, and physical features would not be as indicative of fertility in men. Therefore, males would be expected to place more value on physical attractiveness of a mate than would females. "[T]he adult human male brain contains one or more adaptations designed to produce maximal sexual attraction, other things being equal, to certain physical correlates of human female nubility ..." (Symons, 1990, p. 429).

In contrast to males, female reproductive success is not closely linked to finding fertile mates, because males' availability is not typically a limiting factor. However, reproductive success among females is related to finding a mate who will provide resources appropriate for rearing young. Thus, selection would have favored psychological mechanisms among females for detecting the possession of resources, such as food, shelter, territory, and protection, in prospective mates. The sociobiological explanation of human mate preferences nicely demonstrates Hinde's (1992) conclusion that sociobiology is more an interpretation of already known information and less a prediction about events not yet observed. That is, if it had been discovered that women depended on physical attractiveness for choosing potential mates, it could be determined that men's physical features reflect their access to resources. Indeed, a similar argument is used to account for the fact that females of many species of mammals and birds choose mates on the basis of their preference for particular physical characteristics, such as long feathers or quality of courtship. Furthermore, in the human case, other questions can be raised. For example, do women choose mates with resources because the resources are valued as parental investment, or because of a personal interest in the possession of material wealth?

Daly and Wilson (1988) used Hamilton's theory of inclusive fitness and other sociobiological ideas to generate hypotheses about a variety of human social problems. They predicted patterns of adult homicide and found support for the prediction that child abuse, neglect, and infanticide would be most common in conditions indicating low reproductive value—uncertain paternity or rearing by step-parent, lack of resources, and defects in the child. They also used sociobiological principles to account for the suppression of sibling conflict as part of parental socialization. Parental socialization is traditionally interpreted as the transfer of cultural beliefs, but Daly and Wilson offer a reinterpretation: socialization is the result of a conflict of genetic interests between parents and children. Parents, as the more powerful individuals in the interaction, use this power to establish moral strictures and emphasize their importance so as to reduce the time and effort required to care for their children or to reduce conflict among siblings. Both of these consequences would increase the fitness of the parents. Thus parental behavior usually interpreted as the socialization of children is reinterpreted as enhancing parental fitness.

Sociobiology was designed to explain the evolution of social behavior within the framework of the synthetic theory of evolution, it is not designed to explain developmental phenomena. Nevertheless, sociobiologists formulated postulates about development that are seen to follow logically from their assumptions about the genetic basis of fitness. All social behavior that contributes to fitness must be genetically heritable. Furthermore, it is necessary for the genes to constrain the development of social behavior, because the phenotype must be a reliable vehicle to carry fit genes from one generation to the next. The presumption of a strong genetic influence on the development of adaptive social traits extends to many human characteristics, including cultural phenomena.

In the sociobiological scheme, the primary mechanism through which genes constrain the development of social behavior is by programming the maturation of the nervous system. Of course, this basic assumption is often qualified by disavowing developmental fixity. Sociobiologists often acknowledge that genetically programmed maturation does not inevitably lead to particular behaviors, and that behaviors resulting from such maturation can be modified by extrinsic influences once they appear. Alongside the qualifications, however, is the clear assumption that the development of social behavior has final outcomes that are hard to avoid or to change (Smith, 1987; Gruter, 1986; Alexander, 1979, 1987) *because* these outcomes were established by natural selection acting on genes. The conclusion arises from particular views of how genes work (deterministically), of how characters are transmitted (only those with a genetic basis can have been selected for transmission to future generations), and of how adaptations are achieved (by natural selection of genes, through associated characters, to fit the environment of evolutionary adaptedness).

Despite its successes, sociobiology has a number of serious problems. One of the most telling is that its assumptions about development fly in the face of evidence. For example, many features of human societies point to an exceptional degree of inventiveness and developmental plasticity. Despite their obvious centrality to the human condition, these features must be either ignored or deemphasized before sociobiological principles can be applied to human societies. Nevertheless, these very features have radically and repeatedly altered the human environment and the selective pressures it affords. Different cultures use various technological and social strategies to exploit otherwise unusable ecological resources. The partial buffers created by human inventiveness allow populations to increase beyond the carrying capacity of the immediate ecology and to engage in activities that are ecologically maladaptive. The present environment for humans has been changed beyond all recognition from the evolutionary one (Geist, 1978).

Human beings, with their ability to conceive of their ecological resources as worldwide in scope and virtually limitless with improved technology and management, can achieve complex social organizations that are unlike those of any other animal species, both in terms of complexity and degree of independence from the selective pressures considered by current sociobiological theory. Sociobiologists attempt to address these problems in two ways, by studying traditional societies and by using historical evidence to identify adaptations in early human social and cultural organizations. These research strategies may indeed identify some human adaptations to ecological conditions that were in force during early evolution. However, how does one explain the diversity of contemporary social arrangements among humans? One possibility is to adopt the position of other predeterminists and treat departures from the early hominid adaptations as pathologies, but this raises all the criticisms that have been marshalled against this approach to development (chapters 2 and 3).

Current sociobiological arguments are logical extensions from a set of assumptions. Some of these extensions strike us as absurd caricatures, but they do reveal the underlying assumptions in their starkest form. Once this is done, it becomes clear that some assumptions accepted by sociobiological theory must be discarded, because they are inconsistent with what we know about genetics, development, and the causation of behavior. The two most problematic assumptions are that every measurable aspect of behavior is a character that is determined directly by genes in Mendelian fashion, and that evolution occurs because natural selection shapes each of these atomistically defined characters by progressive changes, over generations, in the frequencies of particular alleles in the underlying gene pool. It is possible to drop both these assumptions, however, and retain an evolutionary explanation of social behavior that includes both adaptation and natural selection as explanatory principles. Furthermore, difficult problems, such as altruism, may drop away as pseudoproblems once the theory is freed of its restricting, flawed assumptions. The example of helping at the nest will illustrate this point.

Several different birds (e.g., some jays, kingfishers, mockingbirds, white-fronted bee eaters, etc.) form extended family groups that are retained during the breeding season, a phenomenon known as cooperative or communal breeding. Nonreproducing, typically younger, group members often help at the nest, particularly by collecting food for nestlings. A great deal of effort has gone into explaining the evolution of helping behavior in terms of individual and inclusive fitness models. This work begins with the assumption that feeding young when not a parent is a different character than doing so as a parent, and the new (altruistic, helping) character is assumed to be under its own selective pressure.

However, it is possible to reconceptualize the evolutionary question (Jamieson, 1989) and consider feeding young as the character (or set of characters) that evolved subject to selective pressure on survival of young. The trait is expressed in nonreproducing individuals in communally breeding species as a secondary result of the evolution of communal breeding: they have access to the stimuli that normally lead to the provisioning behavior. Because of the uninterrupted nature of the social relations between parents and younger group members, which are often the older offspring of the parents, helpers are permitted close proximity to the nest and nestlings.

Jamieson suggests that the evolution of helping may be considered as an example of behavioral heterochrony. Because of communal breeding conditions, the potential helpers are placed in situations that lead to the development of provisioning behavior at an earlier age than is typical. Furthermore, the breeding conditions provide a context in which the behavior can be expressed. Thus, helping is a behavior that is likely to emerge during development, given certain ecological and social conditions, and these conditions occur during an unusually early age in communal breeders. This explanation accounts for the observations that helping can vary from season to season and according to the availability of breeding sites and food resources.

By placing helping in a developmental perspective, the adaptive questions become the more common problems of communal breeding and explaining the origin of bringing food to nestlings (a challenge common to Passeriformes and various other birds) rather than the problem of altruistic helping. Partly because of the reliance on the synthetic theory within sociobiology, this alternative account, where helping behavior arises through no direct effect of natural selection, has received little serious attention (Jamieson, 1986, 1989).

Jamieson's account of helping with care of young by nonparental birds may also be usefully extended to care of young by fathers. In some but not all species of songbirds, the male parent takes turns with his mate in gathering food for the young. It is possible to administer hormones to generate a change in the male's behavioral phenotype, thereby devising an experimental test of the fitness value of his helping behavior. Specifically, testosterone levels are typically high during courtship and the early phases of nesting, dropping to low levels when young appear. This drop in testosterone is associated with the amount of parental care the male provides (Ketterson, Nolan, Wolf, & Ziegenfus, 1992).

Testosterone implants have been used in field experiments to keep the levels artificially high during late stages of nesting. This approach was applied to dark-eyed juncos, a species in which males typically share feeding duties with females (Ketterson et al., 1992). Testosterone severely reduced the amount of feeding that males did, but this reduction was completely compensated by increased feeding activity on the part of the females. Furthermore, at least under the ecological conditions and with the fitness measures used, there was no change in the fitness of either males or females. However, when the males were caught and removed from the study site at the time of hatching, fitness was reduced, as measured by fledgling survival, weight loss in the female, and weight gain by the young (Wolf, Ketterson, & Nolan, 1988).

Another parental activity is nest guarding to defend against predators, typically chipmunks in the case of the dark-eyed junco. A single parent cannot guard the nest continuously because of the need to make foraging trips. Perhaps the functional advantage of the male's presence lies in helping to ward off predators, or perhaps in improving his chances of retaining a mate for the next season (Ketterson et al., 1992). Feeding his young may be under no particular selection in the male: he may engage in this behavior because he remains at the nest site, has reduced testosterone levels, and is exposed to the same stimuli as the female parent.

The importance of contextual factors has long been recognized by social ecologists (Crook, 1970a; Emlen, 1976; Lott, 1984; Rowell, 1972). Reports of variations in social structures for the same species of primates began to accumulate as soon as field studies on the same species were conducted at more than one site (see chapter 2, box 2.2). To take an early example of this structural plasticity, DeVore (1965), working on the open savannah, described the common baboon society as highly structured by a male dominance hierarchy. Rowell (1966), working on the forest's edge, described the same species as loosely structured, with no apparent male hierarchy or special male roles. Disparate descriptions of other species were also made (Fedigan, 1982): in some locales, langurs are found in violently aggressive, unstable groups, whereas elsewhere the groups are stable and peaceable; vervets are territorial in some contexts, but not in others.

Some variations in primate societies can be accounted for by (perhaps random) demographic fluctuations that alter the age and sex composition of a group (Altman & Altman, 1979). The particular pattern of kinship relations that characterizes any given group will also exhibit local differences, perhaps by accident of birth and death, and may be sufficiently different in two groups to cause differences in the way overall group structure would be seen and described.

In addition to these factors, ecological conditions are important sources of variation that can fluctuate rather rapidly in time and space, leading to local, reversible changes in societies as relatively immediate responses to contextual demands. The distribution and richness of food and other resources can cause groups to grow or shrink in size (by immigration, emigration, survival, or death of members) or density (by increasing or decreasing the distance between individuals as a function of individual responses to environmental features—food, water, shade, etc.), can alter time budgets by providing more or less time for social interactions, and can produce different amounts of stress and nutrition status that can alter the quality of social interactions. Changes in these and similar features of a group can have the effect of changing overall group structure.

Contextually based plasticity in social structure is not limited to primates; it was described in various birds and mammals (Emlen, 1976; Lott, 1984). Ground squirrels, for example, have polygynous mating systems in which male-male competition is enacted through dominance hierarchies, territoriality, or scramble competition (Schwagmeyer, 1990). In territorial systems, males defend an area that includes a variable number of female burrows; territory holders win disputes and keep other males from mating with the females on their territory. There is no territory in a dominance-based system, and males differ in their ability to win agonistic encounters that occur near the burrows of females; winners are likely to mate. In the scramble competition system, males do not engage in agonistic behavior. Instead, they spend their time searching for females in estrus; those that find these females at the right time are most successful at reproducing. These systems are associated with different species of ground squirrels, and the species live in different habitats, describable in terms of resource distribution. The distribution of food, in turn, is correlated with the dispersion of females.

Thirteen-line ground squirrels have the most disperse pattern of female burrows. Males in this species spend a great deal of time traveling long distances searching out females. Species, such as the California ground squirrel, whose females place their burrows close together, have the most prevalent system for this group of animals—male territoriality. However, when the burrows are very close, as in Belding's ground squirrel, nonterritorial dominance systems are found. Perhaps dominance systems are the limiting case for territoriality in these animals, present where male density is too high for effective territorial defense.

In ground squirrels and their relatives, males that are best at spatial learning and long-distance running are best adapted to the scramble competition systems, and males that are best fighters are best adapted for the systems that rely on agonism. However, whether these masculine features, or the social systems associated with them, are direct effects of natural selection is an open question. Although members of one species are likely to exhibit a particular social system, this may be only because they are likely to inhabit a particular kind of environment. Developmental and immediate contextual effects of the environment can be hypothesized. In ground squirrels and other small mammals local populations of the same species sometimes live in different habitats and form different social systems (Schwagmeyer, 1990). They may differ because of the accumulated effects of differential selection in the two locales, or because of contextual effects, independent of selection.

The rapidity with which social systems can change is inconsistent with the assumption of genetic determination. It is also unsatisfactory to put the issue off with ad hoc postulations of genetically determined potentials—a singularly untestable idea since anything could be "potential." However, the assumption of genetic determination of development is irrelevant to adaptation. Traits can be adaptive, maladaptive, or neutral regardless of how they develop. Furthermore, within-species diversities in social phenomena can be understood as ecological adaptations.

Despite the assumptions of sociobiologists, the rejection of genetic determination as an explanation of development does not detract from the importance of recognizing that social behavior can be adapted to particular ecological demands, or that certain ecological problems may have only a few behavioral solutions. Of course, once genetic determinism is rejected, it must be replaced with a theory of development that is consistent both with evolutionary adaptation and developmental processes. The incorporation of developmental ideas into evolutionary theory has had the effect of calling many of the assumptions and ideas of the synthetic theory into question.

Problems with the Synthetic Theory

The synthetic theory clearly can claim monumental achievements. Nevertheless, it is important to remember that it is a theory, with hypotheses that must be put to experimental test and data that must be examined critically. Hailman (1982) compellingly argued that the evidence typically presumed to support both the stabilizing and directing effects of natural selection fail to do so. Indeed, he noted that if the evidence of artificial selection obtained from breeding and laboratory studies is ignored, little or no evidence exists that natural selection occurs in naturally occurring populations. Little or no evidence does not mean a wealth of contrary evidence; it means simply that critical data that can rule out competing hypotheses have rarely been collected. Hailman provides us with a critical reexamination of a noted example, industrial melanism, to make his point.

In a series of papers published during the 1950s, Kettlewell (1956, 1961) reported both experimental and correlational data that were interpreted as clear evidence of directional selection on the coloration of moths. When these moths rest on trees during the day, they are unlikely to be detected by their major predators, birds, if their coloration matches the trees. This was verified by direct observation of the foraging behavior of birds with camouflaged moths. In unpolluted regions of Britain, trees are covered with light-colored lichens. However, industrial pollution, which began during the second half of the nineteenth century, killed the lichens and darkened trees in some parts of the British isles.

Like many other moths, *Biston betularia*, the species studied by Kettlewell, has two color variants—one light and the other dark, with the dark variant inherited as a dominant allele. Kettlewell studied collections taken from Manchester, a region that was subjected to industrial growth and pollution. He found that the dark color came to predominate, accounting for almost all (98%) of captured *B. betularia* moths by 1895, whereas they were rare in 1848. Furthermore, at the time of his studies, dark variants predominated in other polluted areas as well, and light variants predominated in unpolluted regions. Experimental release and recapture of marked individuals produced results consistent with differential selection on these two variants: a low percentage of mismatched (light in polluted or dark in unpolluted areas) individuals were recaptured, suggesting that they had been frequently taken by predators during the intervening period.

Despite the carefully collected lines of data converging in support of a selectionist hypothesis, Hailman outlines several problems. Melanism is based on a dominant allele, and it may carry with it advantages apart from predator avoidance in sooty, lichen-free environments. If so, it may have increased in frequency quite apart from the presumed selection from birds. Furthermore, there is some evidence that environmental chemicals may have a direct physiological influence on the development of color. Thus, both selective and nonselective alternatives to avian predation could affect variations in the color of moths.

Another problem has to do with the nature of the data used to support the selectionist argument. Selection acting on changes in the gene pool requires that one variant increases in frequency in a population at the expense of another—there are changes in proportions of alleles. Selection at the species level means that one population replaces another without mixing of gene pools. A change in the proportion of moths bearing a particular phenotype in some particular locale may result from either process, but it could also result from a change in the dispersal pattern of moths from other locales, with no selection occurring. Thus, an influx of dark moths to a particular region would increase the proportion of dark moths even if the numbers of light moths remained constant; more moths simply may be present in the vicinity than previously. Kettlewell's studies show evidence for extensive dispersal of melanic moths.

The methodological point of appropriate counting is important, because many field studies guided by selectionist hypotheses collect data on the change in frequency of individuals bearing some trait in some locale without simultaneously counting the total population bearing this or alternative traits. Such evidence is not evidence of selection.

Hailman's (1982) point was not to reject natural selection as a directing or stabilizing factor in the evolution of species because of the lack of rigorous data. Rather, he urged that we recognize that natural selection is a hypothesis that, like any other, requires empirical demonstration. It is only one of several hypotheses that can be generated to explain evolution. Hailman called for more careful investigation to provide the evidence that would test the operation of natural selection in natural situations.

Of course, extensive data are consistent with the operation of natural selection in both laboratory and field. Controlled breeding studies indicate that it can operate at the microevolutionary level, accumulating gradual change. Like artificial selection, natural selection may be responsible for changes in gene frequencies from generation to generation within a naturally occurring population. These changes could sharpen the adaptive fit of a local population (deme) to the local environment. However, many of these changes initially involve behavioral development and adjustment.

In addition to the challenge of assembling an adequate empirical test of microevolutionary change in response to natural selection, other serious problems must be addressed before the synthesis of genetics and evolution can be completed. We have singled out three such problems that could be addressed by greater attention to the role of development: conceiving of organisms as mosaics of adapted traits; assuming a linear path from gene to trait; and using the niche concept as the driving force of evolution.

Organisms as Mosaics of Adapted Traits

The adaptationist view associated with the synthetic theory, including its most recent version in sociobiology, assumes that the evolution of complex organisms must be understood by the "atomization" of their traits, which are then explained as optimum responses to selection pressures (Mitchell, 1992). The theory does not predict or easily accommodate the appearance or persistence of nonadvantageous or neutral characters, or characters that might have a future use, even though the fact of such characters has been recognized. The label of "preadaptation" has long been in use to describe features at a stage before they become adaptive.

Current critics of the adaptationist view (e.g., Gould & Lewontin, 1979) propose that any feature that an organism possesses may be derived in a number of ways. First, it may have been constructed by the processes of natural selection, or it may have been co-opted for its current use from a different use. In this latter case it would be an **exaptation** (Gould, 1991; Gould & Vrba, 1982). Third, the feature may have arisen with no particular function at all. Hinde (1986) commented that although functional interpretations of behavior may aid in our comprehension of many features already known, they are seldom predictive: hands may be very good for throwing rocks, shooting arrows, and pressing triggers, but that does not mean that manipulative skill arose as an adaptation for success in aggression.

Chance, migration, and mutation can contribute to the presence of a trait in a population. Also, direct environmental modulation can be responsible for the appearance of traits. Lima de Faria (1988) proposed ambient temperature as the reason that tropical birds, insects, fish, and so on tend to be more brightly colored and multicolored than species in temperate and polar regions. Physicochemical dynamics are affected by ambient temperature and can give rise to the bright coloration of tissue. Environmental changes can affect the appearance of a trait and, if an environmental condition continues across generations, the trait may not have to be reinvented in each generation. This is rather similar to the Baldwin effect and to Waddington's (1956, 1975) concept of genetic assimilation (cf. Gottlieb, 1992). Human culture is the most obvious (but certainly not the only) example of the effects of environmental modulation.

The final nonselective explanation of traits concerns the developmental laws of form. Kauffman (1987, 1993) created several dynamic and network models showing that certain kinds of order emerge "spontaneously" in the development of complex systems. Kauffman's theory is an alternative causal model to selection because it shows that traits may be self-organized consequences that emerge from the basic structure of the system itself. Thus, traits can emerge quite independent of the direct or indirect actions of natural selection. This is not to say that natural selection does not act on these traits once they make their appearance. Traits may arise that serve some function, an exaptation (Gould & Vrba, 1982). New traits may also be evolutionarily neutral, neither serving a function nor interfering with reproductive success. Exaptation and neutral features mark the stochastic or unpredictable, random, nondeterministic aspect of evolutionary phenomena among successful species. Of course, new traits may also be maladaptive and

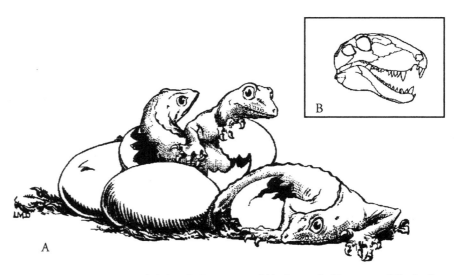

Figure 4.2   Reptiles, which hatch from eggs (A), have skull sutures (B) similar to those of human neonates. Clearly, mammalian skull sutures were not an adaptation for delivery through a narrow birth canal (modified from E. H. Colbert, 1980. *Evolution of the vertebrates*, 3rd ed. Copyright © 1980 John Wiley & Sons, Inc. Reprinted by permission of John Wiley & Sons, Inc.)

either be carried along with a package of other traits that work well enough (Arnold, 1987; chapter 5) or mark the organism for evolutionary failure.

The originator of natural selection was himself well aware of these possibilities. Darwin (1859) stated that nonadaptationist features of organisms must be distinguished from those that were created by natural selection. "The sutures in the skulls of young mammals have been advanced as a beautiful adaptation for aiding parturition, and no doubt they facilitate, or may be indispensable for this act; but as sutures occur in the skulls of young birds and reptiles, which have only to escape from a broken egg, we may infer that this structure has arisen from the laws of growth and has been taken advantage of in the parturition of higher mammals" (p. 197). Therefore, skull sutures are not an adaptive feature of mammals (figure 4.2); they were not created by natural selection (box 4.2). Although they may represent a general adaptive feature derived from natural selection pressures common to reptiles, birds, and mammals, no evidence as yet supports that argument.

Linear Path from Gene to Trait

A second major disadvantage of the synthetic theory is the assumption of **linear causation**; that is, evolution is directed solely by the effects of environments on genes, as mediated by the direct effects of environments on the

Box 4.2   Adaptive, Exaptive, and Evolutionarily Neutral Characteristics

Some troops of Japanese macaques have been regularly given sweet potatoes, wheat, and other food by humans. As a result of this reliable source of concentrated food, the monkeys no longer have to forage. Although not the intent, the provisioning has relaxed selective pressures on foraging and created a "laboratory" for identifying some of the complex ways in which adaptive, exaptive, and neutral characteristics can arise and be maintained.

A heritable developmental anomaly occasionally appears in which the affected monkey is unable to open or spread its fingers and, often, the toes. These individuals seldom survive weaning in most environments, because both locomotion and food handling are impaired. However, the anomaly is seen in a significant proportion of the adult population of the provisioned troops. It has flourished as a novel character because of the joint effects of provisioning and aspects of Japanese monkey society.

A mother's younger sisters or adolescent daughters express great interest in her infant and will carry it and provide it with care whenever she permits. This "aunting" behavior continues after weaning but gradually subsides as the normal infant matures into an active, independent adolescent. However, if the developing adolescent has impaired used of its hands or feet because of the developmental anomaly, it retains the capacity to elicit care from several aunts. The females continue to direct caregiving to adolescents beyond the usual time because of the stimulus properties of the recipients—they are, for example, not as active as normal adolescents—and because they have time on their hands, with food so readily available. In a typical monkey environment that requires a lot of foraging time, aunting behavior would not be able to sustain the affected monkey, because the aunts would be too busy elsewhere. Food provisioning alone would also not support the affected monkeys, because they would be unable to retrieve and use the food. But in a setting with both provisioning and aunting, the anomaly is evolutionarily neutral: it is not an adaptive character, and there is no selective force against it. The aunting behavior, perhaps adaptive for other reasons, serves the function of maintaining in the population a set of characters that were not themselves selected.

It is possible to imagine environmental changes that would make novel configurations of the hand, including inflexible digits, useful for reproductive success. If such a change should occur, the anomaly or novelty might be appropriated as an exaptation, but it would not have been *created* by natural selection.

This argument can be applied to the new aquatic habits of the monkeys that are provisioned on the beach. They have acquired the trait of washing their food, which has led them to spend more time in the sea, which monkeys usually avoid. As a consequence, the numbers and types of marine organisms incorporated into their diet have increased. The animals have also adopted the novel behavioral patterns of swimming and diving. If provisioning were stopped, these land-foraging monkeys would have the exaptive possibility of existing entirely on marine food supplies, or extending their range by swimming to nearby islands. Adaptive as these novel behaviors may eventually prove to be, they were not constructed by natural selection.

reproduction of organisms that carry the genes, and the direct effects of these genes on the reproducing and reproduced organisms. The synthetic theory promotes the notion that environmental consequences of organismic activity, especially behavior, do not contribute directly to evolution. "[T]he modern synthesis has to rule out the possibility that the outputs of active organisms are capable of modifying their own subsequent inputs in evolutionarily significant ways" (Odling-Smee, 1988, p. 75). "Yet developing and behaving organisms routinely select and perturb their own relative environments. Thus, at least some of the selection forces that ultimately select genes are themselves selected and modified by behaviors, and other activities, of phenotypes" (Odling-Smee, 1988, p. 74).

Waddington (1975; figure 4.3) drew attention to the fact that organisms can affect their own evolution by choosing and modifying their environments. He called this the *exploitive system*, which, together with the genetic system, the epigenetic system, and the natural selective system, constitute his four subsystems of an evolution system. What Waddington had in mind is that niches are in part the product of organismic activity. Animals select their habitats, often changing them seasonally or for purposes of reproduction. They modify their environments through behavioral means, by making nests, burrows, pathways and other artifacts. They use resources and create waste products. They select social companions, and change their social environments by modifying the behavior and physiological conditions of mates and other companions. They establish and defend territories, leave odor traces, gather and store food, and otherwise produce changes in selective forces that act on themselves and their offspring (see chapter 3). As Lewontin (1983) put it, "organisms do not adapt to their environments; they construct them out of the bits and pieces of the external world" (p. 280). Thus, the synthetic theory must account for the impact of the behavior of the organism on the environment, and this environment is the same selective environment that is proposed to direct the evolution of the organism (box 4.3).

Recall that, in the synthetic theory, the activity of the organism is assumed to reflect the underlying genotype. With this assumption, it is possible to argue that the environment selects those organisms having genetic programs for altering the environment in ways that are consistent with the constraints of the niche. In other words, the environmental consequences of organismic activities are assumed to be determined by previously selected genes. The adaptedness (fitness) of the genes is measured by numerical frequency in the gene pool across generations. With a focus on the individual, the fitness of an organism's behavior (reflecting its genes) is measured by its effect on the organism's capacity to transmit genes to subsequent generations.

It is interesting to examine how behavioral patterns that are clearly acquired through learning or other forms of experience are handled within this theory. If such behavioral patterns contribute to fitness, then what is as-

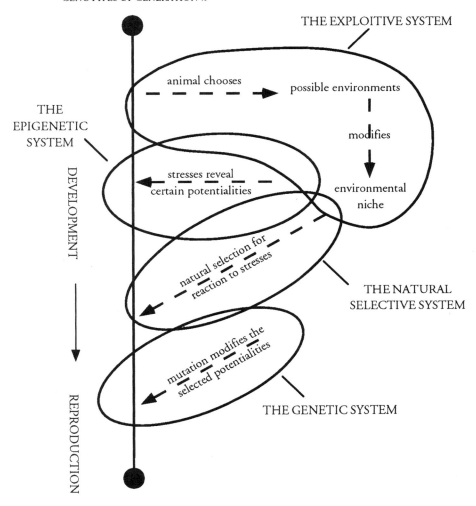

GENOTYPES OF GENERATION *n*

GENOTYPES OF GENERATION *n* + 1

Figure 4.3 Waddington's illustration attempts to integrate processes of development, natural selection, and other factors to account for the changes in genotype between generations (redrawn from Waddington, 1975).

Box 4.3   Niche, Competition, and Natural Selection

In Darwinian theory, competition is the "creator" of the adaptive characteristics of organisms. Evolutionary change occurs by a slow process of competition and displacement. Individuals compete for the resources that represent
the environmental conditions defining a niche. The result of the competition is
represented in reproductive success; the more offspring an individual contributes to future generations, the more successful the individual. Competition
(natural selection) for access to the resources of the niche will hone the characteristics of the population over generations to match the characteristics of
the niche. To help comprehend and communicate the complexity of how the
environment can create adaptive characteristics, Darwin (1859) used the metaphor of a log with thousands of wedges (species) tightly hammered in along its
length (Gould, 1989a). A new species can occur only by entering a crack and
popping another wedge out. Thus, the better a wedge fits a crack, the more
readily it may displace another wedge.

Darwin's metaphor has a certain inherent dynamism. Wedges (species) can
be seen as widening the crack (shaping the niche) as they jam through. This
means that one variation of a species may fill a crack better than another and
therefore displace the current occupant. However, the very process of jamming
a crack and displacing the original occupant creates the conditions (size of the
crack) in which the new occupant may be subsequently displaced by a better
fitting variant (wedge). Indeed, evidence of ecological dynamics supports this
aspect of the metaphor.

Nevertheless, the metaphor can be misleading as well as illuminating. It
creates the impression that some number of potential niches (cracks) may be
filled by only certain limited types of variations (wedges). This sets up the
competition. As variants appear that better fit the crack, the less-fit occupants
will be replaced. The metaphor also creates the impression that the occupant
can affect a crack (niche) only in ways that lead to its potential replacement.
That is, organisms will only affect their environment in ways that make them
less well fit. The metaphor fails to incorporate the ability of organisms to construct their niches and hence contribute to their own evolution. It also fails to
consider the possibility that niches may be created (it is difficult to imagine a
wedge creating a crack in a smooth log).

Of course, all of these problems would be irrelevant were it not that modern
evolutionary biology has begun to examine how organisms play active roles in
directing their own evolutionary changes. The modern evolutionary process is
seen less as a set of specific environmental niches for which organisms compete, thereby leading to the creation of their adaptive characteristics, and more
as a dynamic ecological system in which the niche and the organism participate
in their mutual construction (Odling-Smee, 1988). This change of focus has
profound consequences for developmental psychobiologists (as well as other
scientists) attempting to comprehend and incorporate theories about the processes of natural selection, adaptation, and the identification of adaptive characteristics into their research and theory.

Consider the concept of an ontogenetic niche (West, King, & Arberg, 1988).
These authors make a very persuasive case for the inheritance of specific ecological circumstances in the development of various species of birds and
mammals. That is, the behavior of ancestors provided offspring with ecological

conditions that shape their development in ways more potent than genes. To be even more useful, their concept of ontogenetic niche has to be expanded to capture the dynamics of both organism-environment coevolution and organism-environment interpenetration during development.

sumed in the synthetic theory is that the *capacity* for acquiring the non-genetically encoded behavior is genetically encoded. It is important to note that this assumption is necessary only because the synthetic theory requires that any phenotype contributing to fitness must be determined by genes. Because natural selection works on genes, genes must control the developmental manifestation of the behavior, even if it is only the capacity for the development of the behavior.

However, the study of development provides ample evidence that although genes do contribute to the development of phenotypes, they do not determine them. Moreover, some genes that are associated with the development of phenotypes that contribute to fitness may not be naturally selected; they may be carried by the organism for other reasons. Finally, development itself imposes constraints and direction on the occurrence and expression of organismic activity. To the degree that developmental psychobiological research reveals the processes of development, it will provide evidence relevant for specifying the manner of evolution.

The Niche Concept, Speciation, and Macroevolution

The synthetic theory may be at its weakest when faced with the challenge of evolutionary **novelty**. How do novel forms arise in the course of evolution? The synthetic theory relies on the slow, gradual accretion of changes, but it is difficult to imagine many forms arising in this manner. One of the great strengths of developmental theory is its ability to account for the emergence of novel patterns (chapter 6). Therefore, evolutionary theory can be improved by incorporating epigenetic developmental processes into the explanatory system (Futuyma, 1986; Ho & Saunders, 1979, 1984; Løvtrup, 1987).

Evolutionary theorists (Eldredge, 1985, 1989; Milkman, 1982) often distinguish at least three different levels of evolution: microevolution, speciation, and macroevolution. **Microevolution** refers to the gradual change in, or active maintenance of, phenotypes over time. Speciation refers to the splitting of a population into two separate populations. **Macroevolution** involves evolution above the level of speciation. The synthetic theory accounts for microevolution as the result of directional or stabilizing selection and for speciation as the result of disruptive selection that pushes a divided population in two different directions.

Macroevolution presents an interesting challenge for evolutionists because it calls attention to the hierarchical nature of genealogy, with large, qualitative gaps separating organismic designs at higher levels in the hierarchy and sharing of designs within lower levels. Furthermore, the number of designs for organisms seems to be limited. The synthetic theory accounted for the diversity of species by assuming that the ecological landscape consisted of definable adaptive peaks (Wright, 1932) or niches (Dobzhansky, 1951). But if niches are the driving force of evolution, are they hierarchically organized in ways that can account for phylogeny? Can niches even be identified in advance of their occupancy by some species? The difficulty of doing so is made apparent by intraspecific diversity.

One species is distinguished from another by the fact that **conspecifics** resemble one another more closely then they do members of other species, regardless of ecological setting. However, some species (e.g., coyotes) inhabit an apparently diverse set of ecosystems throughout their range. By criteria likely to be specified in advance, local populations within these species occupy a number of different niches. But if species are shaped by their niches, how can this be? To retain this idea, it is necessary to think of coyotes and other such species as adapted to a higher order of niche organization than can be specified by the usual inventory of economic costs and benefits afforded by the ecosystem.

Evolutionary novelties are most likely to arise during speciation. The fossil record shows that although the transformations of speciation may occur slowly, they often occur rapidly. Most species remain phenotypically stable throughout their existence and then undergo a rapid change, a phenomenon known as *punctuated equilibrium* (Eldredge & Gould, 1972; Gould & Eldredge, 1993). Even allowing for differences in the temporal resolving power of paleontology and population genetics, it is difficult to account for either the stasis or the rapid change apparent in much of the fossil record by the gradual processes of competitive natural selection. This does not rule out important roles for natural selection in deciding which new species survive or in stabilizing the characters of a new species, but it does suggest that other explanatory principles are necessary.

Some modern versions of macroevolution (Eldredge, 1989) find it useful to distinguish natural selection from sexual selection to account for the emergence of diversity within species. Natural selection refers to the economic relation between organisms and their ecosystems, whereas sexual selection is defined in Darwinian terms as the reproductive advantage certain individuals have over others of the same sex. These two forms of selection are intimately intertwined but may be conceptually separated to address specific problems in the synthetic theory. As a result, Eldredge makes the case that sexual selection underlies species formation, and natural selection underlies the adaptive relation of species to their **habitat**.

According to Paterson (1985), members of a species are held together by a specific mate-recognition system, a class of reproductive adaptations formed and maintained by sexual selection. Indeed, Eldredge (1989) proposed that a change in this mate-recognition system leads to speciation by establishing novel attributes as stable entities. It is not natural selection that drives the emergence of new species in evolution, but the emergence of new species that drives natural selection. However, within this view, niches are still conceived as aspects of the ecosystem that are independent of the organism's activity. As we will show later, this assumption has been seriously challenged.

Among the forgers of the synthetic theory, Wright (1932, 1980) was most attentive to the organized nature of organisms. He conceived of natural selection as acting on organisms and the combination of genes they have. Whether or not a particular gene is successful depends very much on the rest of the genes in the same organism. Although not explicitly developmental, Wright's ideas are consistent with a developmental approach, and these ideas were applied explicitly to forge a new synthesis in evolutionary theory (Ho & Saunders, 1982; Løvtrup, 1987).

The developmentalists maintain that an adequate evolutionary theory must take account of the fact that developmental processes, in collaboration with physical, chemical, and biochemical conditions, restrict the number of patterns of organization that an individual might have, because in only some limited set of these patterns will all the components be structurally and functionally compatible. Furthermore, this developmental fact has value in that it helps to explain phenomena that the older synthesis of population genetics and natural selection can explain only poorly, if at all. It provides a means for explaining both evolutionary stasis and the relatively few basic designs that living organisms have.

In addition, the dynamic, generative aspects of development, through which extensive organismic changes can occur by altering relatively simple but key developmental processes, can help to account both for the appearance of novel arrangements in evolution and for the rapidity with which they emerge. Developmental processes affect both reproductive behavior and behavior that fosters the organism's relation to its ecosystem. Therefore, developmentalists, including developmental psychobiologists, have much to offer toward understanding evolution. Perhaps the most helpful contribution will be to show the way to incorporate complex, nonlinear, causal patterns into evolutionary theory.

Alternatives to the Synthetic Theory

Although the synthetic theory is the most dominant Darwinian theory of evolution, it is not the only one. Others working in the Darwinian tradition retained the focus on individual organisms rather than genes as the unit of evolution. This focus has two major implications that distinguish it from the dominant synthetic theory. First, it directs attention to the whole organism as an entity, an attention that leads to the study of development to understand how organic form and function emerge. This in turn identifies genes as parts of organisms, not as separate directors residing within organisms. Second, it directs attention to the context in which organisms live and develop, because organisms and their context form systems that function only when integrated as systems, and not as independent components. Therefore, evolutionary explanations must encompass not only individual organisms, but aspects of their environments. In the remainder of this chapter we present some recent evolutionary theories that address Darwin's ideas of phylogeny, adaptation, and natural selection, while maintaining a developmental and systems orientation.

Organism-Environment Coevolution

A major problem in the synthetic theory of evolution is that it isolates natural selection from other factors, such as the ecology and the physico-chemical properties of organisms (Goertzel, 1992). Several models that avoid this isolation have been proposed to account for the evolution of new forms by incorporating the self-organizing dynamics of organismic and ecological systems (Augros & Stanciu, 1988; Goertzel, 1992; Patten, 1982). They make use of modern mathematical techniques—fractal geometry, castastrophe theory, and dynamic systems—that exhibit nonlinear relations among their components. Therefore, they provide a more precise formulation of the concepts of form, pattern, complexity, organization, and the network of relations among components of a system than was available in earlier general systems models (Miller & Miller, 1992). These models and the computer simulations that they generate will likely form the basis of a new theory of evolution in which organisms and their environments coevolve.

Indeed, Odling-Smee (1988) proposed a model of organism-environment **coevolution** based on Patten's (1982) ecological systems theory. The model allows a bidirectional influence between the organism and the environment, and unites them into a coherent abstract entity so that they coevolve. The pattern of relation between organism and its environment is nonlinear and dynamic. Genes play a role, but they are not the sole source of inheritance. The model incorporates Waddington's and Lewontin's view that organisms alter, in part, their niches. As such, environments can become adapted to organisms. Also, organisms can become more fit by altering their niche to support their offspring.

Animals can select appropriate resources (food, locations, etc.), they can perturb the environment (hoard food, build nests, stake out territories, etc.), and they can predict the environment (acquire knowledge to anticipate environmental changes). Each of these activities allows organisms to affect their environment in ways that feed back onto the organisms. Also, dynamic equilibria can be established. Dynamic equilibria and feedback allow **nonlinear causation** in which the size of events and consequences become dissociated. Thus, the system can buffer large events so that they have small consequences, and it can amplify small events to generate large consequences.

Coevolutionary theory differs from the synthetic theory in a number of ways. In Odling-Smee's model, the organism and its environment are treated jointly as the unit of evolution, and both ecological conditions and genes are considered appropriate units of inheritance. As a result, the concept of fitness includes cultural and social innovation (Odling-Smee, 1988).

If organisms and their environments coevolve and if the unilinear causality of the synthetic theory is inadequate, then much of the basis of the sociobiological program must be reconstructed. Dawkins (1976) proposed that genes are "selfish" in the sense that they commit organisms to reproduce, ensuring the transmission of genes to offspring populations. However, it is a mistake to assume that the only role of phenotypes is to ensure the transmission of genes. That is an idea that stems from "the synthetic theory and not from the existence of 'selfish genes'" (Odling-Smee, 1988, p. 103). Phenotypes are as much a part of evolution as DNA, genes, cell lines, demes, and so on (Eldredge, 1985). As Oyama (1989) and others noted, biological inheritance includes far more than genes. Genes are necessarily carried in germ cells, but stable, reliable, and developmentally useful aspects of the inherited complex extend well beyond these genetic packages. The list includes cellular structure, elements in the intracellular and extracellular environments, aspects of the intrauterine or intraegg environment, self-stimulation from the developing organism, and aspects of the physical and social postnatal environments (see chapters 6 and 7).

Sociobiology, like other theories that rely exclusively on Mendelian genetics as the hereditary mechanism for evolution, can lead to considerable success in the study of function. However, this success cannot be complete, because it is based on an inadequate account of causation, development, and phylogeny, and on a misrepresentation of behavior. To account for behavior in terms of adaptation within the synthetic theory, sociobiology must break a behavioral repertoire into atomistic components, posit an advantage for each component in terms of individual reproductive success, assume a genetic basis for the component, and then infer that natural selection built the component for its implied advantages.

However, organisms are not "packets of atomized parts," each independent of the others (Goertzel, 1992). Adaptive change in one part entails correlated alteration of others, often for structural and developmental reasons unrelated to immediate adaptation (Gould, 1977). Therefore, an ani-

Figure 4.4   A woodpecker finch uses a stick to retrieve insects from beneath the bark of trees, thereby creating a woodpecker niche without a typical woodpecker morphological genealogy (drawn from a photograph in Gould, 1982).

mal's genealogy constrains (Gould, 1989a) the adaptations that it might conceivably achieve in a given environment. Consider the Galapagos woodpecker finches. These birds are not woodpeckers at all. They do not have a woodpecker-like morphology adapted to drilling into trees and feeding on insects that live under the bark. They accomplish these "woodpecker" ends by substituting an unusual behavioral pattern for the long beak and tongue of woodpeckers. They collect a twig or cactus spine and, holding it in their beaks, use it as a tool to extract insects from beneath the bark (figure 4.4). The woodpecker finch has created a woodpecker niche by using tools, not by adopting the morphology of a woodpecker. The birds and their environment are coevolving within the constraints of the Galapagos finch genealogy (Odling-Smee, 1988). These constraints ensure that the finches will never evolve into a species with the bill, tongue, and associated morphology of a typical woodpecker.

The overall form of an animal may involve compromise solutions that make specific functions far from optimal, although the sum total of consequences might approach optimality. Behavioral features are constrained by the requirements of other activities, rather than each one being ideally adapted. Human males and females may differ universally (i.e., independent of their culture) in the features that attract them to potential mates. They may also differ in their parental involvement, marital fidelity, sexual interests, and so on. However, these differences likely derive from universal patterns of sociocognitive development, constrained by features of the complex processes underlying human development, rather than from natural selection acting on specific genes that underlie atomized traits.

Sociobiologists have advanced a particular theory of evolution and have compiled an impressive array of evidence to support the idea that social phenomena, including human societies and cultural phenomena, can be understood within the context of Darwinian evolution. Nevertheless, sociobiology has been criticized frequently, particularly for explaining human psychological development with nothing but provocative speculation. Many of these speculations about human nature include prejudicial language, biased selection of examples, biological reductionism, and the tendency to discount or minimize ecological and social contexts (Travis & Yeager, 1991). They yield what Kitcher (1985) referred to, and justly criticized, as "pop sociobiology." But all sociobiological interpretations of human sociality, whether reckless speculation or sober theorizing, are particular instantiations of a set of assumptions about how evolution works. The difficulty is that these assumptions are often portrayed as following necessarily from an acceptance of Darwinian evolution as fact. Such is not the case.

Hinde urged that we identify what is valuable in the sociobiological approach to human development, because it is unlikely that it is wholly wrong. "We surely now know that no one approach to human development is likely to be wholly correct, and it is also likely that few are wholly wrong. It behooves us therefore, not to discard the baby with the bathwater, but rather ask what is useful in the sociobiological approach and how should it be supplemented" (Hinde, 1992, p. 34). However, if there is no genetic determinism, what do developmentalists have to gain from sociobiology?

Perhaps what developmentalists have to gain are the insights that social behavior has an evolutionary history and that it, like other traits, may perhaps be understood as evolutionary adaptations. These insights derive from the Darwinian legacy, and they are not unique to sociobiological theory. Furthermore, they can be accepted while rejecting those assumptions of sociobiological theory, and its parental synthetic theory, that are incompatible with developmental inquiry. In this way, developmental psychobiology can join forces with behavioral ecology and evolutionary ontogenesis to rescue the baby from the discarded bathwater and provide a basis on which biology and the social sciences may be synthesized (cf. Blass, 1988).

Evolutionary theory is an integral part of any synthesis of biology and the social sciences. However, as Gould (1991) remarked, "the struggle in social science must be to find and use a more adequate evolutionary biology, not to reject proffered aid and genuine partnership because certain previous proposals have been poisoned apples of temptation rather than pipes of peace and shared feasts" (pp. 51–52).

The Union of Developmental and Evolutionary Biology

Over 100 years ago, comparative embryology served as a source of evidence for evolution. Under the influence of Haeckel (1834–1919), the evolutionary history, or phylogeny, of the organism was seen as the cause of its embryonic development, or ontogeny. Therefore, the evidence for evolutionary relationships was sought by comparing descriptions of the embryonic development of various species. However, with the growth of quantitative genetics in the first half of the twentieth century, embryology receded from evolutionary biology, and the two fields grew apart. In recent times, a reunion of developmental and evolutionary biology was sparked by advances that were made in relating the development of organic form to molecular genetics. Evolutionists turned to developmental biology in search of the causal factors involved in evolutionary change (Atkinson, 1992; Gould, 1977). The search focused on the coordination of gene regulation in space and time—morphogenesis (Thomson, 1988). This led to the formation of a new subdiscipline called evolutionary ontogenesis (Raff & Raff, 1987).

Evolutionary Ontogenesis

The single most critical concept in evolutionary ontogenesis is that of **bauplan** (Atkinson, 1992). Bauplan is a German word that captures all at once the idea of an architecturally defined body plan and that of integrated structure and function. "If an organism is to 'work' *all* of its components must be both structurally *and* functionally compatible. The entire organism encompasses a definable *Bauplan*, and the specific organ systems themselves also encompass describable *Baupläne*; in both cases the structural and functional components of the particular plan establish its capabilities and limits. Thus *Baupläne* determine the major constraints that operate at both the organismic and the organ system levels" (Brusca & Brusca, 1990, p. 43).

All animals must perform certain common tasks to survive and reproduce successfully. For example, food must be acquired, metabolized, and distributed throughout the body. Oxygen must be obtained and distributed, and waste products of digestion and metabolism must be removed. Reproduction must occur. Although there are many strategies for performing these common tasks, they are based on a relatively small number of biological, physical, and chemical principles; these contribute to the baupläne. Also, within the constraints of a particular bauplan, the number of options available to accomplish the tasks of living is limited. Thus, baupläne are major constraints on the manifestation and expression of form.

Even evolutionary change appears to have been constrained by the basic baupläne. That is, all animal life since the Cambrian period consists of variations on a very few basic morphological plans (Gould, 1989b; Reid, 1985). These basic patterns depend on specific developmental processes, such as those that determine how symmetry and fundamental cell lineages are established. Thus, some embryonic features of ancestors are present in the embryonic development of modern species.

For example, vertebrates have embryonic stages that are common to all members (the phylotypic stages). These stages seem to be essential for the

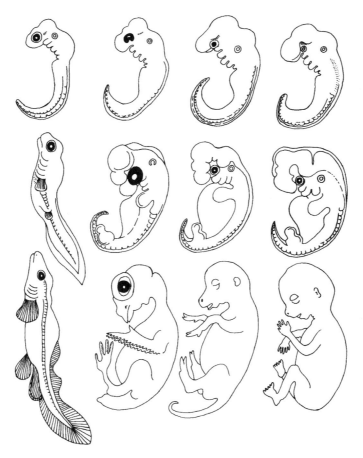

Figure 4.5 Similarities among vertebrate embryos do not reflect the ontogenetic recapitulation of phylogeny. Rather, they demonstrate the ontogenetic constraint on phylogeny. The similarities represent developmental stages that seem to be essential for achieving a coherent and functional individual. Earlier and/or later stages may permit the diversity used in the emergence of species differences (reproduced with permission from Raff & Kaufman, 1983, after Haeckel, 1879).

development of a functional organism. Differences among vertebrate species occur in development before and after the phylotypic stages (figure 4.5). The phylotypic stages remain constant, whereas the other stages permit diversity. The phylotypic stages are consistent with the bauplan theory; they are essential. The baupläne, and the developmental processes on which they depend, determine the means by which homologies may be discerned across diverse types of animals.

Homology has played a very important role in the study of both behavioral and morphological development and evolution (figure 4.6). It was first applied to the observed structural similarities among animals. However, after the advent of evolutionary theory, homologous structures were used as

Figure 4.6 Homology is a concept that provides much controversy in the study of behavior (see chapter 2). However, it does allow the identification of certain forms of similarity among the behaviors of different species. Here, the homologous display of facing away is illustrated in (A) black-billed gulls, (B) laughing gulls, (C) black-headed gulls, and (D) red-billed gulls (reproduced from C. G. Beer, 1973. Species—typical behavior and ethology. In D. A. Dewsbury & D. A. Rethlingshafer, Eds., *Comparative psychology: A modern survey.* New York: McGraw-Hill, by permission of McGraw-Hill, Inc.)

evidence of descent from common ancestry. In 1958 de Beer described how homologous characteristics need not be controlled by identical genes (the eye is homologous throughout vertebrates, yet the genes responsible must be different across species). Some species of amphibia are morphologically virtually identical, yet they differ enormously in their DNA. As de Beer also showed, characteristics associated with the same genes need not be homologous. The genetic differences between humans and chimpanzees are no more than 1% of their genomes despite enormous differences in phenotypic characteristics. Based on such observations, de Beer argued that homology refers to continuity in phylogeny and not to genetic identity or resemblance between structures.

But what is continuous in phylogeny? The homologous pineal eye in reptiles and the pineal gland in mammals are quite different anatomically and histologically. The malleus, incus, and stapes of the mammalian ear are homologous with the bones of the reptilian jaw. The concept of homology is useful for discussing features such as pineal glands and bones, and basic body plans. Although it may be difficult to specify exactly what is homologous, fish are readily classified with humans and distinguished from worms. This is the distinction between vertebrates and invertebrates. Furthermore, invertebrates can be classified into a relatively few distinguishable groups (Gould, 1989b). Thus it is difficult to specify the characteristics of a homologous relationship.

De Beer noted that homologous structures do not arise from similar embryonic cells or parts of the egg. Yet homology does involve developmental processes. The patterns during embryonic development are stable within a relatively small number of groups. The establishment of the embryonic axis, the pattern of cleavage, and the basic morphogenetic movements (e.g., gastrulation) most likely induce a cascade of succeeding events so powerful that only a limited number of modifications of these conditions result in anything other than disaster.

Modern evolutionary embryology seeks to determine whether these basic patterns are real or illusory. Comparative developmental biology is employed to address questions such as what are the molecular processes involved in establishing developmental stability in the presence of mutational variability; are there mechanisms whereby the environment can alter inherited characters in a directed way; what roles do the maternal and zygotic genomes play in the bauplan; does the bauplan passively constrain variation, or does it actively channel such variation; and can the temporal control of development be uncoupled from its spatial control, as suggested by the frequency with which changes in the bauplan are associated with heterochrony (Gould, 1977)? All of these questions reflect a concern for the developmental regulation of evolutionary change.

Another set of questions concerns the relation of evolution to development. How has development itself evolved? There are many conceivable sorts of development. Why are only a few of these possibilities found among multicellular organisms? Did selection occur among baupläne, or are present developmental processes the result of accidents of historical contingency, as posited by Gould (1989b)?

In general, evolutionary embryologists recognize the importance of developmental constraints; that is, evolution is constrained by the complex integrative character of development (Wolopert, 1992a). Embryos cannot make all imaginable forms, and among feasible forms, some are more difficult to make than others. There is simply no reason to invoke the actions of selective pressure to explain the conservation of the basic pattern of the vertebrate limb. It would be extremely difficult, for developmental reasons, to alter the basic pattern. Development also restricts evolutionary novelty because some forms are unattainable. Hence, any theory of evolution must incorporate an appreciation of developmental mechanisms (Wolpert, 1992a).

Changes in regulatory processes early in development can have potentially profound phenotypic effects because of the cascading nature of epigenetic processes; whereas, at other phases of development, similar changes may have little or no effect. According to some (Ho & Saunders, 1979), speciation and large scale macroevolutionary changes involve epigenetic developmental processes and the inheritance of acquired characteristics (box 4.4), whereas natural selection operates only on microevolutionary changes within species. That is, the complex integration of genetic activity with environmental input is thought to provide a direction to evolution that is independent of natural selection. "Organisms both select and alter their environments, and their intrinsic dynamic organization limits the heredity changes that are possible" (Goodwin, 1990, p. 55). Thus, some aspects of evolutionary ontogenesis challenge the synthetic theory of evolution both by providing facts that run counter to assumptions of the theory, and by providing a viable theoretical alternative.

Proponents of the synthetic theory argue that genetic change is necessary for evolution. The evolutionary ontogeneticists maintain that any developmental system has so much phenotypic potential that evolution can occur without changing the gene pool of a population. Changes in developmental phenotypes may eventuate in changes in the gene pool, but that step is not necessary for evolution. Of course, genes are an essential aspect of the developmental system (see chapter 5), but the changes in developmental systems that are essential for evolutionary changes need not involve changes in these genes. Rather, phenotypic changes may result from changes in the patterns of genetic expression during development.

Because organisms themselves have the potential for appropriate developmental adjustment to the environment, much of the variation available for evolutionary change does not have to arise from random genetic mutations. It can arise, instead, from the organism's developmental adjustment to the environment. "Living differently, especially living in a different place,

Box 4.4   The Inheritance of Acquired Characteristics

The inheritance of acquired characteristics was generally accepted, even by Darwin, until it was refuted by a series of experiments by Weismann in 1889 (Barker, 1993). Evolutionary theory had incorporated Lamarck's notion that individually acquired characters could be transmitted to the next generation. Weismann (1894) exposed organisms to environmental events that produced phenotypic changes, but these changes were not passed on to offspring. Weismann proposed that body (soma) and germ line (gametes) were distinct, with the germ line hypothesized to contain the heritable material (genes) used to form the offspring. Thus, a "continuity of the germ plasm" from parents to offspring accounted for heredity. The germ plasm (genotype) was presumed immutable to events happening during the lifetime, whatever their effect on soma (phenotype). Hence, acquired characteristics could not be transmitted from parent to offspring.

Weismann's experiments did not test Lamarck's theory that animals could acquire adaptive characteristics as a result of their efforts. His environmental events were imposed, and not consequences of the animal's efforts. Also, the resulting changes were not adaptive. Weismann's experiments did indicate that hereditary material could be independent of what happens to the individual, and his proposal fit the notion that natural selection acts by inducing changes in gene frequencies. Such changes produce adaptive phenotypes because the development of the soma is directed by the germ line source, the zygote's genotype.

Although Lamarck meant "acquired" in the sense of gain as a result of effort, it can mean simply to gain a characteristic, leaving how it was acquired unspecified. Landman (1991) reported suggestive evidence from molecular biology for the inheritance of acquired characteristics. Although most instances involve single-cell organisms, transitory exposure to physical, chemical, or biological agents may induce heritable changes in multicellular organisms. In some cases, genetic expression was stabilized in a new morphogenetic pattern. In others, DNA modifications had taken place. In yet other cases, loss of nonessential DNA or RNA elements apparently induced acquisition of a new nucleic acid, yielding new proteins with new heritable functions. Some inherited acquired characteristics were adaptive.

Evolutionary theory does not prohibit the inheritance of acquired characteristics (Sober, 1984). Nor would Weismann's proposal topple because of instances of such inheritance under rather rare conditions. However, the work challenges the supposition that nothing other than natural selection and genetic drift can systematically alter gene frequencies. Molecular mechanisms of inheritance are open to many altering influences, some of which occur as a result of individual experience (see chapter 5).

Also, organisms that exhibit prolonged periods of parental care allow offspring to inherit the characteristics acquired by their parents (cf. West, King, & Arberg, 1988). For example, male bullfinches acquire the song of their fathers during their nestling stage. If they are foster-reared by canaries, they pass that song on to their offspring (Immelmann, 1969), resulting in generations of bullfinches that sing canary songs. Transgenerational "grandmother" effects have been reported in rodents (Denenberg & Whimby, 1963; Denenberg & Rosenberg, 1967). These effects can be mediated by maternal hormones that cross the placental barrier to affect fetal development and by predictable differences in maternal stimulation (Moore, 1990).

Exposure to certain physical or social environmental factors can alter the course of development and lead to a new characteristic. Whether the characteristic is then inherited by subsequent offspring may depend on other factors, including the role parents play in offspring development. Thus, developmental psychobiological processes can promote patterns of inheritance formally equivalent to those considered essential for the adaptive relation of the organism to its environment.

Although these examples do not involve changes in the germ line, they are relevant for both developmental and evolutionary theory. Barker (1993) believes that several variants of Lamarck's notions are consistent with modern genetic and evolutionary models (see also Saunders, 1985). Their reconsideration could help forge a synthesis between evolution and development, as they did for Darwin.

will subject the animals to new stresses, strains, and adaptations that will eventually alter their anatomy and physiology (without necessarily altering the genetic constitution of the changing population). The new situation will call forth previously untapped resources for anatomical and physiological change that are part of the species' already existing developmental adaptability" (Gottlieb, 1992, p. 176).

Behavioral adjustment is the initial, directing aspect of much evolutionary change (Larson, Prager, & Wilson, 1984; Piaget, 1978; Reid, 1985). Developmental changes in behavioral phenotypes allow individuals to alter lifestyles, exploit new habitats, and so forth (Gottlieb, 1991c, 1992). Such adjustments reflect the interpenetration of the individual and its environment, with experiential events playing an essential role. For example, an individual's early experiences can structure the pattern of subsequent development, particularly the developmental consequences of subsequent experiences (Gottlieb, 1991a, 1991b, 1991c; Hebb, 1949).

Developmental psychobiology is an important adjunct to evolutionary ontogenesis because it can identify and elucidate the reciprocal processes and mechanisms whereby behavioral development is influenced by the organism-niche interpenetration. Evolutionary ontogenesis, in turn, is valuable for developmental psychobiology because it demonstrates that developmental processes can operate relatively independent of natural selection. The mechanisms that underlie much of behavioral evolution may reside in the processes studied by developmental psychobiologists, rather than in the effects of natural selection. Of course, this observation does not rule out an important role for natural selection. It can weed out bad or poor development-condition relationships. However, this role for selection is very different from its hypothesized, but unlikely, role as director of the development of adaptive traits in individuals.

Summary

We began with an account of sociobiology because it is a popular and influential modern extension of the synthetic theory of evolution. Sociobiology is an attempt to integrate the social and biological sciences by treating many aspects of human psychology and culture as products of naturally selected genes. Two fundamental assumptions of the synthetic theory of evolution are that natural selection underlies all directed evolutionary change and that it acts on genes. We examined the history of evolutionary theory to comprehend and evaluate these assumptions better. We identified and discussed a number of problems with the synthetic theory and sociobiology, arguing that they rely on a limited, outdated conception of genetics, and that they are incompatible with much of what is known about development, mechanisms, and phylogeny.

We presented alternative Darwinian accounts of evolution that can explain the same social phenomena addressed by sociobiologists and that are also consistent with our current understanding of molecular genetics, developmental biology, and developmental psychobiology. In organism-environment coevolution, the organism is considered to be part of a system in which the genes are just one component and in which the organism plays an active role in its own evolution. In evolutionary ontogenesis, which has grown from a merger of phylogenetics and developmental biology, variations in developmental systems, not in gene pools, are seen as the source of evolution. We propose that developmental psychobiology and behavioral ecology provide the foundation for an integration of biology and psychology that can incorporate an understanding of phylogeny and function with an understanding of the mechanisms and development of behavior.

5   Genetics and Development

Consider the fruit fly, Drosophila melanogaster, *which thousands of geneticists have studied. For over 80 years, it has been at the center of genetic research. Tens of thousands of scientist-years have been invested in studying* Drosophila; *billions of dollars of research money have been spent on it; four Nobel prizes have been earned by* Drosophila *geneticists—and more will be coming. That effort has paid off. We can do astounding things: We can clone fly cells, and remove and insert genes at will; we can grow flies with 12 legs instead of six, with four wings instead of two, with legs in place of mouths, and with wings sprouting from their eyes. But after all that investment and knowledge, we still don't know how the fruit fly survives through the winter. We don't understand how a fly's egg transforms itself first into a larva and then into a pupa. We know very little of the mechanisms whereby the flies sense and respond to their surroundings. If scientists learn anything from their studies, it would be how* little, *not how* much, *we know.*

—D. Suzuki and P. Knudston (1989, pp. 21–22)

Conventional wisdom has it that every person is born with an endowment of intellectual and personal capabilities that is unlike anyone else's. The development of these capabilities is also unique to each individual, and is a result of the variations in opportunity provided by society. Consequently, people generally interpret inequalities of accomplishment in any human endeavor as a reflection of some combination of genetic and societal differences among individuals. Furthermore, people believe that it is important to determine which of these two sources of inequality has the stronger influence. In fact, many consider this question to be one of the most important facing a democratic society, because the answer is seen as relevant for setting social policy. Thus a major reorganization of the social, political, and educational structures of society could possibly follow from the resolution of this issue.

Most psychology textbooks reflect tradition in the way that they incorporate genetics into chapters about personality, intelligence, and development. Until recently, a common view was that the role of genetics in individual development is like the role of clay in sculpture. An individual's genetic makeup (genotype) is the clay out of which the environment, particularly through learning processes, sculpts all the substantial and interesting facets

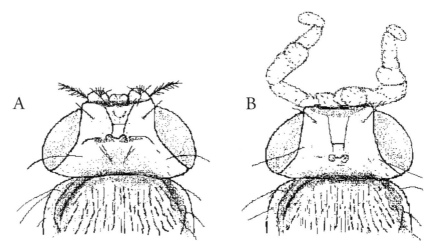

Figure 5.1   (A) A fly with a normal head with antennae, and (B) an *Antennapedia* fly with legs in place of the antennae (after Palka, 1982).

of psychological development. Just as the characteristics of clay limit the free expression of the sculptor, so the characteristics of the individual's genotype limit the impact of the environment.

Of late, interest in this presumed limiting characteristic of individual genotype has been renewed, spurred by claims made on the basis of research in the interdisciplinary field of behavioral genetics. Behavioral genetics applies the techniques of genetics to the study of behavioral traits (Plomin, DeFries, & McClearn, 1990). Media coverage of studies in this field has been extensive, giving wide publicity to conclusions that such psychological traits as intelligence, aggression, sexual orientation, morality, schizophrenia, and even conservatism and respect for authority are determined by genes (Billings et al., 1992; Holden, 1994; Mann, 1994; Marshall, 1994).

We start this chapter with a quotation that acknowledges some of the many exciting advances made by modern genetics (figure 5.1), but that also prompts a critical attitude toward the relation of these advances to the goal of understanding behavior and its development. We examine this relation from several perspectives, providing some of the information necessary to assess the conclusions that are drawn from behavioral genetics. We describe the strengths and limits for application to behavioral development of the different approaches to behavioral genetics. We also address the question of development directly, briefly examining developmental sources of variance in quantitative genetics and developmental mechanisms that involve DNA at the intracellular level.

Many of the ideas and much of the research information that we present violates conventional wisdom about how genes affect behavior. Contrary to usual assumptions (see Jensen, 1969), it is not possible to partition an individual's endowment into genetic and environmental parts. Nor is it possible to identify limits to phenotypic potential by genetic analyses (cf. Turkheimer & Gottesman, 1991). Although the field is a long way from explaining in any detail how genes do contribute to behavioral development and expression, the rapidly growing information from molecular genetics points to dynamic, nondeterministic processes that provide the mechanisms whereby experiential influences can markedly contribute to developmental processes.

We conclude that genetic analyses cannot tell us which behavioral characters are genetically determined and which are not, in the conventional sense of the meaning of "determined." They can, however, help us to describe hereditary processes and to explain how genes function in the systems that underlie behavioral development. We also show how information from developmental psychobiology can be useful to geneticists as they expand their conceptions of hereditary mechanisms at the population level and their conceptions of molecular genetic processes in developing individuals.

Human Behavioral Genetics

Human behavioral genetics combines the techniques of psychometricians and quantitative geneticists (Plomin, DeFries, & Fulker, 1988). It has been hailed as the means by which the relative importance of genetic and social sources of inequalities among both individuals and groups of individuals may finally be ascertained (Plomin, Owen, McGuffin, 1994). Once ascertained, genetic counseling and biomedical intervention can be employed to address identified problems, and educational programs can be tailored to fit identified genetic limitations. Thus, the field has developed with strong ties to pragmatic, public policy goals.

We suspect that much of the interest in behavioral genetics represents a general dissatisfaction with social reform movements that are based on traditional psychological theory and methods, from the rehabilitation of criminals to strategies in the education of typical and atypical children. The identification of a genetic origin for any of the behavioral problems currently capturing the public's attention (e.g., criminal aggression, sex offenses, mood disorders, mental dysfunction) is seized on and used to support one of two arguments: either we must return to traditional methods of dealing with these problems (punishment, isolation of affected individuals) or new biological methods must be used. In recent history, the biological approach focused on anatomy, and psychosurgery was the method of choice to alter "deviant" people. Currently, the focus is on biochemistry, and chemotherapy is the method of choice.

Among the majority of psychologists (and others who think about these matters), two popular positions regarding the role of genetics in human development have emerged. Opinion seems divided between the view that there is little relationship between psychology and genetics, and the view that genes are a major contributor to most, if not all, of the currently most interesting psychological characteristics—mood disorders, intelligence, aggression, and so on. The choice, in other words, is seen as one between the irrelevance of genetics on the one hand and full-blown genetic determinism on the other (Mann, 1994). However, something is wrong with the way the choice has been put. An organism simply cannot function without the involvement of genes, and genes are the major conveyors of heredity and essential sources of organization for the structure and functioning of cells. Genes must be incorporated into a developmental psychobiology, *and this can be done without embracing biological determinism.*

But why has a deterministic view of genetics been so widely adopted in psychology, when nothing in the concepts and findings of contemporary genetics requires it? One answer may lie in the widespread use of the concept of *reaction range* (or *range of reaction*), which has no counterpart in biological genetics, although it does bear superficial resemblance to the biological concept of *norm of reaction* (Platt & Sanislow, 1988). Both deal with the interaction of genotypes with the environment during phenotypic development, but there is a major assumption at the root of the reaction range that is not made regarding norm of reaction. That assumption is that an individual's genotype imposes a priori limits on psychological potential and predisposes the individual toward the development of a restricted set of possible psychological characteristics (phenotypes) (Benson, 1992; Platt & Sanislow, 1988). "The limitation of possible phenotypes to a few rather than many is a fact of genotypes' range of reaction" (Scarr-Salapatek, 1976, p. 63).

The assumption is that something in the genotype determines the outcome of development—not precisely, because the environment can shift the outcome, but within the boundaries of a knowable range that is genetically determined. "A genetic envelope sets the limits on modifiability ... plasticity explains modifiability within those limits" (Rosser, 1994, pp. 6–7). This assumption is apparent in much of the research on genetic contributions to the development of personality and intelligence in humans (cf. Bouchard, 1994), often formalized by explicit use of reaction range as an explanatory concept (Platt & Sanislow, 1988). Platt and Sanislow traced reaction range to Gottesman (1963), who used it to discuss the bases of individual differences in intelligence. In his words, "a genotype determines an indefinite but circumscribed assortment of phenotypes, each of which corresponds to one of the possible environments to which the genotype may be exposed" (Gottesman, 1963, pp. 254–255).

With norm of reaction, it is acknowledged that genotypes may develop differently in different environments. The concept arises from the phenotypic variability that can be observed and measured in experimental studies in which identical genotypes are permitted to develop in different environments. It is then extended as a theoretical concept to cover all the phenotypic outcomes that would arise if a single genotype was developed in all possible environments. It is accepted in a practical sense that there are limits to what these outcomes might be: neither humans nor cows are expected to sprout wings. However, since so much of the genome is shared among species, it may be within the possibility of the human and cow genome to support the development of wings, just as it is within the possibility of chickens to grow teeth. Thus, the developmental limitation is unknowable for any genotype, and consequently it does not enter into the definition of the concept. Compare the language used by Dobzhansky with that of Scarr-Salapatek or Gottesman: "the phenotype observed is the necessary outcome of the development brought about by a certain genotype in a certain succession of environments. We can never be sure that any of these traits have reached the maximal development possible with a given genotype. The performance of a genotype cannot be tested in all possible environments, because the latter are infinitely variable" (Dobzhansky, 1955, p. 77).

In practice, the norm of reaction is estimated by the observed variation of a given genotype within the range of environments, natural or artificial, that are examined in a particular study. It is not presumed that such studies can identify limits on phenotypic variability. The environments to which genotypes are exposed can vary along many dimensions and in many temporal sequences. Thus it is impossible to raise a particular genotype from fertilization in every possible environment to identify the limits on its genetic potential. Even a reasonably large random sample of all available environments presents an impossible task for most animals.

Although some variant of the conventional homily, genes set the limits that cannot be exceeded in any environment, and the environment limits the extent to which a genetic potential can be realized, is frequently encountered in discussions of human behavioral genetics, the fact that the limits of a phenotype are unknowable is rarely pointed out. Instead, the reaction range concept carries with it the implication that genetic potential can be measured by known genetic methods. However, any limits to a phenotype that might be claimed necessarily depends on current knowledge and technological sophistication, and could therefore just as readily depend on the skill of the researcher as the genotype. As Benson (1992) notes, the techniques currently used to describe the reaction range for psychological traits have known deficiencies. For example, they do not adequately estimate the effects of gene-environment interaction and covariation, or changes over the life span in the effects of genes, environments, their interaction or covariation, or other unexplained variation.

Reaction range, like the related notion of genetic determination of traits, is not an explanatory concept that is applicable to development. However, much that is useful can be gained from the study of genetics. This is a fast-moving field that is both technically and conceptually difficult. The following introduction is necessarily brief and incomplete, but will perhaps include enough detail to allow a clear appreciation of the major issues. A complete developmental psychobiology must include genetic information, but it is important to incorporate this material in ways that are conceptually sound and that take us beyond the pitfalls of the conventional wisdom.

The Types of Geneticists

There are really several kinds of geneticists. The *population geneticists'* ultimate concern is with questions about microevolutionary changes and speciation by natural or artificial selection. Using the simple technique of documenting or controlling who breeds with whom, they investigate the nature of a gene and its relationship to other genes and to the occurrence of physical and behavioral characters (phenotypes). They search for more complete understanding of how mutations, selection, population size, environmental conditions, geographical distribution, and other factors concerning a population influence evolutionary processes. Population geneticists assess the operation of natural selection.

A second kind of geneticist—*molecular geneticist*—is ultimately concerned with the role of DNA in the organization of cellular activity, and the relationship between the characteristics of DNA and the characteristics of the gene as defined by the population geneticist. The specific nature of the relationship between population and molecular genetics is the subject of a good deal of philosophical (Ayala & Dobzhansky, 1974; Hull, 1972) and theoretical (Sober, 1984; Mayr & Provine, 1980) debate. Despite this unresolved debate, the *biomedical geneticists* have combined many of the techniques of population and molecular geneticists, primarily for application to clinical issues.

A biomedical geneticist would approach a psychiatric disorder by attempting to identify a link between the expression of the disorder and a marker. **Markers** are biochemical variants associated with particular places on a chromosome. They allow biomedical geneticists to follow the inheritance of nearly any part of any chromosome through families. By linking a disorder to a marker, one can identify where on a chromosome the genes associated with that disorder reside. The linkage also allows the pattern whereby the disorder is transmitted through families to be identified (Torrey, 1992).

These three types of geneticists provide different kinds of information with different kinds of relationships to developmental psychobiology. We present a brief sketch of the historical antecedents of modern genetics as an introduction to the concepts and methods that define these contemporary relationships.

The Origin of the Field of Genetics

The relatively short history of genetics as an independent discipline began with the rediscovery of Gregor Mendel's work at the turn of this century (Carlson, 1966). Mendel had linked a discrete, observable phenotype with a discrete, inherited genotype. William Bateson was the first to see and promote the importance of Mendel's findings, writing a provocative book (*A defence of Mendel's principles of heredity*) on the subject in 1902. Thanks to his encouragements, embryologists took up the challenge of finding a mechanism for the link between particular genes and particular characters. Thus genetics began as part of embryology. This connection seemed apparent because a phenotype can be achieved only through development, and all mutations were understood to affect developmental processes. However, the embryological ideas available at the time were not adequate to account for all the facts of Mendelian inheritance, setting the stage for a split between the fields.

One controversy centered on the location of the hereditary-developmental material. This material was clearly housed in cells, but just where— the nucleus or cytoplasm? T. H. Morgan, who began his career with doctoral research (completed in 1890) on the embryology of sea spiders, was among those embryologists who initially supported a cytoplasmic residence, but his own work was instrumental in disproving that idea. He subsequently abandoned embryology, finding the field too prone to preformationism and other speculative ideas, and championed the separate study of genetics as an area with superior potential to reveal the laws of nature. In 1909 he began to work with fruit flies, an organism that was attractive for work on heredity because of its rapid life cycle. The possibility of cytoplasmic inheritance resurfaced sporadically after Morgan and his contemporaries rejected it, but it was not until the 1950s that acceptable mechanisms of cytoplasmic inheritance were found in the work of Ephrussi and Slonimski on yeast (Carlson, 1966; Gilbert, 1992a).

The research organisms chosen by scientists can have a strong influence on the types of findings that they achieve (Burian, 1992). Had Morgan chosen sea urchins instead of *Drosophila*, he might not have moved so far from embryology, but his achievements in genetics would have been greatly slowed. Molecular techniques now make it possible to do rather spectacular developmental work with fruit flies, but this was not previously the case. *Drosophila*'s egg is not easily manipulated, and the timing of developmental events poses difficulties—some important events occur at such an early age that they cannot be observed by embryological methods, and long delays between the developmental events that determine the fate of a cell line and the manifestation of the fate make it easy for a researcher to miss the connection. Sea urchins are traditional favorites of embryologists because they do not pose these difficulties; however, they are not suitable for genetic studies. Their reproductive life makes it impossible to maintain genetic stocks or to establish pedigrees, goals attained relatively readily with fruit flies. Furthermore, the sea urchin has many small chromosomes that are difficult to tell apart, whereas *Drosophila* has four chromosomes that become so large during some stages that they can almost be seen by eye. Thus the biology of the major experimental animals had a role to play in the separation of embryology and genetics.

Morgan and his most productive student, H. J. Muller, went on to specify the laws of inheritance using the amenable fruit fly. The success of their techniques established genetics as an important discipline. Genetics and developmental biology evolved "their own techniques, rules of evidence, favorite organisms, journals, vocabulary and paradigmatic experiments ... Genetics textbooks stopped discussing embryology, and embryology texts ceased discussing genes" (Gilbert, 1992b, p. 211). Genetics so captivated the thought of biologists from 1900 to 1930 that many biologists asserted that Darwin's theory of evolution through natural selection was not required to explain the diversity of plants and animals. However, the efforts of a small group of biologists in the 1930s and 1940s wedded the discipline of genetics to Darwin's theory to form the synthetic theory of evolution. The synthetic theory subsequently became the major framework for the whole of biological investigation (chapter 4; Handler, 1970).

Although genetics and evolution were synthesized in the 1930s, development was separated from each of these fields until recently. The merger of developmental biology and evolution had intellectually exciting theoretical ramifications for both fields (chapter 4; Raff & Kaufman, 1983). The convergence of developmental biology and genetics has equally exciting and far-reaching implications.

The Search for the Gene

After the rediscovery and promotion of Mendel's work in the early part of this century, genetic investigations were of two kinds: assessments of the generality of Mendel's laws of inheritance, and searches for some material or physical counterpart of his formative elements. Concrete representation of abstract concepts is an important element in human thought. We often find it difficult to accept the idea that many disciplines are built on foundations of hypothetical constructs. The postulation of these hypothetical constructs aids in the organization and coordination of the observed phenomena of the discipline. Genetics is no exception. Even today the gene is still, in part, a hypothetical construct.

Early in the history of genetics, advances in the microscopic examination of cells enabled researchers to discover certain elements in the cell nucleus that appeared to behave as Mendel's formative elements were thought to behave. These chromosomes, so called because they could be readily colored with dye, came in pairs and duplicated themselves before a cell divided in two. Each daughter cell received an identical set of chromosomes. Moreover, when the gametes, or sex cells, were formed, the members of each pair separated and went into different cells in a manner similar to the hypothesized segregation of members of a pair of formative elements.

It was discovered that members of a pair of chromosomes overlap and exchange material (crossover) before cell division. This important discovery enabled Morgan and his colleagues Muller and Sturtevant to perform a series of ingenious and elegant breeding experiments. The results of these experiments suggested that the formative elements, or genes as they were now known, are arranged along the length of a chromosome much like beads on a string. Each gene was found to have its own particular place or locus on a chromosome, with its sister gene (or allele) occupying the identical locus on the other member of the chromosome pair.

Continued investigation led to the mapping of gene positions on the chromosomes and the subsequent discovery that two, three or more different genes (multiple **alleles**) might substitute for one another at the same place or locus on a chromosome. Genes at one locus were also found to affect the action of genes at another (epistasis). Genes were observed to enhance, suppress, enable, mediate, or weaken the action of other genes. Moreover, a single gene could be associated simultaneously with the occurrence of several different phenotypic **traits** (pleiotropism). In addition, changes in gene structure (**mutation**), typically induced experimentally by bombarding the system with X rays, high temperatures, or certain chemicals, sometimes had graded effects, changing the previous phenotype to varying degrees. The degree of disruption depended on the overall genetic and environmental conditions, described as degrees of expression and penetrance. In addition, contingent on certain environmental events during development, quite different genotypes would sometimes result in the same phenotypic trait (phenocopy), with no associated change in the genetic structure. Furthermore, the presence of several different genes were shown to be necessary for the expression of most traits (polygenic traits).

In summary, genes were found to interact with one another, developmental outcome was found to depend on the joint action of environment and genes, and gene-character relationships of a one-to-many or many-to-one type were found to be common. These findings are inconsistent with the all too frequent mental equation of genetic involvement with genetic determination. Inheritance, as measured by the operations of population geneticists, is a statement about prediction. When these geneticists refer to a character as inherited, what they mean is that the percentage of individuals showing that character in an offspring population can be predicted from knowledge about the parental population; that is, the proportion of individuals exhibiting the character in question and information about who mates with whom. This meaning of inheritance says nothing about individual developmental sequences in the ontogeny of the characters. Although this is often done, there is no logical or empirical reason to confuse the genetic concept of *inheritance* with the developmental concept of *innate*, which means developmentally fixed and independent of the environment (see chapter 3; Lehrman, 1970; Lerner, 1976).

Perhaps the confusion of innate with inherited stems from Bateson's introduction, in the early 1900s, of the term unit-character as the name of the hypothesized hereditary material. This term had the unfortunate effect of combining Mendel's differentiating character, the observed differences in a character (e.g., tallness or shortness in plants), with his formative element, that which is passed on in the germ cells from parent to offspring. The new term gave the impression that the character, and not some hereditary material, was inherited. It was a central difficulty for genetics and embryology in the early part of this century to arrive at an adequate conception of heredity that included hereditary material that was not isomorphic with the material of organismic characters.

This is at the core of the debates on preformation versus epigenetics and mechanism versus vitalism (see chapter 6; Gottlieb, 1992). Although the terminology has been transformed, the difficulty continues to plague many who discuss the relations of genetics and psychology (see also Oyama, 1989).

Further contribution to the confusion may be traced to the reliance by geneticists on Mendelian differentiating characters to study mechanisms of inheritance. The ease of counting the individuals possessing particular discrete characters and assigning them unambiguously to different groups within a population made experimental manipulations easy, and statistical predictions more reliable than would have been the case with continuously varying characters. The genetic laws that were established were later extended to the more typical case of continuously varying characters with the important assumption that each of the many genes associated with the character behaved in Mendelian fashion. This choice gave the geneticists sharper predictions and greater mathematical precision than was possible in embryology. Even today, developmental investigations do not enjoy the statistical and experimental sophistication characteristic of genetics. The differences in precision and experimental power undoubtedly contributed to the long tradition among geneticists of ignoring development (Carlson, 1966).

As long as Mendelian ideas predicted the occurrence of individual differences in observed characters within a traditional breeding program, it was simple enough to think of genes as directly determining the ontogeny of the characters. Indeed, if Mendelian analyses of individual differences did not show evidence of predictable major gene effects on behavioral characters, it was often concluded that the differences had no genetic origin (Wilcock, 1969). However, evidence gradually accumulated to indicate that, with few exceptions (notably, those resulting in some abnormal phenotypic mutations), the normal occurrence of a character is attributable to the joint action of a number of genes, each making a small contribution to the total phenotype.

Although a common methodology or conceptual vocabulary no longer integrated the work of genetics and embryology, to varying degrees geneticists remained aware of the general problem of development. Some treated developmental phenomena as nuisance factors that stand in the way of clear interpretation of data, whereas others treated them as challenges that would eventually have to be addressed. This awareness was a necessary consequence of accepting Johannsen's 1909 distinction between genotype and phenotype. The differences between these two conceptual entities forced geneticists to retain some of their embryological beginnings, and to recognize that genes and traits are associated through complex networks of developmental pathways.

Phenotype is defined as any observed characteristic of the individual, such as blood type, eye color, locomotion patterns, or cell structures. **Genotype** refers to the inferred hereditary elements that make the phenotype of one individual different from the phenotype of another individual. Indeed, Sturtevant (1915) argued, "All that we can mean when we speak of a gene for pink eyes is, a gene which differentiates a pink eyed fly from a normal one—not a gene which produces pink eyes." How that gene differentiates a pink-eyed fly from a normal fly is a question for developmental, not genetic, analysis.

Thus many geneticists fully concede that, although all phenotypic **characters**, including behavior, have a genetic correlate, or origin, this does not mean that they are independent of specific organism-environment reciprocal interactions for their development. Even the evolutionary selectionist must acknowledge that the characteristics of any individual organism in a population are determined by the developmental interactions of the organism with its environment (Simpson, 1958). Or, as Dobzhansky expressed it, "Human, as well as animal, behavior is the outcome of a process of development in which the genes and environment are components of a system of feedback relationships. The same statement can be made equally with respect to one's skin color, the shape of one's head, blood chemistry, and somatic, metabolic and mental diseases" (1967, p. 43). In other words, *answers to questions posed by geneticists about individual differences within and among populations are not equivalent to answers to questions posed by psychologists about the development of individuals.*

It is curious that this recognition has been lost in much of behavioral genetics, particularly in research on humans, where correlated behavior in genetic relatives is taken by many to indicate a genetic cause of individual development in that behavior (cf. Mann, 1994; Wolff, 1992). Indeed, human behavioral genetics is valued because of its presumed ability to account for individual differences (Carroll, 1992; Plomin et al., 1994). There is, of course, more than one way to account for individual differences. It is one thing to partition sources of variance in a population, while making a number of assumptions that either ignore developmental sources of variance or hold them constant, and quite another thing to tease apart the different developmental causes underlying individual phenotypes.

As many studies in developmental psychobiology demonstrate, individual differences in behavior emerge from developmental contingencies of particular organisms in particular environments. Individuals reared in apparently different environments may share certain relevant influences or contingencies, sometimes because of shared features in their own characteristics. Conversely, siblings reared in the same family will experience many differences in their social and physical environments, due in part to the pattern of their own characteristics (a consequence of their developmental history) and in part to subtle contingencies in the rearing environment. This is true even for genetically identical individuals. Yet, only recently have behavioral geneticists acknowledged that siblings inhabit different (nonshared) environments or that the individual's characteristics affect the environmental influences that will be encountered or responded to (Plomin et al., 1990). Inadequate knowledge of these environments and organism-environment interactions raises serious complications for interpreting the results of studies in behavioral genetics, such as comparisons of twins reared apart with those reared together.

It is often said that the emergence of a phenotype depends on a developmental interaction with an environment. The term "interaction" in this formulation may be misleading when used in a discussion of genetics, because it implies separate entities that come together at an interface. Clearly, genes and the world do not come together. As was described in chapters 1 and 3, many levels of the individual are comprised by the developmental process. Interactions occur at each of these levels, but interaction between entities cannot skip several levels, as would have to happen for genes to interact with the world outside the organism's skin. Organisms interact with this outside world; genes interact with other entities inside a cell (Lehrman, 1953). Of course, these cellular entities can be influenced by what happens in the outside world.

Psychologists are used to thinking of interactions within a statistical framework. In factorial studies, it is possible to determine the separate effects of individual factors as well as their interaction in producing some measured effect. One is on slippery ground when genes and environments are put into such a framework with the goal of explaining individual development (Platt & Sanislow, 1988; Plomin et al., 1990). Consider the fact that it is entirely possible to eliminate a statistical interaction simply by transforming the scale of measurement that was used. Such a transformation obviously changes nothing about either genes or environments. The unfortunate mistranslation of "norm-of-reaction" to "reaction range," discussed earlier in this chapter, is based to a significant degree on problems of using interaction concepts inappropriately (Hirsch, 1970; Wahlsten, 1990).

Methods of Behavioral Genetic Analysis

The objective of population genetics is to gain access to the genetic system of the species by finding the gene(s) that correlate with the phenotype(s). Population geneticists use quantitative analyses in breeding experiments to evaluate and record the consequences of artificial selective pressures; they use similar analyses in field work to measure the effects of natural selection (Hirsch, 1990). The behavioral geneticist applies the analytical techniques of population geneticists to behavioral phenotypes. The procedures used in population genetics require individual differences in measured phenotypes. If few or no differences exist among individuals, it will not be possible to estimate the relationship of genetic differences to behavioral differences. In addition to their practical use, individual differences are theoretically interesting because natural selection is thought to operate on individual differences in phenotypes. Thus, the researcher must choose behavioral patterns that vary among individuals.

Behavior, like most other traits, can vary in one of two ways. Some traits vary qualitatively: individuals can easily be assigned to mutually exclusive groups according to such qualitative differences as blood type. Other traits, and this includes virtually all behavioral and physiological traits, vary quantitatively: individuals are not easily assigned to or divided among mutually exclusive groups on the basis of differences in behavior. Instead, individuals differ along continuous dimensions that measure the character (e.g., skin color, height, spatial ability).

Reflecting this dichotomy in behavioral variability, two distinct research traditions have emerged from behavioral genetic studies—unifactorial and multifactorial. The *unifactorial approach* focuses on the effects of single genes on behavior. Proponents of the *multifactorial approach* assume that many genes acting together underlie most behaviors. The two traditions require somewhat different methods. The multifactorial approach must rely on sophisticated quantitative procedures; the unifactorial approach can rely on simpler Mendelian techniques (box 5.1).

Unifactorial Methods

One unifactorial method that is common in animal research is to compare the behavior of a normal population with that of an inbred strain (a group of individuals produced by at least 20 consecutive generations of brother-sister or parent-offspring mating resulting in all individuals having essentially the

Box 5.1   The Genetics of Human Handedness

Continuous variation among members of a population in some phenotype (e.g., intelligence, adult height) is thought to reflect the actions of many genes, whereas discontinuous variation (e.g., human A, B, O blood types) is thought to depend on the actions of single genes. But how do we decide whether a behavioral phenotype is continuous or discontinuous?

Consider human **handedness**. It seems to be a discontinuous variable, with individuals either left- or right-handed. The addition of a third ambilateral category (to capture individuals who do not classify themselves with either of the other two categories) seems a sufficient descriptive scheme to cover the phenomenon. However, when the differences between the use of the right and left hand are measured, handedness varies continuously among people. When people report which hand they prefer to use for various tasks, their preference scores vary continuously, especially if the list includes a large number of tasks. Even with only 12 tasks and sophisticated statistical classification techniques, the preference scores in a sample of a few hundred individuals could not be reduced below 8 types (Annett, 1964). It is likely that this number would have been even larger if the number of tasks had been increased. Thus, handedness varies *quantitatively* in the human population; it is not a discontinuous variable.

Does this mean that handedness involves the action of many genes? Yes and no. Annett (1978) demonstrated two aspects of human handedness: in an individual, and the bias in the population as a whole. The phenomenon of handedness itself involves many genes and several randomly occurring developmental events. However, the distinct right-hand bias in the human population is associated with a single gene, which Annett called the right-bias gene.

Annett proposed that if the right-bias gene is not present, the population will be equally divided between left- and right-handers, with most people showing rather small differences between the use of their two hands. If the right-bias gene is present, the distribution of handedness in a population will be shifted to the right. The majority of people are thought to have the right-bias gene, but it is not present in everyone. Having the gene does not make someone right-handed but, for a number of developmental reasons, it does bias the person in that direction. Thus the gene creates a distribution of handedness in the human population with more individuals on the right than left side of the measures. A few of those possessing the gene will show a left hand-use preference, although it will be weaker than if they did not possess the gene. The minority who do not possess the right-bias gene will exhibit an equal distribution of left- and right-handedness.

According to Annett's model, in any random sampling, a majority of those classified as left-handed will not possess the right-bias gene (although some will) and a majority of those classified as right-handed will possess the gene (although a small minority will not). The model accounts for the inheritance of handedness in families, especially the approximately 50% left-handedness among the offspring of two left-handed parents. It also demonstrates the value of accurate and detailed descriptions of the psychological phenomenon for which a behavioral genetic analysis is proposed. Compared with psychiatric disorders, personality characteristics, and intelligence, handedness is a simple and easily measured psychological characteristic. Problems associated with the study of the genetics of handedness should signal caution when the genetics of more complicated psychological abilities is examined.

same genotype, much like identical twins), drawn from the normal population, that carries a known single-gene mutation. Differences in the behavior of the inbred strain and the normal population are assumed to be the consequence of the mutated gene. Figure 5.2 illustrates some of the types of behavioral-genetic analyses used to examine the interactions among a gene and its intragenomic, intrauterine, and maternal environment and how these affect the expression of phenotypic differences between strains. Similar analyses can be done with congenic strains that differ from one another by a mutation of allelic variation, in which the same place on a chromosome may be occupied, in different individuals, by two or more genes or alleles, similar to the A, B, and O blood groups in humans.

Wilcock (1969) criticized much of the earlier work on strain comparisons by noting that the research did not control for intragenomic, intrauterine, and maternal influences, and too often focused on mutations that have little relevance to psychological study. Even when effects of the mutation on an individual's psychological functioning are profound, the genetic effects are trivial with respect to understanding the role of genes in the behavioral phenotype because they are mediated through pleiotropic effects that are remote from the behavior itself. The usual basis of pleiotropism, which refers to the ramifying effects of one gene, is the involvement of that gene in some fundamental developmental process. Thus, when such a gene mutates, consequences are likely to ripple throughout the organism, affecting its general well-being or the functioning of one or more of its systems.

Often to have a qualitative impact on behavior, the mutation of a single gene must result in rather large or widespread anatomical and physiological anomalies. These anomalies in turn can affect behavior simply because they disrupt the organism as a whole: whatever changes in behavior are observed may be pleiotropic effects of the mutated gene on the individual's general well-being. However, it is neither surprising nor illuminating to learn that a sick or physiologically debilitated animal fails to perform in the same way as a well animal. This limitation is what prompted Wilcock to consider the identification of pleiotropic effects to be trivial, although most of what we know about single genes and behavior involve these effects.

To use a well-known example, a severe impairment of human intellectual functioning is associated with a condition called phenylketonuria (PKU). This condition is related to a single recessive gene that, when present in both sister chromosomes, leads to a reduction in the liver's production of the enzyme phenylalanine hydroxase. As a result, the amino acid phenylalanine ingested from the diet is not converted to tyrosine. This failure, in turn, has severe metabolic and anatomical consequences. The problem is treatable by restricting the phenylalanine in the diet of infants diagnosed as phenylketonuric, and significantly reduces the danger of mental retardation.

The discovery that the PKU gene is related to intellectual functioning seems trivial in light of its severe consequences for metabolic and anatomical development (recall the distinction between necessary and sufficient

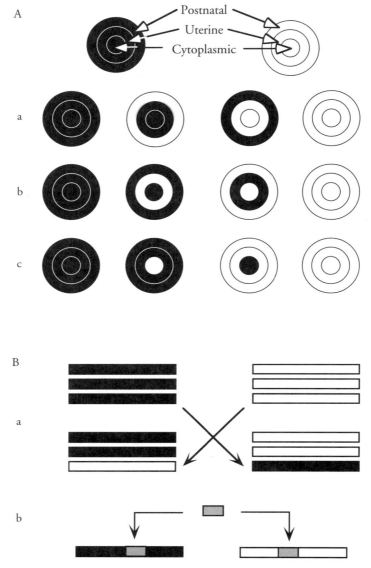

Figure 5.2 Some of the ways by which postnatal maternal influences, prenatal intrauterine influences, and ovarian influences may be examined separately using cross-fostering and ovarian transplant techniques (A). Both breeding and laboratory techniques may be used to examine the influence of a chromosome in relation to other chromosomes and a specific region of a chromosome (gene) in relation to other regions of the chromosome (B).

conditions that was made in chapter 2). Thus, the gene is necessary for normal intellectual functioning only through its contribution to the normal metabolism of food. It is not the cause of, nor the sufficient condition for, intelligence, and it contributes in only trivial ways to individual differences in intelligence. Although knowledge of the pleiotropic gene involved in PKU, like other such genes, is of little use in relating particular genes to particular behavioral phenotypes, knowledge of such genetic conditions is important for understanding why particular individuals may have problems, with intellectual functioning, for example, and for designing efficacious treatment.

Not all pleiotropic genes lead to general debilitation of the organism, but even those that do not often pose interpretive problems. Wilcock noted that performance on behavioral tests used in genetic studies was often affected by some specific consequence of a mutation, such as a change in sensory or motor capacity, that was not a meaningful part of the phenotype of interest. For instance, a gene with a mutation is positively correlated with poor performance by rats on a visual-discrimination learning task. As it turns out, this mutation disrupts the pigmentation of the iris to such an extent that the animal is virtually blind in the test setting. It is not particularly useful to identify the gene in question as a gene for visual discrimination learning.

Recently, sophisticated techniques were employed to examine the effects of single genes. Capecchi (1994) devised a technique that allows the generation of a mouse embryo in which a normal gene is "knocked out" (completely inactivated) and the consequences to the individual of not having that gene product are evaluated. Eventually, genes will be placed under control of a switch that will allow a gene to be activated only at particular phases of development.

At present, the gene targeted to be knocked out is cloned and propagated in bacteria to produce large amounts of the gene's DNA. Then the nucleotide sequence of the gene is changed according to the purposes of the research. The result is called the targeting vector (TV). The TV is introduced into embryo-derived stem (ES) cells from brown mice. If it finds its counterpart (the target) in the DNA of the ES cells, it will line up next to it and replace it. This results in targeted replacement in approximately one in a million ES cells.

To simplify the search for these cells, two selectable markers are inserted into the targeting vector before it is introduced into ES cells. One is incorporated into the middle of the TV and the other is attached to one end. The DNA incorporated into the middle allows those ES cells that have incorporated the TV to grow in a certain medium. The ES cell that have not incorporated the TV will die in that medium. The DNA attached to the end of the TV (the end marker) will also cause the ES cells to die in a certain medium. However, if the TV has been incorporated into the chromosome and effectively replaced the target, the end marker will have become detached and the ES cell will not die. If the TV has been incorporated elsewhere, the end marker will not detach and the ES cell will die. Consequently, only ES cells for which the TV has replaced the targeted gene will remain.

The ES cells are capable of giving rise to all cell types. The ES cells with the knocked out gene are placed in early mouse embryos at the blastocyst stage. The ES cells from brown mice are used because when they are injected into blastocysts of black mice, if they have been incorporated into the blastocyst, they will produce embryos that are chimeric (brown and black) for coat color. When chimeric male mice are mated with black females, their offspring will be brown if the eggs were fertilized by sperm derived from ES cells containing the knocked out gene. These brown siblings are then mated to produce offspring mice with two knocked out copies of the target gene. These offspring are carefully examined for any and all anatomical, physiological, and behavioral abnormalities to reveal functions of the disrupted gene.

In many ways the knockout technique of examining gene-behavior relations resembles the lesioning techniques used to examine brain-behavior relations. At best, they reveal gene products that are necessary for behavioral development or expression without revealing how the behavior is developmentally organized. Also, knocking out a gene and searching for behavioral differences creates a major research problem. What range of behaviors will an investigator examine—learning (and if so, what sorts and under what conditions), exploration, feeding, reproduction? Obviously, all of the potential behaviors of a mouse cannot be examined. Therefore, researchers are likely to be attracted to behavioral tasks that are conducive to the discovery of trivial pleiotropisms. It will require highly sophisticated behavioral research, conducted over a very long period of time, for this technique to provide any insight into the development of behavior.

One recent study (Li et al., 1994) demonstrates the potential contribution of the knockout gene technique to issues in developmental psychobiology. The construction of synaptic connections in the nervous system during development often depends on neural activity. In some cases, N-methyl-D-aspartate (NMDA) receptors in the membrane of the postsynaptic neural cell play a crucial role. Li et al. constructed a knockout mouse missing an aspect of NMDA receptors, rendering the receptors nonfunctional. They then examined the effect of this manipulation on the activity-dependent organization of the developing mouse's brain.

The system they examined is the pathway carrying information from the large facial whiskers to the cortex. A distinct pattern of organization appears at several levels in this pathway (see box 6.1 and figure 6.7). The rows of facial whiskers are represented as rows of neuronal patches that are isomorphic with the pattern of whiskers (Katz, 1994). In the brain stem trigeminal nuclei, the whisker-specific patches are called barrelettes, in the thalamus they are called barreloids, and in the cortex they are called barrels. Controversy has arisen as to whether barrels, barreloids, and barrelettes depend on neural activity for their development. Barreloids and barrels develop after birth, but barrelettes are present before birth (Katz, 1994).

Using knockout mice with impaired NMDA receptors (which die very shortly after birth from respiratory problems), Li et al. (1994) demonstrated that the formation of barrelettes is dependent on functional NMDA receptors. This indicates that prenatal neural activity associated with specific facial whiskers is responsible for the formation of whisker-specific barrelettes in the trigeminal nucleus. It is conceivable that both prenatal and postnatal stimulation of these whiskers are contributing factors to the developmental construction of the barrel organization of the mouse cortical somatosensory system. Thus, the knockout technique for studying single gene effects can be applied to specific issues in developmental psychobiology.

Methods used for the unifactorial genetic study of human psychology differ in several respects from those used with animals. Initially, the methods were derived from those used to study human diseases. Biomedical geneticists would examine the biochemistry associated with some disease, discover a missing enzyme or defective protein, and then identify the gene involved. Thus, for the study of human psychology, biomedical researchers sifted the biochemistry of various psychiatric disorders (e.g., depression, schizophrenia, autism, anxiety), searching for differences from that of psychologically "normal" persons. Unfortunately, it is difficult to disentangle whether the differences are a consequence or cause of the disorder (Martin, Owen, & Morisha, 1987). Moreover, the results of the biochemical analyses are often inconsistent across studies, even those by the same research team (Martin et al., 1987).

In contrast, techniques developed in molecular biology, such as linkage mapping, are now employed in behavior genetics. In 1978 Kan and Dozy identified a normal genetic variant (**polymorphism**) in the DNA molecule itself. This was only the first of a large number of DNA polymorphisms that have since been found and mapped to particular locations on the chromosomes of humans. The practical consequence is that the polymorphisms can be used as genetic markers. Individuals who share the same polymorphic variant for a particular stretch of a given chromosome will share the same characteristic chromosomal appearance. These variants are inherited. Since they can be readily observed in cells taken from anybody, they serve as markers for following how any part of a chromosome has been transmitted through a family.

Linkage mapping studies are done because genes are inherited in blocks, and not necessarily because the observable difference in a chromosome is thought to affect the phenotype. Because of linkage, it can be inferred that someone with one marker polymorphism is likely to have a group of neighboring genes that are the same as those in another individual who has the same marker, and possibly different from those in another individual with a different marker. The underlying logic behind the studies is to seek a relationship between some psychiatric disorder and one of the DNA polymorphisms by examining distributions of these two characteristics in families. If they are linked on a stretch of chromosome, then individuals who have a particular form of the DNA polymorphism will be predicted also to have the disorder. This research strategy first proved its usefulness in tracing the pattern of transmission and predicting carriers of Huntington's disease, which stems from a mutation at a single locus (Wexler, Rose, & Housman, 1991).

Predictable relationships between markers and disorders give researchers information about the chromosomal location of genes that contribute to the expression of a psychiatric or other disorder. For example, consider the genetic disturbance in fragile X syndrome, a common inherited type of mental retardation. Individuals with this syndrome are identified by possessing an X chromosome in which the tip of one long arm is attached by only a slender strand of DNA. In normal individuals, a gene (designated FRM-1) located in this area of the chromosome contains 60 or fewer tandem repeats of a particular trinucleotide base sequence called a codon (see below). Healthy carriers of fragile X syndrome can have as many as 200 tandem copies; individuals with the syndrome have many hundreds to thousands of tandem copies of these base triplets. Since the mentally retarded children are the offspring of healthy carriers, the genes must be expanding between generations. The mechanism for expansion is unknown, but a form of polymerase (an enzyme that adds nucleotides to growing DNA strands) is suspected. Presumably, the syndrome can be prevented once a technique for regulating the polymerase is discovered.

One major assumption of biomedical genetics research on humans is that the psychiatric disorder *must not be multifactorial*. As Kidd (1991) notes, "When dealing with a complex disorder, where we know there is genetic involvement but are not absolutely certain what the mode of inheritance is, we must have what I would call a disbelief in polygenic inheritance. If many different genes are involved and each of them has a very small effect, none of them could ever be found ... For most neuropsychiatric disorders, there is no proof that they are NOT polygenic ... even when the pattern of inheritance is compatible with a major locus, that does not prove a major locus is responsible" (pp. 167–168). In other words, the tendency is to assume single-gene effects, because that is the only type of genetic effect that can be studied with the methods now in hand. Although looking in the only lit area is understandable, the underlying assumption can be faulted (box 5.2). It is estimated (Strohman, 1994) that only about 2% of all human diseases can be related to single gene effects.

Moreover, empirical evidence supports the conclusion that conditions known to be associated with a major locus can be affected by genes at other

Box 5.2   The Medical Genetics of Bipolar Disease

Bipolar disorder is characterized by periods of unreasonable depression occasionally interspersed with bouts of unreasonable euphoria and excitation. The manic phases are less frequent and of shorter duration than the depressive phases. In some cases, evidence clearly shows that the illness runs in families. Thus, the illness has attracted the attention of medical geneticists.

In a much publicized study, Egeland et al. (1987) reported evidence of a linkage of certain DNA markers on the short arm of chromosome 11 and the manifestation of bipolar disease in an Amish population. The evidence seemed to indicate that the gene associated with the disorder was adjacent to the Harvey-*ras* oncogene (H-*ras*). Because the gene (TH) that produces the enzyme for the first step in catecholamine synthesis (tyrosine hydroxylase) had been mapped to that region and because TH was known to have alternative splicing in different tissues, it seemed possible that TH could function normally in some tissues but abnormally in others. Thus, bipolar disease was thought to result from abnormalities of TH in certain brain regions.

However, revised estimates of the position of the TH gene indicated that it was not the candidate gene for this illness. Furthermore, the addition of more family members to the sample (intended to refine the chromosomal localization) and the unexpected expression of the initial onset of the illness in two individuals from the original study group, eliminated all evidence favoring a linkage between H-*ras* and the putative gene. The evidence contributed by the additional family members was all negative, and the onset of the illness in two previously unaffected individuals pointed toward a different pattern of transmission than had been suggested previously. "Thus, there is currently no statistically significant evidence for a gene for manic depressive illness at the tip of the short arm of chromosome 11; the gene that was 'found' has now been 'lost' " (Kidd, 1991, pp. 174–175).

The complexities inherent in the manifestation and diagnosis of psychiatric disorders, the relative primitiveness of current techniques for determining linkage and for estimating patterns of inheritance in humans, and reliance on the assumption of major gene (nonpolygenic) phenotypic expression all warrant caution in applying medical genetics to psychiatric phenomena. There are likely to be many instances in which the apparent genetic cause of a psychiatric disorder turns out to be mistaken. Moreover, even if a major gene were found for some psychiatric disorder, it is likely that many relatives would have the mutant gene without manifesting the disorder. These individuals highlight the weakness of using genetics as the major etiological factor.

Too often, for many psychiatric disorders, genetics is the only clearly defined etiological factor. This may be because genetics is the most important causal factor or because other causal factors have not been identified (Torrey, 1992). The nature of modern genetic techniques is such that if no other causal factors have been clearly defined, then automatically the etiology of the psychiatric trait will be reducible to genetic factors. Many psychiatric disorders are likely exaggerated manifestations of otherwise normal patterns of behavior that emerge from fairly complex developmental events. Some may "run in families" without the necessary mediation of a major gene or gene complex. These phenomena, whether hereditary or not, pose difficult questions for the developmental psychobiologist because alternative causal factors have been neither identified nor clearly defined.

loci. For example, Huntington's disease is a fatal disease that is 100% heritable. Its symptoms include uncontrollable jerking and writhing in various parts of the body, profound intellectual deterioration, emotional disturbances, and occasional delusions and hallucinations. The usual onset is between 35 and 45 years of age, but the observed range extends from 2 to the early eighties. The age of onset is influenced by whether the transmitting parent is the mother or the father, a fact that clearly demonstrates the influence of heritable factors other than the major gene itself.

The fact that the phenotypic expression of the same gene can differ depending on whether the transmitting gamete is egg or sperm is called genetic imprinting, an unfortunate choice of words since this process bears no resemblance to the imprinting concept in ethology. For example, mice embryos with a full set of chromosomes from only one sex exhibit disturbances of embryonic development (Rennie, 1993). Without a maternal imprint on its chromosomes, the embryo becomes abnormal; without a paternal imprint, the placenta fails to develop. Children with Prader-Willi syndrome, a disorder characterized by mental retardation and obesity, often inherit both copies of chromosome 15 from their mother (Rennie, 1993).

Genetic imprinting results from a little understood process by which genes are modified before or during the formation of the gametes (eggs or sperm) in the parents. Gametogenesis of eggs and sperm leads to different patterns of modification, so that a gene originating from the father may be expressed differently in the offspring than the same gene originating from the mother. This change is not carried in the germ line across generations. Thus the genome originating from a female parent will have genes modified to the egg pattern, whether these genes are traced to her mother or her father. The mechanisms controlling genetic imprinting are at present unknown, but may involve methylation of the DNA (Singer & Berg, 1991). Methyl groups can bind chemically to cysteine, one of the bases of DNA, and such methylation seems to inactivate the gene. Since the pattern of methylation is retained when the DNA replicates, imprints in a fertilized egg can be passed to all cells in the body.

In an attempt to deal with the problems associated with many genetic influences, biomedical geneticists are adopting the technique of quantitative trait locus (QTL) analysis (Barinaga, 1994; Crabbe, Belknap, & Buck, 1994; Plomin et al., 1994). This analysis assumes that any gene in a multigene syndrome is neither necessary nor sufficient for the manifestation of the syndrome, yet the genes may vary in the size of their effect. In animals, the analysis involves examining the distribution of a set of different alleles for several chromosomal loci in inbred strains in relation to the manifestation of certain behavioral characteristics (Crabbe et al., 1994). The analysis provides an estimate of risk for differences in behavioral manifestation depending on the presence of specific alleles.

The statistical analyses of such associations in humans require both the adoption of very stringent and conservative levels for identifying an association between an allele and the syndrome, and the use of very large samples. Also, at present, since there are few candidate genes for human behavior, the technique involves screening a relatively random assortment of DNA polymorphic markers in the hope of finding associations (Plomin et al., 1994). Thus, in human research there is little, so far, to distinguish QTL from unifactorial analyses.

In addition to genetic imprinting, phenotypes traceable to unifactorial genetic effects can be influenced by diverse prenatal and postnatal developmental events. Consider the hypertensive rat. Lander and Botstein (1986) found that the hypertension was linked to a mutation at the angiotensin-converting enzyme (ACE) locus. The ACE gene produces an enzyme that converts renin to angiotensin. Angiotensin is a protein involved in regulating blood pressure. If newborn rats are taken from mothers with the ACE mutation and nursed by normal mothers, the pups show decreased levels of hypertension (Myers et al., 1989). Thus, early developmental events affect the phenotypic outcome in individual organisms with a mutated ACE gene.

Unifactorial genetic methods are interesting to developmental psychobiologists because they may help identify certain necessary conditions for the development of some psychological characteristics. However, they are unlikely to reveal sufficient conditions for the development of any psychological trait. Most of the behavioral and physiological traits studied by psychobiologists require many genes, functioning in both direct and indirect pathways, for their development and expression. A different, quantitative approach is required for their genetic analysis. Most quantitative geneticists start with some phenotype of interest and use predictable variation in the phenotype to examine genetic contributions.

Multifactorial Methods

Heritability

The multifactorial approach relies on various statistical procedures to estimate how much of differences in performance of some behavior can be assigned to genetic differences among the individuals. These estimates measure heritability, which is essentially a statement of how well parental attributes can be used to predict offspring attributes. Heritability estimates are useful in animal and plant genetics because they can tell one whether and how readily some character will respond to selection. They are used to construct and evaluate breeding programs designed to decrease or increase the frequency of occurrence of some trait in a population. The estimates are also useful in natural populations, where they can be applied to the study of natural selection.

However, several features about heritability as a measurement of genetic involvement must be kept in mind when exporting the concept from its original domain. Three features stand out as important for developmental work. First, heritability estimates do not indicate how the characteristic is inherited (Hirsch, 1970). Second, the statistical techniques that are used depend on a number of important assumptions; if these assumptions are not met in a given case, the measures are useless. Third, measures of heritability severely underestimate the interaction between genes and environment (Wahlsten, 1990).

Certain assumptions must be made when calculating heritability estimates. The first is that any particular behavioral characteristic of an individual (e.g., intelligence, personality traits) can be reliably and validly described and represented by a single score or measurement. The value of this score depends on both genotype and environment. A second assumption is that the behavior of a population of individuals can be characterized by group averages and by measures of the differences between individual scores (variance measures). This assumption is usually represented by the equation $V_p = V_g + V_e$, which means that the differences in the behavioral phenotype in the population (V_p) are equal to the genotypic (V_g) plus the environmental (V_e) differences among its members. This equation in turn rests on the assumption that the different genetic influences making up V_g are additive; that is, that there is no interaction among genes. This last assumption is made for practical reasons, and not on theoretical grounds. Some geneticists question whether it is ever valid.

The equation rests on yet another assumption that the genetic and environmental circumstances of the individual are additive, independent, and not covarying. This assumption is extensively violated in human genetic research (Cavalli-Sforza & Bodmer, 1971). That is, humans do not mate randomly, but with people who are like them with respect to background, socioeconomic status, education, and so forth.

Of course, statistical techniques (analysis of variance, multiple regression) are available to determine whether there is an interaction between heredity and environment, and other techniques estimate gene-environment covariation (Plomin et al., 1988). Unfortunately, they are relatively insensitive to detecting the presence of interactions (Bateson, 1987a; Wahlsten, 1990). In agricultural research, population geneticists recognize the problem and attempt to overcome the insensitivity of the statistical techniques by using sample sizes very much larger than those employed in behavior-genetics and medical genetics research (cf. Mann, 1994).

Despite its problems, the heritability equation can derive a common heritability estimate (h^2) in the following way: $h^2 = V_g/(V_g + V_e) = V_g/V_p$. This equation gives an estimate of the proportion of individual differences in phenotype that is due to differences in genotype. Note that heritability is never estimated for whole behaviors or behavioral complexes such as aggression, intelligence, or fear, but only for one feature of the pattern, such as the frequency, *or* the intensity, *or* the duration of fighting in a specific context.

The most straightforward way to obtain the necessary estimates of the separate genetic and environmental influences on a score is to use inbred strains. Because the members of an inbred strain are genetically identical, any differences in their scores on some test must be due to environmental influences. By comparing the differences in scores of an inbred strain with differences in scores of a normal or randomly bred population, researchers obtain an estimate of h^2.

Using the example of fighting in mice, the logic of the h^2 estimate is as follows.

1. The score differences (phenotypic variance, V_p), on some aggression test, for a randomly bred population are assumed to reflect both genotypic and environmental influences. This is expressed by the equation $V_p = V_g + V_e$.

2. The score differences on the same test for an inbred strain are assumed to reflect only environmental influences. This is expressed V_e (environmental variance).

3. One estimates the genetic component of the score difference by subtracting the result of step 2 from the result of step 1: $V_p - V_e = V_g$ (genetic variance).

4. Finally, one estimates the heritability of aggression in mice by dividing the result of step 3 by the result of step 1: $V_g/V_p = h^2$.

Inbred strains are unusual laboratory phenomena. They give researchers powerful tools for testing genetic hypotheses, and they reveal the underlying logic of heritability estimates without the complications that natural populations or even selected strains would have. Human behavioral geneticists, quantitative geneticists interested in questions of population biology, and applied geneticists all use heritability estimates, and all have to contend with less than optimum conditions for their measurements.

Population biologists and applied geneticists start with a phenotype and are interested in its response to selection. Population biologists are concerned with measuring the effects of natural selection and use quantitative genetics, including modeling approaches, to that end. The logic underlying their work has much in common with that of the applied geneticist, who has the practical goal of improving some phenotype for agricultural purposes.

The applied geneticist has access to experimental methods that are often not available to population biologists. In a typical experiment, artificial selection will be applied, and response to that selection will be measured in subsequent generations. If response is rapid, heritability is high. If there is no response, heritability is zero. Using correlational procedures, heritability is measured by the slope of the line that predicts the value of some pheno-type measured in offspring from the value of the same phenotype in parents. A measure of heritability obtained in this way is mathematically equivalent to that described for inbred strains.

It is instructive to examine some of the explicit assumptions that are rou-tine in applied genetics research. For example, the fact of gene-environment interactions (i.e., the phenotypic outcome of a particular genotype may change if the environment is changed) is explicitly acknowledged by the simple, practical expedient of incorporating the environment into the op-erational definition of the trait. This is possible because of the relatively limited and relatively controlled environments within which the plants or animals will be allowed to develop. If the objective is to increase milk yield in a population of cows, for example, selection is readily applied by allowing only high-yielding cows to reproduce. However, the cows must live, repro-duce, and be selected in a pasture that has particular characteristics. If this pasture was, let us say, relatively good, the cows selected for high yield in this pasture may not be the ones with high yields in a poor pasture. There may be no correlation or even a negative correlation between the two phe-notypes. This is handled by treating "yield in good pasture" and "yield in poor pasture" as separate traits, selecting on one, and measuring whether there is correlated response in the other.

Similarly, homologous traits at different ages are treated as different traits. For example, if selection for body weight is applied at one age, this age becomes part of the operational definition of the trait. Weights at other ages are treated as different traits, and it becomes an empirical question as to whether selection at one age has positive, negative, or no correlated effects at other ages. These procedures have been adopted because of em-pirical necessity: there are numerous examples of selection applied at one age or in one circumstance having either no effects or effects of opposite sign on the "same" trait at different developmental stages or in different circumstances (Arnold, 1987).

Twin and Adoption Studies

Neither inbred nor selected strains of humans exist. Investigators have had to develop other methods to estimate heritability within our own species. For obvious reasons, these methods are far from ideal. The most powerful technique is an extension of the inbred strain method used by experimental geneticists: studies of genetically identical twins. The contribution of en-vironmental variance is measured by comparing identical twins who have been reared apart. Because these twins are genetically identical, the only source of variance is the environment (given the assumptions of heritability measurement outlined earlier). When the environmental variance estimated from twins is subtracted from the variance exhibited by people who differ both in their genetic makeup and in their environments, what is left is the variance due to genetic factors. Essentially, what this boils down to is that the similarities (concordances) between twins reared apart are used to estimate genetic contributions to individual differences (Bouchard, 1983, 1984, 1994).

Twin studies are the foundation for a number of controversial assertions in behavioral genetics. Of these, none has been more controversial than the heritability of intelligence. The argument has many angles. First, serious questions exist about the data base. Careful examination of early twin studies (Bronfenbrenner, 1972; Kamin, 1974) revealed major inconsistencies and contradictions in the data.

Closer to developmental issues, it also became apparent that many of the twins who were "reared apart" were often raised by close relatives, lived in the same or similar neighborhoods, and even attended the same schools. Moreover, when twins did not live with relatives, the adoption agencies, in keeping with standard policy, placed them in home environments similar to their original family environments (Billings et al., 1992). For all these reasons, even in a carefully done study, the discordance in twins reared apart provides an inadequate estimate of the variance that can be attributed to environmental influences in the population as a whole. Given the structure of human society, it is unlikely that any group of twins would ever be brought up in environments that were different enough to represent even vaguely the range and diversity of environmental conditions found in a typical modern society.

Although some more recent work purports to address some of these difficulties (Bouchard, 1983, 1984, 1994), Billings et al. (1992) provide a critique that applies to all studies of twins reared apart. Among their criticisms is that people use physical appearance as a basis for their behavior toward others. The way that people are treated by others contributes importantly to the development of personality characteristics. Because identical twins are physically more similar than nonidentical twins, they will be treated more similarly even when reared apart. In assessing the implications of twin studies, it is important to bear in mind exactly what is included in the genetic term of the heritability equation. For example, the implications of Bouchard's findings take on a different hue once it is realized that he treats all gene-environment covariations as genetic!

These studies are useful because identical twins share all the same genes; however, this very fact presents another problem for interpreting the results. Identical twins share identical gene-gene covariation and interaction. The similarities for polygenic traits, for epigenetic pathways for indirect genetic effects, and for prenatal maternal effects are also maximized. Because all these effects are confounded with direct genetic effects, twin data overestimate the genetic contributions to psychological variability (Plomin, 1990). It is worth remembering that such interpretative complications and genetic nuances are rarely retained in media coverage of such studies.

Thus the most powerful human genetic tool is limited in what it can accomplish. Concordance of twins on psychological measures provides a weak foundation for estimating genetic influences, because the concordance may arise from other sources. At best, the study of the dissimilarities (discordance) between twins reared apart might be used to identify environmental contributions to individual differences (Hinde, 1968; Billings et al., 1992).

Twins represent a small segment of the human population. Therefore, geneticists employ other techniques to estimate genetic influences on human psychological traits. One frequent approach is to compare the correlations on some phenotypic measure of adopted offspring with their two sets of parents, biological and adoptive (Plomin et al., 1988). Correlation with the biological parent is taken to represent genetic contributions to the individual differences in expression of the psychological trait. Bateson (1987a) demonstrated that these techniques are insensitive to patterns of difference between parents and offspring in the rearing environment. For example, adoptive parents may be bright or less than bright. Either way, however, they set challenges for adopted children that are achievable or non-achievable. The nature of the match between relevant aspects of the environment that parents set and characteristics that their offspring bring to the interaction is probably far more important to intellectual development than is parental brightness. Standard correlational studies do not measure this match.

Even though correlational studies may not measure the most interesting kinds of things from a developmental perspective, it is nonetheless necessary to explain why the correlations within biological families are consistently higher than correlations within adoptive families for many psychological characteristics (Bouchard & McCue, 1981). One answer may have to do with the nature of the comparisons. Using data from measures of psychological traits, it has been pointed out that the relative ranking of adopted children may be more closely correlated with the relative ranking of their biological parents than that of their adoptive parents. However, correlations based on absolute scores may demonstrate a closer correspondence between the children and their adoptive parents (Schiff & Lewontin, 1986). Indeed, several studies of the effect of biological versus adoptive parents on IQ and school success of adoptive children in France demonstrate a powerful influence of adoption (summarized in Duyme & Capron, 1992). Adoption can produce an 11.6-point difference in IQ. Thus, adoption studies raise a number of interesting questions that can be pursued developmentally, but they do not provide unambiguous data for drawing genetic conclusions.

Benson (1992) called attention to another characteristic of families that is a likely confound in both twin and adoption studies. "Deidentification," which is a mechanism for reducing family tension, refers to the processes underlying the development of contrasting personalities within the same family group. Deidentification includes differential parental treatment of children, differential treatment of siblings by each other, the active adoption of a particular role by the individual, and the responses of others outside the family toward the adopted role. The dynamics of these interactions lead to divergence among personalities within the family. Although siblings reared together share an environment, it is also clear that this environment differs in important ways among siblings in the same family (Plomin & Daniels, 1987).

Children are very attentive to their social environment, and pay close attention to their own as well as those of others in the family group. They are adept at identifying differences from a very early age (Dunn, 1988; Dunn & Plomin, 1985, 1990, 1991). Indeed, siblings of different ages will readily note differences in parental care, even when what the children categorize as differences are seen as age-adjusted equivalences from an outside perspective. For example, when a parent treats a second-born child who is three years old in exactly the same way that its five-year-old sibling was treated when he or she was three years of age, the two children will perceive and respond to this as differential treatment. The perceived difference has the effect of accentuating the development of personality differences between the siblings, even when, from the parent's perspective, treatment has been identical (Baker & Daniels, 1990).

The family is a rich and incompletely analyzed source of developmental influence on psychological development but, as Benson (1992) reminds us, the relevant environment extends well beyond the family (Bronfenbrenner, 1986). Bronfenbrenner's list of potential contributors to psychological characteristics include the neighborhood, schools, recreational and sports activities, adults from outside the family, peer groups, acquaintances, friends, enemies, religious groups, and the media (radio, television, computer games, books, etc.). Although both known and unexamined effects on psychological development come from such sociocultural sources, these environmental effects have not been incorporated into the kinds of questions asked by behavioral geneticists, nor are current genetic methods designed to measure them. They are, however, appropriate effects to be incorporated into the kinds of questions posed by developmental psychobiologists.

It is difficult to summarize the current status of human behavioral genetics without concluding that the field is in serious trouble. It is unable to use the experimental methods that are open to animal genetics. The approximations to these methods, twin and adoption studies, run into problems that seem unsolvable. Bodmer and Cavalli-Sforza (1970) concluded that these difficulties kept the requirements of genetic analysis from being met adequately and that, therefore, there could be no science of human behavior genetics. Since that time, there is little to suggest that the serious limitations have been overcome. In assessing the field, it is important to ask what it is attempting to achieve. It does not share the goals of applied animal genetics or theoretical populations genetics. Eugenics movements have occurred in human history, but this is not an accepted element in our society. Unlike applied animal genetics or population biologists, human behavioral geneticists are not attempting to improve a response to artificially applied selection or to measure a response to natural selection. The goals seem clearly related to development: to identify genetic contributions to development and (in an applied vein) to inform public policy on education and other developmental issues. (See Gould, 1981, for a cogent historical discussion of this topic.)

We can react in three ways to the current status of human behavioral genetics. One way is to reject the whole enterprise and cease trying to do human behavioral genetics, as several critics suggested. This is not satisfactory to a psychobiologist, for the obvious reasons that humans have genes, and genes are involved in the development and expression of behavior. A second reaction is to retain the dichotomy between biologically and environmentally caused development. Behavioral geneticists who defend their work in this manner argue that genetic influences are indeed special: they limit responses to environmental influences, and they can and should be identified (Turkheimer & Gottesman, 1991). Twin and familial heritability data are thought to identify the presence of these influences, even if only imperfectly, and evidence from single-gene and chromosome marker studies is seen to support the same idea. However, this position can be adopted only by also adopting a flawed view of development (chapters 2 and 3) and by ignoring a tremendous amount of developmental evidence. Furthermore, the argument is too often couched in terms of such questionable genetic concepts as reaction range and genetic potentials.

The third reaction is to expand behavioral genetics to include developmental phenomena within a sound theory. To see how this might be done within a multifactorial genetic framework, it is helpful to know how applied animal geneticists, population biologists, and experimental behavioral geneticists have dealt with developmental contributions to individual differences.

Developmental Sources of Variance

Generally speaking, the goal of behavioral genetics is to explain individual differences on some behavioral trait by identifying correlated individual differences in the allelic form of a particular gene. This task is complicated by the fact that particular alleles may be correlated with a number of other factors, each of which may make additive or interactive contributions to the same trait. We refer to these factors as developmental sources of variance, because they can alter the phenotypic value of a trait by changing the developmental contingencies for some allele under study.

Heritability estimates have been frequently criticized (e.g., Hirsch, 1970, 1976; Wahlsten, 1990) because they can only partition variance into additive genetic and environmental sources, arbitrarily setting interaction terms to zero by lumping them into one of the other terms (typically the genetic one). This practice obscures an important source of variance in populations: developmental phenomena. As Hirsch (1970) indicated, heritability is a convenient but fleeting statistic. Any estimate of it is completely dependent on the environmental circumstances and genetic differences that were present in a specific population at the time of testing. An estimate obtained from such a set of measures cannot be extrapolated to another population or to the same population under different environmental circumstances, at different developmental stages, or in different generations. Heritability measures allow us to predict phenotypic outcome in a population only under restricted conditions that prevent a change in variation from developmental sources.

Natural populations exist in varied circumstances. To measure the direct contribution of a particular genetic difference to phenotypic variance in natural populations, it is necessary to address correlated (confounded) differences in other factors. These factors may be other genes that have either direct or indirect effects on the trait, or they may be environmental factors that are nonrandomly associated with a particular allele. It should be remembered that in genetic work based on Mendelian principles, a gene is recognized by a heritable trait. Therefore, to study correlations among genes, one starts by examining correlations among heritable traits.

Two mechanisms at the level of an individual genotype, pleiotropism and linkage disequilibrium, can lead to the correlation of traits within a population (Arnold, 1987). As we have seen, most traits are affected by the joint action of many genes, and pleiotropic effects of individual genes are rather common. Imagine such a pleiotropic gene that affects both the timing of migration of cells within a particular part of the nervous system and the timing of prenatal testosterone secretion. Such a gene may speed or slow each of the two developmental events. It is possible to imagine four different alleles at the same genetic locus: one speeding both processes; one slowing both processes; one speeding migration but slowing testosterone secretion; and one slowing migration but speeding testosterone secretion. Thus, the two phenotypes may be either positively or negatively correlated in the population, depending on which of these alleles is most numerous.

Pleiotropism is a common source of genetically correlated phenotypes, but correlations can also arise because of **linkage disequilibrium**, a nonrandom pattern of linkage between alleles at two different loci (Arnold, 1987). If a gene at one locus affects trait A and a gene at a second locus affects trait B, then phenotypic correlations between two traits may result when a particular allele at one locus is likely to occur along with a particular allele at a second locus. These correlations can be either positive or negative, depending on the most numerous pattern of linkage in the population.

Correlations can also arise through indirect epigenetic effects within individual development (Atchley & Hall, 1991). A gene may produce an effect in one set of cells that, in turn, sets conditions that bias the course of development for another set of cells. Such indirect effects should be distinguished from pleiotropism, because the same gene(s) do not directly affect the two phenotypes. An example would be the inductive effect of neighboring cells on the morphological differentiation of a cell. Chapter 6 examines many such location-dependent interactions during embryogenesis.

In addition to correlations arising from within an individual, phenotypic correlations can arise because of correlations between an individual's genes and its environment (Arnold, 1987; Atchley & Hall, 1991; Kirkpatrick & Lande, 1989). Experimental geneticists are particularly concerned with examining what they refer to as maternal effects, by which they mean effects of the maternal phenotype on offspring phenotype. Because of the relation between mother and offspring, maternal phenotype (whatever its source) forms part of the inheritance of the offspring and may be correlated with offspring phenotype. When the maternal phenotype is due if only in part to her genotype, it is possible for genetic correlations to be expressed phenotypically in two different generations.

It is important to remember that all these correlations can be positive or negative. It was, in fact, the negative correlations that forced applied geneticists to attend to these developmental sources of variance. A concrete example may clarify the kinds of relationships that can occur. Consider artificially applied selection for increased body size in some animal that has numerous offspring. A large dam will be likely for developmental reasons to have a large litter. Again, for developmental reasons, individual pups in a large litter will be smaller than individual pups in a small litter. Thus, selection for large body size in one generation is likely to have the paradoxical effect of small body size in the next, because of the positive correlation between body size and litter size within the dam, and the negative correlation of the maternal factor (litter size) with body size in the offspring generation. (See Arnold, 1987, for additional examples and a clear discussion of these points.)

We now have many examples illustrating both positive and negative maternal effects with respect to selection for some characteristic. Depending on the nature of the correlation, these effects can augment the rate of phenotypic change in the same direction as selection, or they can produce phenotypic changes opposite to the direction of selection; they can also produce continuing evolution after selection ceases (Kirkpatrick & Lande, 1989). Because of the intercorrelations among characters, selection that produces change in a particular character can lead to changes in a second. This second character may not be under selection, in which case the change would be neutral, or it may be under selection in the opposite direction, in which case the change would be maladaptive. If the environment were to change, the changed second character may turn out to be adaptive, in which case it would fit the definition of an exaptation (chapter 4). In any event, the second character can be thought of as simply being dragged along because of selection on the first.

Positive or negative correlations among phenotypical traits may exist within an individual at a given age (e.g., **allometric growth** of two body parts), between different ages of the same individual (e.g., weight at weaning and weight as an adult), between the sexes (e.g., mounting in female as well as male rats), and between parent and offspring (e.g., litter size and body size). The positive correlation between body size and antler size in Irish elk is an example of allometric growth with dire evolutionary consequences; it is thought that the elk grew themselves to extinction because the correlated increase in antler size exceeded the capacity of the animals to support them (Gould, 1977).

Correlations also may be seen between traits and aspects of the biotic (e.g., food) or physical environment selected or modified by an individual or its parents (e.g., nest site, ambient temperature). They may arise because of correlations among genes or between genes and environments, with environments inherited through either genetic or nongenetic means. Thus, correlations exist between the genes through which particular traits are thought to be inherited and a host of other factors, producing individual differences in these traits. Although derived from a different starting point, these gene-gene and gene-environment correlations illustrate the developmental constraints on evolution discussed in chapter 4.

The applied geneticist deals with these developmental complications empirically. For example, selection may be applied on a trait (body weight) exhibited at one age and the response to this selection on the same trait at a different age may be measured. Or the response to selection applied in one environment may be measured in a different environment. Or selection may be applied to a maternal trait (milk yield), and the correlated response in a second offspring trait (proportion of fat) may be measured. These procedures are available because of the relatively small number of variables, with values that are identifiable and relatively circumscribed in range, that are of interest to the applied geneticist and their ability to control other sources of variance in these domestic or laboratory settings.

The quantitative geneticist responds by complicating the predictive model (Atchley & Hall, 1991; Atchley & Newman, 1989; Cheverud, 1984; Kirkpatrick & Lande, 1989; Lande & Arnold, 1983). Efforts are made to measure or to model the contributions of correlated genes and environmental variables, including direct and indirect effects. Although research of this nature is now in a growth phase, it is not new. Wright, in fact, devised path analysis to deal with just these complexities in work dating back to the 1920s (1968). When put into the type of equation that is familiar from heritability estimates, the additional terms uncovered by analysis of correlated variables take the form of additive covariates having either positive or negative sign. (The separate contributions of interactions among the variables remain elusive with this type of analysis.) The underlying objective of the population geneticist is to measure the response to selection of some phenotype, and the necessary predictions cannot be made without extending the models beyond direct genetic effects to include the covariates.

When experimental procedures are available, geneticists may attempt to identify the separate contributions of different correlated variables. These studies, which are typically done with mammals, usually proceed by dividing maternal effects into prenatal (intrauterine) and postnatal (nursing) components. A study might therefore examine for genetically correlated postnatal effects by using two strains of mice, comparing young reared after cross-fostering to a different maternal environment with those reared after fostering within their own strain. Similarly, intrauterine effects can be examined using ovarian transplants in an analogous fashion. These studies permit one to identify the separate effects of maternal and offspring genotypes during each of these developmental stages.

Elaborate breeding programs can be used to place a known stretch of chromosome, containing a gene that has been linked to some heritable phenotype, in different backgrounds, systematically testing each of several compartments that are in the usual course of events correlated with the gene. Tools have been developed to examine separately the contributions of other parts of the same chromosome, other chromosomes, genetic imprinting (whether the gene originated from the mother or father), maternal cytoplasm, uterine environment, and postnatal maternal environment. These studies can yield surprising results (box 5.3, figure 5.3), including interactions between genes, between genes and each of the environmental compartments, and between environments.

Geneticists working in a Mendelian tradition have procedures for identifying, measuring, and incorporating developmental sources of variance into explanatory models. These procedures are useful to population biologists and applied geneticists as they seek to improve their predictions and measurements of response to selection. However, nothing in the procedures requires retention of the concept of genetic determination. In fact, such a concept is contrary to the data collected by the geneticists themselves.

Although information gathered by quantitative geneticists is consistent with developmental inquiry, there are sharp limits to how far such methods can go toward illuminating developmental processes. As the contribution of separate correlated factors multiplies, so must the number of covariates in the quantitative models. Similarly, the number of variables in the complex experimental designs required by experimental geneticists as they attempt

Box 5.3   Interpenetration of Gene and Environment in Mouse Aggression

Males from the N (NZB) strain of mice are more likely to attack an unfamiliar docile male intruder from a third strain than are males from the H (CBA/h) strain. The difference in threshold to attack has been linked to differences in a region of their Y chromosome. However, this region co-occurs in development with other parts of the Y, the X chromosome, the autosomes, maternal cytoplasm from the fertilized egg, and particular prenatal and postnatal maternal environments, all of which vary with strain (see figure 5.2). Carlier, Roubertoux, and Pastoret (1991) disentangled the influence of some of these factors to determine the effect of variation in overall background of the Y chromosome, and to separate the effects of the uterine and postnatal maternal environments from ovarian contributions (X chromosome, autosomes, cytoplasm).

The F_1 female offspring, created by crossing H × N strains, were given ovarian grafts from either H or N females. Grafted females were mated to males from each strain or to F_1 males. These matings resulted in groups of males with a Y from either N or H strain, an X from either strain, and autosomes that were all from either strain, half from each strain, or three-fourths from either strain.

The same mating procedures were also followed for females that retained their own ovaries. All mothers then reared their own offspring, creating 16 different types of mother-offspring genotype relations. The strain of origin for the cytoplasmic environment was always confounded with that of the X chromosome, but the uterine and postnatal maternal environments were kept constant in half of the groups by the ovarian graft procedure. In the remaining groups these maternal environments varied with the X chromosome. The manipulations placed the Y chromosome from the H and N strains in each of eight different backgrounds (see figure 5.3).

Although N males are more likely to attack than H males when born to and reared by dams from their own strains, this is not simply due to the Y chromosome carried in the N strain. Males with this Y will show a moderate or low probability of attack when the Y co-occurs with other chromosomes from the H strain or with the F_1 maternal environments. Conversely, males with a Y from the H strain (i.e. with the putative low-aggression gene) are more likely to be aggressive occurs in a background of other factors from the N strain. Th Y chromosome on agonistic behavior depends on cluding other chromosomes (autosomes), the X aternal components (cytoplasm of the egg, pretal conditions).

t males with H ovarian mothers and N fathers f born to and reared by H females, but low ed by the H × N F_1 females. A follow-up offspring of N fathers and H mothers that oster H mothers or by H × N-crossed enteenth condition, disentangling the he F_1 mothers. As it turned out, the nsible for the lowered probability of in.

ne gene has different phenotypic g postnatal maternal influences.

> Intriguing developmental questions remain. How does either the Y chromosome or background genetic factors contribute to the development of the behavior? What are the relevant maternal differences, and how do they exert their effects?

to tease apart the separate and interactive contributions of different maternal effects is already quite high. Yet, for a developmental psychobiologist, categories such as postnatal maternal effect are far too global to reveal the details of mother-infant interaction that contribute to development. Thus, at some point genetic methods must give way to developmental methods, if understanding development is the goal.

Molecular Genetics and Development

The relatively recent association of the molecule DNA with the gene concept, and the subsequent emergence of the field of molecular or biochemical genetics have made available new ways of studying the developmental pathways associating genotypes with phenotypes. Both developmental psychobiology and molecular genetics use concepts that are aimed at understanding developmental processes within individuals. Therefore, a convergence of the two fields is possible, although the fields are far apart in their typical levels of analysis. Their closest link is currently found in the study of the developing nervous system (chapter 6).

It is possible to divide the work of molecular geneticists into two broadly defined lines of investigation. The first is concerned with redefining Mendelian genetics in terms of physicochemical events and structures found within cells. This may appear to be an excellent case of reduction in the sense discussed in chapter 2. However, as Hull (1972) demonstrated, before the relationship between molecular and Mendelian genetics could be satisfactorily stated, the two approaches had to exchange concepts and notions. It is more accurate to characterize the relation of the two subdisciplines as a growing-together or synthesis, rather than a reduction of one to the other.

The second line of investigation traces the biochemical pathways of development leading from the activities of DNA in the cell nucleus to the appearance of phenotypic traits. This is a rich and significant source of information about developmental phenomena. It is unfortunate that so many behavioral scientists have either largely ignored the findings of developmental genetics or assimilated them into old ideas about development. In fact, the success of molecular genetics prompted a resurgence of the preformationist and predeterminist notions of development among psychologists. However, nothing inherent in the concepts of molecular genetics

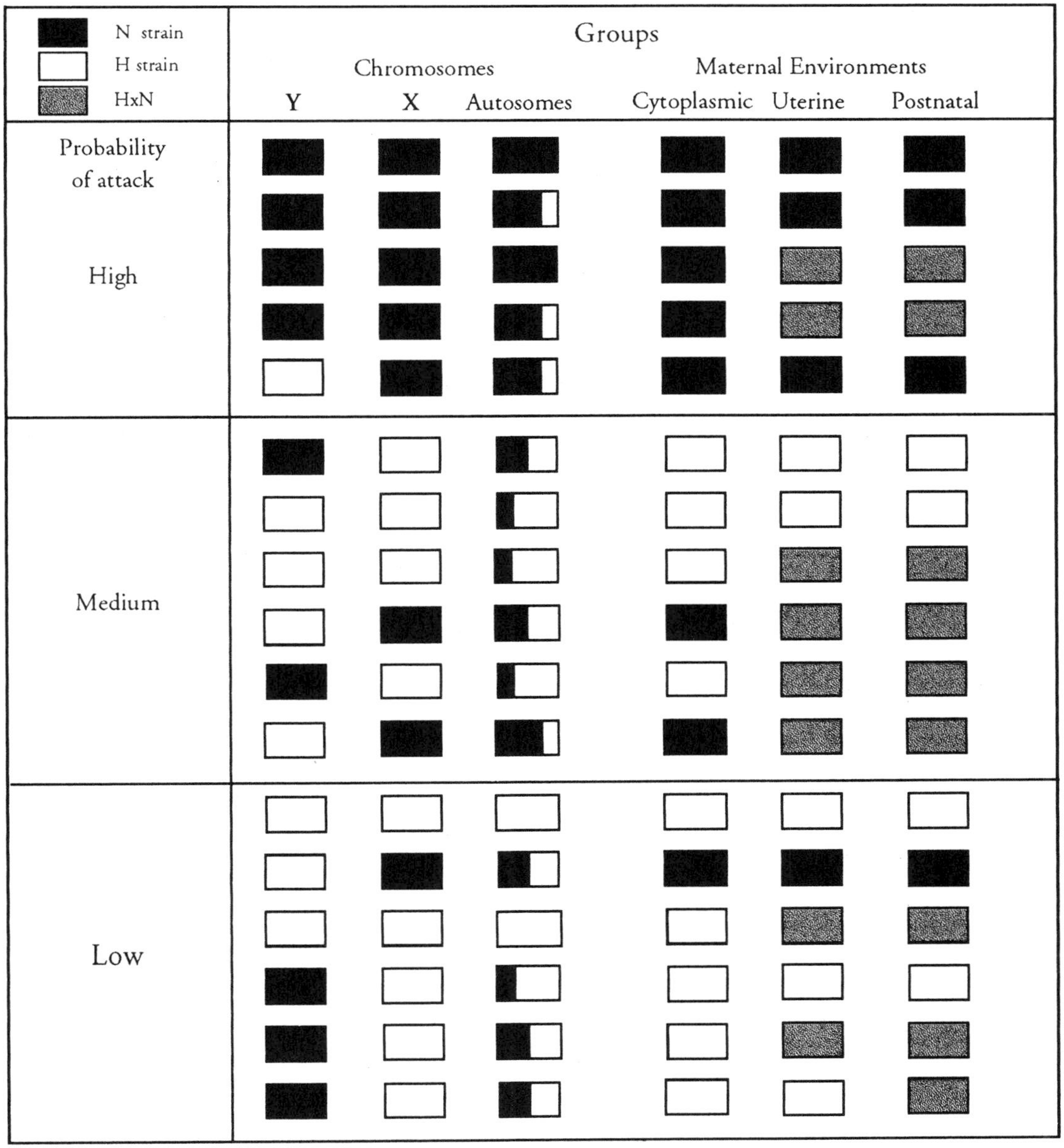

Figure 5.3 A genetic-environmental analysis of aggression in mice. The diagram identifies the strain of origin of the Y and X chromosomes, the autosomes, and three components of the maternal environment as manipulated in a multifactorial breeding study. The greater aggressiveness of males from the N strain when all of these factors are confounded could not be located in any one factor by this analytic study (after Carlier, Roubertoux, & Pastoret, 1991; see box 5.3 for details).

warrants such a revival of outdated notions about development. Indeed, molecular models of the gene at work in developing and functioning organisms require a large, hierarchically ordered set of environmental influences.

A sharp distinction should be made between two parts played by DNA: its role in heredity and its role in cellular function. The capacity of DNA to replicate itself rather faithfully and the cellular mechanisms that ensure that these replicates are lodged in gametes have unquestioned and fundamental importance to heredity. The acknowledgement that there are hereditary factors in addition to DNA (chapter 4) does not detract from this importance. However, what appears from the perspective of heredity as a codelike, informative relationship between DNA and traits is revealed to be an illusion when the details of cellular functioning are examined. It is an illusion because a multitude of intervening steps have been glossed over and because other necessary elements have gone unnoticed. As research in the rapidly advancing field of molecular genetics accumulates, an alternative picture emerges of DNA as a material participant among other material participants in a dynamic and hierarchically ordered system (Stent, 1981).

The distinction between DNA as a self-replicating structure that can carry "information" from one generation to the next and DNA as part of the cell's machinery is recognized in a recent textbook by the appropriation of the word "genome" to refer to the latter: "The term **genome** is used to describe the totality of the chromosomes (in molecular terms, DNA) unique to a particular organism (or any cell within the organism), as distinct from genotype, which is the information contained within those chromosomes (or DNA)" (Singer & Berg, 1991, p. 22). Although we go farther than these authors and also reject the informational definition of genotype to characterize heredity (as does Oyama, 1985), it is instructive that they define genomes and genes (p. 440) in material terms that do not include reference to information.

Genetics and Conception

The story of molecular genetics can begin with the processes necessary for conception. The female and male of sexually reproducing species each has specialized cells (**gametes**) that possess only half the total number of chromosomes typical of the species. For example, whereas most cells in the human body contain 46 chromosomes arranged as 23 homologous pairs, human gametes (egg and sperm cells) each contain only 23, 1 member of each chromosome pair. The primary constituent of each chromosome is one very long molecule of deoxyribonucleic acid, **DNA**, which can be thought of as a string of genes. Gametes are formed when cells divide in such a way that the end result is daughter cells having only half the chromosome complement of the parental cell. This is called **meiosis** to distinguish it from the usual cell division, **mitosis**, which duplicates the full set of chromosome pairs. Each chromosome pair divides independent of the other pairs during meiosis, which means that many gametes produced by the same individual will vary in their particular combination of chromosomes and, consequently, of genes.

In addition to the genetic shuffling that occurs during the independent division of chromosome pairs, there is another source of genetic variability during meiosis. Each member of a homologous chromosome pair originates from a different parent. Homologous chromosomes can join together and interchange part of their length, called *crossing over*, to form new chromosomes having a block of maternal and a block of paternal genes on the same molecule. Each chromosome still has exactly one copy of all genes, but the ancestral origins of the genes residing on the same chromosome are mixed. (As we noted earlier in this chapter, the discovery of DNA polymorphisms in 1978 enabled human geneticists to identify the maternal and paternal origins of the parts of chromosomes. These polymorphisms allowed any part of any chromosome to be traced through families to reveal how it has been transmitted.) Crossing over leads to variation in the combination of allelic forms of genes residing on the same chromosome and therefore transmitted as a package to the next generation. The shuffling of genes during meiosis is known as genetic *recombination* (Dobzhansky, 1955).

Conception, or fertilization, occurs when the chromosomes of a male gamete enter the nucleus of a female gamete, forming a new cell (**zygote**) that has the number of chromosomes typical of that species, with one member of each homologous pair from each parent. Chromosomes within a pair are morphologically similar, with the exception of the sex chromosome pair in many species. In mammals, males have one X and one Y chromosome, which differ in size and shape; each sperm cell has only one of these chromosomes, a fact that underlies sex determination at fertilization. After conception, the zygote begins to grow and divide (by mitosis) into 2 cells, each of which divides, yielding 4 cells, then 16 cells, and so on. Barring mutations that might occur in somatic cells, each new daughter cell formed by these divisions contains identical reproductions of the original chromosome pairs and their constituent genes that were present at fertilization.

Genetics and DNA

In a paper that revolutionized genetics, Watson and Crick (1953) proposed a model for the structure of the DNA molecule that accounts for its identical duplication during cell division. They characterized the DNA molecule as a long chain composed of two strands of sugar phosphate molecules linked together in a twisting parallel, or double helix, by a series of chemical bases. These chemical bases are adenine, cytosine, thymine, and guanine (ACTG).

Some accounts name the four nucleotides adenylate, cytidylate, guanylate, and thymidylate, which include the sugar phosphate molecules with the bases. The bases or nucleotides are attached to one side of each strand. Humans and mice have 3 billion nucleotides, and they share over 99% of the same genes.

Within each strand of DNA, the bases are linked by strong chemical bonds. However, the bonds across the two strands are weak, which allows them to separate readily under the right conditions, such as the presence of specific enzymes. Although the order of the bases can vary along the DNA molecule, the same is not true for connections across the two strands. Across strands, thymine can unite chemically only with adenine, and guanine only with cytosine. No other connections are possible. In this way the order of bases on one strand controls the order of bases on the other strand. For example, if one strand contained the base sequence CTCATC, the other strand must contain the sequence GAGTAG, or else the two strands would not unite to form a DNA molecule.

The dual strands of the DNA molecule and the restriction on the pairing of the bases make it possible for DNA to be duplicated exactly. One strand is used as a template to form a complementary strand, and all strands formed on the same template are identical. Replication begins when the two strands unravel and separate during cell division. As soon as they begin separating, duplicate strands are built by the attachment of nucleotides to specific sites that become available on each of the separating strands. Nucleotides, which are sugar phosphate molecules attached to a single base, are usually present in sufficient supply in the cell nucleus. Special enzymes catalyze the linkage between one base and the next in the strand being formed. Because the order of bases in a strand is determined by the pairing of the correct base with its complementary partner in the opposite strand, two identical and separate molecules of DNA are formed. After cell division, each replicated molecule becomes part of the nucleus of one of the two newly formed daughter cells.

The ability of DNA to replicate itself faithfully has very different implications for heredity and development. DNA is a useful medium for heredity precisely because of its ability to generate replicas of itself. This characteristic is also useful in development, because it is important for cells within the same individual to share properties. Yet, it also poses serious difficulties, because cells differentiate during development, taking on different shapes and functions. It is a challenging developmental and genetic problem to explain how cells that differ from one another in morphology, biochemical constitution, and physiological processes do so despite identical genetic material. Pursuit of this question has uncovered a panoply of intracellular and extracellular factors that regulate the function of DNA molecules as a function of spatial, temporal, and other contextual constraints.

DNA, the Gene, and Proteins

Whereas the genes studied by Mendelian geneticists are typically associated with phenotypes of the organism, such as gross anatomical or behavioral characters, stretches of DNA studied by molecular geneticists are associated with phenotypes of the cell, namely, proteins. Proteins are arguably the most important class of physicochemical substances in a cell, functioning as structural elements, catalysts, and regulatory agents for all aspects of cellular activities. They are large **molecules** made of folded filaments called polypeptides. Polypeptides, in turn, are composed of strings of different types of amino acids. The types, numbers, and sequences of amino acids in a protein determine its physicochemical shape and other properties. These properties define the functional role of the protein.

One of the great achievements of molecular genetics has been to relate the sequence of nucleotides on the DNA molecule—the genetic code—to the production of particular proteins (Singer & Berg, 1991). As originally formulated, the code consists of a strict parallel between the sequence of nucleotides in DNA and the sequence of amino acids in the polypeptide. Because DNA has only four nucleotides, it is necessary to use sequential strings of them to code for a particular amino acid. There are exactly three nucleotides in each meaningful string (codon) and each codon specifies only one amino acid. For example, the codon GGC (guanine, guanine, cytosine) represents the amino acid glycine. These basic properties of the genetic code apply generally to all organisms.

Four nucleotides taken 3 at a time yield 64 (4^3) possible codons. Because a DNA molecule is one long string of nucleotides, punctuation is necessary to indicate where codons (and genes) start and stop. Most (61) codons code for amino acids, but one of them also indicates where to start "reading" for a particular gene. The remaining three are used to mark the end of the coding sequence for a gene. Only 20 codons are required to specify the 20 amino acids in proteins, but each of the 64 codons can be read. Some amino acids are therefore coded redundantly by two or more codons (figure 5.4).

By analogy with language, proteins can be thought of as sentences and amino acids as words that can be combined in various numbers and ways. As the analogy makes apparent, the very large number of proteins necessary for diverse cellular function in diverse organisms, tissues, and cells can be produced by drawing from a set of only 20 amino acids in particular, varied sequences. The genetic code was initially investigated in prokaryotes (single-cell organisms such as the bacterium *Escherichia coli*). In these organisms, the order of codons in the DNA molecule exactly specifies the order of amino acids produced in a polypeptide chain and, consequently, the kind of protein that is produced. Based on this regular relationship, a gene was defined as a piece of DNA having the base sequence to code for a protein plus the start and stop codes.

A

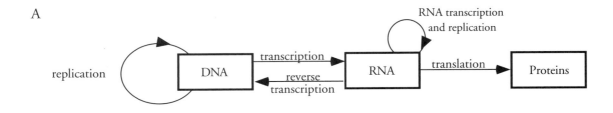

B

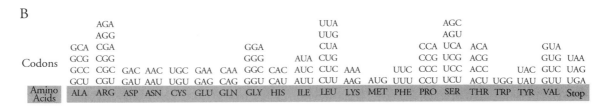

Figure 5.4 (A) The informational relationships among DNA, RNA, and proteins include feedback. (B) Each of the 20 amino acids (represented by their three-letter abbreviation) and the stop coding signal are represented by one or more codons (redrawn from Singer & Berg, 1991).

The linear relationship between the codon sequence and the amino acid sequence observed in prokaryotes does not generally apply in eukaryotes (multicelled organisms). Instead, the nucleotide sequence in the DNA molecule consists of coding sequences interrupted with noncoding sequences (i.e, codons that are not used when forming the protein). These intervening sequences of noncoding DNA, called *introns*, are removed before the coding sequence can be used to form protein. Their presence in DNA complicates the definition of a gene, making it necessary to incorporate into the definition processes that intervene between transcription of the code from DNA onto RNA and translation of the code into protein (Singer & Berg, 1991).

Transcription and Translation

Protein synthesis takes place on *ribosomes*, which are located in cytoplasm, yet the DNA of eukaryotes is confined to the nucleus. How, then, does the DNA code get to the ribosomes? The process is known as **transcription**, and it is carried out by a special kind of ribonucleic acid, messenger RNA (*mRNA*). The mRNA is a single strand of nucleotides that is constructed on a strand of DNA by the same template principle used to duplicate DNA. Messenger RNA copies all or part of a single strand of DNA, transcribing the code for the amino acid sequence of a particular protein from the DNA into an mRNA code (see figure 5.3). The strand of mRNA then moves from the nucleus to ribosomes in the cytoplasm, where the sequentially ordered nucleotides in the strand are used to build polypeptide chains (**translation**). Transcription processes are used to construct two kinds of products from DNA: proteins, with mRNA as an intermediary that carries the base pair coding sequence, and other RNAs that are used in translation.

The process of transcription begins when an enzyme, *RNA polymerase*, binds with a small *core-promoter* region on the DNA molecule. The promoter marks the start site for transcription. A variety of other proteins must work jointly with RNA polymerase before transcription can occur. Proteins that affect transcription by binding to **regulatory** (or *enhancer*) **elements** on DNA, or by interacting with other proteins that do, are called **transcription factors**. Regulatory elements can be located within or near the transcription sequence for a gene, or at a more remote site on DNA. Transcription factors are a heterogeneous group of proteins that regulate by both activation and inhibition whether and to what extent genes will be expressed. Some transcription factors are generated or modified by extracellular agents such as hormones (Singer & Berg, 1991).

The template method of producing mRNA means that when genes are split into segments of coding regions (*exons*) and noncoding regions (*introns*), the initial strand of RNA to be formed will include both types of sequences. Therefore, the initial RNA transcript (pre-mRNA) must be transformed into a mature mRNA that will be used to construct a polypeptide. This is accomplished by splicing out the introns from the initial RNA to leave an uninterrupted code; this is called RNA editing. Each end of an intron is marked by splice sites, which are recognized precisely by elements in the splicing machinery. This machinery consists of small nuclear RNAs (snRNAs) and specialized nuclear proteins that form ribonucleoprotein complexes or snRNPs (nicknamed "snurps"). The immature RNA, the snRNPs, and other proteins together constitute a transient structure called the *spliceosome*, which is functionally similar to a ribosome (Lemke, 1992; Singer & Berg, 1991).

The fact that many genes are interrupted and must undergo splicing of RNA to create a usable code is remarkable enough. It is even more remarkable that sometimes crucial information that is not specified in DNA is added to the RNA molecules. Moreover, the very same precursor to mRNA can be spliced in more than one way to create very different forms of mature mRNA (Singer & Berg, 1991).

The patterns of *alternative splicing*, include, but are not limited to, differential exclusion of introns or retention of exons, and variation in recognized promoter sites (Lemke, 1992). If the metaphor of language or code is applied to alternative splicing, the spliceosomes can be described as "deciding" how to parse the DNA "sentence," with different spliceosomes arriving at very different meanings.

One example of an alternatively spliced gene that makes this point is a gene that codes either calcitonin, a circulating peptide involved in calcium

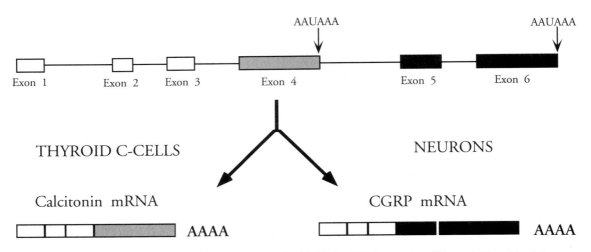

Figure 5.5 The same strand of initial mRNA may be differentially spliced, in part according to the cellular milieu, to produce quite different proteins. Here, exons 1, 2, 3, and 4 are spliced to form calcitonin mRNA in thyroid c cells, whereas in neurons, exons 1, 2, 3, 5, and 6 of the same initial mRNA will be spliced to form calcitonin gene-related peptide (CGRP) (modified from Emeson et al., 1992).

regulation, or a neurohormone (calcitonin gene-related peptide) that is widely distributed in the nervous system (figure 5.5; Emeson et al., 1992). The neurohormone (calcitonin gene-related peptide) is formed when mature mRNA has been spliced in neurons, and calcitonin is formed when the mature mRNA has been spliced from the same precursor RNA in the cells of the thyroid gland or other nonneural tissue. When the gene is located in a neuron, it is exposed to regulatory factors that cause the splicing mechanism to excise an exon that is retained by nonneuronal cells and to recognize a different terminus to the coding sequence, which has the effect of retaining two exons that are cleaved from the final mRNA in nonneuronal cells.

As this example indicates, alternative splicing is regulated by factors in the cellular milieu. It increases the diversity of products that can be encoded in a single gene, and its regulation makes it possible to select from this diversity in tissue-specific or other contextually determined ways. Clearly, any factor that can regulate spliceosome formation can have profound effects on the structure of mRNA and the type of protein it helps to construct. The resulting cellular phenotype does not, therefore, inhere in the DNA code, but emerges from the interaction of many parts of the cellular machinery.

To translate mRNA into a protein, mRNA must bind with a ribosome. The ribosome must add a particular protein or stop lengthening the protein according to each codon (three base sequence) in the mRNA. The mRNA is morphologically distinct on its two ends. The 5′ end has gone through a process called capping, which marks the point at which translation will begin. The tail of the strand, the 3′ end, includes markers to terminate the translation sequence. These distinctions allow polypeptides to be assembled in a unidirectional manner by the combination of ribosomes, various participating proteins, mRNA, and a second kind of RNA—transfer RNA (*tRNA*).

The three stages in the assembly process are initiation, elongation, and termination, each of which is subject to regulation. To initiate assembly, a start codon (AUG) must be available, and it can be sequestered in various regulated configurations of mRNA. Elongation refers to the actual construction of the polypeptide chain. There is no direct complementarity between the nucleotides in mRNA and the amino acids that are strung together into polypeptides. To overcome this difficulty, tRNA serves as the necessary intermediary. It has three nucleotides at one end and an amino acid, activated by attachment to certain phosphoric acid groups, at the other. The attachment of a series of these tRNAs to the appropriate parts of mRNA allows the sequential construction of a polypeptide. The codons in mRNA are processed one by one, with tRNA released and replaced with a different tRNA once an amino acid has been placed in the sequence.

Of interest, not all meaningful codons are side by side. Ribosomes must occasionally "frame-shift," skipping forward or backward over one or more bases (in some cases as many as 50) to find a codon; this is called RNA recoding (Rennie, 1993). When a stop codon (UAG, UAA, or UGA) is encountered, construction terminates. The mRNA is broken down into individual nucleotides and recycled, and the polypeptide is freed from the ribosome for further processing (Singer & Berg, 1991).

Translation is also affected by cytoplasmic events that regulate the availability of mRNA to interact with the protein synthesis machinery. For example, after fertilization, maternally inherited mRNAs that are localized in distinct regions of the egg are important for germ layer formation in the early embryo of a wide variety of organisms (Richter, 1993). However, before fertilization, these egg mRNAs are masked by RNA-binding proteins. Fertilization may stimulate the mobilization of several mRNA polysomes. Thus, translational control can be very important during early development.

After translation, polypeptide chains fold into compact two- and three-dimensional structures with the order of the amino acids in the chain determining the shape. Often the primary translation product is altered by putting together different polypeptide chains to form a larger protein with a different morphology, by cleaving the chain into several proteins and peptides, or by other processes, such as phosphorylation, that changes its shape (Singer & Berg, 1991). The shape of the mature protein constrains its functional properties by affecting its ability to bind with other structures. Structural proteins are those with shapes conducive to binding with other proteins of this type to form structural elements in cells. Other shapes allow proteins to bind with chemicals, where they can serve as enzymes, regulating the speed of biochemical reactions. Yet other proteins act as regulators of various cellular activities after binding with diverse cellular components, including DNA and RNA. Indeed, some proteins can autoregulate their own levels through feedback relations with either translation or transcription processes.

Once the complex, multistep process of protein synthesis is completed, the finished protein must be transported to an appropriate intracellular or extracellular locus before it can carry out its function. These steps engage other aspects of the cellular machinery, and they are also subject to regulation (Singer & Berg, 1991).

Regulation of Gene Expression

As the brief summary of transcription and translation indicates, the expression of a particular gene into a cellular phenotype is regulated in numerous ways. Regulation determines whether a gene will be expressed, the degree to which it will be expressed, when it will be expressed, where it will be expressed, what phenotype will be expressed from a given gene, how the resulting protein will be modified, and where it will be located. Regulation can occur at any of the steps in the expression of genes and the modification of the primary products (figure 5.6), but most occurs by determining whether transcription will occur and, if so, what its rate and duration will be. Therefore, most regulators are known as transcription factors.

Of all the tissues in the body, those making up the nervous system have the greatest diversity of cellular types and cellular products. This diversity can be accounted for in two nonexclusive ways: each cell expresses only a small subset of the genes in its genome, or the cells have devised means to use the same set of genes in original ways. Either way requires high levels of genetic regulation, and the nervous system is particularly rich in regulatory processes (Lemke, 1992).

One kind of regulation is provided by the configuration of the chromosome, which determines whether or not genes are available for transcription. The inactivation of one of the two X chromosomes in genetic female mammals is a striking demonstration of this fact. The inactive X is tightly folded and remains in a highly condensed form, which can be observed as the Barr body. Which X is inactivated varies randomly from one cell to the next in the individual. Very few genes of the condensed X chromosome are transcribed, which renders this chromosome functionally similar to the smaller Y chromosome present in males. If alleles on the two X chromosomes differ, the random pattern of inactivation across cells means that females are somatic mosaics for certain traits, a phenomenon that underlies the tortoiseshell coloration in some female cats (Wolpert, 1992b).

It is only at certain times in a cell's life that chromosomes are straightened into the rodlike formations that are usually represented in photographs of karyotyping, providing the clear representation of the X and Y chromo-

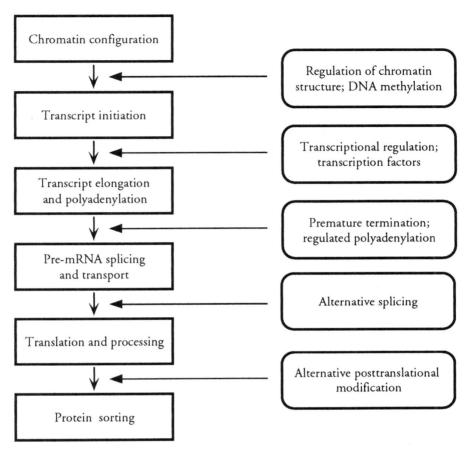

Figure 5.6   Some of the various ways by which gene expression can be regulated at the cellular level (redrawn from Lemke, 1992).

somes, for instance. A DNA molecule resides in a structure called *chromatin*, which also includes proteins, such as histones, that bind with DNA and form part of the structural matrix. Most of the time, chromatin is coiled into a tangle, and it is difficult to discern the chromosomal shape. In addition, over 90% of DNA is typically wrapped around histone complexes, forming beadlike structures called *nucleosomes*, with approximately 150 to 200 base pairs of DNA in each nucleosome. The location of nucleosomes may regulate transcription, by affecting availability of binding sites, for example. In addition to structural changes in chromatin, structural changes in the DNA (e.g., methylation) may reduce the likelihood of transcription (Lemke, 1992; Singer & Berg, 1991).

The expression of genes is often regulated in a tissue-specific fashion. The alternative splicing of an RNA transcript in neuronal and nonneuronal cells to produce either calcitonin gene-related peptide or calcitonin is an example of tissue-specific regulation of a posttranscriptional event. The resulting phenotype is morphologically and functionally quite different. A dramatic example involving transcription and perhaps various other events is provided by changes in cytoplasmic regulatory factors from the undifferentiated zygote to differentiated adult cells.

In amphibians and other nonmammalian species, the nucleus from an adult cell may be extracted and placed in an enucleated egg, and a normal embryo will develop. This means that the DNA has not changed during differentiation; what have changed are the cytoplasmic factors that regulate transcription. When DNA is moved from a differentiated cell to the cytoplasmic environment of an egg, proteins are expressed that are characteristic of that early developmental stage and not of the adult cell type. However, the nuclear transplantation experiment does not work in mammals: no embryonic development will occur. As Gilbert (1992b) remarked, "genes are changing in some way during development" (p. 214). Development apparently entails changes in both the genome and the regulatory processes of cells. Perhaps an even more dramatic example of genomic change is provided by red blood cells, from which the entire nucleus of the cell has been lost (Wolpert, 1992b).

A great many transcription factors are proteins, often the primary products of translation. Therefore, the product coded by one gene can regulate transcription of other genes, and sometimes of the same gene that expressed the product. Thus, activity in one part of the genome can affect activity in other parts. This phenomenon lies behind such concepts as "master gene," because some transcription factors expressed by genes can have widespread effects on genomic activity.

Immediate Early Genes

Of all the genes that can express transcription factors, the *immediate early genes* (IEGs) have captured the most attention of behavioral and neuroscientists. This is because these genes can act as transducers of extracellular signals, allowing extracellular events to regulate genetic activity (box 5.4).

In normal cellular functioning, IEGs are characterized by rapid but transient expression in response to diverse signals from the extracellular domain, such as polypeptide growth factors or neurotransmitters. The IEGs were initially discovered as oncogenes, because they can be usurped by retroviruses and undergo mutation, or be freed from normal regulation, which can result in uncontrolled cancerous growth. For this historical reason, IEGs in their normal cellular state are also called protooncogenes. The proteins expressed by IEGs are involved in diverse intracellular and intercellular regulatory functions, including the regulation of transcription (Morgan & Curran, 1991).

Box 5.4   The Experiential Induction of Gene Expression

The development of the cat's visual cortex is guided by the kitten's neonatal visual experience. This can be demonstrated by comparing the development of kittens with normal binocular vision with that of kittens restricted to monocular vision. When kittens are reared with one eye sutured closed after the other eye opens, extensive anatomical and physiological alterations in the visual cortex are found. Sensitivity to such monocular deprivation is limited to a stage of development that begins within two weeks after birth, peaks at five to six weeks, and gradually declines over a period of several months. The time course of this developmental stage is also regulated by visual experience. Dark rearing extends the stage beyond the normal few months. However, a brief, six-hour period of visual experience during the course of dark rearing allows development to occur and sensitivity to decline.

Rosen and colleagues (1992) examined the capacity of the visual experience to influence the expression of cellular immediate early genes (IEGs) in the kitten's cortical cells. The IEGs transmit information between and within cells. They are involved in the production of cell surface receptors, protein kinases, G proteins, polypeptides to be secreted as extra cellular messengers, and factors affecting DNA transcription (Morgan & Curran, 1991).

The IEGs are transiently active in response to stimulation arising from outside the cell (e.g., postsynaptic activity in a neuron in response to afferent input). Immediate early gene activity can thus transduce sensory input within a cell nucleus (Morgan & Curran, 1991).

Rosen et al. measured mRNA associated with immediate early gene activity in the visual and frontal cortex of dark-reared cats exposed to brief periods of visual experience. One hour of light exposure was sufficient to increase dramatically the activity of specific immediate early genes in the visual cortex but not in the frontal cortex. Furthermore, this activity was higher when the exposure occurred at 5 rather than at 20 weeks of age. The researchers speculate that the activation of IEGs within cells of the visual cortex in response to normal visual experience may initiate gene-regulated processes that contribute to the development of mature cortical cells and to the repression of genes whose continued expression is necessary for maintaining the stage of development beyond its normal time course during dark rearing. In this manner, experience may regulate molecular genetic activity.

The transient activity of immediate early genes in response to stimulation arising from outside the cell allows genes of this type to transduce extracellular input, including sensory input that originates outside the organism, into a crucial step in a cascade of gene-regulated activity within the cell. The IEGs are therefore an important link in the cellular machinery that can convert brief environmental input into enduring cellular changes, thereby contributing both to the construction of the developing nervous system and to its plasticity throughout life (Lemke, 1992; Morgan & Curran, 1991). One immediate early gene that has attracted intensive study by neurobiologists is c-*fos* (Lemke, 1992; Morgan & Curran, 1991; Schilling, Curran,

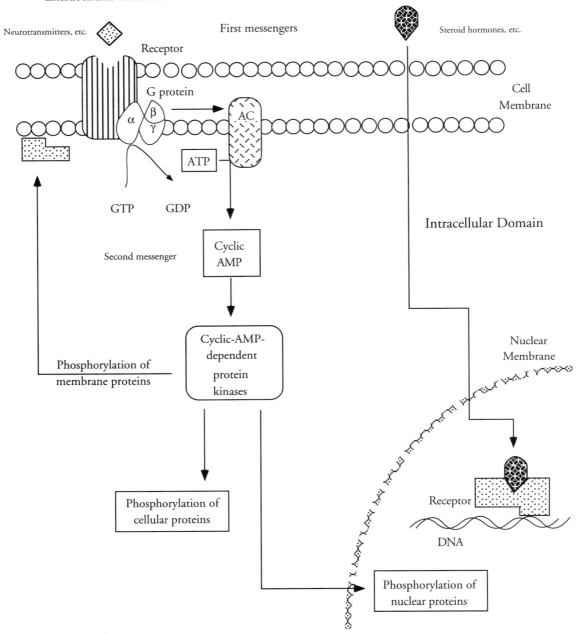

Figure 5.7 Steroid hormones pass through the cell's membrane and join with receptors to affect cytoplasmic processes, and through the cell's nuclear membrane to affect transcription directly. Neurotransmitters and peptide hormones may affect cellular processes by binding with G protein receptors and initiating second messenger activities that affect cytoplasmic processes and/or nuclear processes. Thus,

& Morgan, 1991). The viral form of this gene, v-*fos*, is an oncogene that induces bone tumors in mice. The normal cellular form, c-*fos*, is very active in neurons, expressing a protein, Fos. Fos can bind to regulatory elements on the DNA molecule, where it can serve as a transcription factor for other genes. The structure of Fos can be changed by various posttranslational events, such as phosphorylation (see below). Furthermore, Fos functions in combination with various other proteins, including those expressed by other immediate early genes, notably those in the *jun* family. Thus there are numerous pathways through which c-*fos* and other IEGs can both regulate and be regulated by transcription events and other cellular activities in the nervous system.

In comparison with other physiological systems, the nervous system has an extreme degree of temporal and spatial variation in the activity of its cells. This variation is highly orchestrated, calling for a high degree of intercellular communication. The immediate early genes and their products are one mechanism through which certain genetic activity can be confined to particular cells and coordinated temporally with other events in the nervous system and in the external environment. Indeed, one reason for the intense interest in the IEGs is that it is possible to construct maps of neural activity at particular times or in particular situations using immunocytochemistry to visualize the proteins, such as Fos, expressed by the genes (Schilling et al., 1991). Two other intensively studied mechanisms that are involved in gene regulation and intercellular communication are the hormones and their receptors and the G proteins that mediate between extracellular and intracellular signals.

Hormones and Their Receptors

Steroid hormones (e.g., estrogen, testosterone, progesterone, glucocorticoids, aldosterone) are lipid-soluble molecules that can diffuse across the plasma membrane and into the cell nucleus. The hormones regulate differentiation and activity of many neurons and other cells at the genomic level (figure 5.7). Steroids, thyroid hormones, retinoic acid, and vitamin D bind to intracellular receptors that contain a DNA-binding domain, a hormone-binding domain, and a domain responsible for transcriptional regulation. Once a steroid hormone (or other factors that have a similar action) becomes bound to its receptor, the resulting complex is able to attach to acceptor sites on the chromatin and regulate transcription of DNA into RNA. The regulation can include whether or not transcription will occur, the rate at which it occurs, and the site at which it will begin. Thus, steroids can act

environmental factors that affect hormonal milieu and neural activity can have profound effects on cellular functioning, including regulation of genetic expression (redrawn from Brown, 1994).

as transcription-enhancing factors in cells with the appropriate receptors, thereby regulating protein synthesis through their effects on genetic activity (Brown, 1994).

Because they are lipid soluble, steroids can pass freely through cell membranes, but only *target cells* have receptors for a given hormone. Various agents, including hormones, can induce the production of receptor proteins. Therefore, a hormone such as estrogen can regulate the responsiveness of cells to other hormones such as progesterone (recall the ring dove reproductive cycle described in chapter 2). Hormones can also regulate their own effectiveness through feedback processes that *up-regulate* or *down-regulate* the number of receptors in target cells. Thus, female rats that are ovariectomized for a prolonged period require estrogen to be replaced for some time before target cells are primed by increasing the number of estrogen receptors to respond appropriately to the estrogen (Brown, 1994).

Environmental stimulation can affect the production and secretion of hormones. Therefore, genetic activity in target cells can be affected by environmental input that changes hormone availability. In this way, experiential effects can interpenetrate with molecular genetics to regulate both developmental processes and more transient changes in cellular functioning. The gonadal steroids (testosterone, estrogen, progesterone) are open to environmental stimulation through the brain-pituitary-gonad axis (chapter 3). The effects of these steroids, particularly those of testosterone, on the development of the nervous system and behavior have been especially well studied (Breedlove, 1994; chapter 6). The fact that males and females secrete different amounts of testosterone during particular developmental periods makes it readily accessible for study. Testosterone has extensive effects on the developing nervous system and other parts of the organism, some of which have been traced to genetic mechanisms.

G Proteins

Many hormones, neurotransmitters, and neuromodulators regulate the activity of neurons by binding to special receptors on the cell's surface, the G protein receptors (Ross, 1992; Spiegel, 1989). Activation of these receptors initiates a cascade of biochemical events that modify the enzymatic phosphorylation of various structural and enzymatic proteins in the cytoplasm and membrane of the cell (Nestler & Duman, 1994). The G protein receptors are called second message systems to distinguish them from receptors whose activation takes the form of immediate fluctuations of ions (e.g., Na^+, K^+, Cl^-) across the cell membrane.

The G protein receptors are so called because they couple to intracellular guanosine triphosphate (GTP)-binding regulatory proteins. The proteins are formed from a complex of three membrane-bound proteins. When the receptor is activated, the alpha unit binds GTP and dissociates from a complex of the beta and gamma subunits. Both alpha and the beta-gamma subunit complex may go on to trigger subsequent events. Activated G proteins have a lifetime of seconds to minutes during which the activated receptor may couple with additional G proteins, enhancing the effect of the stimulus (Manji, 1992). G-alpha autoinactivates by hydrolyzing its bound GTP, after which it reaggregates with G-beta-gamma and returns to the state that allows it to bind with the receptor.

The G proteins are the first link in signaling cascades that achieve their effects either by activation of protein kinases (enzymes that phosphorylate cellular proteins) or by changes in the level of intracellular calcium (Ca^{2+}), which in turn can trigger protein phosphorylation (Nestler & Greengard, 1994).

The G proteins affect cellular activity in at least four ways (Nestler & Duman, 1994; figure 5.8). First, they may link directly to nearby membrane channels to regulate their permeability. Second, they may either up- or down-regulate adenylate or guanylate cyclase to change cyclic adenosine monophosphate (cAMP) or cyclic guanosine monophosphate (cGMP) levels that in turn may directly modulate membrane channels. However, cAMP more commonly binds with the regulatory subunit of cAMP-dependent protein kinase (A-kinase), releasing the catalytic subunit that phosphorylates membrane channels or other intracellular proteins. In the latter case, transcription, translation, and posttranslational cellular events can be affected (Nestler & Greengard, 1994).

For example, changes in level of cAMP can have profound and nearly instantaneous effects on the expression of a variety of neural genes. An area of the DNA (CRE) has many properties of an enhancer element. Also, a CREB (CRE-binding) protein has been identified. Cyclic AMP activates protein kinase A (PKA), which phosphorylates a wide variety of proteins including CREB. This allows cAMP to activate CREB, which initiates processes that lead to transcription. This is one mechanism whereby environmental effects can directly regulate DNA transcription in neurons (see box 5.4).

Third, G proteins may activate the inositol phospholipid system. In this case two second messengers are generated, diacylglycerol (DAG) and inositol triphosphate (IP3). Inositol triphosphate stimulates the release of Ca^{2+} from intracellular stores, which in turn may activate Ca^{2+}-dependent enzymes, including kinases. Also, Ca^{2+} triggers translocation of C-kinase from the cytoplasm to the membrane. Once this translocation has occurred, membrane-bound DAG activates the C-kinase (which phosphorylates membrane channels).

Finally, G proteins may couple to phospholipase A_2, forming arachidonic acid by hydrolysis of membrane phospholipids. Arachidonic acid may act either as a second messenger or as a precursor for several enzymes, some of which affect the production of neurohormones.

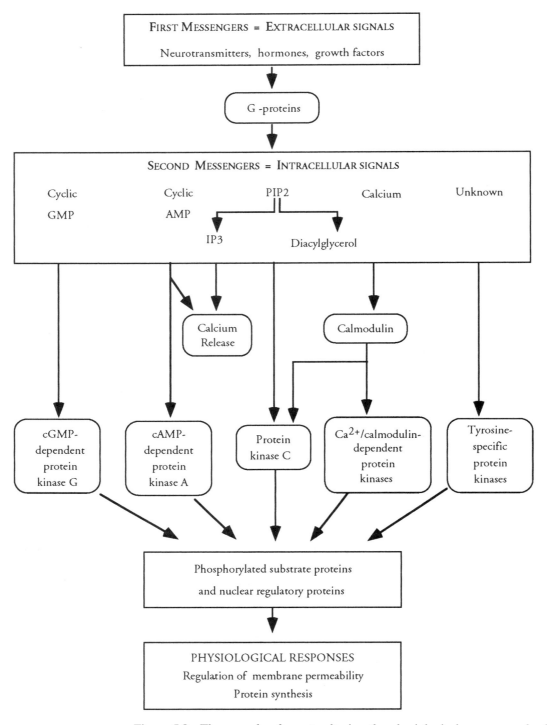

Figure 5.8 The cascade of events altering the physiological processes of cells that are initiated by first messenger activation of G proteins (redrawn from Brown, 1994).

Thus G protein receptors are one means by which environmental events can directly influence both DNA transcription and translation, as well as posttranslational changes in neural cell activity. All such consequences represent the developmental psychobiology of experience.

DNA and Development

Organisms are not built from proteins but from cells. Cells interact with one another to give shape to an organism and its organs (Edelman, 1988, 1992; Wolpert, 1992b; chapter 6). These interactions determine the location of a cell with respect to other cells, and this relative position has a profound effect on cellular phenotype. An organism's shape and that of its tissues (including the brain) is derived from the shapes of collections of many types of cells. Each type represents different proteins, because different combinations of genes are expressed in different types of cells. These changes occur only when a cell is surrounded by other cells in a particular place (Edelman, 1992).

Cells accumulate by dividing and passing the same amount and kind of DNA to their daughter cells. The cells adhere to each other, and when they accumulate they eventually form sheets, or **epithelia**. As division continues, the sheets curl into tubes without loss of contacts between cells. If contact is lost, cells migrate along the surface of other cells to form layers, or they migrate along a matrix of molecules released by other cells. After migration, readhesion forms new combinations of cells. Cells also migrate by separating from their connections in sheets to form loose, moving collections, called **mesenchyme**. All of these processes change the relative location of cells.

The location of cells is important for the processes of differentiation. Cells differentiate when different combinations of genes are transcribed, and hence different patterns of proteins are expressed. The process depends on receiving the right cues at the right place in the embryo. Cells also die in particular locations more than in other locations. Differentiation and differential cell death are processes of morphogenesis. They imply that the action of combinations of genes depends on the relative position or spatial location of cells (Edelman, 1992).

Certain genes produce molecules that regulate cell adhesion and movement. Cell-adhesion molecules (CAMs) link cells together, surface-adhesion molecules (SAMs) link cells indirectly by providing a matrix (base) on which cells can move, and cell-junctional molecules (CJMs) link cells that are bound by CAMs into epithelial sheets. *These proteins are specified by certain sets of genes that are activated at particular places in the embryo.*

Thus genes control the processes of development indirectly by governing which morphoregulatory protein will be produced, but "the actual microscopic fate of a cell is determined by epigenetic events that depend on developmental histories unique to each individual cell in the embryo"

(Edelman, 1992, p. 62). This means that mechanical events leading to the rearrangement of cells affect the sequential expression of genes. Also, the genes specifying the shape of cells (differentiation) are not enough to produce morphogenesis, "making proteins or cell surfaces that latch onto one another, each specific for a given cell, cannot account for how genes specify shape" (Edelman, 1992, p. 60). Edelman suggests, rather, that the unpredictable movement and death of individual cells are the basis of morphogenesis.

Although the cells of an embryo resemble each other on the average, the movement and death of any particular cell at any particular place is a matter of probability. This eliminates any notion of genetic instruction for morphogenesis, because a cell's exact position cannot be prescribed by a code in a gene. "Events occurring in one place require that previous events have occurred at other places. But it is also inherently dynamic, plastic, or variable at the level of its fundamental units, the cells. Even in genetically identical twins, the exact same pattern of nerve cells is not found at the same place and time. Yet the collective picture is species-specific because the *overall* constraints acting on the genes are characteristic of that species" (Edelman, 1992, p. 64). Thus, Edelman introduces the concept of historical contingency into theories of embryological development (see chapter 10).

One component of the processes involved in the regulation of morphogenesis is a set of homeotic genes (*HOM*) in the fly *Drosophila*, and the potentially homologous *Hox* genes in mice and humans (figure 5.9). These genes specify the production of proteins that bind to portions of other genes in other cells and subsequently regulate the production of the proteins specified by those genes (McGinnis & Kuziora, 1994). Thus they contribute to the regulation of the activation or repression of DNA transcription.

The genes that make up the HOM complex are expressed in gradients according to particular region of the fly. Their order on the chromosome reflects the order of boundaries of gene expression along the anteroposterior axis of development. Thus the homeotic genes regulate differentiation in *Drosophila* by specifying which organ will form in a particular body segment (figure 5.10). The Hox genes may also specify the anteroposterior pattern of organ development in vertebrates such as the mouse and human. The fruitfly HOM gene complex and the mouse Hox and the human Hox gene complex are quite similar in structure and function (McGinnis & Kuziora, 1994). They are all members of a homeobox gene family. Homeoboxes refer to DNA sequences that provide the code for the transcription of a related group of regions on proteins called homeodomains. The conservation of these homeodomains across widely divergent species provides support for the theory that extensive changes in phenotypic evolution can occur with little change in genotype (Gottlieb, 1992; see chapter 4).

A

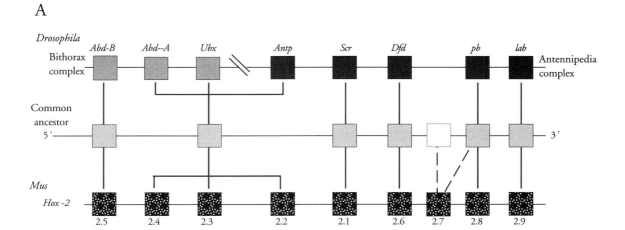

B

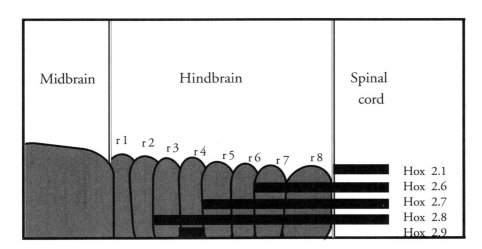

Figure 5.9 The homologous areas of HOM and Hox homeobox genes of the fly *Drosophila* and the mouse *Mus*, respectively (A), contribute to the regulation of the development of segmentation of the fly's body and the mouse's brain (B) (redrawn from Anderson, 1992).

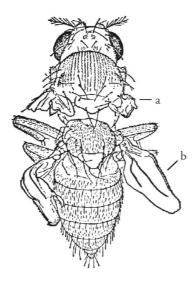

Figure 5.10 Manipulation of the HOM genes can result in the development of a bithorax fly with a double set of wings (reproduced with permission from Waddington, 1956).

Of course, this does not mean that development occurs without coordination of gene expression; however, very little is known about the mechanism responsible for that coordination. Consider the various ways that many developmental anomalies can arise from the malformation of a single gene pair. The gene product may be necessary for the development of a structure that directly or indirectly influences several other tissues. For example, production of the H-Y antigen promotes the differentiation of the primordial gonad into a testis capable of secreting testosterone, which, in turn, affects the development of cartilage, bone, nervous system, and so on. Or, the gene may produce a protein that is essential for the function of a structure that forms portions of several organs. Any gene product that affected the development of cellular receptors for norepinephrine would have widespread consequences involving the nervous, endocrine, digestive, and other systems. Or, the gene may produce a protein that is necessary for the morphogenesis of several different organs. Nerve growth factor may be involved in the development of organ systems in addition to the nervous system. Obviously, molecular genes are important contributors to the development of the individual. Nevertheless, the nature of that contribution is not one of either programming or instruction.

The Concept of Environment in Development

For the geneticist, the environment is everything external to the DNA or genome (complete set of genes) of an individual that mediates and influences the timing and concentration of enzyme production involved in phenotypic development. The environment includes the substances in the cell that are produced by that cell; that are incorporated from other cells, tissues, and organs; or that are the metabolites of ingested food. All these substances together can be considered the chemical milieu influencing DNA regulation of protein synthesis. Models of gene action detail the means by which alterations in the chemical milieu can lead to changes in the amounts and kinds of proteins and enzymes produced by a cell and consequently, its biochemical properties. Of course, changes in the biochemical properties of nerve cells or cells involved in hormone secretion may ultimately be reflected in changes in behavior.

For the psychologist, in contrast, the environment is all of those factors (physical energies, material objects, social companions, etc.) outside the boundary of the individual's skin. These environmental factors can influence the activity of DNA and the cell primarily through their effects on the individual's internal chemical milieu. In multicellular and many noncellular organisms, specific organs or organelles have evolved to enhance and control the effects of the environment on the chemical milieu. These special structures are called biological transducers because they change environmental energies (light, sound, gravitation, etc.) into biochemical substances.

As yet, science is far from understanding, even for the simplest of organisms, the sequence of events that alters the chemical milieu that, in turn, affects enzyme production during development.

Genetics and Developmental Psychobiology

Developmental psychobiology provides information about the character of organism-environment relations. This information can illuminate how inheritance contributes to both the progression and the outcome of development. Inheritance tends to reduce the variability of developmental phenomena. Thus it becomes important to understand the developmental mechanisms through which this occurs. Developmental psychobiology also provides information about noninherited contingencies that occur during development. These events tend to increase the variability of developmental phenomena and contribute to the emergence of the individualistic character of development.

Atchley and colleagues (Atchley & Newman, 1989; Atchley & Hall, 1991) developed a model for integrating quantitative genetics with developmental analysis to explain the formation of complex morphological structures. Their problem has much in common with the problems that face developmental psychobiologists, and their work is relevant for integrating genetics with developmental psychobiology. They identify several kinds of historically contingent factors that affect the variability of developmental phenomena:

1. Contingencies in mating, which create the individual's genome
2. Contingencies of the epigenetic processes within an individual's ontogeny
3. Contingencies of the particular maternal environment in which the individual develops
4. Contingencies of the nonmaternal environment in which the individual develops

Heredity enters into each of these factors (cf. figure 5.2). The genome is inherited from parents. Different genes can have different consequences for development by virtue of their effects on structural or regulatory elements within cells. Atchley refers to these types of genetic effects as intrinsic because changes in cells can be traced directly to transcriptional events within the cells. Other consequences of an individual's genome are indirect, and are referred to as epigenetic. From the point of view of the cell, they result from interactions with other cells. Effects may be local, as in embryonic induction, or global, as in hormonally mediated effects. Genes from the epigenetically acting cells are not directly engaged in the developmental event; their effect is indirect, mediated by the activities or products of cells (which are, of course, also subject to intrinsic regulation by genes and whose effect on other cells may involve genetic activity). Epigenetic processes are stochastic, open to influence from the organism's environment, and therefore subject to historical contingencies.

Mammals have mothers that provide prenatal (uterine) and postnatal (nursing) environments that can affect offsprings' development. Some aspects of these effects are influenced by the maternal genome, which is partially shared with offspring. Therefore, a genetic mechanism is in place through which maternal environments can be inherited. Maternal environments are another source for the control of developmental variability that is sensitive to historical contingency. As research in developmental psychobiology abundantly demonstrates, their numerous prenatal and postnatal effects can easily be extended to include paternal and sibling effects, as well as effects from other conspecifics. As for maternal effects, shared genetic factors provide a Mendelian mechanism for the inheritance of other socially mediated effects.

Nonmaternal environmental factors also can affect developmental variability. These include factors that are shaped or selected by the individual, parents, and other conspecifics, such as nests and other shelters, food, and tools. To the extent that these activities are influenced by genes, Mendelian mechanisms exist for their inheritance.

Thus, to use Atchley and Hall's (1991) taxonomy, there are genetic mechanisms for the inheritance of intrinsic genetic effects, epigenetic effects, maternal effects, and environmental effects. There are also nongenetic mechanisms for the inheritance of aspects of maternal and other social environments as well as for some environmental effects (traditions, phenotypic effects that reverberate across generations, etc.). Inherited contributions to development reduce variability in phenotypic outcome across generations, whether inherited by genetic or nongenetic means, and whether mediated in development at the level of intrinsic genetic mechanisms or epigenetic mechanisms (cell-cell interactions), or through organism-environment interactions.

It is also the case that development is affected by noninherited factors. This is most obvious for environmental features that are unrelated to the alterations imposed by the behavior of the developing individual or its companions. These may be random, but often are not. They can be cyclical (diurnal, lunar, seasonal, etc.), ubiquitous (gravity, viscosity of the media, etc.), or predictable (barometric pressure, ambient temperature, etc.). Noninherited factors are also present in the maternal and other social environments, for example, quality of maternal diet, level of maternal stress, number of individuals in the local group, sex of siblings, and a host of other possibilities. Finally, noninherited epigenetic factors can arise because of normal stochastic processes (chapter 6) or because these epigenetic processes are open to effects from the social and physical environments. Randomly or systematically fluctuating epigenetic and environmental events promote variation across generations.

All of these factors together create the conditions governing the progression and finality of individual development. They represent the fluctuations on the microlevel by which developing systems can organize and reorganize to reestablish coherence in the presence of perturbation. This description provides information about the initial starting conditions, both within the system and in its context, from which the system grows. From the system's point of view, it makes no difference whether or not a starting condition is inherited; whether it originates in the individual or in the maternal uterus; whether it results from epigenetic interaction among cells; whether these cells have the characteristics they have because of intrinsic genetic activity or because of local environmental perturbations; whether intrinsic genetic activity is in response to events that originate inside or outside a cell; and so forth. Genes enable development, but so do many other components in the system; there is no basis for granting a unique status to genes (Nijhout, 1990).

Summary

Population geneticists are restricted by their concepts and methods to the study of groups. They have made important contributions to the study of inheritance and to the measurement of phenotypic response to natural and artificial selection. Quantitative geneticists have uncovered developmentally interesting contributions to inheritance apart from direct effects of an individual's genotype. These include covariation both among genes and between an individual's genes and aspects of its prenatal, postnatal, and physical environments. It is essential to include information from these developmental sources in models predicting response to selection. In fact, these effects sometimes produce phenotypic change contrary to the direction of selection. Experimental analysis also reveals gene-gene and gene-environment interactions: the phenotypic outcome of a particular allele may differ depending on its genetic or environmental context. Human behavioral geneticists use quantitative techniques to identify genetic correlates of psychological traits. Although there is interest in drawing developmental conclusions from this information, little attention has been devoted either to measuring developmental sources of variance or to developmentally informed analyses.

Molecular genetics, unlike population genetics, involves the study of individuals. Molecular geneticists are concerned with genes as biochemical units in the cells of individuals. They study the processes through which genes and other constituents of cells interact to affect the functioning and development of cells and, ultimately, of the organism. Recent research revealed so much unsuspected complexity in the regulation of transcription, translation, and protein synthesis that Lederberg, a leading molecular geneticist, noted that "a great deal of genetics and evolutionary theory has not yet caught up with the implications of the dynamic chemistry of DNA" (Rennie, 1993, p. 124).

The work of the molecular geneticist is qualitatively continuous with that of the developmental psychologist because both seek to understand the functioning and development of individual organisms. However, the levels of organization on which the members of these two disciplines focus their attention are different. Recent advances in understanding the regulation of genes by extracellular events during development and in mature functioning have expanded the purview of molecular genetics beyond the cell to include whole-organism processes. Understanding the developmental pathways of behavioral organization requires knowing the ways in which individual experiences affect the structure and biochemistry of cells, as well as knowing the biochemical activities themselves. The study of neuroembryology is one area that may form a meaningful bridge between molecular genetics and developmental psychobiology.

6   Neuroembryology and the Ontogenetic Origins of Behavior

It seems to be, that some look for the determinants mainly in the germ [fertilized egg], while others search for them mainly in external influences. No one identifies determinants with future organs. Both sides maintain that the organs of the developed form have to be made, and that they must be made in orderly succession as epigenesis affirms. Both sides recognize the germ as something determined, and as determining something. Both sides claim ultimate units of organization within the germ, and both agree that external influences are responsible to some degree, for what results. Our difference, then, is not one of mutual contradictions, each excluding the other, but one of mutual concessions diverging only as we estimate the two classes of complementary causes unequally. The intra- *and the* extra- *do not exclude each other but coexist and cooperate from beginning to end of development.*
—C. O. Whitman (1894, pp. 221–222)

As may be discerned from the date of Whitman's comment, embryology has had a long history of trying to conceptualize how the various features and structures of development are achieved. It is generally agreed that the sperm and egg jointly provide a set of determinants for development; however, exactly what these determinants determine and how they do it is not clear. Perhaps the answers to these questions will provide insight into the development of psychological processes.

Embryological Development

Embryological development of most sexually reproducing animal species consists of four basic stages (Wolpert, 1992b): fertilization, cleavage, gastrulation, and organogenesis. **Fertilization** refers to the union of the male's **sperm** and female's *egg* to form a zygote, the first stage of a new organism. **Cleavage** is the rapid division of the zygote to form a ball of cells (the *morula*), which becomes a hollow sphere (the **blastula**). **Gastrulation** marks a decline in the rate of cell division and the increase of cell movements as they change positions. This begins when the blastula caves in on itself, creating three cellular regions (germ layers): the ectoderm, mesoderm, and endoderm. During gastrulation, front-back, top-bottom, and the basic body plan

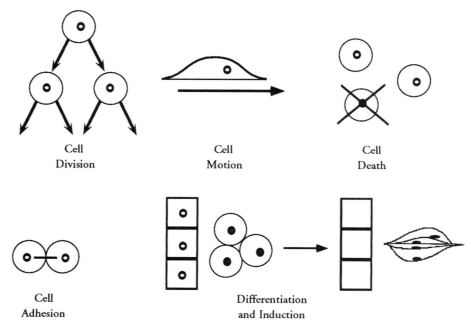

Figure 6.1 The primary processes of development at a cellular level include the driving forces of cellular division, movement, and selective death, and the regulatory processes of adhesion, differentiation, and induction (redrawn from Edelman, 1987).

become apparent. **Organogenesis** occurs after the germ layers are formed, when the cells interact and rearrange themselves into various bodily organs. Further development consists of the molding of form associated with differential growth (figures 6.1 and 6.2).

Gastrulation is considered the most important embryonic stage because it creates the cell layers from which all bodily structures will develop. The ectoderm produces cells that eventually form such structures as the outer skin layer, lungs, and nervous system. The endoderm produces cells that eventually become the lining of the digestive tract and associated organs (e.g., pancreas, liver). The mesoderm produces cells that give rise to other organs (e.g., heart, kidneys), blood cells, and connective tissue (e.g., bones, muscles, tendons). However, many organs are created by cells from different germ layers. Throughout the organism, most cells have to migrate long distances to establish the basic structural organization that is characteristic of any organ system.

As noted in chapter 5, the stages of embryonic development reflect two separate kinds of developmental processes. Differentiation refers to the process whereby cells change from an "uncommitted" state in which they could participate in the formation of any tissue, to a state in which they become specialized to be a blood cell, heart cell, neural cell, liver cell, and so on. In humans, the single fertilized egg differentiates into 350 distinctly dif-

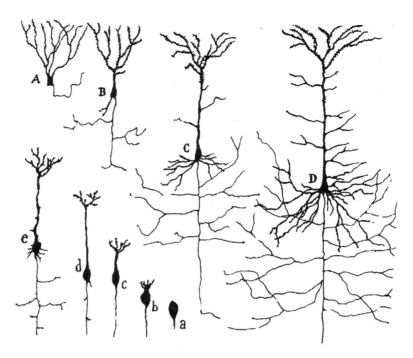

Figure 6.2 Differentiation of pyramidal cortical neurons as drawn by Ramón y Cajal (1894/1990). The stages of differentiation (a–e) in particular cortical layers yield a characteristic pyramidal morphology that is similar in diverse vertebrates: (A) frog; (B) lizard; (C) rat; (D) human (reproduced with permission).

ferent cell types. The second process, morphogenesis, involves the migration of cells to new locations, resulting in the structural organization of the individual.

Morphogenesis

Until fairly recently, morphogenesis was considered an epiphenomenon of differential gene expression by particular cells. However, modern research has shown that knowing how cells differentiate into different types does not really address morphogenesis (Gilbert, 1992b). For example, both the biceps muscle and the distinctly different muscles stretching across the shoulder blade are composed of striated muscle cells. Yet, knowing how striated muscle cells differentiate does not reveal how these different muscles manage to occur in their proper spatial locations.

All changes in early embryonic form reflect a changing pattern of cell contacts involving the **folding** and unfolding of cell sheets (figure 6.3; Edelman, 1988; Wolpert, 1992b). Pattern formation is the regulation of contraction, movement, and change in adhesion of cells in space and time. Spatial and temporal differences in this regulation can generate very different

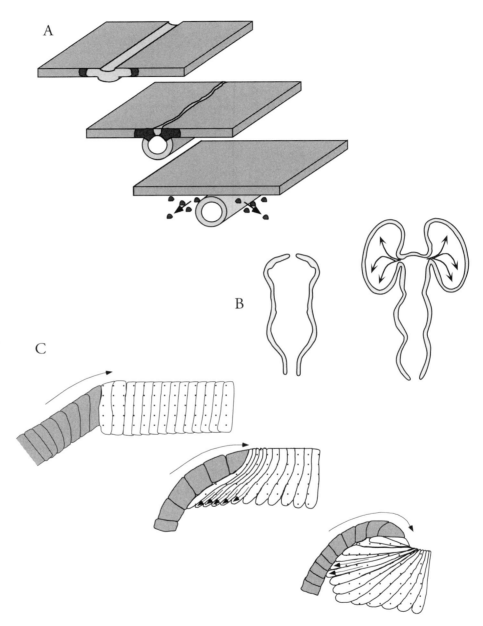

Figure 6.3 (A) Neurulation originates during gastrulation by folds in the dorsal epithelial sheet at the boundaries between neural plate and epidermis. The neural plate then rolls into a tube and separates from the overlying epidermis. Neural crest cells, formed at the epidermal-neural plate boundaries, migrate to form diverse structures. (B) The ventricles of the brain are formed by the rostral expansion of the neural tube, including its lateral outpouches (A and B redrawn from Lund, 1978). (C) Diagrams of newt neurulae at stages 15 through 17 illustrate a model of folding as a result of cell motion. Epithelial neural plate cells undergo cycles of cytogel mo-

forms. Thus, production of morphological structures is a complicated "developmental choreography" (Atchley & Hall, 1991) in which the ontogenies of the separate components are spatially and temporally coordinated.

The final form of a complex structure results from the integration of a number of separate component parts. Each of these components may develop at their own rate and have separate causal factors. Thus the fundamental problem of embryology is how the developing organism achieves the spatial and temporal arrangement of cells appropriate for the species to which it belongs. Indeed, the history of developmental biology reflects the different positions taken in an attempt to resolve this fundamental problem. An enduring theme in this history is the dispute between **vitalists** and **mechanists**.

Hans Driesch (1867–1941) proposed that plants and animals have inherent organizing principles (vital factors, or entelechies) that are not explained by the natural forces of physics and chemistry. He thought of these organizing principles as a sort of overall plan for growth that could keep development on track, according to the "prospective potency" of the embryo, even if perturbed by various environmental insults. Driesch was persuaded that an organism's entelechy—the plan or force behind development—was not part of the matter constituting the organism, as proposed in Weismann's germ plasm theory (Driesch, 1914).

Driesch's experimental work on sea urchin embryos was extremely important in the germ plasm controversy. He bisected the embryos at the gastrula stage and observed that a complete adult developed from each half of a bisected embryo, demonstrating that each newly divided cell has the same, full spectrum of determinants, what we now call genes, as the parent cell. If these determinants are used as material components of the developing organism, two partial sea urchin monsters would have been expected because each half-embryo would have had only half of the organism's genome. These experimental findings, later extended to vertebrates by Spemann (1938/1967), had a lasting impact on developmental biology. They ended the preformationist view of genes as miniature organs and contributed to the rise of epigenetic theories. Unfortunately, the entelechy concept was too readily assimilated into philosophical vitalism. As Reid (1985) deserved, many of the attributes of Driesch's entelechy also apply to DNA and many are familiar principles of modern epigenesis. Therefore, it was quite unnecessary to reject materialistic conceptions of embryogenesis because of the inadequacies of the materialist germ plasm theory.

tility analogous to those of mesenchymal cells, but remain anchored at their apical surfaces. Adhesion mechanisms permit movement along the basal surfaces of neighboring epidermal cells, which has the effect of pulling the epidermal sheet into a fold and stretching the neural plate cells into flask-shaped cells with contracted apices (redrawn from Jacobson, Odell, & Oster, 1985).

Organicism

Driesch's vitalism was a peculiar variant of organicism, a position that was common in the nineteenth century. **Organicists** proposed that Plato's eternal laws of form and organization were reflected in the structural features of organisms (Casti, 1990). Consequently, each organism as a whole represents transformations of idealized forms. For organicists, the main objective of biology was to classify the types of forms that could occur. These efforts led to the discovery of some interesting regularities among species and to the observation that differences in form can arise from relatively simple transformations. Thompson (1917/1961) developed an intriguing system for comparing species that continues to be useful for understanding the relationship between development and evolution. He used a mathematical coordinate system, elegant in its simplicity, to demonstrate how the forms of different species could be related to one another (figure 6.4). Applied to evolution, it illustrated how novel forms could be generated from a given archetypal species by simple alterations in the coordinates.

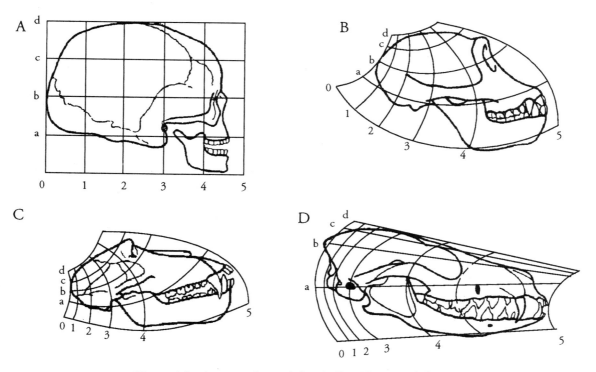

Figure 6.4 A comparison of the skulls of humans (A), chimpanzees (B), baboons (C), and dogs (D), using a grid drawn on the human skull for reference. Deformations in the grid can be used to describe transformations in form resulting from differential rates of growth of component bones. Note that the baboon and dog skulls, although superficially similar, are achieved by very different transformations (modified from Thompson, 1917/1961. Reprinted with the permission of Cambridge University Press).

Both vitalists and organicists were seeking an organizing principle that would deal with form as a whole. However, as the modern organicist Waddington (1966) noted, "vitalism amounted to the assertion that living things do not behave as though they were nothing but mechanisms constructed of mere material components; but this presupposes that one knows what mere material components are and what kinds of mechanisms they can be built into" (p. 19). In contrast to the vitalists, Waddington argued that the assembly of organisms is subject to physical laws. However, the organization of the assemblage cannot be derived from the laws—it is an emergent property.

For many organicists, the essential organizing feature in embryology was a morphogenetic field that would guide the general developmental plan. Genes, on the other hand, accomplish the secondary but vital role of constraining the specifics of the field. Morphogenetic field describes morphogenesis, but systematic empirical investigation of its particular instantiation in the development of individual species is required before the concept can explain morphogenesis. In a sense, the morphogenetic field shares the same reality as electric and gravitational fields: it is a useful abstract concept potentially represented by a mathematical formula.

Mechanists

In contrast to organicists and vitalists, mechanists argued that the development of form can be understood through the action of physicochemical influences (morphogens) on cells. *Morphogens* exert their effects by inducing cells to produce the right proteins at the right time in the right place. Spatial variation in concentration of morphogens would provide positional information in developing tissue. Mechanistic embryologists (e.g., Wolpert, 1992b) focused on how cells might obtain positional information. One idea is that chemical gradients might provide a coordinate grid.

If cells could read their position on a gradient with respect to a set of boundaries, then cell position could determine morphogenesis. Since morphogenesis begins very early in embryonic development, positional fields would never have to be larger than 30 to 50 cells. Therefore, simple diffusion of chemicals could provide signals regulating morphogenesis. Indeed, Turing (1952) demonstrated that the distribution of two interacting chemicals will spontaneously organize into specific spatial and temporal patterns of concentration. Several reaction-diffusion models involving the interaction between two chemicals (an activator that stimulates its own production, and the production of an inhibitor that inhibits the production of the activator) spontaneously generate spatiotemporal patterns that can account for several aspects of morphogenesis (Wolpert, 1992b).

One problem with the theory that positional information is important for morphogenesis is that in any positional grid the boundaries must be specified. Fortunately, animal-vegetal differences in the embryo provide one boundary region for positional information. In many frog species, the site at which the egg is attached to the ovary becomes the animal pole and the other end becomes the vegetal pole. The vegetal pole is a region where cells of the gut form and where skeleton-forming cells enter. The first two cleavages of the fertilized frog egg are parallel to the animal-vegetal pole, and the third is orthogonal to that pole. The animal-vegetal regions establish the anterior-posterior organization of the embryo, and the dorsal-ventral boundary is specified by the point where the fertilizing sperm enters the egg. That site becomes the ventral side. Thus, a morphogenic field specified by anterior-posterior and dorsal-ventral boundaries would work for the frog embryo.

It is unknown how anterior-posterior and dorsal-ventral are specified in developing mice (Wolpert, 1992b). Mammalian embryos do not exhibit polarity even up to the 16-cell stage. Moreover, the cell divisions of a mammalian egg are unlike those of other animals in which planes of division are distinctive. By the 32-cell stage, the mammalian embryo consists of a single layer of cells enclosing some cells on the inside. Those on the outside form the trophoblast, which enables implantation of the embryo in the uterus and the formation of the placenta. The embryo develops from the cells within. The determination of which cells form the trophoblast results from chance differences in the position of the cells—their different environments.

In many species of invertebrates, the egg has local variation within the cytoplasm. Hence, cleavage will separate these local cytoplasmic differences into different cells lines. Depending on the timing and orientation of cleavage, a cell line will be established with a particular cytoplasmic constituency that promotes the formation of one type of cell. Thus, cell types can depend on their lineage. Unfortunately, lineage fails to account for most aspects of differentiation and morphogenesis.

Edelman (1988, 1989) proposed an alternative to the morphogenic chemical grid model that involves the surface interactions between cells. Edelman contends that small collectives of cells act as a group on their immediate neighbors. These local interactions determine the motion, division, differentiation, and even death of cells. All of this local activity merely gives the appearance of overall coordination because it works. There is no overall controller making sure that each cell is playing its appointed role in some overall plan. In this sense, Edelman's view is similar to that of modern organicists (e.g., Gilbert, 1991; Goodwin, 1990).

Genes and Embryology

So how do genes contribute to development? From the perspective of developmental genetics, genes act as switches in a spatiotemporal cascade of

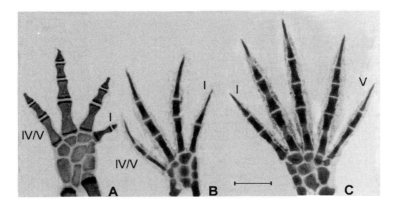

Figure 6.5 (A) The left foot of *Hemidactylium scutatum*, a salamander that normally has four toes and fewer phalanges on each toe than ancestral salamanders. (B) The left foot and (C) right foot of *Ambystoma mexicanum*, an axolotl that normally has five toes and the bone structure illustrated in the right foot. The left foot of this specimen was treated with colchicine, a mitosis inhibitor, at the limb bud stage. Not only is the treated foot smaller, but its structure is rearranged relative to the untreated right foot, and resembles that of the four-toed species in both number of phalanges and number of toes (digits are numbered I–V, with I = thumb; calibration bar = 1 mm) (reproduced with permission from Alberch & Gale, 1985).

choices that underlie differentiation. Because the *origin of differences* is taken as the question of interest, developmental geneticists search for mutations that produce a change from one organism to another in the product of differentiation or morphogenesis (van der Weel, 1993). As van der Weel puts it, these genes are considered the crucial causal factors in development because it is their activity that "makes a difference." However, other questions are of interest to developmentalists. As Goodwin (1984) proposed, identification of a genetic factor that is sufficient to account for the difference in two morphological variants, such as the number of digits on a foot, is not the same as identifying the factors sufficient to explain the form of the foot. For example, amphibian species vary, with some having four digits and some five. It is possible to cause an individual from a five-toed species to develop a foot with only four toes and other morphological features found in four-toed species by applying an inhibitor of mitosis at the limb bud stage (Alberch & Gale, 1985; figure 6.5). The inhibition of mitosis at the right developmental stage may account for the origin of morphological differences in ways that can be related to genetic differences between the species, but this inhibition is only one of a set of factors required for a sufficient developmental explanation of the morphology (Goodwin, 1984, 1990).

Van der Weel (1993) notes that the issue at the heart of Goodwin's criticism of developmental genetics concerns the meaning of causation in developmental biology. Developmental geneticists apply causation in much the same way as it is applied in daily life explanations and in Western legal contexts, identifying the "difference that makes a difference" in what is generally regarded as a self-evident explanatory ideal. Following John Stuart Mill (1843/1973), however, science is often described as concerned with identifying complete causes, the whole set of antecedent conditions. Nevertheless, Mill and others (e.g., Mackie, 1974) recognized that in practice, causal statements do not usually address complete causes but are answers to implicit causal questions selected from the set of sufficient conditions.

This selectivity allows developmental geneticists to acknowledge that there are many nongenetic factors among the antecedent conditions for differentiation and morphogenesis, yet they relegate these conditions to background "housekeeping" roles because they do not make a difference, or a difference of significance, among individuals. At best, it is allowed that background conditions can constrain the possibilities for the development of form, but they cannot explain its diversity. The heuristic power of mutations to generate differences among individual organisms and the seductive character of metaphors such as "master genes" and "genetic programs" have contributed to the persuasiveness of the developmental geneticist's argument. Even when factors other than genes (e.g., teratogens) are found to make specific differences in embryological development, developmental geneticists can readily include these into their causal framework because of the simplicity of its form. However, the discovery of such factors does not change their general strategy of treating many antecedent conditions as causally irrelevant background conditions, because that strategy arises from their primary interest in the origin of differences rather than developmental explanations of transformations in organic form (van der Weel, 1993).

Other developmentalists (e.g., Goodwin, 1988; Atchley & Hall, 1991) take these transformations as their primary interest and seek a more complicated causal framework that would yield a complete explanation of the development of form. Genes assume a different role in the set of sufficient conditions for these developmentalists because genes are not determinants of form (Atchley & Hall, 1991). Their role, however important, is different because gene products are created and operate only within the field effects that construct the actual morphology. From the organicist's perspective, genes contribute to the forms that any organism can achieve by providing the biochemistry that promotes cooperative interaction among cells (Gilbert, 1992a). Gilbert proposes that the biochemical communication systems employed by individual cells to promote cooperation were selected during evolution for use during development to construct an integrated organism. This would account for how the fusion of cell lines from related species can produce a single chimeric organism. Although the cells differ genetically, they manage to cooperate to produce an organism that may or may not be a mosaic.

Embryology and the Nervous System

Developmental biology is a long way from providing a full account of morphogenesis for any, much less each, species. Nevertheless, a fair amount of information is available to describe the processes underlying the development of certain organ systems, particularly the nervous system. Although such research is still in its infancy, it does provide information important for understanding morphogenesis and for constructing an interdisciplinary developmental psychobiology. In this chapter we examine the development of the nervous system and its relation to the origins of behavior.

The central nervous system consists of a vast number of cells that form intricate and functionally meaningful connections with one another and with the rest of the body. Both individual cells and regional populations of cells are morphologically heterogeneous. All of these features reflect common embryological problems. How do cells that begin life with the same genetic endowment differentiate into such different types? How do neurons segregate themselves into functionally distinct, appropriately sized, and appropriately interconnected populations?

Moreover, at the level of the whole organism, the central developmental puzzle is how adaptive matches between structure and function are achieved. It is clear enough that the process is dynamic and epigenetic, but it is often the case that neurobehavioral systems are present and in good working order at the first opportunity for their use. This is the principle of **forward reference**. How is it achieved? As we will discuss in chapter 8, the concept of maturation is employed in developmental psychology to solve this problem. This concept is endowed with an assumption that a directing control system foresees future use.

Species, even closely related ones, differ from one another in ways that fit with the selective pressures of their environments. They differ in size and shape, in receptors and effectors, in form and function of the central nervous system, and in behavioral capacities and probabilities. Sometimes polymorphic variations occur within a species, such as the differences distinguishing males and females, as well as major changes at different life stages of the same individual.

Consider the differences between the tadpole and the frog, the caterpillar and the butterfly, or the infant, child, teenager, adult, and senior citizen. Some of these variations can be understood as adaptive responses to sexual selection within a species or as ontogenetic adaptations to selective pressures that operate only at particular stages of the life cycle. But from an embryological point of view, these adaptations pose an intriguing problem because they mean that individuals with identical or very similar genotypes develop morphologically and functionally different phenotypes. How do these differences arise? Also, how do epigenetic regulatory processes produce matches between the form and function of the nervous system and the demands of the body and external environment?

We will consider each of these questions in the present chapter, focusing on the development of the nervous system. Although the same general principles underlie development of the nervous system and other parts of the body, the nervous system is notable for the degree of its internal specialization, the complexity of its organization, and the extent of its plasticity. These features have captured the imagination of many, and developmental neuroscience is currently in a very active growth phase. This chapter will introduce some of the findings and ideas from this field.

Neuroembryology

The size and form of the nervous system are gradually established during embryonic life. Anatomical changes within the nervous system are coordinated with similar changes in the rest of the body and with the emergence of function. It is now understood that this coordination is achieved through reciprocal interactions between the nervous system and the rest of the body (Purves, 1988). These interactions result in the construction of a nervous system that is appropriate to the tasks it has to accomplish. Dynamic processes underlie the developmental outcome of individual cells. Dynamic processes also underlie the local arrangements of cells into architecturally and functionally distinct regions. Development of each of these two levels will be considered in turn. Then, the ontogenetic origins of species differences and polymorphisms within a species will be discussed.

The Number, Movement, Form, and Connectivity of Cells

The developmental events that can be observed at the level of individual cells include birth, death, migration, differentiation, and connectivity (Jacobson, 1991; Purves & Lichtman, 1985). **Neurons** increase in number by mitosis, which involves birth of new cells by division of existing cells. In vertebrates, most neurons are born during early developmental stages by division of cells in the neural epithelium, which is a layer of cells that lines the neural tube. Formation of new neurons can occur after the embryonic period, but this is not the rule. In some species of fish and amphibians **neurogenesis** continues throughout life and results in progressively larger nervous systems (Fine, 1989). Also, some cell populations within the nervous system of birds and mammals retain the capacity for neurogenesis. Notable among these are the dentate gyrus of the hippocampus and the olfactory bulb of mammals (Kaplan & Hinds, 1977), and the songbird neostriatum, where newly divided cells are found on an annual cycle (Nottebohm, 1981).

The rate and duration of neurogenesis contribute to the number of neurons in a nervous system, but this number is also determined by the natural death of "overproduced" neurons. Natural **neuronal death** plays a major role in the neuroembryology of birds and mammals. It is regulated by local conditions in particular regions of the nervous system and is a relatively late embryonic event, typically occurring after the initiation of synapse formation. Between the time of its birth and the decision of whether it will survive the embryonic period, a neuron moves to its final location, undergoes differentiation, and establishes its initial efferent and afferent connections.

Location

Most of the established neurons in a functioning nervous system are located at a distance from their place of birth. Thus, cellular movement is a major component of embryology. To understand this movement, it is useful to divide embryonic cells into epithelia and mesenchyme. Epithelia are sheets of polarized cells, joined to one another at their lateral surfaces through the actions of cell **adhesion molecules**. The surface at the apical pole of epithelial cells is free to interact with the outside world, and the basal surface lies over the **extracellular matrix**. The extracellular matrix consists of cellular products, including a number of large proteins that serve as substrate adhesion molecules. Aggregates of cells, mesenchyme, that are neither joined together nor markedly polarized are present within the extracellular matrix. Epithelial sheets can break up into mesenchyme, and mesenchyme can coalesce into sheets. These transformations are epigenetically regulated with respect to both time and place by interactions that include signals from molecules in the extracellular matrix (Edelman, 1988).

Most early movement of cells occurs as a result of folds that are produced in epithelial sheets by the mechanical dynamics of growth in a restricted space. Individual cells within the sheet maintain position with respect to one another and are carried along passively by forces acting on the sheet as a whole (Edelman, 1988). As development continues, movement is more likely to involve active **migration** of individual mesenchymal cells. Movement of migrating cells is accomplished primarily by gliding along surfaces (Abercrombie, 1980). Gliding involves the extension of membranous processes that adhere to a substrate, followed by the generation of force by contractile proteins within the cell. This force pulls the body of the cell over its leading edge.

One of the most intriguing puzzles in neuroembryology is how migrating neurons find their appropriate destination. Some directionality may be imparted by intrinsic asymmetries that can polarize a newly divided cell (Albrecht-Buehler, 1978), but the major source of guidance comes from surfaces surrounding the cell. These surfaces differ in their adhesiveness, and it is this property that is apparently most important for establishing a migratory pathway (Edelman, 1988). A large part of the adhesive substrate for neurons in some parts of the developing central nervous system is provided by **glia**, the other major type of cell in the central nervous system.

In the cortex, for example, glia with cell bodies in the ventricular zone extend radial processes through all the developing cortical layers to the pial surface. These **radial glia** form roadways along which neurons, after having divided in the deepest layers near the ventricle, glide into position at more superficial layers of the cortex (Rakic, 1971, 1981; figure 6.6). Radial glia manifest their radial shape only transiently during development, after which they retract their radial processes and assume the shape of astroglia. Radial glia are best known for their developmental role in laminated brain regions such as the cortex, but they may also contribute to the migratory route of neurons in unlaminated regions, such as the hypothalamus (Tobet & Fox, 1989). Nevertheless, glial roadways do not account for all migratory routes. Other cells and adhesive surfaces in the extracellular matrix also serve in similar ways as guides for moving cells.

Gradients of adhesiveness are not the only source of directional information in the surround of a cell. Some chemical gradients could in principle direct migration, but currently no evidence exists that neurons follow them.

Differentiation

Another captivating puzzle in neural development is that cells divide with identical genetic makeup yet differentiate into a panoply of morphologically and functionally distinct neurons in the mature nervous system. Cells become either glia or neurons. Neurons differ in size, in the extent, shape, and orientation of their dendrites and axons, and in the neurotransmitters that they use. These differences emerge through processes that are not fully understood but that involve both contextual effects and the differential activation and suppression of genes at particular developmental stages. As cells develop through successive stages, they acquire properties that bias developmental possibilities of the next stage. It seems generally the case that these properties are acquired through interactions with other cells. The progressive constraints on a cell are often described as *determination of "fate" from an original multipotency.*

For example, cells that originate in the neural crest, an early embryonic structure that lies alongside the neural tube, differentiate to form various nonneural cells, such as melanocytes, cartilage and connective tissue, and the glia and neurons of the peripheral nervous system. The differentiation of neurons from other cell types occurs in early stages, perhaps before migration is complete. Differentiation of neuron type occurs in a second stage, after the migrating cell reaches its destination. This differentiation is regulated, at least in part, through interactions with the targets that they

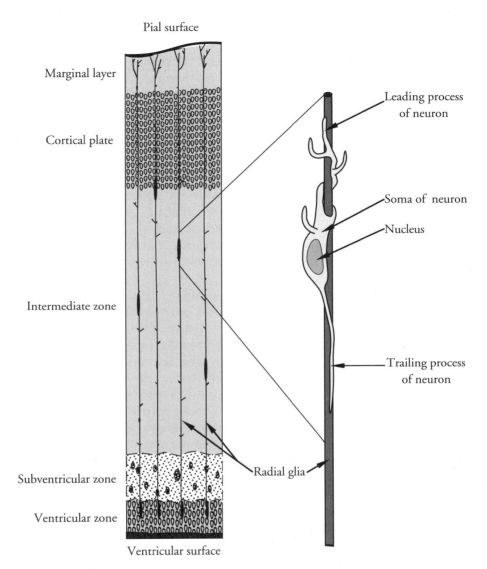

Pial surface

Marginal layer

Cortical plate

Intermediate zone

Subventricular zone

Ventricular zone

Ventricular surface

Leading process
of neuron

Soma of neuron

Nucleus

Trailing process
of neuron

Radial glia

Figure 6.6 Neuronal migration in the telencephalon of a rhesus monkey at mid-gestation. Radial glia form roadways that guide migrating cortical neurons from the ventricular zone, where they divide, to their layer of residence. The migrating neurons send out processes and creep along surfaces, as in the neuron shown in the enlargementt, which is moving along a radial glial cell (after Rakic, 1971, 1978).

innervate, and is therefore concurrent with the initial formation of connections.

Consider, for example, the peripheral autonomic system, which is divided into sympathetic ganglia, where most neurons are adrenergic, and parasympathetic ganglia, where most neurons are cholinergic. Adrenergic neurons rely on norepinephrine as a neurotransmitter, whereas cholinergic neurons rely on acetylcholine. The neurotransmitter specificity of neurons in the autonomic system differentiates during interaction with the cellular context. Substances produced by target cells normally innervated by these neurons are capable of changing neuronal specificity; for example, substances from cardiac cells can induce neurons to be cholinergic (Patterson, 1978; Potter, Laudis, & Furshpan, 1980). Another relevant factor in differentiation may be synaptic activity. Cells that are cultured in a medium mimicking electrical synaptic activity become adrenergic neurons, whereas the same cells without such activity become cholinergic (Patterson, 1978; Black, 1982).

Many neurons are polarized cells with one axon and one or more dendrites extending from the cell body. In early stages, the cell extends a number of processes called neurites. One of these becomes an axon. Once this is established, other neurites differentiate into primary dendrites. Perhaps the most distinctive feature of a neuron is the shape and orientation of its dendritic arbor, which reflects the number and location of primary dendrites and the nature and extent of their branching. Neurons in the same architectural region of the nervous system often resemble one another and differ, sometimes strikingly, from neurons in a different region. The general shape of the cell body and dendritic arbor is acquired during early developmental stages, but many features (e.g., cell size) are open to change throughout life. However, the most dramatic changes in later stages of ontogeny occur through the growth or retraction of axonal and dendritic processes.

Both the stability and plasticity of neurons are rooted in the cytoskeleton, a matrix of microtubules, neurofilaments, and actin microfilaments that fills the cell (Vale, Banker, & Hall, 1992). The cytoskeleton forms a stable, cross-linked gel within the cell that provides both mechanical strength and a system of intracellular transport. It also forms growth cones, dynamic structures that serve as the leading edge for growing neurites (axons and dendrites). Membrane is added to the tip of the elongating neurite at the growth cone.

The pathways taken by growing dendritic and axonal branches determine the connections that a neuron can have with other cells. And the functional roles that a neuron can assume are defined by the connections that it makes with other neurons, sensory cells, muscle fibers, and glandular cells. These connections serve as conduits for the neurotransmitters and hormones that regulate functioning within the nervous system and between the nervous system and other parts of the body. In addition, connections between neurons and other cells allow for the transmission of trophic factors that are essential for neuron survival (Purves, 1988).

Survival and Death

The importance of **trophic factors** for neuronal survival is dramatically revealed when the targets to which the neurons are connected are removed. If, for example, a limb bud is removed from a developing chick embryo, the lumbar spinal cord, which would normally have innervated the limb, will have many fewer neurons. Currently, it is thought that the mechanism underlying this neuronal response to embryonic target ablation also underlies the natural embryonic death of neurons (Hamburger & Oppenheim, 1982). Cell division during early embryonic stages results in roughly two or three times the number of neurons that will survive in later stages. Normal neuronal death occurs shortly after afferent and efferent connections with other cells are made, and is thought to result from competition among many neurons for a finite supply of trophic factors. However, the exact nature of this competition is not understood.

Neurons that interact successfully with targets obtain the necessary trophic factors, and those that fail to interact successfully do not. The net results are the adaptive elimination of excess cells, and the survival of an appropriate number of functioning neurons for each target. Evidence for this interpretation comes from studies that increase the size of the target for a regional population of neurons. For example, the number of surviving motor neurons in the relevant part of the lumbar spinal cord is increased by transplanting an extra limb bud in chick embryos (Hollyday & Hamburger, 1976).

The regulatory processes through which target muscles provide trophic support to motor neurons must involve interactions between the neuron and muscle at the neuromuscular junction, since the number of surviving motor neurons innervating particular muscles can be experimentally manipulated by changing activity at the neuromuscular junction. When activity is blocked with such pharmacological agents as curare, the number of surviving neurons is increased; when activity is increased, fewer neurons survive (Oppenheim & Nunez, 1982; Pittman & Oppenheim, 1978, 1979). These counter-intuitive findings demonstrate that trophic factors are not gained as a straightforward consequence of synaptic activity, although such activity is an important regulator of the processes through which only some motor neurons within a pool gain sufficient trophic factors to survive.

The sensory as well as the motor periphery is an important source of neurotrophic factors. Trophic factors can be transmitted to a neuron through both afferent and efferent connections. Even the survival of motor neurons can be affected by afferent input from sensory neurons (Okado & Oppenheim, 1984). In addition to the periphery, neurons, glia, and the extracellular matrix within the central nervous system can provide trophic support that affects neuronal survival (Jacobson, 1991; Oppenheim, 1991).

The best known of the trophic factors is **nerve growth factor** (NGF), which was characterized by Levi-Montalcini (1975) in an elegant series of studies. The search for NGF began when it was noticed that the dorsal root and sympathetic ganglia developing near mouse tumors that had been grafted into chick embryos grew much larger than normal. During an experiment aimed at isolating NGF from the mouse tumor, snake venom was added as a step in breaking down a fraction of the tumor. It was serendipitously discovered that the venom was a far richer source of NGF than the tumor, which in turn led to the discovery that the salivary gland of mice, which is a homolog of the snake venom gland, is an excellent source of NGF. Although NGF is only one of several agents that contribute to the survival and growth of neurons, it is an important one. Furthermore, its accessibility set the stage for intensive research on its role in nervous system development.

Nerve growth factor is produced naturally within the nervous system and its peripheral targets, and certain populations of neurons require it for their survival and growth (Levi-Montalcini, 1975). These include sympathetic ganglia, sensory cells in the dorsal root ganglia, and some populations of brain cells. Injection of NGF into developing embryos increases the survival of these neurons during the period of normal cell death. Conversely, injection of an antiserum to NGF greatly increases the number of neurons that die. Although many neurons do not have receptors for NGF and are unaffected by it, they may be affected by other trophic factors. It now looks as though the regulation of neuron survival by various trophic factors is widespread in the vertebrate nervous system (Purves, 1988; Jacobson, 1991).

Connectivity

The essence of neuronal function is to integrate input from one group of cells and to transmit the resulting activity to yet other cells. The pattern of connections that a neuron maintains with other cells defines, to a very great extent, the nature of its functioning. However, this aspect of development remains plastic for an extended period, with some features that are malleable throughout life.

Many of the explanations underlying migration of whole cells apply also to the movement of **axons** and **dendrites** (Patterson, 1992; Purves, 1988). Axons and dendrites move toward targets as they grow out from the cell body. A specialized structure called the **growth cone** is formed at the leading tip of a **neurite** (dendrite or axon). The growth cone is responsible for adding new membrane to the elongating neurite, but it is also the mechanism by which neurites move toward their targets. The growth cone responds to cues in the local environment that are provided by other cells and the extracellular matrix. A variety of factors have been identified, including such diffusible proteins as NGF, which can attract and guide growth cones, and several adhesive proteins. Movement is achieved by the extension of fingerlike or membranous processes from the growth cone. When these adhere to a substrate, traction is produced that pulls the neurite along.

As is the case for migration, a variety of neural and nonneural surfaces can serve as roadways for growing axons and dendrites. One of the more curious of these is provided by a transient population of cortical neurons, called the subplate, that is present in some mammals. These neurons differentiate at an early stage into mature neurons with functional synapses. They extend their axons from the cortex to the relatively remote thalamus and tectum. Because of the continued growth of the brain, the axons of these early maturing subplate neurons have to travel a shorter distance before reaching their targets than those of the cortical projection neurons that appear later. However, cortical projection neurons use the axons of subplate neurons as roadways to their targets. Once this has happened, the subplate neurons die (McConnell, 1991). There are other similar examples of transient "pioneer" axons; although their usefulness is clear, it is unclear whether this use is necessary for the axons that follow to find their way.

Trophic factors obtained from the local cellular environment are important regulators of the formation, growth, and remodeling of axons and dendrites. The initial stage of neurite formation is characterized by exuberant growth, or the production of more branches than will be retained. In a later stage, some branches are retracted and others are retained. Although this is often called synapse elimination, the number of synapses usually increases or does not change (Murakami, Song, & Katsumaru, 1992; Purves, 1988). Synapses may, however, be redirected to other targets through **remodeling**. For a motor neuron, remodeling typically takes the form of first extending a number of axonal terminals to make synaptic contact with several muscle fibers. Then, a systematic shifting of contacts occurs so that each muscle fiber is innervated by only one adult motor neuron, although there will usually be many synaptic contacts between the neuron and that fiber (Purves, 1988).

Loss of dendritic or axonal branches after a period of extensive growth has been observed within many parts of the central nervous system. This is often described metaphorically using gardening terms such as pruning of exuberant growth. For example, the corpus callosum of cats experiences a striking loss of axons during the neonatal period (Berbel & Innocenti, 1988). The corpus callosum is a tract that carries cortical axons from one hemisphere to the other. The loss of axons in this tract is coincident with a major reorganization in the pattern of projection of cortical neurons. In early stages, these neurons project over a wide range of the cortex; in later stages, the projection is restricted to a relatively small part of the contralateral hemisphere.

Similar patterns have been observed elsewhere in the central nervous system and in other species. It is assumed that the remodeling that takes place reflects the outcome of cellular interactions. The net result is a nervous system that has a relatively high degree of specificity in its interconnections. It may be that connections that are functional are retained, whereas those that are not are lost. This may be explained metaphorically in terms of competition for limited resources (Edelman, 1987, 1988). It should be remembered, however, that the repertoire of connections continues to change throughout life, which suggests that the pattern of trophic support also changes (Purves, 1988). Therefore, cells may have more than one opportunity to compete, and can compete in more than one arena.

Gradients of NGF surrounding a cell can play an important role in shaping the morphology of cells that are sensitive to this substance. For example, the number of primary dendrites, those that grow directly from the cell body, can be increased in the sympathetic ganglion cells of mice by administering NGF during the neonatal period. Conversely, they can be decreased by administering NGF antiserum during the same period. When NGF is administered at later stages, however, it leads to growth and higher-order branching, but does not affect the number of primary dendrites (Ruit & Snider, 1991). Therefore, the effect that trophic substances can have on a cell is constrained by the state of differentiation of the cell at the time of the effect. The number and general orientation of dendrites are related to the general size and shape of the cell body, and are therefore relatively stable features of a neuron. Other aspects, such as branching of primary and higher-order dendrites, their length, and such morphological features as the number of dendritic spines, are more likely to change.

Hormones, such as the gonadal steroids, can exert trophic effects on developing neurons that have protein receptors for that hormone. For example, hypothalamic neurons from embryonic mice show an astonishing degree of neurite outgrowth when cultured in the presence of testosterone or estrogen (Toran-Allerand, 1976). Testosterone affects the pattern or rate of dendritic growth in the preoptic area of hamsters (Greenough, Carter, Steerman, & De Voogd, 1977) and rats (Hammer & Jacobson, 1984) during early development. These findings may reflect a direct effect of the hormone on dendritic growth, or an effect of the hormone on the availability of other trophic factors in the local environment.

Finally, stimulation from the external environment and self-generated feedback from behavior can have profound effects on the pattern of connectivity in the nervous system. These effects are often detected by changes in the functional properties of the nervous system, but many studies demonstrated changes in dendritic branching and extent, synapse formation, and axonal branching as a function of experiential influences. Many of these effects occur during late embryonic or early neonatal development (Rauschecker & Marler, 1987), but they also occur during later juvenile and adult life (Greenough, 1986; Greenough & Black, 1992; Greenough & Juraska, 1979; Juraska, 1986, 1990).

Regional Patterns Within the Nervous System

The general principles of development at the cellular level—division, migration, differentiation, selective survival, neurite outgrowth, and synapse formation—underlie development in all parts of the nervous system. Nevertheless, marked regional differences in both form and function are seen within an individual nervous system. The retina, for example, consists of layers of cells, with the retinal ganglion cells that occupy one layer being very different in both form and function from cells in other layers, such as the rods and cones in the outer layer. The hypothalamus has a very different structure from the cortex, but each has a regular structure that can be described in cytoarchitectural terms, and so forth for each part of the nervous system. How does this patterned diversity arise? Why does an individual retinal ganglion cell assume the morphology that it does, rather than that of a photoreceptor or a cortical pyramidal cell?

Much of the gross form of a nervous system results from the rate of cell division in particular regions and from mechanical forces that result in the folding of sheets of cells (Edelman, 1988; Lund, 1978). However, individual cells grow to a particular size, extend neurites in particular patterns, and form particular connections with other cells. Moreover, they are likely to resemble their neighbors in these attributes, thereby producing regional differences in the microscopic character of the nervous system.

One theory about how such patterns might arise is that cells with a common lineage have a common **fate**. Developmental outcome or fate may be determined before mitotic division, and the new cell may then find its appropriate location. There is little support for this idea, at least in vertebrates. However, the fate of each individual cell in the 959 cells that compose the tiny nematode worm *Caenorhabditis elegans* is predicted invariably by its lineage—the cell line that gave rise to it and the number of prior divisions. Whether this invariance results from autonomous, intracellular responses to instructions set in motion at the first division or from invariant interactions among cells is at present undecided (McConnell, 1991). Whatever the resolution of this issue for these simple invertebrates, lineage holds limited predictive value in vertebrates. This was demonstrated by marking a precursor cell and then observing that cells arising from the precursor are often highly variable; even glia and neurons can emerge from the same precursor (McConnell, 1991). Furthermore, neuronal clones are widely dispersed across the mammalian cortex in no clear, predictable pattern (Walsh & Cepko, 1992).

The currently favored alternative for vertebrates is that a newly divided cell can take on a number of possible fates, with the one ultimately chosen dependent on interactions with its neighbors. This idea is supported by studies that have altered the environment of a developing cell and changed developmental outcome in predictable ways. The environment refers to the local cellular context, and its alteration includes such manipulations as transplanting cells to a new site within an organism, destroying or disrupting neighboring cells, and transplanting cells to a host with different characteristics. Experimental manipulations such as these have a long and important history in embryology. Their use at the turn of the century led to the following major conclusions, still generally accepted (Gottlieb, 1992; Oppenheim, 1982a; Oppenheim & Haverkamp, 1986).

1. Each cell retains the complete genome. Therefore, genetic contributions to differentiation must involve processes that selectively activate or suppress different genes in each cell. An earlier idea, held by August Weismann (1834–1914) and other prominent embryologists in the late nineteenth century, was that cells differed in their genetic makeup because of the progressive loss of genes (or germ plasm) during successive divisions. Hans Driesch (1908) put this concept to rest in 1891 by demonstrating that each daughter cell can become a full organism if experimentally separated from one another at the blastomere stage.

2. Developmental outcome for particular cells is determined by their location. This was convincingly shown by demonstrating that a normal organism will develop even when its tissue has been rearranged. For example, when the locations of tissues that would ordinarily become skin and brain were exchanged during the early gastrula stage of frogs, a normal frog developed nonetheless (Spemann, 1938/1967). Studies such as these led to the idea that signals from the local environment induce cells to adopt a particular fate.

3. As development proceeds, however, regionally identified tissue becomes committed to a particular outcome. This conclusion followed from the results of experimental tissue rearrangements undertaken in later developmental stages. These manipulations lead to an aberrant organism because development of transplanted tissue continues as if it had not been transplanted. If, for instance, presumptive skin is transplanted to the brain region of frogs during the late gastrula stage, patches of inappropriately located skin will continue to develop (Spemann, 1938/1967). Such findings gave rise to the concept of determination or commitment to a particular fate. They are also the foundation for the concept of critical period, which has had such a profound impact on developmental psychobiology, because inductive signals apparently have their effect only during a restricted period of time.

Continued study refined the questions and led to the realization that cellular phenotype is not induced all at once, but is attained through a series of steps that sequentially limit choices. These steps differ in kind, and can vary from place to place in the nervous system. Some constraints are inherited from ancestral cells, some occur in particular cell phases during mitotic division, and some occur after cells have migrated.

Box 6.1 Plasticity in the Somatosensory Cortex

The somatosensory cortex of mice and other rodents has a characteristic barrel arrangement, so called because of the three-dimensional shapes created by patches of neurons and neuropils. Individual barrels receive tactile input by way of a thalamic pathway from individual facial vibrissae. There is a topographical correspondence between the vibrissae and the projection pathway at each stage beyond the trigeminal ganglion. This correspondence can be detected anatomically, with rows of cortical barrels and rows of two-dimensional thalamic barreloids that mirror contralateral rows of whiskers. In addition, topographically arranged patches (barrelettes) in trigeminal brain stem nuclei reflect ipsilateral whiskers.

The anatomical arrangement develops prenatally in the brain stem, but that of the thalamus and cortex develops over the first few days of life and can be modified by changes at the periphery. Removing the whiskers before seven days of age leads to reorganization of the somatosensory cortex, including elimination of barrels. Similar changes are observed in the thalamus when removal is done before four days of age (Woolsey et al., 1981). Furthermore, genetic selection for extra whiskers in mice results in a numerically appropriate addition of barrels in the somatosensory cortex (Van der Loos, Welker, Dörfl, & Rumo, 1986). These dramatic findings add to an emerging picture of the central nervous system as constructed in large part by input from the periphery.

Somatosensory plasticity does not end in early development. Functional reorganization in the primary somatosensory cortex that receives projections from the hand was studied in an extensive series of experiments in adult owl monkeys. These results reveal a high degree of plasticity in the size and location of cortical maps that represent particular tactile regions on the hand. For example, the map becomes reorganized after median nerve damage, with other hand regions temporarily taking over zones that no longer receive their previous input; however, there is a return to the original map after the median nerve regenerates (Kaas, 1991; Wall, Huerta, & Kaas, 1992). Furthermore, removal of a digit results in the expansion of zones representing contiguous digits (Merzenich et al., 1984).

Equally dramatic changes can be observed after a change in use of the hands. Stationary tactile stimulation of the second and third digits results in a significant expansion of their cortical maps (Jenkins et al., 1990). Changes in cortical somatosensory representation as a function of manual experience are widespread, with moving inputs decreasing the zone of representation, thereby increasing discrimination (Merzenich, Recanzone, Jenkins, & Nudo, 1990). Similar changes are found in other somatosensory systems. Stimulation of the ventrum by suckling pups results in extensive reorganization of the lactating rat's cortex (Xerri, Stern, & Merzenich, 1994).

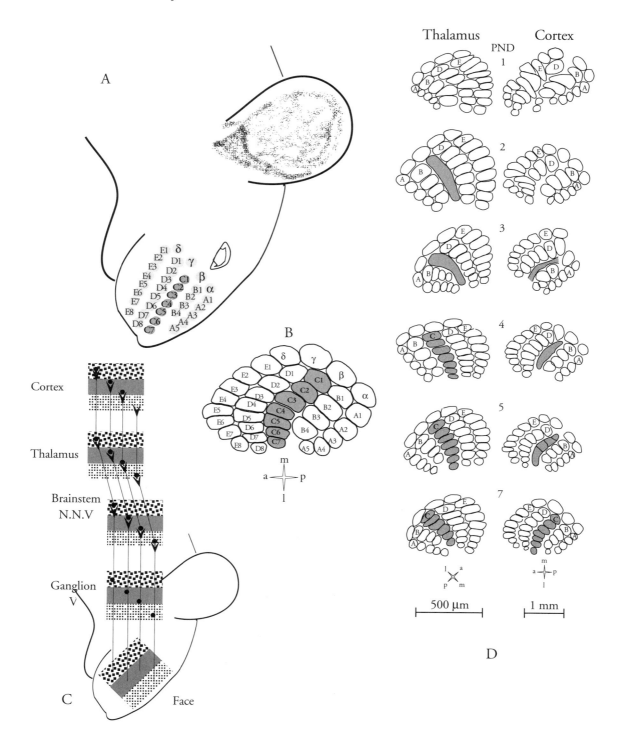

A

B

C

Cortex

Thalamus

Brainstem
N.N.V

Ganglion
V

Face

δ   γ
E1   D1   β
E2   D2   C1
E3   D3   C2
E4   D4   C3   B1   α
E5   D5   C4   B2   A1
E6   D6   C5   B3   A2
E7   D7   C6   B4   A3
E8   D8   C7   A5   A4

Thalamus   Cortex
PND
1
2
3
4
5
7

500 μm   1 mm

D

For example, the description of how a cortical neuron's final fate is achieved must include the following steps (McConnell, 1991). During very early stages, ancestral cells become committed to an anterior, as opposed to posterior, neural fate through interactions between the ectoderm and chordomesoderm. Then, during formation of the neural tube, ancestral cells become committed to the forebrain segment, instead of midbrain, and so on. At later stages, a precursor neuron becomes committed to a particular layer of the cortex. In an even later step, the neuron becomes committed to a phenotype appropriate to its target. Each of these steps involves interactions between the developing cell and its neighbors, but the nature of these interactions differs markedly. Although the completion of each step may restrict the cell's ability to reverse a choice, it need not affect subsequent steps.

Transplantation of presumptive cortical neurons between rat embryos of different ages showed that the layer in which a cell will take residence is decided during a particular phase of its mitotic division. Therefore, the migratory destination of a cell is predicted by its birth date. However, the signal for this laminar destination originates from the cells that surround the dividing cell, perhaps having its effect by activating particular adhesion molecules (McConnell, 1991). Although the layer in which the neuron resides constrains possible targets, the target is decided through cell-cell interactions. Furthermore, the functional division (visual, somatosensory, etc.) of the cortex occupied by a neuron is not predicted by the part of the ventricular zone that gave rise to it (O'Leary, 1989). Clones arising from the same cellular lineage are widely distributed in the cortex (Walsh & Cepko, 1992). It seems as though cortical cells are capable of doing broadly similar kinds of things, and the specialized function they ultimately perform is a matter of the specific connections that they make.

Experiments that rearrange embryonic cells demonstrate that both functional and morphological phenotypes emerge from the interactions among cells. For example, if visual input is artificially rerouted to somatosensory cortex, the cells will respond appropriately to visual input. Furthermore, when embryonic visual cortex is transplanted into the somatosensory cortex of rats, it will take on the distinctive appearance of this new region (O'Leary, 1989; box 6.1; figures 6.7 and 6.8).

Figure 6.7 Schematic maps of (A) facial whiskers and (B) anatomically defined barrels in the somatosensory cortex of mice, showing the topographical relationship between them. (C) The sensory pathway from facial whiskers to cortex includes a similar topography in the ipsilateral brain stem and the contralateral thalamus. (D) Anatomical consequences in the thalamus and the somatosensory cortex of removing the whiskers in row C (shaded in the diagrams) on postnatal days one through seven demonstrate that the arrangement develops postnatally as a consequence of input from the somatosensory receptors associated with whiskers (see box 6.1; redrawn from Woolsey et al., 1981).

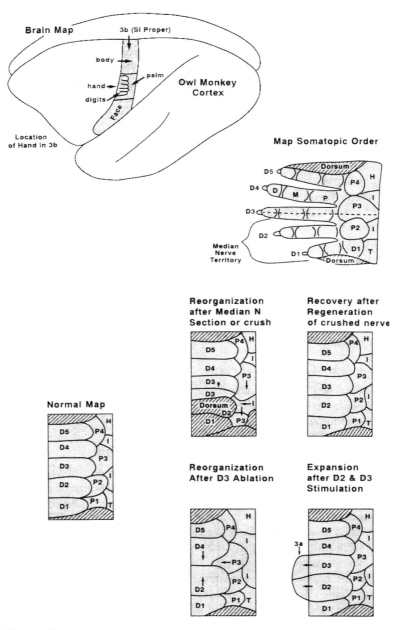

Figure 6.8 Reorganization of the primary somatosensory cortex representing the hand of adult owl monkeys after various experimental manipulations (see box 6.1 for details; adapted from Kaas, 1991. Reproduced, with permission, from the Annual Review of Neuroscience, Volume 14, © 1991, by Annual Reviews, Inc.).

Generally speaking, attaining a new developmental state restricts the ability to respond to particular environmental signals, and this is what progressively constrains cellular phenotype. However, this restriction need not be absolute, and may vary with the nature of the change that is made. Therefore, concepts of irreversible fate and critical periods cannot be applied uniformly, but must be examined separately and perhaps interpreted differently for each embryonic event. Clearly, cellular division requires an undifferentiated neuronal precursor cell, and events that lead to cell death are irreversible for that cell. When cells stop migrating, their interactions with other cells may lead to a state that precludes further migration. However, this does not prevent connections with other cells from changing through growth and remodeling of axons and dendrites, or through neurochemical changes, such as in neurotransmitter production.

The identities of the signals that contextual cells provide to differentiating cells are not well characterized at present, but they are undoubtedly heterogeneous. Furthermore, the intracellular events triggered by the signals are also poorly understood, but undoubtedly also heterogeneous. It is possible that some of the major morphological changes during the early development of the nervous system involve homeobox proteins, a group of nuclear proteins that bind DNA (Anderson, 1992; chapter 5). These proteins are highly conserved throughout the animal kingdom. They were first identified as transcription factors in homeotic mutations in *Drosophila*. **Homeotic mutations** transform a part of one body segment into a homologous part of another segment. They underlie the normal diversity of segments within an organism, and such bizarre developmental outcomes as flies with two pairs of wings, or with legs instead of antennae. Homeobox proteins are also involved in the normal genetic regulation of segmentation of the body in *Drosophila* and, apparently, of the segmented development of the vertebrate brain.

These proteins are only one variety of many that bind DNA and that might be involved in neuronal differentiation. Furthermore, their activity is regulated by unidentified signals arising from other cells, acting through receptors at the cell surface that have yet to be characterized. Although the appropriate questions have been framed for investigating the molecular basis of neuronal differentiation and some exciting advances have been made, the experimental work is still in an early phase.

Variations Within and Among Species

Generally speaking, the neural development of members of the same species is very similar. This generalization holds despite the fact that numerous small variations occur from individual to individual, even genetically identical ones (Purves, 1988). The fact of this variation has important conceptual implications, for it points to the nonlinear relation between genotypes and phenotypes and to the many developmental events that distinguish the zygote from the functioning organism. Given the stochastic nature of many of the relevant processes that underlie neural development, some degree of individual variation is hardly surprising. What is perhaps more surprising is that variation is sometimes predictable and discontinuous, so that some individuals share neural features that differ from those of others within the same species. There are, in other words, polymorphisms in neuroanatomy. The best known of these are differences that are related in some way to reproduction. They range from subtle to dramatic.

Sex differences account for the largest number of known neural polymorphisms. Because of the ease with which they can be identified, the two sexes provide a ready starting point for studying divergent neural development. Furthermore, it is relatively simple to manipulate the developmental hormones that underlie development in the two sexes, which opens the study of dimorphic neural development to experimental analysis. The study of sex differences in neural development cannot tell us how males and females ought to behave, how they should be raised, how they should fit into society, or what their separate capacities might be (chapter 2). It does, however, provide a powerful means for investigating basic processes of neural development.

Neuroanatomical Polymorphisms and Reproductive Function

Perhaps the clearest examples of polymorphic neural development are those that are directly related to peripheral differences. Some animals have striking sex differences in effector organs that are used in courtship and copulation. In some species of fish, for example, males set up mating **territories** and then vocalize to attract females to spawn in their nest. As part of their territorial courtship, male oyster toadfish produce a boat whistle sound by contracting paired muscles associated with the swim bladder. Females do not produce the sound. Males have a larger sound-producing organ than females, with about 47% more fibers in each muscle. There are no sex differences in the number of neurons innervating the muscles, but the motor neurons are substantially larger in calling males. The difference in musculature occurs because the muscle grows at a faster rate in males than in females after the onset of puberty. It is interesting that not all males hold territories and produce boat whistles. These silent males are smaller and have sonic motor neurons that are as small as those in females. However, the muscles in their sound-producing organs are similar to those of calling males. Therefore, the larger size of motor neurons in calling males is likely the result of their increased use (Fine, 1989).

The plainfin midshipman is a related fish that also has two types of reproductively mature males. The large, territorial males produces courtship sounds and the smaller, nonterritorial males do not. The silent males reproduce by approaching the nest of a large male when a female is present and depositing sperm into the nest. The calling males have larger sonic organs than females as well as larger motor neurons, although there is no sex difference in motor neuron number. However, small, reproductively mature males resemble nonreproductive juveniles in body size, in the size of their sonic organs, and in both size and number of sonic motor neurons. Although they are reproductively mature and have gonads equivalent to those of territorial males, the small males have fewer muscle fibers and fewer motor neurons innervating the sonic organ than territorial males (Bass & Andersen, 1991).

Heterochrony refers to dissociations in the timing or rate of development of two different parts of the same organism. It is a powerful ontogenetic agent for producing new phenotypic variants during speciation (chapter 4). Vocalizing fish, with their two distinctively different male morphs, represent an interesting case of within-species heterochrony, with gonadal maturity shifted in time with respect to other maturational processes. The smaller, nonterritorial, noncalling variants apparently reach sexual maturity at an earlier age than the slowly maturing, larger fish. Other differences in morphology and behavior follow from this simple difference. With respect to brain development, the ontogenetic shift in the timing of gonadal maturity led to differences in the size of brain nuclei that control calling. In one species, the brain difference is entirely one of motor neuron size, which probably reflects differential use, and in the other species it is one that combines motor neuron size, again a probable consequence of differential use, and motor neuron number, which is a consequence of differences in the number of muscle fibers in the sound-producing organ.

Hormones are major regulators of polymorphic neural development. In most vertebrates, there are only two morphs to consider—males and females—and differences between them can often be traced to differences in the gonadal hormones they secrete. Hormones can affect neural development in a number of ways: through a variety of direct actions on neurons; indirectly, through altering peripheral structures, such as muscles and sensory receptors, that in turn directly affect neurons; and, even more indirectly, through producing changes in organismic properties that alter the probability or salience of external stimulation that in turn affects neurons. Effects can be exerted at all stages of neural development—neurogenesis, migration, differentiation, death, and connectivity.

One system that has been well studied are motor nuclei that are involved in the copulatory behavior of rats. These nuclei are located in the lumbar spinal cord and innervate muscles that control penile reflexes. The penile reflexes are used during copulation to achieve intromission and ejaculation. Less obviously, they are also used to form a sperm plug and set it firmly against the female's cervix so that sperm can be transported into the female's reproductive tract. Finally, they are used to remove sperm plugs that have been placed there by other males. Therefore, the reflexes are important in a number of ways to the males' reproductive success (Sachs, 1982; Wallach & Hart, 1983).

Female rats have far fewer motor neurons in these lumbar nuclei than males, and this difference results from the fact that males secrete testosterone during the perinatal period, whereas females do not (Breedlove & Arnold, 1983). The difference can be reversed by providing females with testosterone during the early neonatal period or by removing the testes of males. Testosterone regulates the size of the sexually dimorphic spinal nuclei by increasing the number of motor neurons that survive the period of natural cell death. The major route by which testosterone has its effect is indirect, mediated by an effect of the hormone on sexually dimorphic muscles. Embryonic males and females both form the small perineal muscles that are later used in penile reflexes of males. However, the muscles continue to develop in males as a result of the action of testosterone, whereas they atrophy in females. These changes in musculature occur during the neonatal period and are coextensive with the period of natural motor neuron death. Most of the sex difference in size of the spinal cord nuclei can be explained by differences in surviving musculature and the trophic factors that they provide (Rand & Breedlove, 1988).

In fact, another dimorphic nucleus located more rostrally within the lumbar spinal cord owes its dimorphism to a muscle that forms in males but not females (Newton & Hamill, 1989). This muscle, the cremaster, is used to retract the testes from the scrotum into the abdominal cavity. The origin of the cremaster is not affected by testosterone; rather, it is induced in males by the presence of the testicular mass quite apart from the hormonal activity of the testes. Trophic effects of the muscle or its afferents on the motor neurons in this motor neuronal system lead to greater neuron survival in males.

The presence of dimorphic muscles is sufficient to account for most of the sexual dimorphism in the number of motor neurons in the sexually dimorphic lumbar nuclei. However, other contributors to this phenotypic variation include direct effects of testosterone on the developing neurons (Breedlove, 1992) and other indirect effects of testosterone (Moore, 1992).

Infant rats receive extensive afferent input to the lumbar region of the spinal cord as part of normal interactions with their mother. Mother rats lick and handle their pups extensively, beginning at birth and continuing throughout the first few weeks of life. Much of the maternal licking is directed to the perineum, where it has the necessary immediate consequence of eliciting urination and defecation from the pups. Males receive more of this perineal stimulation than their female siblings. This difference in input results from a hormone-dependent difference in the functioning of the preputial gland, a source of chemical stimuli that elicit maternal licking. In addition to the immediate consequences, the stimulation has long-term effects on behavioral development. Males exposed to experimentally reduced levels of maternal stimulation exhibit some deficiencies in their masculine sexual behavior in comparison with those receiving the normally high levels of stimulation (Moore, 1992). When pups receive less than normal amounts of perineal stimulation during the neonatal period, they also have fewer neurons in the sexually dimorphic lumbar motor nucleus that controls reflexes used in intromission and ejaculation (Moore, Dou, & Juraska, 1992).

The sex differences in the morphology of motor nuclei underscore the importance of keeping the whole organism in mind when attempting to understand the development of phenotypic variants. The rest of the body and the external environment in which the organism lives are major contributors to development in the central nervous system. It is not necessary to hypothesize a central organizing factor to account for phenotypic variants in neuroanatomy, even when these variants have clearly adaptive functional consequences, as they do with copulatory reflexes and courtship vocalizations. The nervous systems of males and females can become different while following the same neuroembryological rules; in fact, they can become different even with no direct action of hormones on the nervous system. This is because a relatively minor difference at the periphery (size or presence of a muscle, reliable input of some stimulus, etc.) can be reflected in substantial changes in neural development.

It is well established that the early hormonal environment can produce morphological changes in the brain as well as the spinal cord, leading to reliable sex differences in the structure of some brain regions because of sex differences in early hormone secretion. In general, the research on sex differences in neuroanatomy has focused on two goals: describing the location and extent of the differences, and establishing the hormonal basis of the differences by experimental manipulation of the steroid environment during early development. It is likely that research into the mechanisms by which the hormones have their effect will reveal at least as much heterogeneity as has been found for spinal cords. There is no reason to presuppose that all structural dimorphisms have arisen in the same way. Some may result from the direct, and others from the indirect, effects of gonadal steroids on neurons.

Observable morphological differences may arise from a wide variety of conditions (Breedlove, 1992; Tobet & Fox, 1992; Yahr, 1988): local differences in the number of neurons or glia because of differences in mitosis, migration, or cell death; differences in the size, shape, or orientation of cells; differences in the extent and direction of axonal outgrowth and the degree of **myelination** of axons; differences in the extent and pattern of dendritic growth; differences in the extent of synaptogenesis and pattern of connectivity among cells; differences in the degree of packing density; differences in neurochemistry or physiological activity that may affect the visualization of a region after staining; or differences in a host of other cellular and regional properties. Any one or combination of these factors may produce morphological differences that can be observed in the gross or fine structure of the brain.

The direct and indirect effects of hormones on cellular functioning are so various that they can, in principle, produce observable differences in brain structure by changing any one or combination of these eight factors. In fact, when all of the sexual dimorphisms that have been studied are considered as a whole, evidence can be found for contributions to dimorphic appearance from all these sources (Breedlove, 1992; Tobet & Fox, 1992; Yahr, 1988; box 6.2; figure 6.9). Some, but not all, hormonal effects must be confined to early embryonic periods, because that is when particular developmental events occur. If the developmental event has a stable end point that is not readily reversed (e.g., attaining a particular cell number through cell death), then the hormonal effect will endure. However, other effects may occur at later stages of the life cycle, and some of these may be transient (Arnold & Breedlove, 1985).

Despite its relatively long history, neuroanatomy has only recently begun to quantify its descriptions in a manner that allows one to identify the basis of observed differences in morphology. Indeed, earlier methods led to reports of differences that proved illusory or failed to detect differences that are present (Gundersen et al., 1988). The new quantitative techniques provide more accurate descriptions because they address the realities of three-dimensional structures, including those of the cellular elements that constitute such larger structures as nuclei, layers, and tracts. Accurate descriptions are necessary for developmental study and for relating structure to function.

The importance of attending to the cellular basis of gross anatomical measurements is well illustrated by some intriguing studies of the **corpus callosum**, a large fiber tract that connects the two cerebral hemispheres. The gross size of this structure can be measured by calculating its area in a section through the midsagittal plane. The report (de Lacoste-Utamsing & Holloway, 1982) that this area is larger in human males than in females generated a great deal of interest and several failed attempts to replicate the finding (e.g., Bleier, Houston, & Byne, 1986; Clarke, Kraftsik, van der Loos, & Innocenti, 1989). One possible basis for the discrepant results is that the size—and shape—of the corpus callosum is extremely variable from one individual to another (e.g., Bleier et al., 1986).

More important, however, two individuals can achieve the same gross size in very different ways. This point was made in an experiment with rats that is both elegant and provocative (Juraska & Kopcik, 1988). These authors found that the gross size of the corpus callosum was the same in the two

Box 6.2   Do Dimorphic Hypothalamic Nuclei Control Sexual Orientation?

Large numbers of nuclei are clustered in the anterior hypothalamus and pre-optic area of mammals, a region of the brain that is located just above the optic chiasm. Many of these nuclei have been implicated in the regulation of reproductive behavior and physiology, although the pattern of regulation has not been easy to discern. Studies report several functions for a particular nucleus, as well as numerous sites for specific functions. Neurons in this brain region are richly supplied with receptors for gonadal steroids, and these hormones are an integral part of the reproductive functions. Of interest, the volumes of some of these nuclei differ for males and females (Tobet & Fox, 1992).

The first sex difference in the volume of a hypothalamic nucleus, the medial preoptic nucleus, was found in rats. Both the nucleus as a whole and a cell-dense central portion, called the sexually dimorphic nucleus of the preoptic area (SDN-POA), are considerably larger in males, a fact that was traced to the effects of testosterone secreted endogenously by males during late embryonic and early neonatal life (Gorski, Gordon, Shryne, & Southam, 1978; Gorski, 1984). Similar dimorphic nuclei were reported in other rodents, ferrets, and humans. Sex differences in perinatal testosterone secretion also underlie sex differences in the neuroendocrine regulation of gonadal secretion and aspects of reproductive behavior. Although some correlations between nuclear volume and behavior have been found, functional consequences are not always related in a straightforward way to the size of nuclei (Gorski, 1984; Yahr, 1988).

In rats, for example, experimental interventions can alter the size of the SDN-POA while having no effect on either behavior or endocrine regulation, and vice versa. Furthermore, the volume or other aspects of some dimorphic nuclei can change in adulthood. A change in circulating hormones sometimes produces a change in neuronal size, dendritic extent, synapse number, or biochemical properties. Some sexually dimorphic nuclei do wax and wane in volume as gonadal steroid levels fluctuate (Tobet & Fox, 1992; Yahr, 1988). These reversible volumetric changes probably reflect either the size or staining properties of cells that are used to identify the perimeter of the nucleus, or the density with which cells are packed within the nucleus.

Experimental work with animals provides a useful context for evaluating hypotheses about the functional meaning of sexually dimorphic hypothalamic nuclei in humans. A great deal of interest was generated by the suggestion that one of these nuclei, the interstitial nucleus of the anterior hypothalamus-3 (INAH-3), is responsible for sexual orientation (LeVay, 1991). LeVay compared nuclear volume in the anterior hypothalamus of women, heterosexual men, and homosexual men. He found that INAH-3 is larger in men than in women, and larger in heterosexual than in homosexual men. No differences related to either sex or sexual orientation were found in the three other nuclei within the same cluster. An earlier study in which the cytoarchitectural divisions used by LeVay were first described, however, revealed that both INAH-2 and INAH-3 were larger in men (Allen, Hines, Shryne, & Gorski, 1989).

A sexual dimorphism in the same region of the anterior hypothalamus was originally reported even earlier (Swaab & Fliers, 1985). However, no differences between heterosexual and homosexual men were seen in this region (Hofman & Swaab, 1989). Although there were differences in the way that the two research groups delineated the region, the dimorphic area studied by Swaab and colleagues is probably either the same as INAH-1 or a combination of INAH-1 and INAH-2 (Allen et al., 1989; Tobet & Fox, 1992). The sexually dimorphic nuclei in humans and in other mammals that have been studied are all in the same general region of the hypothalamus, but species differences in anatomical details and in the number of nuclei that were observed within the same region leave homology an open question.

In a further complication to the pattern of findings, Swaab and Hofman (1990) observed that homosexual men have larger suprachiasmatic nuclei than heterosexual men, although this hypothalamic nucleus (which contains neural mechanisms underlying circadian rhythms) is apparently not sexually dimorphic in humans.

One possibility that must be considered is that the volume of a hypothalamic nucleus, including the INAH-3 studied by LeVay, may reflect the hormonal status of the individuals at the time of death. It is possible that the two male samples examined by LeVay differed in their behavior (e.g., frequency of sexual activity), level of stress, health, or a variety of other factors in ways that may have produced relevant hormonal differences. For example, one known confounding factor is that all of the homosexual men but only some of the heterosexual men died of the acquired immunodeficiency syndrome (AIDS). Testosterone levels are known to be low during the final stages of human immunodeficiency viral infection. If the infected homosexuals had better health care than the infected heterosexuals, who were likely to have been drug addicts, they may have survived longer with consequently longer periods of low levels of testosterone. Either this or other confounds related to the disease course in homosexuals and heterosexuals with AIDS provide a plausible basis for the difference in nuclear volume that has nothing to do with sexual orientation (Byne & Parsons, 1993).

Interpretation of the observed differences would be aided by information about the structural basis for the differences in volume as a function of sex and sexual orientation. For example, either the sex difference or the sexual orientation difference, or both differences reported by LeVay, may have resulted from a difference in neuron number within INAH-3, but cells were not counted, and it cannot be assumed that this was the case. Volume differences may just as readily reflect attributes, such as cell size, that can change after cell number is established. If so, the smaller size of INAH-3 in the homosexual men (or, independently, in the heterosexual women) may have resulted from some aspect of their lives that differed from the heterosexual men in the sample.

It is known that at least some of the human hypothalamic sex differences reflect features that change with age (Swaab & Hofman, 1988; Hofman & Swaab, 1989). When these researchers both measured volume and counted cells, they found that males had a larger nucleus that contained more cells. The dimorphism was first apparent in their sample after age four years and it resulted from a greater cell loss among girls. A second phase of cell loss began between 45 and 50 years of age, at which time loss was more accelerated in men than in women. The net result of these changes was that the degree of dimorphism was reduced among older adults. If the smaller volumes of INAH-3 among the homosexuals who were measured by LeVay could be attributed to cell number, it would raise the important developmental question of when the differences first arose. Perhaps something related to sexual orientation in at least a subsample of the homosexual men led to an earlier onset of the adult decline in cell number.

The pattern of human sex difference has not been consistent from study to study, with some differences reported in one study but not another. Furthermore, there is great individual variation and overlap of groups within each study. In the report by Allen et al. (1989), women had a smaller INAH-2 on average, but the INAH-2 of women of childbearing age was equal in size to that of men. Perhaps ontogenetic shifts in the sizes of nuclei as a result of hormonal, experiential, or other factors associated with age account for some of the variability both within and across studies.

The substantial overlap in the size of INAH-3 among individual men of different sexual orientation eliminates the possibility of a simple causal relation—some men with a relatively large INAH-3 choose male partners whereas others with the same nuclear size choose females. Furthermore, the sizes of both INAH-3 and the suprachiasmatic nucleus are correlated with sexual orientation among men. Which is the biological substrate for sexual orientation? Should one assume that sexual dimorphism is a logical necessity for hypothesizing that some structure is the substrate for sexual orientation within one sex? Male homosexuality and female heterosexuality are not the same thing, and the preference for male partners may have very different mechanisms in the two cases.

Whether either nucleus is involved in any way with the causation of sexual orientation remains an open question. Even apart from the obvious constraints of working with autopsy material, it is unlikely that an answer will be found without rephrasing the question. In contemporary social usage (and in the LeVay study), sexual orientation is a cognitive self-categorization and therefore a totally human trait. It is bound up in ways that are only partially known but clearly individually variable, with a variety of behavioral predilections and perceptual preferences, only some of which may have mechanisms that are continuous with those underlying sexual behavior in other species. Hypothalamic nuclei are far more likely to be associated with these specific behavioral mechanisms than with identification of oneself as heterosexual or homosexual.

sexes, but females had more callosal axons crossing through the midline than males. Although the males had fewer axons, these were more likely to be larger and myelinated. Some of the rats in the study were allowed to live with social companions in a large, object-filled cage for 30 days after weaning; others lived alone in standard cages for the same time. The axons in the corpus callosum of rats from the complex environment were greater in number and larger in diameter. This finding demonstrates that the cellular composition of the corpus callosum changes after weaning in ways that vary with the environment. Furthermore, the two sexes did not respond identically to the same environment: among males, but not females, myelinated axons were larger after rearing in the complex environment; and among females, but not males, the number of myelinated axons (not their size) was greater in the complex environment (figure 6.10).

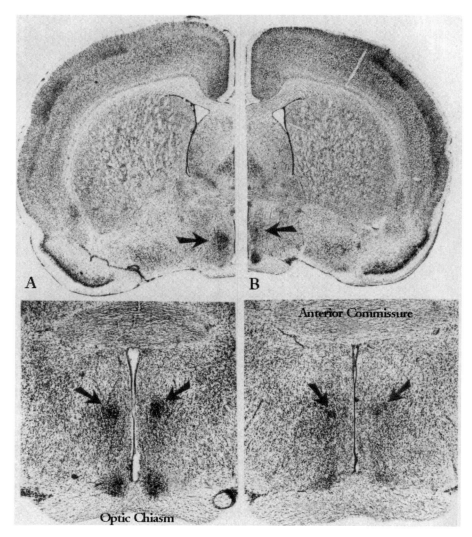

Figure 6.9   The medial preoptic nucleus of a male (left) and a female (right) adult rat (Nissl-stained sections). The nucleus as a whole and its denser medial and central components are larger in males than in females (see box 6.2). (Reproduced with permission from Gorski, 1979.)

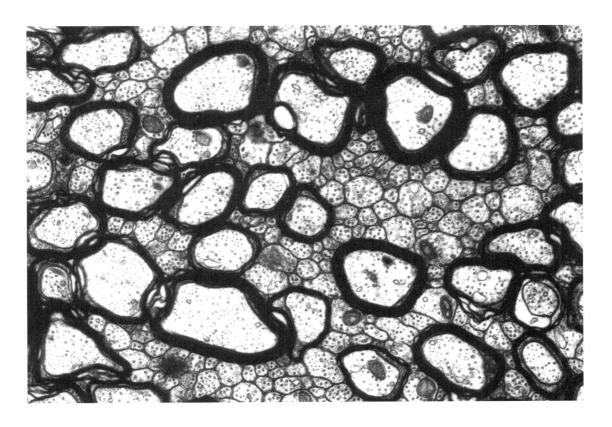

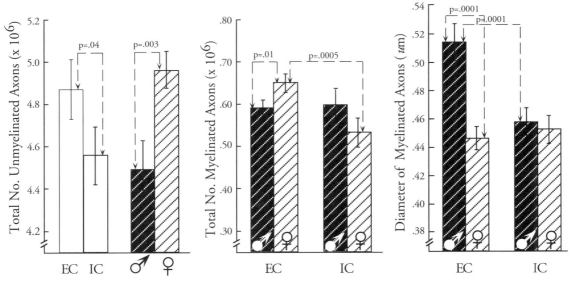

Figure 6.10 (Top) A cross section through the corpus callosum of the rat shows both the relatively more numerous unmyelinated axons and the larger, myelinated axons (approx. 39,600 ×; micrograph provided by Janice Juraska and Jan Kim). (Bottom) The effects of rearing environment and sex on the number and size of axons in the corpus callosum of rats (see text; redrawn from Juraska & Kopcik, 1988).

These findings place the human data in a new light (Juraska, 1990). Those who failed to find a sex difference in gross size may have overlooked a difference in cellular composition. Furthermore, those who identified a difference will not have found its developmental basis or, necessarily, a static end point. The structure can grow to different extents and in different ways, depending on characteristics of the environment, and the morphology is remarkably plastic for an extended period of life. To complicate issues even further, the functional consequences of the sex difference in rats are unknown: do the two sexes achieve functional equivalence through different mechanisms, or can they achieve different kinds of interhemispheric communications?

Speciation and Neuroanatomical Changes

The number of ways in which differences in developmental end points can be achieved suggests the number of ways in which input from peripheral organismic sources, including the environmental surround of the organism, can influence these differences. These sources of variation can underlie neuroanatomical differences that are present within a species. They can also underlie differences between closely related species.

This insight offers an enormously useful explanation of how speciation can produce an adaptive complex of brain mechanisms and peripheral structures, or of brain mechanisms and species-typical behavior (Edelman, 1988; Gottlieb, 1992; Gould, 1977; Purves, 1988). If many of these changes occur in ontogenetic as opposed to phylogenetic time, it is unnecessary to hypothesize the slow, independent accretion of numerous changes as a result of directional natural selection. One difficulty with the natural selection theory is that numerous changes must be correlated before any one of them offers a selective advantage. What is the good, for example, of a peripheral change in a limb without the necessary neural mechanism to use it? However, if that neural mechanism follows from the peripheral changes because of peripherally regulated ontogenetic processes, then the statistical odds of evolving an adaptive system are greatly increased. This argument can also be extended to behavior. Although the relevant studies have not been done to test the idea, it is possible that some of the brain differences that correlate with behavioral differences among closely related species do so through ontogenetic as opposed to selection processes (chapter 4).

One of the more useful techniques in embryological study is the formation of **chimeras**, organisms that are mosaics of tissue from two different species. Chimeras are formed by transplanting tissue from the embryo of one species into an embryo of a second, related species. The idea is to be able to identify the transplanted tissue at later stages of development. The technique is an old one, and it was very useful in studies designed to determine whether differentiation is regulated by factors intrinsic to the cells or by factors obtained from the surrounding environment (Oppenheim & Haverkamp, 1986). These experiments also offer some interesting insights into the nature of species differences and the developmental processes through which the differences might emerge.

Remarkably enough, chimeras can develop into complete, integrated organisms. Transplanted tissue can make use of inductive signals from the host to continue their development, but the outcome can be rather novel. If, for example, the belly skin of a newt is moved to the mouthpart region at the early gastrula stage, it will become mouthparts. The same is true of frogs. When the belly skin is transplanted in a similar fashion across the two species, it will also form mouthparts. However, the belly skin of a newt moved to the mouth region of a frog will develop into newt mouthparts, and vice versa. Newts have balancers in this region, whereas frog tadpoles have suckers that they use for adhering to the substrate. Balancers and suckers are anatomically very different structures. Nevertheless, the cellular interactions underlying mouthpart development in newts and frogs are equally capable of regulating a normal developmental process for either balancers or suckers. However, some difference in the cells of the two species at the early gastrula stage results in different morphological outcomes on transplantation to a locality appropriate for mouthpart formation (figure 6.11). It is possibly a difference intrinsic to the cells, such as in structural genes, or a difference in local factors emerging from very early cellular interactions that are transplanted together with the block of tissue.

Whether the source of the species difference involves a change in some structural gene or in gene regulation, the experimental formation of chimeric newts with suckers and chimeric frogs with balancers illustrates rather nicely how a small change can be incorporated into a system and lead to a remarkable degree of morphological change in a well-organized animal. Much of the system is apparently identical for newts and frogs, yet the final outcome looks radically different to us and functions in very different ways for the two organisms. Although it would be interesting to track down the singular difference in cellular biochemistry that marks the species difference, doing so will not explain the developmental formation of either balancers or suckers. Those are processes that involve many steps, some extrinsic to the differentiating cells and some not at all specific to the species.

The rules revealed by chimeric development of mouthparts apply as well to species differences in neural development. Differences in developmental outcome can result from a small difference in any one of many developmental steps. The gonadal hormones are useful for illustrating this point, both because they play an important regulatory role in the development of many parts of the organism and because they are so readily manipulated in experiments.

Generally speaking, mammals follow similar processes in their sexual development. The sexes differ because of differences in the availability of

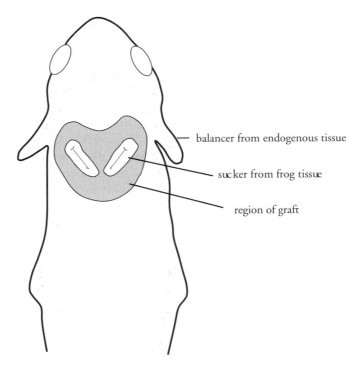

balancer from endogenous tissue

sucker from frog tissue

region of graft

Figure 6.11 Induction of heterospecific frog mouthparts in a newt after transplantation of ectoderm from the belly region of a frog donor. Factors in the prospective oral region of the host induced the formation of mouthparts rather than belly skin. However, the mouthparts included suckers typical of frog tadpoles rather than newt-typical balancers. The illustrated chimeric larva has both the more lateral balancers from endogenous tissue, and the more medial suckers from transplanted frog ectoderm (redrawn from Spemann, 1938/1967).

testosterone during early stages. This is true for some behavioral patterns as well as for some aspects of morphology. However, the nature and degree of sex differences vary from species to species (Baum, 1979; Beach, 1971). For example, mounting, which is a typical male copulatory pattern, is relatively common in female rats but rare in female hamsters. Many of the other differences between the species are similar in character, yet, they can be understood by knowing the difference in the degree to which males and females are exposed to testosterone during particular developmental periods. For both species, differences can be increased when the amount of testosterone available to females at a particular time is decreased relative to that in males. The differences will also be greater when the timing of particular developmental events is changed to correspond to low points in the endogenous fluctuation of the hormone in females; converse changes decrease the differences.

The hamster-rat difference can be understood by knowing that female rats are exposed to more testosterone than are hamsters during the last few days of gestation, at least in part because hamsters have a shorter gestation, with birth occurring before the testosterone surge in fetal males (Vomachka & Lisk, 1986). Testosterone does not operate alone as an independent causal agent, but rather is a component in a spatially and temporally organized developmental system.

Changes in hormone availability during particular stages have also been linked to neural changes. In many mammals, the lumbar nuclei that innervate muscles involved in copulatory reflexes are all located in the more lateral part of the spinal cord. In rats, however, a population of these motor neurons migrates to a medial location of the same cord segments and creates a separate nucleus (Breedlove, 1992). The medial and the lateral neurons innervate different muscles and control different reflexes.

When females are treated with an androgen during the relevant prenatal period, they will retain both sets of muscles and the motor neurons to innervate them. However, the neurons do not migrate to the medial location, but remain in the lateral location, as is the case for some other mammalian species. This developmental aberration is probably the result of some slight difference in the timing of the artificially administered androgen relative to the species-typical course of events as experienced by males. It results, nevertheless, in a rather striking difference in neuroanatomy: the males have a large motor nucleus in the medial part of the spinal cord, whereas the treated females do not. This difference is related only to the location of neurons, for the same muscles are innervated in both cases. Neuroanatomical differences between species could arise in the same fashion. Some of these differences may result in systems that function differently, whereas others may result in systems that look different but function in a similar manner.

In some instances, species differences in neuroanatomy may result from species differences in sensory input from the external environment. The naked mole rat provides a dramatic example. This odd rodent has many features that differ from other rodents but seem to fit its completely subterranean existence, and reflect a high degree of **neoteny**. Among these neotenic features is the retention of the closed eyes of infancy throughout life, an adaptation suited to life in dark, earthen tunnels. Correlated with this peripheral adaptation, the visual cortex and associated subcortical regions of mole rats are markedly different from those of other rodents. However, they have features observed in the central visual system of rodents that develop while experimentally deprived of visual input (Cooper, Herbin, & Nevo, 1993).

Neuroanatomy and Function

The nervous system develops through interactions at several different levels of organization. Cells interact with other cells and the extracellular matrix;

regionally different groups of cells interact with one another; the nervous system interacts with the rest of the body; and the organism interacts with its environment. Each of these levels is marked by patterns of dynamic equilibria, which in turn contribute to the equilibria of each of the other levels. Hence, nonlinearity is inherent in the mechanisms of causality promoting change and stability. A small change can be multiplied into a major effect or it can cascade into many effects. Conversely, a large change can be buffered, muted, or counteracted by other changes.

Because the nervous system builds itself in ways that reflect earlier ontogenetic steps, and because some of these steps produce sex or species differences, it is likely that structural changes will occur in the nervous system that have no functional meaning, but merely **cascade** from an earlier event. If these cascading changes are consequential, in the sense of altering the behavioral functioning of the individual, several possibilities are opened. The behavioral consequence may be neutral, or it may turn out to fit with the environment. In either case, the behavior would be retained. If, on the other hand, the consequence does not fit with the environment in which the individual resides, the phenotype may be eliminated by natural selection.

One other possibility is that compensatory events during ontogeny may ensure that the behavior initiated by the cascade is negated by additional developmental steps. This is just another way of saying that there is more than one way to reach the same developmental end point, a principle that is well established in neural development (Purves, 1988). With respect to neuroanatomy, the implication is that not all brain differences will have consequences for behavioral performance, and that the same behavior may be achieved through somewhat different mechanisms. Thus, a direct relation between neural mechanism and behavior is not a necessary condition of developmental biology. This insight challenges theories that depend on localization of function.

The study of sex differences led to the identification of several neuroanatomical differences between males and females, but functional correlates of these differences are often lacking, despite extensive efforts to find such correlates. The sexually dimorphic nucleus of the preoptic area of rats is the first dimorphic brain region to receive intensive study. Despite large, reproducible, hormone-dependent sex differences, there is no clear functional correlate to the size of this nucleus (Gorski, 1984; Yahr, 1988). Males that are castrated neonatally and females that are injected neonatally with testosterone both have nuclei that are intermediate in size to those of normal males and females. Yet, in a sexual context, the castrated male behaves like a female and the injected female behaves like a male. The meaning of the anatomical difference and the appropriate interpretation of the failure to find a correlate of the difference in behavior are far from clear. One conclusion that can be drawn, however, is that a structural difference in one part of the nervous system need not imply that the function normally subserved by that part will be different.

In conclusion, species differences and polymorphic differences within a species may arise rapidly in the nervous system as a result of ontogenetic events linking neural changes to those in the periphery and environment. Some of these changes may be both adaptively and causally related to the environmental or peripheral change, whereas others arise secondarily and may be causally but not adaptively related. The behavioral consequences of these secondary changes may be neutral, adaptive in a different context, or maladaptive. If maladaptive, they may be counteracted by other developmental events so that the original behavioral outcome is reached through different mechanisms. It follows that not all brain differences will have adaptive behavioral correlates.

Neuroembryology and Behavior

There is no clear ontogenetic stage at which neuroembryology ends. The cellular and regional processes described in this chapter continue after the organism begins to exhibit behavior; indeed, many of the processes continue throughout life. However, when the organism develops to the point at which it engages in activity that involves coordination among its various parts, a shift has taken place in the level that requires explanation, and a new set of terms and explanatory principles becomes necessary. This is due in part to the whole-organism quality of behavior, but it is also due to the increasing importance of the external environment as a major contextual element. Factors from the external environment, such as chemicals and thermal changes, can affect the nervous system at all developmental stages, of course, but the range of such factors and the degree to which they can exert an influence are markedly increased by the emergence of functioning sensory systems.

We use **behavioral embryology** to refer to developmental processes during embryonic, perinatal, and early neonatal life that involve sensory or motor activity of the organism. Self-generated experience and stimulation from the external social and physical world affect the developing nervous system through processes that are continuous at the cellular and regional levels with those that were described for neuroembryology. Although the processes do not differ when considered at the level of neurons and their interconnections, the addition of sensory inputs from external and self-generated sources provides a new element to the system. This creates a new level of organization. At this new level, contextual effects continue to be important, but are best described in terms of the interaction between the organism and its environment (see chapter 3; Lehrman, 1953; Schneirla,

1957), and the organism's environment is predominantly a sensory one, including proprioceptive and kinesthetic sensations.

For the organism's environment to affect cellular and regional processes within the nervous system, it is necessary for environmental factors first to be translated into agents that have contextual efficacy at the level of individual cells or groups of cells. Many examples of environmental effects on nervous system development have been followed experimentally to the cellular level. However, this reductive step cannot be taken without understanding developmental processes at the whole-organism level. This understanding has been impeded by the conceptual dichotomization of development into processes that are open to environmental influences and those that are not (chapter 2).

The problem hinges on identifying what constitutes an environmental influence. One difficulty arises when relevant influences are formally or functionally discontinuous with the developing system. Another difficulty arises when the environmental influence is so ubiquitous that it is not noticed by the investigator.

When sensory and motor systems become functional, their functioning raises the possibility of such intuitively apparent influences as rehearsal, practice, correction, and familiarization. These processes do occur, and are an important part of early development. The use of a system often improves the efficiency or competence with which the system can be used, extends or restricts the range of its use, or converts a vaguely specified system into one that is more precise or detailed. The intuitive appeal of such processes stems from the underlying formal or functional continuity between the developmental process and the use of the developed system. This makes them relatively easy to identify and understand.

For use to contribute to further development, it is necessary first to have a nascent system that has developed to a usable state. This raises the more difficult developmental question of how this initial system was achieved. Some resolved the difficulty by labeling the initial system as innate, and suggesting that it is an appropriate research topic for genetics and embryology, but not for behavior (e.g., Lorenz, 1965). Others disagreed, and grappled with this question within a broadly epigenetic approach to behavioral embryology (e.g., Gottlieb, 1973; Kuo, 1967; Lehrman, 1953; Schneirla, 1957). What emerged from their efforts is the understanding that many aspects of behavioral and neural development are explained by experiential factors that are not intuitively obvious and that are functionally discontinuous with the behavioral system under study. Nevertheless, these experiential factors may have effects on the nervous system that are similar to those of the more readily identified, functionally continuous factors of practice, reinforcement, and familiarization. The categories that human observers use to distinguish among different sorts of experiential influences have no meaning for the developing nervous system, because all forms of experience encountered by an organism must first be translated into agents that can affect cells. At that level, new forms of experiential influences that are not intuitively obvious may be identified.

Developmental psychobiologists devised a number of strategies that proved useful for identifying potentially important but nonintuitive developmental influences. Four of these strategies seem particularly important, and go a long way toward defining the field. First, *the descriptive methods of natural historians and ethologists* are applied to the natural course of behavioral development and to correlated aspects of the environmental context. This descriptive material is then used to generate hypotheses for experimental test.

Second, terms in the description are varied so that *the same phenomenon is described in more than one way*. For example, a behavioral pattern may be described in terms of both its immediate consequences and its movement patterns, or motor activity may be described both as temporal patterns of movement and quiescence and as the relative location of elements around shared joints. No description is complete. Many qualitatively different descriptions can suggest hypotheses that would not emerge from only one. They can also provide alternative perspectives from which insight into the factors contributing to the stability and change in the developing system can emerge.

Third, *various species are studied*. Again, the diversity of perspectives that cross-species comparisons have to offer promote understanding of the web of causality. These comparisons often suggest possibilities for some species that might not otherwise be considered. For example, a surprising developmental relationship between two variables may loom large in a particular species, and prove on examination to be present in another species albeit in a more subtle, easily missed, manner.

Finally, there is *willingness to examine many parts of the organism*, not just its nervous system, in constructing developmental explanations of the manifestation of behavior. These four strategies prompt our expectation that developmental psychobiology will become the foundation for the integration of biology and psychology in the study of behavioral development. The remaining chapters include many examples that applied one or more of these strategies.

Summary

The nervous system is constructed primarily during embryonic life as cells divide, migrate, differentiate, form connections, and survive beyond the period of natural cell death. The nervous system continues to change form as the connections among neurons are remodeled throughout life. Synapses are formed and lost, and both dendrites and axons retain the capacity to branch and to extend or retract their leading edges throughout their lifetime. Initial development and continued plasticity in the nervous system reflect events in the rest of the body and its surround. This leads to an adaptive fit between the nervous system and other parts of the organism, particularly the sensory and motor systems through which interactions with the external environment are achieved. The principles underlying neuroembryology are useful for understanding how integrated changes can occur synchronously in behavior, peripheral morphology, and the nervous system during both speciation and polymorphic development within the same species. These principles can also help to understand how the capacity for some behavioral patterns develops in advance of opportunity to practice.

The study of embryology alerts us to the fact that, at any moment, the physical form of an organism is the result of interactions among thousands of variables, including regulatory genes, chemical reactions involving proteins, environmental factors, and a host of others. Although the organic form is a well-organized whole, it is the product of numerous discontinuous and frequently changing interactions. The relation between the organism and the causal elements through which it is constructed can be understood within the framework of dynamic systems theory. Thus, the various resultant forms are the "attractor" states of the dynamic system. The emergence of new tissues, organs, and features occurs in three-dimensional space plus time called the parameter space. Continuous alterations in any or all of these parameters will be marked by discontinuous shifts from one attractor to another as the consequences of changes are initially buffered and then enhanced. Therefore, the complexity of thousands of interacting variables may be observed as relatively few discontinuous shifts in organic form. It is the work of developmental psychobiologists, in collaboration with developmental biologists and psychologists, to identify the factors that typically promote the orderly course of behavioral development.

7   Behavioral Embryology

Development is not always progressive and constructive. For example, immature animals (embryos, fetuses, larvae, neonates) frequently inhabit environments that are markedly different from those of the adult. Consequently, each of these stages may have required the evolution of specific morphological, biochemical, physiological, and behavioural mechanisms which are different from the adult, and which may require modification, suppression or even destruction before the adult stage can be obtained.... I recognize that in many cases ontogenetic events may serve immediate needs, as well as influence future goals. Furthermore, I do not want to leave the impression that the development of an ontogenetic adaptation—even of completely transient traits—is fundamentally different from the development of an adult trait. At some level of organization, both represent the end product of a previous, gradual epigenetic process."
—R. W. Oppenheim (1981b, pp. 74–75)

All vertebrates must grow from a tiny zygote and differentiate into adult form. But the vertebrate classes differ markedly in how these changes are achieved. Amphibians go through a free-living larval stage that is morphologically and behaviorally discontinuous with the adult form. Fish and reptiles emerge from their embryonic stages as miniature adults. Except for the difference in size, they are morphologically and behaviorally similar to adults. Birds and mammals undergo more gradual transitions that include postnatal immaturity. The degree of immaturity at hatching or birth is variable, giving rise to the terms **altricial** and **precocial** to describe these differences. Nonetheless, all birds and mammals, unlike most of the reptiles from which they evolved, have a period of neonatal dependency on parental care. Life during the prenatal and, for birds and mammals, early postnatal periods is very different from life in later periods, involving differences in neural organization, sensory and motor capacities, physiological requirements, and environmental context. Behavioral embryology is the study of behavioral development in these young organisms.

Ontogenetic Adaptations

Immature organisms frequently inhabit environments quite different from those of the adult, and this is clearest for the conditions of embryological development. Oppenheim (1981b, 1982b, 1984) drew attention to this fact and proposed that phases in development are often fully understood only when they are considered as adaptations to current conditions and not solely as preparations for later phases. Although in some sense all steps in development are necessary for adulthood, ontogeny must serve immediate as well as future needs. Therefore, developmental psychobiologists seek to determine the extent to which early phases are preparations for adult features, and the extent to which they are adaptations to current conditions—*ontogenetic adaptations* (Oppenheim, 1981b, 1982b, 1984). When combined with modern evidence on the embryological development of the nervous system, the concept of ontogenetic adaptation requires reconceptualization of both embryonic behavioral development and the transition from embryonic to postembryonic development.

The differences between intrauterine and extrauterine environments for mammals, and the differences between in ovo and ex ovo environments for other vertebrates, surely require separate ontogenetic adaptations. However, it is also true that the study of embryonic events can help us comprehend postembryonic neurobehavioral organization. Neurobehavioral development during embryonic life consists of two classes of features and processes: those that are primarily adapted to embryonic conditions and those that serve primarily as preparation for the eventual development of features and processes that are adapted to postembryonic life (Hall & Oppenheim, 1987). Of course, any particular aspect of neurobiological development may embody both of these attributes.

Birth and hatching are in many ways arbitrary time points. Despite some radical changes entailed by these dramatic events, there are many developmental continuities. Furthermore, birth and hatching occur at different developmental stages in different species. Therefore, for certain species, we include in behavioral embryology (and use the term "embryonic" to refer to) the period of development confined by an egg, and the one immediately after it that encompasses hatching and early posthatching behavior. For mammals we include the period of development confined to a uterus and the one immediately after it, which encompasses birth and early neonatal behavior. Information about postembryonic development from the period when caregivers form a necessary part of the developing organism's milieu will also be included when it seems appropriate.

Clearly, many technical difficulties must be overcome before embryonic behavior can be studied. For this reason, early studies were confined to amphibian species with an aquatic larval stage, or to embryos or fetuses that

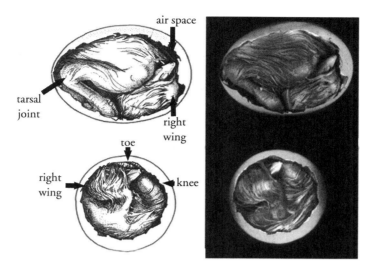

Figure 7.1 The embryo of the domestic chicken shortly before hatching. (Top) Side view of the embryo shows the characteristic hatching position, with the head tucked under the wing. (Bottom) View of the embryo from the air space (reproduced with permission from Oppenheim, 1973).

were removed from their natural environment (Carmichael, 1970). In recent years, methods have been developed for visualizing embryos and their spontaneous behavior while maintaining an intact support system. Avian eggs are far more accessible than mammalian uteri, and techniques for observing and manipulating embryos were first developed for birds (Kuo, 1967; Oppenheim, 1973; figure 7.1). Consequently, much of the information in behavioral embryology comes from avian species. Studies of exteriorized fetuses in the earlier work with mammals were often complicated by anesthesia or by disruptions in the prenatal support systems, such as inadequate oxygen or altered temperature (Carmichael, 1970). Improved experimental techniques avoid some of these complications (Smotherman & Robinson, 1991). Furthermore, the use of external monitoring devices and ultrasound to observe human fetuses and advanced methods to support very young, premature infants have extended our knowledge of early human development (Birnholz, 1988).

It has been recognized for some time that movement begins very early in fetal life (Carmichael, 1970; Coghill, 1929; Hooker, 1952; figure 7.2). Much of the research in behavioral embryology has been directed toward understanding this movement. Is it useful, or is it merely a byproduct of the developing motor system? To what extent is it controlled by processes endogenous to that system, and to what extent is it reactive to stimulation? One of the things to emerge from recent studies is an appreciation of the fact that very young organisms do have behavioral patterns that are

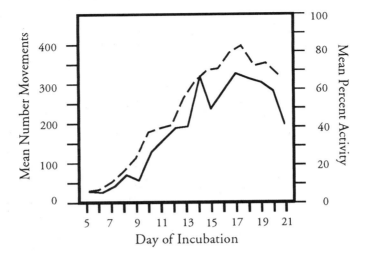

Figure 7.2 Movement in the duck embryo increases until embryonic day 18 and then declines. Hatching occurs on day 27 (redrawn from Oppenheim, 1970).

organized and reactive to specific aspects of their natural intraegg, intra-uterine, or early social environments. Nevertheless, much of the motor activity seen in young organisms does not seem to fit this description. In fact, it is often described as jerky and disorganized (Hamburger, 1970). Is this activity useful in the early stage, is it useful as preparation for later life, or is it both? One consequence of improved access to ever younger organisms is that these questions have been pushed back to the very beginnings of fetal movement.

Features of Embryonic Neurobehavioral Organization

For many decades, reflexive behavior was the only feature of embryonic neurobehavioral organization thought worthy of examination, in part because of its practical importance in neurology (Gordon, 1976). Neurologists traditionally used the character of reflexes to assess the developmental status of the nervous system. Reliance on procedures that were designed primarily for diagnostic purposes may have contributed to the impression that fetal and neonatal motility lacks spatiotemporal coordination. However, research has moved toward the spontaneous behavioral repertoire of the undisturbed embryo as a valuable source of information about neurobehavioral organization.

Spontaneous human fetal activity begins at about eight weeks postmenstrual age and rapidly increases in both frequency of occurrence and differentiation of movement patterns (de Vries, Visser, & Prechtl, 1984;

Prechtl, 1986). By 15 weeks, 16 different movement patterns may be observed, such an independent movement of the arms and legs, retroflexion of the head, rotation, breathing, yawning, and swallowing (de Vries et al., 1984). Interjoint coordination within a single limb is observed after 12 weeks; for example, the independent extension of an arm is frequently accompanied by extension of the fingers on that limb. Rotation of the head begins to occur between 10 and 13 weeks. The frequent association of head rotation and hand-face contact around this time represents another level of motor coordination.

Complete changes in fetal position begin at about 10 weeks, increase in frequency to about 15 weeks, and thereafter decline in frequency (de Vries et al., 1984). This decline is not due to a decrease in activity but seems to result from the reduction of free room in the uterus, which makes it difficult for the fetus to shift position. Thus the uterine environment begins to act as an identifiable constraint on fetal movements early in the second trimester of pregnancy (box 7.1). Positional changes around the transverse axis are usually achieved by a backward somersault involving general movement of head and torso, and alternating leg movements (Prechtl, 1986). Alternating leg movements involve coordination between the limbs. Positional changes around the longitudinal axis are typically executed in one of two ways, a combination of hip rotation and leg movements, or rotation of the head followed by the trunk. Thus, very early in development head rotation movements or head orientation influence motor patterns of the trunk and limbs.

Sensory Input and Spontaneous Prenatal Behavior

In humans, as in other mammals, spontaneous activity begins to occur only after afferent connections have formed in the spinal cord (Hamburger, 1970; Humphrey, 1964, 1969). This temporal sequence was used to argue that spontaneous activity depends on and is regulated by sensory input (Windle, 1940). However, the temporal sequence is different in birds. In chickens, spontaneous activity precedes the connection of afferents with either spinal interneurons or motoneurons. Moreover, deafferentation does not alter the normal developmental changes in the temporal character of the spontaneous activity of chick embryos. Even complete elimination of sensory input on the second embryonic day, by isolating the lumbosacral cord from more rostral regions, removing its dorsal part, and removing the neural crest cells that would form the dorsal root sensory ganglia, has no effect on the normal spontaneous leg movements of avian embryos (Hamburger, 1970, 1973; Hamburger, Wenger, & Oppenheim, 1966). This surgical procedure severely impairs posthatching walking (Narayanan & Malloy, 1974), however, and less drastic deafferentation procedures also disturb some aspects of the transitions to prehatching behavior and hatching behavior (Bekoff,

Box 7.1   Intrauterine Environmental Influences on Fetal Behavior

Robinson and Smotherman (1992) demonstrated that the intrauterine environment influences fetal behavior in rats. Using recently developed techniques, they observed the behavior of the rat fetus while in the uterus, while removed from the uterus but still in the amniotic membranes, and after removal of the membranes. In each case, the umbilical cord was still functional and the fetus was not physiologically compromised or stressed. They found that when the fetus was removed from the uterus, it had more spontaneous activity, behavioral diversity, and greater temporal organization among movements than when it was in the uterus. Indeed, the behavioral organization outside of the uterus was similar to that after birth.

The authors proposed two explanations for the difference in behavioral organization manifested by a fetus in versus out of the uterus. As the fetus grows, the uterine space diminishes and amniotic fluid decreases, resulting in a physical restraint on fetal movements. Thus, one explanation for the behavioral differences is that the elastic walls of the uterus essentially prevent all but the strongest and most vigorous movements. The nervous system activates the muscle system, but the muscles lack the power to distend the uterine wall to execute the movements.

A second potential explanation is that, by particular proprioceptive feedback from joints and muscles that results from constrained movements, the fetus detects the restraint imposed by the diminishing space and adjusts to it by altering its behavior. Robinson and Smotherman have demonstrated that the fetus is responsive to external stimulation, and that the fetal nervous system is capable of processing tactile and proprioceptive sensory information. Therefore, sensory feedback of movements constrained by the uterus could modify the neural systems governing motor activity, resulting in a behavioral adjustment to these environmental circumstances. Such adjustment would certainly be an example of an ontogenetic adaptation to the uterine conditions that would not be applicable after birth. Given the sensitivity of the nervous system to the effects of sensory experience, however, the feedback modification of the neural systems that govern movement could also produce changes that could last beyond the conditions of the uterus.

Casaer (1979) reported that the postural characteristics of newborn humans represents a continuation of those achieved in the uterus during the last trimester of pregnancy. These neonatal postural characteristics themselves contribute to the infant's neurobehavioral development. Thus, the decline of fetal movements can be both an ontogenetic adaptation to the conditions of the uterus and a bridge for postnatal development.

Nusbaum, Sabichi, & Clifford, 1987; Oppenheim, 1975). If a similar developmental pattern underlies spontaneous fetal behavior in humans and chickens, then one would conclude that much of the spontaneous behavior of fetal humans is neither initiated nor regulated by somatosensory input.

Of course, other important roles for sensory input are not excluded by this conclusion. The mammalian fetus is certainly responsive to chemical (gustatory-olfactory), tactile, and auditory stimuli (Carmichael, 1970; Hooker, 1952; Humphrey, 1964, 1969; Robinson & Smotherman, 1992), and it can retain prenatal experiences into postnatal life (Robinson & Smotherman, 1992). Sensory input can have organizational effects on neuromotor development that are independent of regulatory effects. For example, bilateral deafferentation of fetal forelimbs as early as the end of the second trimester of gestation eliminates postnatal prehensile abilities in monkeys (Taub, 1976). However, the same procedure performed on neonatal monkeys does not result in permanent loss of prehensile abilities. Therefore, somatosensory input may be important for the organization of neuromotor patterns essential for certain postnatal motor skills, even though the input may not regulate the spontaneous prenatal behavior of humans.

Descending Control and Spontaneous Prenatal Behavior

The mammalian fetus and chick embryo continue to produce qualitatively normal behavior when the spinal cord is surgically separated from the brain (Stelzner, 1986). Leg movements in spinal chick embryos appear normal between 4 and 19 days of incubation, although some quantitative differences occur (i.e., they have shorter activity periods after 10 days of incubation than do normal embryos). Oppenheim (1975) interpreted the quantitative differences as indicating that a **descending pathway** modulates the activity circuits in the spinal cord, producing longer periods each time the circuit is active. This would have the effect of extending the activity period.

Descending control develops in a **rostral** to **caudal** direction within the spinal cord and from a caudal to rostral direction within the brain (Stelzner, 1986). That is, descending input from the forebrain appears later than input from the midbrain, and input to the forelimbs occurs earlier than input to the hindlimbs. Midthoracic spinal transection performed in the first few days after birth has no apparent effect on the hindlimb movements of rat pups, although the same procedure is severely disruptive when performed after about two weeks of age. Neonatally transected animals continue to develop into adulthood, and they exhibit coordinated locomotion. However, if neonates have only half of the spinal cord transected so that descending control to the lumbar region develops on one side but not the other, movements involving the hindlimbs are greatly impaired. This suggests that connections intrinsic to the lumbar spinal cord continue to develop in neonates at the same time that descending control is integrated into the system. A functional spinal cord can be organized with or without the descending input, but this organization will be different in the two instances, even though both support coordinated locomotion (Stelzner, 1986).

Midbrain and forebrain lesions indicate that the midbrain circuits are involved in organizing the hatching behavior of chicks, whereas the forebrain is involved in triggering the onset of hatching (Oppenheim, 1972). In all birds and mammals that have been studied, the decrease in spontaneous activity normally seen toward the end of incubation or gestation is at least partly the result of supraspinal inhibition (Bekoff, 1981b).

Inhibition and Spontaneous Prenatal Behavior

Behaviorally relevant inhibitory mechanisms appear very early in all vertebrate embryos. They may be responsible for regulating the periodic or rhythmic nature of spontaneous activity as well as for the coordination manifested within and between joints and limbs. The presence of these mechanisms led to idea that new patterns of behavior can be explained by changes in inhibition. However, pharmacological antagonists of inhibitory neurotransmitters result in uncoordinated behavior, but do not produce new patterns of coordination. For this and other reasons, it is unlikely that supraspinal inhibition produces appropriately coordinated postembryonic behavior either by selectively inhibiting particular preexisting circuits or by gradual withdrawal of inhibition from previously constructed circuits to reveal progressively more coordinated behaviors. Instead, it is likely that new circuitry is constructed with development (Bekoff, 1981b)

Drawing on the admittedly limited research on other animals, we might propose that human prenatal activity is well coordinated. Intrajoint coordination appears first, followed by interjoint coordination within limbs, and coordination between limbs. The coordination between homologous limbs (leg with leg, arm with arm) occurs earlier than the coordination between homolateral limbs (right leg with right arm, left leg with left arm). In addition, limb movements are coordinated to torso and head movements very early in gestation (Bekoff, 1981b; de Vries et al., 1984; Prechtl, 1986).

Human fetal activity is primarily organized and activated by spinal and lower brain stem circuits that may be modulated in activity by supraspinal systems. However, supraspinal mechanisms may play more of an integral role in those behavioral transitions that are preparatory to birth. Inhibitory mechanisms always play a role in the expression of fetal activity, but supraspinal inhibition does *not* prevent the premature expression of postnatal patterns of neuromotor organization. Furthermore, there does not seem to be a gradual decrease in inhibition that can account for the temporal pattern of emergence of postnatal behavior (Prechtl, 1982).

Significance of Spontaneous Fetal Activity

Three general hypotheses have been advanced to explain why fetuses exhibit spontaneous patterns of activity (Hall & Oppenheim, 1987; Oppenheim, 1981a, 1981b; Smotherman & Robinson, 1988, 1990). One of these is that the activity serves no developmental role, but is merely an epiphenomenon of nervous system development. A second is that the activity serves no role for the fetus, but is important preparation for the development of postnatal behavior. The third is that the activity is an ontogenetic adaptation to fetal life.

Fetal Activity as an Epiphenomenon

Fetal activity may be an overt manifestation of neural maturation with no intrinsic significance to the organism, although it can be useful to researchers as an indicator of morphological development. It is frequently observed in developmental biology that a system becomes functional before it is necessary. For example, human preterm infants have the capacity for pulmonary respiration and sight long before these functions are relevant to survival. Spontaneous fetal movements may be another example of this forward reference, with no developmental role of their own.

Experimental efforts to address this hypothesis by using drugs to prevent movement are provocative, but limited. When the onset of movement was delayed for 36 hours in salamander larvae, normal swimming was not prevented, although some transient deficits were detected (Oppenheim & Haverkamp, 1986). Similarly, some apparently normally motor patterns occur in young chick embryos that previously had their movement blocked. Therefore, earlier motor activity is not essential for some aspects of motor development to occur. However, these studies were limited to motor patterns that are rather simple in form and that rely on slow, rhythmical cycles of motor activity (Bekoff, 1992). Furthermore, it is not possible for normal joint or muscle development to occur in chick embryos that sustain extended immobilization (Drachman & Sokoloff, 1966). This points to an important role for movement in morphological development, but restricts the usefulness of motoric deprivation as a method for asking questions about motor behavior (Provine, 1986).

Of course, systems that develop in advance of their use may undergo further development once in place. This further development is usually dependent on their function, and may be rather extensive. Even the swimming pattern of amphibian larvae may improve with practice. Other kinds of continued development are often difficult to detect, as they involve the incorporation of previously developed elements into new patterns that differ qualitatively from the old (Bekoff, 1992; Fentress, 1991, 1992).

Fetal Activity as Preparation for Postnatal Behavior

The exercise of specific motor units or combinations of motor units over time facilitates their expression and coordination in postnatal conditions. For example, frequent contiguous head-hand activity and thumb-mouth-sucking activity may facilitate the postnatal coordination of these activities into self-comforting patterns during distress. Episodic spontaneous breathing may be important for adequate differentiation of lung tissue and perhaps for achieving correct innervation of intercostal muscles. In the rat, aberrant connections of intercostal nerves with "wrong" segments of the muscles are eliminated during fetal development after the onset of nonfunctional fetal breathing (Dennis & Harris, 1979).

Prenatal activity may provide sensory experience relevant to the molding of postnatal behavior. The neonate's posture represents a pattern organized in part by the intrauterine constraints on posture during the last months of gestation (Casaer, 1979). Prechtl (1965) found that the leg withdrawal reflex and the spontaneous flexed posture of the legs in neonates are reversed in neonates delivered in a frank breech presentation. Other breech presentations, without leg extension, did not result in reversed neonatal motor patterns. In addition, the directional preference of neonatal supine head orientation seems to be affected by intrauterine position (Michel & Goodwin, 1979; Michel, 1983).

Fetal immobilization studies are even more limited in mammals than in birds because immobilization can be produced only for a relatively short period and does not affect neural activity (Provine, 1988). Nevertheless, the studies that have been done have not demonstrated any obvious effect on postnatal behavioral organization. The role of fetal activity as preparation for postnatal behavior must be considered as unknown.

Fetal Activity as Ontogenetic Adaptation

Movements in fish and amphibian embryos aid respiration. The repeated flow of amniotic fluids in and out of the lungs in response to embryonic movement is also important for lung and respiratory development in mammals. In avian embryos, movement is essential for the formation of joints between bones, for attaining the appropriate position for hatching, and for stimulating parental interactions with the eggs. In rats, swallowing amniotic fluids may serve both to produce appropriate adjustments in the intrauterine environment by decreasing the volume and increasing the viscosity of fluid as the embryo increases in size, and to incorporate important nutrients, hormones, and immune factors. These movements may also set the stage for the transition to suckling and ingestion of milk in mammals. The flow of fluids over taste and olfactory receptors provides chemical stimuli that may play an important role in identifying food and its source on the mother's body (Smotherman & Robinson, 1988).

Rats were exposed to specific odors during the last few days of gestation by injecting a tasteless odor, citral, into the amniotic fluid (Pedersen & Blass, 1981). If exposed to this same odor postnatally, while having the skin stroked in a manner similar to maternal handling and licking, the pups suckled from citral-scented nipples. Pups that did not have the intrauterine experience avoided the scented nipples. Rat pups require particular familiar odors before they will suckle, and they apparently acquire the initial familiarity prenatally. Under natural conditions, the odors on the mother's nipples have elements in common with odors in amniotic fluid.

In general, spontaneous neuromuscular activity is important for normal differentiation of muscle, for preventing muscular atrophy, and for normal development of joints in limbs (Drachman & Sokoloff, 1966; Oppenheim, Pittman, Gray, & Maderdrut, 1978). In humans, joint development can be normal in infants with spina bifida or fetal paralysis (Casaer, 1992). However, achieving the vertex (head down) presentation of the human fetus before delivery may require particular activities, such as stepping and crawling movements. Also, changes in the mother's psychological and, perhaps, physiological condition occur with the onset and progression of quickening. As yet, however, the ontogenetic adaptation for human fetal activity remains undemonstrated.

Continuing Questions

Although human fetal activity is complexly organized with interesting developmental changes in its patterns, its significance is unknown. The details of the circuit formation and of the development of the longitudinal, integrating neural pathways that are obviously involved in the spinal coordination of these activities are also unknown. We do not know when, how, or even if specific brain parts are important for the emergence of specific prenatal activity patterns. In fact, little is actually known about the normal sequence of intrauterine behavioral events. Therefore, it is not too surprising that the significance of fetal activity eludes us. With technological advances in noninvasive monitoring of fetal development, and with more investigations concerned with exploring both the ontogenetic adaptiveness as well as the developmental preparatory character of fetal activity, we can expect our current ignorance to be replaced by more sophisticated levels of ignorance.

One of the challenges to finding a relationship between prenatal and neonatal behavior is that differences between the two environments may be responsible for qualitative differences in behavior. This can create the impression that embryos and neonates are more different than they are. One of the most striking differences between prenatal and postnatal environments is the amount of space available for movement. The effect of confinement in a restricted space has been studied in two ways: by placing rat embryos into a bath outside the uterus and its layers of membranes, and by placing hatched chicks into a glass egg.

Beginning on day 17 of gestation, rat fetuses show the least amount of movement if left in the uterus; intermediate amounts of movement if removed from the uterus into a warm saline bath, but left in the amnion; and the most movement if removed from the amniotic membranes. Furthermore, more complex movements are performed in the less restricting conditions (Smotherman & Robinson, 1988). It is unknown whether these contextual differences in rat fetal movements result from differences in global stimulation from the restricting membranes, or from some more specific stimulus associated with them (see box 7.1). The latter possibility is suggested by studies in chicks.

During hatching, chicks have characteristic behavior patterns, including a hatching vocalization, rotation, head movements that strike the beak against the shell, and synchronous extensions and flexions of their legs. These behaviors can be reinstated well after hatching by placing the chick into the confined, tucked, hatching posture (Hamburger & Oppenheim, 1967). This involves a specific type of sensory input that can be achieved by bending the neck to one side or the other and restraining it (Bekoff, 1992; Bekoff & Kauer, 1982). Other types of restraints or sensory inputs are not effective, and local anesthesia applied to the neck region, but not to the thigh, stops the synchronized leg movements. In normal hatching conditions, the typical tucked posture provides the appropriate sensory input. Successful hatching frees the neck, and consequently the behavior ceases. The underlying motor circuitry remains in place, but the specificity of the stimuli required for the behavior makes it unlikely that it will be used at any time other than at hatching.

Ontogenetic changes in context can also arise from changes within the developing organism. For example, the metamorphosis of tadpoles involves morpological changes that can support transitions in behavior through purely mechanical routes. The presence of newly formed forelimbs can make undulatory swimming more difficult, by increasing drag, for example, and the degenerating tail can make pedal locomotion easier by getting rid of dead weight. However, these bodily changes can also support behavioral transitions through a neural route. This was demonstrated by removing the tail before metamorphosis was complete and measuring effects on stepping behavior in response to light touch (Stehouwer, 1986, 1991). When removed at stage XIV, there was no difference between intact tadpoles and those with amputated tails: neither performed stepping. However, if removed at stage XVII (still eight stages before metamorphosis is complete), the amputated tadpoles displayed stepping behavior and the intact ones did not. The change in sensory input from the loss of the tail led to an immediate shift in neural control so that stepping was expressed. However, this shift was possible only when the neural circuitry had achieved some necessary organization.

In sum, the research on behavioral embryology demonstrates that many aspects of behavioral development have their origin in embryological behavioral and experiential events.

Features of Neonatal Neurobehavioral Organization

Traditionally, neonatal behavior was considered to be heterogeneous, uncoordinated, and primarily reactive to simple stimuli. As with fetal activity, however, observation of spontaneous behavior revealed patterns of action involving all or several body parts, usually coordinated with the postural position of the neonate (Butterworth & Hopkins, 1988; Hopkins et al., 1987). Neonates adopt a limited number of different postures when supine, prone, seated, or carried. These postures, which reflect in part a continuation of the patterns of behavioral organization in utero, affect motoric interactions with objects and caregivers.

Although neonates can be induced to perform reflexlike behavior under specific conditions, these conditions of assessment are rather different from the conditions under which the behaviors typically are expressed (Prechtl, 1983). When the reflexlike patterns occur in conditions of self- and social stimulation, they are more variable in form and more coordinated with other actions. For example, during typical nursing, rooting, sucking, swallowing, and breathing become interdependent responses rather than independent reflexes. They also seem to be coordinated to alterations in posture, muscle tonus, and changes in state in very specific ways (Prechtl, 1983). Thus, spontaneous neonatal behavior is coordinated, and it is well organized for the conditions of early postnatal life.

Prechtl (1982, 1983, 1984, 1986) maintained that reflexes play only a minor role in the organization of neonatal behavior. Contrary to an earlier idea, behavioral development is not equivalent to the progressive inhibition of reflexes by cortical mechanisms. Although the earlier idea was supported by the observation that cortically damaged adults exhibit reflexive behavior, this behavior is qualitatively different from that of neonates (Prechtl, 1982). Neonatal behavior is neither reflexive nor random. It is coordinated, and this coordination represents the pattern of organization and functioning of the neonatal nervous system.

As the infant develops, later-developing neural structures become integrated into the existing neural organization, with the result that new patterns of function become possible. Neural development during this stage is more accurately described as an integrated, patterned reorganization, than as the addition of layers of cerebral control over intact circuits and reflexes that were previously developed in the brain stem and spinal cord. Of course, cerebral neural systems do become more and more integrated with brain stem and spinal systems during development. However, this involves reorganization of circuits, not simple suppression or inhibition of primitive reflexes.

One prevalent characteristic of the neonate's behavior is an asymmetrical posture that includes a preferred direction of head orientation (Michel, 1983; Turkewitz, 1977). This preference influences limb movements. For example, when placed supine, the neonate will turn the head to one side (the right more often than the left, for most infants). The arm and leg on the side to which the face is turned are likely to be extended, whereas the other arm and leg are likely to be flexed. The face-side arm is more active than the other in both its range and frequency of movement. During the first few weeks, the face-side hand will be fisted more often than the other, and later the fingers will be more active.

Placing a neonate in a semiinclined infant seat will elicit behaviors similar to those exhibited when supine. Any orientation of the head to the direction of a sound or visual stimulus will increase the likelihood of arm movements such that the hand often will be positioned into the same spatial vector as that of the object of attention for the head/eye. The specific character of this coordination demonstrates that these are not incomplete or poorly controlled reaching actions (Michel, 1987); however, they may be the patterns of coordination from which prereaching behaviors emerge.

Additional examples of the systematic nature of spontaneous neonatal behavior have been and will continue to be discovered. However, it is clear that neonatal reflexes are not independent components of a primitive nervous system that either must be suppressed or orchestrated into functional sets or systems during development. They already operate in functional systems. The so-called reflexes are an important element in the organization of spontaneous behavior in neonates, but they are not stereotyped, inflexible modules. They are aspects of the modulating or biasing mechanisms that affect the relative probabilities of specific postures and movements. As in adults, the units of motor action in neonates are postures and movements, not reflexes.

The Role of Descending Control

The movements of the human neonate may entail cortical participation. The inner cell layers of the sensory and motor cortical areas are well developed at birth. Electrophysiological evidence suggests that the cortex may modulate and regulate neonatal movements through processes of both selective inhibition and activation (Schulte, 1974). Although descending motor pathways are present at birth, they continue to expand and refine their connections with spinal interneurons and motor neurons throughout the first year.

The corticospinal pathway that creates the pyramidal tracts is the descending motor control system that exhibits the greatest postnatal development (Stanfield, 1992). As this system develops, many of the cortical neurons that contribute their fibers to the pyramidal tracts, project directly to those motor neurons that control the muscles of the hand and fingers. These cortical neurons are the corticomotoneuronal cells. In chimpanzees and humans, the motor neurons controlling the muscles of the shoulder and arm receive innervation from corticomotoneuronal cells as well.

In newborn monkeys, the direct corticomotoneuronal connections are not present, but they gradually appear during the six to eight months after birth (Lawrence & Hopkins, 1976). Paralleling their appearance in monkeys is the development of relatively independent finger movement and precision grasping. Bilateral lesions of this pathway in adults produce monkeys that cannot execute either the independent finger movement of precision grasping or abduction-adduction of the wrist (Lawrence & Kuypers, 1968). Therefore, the corticospinal system that connects the cortex with spinal motor neurons subserves highly sophisticated modes of motor control.

The development of precision grasping in human infants is not simply a matter of developing the corticomotorneuronal connections. Several descending brain stem pathways also distribute fibers to the same motor neurons (Kuypers, 1982). Unlike the fibers that descend from the cortex, these fibers usually extend collateral branches and form synapses with several motor neurons and several spinal interneurons. Thus, a motor neuron receives input from several spinal interneurons, several brain stem fibers, and corticospinal fibers projecting from many different places in the cortex. The activity of a motor neuron is determined by the patterned relation of the input from these various pathways. The cortex can exert a powerful influence on the motor neuron through its corticomotoneuronal fiber system, but this influence is always relative to the level of development and pattern of activation of other descending systems.

The programmatic work of Kuypers (1982) and his colleagues showed that some brain stem pathways act as "gain-setting" systems that determine the overall responsiveness of motor neurons and interneurons to the influence of descending and interneuron input. Other brain stem systems seem to be involved in the coordinated control of the body as a whole and the integration of limb-body movement and the synergistic movements of a whole limb. Still other descending systems provide for the capacity to execute independent movements of individual limbs, especially their distal parts. The corticospinal system amplifies and modulates all of these functions and enables the independent control of the individual muscle action that is involved in the fine control of movement. Of course, all of these systems continue their developmental control of spinal systems after birth.

Therefore, changes in the behaviors of the infant do not signal the maturation of a specific descending system. Rather, they mark developmental changes in the relative influence of each of the descending systems on spinal mechanisms. Moreover, during the first year many cortico-striatal-cerebellar-thalamic-brain stem-cortical connections are formed and expanded. These provide a network of loops, or circuits, involving the cortex, basal ganglia, cerebellum, thalamus, vestibular system, and other elements, that function in the coordination of fine movements and skilled motor acts. The complexity of this network continues to expand during development, belying any simple reduction of developmental changes in behavioral competence to changes in the status of the nervous system. Consequently, although much is now known about the sequence of postnatal behavioral events, knowledge about the details of circuit formation, the development of integrating pathways, and the specific brain areas that are involved in the emergence of behavior has not progressed much farther than for embryonic behavior.

Significance of Spontaneous Neonatal Activity

Just as for fetal activity, three hypotheses have been advanced with respect to neonatal activity. It may be epiphenomenal, with no significance of its own; it may prepare the organism for postnatal life; or it may be an ontogenetic adaptation to the neonatal habitat.

Neonatal Activity as an Epiphenomenon

One possibility is that neonatal activity is simply a reflection of the current level of neural development. Indeed, it was theorized that human behavior in the first two months after birth is nothing more than the continuation of prenatal patterns, altered by the changes in such physical constraints as the pull of gravity in the new terrestrial medium (Prechtl, 1983, 1984, 1986). Prechtl proposed that the human infant is born too soon, and that real postnatal neurobehavioral development does not begin until some three months postpartum.

The difficulty of ruling out the epiphenomenal argument is illustrated by the spontaneous arm movements of the newborn human. These movements may result in contact of the hand with the head, face, or mouth. It is known that older infants employ hand-to-mouth movements for self-regulation of state. After the emergence of prehension, moreover, hand-to-mouth movements become components of actions used to manipulate objects. It is possible that these movements are a form of tactile self-exploration, and that mouthing objects provides information about their properties. Therefore, it might be supposed that the hand-to-mouth pattern is either an ontogenetic adaptation for self-soothing, or a precursor for the subsequent development of more functional hand-to-mouth activity.

These hypotheses face difficulties, however. Hand-to-mouth is a rather infrequent activity of neonates (Blass et al., 1989). A number of studies showed that a specific set of constraints is necessary to increase the likelihood that spontaneous hand movements of the neonate coalesce into the hand-to-mouth pattern (Butterworth & Hopkins, 1988; Schwartz & Michel, 1992). Among these are a distinct asymmetrical posture that includes a particular directional orientation for the head, and this head orientation induces more frequent flexion of the arm on the face side. Some of these flexions result in contact with the mouth when the mouth is open. Since hand-in-mouth is a frequent prenatal pattern, the rudimentary, neonatal movement could derive from prenatal experience and depend on proprioceptive information for its organization. Finally, Blass et al. (1989) found that hand-to-mouth was not related to states of distress in neonates, and therefore does not appear to be an ontogenetic adaptation. Rather, it is likely that it is an epiphenomenon of the effects of posture on arm movements.

Neonatal Activity as Preparation

It is a cardinal rule of developmental psychology that early sensorimotor experience forms the basis for later abilities. However, surprisingly little evidence demonstrates the contributions of neonatal activity to later behavior. Indeed, assessment of neonatal reflex performance is a disappointing predictor of later functioning. Exercise of the neonatal stepping response pattern facilitates the development of walking (Zelazo, 1983). Indeed, some cultures typically employ such techniques to engender motoric precocity (Super, 1976).

However, adult-controlled exercise of neonatal stepping patterns is a relatively unusual event. Under normal conditions, stepping disappears rather early from the infant's behavioral repertoire. Therefore, the contribution that it normally might make to the development of walking is unclear.

Detailed analyses of the coordination of leg movements in neonatal stepping, neonatal supine kicking, and infant walking (Thelen & Cooke, 1987) show that the same fundamental pattern is present in all three. Therefore, stepping during spontaneous rhythmical kicking of a neonate may be a self-generated exercise for the natural facilitation of infant walking. Of course, it remains to be demonstrated that interfering with neonatal kicking delays the onset of walking.

There is little doubt that eye-hand coordination in accurate reaching depends on visual experience of the hands (Jeannerod, 1988). This experience may be provided by the spontaneous neonatal behaviors that bring the movements of the hands into the visual field. Certainly, the right-sided bias in head orientation preference of neonates sets a lateral bias to both hand visualization and the action patterns of the hand.

This lateral bias in sensorimotor experience of the hands among neonates predicts subsequent hand-use preferences in reaching for and manipulating objects during the age period 6 to 18 months (Michel, 1991a). A hand-use preference in turn affects the infant's ability to solve simple sensorimotor problems, such as how to coordinate two-handed reaching for a desired object when the trajectory of one hand is slightly impeded by a small barrier. Because infants seem not to transfer certain haptic experiences between the

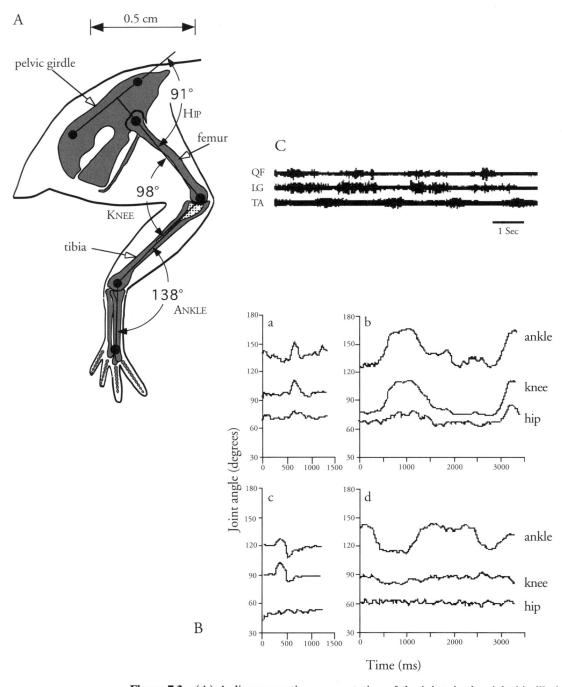

Figure 7.3 (A) A diagrammatic representation of the joints in the right hindlimb of a chick embryo. (B) Changes in the angles of the ankle, knee, and hip joints as a function of time in examples of different movement patterns observed in 9- to 10-day-old chick embryos. (C) Embryonic motility of 9-day-old embryos as measured by electromyographic recordings from three muscles in the right leg: a knee extensor,

hemispheres before 10 to 12 months postpartum, the sensorimotor skills that are created during play can be restricted to the hemisphere that is contralateral to the playing (preferred) hand. Thus, the spontaneous behavior of neonates both reflects and contributes to the development of neurobehavioral organization during infancy.

Neonatal Activity as Ontogenetic Adaptations

Mammalian young will survive and grow only if they elicit the proper nursing repertoire from the caregiver. Therefore, it has been argued that the behavioral repertoire of mammalian young evolved to ensure proper caregiving from parents and may not contribute directly to later development (Galef, 1981). During nursing, the complex coordination of crying, rooting, sucking, swallowing, and breathing facilitates ingestion of nutrients. However, these patterns may not play any role in the developmental organization of subsequent ingestive behavior. For example, infant rats fed through cannulas and deprived of suckling exhibit no disturbances in making the transition to independent ingestion, or in later-appearing behavior patterns (Hall & Williams, 1983). It is conceivable, then, that many of the behaviors of neonates are required for immediate conditions and are not preparations for later development. In this sense, the organization of the neonate's nervous system may be viewed as an entity with its own properties. Assessment of these properties may reveal disturbances that can affect neonatal survival but may reveal little about later functioning.

Similarly, Thelen and Fisher (1982) reported the presence of many different stereotypies in the behavior of infants that seem to disappear in childhood. It is conceivable that these stereotypies reflect ontogenetic adaptations to the conditions of infancy, and hence the neural organization underlying their expression does not contribute to the neural organization of later development.

On the other hand, discontinuous behavioral patterns may share some of the same neural bases (figure 7.3). For example, the movements of the chick's legs during hatching appear quite distinct from their movement during posthatching walking. Nevertheless, the neural circuits regulating these different movements are apparently the same (Bekoff, 1981a, 1992; Bekoff et al., 1987). Similarly, the neural circuits that are developed for effective performance during nursing may contribute to the development of behavioral events that are phenomenologically quite different from nursing. The same is possible for the neural underpinnings of stereotypies that disappear after infancy.

quadriceps femoris (QF); an ankle extensor, lateral gastrocnemius (LG); and an ankle flexor, tibialis anterior (TA) (A and B redrawn from Watson & Bekoff, 1990; C redrawn from Bekoff, 1988).

Robinson and Smotherman (1992) point out another class of transient developmental conditions that are not ontogenetic adaptations. Often in embryological development, anatomical structures appear and then disappear. However, when they are present they do not subserve the adaptation of the embryo to its environmental conditions. Nor are they simply epiphenomena. Rather, they subserve important developmental processes.

For example, early in human fetal development, a set of cells forms in the brain and migrates to a midline position to form a bridge by which axons from neurons in the right and left halves of the cortex may cross to make connections with neurons in the opposite half. These axons make up the corpus callosum, and they enable levels of neural coordination underlying certain psychological abilities. The bridge cells are only present for a short time during fetal development. If anything delays axonal growth, or bridge cell formation or migration, the corpus callosum does not develop. Thus the bridge cells act as "scaffolding" in that when they are present at the right place and at the right time, they enable development to proceed. However, once their developmental function has been achieved, they disappear.

Robinson and Smotherman (1992) believe that the metaphor of scaffolding is appropriate for understanding the disappearance of certain behaviors during development, and may reveal important processes in behavioral development. They note that the chronology of movement synchrony in the fetal development of rats provides evidence of scaffolding. Initially, movement synchrony is produced by the random association of simple movements. Then, specific patterns of coordination appear, disappear, and are replaced by more sophisticated patterns. The transient pattern of coordination served no function other than to be used in the organization of the more sophisticated pattern. Golani and Fentress (1985) reported similar transient patterns in the postnatal development of facial grooming patterns in mice that enabled the emergence of more sophisticated patterns. Therefore, transient behavioral events in neonates may reflect ontogenetic adaptations or scaffolding processes contributing to the further development of behavior.

Clinical Implications

If the nervous system of the neonate is conceived of as an intricate system subserving biologically relevant functions, the prenatal-neonatal continuum and the neonatal-infant transition must be reconceptualized (Prechtl, 1981). This reconceptualization will have implications for clinical practice as well as for basic research and theory. For example, the choice of behaviors during clinical evaluations of the condition of the neonatal nervous system will change. Assessment of the neonate's spontaneous behavioral repertoire holds greater promise for revealing the state of the nervous system than does the examination of reflexive behavior.

If neural development involves not only preparation for later phases but ontogenetic adaptations, peculiarities observed at early ages may not be predictive of peculiarities of later ages. However, early signs may have important consequences for immediate functioning, especially for social interaction. Therefore, their diagnostic value for infants may be similar to that for adults; that is, they are not diagnostic for long-term consequences, but for immediate, continuing functions.

Finally, we might conclude that the growing nervous system responds differently to damage than the adult system (Kolb & Whishaw, 1989). These differences are not just a matter of differential plasticity. Rather, the response to early damage may be the establishment of incorrect neural connections by compensatory axonal branching, dendritic sprouting, and unusual synapse formation on appropriate neurons, as well as synapse formation on inappropriate neurons. Brain damage during development does not simply result in the loss of tissue. It involves changes in the functional and structural organization of the remaining tissue. Within limits, a new brain is formed, intact but different, possessing a different functional repertoire (Prechtl, 1982). Thus, developmental neurobiology requires concepts and principles derived from information provided by investigations of the developing, not the adult, brain. Behavioral embryology and developmental psychobiology will be major sources of that information.

Sources of Embryonic Experience

Sensory systems develop in a sequence that is common to all vertebrates (Gottlieb, 1971). Birth or hatching occurs at different points in this sequence for different species, but most systems are functional prenatally. In the altricial rat, for example, olfaction, taste, and thermal, tactile, and vestibular sensitivity are all present before birth (Alberts, 1984). The movement of the mother and her internal organs, the movements of the fetuses themselves and of their siblings, and the chemicals carried in the fluids that bathe the fetuses together make the intrauterine environment a stimulating place (Alberts & Cramer, 1988). The same is true for other species, although the type of stimulation differs, as do modalities that are available to receive it. In humans, all the sensory systems achieve functional status before birth. There is no evidence that sufficient light reaches the fetus to play a significant role, but sounds do. Some relevant auditory stimuli originate from the external environment, but the mother is a particularly rich source of these stimuli in the movements of her internal organs and her voice (box 7.2).

We gave many examples of prenatal influences of naturally occurring stimulation in earlier chapters. Recall, for example, the auditory communication that takes place between laughing gull parents and their unhatched chicks, and the importance of prenatal auditory input from the duckling

Box 7.2   Auditory Experience of the Fetus

Examination of the auditory environment of the womb reveals that hearing the mother's voice is a prominent and common experience. Ambient voice sounds are progressively attenuated by transmission through maternal tissue and amniotic fluid, but the mother's voice readily penetrates. It can be demonstrated that the fetus is responsive to the mother's voice and other sounds in the extramaternal environment. However, unlike other sounds, the mother's voice is accompanied by kinesthetic and tactile stimulation to the fetus from the muscle movement of the diaphragm as the mother speaks. Thus, the mother's speech provides the fetus with auditory experience that is correlated with vestibular and tactile stimulation.

Prosody is the most common feature of the maternal speech that the fetus is likely to experience. Prosodic characteristics of speech are attended to by very young infants and may account for the ability of two-day-olds to recognize the mother's voice. Moreover, prosody carries information about emotional state. Attention to prosody may be important in the development of emotional sensitivity. The repeated prenatal exposure to auditory experience may account for the positive value that neonates attach to a story that their mother read prenatally, a melody that she sang prenatally, and the sound of her voice. The auditory system of the fetus is exposed to many kinds of maternally generated sounds, including low-frequency digestive sounds (borborygmi). Thus, the mother provides the fetus with a relatively rich auditory environment that may provide the experiences that are very important for the manifestation of many of the neonate's cognitive, social, and emotional abilities (Fifer & Moon, 1988).

Very young infants, like adults, discriminate categorically the various stop consonants of speech, such as [d] and [t], even though the differentiating acoustic signals vary on a continuum. Some consider this ability, which is vital to speech comprehension, too complex to arise from prenatal or postnatal experience and interpret categorical perception of speech sounts among infants as evidence for innate neural mechanisms tuned to the acoustic features of speech (Lieberman, 1984). However, Seebach, Intrator, Lieberman, and Cooper (1994) used as unsupervised neural network computer program to demonstrate how such categorical discrimination can arise from prenatal auditory experience. They exposed the program to natural speech sounds that were altered to match both the kinds of stimuli available to fetuses and the processing constraints of the fetal auditory system. The program acquired categorical perception of speech sounds from the source language, English. Furthermore, it could use its categorical perception to detect and discriminate Hindi stop consonants, even though the requisite acoustic signals occur only occasionally in English and are not used to discriminate English stop consonants. Thus, as with infants, the program exhibited categorical perception of speech sounds not prevalent in the native language. These results reveal one of the ways by which prenatal auditory experience can become a source for the initial development of language skills.

mother, siblings, and self on the development of posthatching species recognition. Stimulation that is transduced through the sensory systems can have an effect on the developing young in several different ways. Just as is true for adults, it may elicit and guide embryonic behavior. It may also play an important role in further constructing the sensory system by which it is transduced. Over the past three decades an extensive literature has been generated on sensory capacities that require sensory input for their development. Much of this work was conducted on vision (e.g., Hirsch, 1986), but similar stories are found for somatosensation and the chemical senses (Clopton, 1986).

It is well recognized that the capacity for learning is present in embryos. This provides another route by which embryonic sensory input can affect behavior. Rat fetuses, for example, form both positive and negative conditioned associations to chemical stimuli (Smotherman & Robinson, 1988). Finally, sensory input can affect the development of parts of the nervous system other than the sensory systems that are directly activated by the input. The development of motor systems, for example, may be affected by sensory input. The possibility that sensory input can play a constructive role in functionally discontinuous parts of the nervous system raises the interesting possibility that early-developing sensory systems may be the foundation for later-developing systems (Turkewitz & Kenny, 1982). The invariant sequence in which the sensory systems develop is consistent with this possibility.

One fruitful direction for future work is suggested by the observation that embryonic environments have features that are both salient to the developing organism and reliable in their occurrence. In combination with the orderly sequence with which sensory systems become functional, these environmental features may account for some of the universality of development within a species (chapter 5), as well as for some individual differences (box 7.3, figure 7.4).

Continuity and Qualitative Change

As important as the concept of ontogenetic adaptations is to behavioral embryology, it is necessary to recognize that developmental events may seem quite unrelated when described in one way, but with a change in the mode of description, a relationship becomes evident. The metamorphosis of tadpole to frog is so striking that it is often used to symbolize qualitative change in development. Nevertheless, continuities in neural patterns underlying locomotion are present, although the swimming of tadpoles and the terrestrial locomotion of frogs are very different behaviorally (Stehouwer, 1991). Similarly, the temporal and spatial patterns of movement in early

Box 7.3   Prenatal Vestibular Experience and Hemispheric Specialization of Function

The left and right hemispheres of the human brain are specialized to perform somewhat different psychological functions. This asymmetrical functioning of the left and right halves of the forebrain achieve final status early in the school years. Several neonatal postural, manual, and auditory asymmetries may provide experiences that contribute to the development of hemispheric specialization (Michel, 1987), but what is the developmental source of these neonatal asymmetries?

Previc (1991) provided a provocative account of the role of prenatal vestibular experience in the development of the neonatal postural asymmetries. Although fetal position varies throughout pregnancy, the asymmetrical character of the human uterus in combination with the specific gravity of the fetus create conditions that result in one position being more probable than any other (i.e., inverted fetus with the back to mother's left side). As a consequence of this predominant position, the typical forward motion of an active mother will provide an asymmetrical vestibular experience for the fetus. Since humans, unlike other primates, move around in an upright posture, and since the fetus typically is oriented in one way, the mother's forward movements are differentially registered by the left and right otolith organs (a vestibular apparatus) of the fetus (figure 7.4).

The lateral asymmetry in stimulation can result in the left otolith organ being more sensitive than the right. Since the left otolith organ projects to the right hemisphere, it provides that hemisphere with a different pattern of activation than the left hemisphere. Moreover, activation of the left organ results in motoric activation of the muscles that turn the head to the right and curve the trunk to the right. Thus, asymmetries in prenatal activation of the left and right sides of the vestibular system (induced by the combination of the mother's upright posture and forward mode of locomotion, and the fetus's asymmetrical orientation in the uterus) can promote vestibular asymmetries in sensitivity to postnatal gravitational and other influences. Such differential sensitivity, in turn, contributes to the manifestation of asymmetries of neonatal posture that contribute to the development of asymmetries in infant hand use.

The vestibular system is one of the earliest sensory systems to develop and appears to be quite active during fetal development. However, previous to Previc's analysis, there was no intuitive connection between its development and hemispheric specialization. Subsequent to Previc's analysis of factors affecting prenatal development of the vestibular system, it has become possible to examine other factors that may contribute to the development of hemispheric specialization. For example, Previc notes that there seems to be more noradrenergic and serotonergic innervation of the right hemisphere and more dopaminergic and cholinergic innervation of the left hemisphere. There is extensive otolith organ input to the locus coeruleus and the raphe nucleus. Thus asymmetries in activation of these structures by vestibular inputs could be responsible for the asymmetries in these major neurotransmitters and the activation of these midbrain structures.

The experiential factors that contribute to the development of various psychological abilities often bear little intuitive connection to those abilities. Consequently, the connections between experiential events and the development of psychological abilities will have to be discovered by ingenious experiments prompted by broad knowledge of the research on other animals.

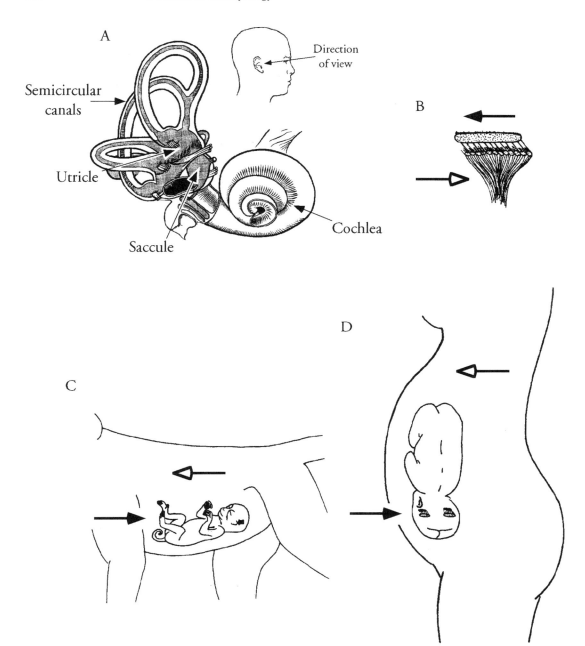

Figure 7.4 (A) Labyrinth anatomy, indicating locations of the otolith organs, the utricle and the saccule. (B) A schematic representation of shearing forces on the otoliths (solid arrow) in relation to direction of movement (open arrow). (C) and (D) Vestibular stimulation during embryonic development has a left-right symmetry for most primates, but is asymmetrical for humans because of the posture of the fetus and the upright locomotory posture of the mother (open arrow indicates direction of locomotion and closed arrows indicate shearing forces) (modified from Previc, 1991; see box 7.3).

ontogenetic stages of chicken development have been described by many observers as uncoordinated and disorganized, in contrast to the coordinated behaviors of hatching and walking. Indeed, Hamburger (1970, 1973; Hamburger & Oppenheim, 1967), was so struck by the apparently qualitative differences between the embryonic movement and the coordinated behavior that occurs at later stages that he called the embryonic movement *motility*.

In one description of chick embryos, limbs are seen as moving independent of one another, and the temporal sequence of the movement seems random. However, if a kinematic analysis is employed to examine the pattern with which joints of the same limb move, regular patterns are found in embryos that are continuous with those exhibited by hatchlings. In fact, the neural circuitry underlying the patterns that are kinematically similar before and after hatching is present from the beginnings of embryonic movement (Bekoff, 1988, 1992; Watson & Bekoff, 1990). An important message behind these findings is that two very different conclusions about the nature of development will be reached, depending on the description that is used. When movement is described in one way, development seems discontinuous; described in another way, it seems continuous.

Gottlieb (1976, 1992) suggested that experiential events can have one of three different kinds of influence on organismic development: maintaining, facilitating, and constructive (see chapter 3). It is likely that the choice of which influence is to be applied to a particular pattern of development will depend greatly on the descriptive terms that are used to characterize it. The rules that are used to understand changing patterns in development will also be radically different, depending on the description. Complex rules have to be generated to capture developmental changes in social interactions when these interactions are described in terms of postures, communicative displays, and other movement patterns. However, rather simpler rules can be used to capture these transformations if the focus is placed on relative movements of individuals with respect to each other (Fentress & McLeod, 1986, 1988).

Ontogenetic adaptations may have a functional role during an early stage and also become incorporated into patterns of organization that are adaptive in later stages. As Oppenheim (1981b) noted, these are not mutually exclusive possibilities. Indeed, development is likely to build on whatever raw materials are at hand. There is no logical or biological reason that this developmental recycling of earlier achievements should be compartmentalized into functionally similar categories. This calls for some ingenuity on the part of researchers to hunt for precursors of adult abilities that are not intuitively obvious. It also calls for some caution when adultlike patterns are elicited from embryos or neonates. Similarities need not indicate that the adult neurobehavioral organization is already present, although elements that enter into this organization may be.

For example, neonatal rats can be induced to perform a response that looks like the sexually receptive lordosis assumed by adult females (Williams, 1991). This is achieved by rubbing the flanks of a prone pup to provide artificial tactile stimuli similar to that provided when an adult male mounts a female. The rump elevation and spinal dorsiflexion are similar in both cases, and it is very likely that much of the same neural circuitry is involved. Furthermore, the probability of responding is increased by estrogen treatment in pups, as it is in adults. Despite these similarities, the threshold to respond is high even in hormone-treated pups, and the pups require special circumstances, such as several hours removed from the mother in a warm environment, before they will exhibit the response. However, very similar movements of the legs and rump (perhaps involving much of the same neural circuitry) can be elicited reliably by stroking the perineum of a supine pup, at room temperature and within seconds of removing the pup from its mother (Moore & Chadwick-Dias, 1986).

The response to perineal stimulation can be considered an ontogenetic adaptation, because it is involved in the maternal elicitation of urination and defecation. These processes require tactile stimulation of the perineal skin in neonates. Although they are functionally different, perhaps the neonatal behavior and adult lordosis share some of the same neural elements. The neural control does not seem to be identical, however, as the most effective posture and locus of tactile stimulation are different. Of interest, maternal stimulation of the perineum (and perhaps the pup's response to it) apparently plays no preparatory role for the adult lordosis, but it does contribute to adult masculine sexual behavior, with movements that are very different from lordosis (Moore, 1984, 1992).

Like other mammals, newborn rat pups obtain their food by suckling. Weaning refers to the gradual replacement of this source of food with ingestion of solid food in the manner of adults. Both are ways of obtaining food and, although one gives way to the other in the usual course of ontogeny, they are not mutually exclusive. During a transitional period pups both suck milk from the nipple and eat solid food. This period can be extended artificially by continued permissive behavior on the part of the nursing mothers. When rat mothers nurse their young, they adopt a crouching posture and then fall asleep. Their willingness to crouch declines as the litter grows older. However, if the litter is repeatedly replaced with a younger foster litter, a mother will continue to nurse for an indefinite period (Wiesner & Sheard, 1933). If a single older pup is kept with successive, young, foster litters, it will continue to suckle alongside its perpetually young foster siblings into adulthood (Pfister, Cramer, & Blass, 1986). Once weaned, however, it will not resume nursing when given the opportunity.

Neonatal rats are altricial and cannot chew solid food. They do not ordinarily take food except from the nipple but, with special environmental support, they can be induced to lap milk from puddles. Thus, just as suckling can be extended beyond its usual developmental course through appropriate modifications of the environment, nonsuckling ingestion can be induced prematurely. The two methods of obtaining food differ in their sensory control and their motor patterns (Hall & Williams, 1983). It has also been suggested that they differ in the mechanisms that regulate the amount of intake. Specifically, postingestion feedback from the amount and quality of food that has been eaten is important for regulating adultlike ingestion, but does it regulate suckling?

When milk is provided to young pups either from a cannula that is placed at the back of the tongue, where the tip of the mother's nipple would rest (Hall & Rosenblatt, 1977), or from repeated, hormonally induced ejections of milk from anesthetized dams (Cramer & Blass, 1983), the pups will ingest enough to overdistend their stomachs, stopping only when they are unable to breathe. Findings such as these led to the conclusion that, for pups less than 10 days of age, the amount of food obtained through suckling was controlled primarily by the mother's nursing behavior and the amount of milk she had available. Indeed, pups are attached to the nipple almost continuously whenever the dam is in the nest; however, milk is ejected only periodically. Most suckling behavior involves nonnutritive sucking.

Further attention to the details of sucking led to the discovery that young pups adjust the amount of milk that they extract from a particular milk ejection on the basis of such variables as length of time since last suckling and whether they received a preload of food—provided that the milk was delivered to them at a rate that they could handle. When provided too rapidly, as in earlier studies, the regulation breaks down. In other words, young pups do regulate their intake on the basis of feedback from previous ingestion under natural feeding conditions. This regulation does not alter the probability of attaching to the nipple and sucking, but it does alter the amount of milk that they extract and ingest (Brake, Shair, & Hofer, 1988). Thus suckling exhibits some of the same characteristics as lapping milk and ingesting solid food. Although it is reasonable to conclude that suckling is an ontogenetic adaptation to mammalian lactation, it is not a system that is completely separate from adultlike ingestion.

Rat pups can engage in adultlike ingestion when induced to lap milk throughout the ontogenetic period when suckling is their normal feeding route. The behavior appears similar: ingestion is increased by length of time since last feed and decreased by directly filling the stomach with milk. However, closer examination of the underlying controls indicates important differences between rats examined at 6 days of age and those examined at 15 days (Phifer, Ladd, & Hall, 1991; Hall, 1990).

The relevant internal state for the younger pups to initiate ingestion is dehydration alone; for the older pups, nutritional deficits are also important. This was demonstrated by infusing isotonic saline directly into the stomach.

Young pups kept in hydrational balance by this method behaved like those maintained on milk infusions, and quite unlike dehydrated pups that consumed a great deal. The hydrated pups ingested little milk, even though they had not eaten for 22 hours and had an empty stomach at the time of testing. Older pups treated in a similar fashion ingested the same amount after milk had been withheld, whether or not they had received isotonic saline. Thus, younger pups have a regulatory system to initiate intake that is the same for food and water, but this is no longer the case by at least 15 days of life. The termination of a meal also undergoes developmental changes in its regulation. For younger but not older pups, gastric distention is a sufficient stimulus, regardless of nutritive content of the load (Hall, 1990). These studies demonstrate that the underlying regulation of behavior can undergo marked reorganization, even when the superficial aspects of the behavior appear similar.

Some Special Features of Mammalian Behavioral Embryology

Physiological Regulation in Neonates

In mammals, including humans, the mother and her offspring share a physiological intimacy from the moment of conception through weaning. Mammalian physiology is characterized by a large number of systems devoted to keeping the individual alive and regulated within rather narrow homeostatic limits, despite often wide environmental fluctuations. The levels of temperature, oxygen, water, electrolytes, and nutrients within the **milieu interieur** must all be regulated. During prenatal life, this is accomplished for the fetus by tapping into the maternal blood supply and by maternal regulation of the intrauterine environment. The transition at birth places new demands on the young organism: other ways must be found to achieve a regulated interior environment. Although immature in some respects, the respiratory, metabolic, circulatory, excretory, and other internal regulatory systems of the neonate must swing into action.

No mammal is fully independent at birth, however (figure 7.5). Unlike their reptilian ancestors, the neonates continue to receive support from a maternally regulated milieu. In fact, nursing their young is one of the defining characteristics of the mammalian class. Particularly in altricial species in which regulatory systems are often inadequate at birth, maternal support may extend beyond nursing. Since milk is not involved, these forms of support may also come from fathers, siblings, and others in the social nexus. The mother is typically the major source of other adjustments as well, perhaps only because she is available for nursing.

Milk is the most direct and the most universal vehicle through which mammalian mothers contribute to the regulation of neonates. This complex

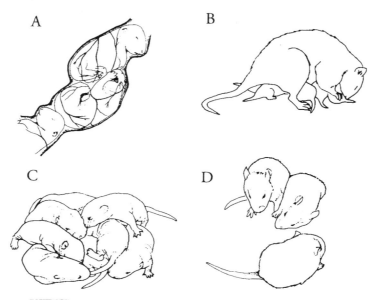

Figure 7.5 Four habitats characteristic of developing rats: (A) intrauterine; (B) the mother in nest with littermates; (C) the littermate huddle; (D) the social group (reproduced with permission from Alberts & Cramer, 1988).

fluid provides nutrients, water, electrolytes, hormones, and immune factors (Kon & Cowie, 1961). Both mother and neonate develop adaptive mechanisms (lactation, nursing, suckling) to ensure that milk is produced, delivered, and ingested on an appropriate schedule, in appropriate amounts (Lincoln, 1983; Stern, 1989).

The delivery of milk to an infant can have unexpected physiological effects (Hofer, 1983). When young rat pups are isolated from their dams, even when maintained in a warm nest with littermates, heart rate begins to decline within about 4 hours to about 60% of the normal rate by 18 hours of separation. There is also a correlated decline in respiratory rate. The underlying cause of these changes is a change in blood pressure that can be reversed with an appropriately scheduled delivery of milk through an intragastric cannula (Hofer, 1983). Careful, simultaneous monitoring of blood pressure and heart rate in individual pups and the milk ejections of their mothers during normal nursing episodes reveals repeated microchanges in the pup's physiology in response to milk ejections (Shair, Brake, Hofer, & Myers, 1986). Rat dams nurse their young about once an hour, with several ejections in a session. Thus these changes occur frequently during early life. They may have lasting effects on the organism's physiology (Myers, 1991).

Some mammals are born before the neural systems that permit internal control of elimination are ready to function. These neonates require maternal help in the form of tactile stimulation of the perineum to urinate and defecate. The dams lick the perineal skin of their pups, eliciting reflex release of urine and feces. These substances are ingested by the dam, which has the obvious consequence of keeping the pups and nest clean and the less obvious consequence of recycling fluids and electrolytes to the dam that, because of her lactational state, has increased need of water and salt (Alberts & Gubernick, 1983; Gubernick & Alberts, 1983). The dynamics of this interaction raise the interesting and important point that regulatory processes in two individuals, mother and neonate, must be kept in mind when explaining events during the postnatal period. Some used the term *symbiosis*, perhaps metaphorically, to capture this fact (Rosenblum & Moltz, 1983).

In addition to specific effects on elimination, licking is one of the ways that mothers provide stimulation to their neonates. The intrauterine and nursing environments are a rich source of somatosensory and vestibular stimulation. In rats, this stimulation is self-generated or it originates from the siblings and the dam. Maternal licking of the perineum occurs reliably when dams enter the nest to initiate a nursing session, is relatively prolonged, and involves manipulating and turning the pup to adjust its posture and orientation, local heating and cooling of the skin from paws and saliva, and tactile stimulation over much of the body (Moore & Chadwick-Dias, 1986). However, dams also lick and nuzzle other parts of the pups' bodies and, while moving about the nest, brush them with their fur, step on them, and so forth. Such stimuli are essential contributors to the growth of the rats. When isolated from such stimulation, growth hormone levels fall rapidly, as do the levels of a tissue enzyme ornithine decarboxylase that is involved in protein formation. After a short period of interacting with a stimulating mother, or after artificial brush stimulation in isolated pups, these isolation-related changes are reversed (Kuhn, Butler, & Schanberg, 1978; Evoniuk, Kuhn, & Schanberg, 1979).

These findings are illustrative of a large body of evidence from animal studies that links typical patterns of early stimulation to physiological aspects of development. They demonstrate that the quality, intensity, amount, and patterning of stimuli can influence a variety of developing systems. The animal work was an incentive to explore similar effects in humans, often with the clinical goal of improving the stimulating aspects of atypical environments, such as hospital wards. For example, Schanberg and Field (1987) applied the growth hormone work to low-birthweight, premature human infants with promising results. Infants who were regularly given gentle stroking gained weight more rapidly and were released from the hospital sooner than controls.

Prematurity raises a number of intriguing questions about early stimulation. The premature infant is kept from the patterns of stimulation that it would have received by remaining in the intrauterine environment, such as vestibular stimulation from maternal and self-generated movements. That is not all: the infant is also exposed to stimulation, such as light, that infants born at term first encounter at a later age. Both may be important.

Patterned vestibular stimulation on a waterbed reduces the frequency of prematurity-related apnea in human infants, and also has other beneficial physiological effects (Korner, 1980). Turkewitz and Kenny (1982) maintained that the temporal sequence with which sensory systems become functional is an important developmental contributor to the organization of these systems. The onset of visual functioning by premature exposure to light can therefore alter the organization of systems that develop earlier, which, in the usual course of events, have some time to function in the absence of input to the visual system (Lickliter, 1993). Evidence for these effects exists in rats (Kenny & Turkewitz, 1986) and quail (Lickliter, 1990).

One of the obvious but nevertheless important differences between a neonate and an adult is size. The smaller an animal, the larger is the surface to volume ratio. Therefore, young mammals are more likely to lose heat than are their older counterparts. Particularly when coupled with immature thermoregulatory systems, this poses a significant challenge to homeostasis. In addition to providing the food that can be converted to metabolic heat, maternal animals assist their young by providing heat directly through conductance, by building insulating nests or other shelters, and by keeping their young clustered in one place.

Adult mammals are **homeotherms**: they regulate their internal temperature within a homeostatic range primarily by endogenous mechanisms (*endothermy*). The young of many mammalian species, including rats, also use endogenous mechanisms, especially metabolism of brown fat, to thermoregulate, but neonates are successful in achieving homeostasis only in a narrow range of ambient temperatures. They therefore resemble **ectotherms** by using behavioral means to collect heat from the environment. When adequate environmental heat is denied, they are unable to compensate; like reptiles, their body temperature drops to ambient levels.

In thermoregulation as in suckling, the behavior of a newborn rat complements the maternal contributions. Although their locomotory competence is limited, pups are able to move short distances toward a source of heat. This keeps them in the nest, which is warmer than the surround because of heat deposited by the dam and the insulating properties of the nest. Furthermore, the simple behavior exhibited by individual pups of moving toward a warmer spot keeps the litter organized into a huddle, which can expand and contract in adaptation to changes in the ambient temperature (figure 7.6). This was examined in a series of ingenious studies (Alberts, 1978; Alberts & Brunjes, 1978; Alberts & May, 1984).

Dams cluster their pups into a nest that has a rim or walls that restrict dispersion. Once the dam leaves the nest, the pups do not position themselves randomly within its confines. Instead, they form a huddle, that maintains a particular shape because of the summed, independent actions of each pup. Pups on the surface of the huddle become cooler than their siblings, which stimulates them to burrow into the huddle, thereby moving others to

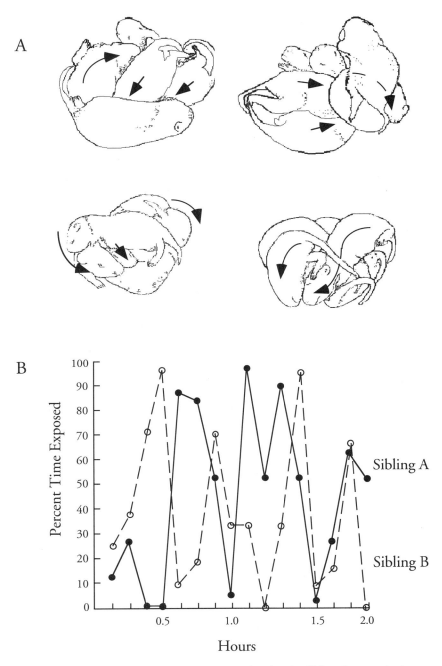

Figure 7.6 (A) The littermate huddle maintains itself by the constant movement of cooler rat pups on the outside of the huddle into the warmer central regions (arrows). (B) This continual movement can be seen in the locations of two 10-day-old littermates measured in successive 7.5-minute blocks (modified from Alberts, 1978).

a surface position. Once these pups cool, they will be the ones to burrow below the surface. If an individual pup is anesthetized and placed in the huddle, it will remain on the surface; thus, an individual pup's location in the huddle depends on its own actions. Given a particular environmental temperature, the huddle will be maintained in a particular organization, but each pup will have changed its position numerous times. Participating in a huddle leads to great metabolic savings—up to 40% in one study with a litter of eight pups—because of the insulation provided by siblings (Alberts, 1978).

Ultrasonic vocalizations in small mammals were first studied in bats, which use echoes from the sounds they emit to detect insects to eat or obstacles to avoid as they fly in the dark (Griffin, 1958). Soon after bat detectors, devices that convert ultrasound into the humanly audible range, were brought into the laboratory, it was discovered that rodents use ultrasonic vocalizations in social interactions such as aggression and courtship (Barfield & Thomas, 1986). Furthermore, young rodents emit ultrasound in response to being scattered outside the nest, and their dams respond to these sounds by approaching and retrieving them back to the nest (Noirot, 1972).

The ultrasonic emissions of pups were thought of as isolation vocalizations, having the function of communicating a state of distress to the mother. They were subsequently used by many investigators as indicators of distress in analytical studies designed to identify situational or physiological mediators and alleviators of this hypothesized state. However, an intriguing series of studies demonstrated that the ultrasound produced by young rodents is an audible byproduct of physiological maneuvers related to respiration and thermoregulation (Blumberg & Alberts, 1990; Blumberg, Efimova, & Alberts, 1992; Hofer & Shair, 1992).

Neonatal rats are very sensitive to cooling of the skin. Shortly after exposure to a cool ambient temperature, they begin to metabolize brown adipose tissue to generate heat. This increases the amount of oxygen they require, which stimulates increased intake of air. In a cool environment the external air is cooler than the air in the lungs, and increased exchange of air leads to further cooling of the body. The system responds to this set of conditions by constricting the larynx so that air is released more slowly, a phenomenon that was described as laryngeal braking in human infants under similar physiological conditions. The audible result is a grunt in human infants and an ultrasonic squeak in rat pups (Blumberg & Alberts, 1990). Still comatose rat pups also exhibit laryngeal braking and produce ultrasonic sounds during recovery from deep hypothermia, a phenomenon that can increase oxygenation and maintain lung structure under conditions of severe compromise (Hofer & Shair, 1992). Very careful control of the thermal environment while young pups are isolated from other aspects of the maternal, sibling, or nest environment demonstrate that thermal cues alone are sufficient to account for ultrasound production (Blumberg, Efimova, & Alberts, 1992).

Of course, as Hofer and Shair (1992) point out, ultrasonic vocalizations can still function as communication. Even the passive release of odorous substances or visual stimuli provides information to the mother. The debate over what it is that ultrasonic vocalizations signify about the young animal and what they communicate to the dam can best be resolved by keeping in mind two important distinctions that were discussed in chapter 3: that between proximate and functional questions, and that between different levels of developmental complexity.

Clearly, dams can and do quickly become able to use ultrasound to locate and retrieve pups, and this has the effect of both warming them and returning them to other aspects of the home nest environment. However, neither the proximate control in the pup nor its evolutionary history need have anything to do with this informative role: ultrasonic vocalizations may serve as an exaptation. It is also clear that pups eventually seek aspects of the social and nest environment other than warmth. Nevertheless, that need not be (and apparently is not) the case initially. It is yet to be determined whether a linkage at the level of internal control mechanism is ever formed between the production of ultrasounds and the absence of nonthermal, socially provided stimuli.

The Biosocial to Psychosocial Transition

It is sometimes implied that infants start life unattached and must become attached to a mother. This is a key idea behind the concept of **attachment**. However, a young mammal begins life as part of a system that includes very intimate connections with the mother, and despite changes in the mother-young system at birth, the neonate maintains those obligatory connections. During both the prenatal and neonatal stages, these connections are predominantly physiological. It is possible, therefore, to characterize the progress in social relationship between the young mammal and its mother as moving gradually from a biosocial to a psychosocial level (Schneirla & Rosenblatt, 1963). From this point of view, development consists of the progressive loosening of ties, or the substitution of more flexible ties for those that characterize earlier stages.

To expand on an example from the previous section, when the ambient temperature falls below the optimum range, the behavior of young altricial mammals that have difficulty regulating their own body temperature through physiological means is disrupted. The mother is an important source of heat for these animals, and the young may regulate their body temperature behaviorally by adjusting their position along a heat gradient that extends from her body. In other words, young mammals adjust their proximity to the mother in the same way that they would adjust themselves along a heat gradient created by a heat lamp (Alberts & May, 1984; Rosenblatt, 1976). The same is true of their responses to littermates (Alberts, 1978).

Thus in the early neonatal period it is misleading to maintain a sharp distinction between social and nonsocial processes. In rat pups, the nest plays an important mediating role in the development of behavioral patterns that are later addressed to the mother and siblings. As soon as the pup is able to show oriented locomotion, which is at first a rather primitive crawl, it can get itself to the nest by moving along thermal and odor gradients. The nest is warmer than surrounding areas, creating a temperature gradient that the pup follows. In addition, an odor gradient terminates in the highly concentrated odor deposits found in the nest. By its behavioral adjustments to odor and temperature, the pup keeps itself in the nest, where, because of the mother's attraction to the nest and young, all interactions with the mother occur.

The young pup responds to its mother and to its siblings in ways that are at least partly identical to its responses to the nest. All of the inhabitants of the nest share odor characteristics of the nest and therefore elicit approach responses. Because the mother and siblings are warmer than the nest and have attractive tactile properties, the pup will further adjust itself to maintain contact with them while in the nest (Rosenblatt, 1976). When the pup begins to walk in a coordinated fashion, it makes excursions from the nest. At this time, it can go directly to the mother by following her odors, which are particularly strong and salient during the latter half of lactation (Leon & Moltz, 1971). The pup can therefore initiate contact with the mother, to suckle, for example, whether she is in the nest or not. When the eyes open, visual cues become incorporated into the pup's social behavior, and social behavior continues its progressive reorganization (Rosenblatt, 1976).

Around midway through the nursing period, the social interactions between the dam and her young can be described in terms similar to those used for interactions among adults. The same is not true of the early neonatal period, which is characterized by thermotactile behavior. Indeed, it is only by sustained experience with concurrent thermotactile and olfactory cues that pups come to direct their approach responses preferentially to the dam and littermates, as opposed to warm, inanimate objects such as plastic tubes filled with warm water (Alberts & Brunjes, 1978); Alberts refers to this as filial huddling.

It is thermotactile stimulation that is important for the formation of filial responses to particular odors. An equal attraction to an odor was formed in pups given experience with an odor paired either with an active, lactating mother or with a warm tube (Alberts & May, 1984). The addition of milk or suckling opportunities did not increase the filial response. Furthermore, attraction to a novel odor can be formed in neonatal rat pups by pairing the odor with a mild electric shock (Camp & Rudy, 1988). Older pups, like adults, learn to avoid odors paired with the same level of shock. Clearly, profound differences exist in the internal organization underlying the socially directed behavior of neonatal and older animals. This is true even when the overt behavior or behavioral consequence (huddling or contact with the mother) looks the same (Alberts & Cramer, 1988).

The transition seems to be one that moves from social interaction as a part of the homeostatic regulatory processes in the young animal to greater emancipation from direct involvement in these regulatory processes: from biosocial to psychosocial, in Schneirla and Rosenblatt's (1963) terms. This terminology should not imply that social processes in older animals are free of physiological components, including those that serve homeostasis in nonsocial realms. Indeed, Leon and colleagues (Adels & Leon, 1986; Leon, Crosskerry, & Smith, 1978) made the case that some aspects of maternal behavior are mediated by thermoregulatory processes, and Alberts and colleagues (Alberts & Gubernick, 1983; Gubernick & Alberts, 1983) proposed that some aspects of maternal behavior are mediated by water and salt appetite.

The most familiar physiological changes to accompany maternal condition are hormonal. The openness of the neuroendocrine system to external stimulation allows stimulation from the young to influence the mother's hormonal condition and vice versa. Furthermore, hormones secreted by the mother can pass through the placental blood connection to developing embryos and through the milk supply to neonates. Thus they have a direct, behaviorally relevant link between maternal and embryonic physiologies.

Lactation requires hormonal changes, but the importance of hormones to maternal behavior varies in extent and qualitative detail across species. In some species, the onset of maternal care requires hormonal support. The sequence of progesterone elevation and decline followed by estrogen elevation promotes the rapid onset of maternal behavior in laboratory rats and some other mammalian species (Rosenblatt & Siegel, 1981). Other hormones may also be involved. In sheep, for example, there is also a dramatic, necessary effect of oxytocin, which is secreted in response to the vaginocervical stimulation that accompanies delivery. Without this stimulation, or injected oxytocin, the mother will reject her lamb. In the presence of oxytocin, the mother quickly develops an attraction to the lamb, and learns its individual characteristics so that her subsequent behavior is directed exclusively to her own offspring (Keverne & Kendrick, 1992).

Once delivery is complete and maternal behavior has been initiated, the infant's behavior can continue to affect maternal physiology and behavior. To take an important example from studies in rats, suckling stimulates prolactin and oxytocin secretion, thus maintaining the lactational state and regulating the delivery of milk (Grosvenor, Maiweg, & Mena, 1970). Tactile stimulation of the mammary region by the rooting behavior of pups also leads the mother to adopt a nursing posture over the litter, which permits the pups to attach to her nipples and initiate suckling (Stern, 1990).

The prolonged and intensive stimulation of the ventral region of a nursing dam by her pups also leads to a reorganization of the dam's somatosensory cortex (Xerri et al., 1994). Specifically, the primary somatosensory representation of the ventral, nipple-bearing skin enlarges to about twice its original size after several days of nursing. Furthermore, the receptive fields of individual neurons driven by tactile input to the hairy skin surrounding the nipples become smaller. These changes provide a basis for increased acuity and sensitivity to further stimulation by pups (Xerri et al., 1994).

The human infant, like other mammals, is born into an intimate social setting involving one or more adults. Its social contacts contribute an enormous proportion of what might be called its Umwelt, or personal environment. Because this environment is social, that is, provided by other living individuals, it is not static. The caregivers and other companions of infants also undergo development, sometimes as dramatic as that of the infant. Like other mammals, the early postnatal behavioral development of humans is best characterized within the framework of parent-young reciprocity.

The nature of the parent-young interaction can also affect the course of infant development. Hinde and Spencer-Booth (1967) showed that mother rhesus monkeys living in social groups are more likely to prevent the departure of their young from them and to retrieve them when they have departed than are rhesus mothers living alone with their infants. Consequently, weaning, or the attainment of independence as evidenced in willingness to spend more time exploring away from the mother, occurs both sooner and in a different fashion in the solitary dyads.

The nature of the reciprocal relationship between parent and offspring can be rather well meshed and synchronous or disordered and disruptive. For example, Brazelton, Koslowski, and Main (1974) observed that the behavioral interaction of human mothers and their infants during the first 4 to 20 weeks postpartum can be characterized as the establishment of a routine. The infant appears to go through cycles of attention and inattention during which it is either responsive, initiating social exchange, or unresponsive. Because of their sensitivity to their infants, mothers quickly adjust their interaction to coincide predominantly with the infant's attention phase. Presumably as a result of establishing this rhythm, the infant gradually extends the duration of its attention phase, thereby providing for and engaging in longer and more complex social exchanges.

Sander (1970) reported that the infant and its caregiver can have established reciprocal routines of interaction—albeit very simple ones—as early as 15 days postpartum. Klaus and Kennell (1970) observed that the normal hospital obstetrical routines of the 1950s and 1960s may have interfered with the initial establishment of parent-offspring reciprocity, particularly in the case of infants restricted to incubators. If, as was usually the case, the mother was not allowed to care for her infant while it was in the incubator, a reciprocal social relationship was not established, and the child's development was adversely affected. Children whose mothers were allowed to care for them while they were restricted to incubators did not show these disruptions in psychological development (Ringler et al., 1974).

Because of the reciprocal nature of the parent-young relationship, any effects that an event has on the development of young while they are still dependent on their parents may be due either to the direct effects of the event on the young or to the response of the parent to changed characteristics of the young. For example, animal studies of the effects of early experience showed that rats that were handled by humans during the first three weeks after birth were more exploratory and less "emotional" as adults, even when this handling was limited to a three-minute episode. Initially, it was presumed that this effect of early experience on the adult's behavior was a direct consequence of the handling. However, subsequent work called this presumption into question.

The behavior of mouse (Priestnall, 1973) and rat (Lee & Williams, 1974) mothers was observed after their young had undergone a typical handling procedure. In both species, mothers licked young pups that had been handled more than pups of comparable ages that had not received the treatment. It is therefore likely that handling exerts its long-term effect on the young at least partly by altering the nature of parent-infant interaction.

The consequences of the reciprocity of the parent-young relationship can extend beyond the boundaries of parental care. The primate literature, for instance, abounds in examples of mothers acquiring new skills and habits through observing the skills that their offspring acquired by themselves (Hinde, 1974). Remember the transmission of the potato-washing skill of Japanese monkeys that was mentioned in chapter 2.

The animal studies directed attention not only to the influence of the parents on the development of the young but also to effects of the young on the performance of the parents (Bell, 1968, 1974). The results of these studies stimulated attempts to describe precisely and to characterize the reciprocity in the parent-young relationship (cf. Fogel, 1991) and its changes with time (cf. Cairns, 1979).

It is important to recognize that the character of that relationship varies with the development of the infant and changes in the state of the parent and with circumstances. That is, at times and under certain circumstances, the parent will dominate and control the relationship in a supportive, disruptive, authoritative, or autocratic manner. There is no generally appropriate pattern in the relationship. A parent who supplies the appropriate adjustments in action to support the actions of the infant is providing the social scaffolding necessary to obtain new levels of achievement. However, being more sophisticated, the parent will encounter circumstances in which either an authoritative or an autocratic relationship will have to be imposed.

Yet, too much or inappropriate imposition by the parent can disrupt development in the infant. The results of animal behavior research suggest that it is the pattern of reciprocal relationships in which the child participates that contributes to the development of later psychological characteristics.

Transgenerational Effects of Life Events

Parental care systems have certain stable features that form part of the inheritance of the offspring (chapter 4). Some of these features are shared broadly within a species, whereas others are idiosyncratic to particular parents. Species-universal features can be passed on from generation to generation in much the same way for each parent-offspring unit in the species. Idiosyncratic features add to the diversity within a species, perhaps washing out after one or two generations, perhaps becoming traditions in local populations. In short, parental care allows the offspring to inherit the characteristics acquired by their parents (West et al., 1988). For example, male bullfinches acquire the song of their fathers during their nestling stage, even if they are fostered-reared by canaries, and they then pass that song on to their offspring (Immelman, 1969). As a result, there can be a line of bullfinches that sing canary songs.

A wide range of transgenerational effects have been uncovered through cross-fostering studies or through experiments in which the effects of manipulations imposed on one generation are traced through one or two subsequent generations. Transgenerational grandmother effects were reported in rodents (Denenberg & Whimbey, 1963; Denenberg & Rosenberg, 1967). Specific types of experiences encountered during infancy can affect not only the adult animal's patterns of coping with environmental stressors, but also those of their daughter's offspring. Effects such as these can be mediated by regularities in maternal hormones that cross the placental barrier to affect fetal development, and by predictable differences in maternal stimulation (Moore, 1990).

An individual's exposure to certain physical or social environmental factors during development can alter the course of development and lead to a new characteristic, provided that there is some match between the individual's characteristics at that point in development and the environmental factor. Whether the characteristic is then inherited by subsequent offspring may depend on any of a number of factors, including the role that parents play in regulating the offspring's development.

Regularities in the social environment at particular ontogenetic stages can provide the kinds of developmental stability and predictability typically associated with population genetic analyses of inheritance. Thus, developmental psychobiological processes can promote patterns of inheritance formally equivalent to those considered essential for the establishment of the adaptive relation of the organism to its environment. They may even be important influences in the origin of species, as well.

Normal development of the embryo is dependent on the occurrence of many physiological events within the mother's system. These include, but are not limited to, neuroendocrine events. Evidence from animal behavior studies demonstrates that idiosyncratic socioenvironmental factors can have profound effects on the postnatal development of offspring, mediated by physiological changes in the mother. Social environmental factors, including those that produce stress, emotional disturbances and disorders, frustrations, satisfactions, and elation, can affect the neuroendocrine system of human mothers, resulting in changed proportions of specific hormones.

Many of these hormones pass the placental barrier and enter into the fetal blood system, where they may eventually affect the developing fetal neural and neuroendocrine system. Since the neuroendocrine system is responsible in part for an individual's reactivity to stimulation, activity rhythms, and the ability to cope with situations and to organize behavioral responses (Levine, 1969), the neonate's behavior and course of development may show the consequences of social environmental factors that affected the mother's physiology during pregnancy. The effects of endocrine changes in response to idiosyncratic life events, particularly those associated with prenatal stress, have received extensive attention in animal studies (e.g., Ward, 1992).

Malnutrition is another well-studied event that has transgenerational effects. Clearly, direct, physiological mechanisms can mediate the effects of both stress and the nutrition status of the mother on the developing embryo and nursing neonate. However, Birch (1972) suggested that these social environmental factors need not be present during the pregnancy to affect the development of offspring. Female rats that were malnourished when young, but not when adult or when pregnant, bore offspring that were smaller and behaviorally less competent than rats born to normally nourished females. Third-generation young also showed the effects of their grandmothers' malnourishment, even though they and their mothers had never been malnourished. Birch suggested that malnourishment early in a female rat's life disrupts her neuroendocrine physiology, with the result that later she provides a less than optimum intrauterine environment for her offspring. This changed intrauterine environment so affects the offspring that their intrauterine environments are also less than optimum, despite the fact that they have never been malnourished. Thus, a cross-generation social environmental effect can be established, mediated by neuroendocrine and intrauterine conditions.

Birch (1971) extended these findings to the analysis of a human development issue. Hospital studies conducted in the 1950s and 1960s had indicated that the condition of the infant (birthweight, mortality, morbidity) was more highly correlated with the mother's race than with her socioeconomic status.

These results were particularly perplexing because the birth condition of the infant ought to reflect the quality of prenatal nutrition and care received by the mother during pregnancy, and these factors were expected to vary according to socioeconomic status rather than to race. Yet the condition of neonates born to middle-class African-American mothers was not better than that of neonates born to lower-class European-American mothers. The condition of neonates born to middle-class European-American mothers, however, was significantly better than that of neonates born to either lower-class European-American or middle-class African-American mothers.

Birch decided to divide the middle-class African-American mothers into two groups: those who had been born into middle-class circumstances and those who had been born into lower-class circumstances. If lower-class circumstances result in poorer prenatal and postnatal nutrition and health care, they may result in an intrauterine environment that is less than optimal for the next generation despite the good nutrition and health care available to the adult as part of her new, middle-class circumstances. Indeed, this division revealed the expected correlation of the infant's birth condition with the mother's socioeconomic status. It was her socioeconomic status at the time of her birth, and not at the time of her pregnancy, that was relevant.

Many animal behavior studies have demonstrated the influence on the behavioral development of the young of socioenvironmental factors directly affecting the mother (Bell & Smotherman, 1980; Smotherman & Bell, 1980). The effects of such events on the psychological development of humans deserves more attention. Such research, when considered seriously, would lead to profound changes in the infrastructure of most societies.

Summary

Behavior is the predominant function of the nervous system. Therefore, neuroembryologists have used behavior as a way to investigate neurogenesis, and developmental psychobiologists have often turned to the study of neural development. Their joint efforts formed the specialty of behavioral embryology. An important idea guiding much of the work is that some embryonic behavior may be the result of adaptations to the embryonic environment. Previously, embryonic behavior was thought to be either a functionless epiphenomenon or preparation for adult behavior. Although most of the knowledge about embryonic neural development and behavior is about nonhuman animals, the processes seem quite similar to those occurring in humans. Our principal aim in this chapter was to examine human behavioral embryology by illustrating some of the conceptual advances that have occurred and indicating the problems that still remain.

Close physiological ties exist between mammalian mothers and their young offspring. These ties provide a foundation for bidirectional developmental effects between caregiver and young. The initial interactions between the developing embryo and its caregiver center on homeostatic regulation and growth processes. The behavioral capacities of the neonate expand in parallel with increasing internal regulation of physiological processes. Initially qualitatively different, social interactions between the developing offspring and caregiver increasingly resemble those that characterize older individuals in the species.

8   **Cognitive Development and Developmental Psychobiology**

An examination of infant behaviour is essentially an examination of the central nervous system.
—A. L. Gesell and C. S. Amatruda (1947, p. 184)

In trying to understand the functional principles governing the human nervous system, we must remind ourselves that our brain has evolved from earlier kinds of brains— that our kind of brain was not built from scratch especially for us, but has capacities and limitations that are due to its historical origins.
—P. S. Churchland (1986, p. 14)

The relationship between the developing **cognition** and the developing brain of a growing child has intrigued more than a few developmental psychologists (Case, 1992; Gibson & Peterson, 1991). However, much of the thought and work on this issue has taken place within a tradition different from that of developmental psychobiology. Because of the differences in tradition, it is instructive to compare the approaches that these two branches of inquiry have taken. Such comparison allows the possibility, on the one hand, of making explicit to the biologically oriented investigator those aspects of human development in need of explanation and, on the other hand, of introducing to the developmental psychologist new and potentially useful ways to approach their explanatory task.

The domain of human cognition is too broad to discuss in its entirety, so we have chosen to examine three aspects of infant development: motor skills, with a particular focus on manual skill; sensorimotor intelligence; and language. These three aspects do not exhaust the range of psychological research on human infancy, but they are areas where significant effort has been directed toward relating brain and cognition. Furthermore, they are three of the most distinctive psychological features in human evolution.

Two troublesome trends in the developmental study of brain and cognition strike an all too familiar chord with developmental psychobiologists. One is the use of brain maturation as an explanation for cognitive change: "During the infancy period, bursts of change in behavioral functioning coincide with the maturation and involvement of implicated brain regions (e.g., the frontal cortex, visual cortex, and hippocampus)" (Rosser, 1994, p. 317). The other trend is the acceptance of some form of **nativism**. It stems from the former trend because it is assumed that an explanation of cognitive development in terms of neural development requires nativism: "[B]rain development continues after birth, but the initial foundation already established before birth will place limits on what can happen later. And, indeed, even what happens later may be endogenously controlled.... This is what tips the scales toward nativism" (Rosser, 1994, p. 314). Both of these trends have logical and empirical problems associated with them. We propose that the advances made in developmental psychobiology provide theoretical and empirical tools for avoiding the trends while maintaining the important focus on understanding the relation between brain development and cognitive development.

Developmental psychologists have turned to physiological and neuro-anatomical explanations of cognition because explanations that exclude some attention to the contributions from the developing organism, particularly its nervous system, have been unable to account for the full range of cognitive development. As reported in chapter 1, psychology has a long history of couching biological explanations in terms of maturation or nativism. However, before modern uses of these ideas are rejected, it is necessary to demonstrate how they can be replaced with more adequate conceptions that we believe are available within modern developmental psychobiology. Once incorporated into the discussion, the older, flawed concepts, such as maturational unfolding, or innate faculties, concepts, first principles (Gelman, 1990), beliefs (Spelke, 1988, 1991), and devices put in place by natural selection will no longer seem necessary.

We believe that four conceptual contributions from developmental psychobiology are particularly useful to contemporary cognitive neuroscience. The first is that *new psychological achievements grow out of raw materials present at earlier phases* of development. Unlike previous ideas that were similar, this one recognizes that this process is not constrained by *functional* categories as they may be exhibited by the developing individual or that we, as researchers, perceive. The achievements of earlier phases of development become the recyclable raw materials for the achievements of subsequent phases. The processes and mechanisms underlying the earlier achievements need not retain the same functional tag. Thus the phenomena we recognize as **syntax** may grow out of processes and mechanisms underlying earlier achievements that are functionally independent of language, and the phenomena characterized as rules for reasoning can emerge from achievements associated with the control of manual skills. The developing system has no respect for functional boundaries.

The second contribution from developmental psychobiology is the recognition that *the development of the nervous system is intimately dependent on contextual effects* originating from both within and without the individual.

These effects include the consequences of using the nervous system at earlier phases of development. Thus, brain development and cognitive development are reciprocal and interdependent. The structural underpinnings of behavior do shape behavior, but behavior also contributes to the construction of the nervous system.

The third important idea is that *the individual is part of a structured system that also includes the immediate social and physical surroundings*, and this is true throughout development. What is adaptive and stable about this system at one point in development (e.g., infancy) may be very different from what is adaptive and stable at another point (e.g., adulthood). Thus to argue that an infant is competent does not mean that it is adultlike, because contextual requirements may differ for the infant and adult competencies. This is the idea of ontogenetic adaptations. The important developmental question is how the earlier competency relates to the development of the later competency.

The fourth contribution is the recognition that since both internal and external elements to the system are important for its achievements, *different combinations of internal and external elements can form similar-appearing achievements*. Thus, external support can be used to create the impression that infants have adult capacities when they do not. This is a methodological point with important theoretical implications. These four ideas can be used to begin the task of replacing some of the more problematic biological conceptions currently used to explain motor skills, sensorimotor intelligence, language, and other aspects of human cognitive development.

Maturation and Cognition

Child psychologists typically use the concept of neural maturation to account for changes in behavioral capacities, the disappearance of some patterns of behavior, and the emergence of others over the course of time (see Segalowitz & Rose-Krasnor, 1992). The criterion of *universality* distinguishes maturation from other potential explanatory factors. Thus, research is directed toward identifying those features of psychological development that are universal (i.e., age-related patterns that are apparent across all cultures). When universality in the face of cultural diversity is found, it is concluded that it is sufficient to exclude the influence of learning and to accept the presumption of neural maturation as the underlying cause of the feature. However, the universality of achievement or pattern of development can be a consequence of ubiquitous features of human existence (e.g., adult care of offspring) within which cultural diversity may represent only minor variations on a theme.

Chronological age is all too often the sole measure of maturation. This practice is based on the strong assumption that maturation is clocklike, proceeding in an invariant fashion regardless of circumstance; thus it can be measured by the passage of time. As a practical matter in developmental research, age is often the independent variable, serving as a shorthand for maturation of the nervous system.

However, the development of any biological system is a complex process. The different components of the nervous system vary in their rate of development, and since they are interdependent, the rate of development of each component can alter the development of the other components. Moreover, the development of the nervous system is affected by and, in turn, affects, the development of other systems in the body (e.g., endocrine, immune, digestive). Finally, since the nervous system is especially open to environmental influences, the rate of its development will also be influenced by various environmental factors. Thus, maturation does not occur at an invariant pace: it is not clocklike. This makes the passage of time a very poor measure of the state of development of the nervous system. Given these complications, it can be concluded that age is not an appropriate independent variable in developmental research (Wohlwill, 1970).

If age is unreliable, then some other measure of the status of neural development must be employed. Human research has two types of assessments to document the status of neural development independent of behavioral evidence or age: **myelination** and electrophysiology. A certain proportion of neurons of the central and peripheral nervous systems have their axons wrapped by glial or Schwann cells. This wrapping facilitates the manifestation of the action potentials that enable one neuron to affect the state of another neuron or a muscle fiber. The extent and pattern of myelination in different parts of the nervous system occur in a time-dependent manner (figure 8.1). Since myelination affects the timing of neural activity, it is an important contributor to the sequencing and timing of behavioral events.

However, several problems are associated with myelination as a marker of neural maturation in relation to psychological development. Too often, research uses fairly gross assessments of the degree and pattern of myelination to associate with very complex psychological abilities. For example, the degree of myelination of the frontal lobes may be associated with the achievement of rather complex intellectual abilities, without any means of determining how the facilitation of the transmission of action potentials in the frontal lobes would contribute to the development of that ability. Also, at what point in the prolonged period of myelination is the function manifested? Does the function occur as soon as one-half (or two-thirds, or three-quarters) of the structure is myelinated? Or does the function become manifest slowly, in direct proportion to the amount of myelination of the structure? There is no evidence that any of these relations between myelination and function apply.

Another problem is that many parts of the nervous system function appropriately before they are myelinated, and the majority of neurons in the

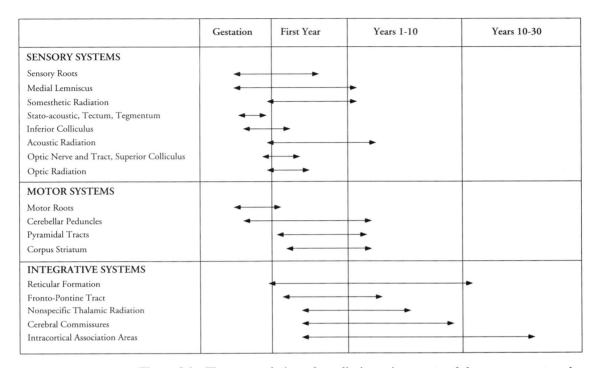

Figure 8.1   The accumulation of myelin in various parts of the nervous system has been used as a measure of their functional maturity. As this figure reveals, myelin accumulates over fairly prolonged periods, and often it is difficult to specify exactly when it has achieved the mature level (redrawn from Lou, 1982).

central nervous system are unmyelinated. Therefore, myelination patterns are too coarse a measure to provide insight into the developmental status of the nervous system.

Electrophysiological techniques may provide some account of developmental changes in neural activity that may be used independent of behavioral evidence. Changes in the electroencephalogram and evoked potentials do correlate with some changes in neural development (particularly myelination), and also with changes in psychological phenomena. However, electrophysiological techniques suffer from the same limitations associated with myelination. They are rather gross measures of neural status, and often there is no clear way in which the changes that they measure may be translated into physiological mechanisms that could account for the changes in psychological phenomena.

Nevertheless, myelination and electrophysiological information can provide additional insight into the development of psychological abilities. For example, Salamy (1978) demonstrated in humans that changes in electrophysiological status of the brain with age correlate with changes in the myelination of the corpus callosum. The corpus callosum is composed of axons from neurons in one hemisphere of the brain. That is, neurons in one hemisphere project axons to make connection with neurons in the opposite hemisphere. The corpus callosum is those axons. Most of the projections are established during the last trimester of human pregnancy. Myelination of these axons continues for 14 to 21 years after birth. The axons are functional at birth, but electrophysiological evidence reveals no alteration of the status of one hemisphere by the activation of the other. Thus, it appears that the information that is passed between hemispheres may have little consequence in infants.

Salamy (1978) showed that the ability of one hemisphere to affect the other (as measured electrophysiologically) increased in direct correspondence with the myelination of the corpus callosum. Others (Quinn & Geffen, 1986) demonstrated that the ability to transfer tactile information between the left and right hands was also associated with the changes in electrophysiological measures of callosal functioning. Thus, when combined with detailed accounts of myelination and behavioral information, a clearer understanding of the developmental changes associated with psychological phenomena may be obtained with electrophysiological assessment.

However, the changes in myelination and neural functioning must not be perceived as independent of the activity of the neurons involved. The experiences of each hemisphere may be contributing to the manner of interhemispheric communication. Since callosal neurons are active before myelination, they must both represent the activational status of the hemisphere from which they originate, and contribute to the activational status of the hemisphere to which they project. Thus experiential processes are as much contributors to the developmental changes associated with myelination and evoked potentials as they are a consequence of those changes. Indeed, experimental evidence indicates that rats given postweaning experience with a complex physical and social environment have substantially more myelinated axons in their corpus callosum than controls that develop in standard laboratory cages (Juraska & Kopcik, 1988; chapter 6).

Although myelination and electrophysiological condition may give relatively independent assessments of the developmental status of the nervous system, all too often human research makes no attempt to assess neural development separately from the behavioral process that is meant to be related to neural status. Because the degree of neural maturation can be known only through measures of behavioral development, the inferred neural maturation cannot explain the behavioral development. Maturation as it is currently measured and understood must be rejected as a useful causal concept in developmental psychology, but it can continue to be an appropriate descriptive name for various growth processes (Connolly, 1981).

Despite the conceptual difficulties with neural maturation, it is important to keep in mind that for humans, as for all vertebrates, there can be no coordinated behavior without patterned organization to the nervous system. Both the nervous system and behavioral processes change in their organization during development, and these changes are causally interrelated. Understanding the interrelationships is a central goal of developmental psychobiology. As we have seen, an ontogenetic chart of behavioral development is not a reliable guide to the development of the nervous system. It is also unlikely that a description of gross anatomical or electrophysiological changes in the nervous system will provide explanations for psychological development. These time-honored strategies rely too heavily on old assumptions that have since been discarded: neural changes do not follow an invariant, age-related program, but are subject to variations from several sources; the direction of causation in not just from structure to function, but also from function to structure; and many universal aspects of development require ubiquitous input from the environment.

What is likely to be useful is a joint, mutually informed study of neural and behavioral development. Two areas of research seem particularly promising in this regard. One of them is behavioral embryology, which was discussed in chapter 7. The other is cognitive neuroscience, which is the subject of the present chapter. Each of these two areas permits us to examine several issues of prenatal and postnatal development that demonstrate some of the advances in, as well as some persisting limits to, our understanding of the relationship between behavioral and neural development.

The first thing to do is to examine the meaning of cognition. Osherson and Lasnik (1990) offer the following: "*cognitive science* is the study of human intelligence in all of its forms, from perception and action to language and reasoning. The exercise of intelligence is called cognition" (p. xi). Unfortunately, this definition requires one to know what another vague term, intelligence, means (Gould, 1981). Note that Osherson and Lasnik (as do most other cognitive scientists) rely on the intuitive concepts prompted by the word "intelligence," although they go a bit farther by noting that intelligence includes perception, action, language and reasoning. Rosser (1994) defines cognition as "... thinking and knowing. It is knowledge and knowledge acquisition. It is all the mental activity entailed in transforming stimulation from a physical source to a representation of reality that will guide behavior" (p. 2). Her book contains chapters on perceptual, spatial, conceptual, semantic and language development, development of reasoning, problem solving, and memory, as well as chapters on issues of knowledge about mechanics, number, and folk theories of mind and biology. Despite its vagueness, we may conclude that the meaning of cognition must at least include these aspects of psychological functioning.

Osherson and Lasnik propose further that knowledge obtained through cognitive science is relevant for resolving problems in education, medical treatment, and the organization of social institutions. However, since they expanded the domain of cognition to include the thoughts, perceptions, utterances, and actions created by cognitive processes, without rules for distinguishing cognitive processes from other kinds of processes, the risk is that everything is labeled as cognitive.

Even if it could be narrowly defined, human cognition would still be a broad and complicated phenomenon. Therefore, it must be broken into smaller chunks for analysis. There are no natural lines of segmentation to ensure that these chunks are meaningful units. Consequently, conventional notions of human **faculties** (e.g., language, perception, motor control, thinking) were used, perhaps only out of convenience, to carve cognition into manageable pieces. This practice carries with it no guarantee that such division mirrors the fundamental organization either of cognition or of the brain processes associated with it. Nevertheless, independent investigation of perception, motor skills, language, and reasoning abilities has been a dominant feature in the history of cognitive psychology, and it is likely that such research will continue to influence our conceptions. These traditions provide no reason, however, to reject the idea that cognitive processes cut across some or all of these psychological faculties.

Systematic examination of the conventionally accepted cognitive faculties has been quite difficult. It is no wonder, then, that researchers frequently fall back on maturational explanations of development. For example, Fodor (1983) proposed that cognition is meaningfully divided into a set of functional modules that are the correlates of separate brain structures. Fodor's modules are innate, "hard-wired" in brain structure, and specific to a particular cognitive domain. They emerge fully formed, operate with automatic, involuntary processes, and function separately from other cognitive modules. Thus, no provision is made for functionally guided assembly during development or for general properties shared across modules.

A surface similarity exists between some aspects of Fodor's idea of functional modularity and certain aspects of the neurophysiology of brain organization. However, such functional modularity in the brain may well be a product of development (Changeux, 1985), not an antecedent condition. There is also an apparent modularity to the structural organization of the brain, but this may arise as an epiphenomenon of simple, developmental growth processes (Purves, Riddle, & LaMantia, 1992, 1993) and have little relation to the functional divisions that interest cognitivists. Moreover, the kinds of functions affected by brain modularity may be very low level, bearing little similarity to the psychological faculties. Fodor's theory of cognition is an example of modern nativistic theories with all of the difficulties of earlier nativistic theories. Furthermore, his reliance on functionally defined divisions does not allow integration with promising lines of research in developmental psychobiology.

Many contemporary developmental psychologists reject nativism, especially in forms such as that advanced by Fodor. They are likely to argue that it is necessary to integrate physiological and experiential factors so as to comprehend development. They propose that both specific experiences and specific brain structures are necessary for the ontogenesis of psychological functions (Segalowitz & Rose-Krasnor, 1992). Too often, however, these two classes of factors are separated, and brain growth alone is allowed to account for at least some developmental change in behavior (cf. Johnson & Karmiloff-Smith, 1992; Rosser, 1994; Segalowitz & Rose-Krasnor, 1992). A developmental psychobiological perspective is not consistent with the idea that internal and external causal factors can operate independently in development.

Plunkett and Sinha (1992) present an interesting analysis of modern cognitive science; that is, that the field is committed to certain methodological imperatives that ensure adoption of some form of nativism. These imperatives stem from two notions: adult cognition is a symbolic computational system that represents reality, and the developmental task for the child is conceived in terms of the adult cognitive system (i.e., the symbolic system as currently conceptualized by theorists). For cognitivists, the representation of reality involves an organized symbol system in which the meaning of symbols derives from the rule-governed combinatorial relations with other symbols. However, there is no logical way to achieve symbol systems with combinatorial rules that are specific to each cognitive function (perception, memory, motor control, language) without beginning the developmental process with certain givens built into the system. Specifically, a basic set of symbols and rules must be built into the individual that enable effective interaction with the world. With these presuppositions as givens, cognitive scientists are forced to conclude that cognitive abilities are driven by innate mechanisms (e.g., biological constraints, innate ideas) that are designed to achieve the mature state. This conception is formally equivalent to that of the early, nativistic ethologists and other genetic determinists: an encoded adult state informs the maturing system.

Once this idea is rejected, as it has been by developmental psychobiology, it is necessary to consider development in terms other than those by which the finality of the competent, mature system is defined. Consequently, representational symbolic systems may emerge during development from processes that do not include basic symbols and rules (see also Ballard, 1993; Olson, 1993). This is a liberating perspective that opens interesting possibilities as to what these processes might include.

In the remainder of this chapter we examine selected aspects of the development of motor skills, sensorimotor intelligence, and language during infancy. We point to some of the contributions that developmental psychobiologists can make to the challenging task of relating cognitive development to brain development.

Development of Infant Motor Skills

Human infants are not devoid of motor abilities when they are born. Their motor capacities are sufficient for functioning well within the microhabitat that is defined and provided by caregivers, but are severely limited in other contexts. Over the course of the first year of life, the infant develops the ability to interact with its environment in an astonishing variety of ways. The acquisition of locomotor skills widens the range of this environment, and progressive changes in manipulative skills provide the infant with increasing capacity to change the environment that it encounters. The developing motor skills are clearly related to the developing nervous system, but the nature of this relationship is a puzzle that has occupied many. Both historically and currently, the answers proposed have often been bound up with the concept of neural maturation (cf. Connolly, 1986). In recent years, we have witnessed increasing skepticism about how far this concept can take us, and increasing interest in more dynamic approaches to the question.

Maturation and Neurobehavioral Elements

The conventional view of neurobehavioral development has embedded within it three separable but overlapping orientations that have guided most of the research. These orientations share the idea that the nervous system is best approached as a set of separate elements that develop rather independent from one another. They differ in the focus of their research strategies. In one, the focus is on the *age of appearance* of particular motor capacities. The other two start with the idea that the earliest stage of behavior is dominated by reflexes, which are considered to be the basic neural elements for behavior. For some researchers, the focus is on following the disappearance of these primitive reflexes as an index of the maturation of higher brain structures. For others, the focus is on primitive reflexes as components in the construction of more complex behavior.

Age of Appearance

The nervous system is portrayed as comprising components or modules that are independent of one another, with each module having different consequences on motor and sensorimotor ability. Because they are independent, each of these components may mature at a different age. Consequential to maturation, specific sensorimotor abilities appear at different ages. Methodological tools favored in the research and the clinical assessments that emerge from this view emphasize the age of appearance of specific motor acts or skills. In its most extreme form, age of appearance is used as an indicator of functional maturity of the neural elements underlying the motor act. For example, the performance of precision grasping by an infant might be used to indicate maturation of the pathway connecting particular cells in the motor cortex to the motor neurons in the spinal cord that control the movement of the muscles in the hand.

A modern variant of this view considers reaching and grasping to represent separate action systems (von Hofsten, 1990). Research with monkeys demonstrated that both reaching movements and the maintenance of balance during reaching depend on the descending ventromedial spinal pathway. Grasping depends on the descending dorsolateral pathway. Extrapolating from the monkey research to humans means that before an infant can perform precision grasping of an object, the ventromedial and the dorsolateral pathways must be functional, and the reaching system must be coordinated with the grasping system. Therefore, the neural mechanisms underlying each of these separate actions must develop, as must some additional mechanism that integrates the two actions.

Unfortunately, von Hofsten's proposal is complicated by the fact that, in humans and great apes, reaching depends on both ventromedial and dorsolateral descending systems (Kuypers, 1982; Stanfield, 1992), and by the observation that grasping depends on a larger set of neural mechanisms (Johansson & Edin, 1992; Forssberg et al., 1991, 1992; Gordon et al., 1992) than von Hofsten supposed. Thus for the human infant, many different neural mechanisms may be employed in the organization of reaching and grasping at any particular point in development.

Primitive Reflexes

In the second orientation the infant is portrayed as dominated initially by **primitive** reflexes. Because anencephalic and hydrocephalic infants seem to show the same reflex development as normal infants during the first two months postpartum, the neonate is often described as a subcortical creature (Capute et al., 1978; Woodruff, 1978). Neuromotor development is thought to consist of the suppression or inhibition of these lower-order mechanisms by the maturation of higher-order, voluntary, cortical structures.

Research and clinical assessment emphasize the description of the disappearance of reflexes as an index of the maturation of higher brain structures. Since some of these neonatal reflexes seem to reappear in adults when higher (more rostral) brain areas are damaged, adult brain pathology has been used as a model for identifying the structures of the brain whose maturation is thought to suppress these reflexes. Taken in extreme, the disappearance of a reflex, such as the palmar grasp, signals the maturation of a specific neural structure such as the supplementary motor area of the cortex.

There is no doubt that developing processes of neural inhibition contribute to developmental changes in the organization and expression of behavioral patterns. However, so do developing processes of neural excitation.

Moreover, higher-order (more rostral) control mechanisms, including in-hibitory processes, are present in the newborn (Schulte, 1974). Therefore, it is unlikely that simple maturation of inhibitory control mechanisms accounts for developmental changes in behavioral organization during infancy. It is much more likely that changes in patterns of behavioral organization emerge from alterations in the balance of both inhibitory and excitatory neural processes. Also, Prechtl (1981, 1982) believes that since the adult nervous system is organized differently from the young nervous system, the study of brain-damaged adults will not provide an adequate basis for un-derstanding the developing brain.

Construction from Reflexes

In the third orientation the neonate is portrayed also as a bundle of re-flexes that are considered to be the building blocks for the construction of more complex patterns. As higher-level control mechanisms develop, goal-directed actions can be generated by appropriate selection, coordination, and timing of the performance of the simpler reflexive patterns. Research and clinical assessment emphasize detailed descriptions of motor actions as they occur to determine which simpler patterns are employed and the pro-cess of their organization and execution. Taken in extreme, complex acts of prehension, such as those involved in taking a toy from a box, might be considered to depend on the orchestration of reflexes of the motor cortex and spinal cord by structures in the frontal lobe.

Certainly, developmental changes in the functioning of many different subsystems of the nervous system (cerebellum, basal ganglia, vestibular system, etc.) contribute to the changes in the range and complexity of be-havioral organization that may be achieved. However, the neonatal nervous system is already organized and is not simply a bundle of reflexes (Prechtl, 1981, 1982). It is spontaneously active and has a behavioral organization in which it is possible to elicit reflexes. However, in the manifestation of spontaneous activity, the reflexes are already smoothly incorporated in complex patterns of coordinated actions (Michel, 1987). Development con-sists of changes in behavioral organization that occur as structures active in earlier organizations contribute to the development of new structures and their eventual integration into new patterns of organization. This theory is consistent with the dynamic systems perspective as articulated by Thelen and Fogel (1989).

The dynamic systems perspective describes the infant's motor skills as the consequence of a dynamic combination of components, some belonging to the infant and some belonging to the environment, that are organized in a fluid, task-specific manner. Each element of these components has the potential of functioning as a **control parameter** (an agent for changing the organization of the system). Changing the status of neural mechanisms, skeletomuscular systems, social interaction, or object properties (alone or in combination) may allow the infant to do things that it was not previously able to do.

Perhaps one reason why all of the three conventional concepts about neurobehavioral development are so common is that they are consistent with two conventional theories of motor development. The first concept is that development consists of a gradual and continuous progression in which the individual takes on more of the features of the adult. Each phase or step in the developmental progression is thought to be a quantitatively less perfect version of the adult and an integral antecedent for subsequent phases. The second idea describes an orderly sequence in the development of such motor skills as posture, locomotion, and manipulation.

However, as our examination of behavioral embryology revealed, phases in development may be understood fully only when they are considered also as adaptations to current conditions and not solely as preparations for later phases. Therefore, the first theory has to be modified in light of modern research in behavioral embryology. The second notion, in contrast, may require more than any simple modification can achieve. Indeed, no one of the three orientations, nor any combination of them, can adequately account for the relation between behavioral and neural development. Thus, the stage is set for a great deal of empirical and theoretical work by developmental psychobiologists.

Gesell's Maturational Theory

To understand the problems inherent in the conventional view of an orderly sequence in motor development, we must examine briefly Gesell's theory of neurobehavioral development. Gesell (1946) defined human behavioral development as a unitary process governed by endogenous biological processes. After observing the behavioral development of infants and children, he was struck by the relatively invariant sequence of accomplishments for each aspect of posture control, locomotion, and manual skill. Each of these activities was considered to be essential for the survival of the species (figure 8.2). Cross-cultural studies also yielded observations that took on great importance. Namely, the order of motor development followed the same sequence in children from different cultures. These data were interpreted as confirmation of Gesell's theory of maturation. The orderly sequence of development and the cross-cultural universality of this sequence led Gesell to propose that the basic sequential form of motor development is determined by endogenous factors. In his scheme, the environment can support, reflect, or distort the behavioral form, but it cannot produce the developmental sequence.

In addition, Gesell proposed that all psychological capacities have their developmental origin in the motor system. "Is any psychic state ever so

Motor Sequence

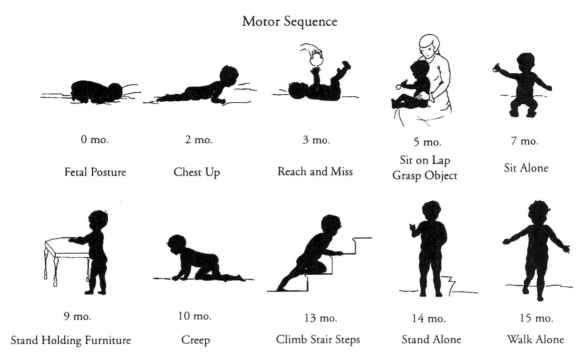

Figure 8.2   An example of motor milestones typically used to assess infant development (modified from Shirley, 1933).

attenuated that it is devoid of some bodily tension, some active motor content, or motor derivation? Is not all thinking dependent on motor set and postural adjustment and readjustment? In any event, we must explore the postural behaviors of fetus and infant if we would know the embryogenesis of the mind" (Gesell & Amatruda, 1945, p. ix). Therefore, the study of motor development was fundamental to understanding psychological development. Motor development itself reflected progressive differentiation along three axes: cephalocaudal (from head end to tail end), proximodistal (from the center of the body outward), and ulnar-radial (from control of the hand as a whole to relatively independent finger control and thumb-finger opposition).

Since most structures of the body are paired, Gesell and Amatruda (1945) proposed that development must be marked by phases of progression and regression. This produces a reciprocal interweaving as structures on opposite sides of the body compete for control. For example, the reciprocal antagonism between flexor and extensor muscles results in an early flexor phase being superseded by an extensor phase, which in turn is superseded by a phase in which these opposites are coordinated. Thus development should be nonlinear because of successive shifts in the ascendancy of one function over another as organs compete for control. One end result of the sequence of reciprocal interweaving is the adult lateral asymmetry exhibited by hand, eye, foot, and even cerebral hemispheric dominance.

Gesell considered motor development as self-regulatory because the system moves from instability to stability by establishing new behavioral patterns. Indeed, there is an ultimate pattern of stability toward which the system tends. This tendency toward stability allows compensation to occur even after significant perturbations or insults to the developmental sequence.

To support his theoretical proposals, Gesell embarked on a series of observational studies that determined the focus of modern research. The motor skills examined included manual skill developed during infancy, focusing on patterns such as grasping, reaching, prehension, bimanual manipulation, and handedness. One difficulty with Gesell's theory was that many of the features that supposedly account for the sequential character of motor development are present in the acquisition of many skills, even in adults (Newell and van Emmerik, 1990). That is, careful analyses of the movements of adults as they practice while acquiring new skills reveal a cephalocaudal, proximodistal, and ulnar-radial pattern. This is true, however, only for tasks that require the individual to maintain posture in relation to the center of gravity and/or manipulate an object. Reversals in the direction of development will occur when adults are acquiring new skills in which their body must maneuver in relation to a fixed object and/or independent of maintaining a center of gravity. This raises the issue of whether such reversals would be apparent developmentally if the tasks facing the developing child were different (e.g., zero gravity conditions).

Reciprocal interweaving (progression and regression in development) also is characteristic of changes in performance that occur during the practice of any skill. Acquiring the skills of any sport (skiing, tennis, etc.) is marked by prolonged periods of little or no progress superseded by rapid and apparently qualitative advances that are then followed by apparent regressions, and so on (cf. Siegler & Munakata, 1993). Again, depending on the task, coordination of flexor-extensor muscles by adults goes through a sequence of control much like that during development. Moreover, the self-regulatory character of development is characteristic of motor skill in general (Kugler, Kelso, & Turvey, 1980). Finally, the acquisition of motor skills in adults is marked also by omissions, commissions, and reversals in the sequential pattern of movement. Thus, the principles on which Gesell's maturational theory depended appear to be general for the acquisition of skills appropriate for certain types of tasks, no matter what the age of the individual (Newell & van Emmerik, 1990).

Manual Skills

With few exceptions, mammals locomote on four limbs. Many other species also make secondary use of their forelimbs to manipulate their environments.

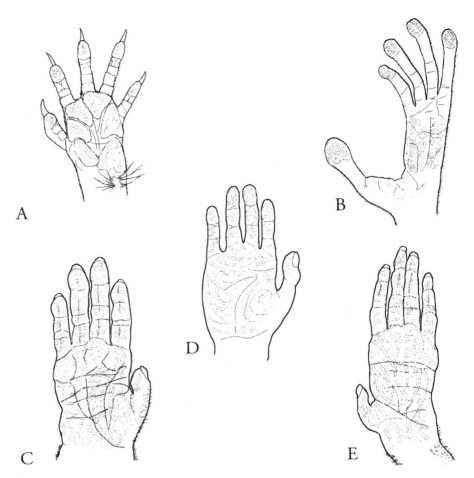

Figure 8.3   The evolution of the hand has had major consequences for human cognitive development. Extensive differences in the primate hand are related to its phylogenetic history, with the human hand particularly specialized for touch, manipulation, and fine motor control. Depicted here are the hands of (A) the most primitive primate, the tree shrew, (B) a prosimian, (C) a chimpanzee, (D) a human, and (E) a gorilla (redrawn from Campbell, 1966).

Humans adopt bipedal locomotion and devote their forelimbs more or less exclusively to manipulation. This evolutionary step includes anatomical changes in the arm and in the hand (figure 8.3). Changes in the arm are adapted to reaching (Simpson, 1976), and changes in the hand are adapted to **prehension** (Napier, 1956, 1976). In reaching, the arm moves the hand relative to the body and to objects in the environment. In prehension, a reach culminates in seizing an object by grasping it and retaining it in the hand.

   Objects are often located visually. Thus prehension typically entails coordination of the hand with the eye. Once an object is grasped, it is often

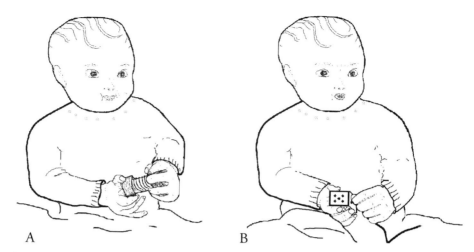

Figure 8.4 Bimanual manipulation is an important skill that develops during the latter half of the infant's first year. (A) The right hand exhibits a more flexible grasp for turning as the left hand maintains a solid supporting palmar grasp. (B) The right hand provides support as the left hand pulls on the lace (drawn from photographs in Connolly, 1973).

manipulated by the joint action of two hands. Thus, another manual skill of great importance is **bimanual coordination**. Bimanual activities often entail specialized tasks for each hand. This is called role-differentiated *bimanual manipulation* (figure 8.4). Humans typically prefer to use one hand for particular kinds of actions and the other hand for other actions. Thus handedness is another important feature of both unimanual and bimanual skills.

Prehension, bimanual coordination, and handedness all undergo extensive development during infancy. They are substantially complex, and the fully realized skill is not achieved all at once, nor is it a gradual accretion. Instead, it is characterized by progressive reorganization. The detailed developmental study of manual behavior has fostered a reconsideration of the underlying neural processes. The evidence that has been gathered is more consistent with dynamic systems approaches than with earlier ideas of the sequential maturation of discrete reflexes and higher control modules (Michel, 1991a).

Prehension

In motor skill theory, movements are defined as the sequential activity of a particular set of muscles over time. Actions are defined as sequences of movement. Prehension, therefore, is categorized as an action that includes both reaching (arm movements) and grasping (hand movements). The development of prehension includes the development of each of these movements and organizing them into a single, smooth action.

The deceptively simple question of whether neonates reach for objects has been the subject of quite a few studies and some debate. Actually, two questions are embedded in one: one involves the nature of the arm movement, and the other involves the relation of this movement to an object. Clearly, newborns' arm movements are not random thrashings (White, Castle, & Held, 1964), but are they reaching in the sense used for adults?

It is helpful to start with an idea of what reaching for objects includes when this is done by adults. To direct a reach to an object, three pieces of sensory information must somehow be mapped onto the same coordinates: the visual location of the object, the visual location of the hand and the kinesthetic or proprioceptive location of the hand. Then the arm must move through a series of locations to bring the hand and object together. In adults, this movement is accomplished by stringing together a series of "virtual positions" between the position of the hand and arm at the beginning of the reach and the final, contact position when the object can be grasped (Bizzi & Mussa-Ivaldi, 1990).

From the point of view of the nervous system, the trajectory of a movement is a sequence of postures involving the joints of the arm, appropriately timed and spatially adjusted with respect to one another and the target. Proprioceptive, visual, and tactile feedback are applied to make these adjustments. Thus, the arm movement of a reaching adult is guided by the location of the target, corrected with changes in the target, and coordinated both within the arm and with respect to the rest of the body.

Researchers have focused on three issues in an effort to determine whether the arm movements of neonates are reaches: eye-hand coordination, the motor quality of the movement, and correctability of the movement (Bushnell, 1985). Although older infants make appropriate adjustments to reach a target when they wear goggles that impose a lateral displacement of that target, neonates do not. Thus, neonatal reaches, unlike those of older infants and adults, are not corrective. Neonatal arm movement also has a swiping quality suggestive of a ballistic rather than visually guided motor control. Straight reaches involving adjustments in both shoulder and elbow joints are not apparent until around age nine months (McDonnell, 1979). The most controversial of the three issues is whether eye-hand coordination is involved in infant arm movements.

Neonates are not very successful in making contact with a target (Bushnell, 1985). In contrast with five-month-olds, who make contact over 80% of the time (Bower, 1974), neonates make contact less than 10% of the time (von Hofsten, 1982; Ruff & Halton, 1978). Yet, they came closer to a target when they visually fixated it than when they looked elsewhere or closed their eyes. This suggests that eye-hand coordination is already present.

Beginning with Piaget (1952), others argued that eye-hand coordination depends on correlated visual and tactile experience with the hand and object. For Piaget, coordination emerges from the mutual assimilation of three schemas: looking at the object, looking at the hand, and feeling with the hand. Young infants do spend a lot of time looking at their hands, and this experience may contribute to the clear ability of three- to five-month-olds to guide their reaches with visual input (Bower, 1974; Bruner, 1969; Bushnell, 1985; McDonnell, 1979; White et al., 1964). Indeed, a lateral bias in the visual regard to the two hands may contribute to the hand bias of manual skills (Michel, 1987).

If the eye-hand coordination underlying visually guided reaching requires postnatal experience with the sight of moving hands, what might account for the apparent coordination that von Hofsten concluded was present at birth? One possibility is suggested by attending to the posture of the infants (Michel, 1991a). Posture is a major contributor to the organization of movement patterns. Neonates exhibit postural asymmetry when seated or supine, with the head oriented to one side. Most prefer the right side (Michel, 1981, 1987). When in this posture, the hand on the side toward which the face is oriented is more active than the hand on the other side. This increases the probability that arm movements will be correlated with the direction of gaze. This correlation, together with the increased activity of the hand and arm on the preferred side, may create the spurious impression of eye-hand coordination.

Indeed, von Hofsten reports that eye-hand coordination during arm movement disappears around seven weeks of age, only to reappear at about four months. The disappearance corresponds in age to the appearance of the asymmetrical tonic neck reflex. This reflex is a component manifestation of neonatal postural control; its appearance indicates a change in postural control. Therefore, the arm movements of neonates may reflect a reaching-like pattern that is coordinated primarily by the biomechanics of their posture and not by visual input. As the neuromotor mechanisms underlying posture change, the constraints that shape the arm movements change, thereby accounting for the apparent disappearance of eye-hand coordination noted by von Hofsten. Visually guided reaching may represent a new pattern of neural control that coordinates early arm movements with information gained through visual, tactile, and kinesthetic experience. At this level of organization, reaching is no longer so constrained by posture; on the contrary, posture is changed to support the reach (Michel, 1991a).

For about the first two months of life there is a synergy among the joints of the arm and hand. When a newborn extends its arm, the hand opens because of the synergistic extension of the digits. Because of this synergy, reachlike extensions of newborn infants are incompatible with grasping. Grasping can occur only if synergistic flexing along the arm and hand is initiated at the shoulder level. Independent flexion or extension of the arm and hand begins after two months, and reaching behavior begins to increase at about three months. At this age, reaches can be accompanied by an open hand that has the capacity to close, independent of the movement in the arm. By the end of the first year, the hand is shaped in preparation for grasping before or during reaching with the arm (Newell, Scully, McDonald, & Baillargeon, 1989).

A number of patterns can be used to grasp an object, and they appear in an orderly developmental sequence (Halverson, 1931, 1932, 1937). The most primitive grasp, observed in the youngest infants, involves circle clawing. This is followed by a power grip squeeze by 20 weeks, a superior palm grasp by 32 weeks, and a precise grasp with opposition of thumb and index finger by 52 weeks. Manipulative patterns continue to improve throughout the first five years of life (Connolly & Elliot, 1972; Connolly, 1973).

Controversy surrounds how much these developmental sequences reflect changes in the underlying neuromotor control. An alternative interpretation is that **constraints** may account for differential performance, because the same objects may pose different tasks for younger and older infants. For example, the size and shape of objects must be considered in relation to the size of the infant's hand. When the grip configurations used by infants age four to eight months across a variety of tasks were examined, task constraints accounted for much of the differences in the configurations that were selected, independent of age (Newell et al., 1989). However, the four-month-olds were more variable than older infants, and they did not shape their hands until after contact was made. Although task constraints can account for shifting from one grasping pattern to another, infants of different ages also use different grasp patterns when constraints remain constant. The tasks in Halverson's studies were a small pill-shaped object and a 2.54-cm cube, and it is unlikely that changes in the size of the hand could account for the age-related transitions in grasping patterns. Nevertheless, at least some transitions in grasping may reflect changes in neuromotor organization.

This issue takes on added significance when the movements preparatory to grasping are used to assess the infant's knowledge of the physical world. Adults adjust both the shape of the hand and the force of their grip in relation to the visual size and shape of objects. Force is also adjusted by the felt size, tensile strength, and other properties of an object once the grasp is initiated. The preparatory adjustments made by infants change with age. For example, the distance between thumb and index finger is adjusted to the visually perceived size of an object after nine months, but not at five months (von Hofsten, 1990). The force that is used to grasp an object will not be adjusted to the size of an object before age three years (Gordon et al., 1992). These changes indicate that a long period of development exists in which the motor processes underlying prehension become integrated with expanding knowledge of objects.

Clearly, the properties of the tasks that are used to examine reaching behavior can influence the nature of the reach, and it is important to determine whether they are equivalent for infants of different ages before drawing conclusions about differences in underlying processes (Newell et al., 1989). It is also important to remember that the state and posture of the infant provide constraints that influence reaching behavior, and that the nature of these constraints changes over the course of development (Michel, 1991a). It is possible for different research protocols to arrange these internal and external constraints incidently in such a way that similar-appearing behavior can be performed through very different neuromotor mechanisms. Thus, two problems have to be avoided. On the one hand, experimental conditions must not allow the relatively trivial age-related features such as hand size to create the false impression of underlying neural differences; on the other hand, differential support from the experimental conditions must not be used to create the false impression that younger infants have the same neural organization and behavioral competency as older infants. These problems may be best approached through a variety of experimental interventions. For example, the similar behavior of younger and older infants may be challenged with various perturbations to reveal potential differences in organization.

Bimanual Coordination and Handedness

The coordinated use of the arms is seen in a variety of locomotor and manual patterns during the second half of the first year. Bimanual coordination implies linkage of left and right arm movement in both time and space (Kelso, Putnam, & Goodman, 1983). From the point of view of neural control, linkage provides an efficient way for many joints to be controlled simultaneously during complex movement.

Infants exhibit temporal and spatial linkage of the two limbs during bilateral reaching. However, the nature of this linkage differs at 7 and 11 months of age (Goldfield & Michel, 1986a). The arms are more tightly linked at the earlier age: the movements are more linked in time, and they are also more likely to move in the same direction. At 11 months movement is more likely to be complementary than isomorphic. This complementarity is expressed as convergence on a target—if one hand moves leftward, the other moves rightward toward the same object.

Bimanual coordination cannot be considered without also attending to the handedness of the infant. Infants do have hand use preferences that can be revealed with the appropriate assessment procedures. Their differential hand use may stem from the postural bias of orienting toward one side. The postural bias can be used reliably to predict later hand preferences. By four months of age, a hand preference is manifested in differential use of the two arms for reaching from midline. The reaching preference predicts hand use for object manipulation at later ages. When appropriate adjustments are made for changing behavioral capacities, handedness remains stable for most infants through at least 18 months of age (Michel, 1987, 1991a).

Bilateral reaching can be elicited by using an object such as a large ball that requires both hands to grasp. Here, handedness affects the infant's bilateral reaching, particularly when barriers are used to complicate the task (Goldfield & Michel, 1986b). In barrier-free reaching, the preferred hand is the leading hand. When a low, opaque barrier is placed in the pathway of one hand, a disruption in reaching occurs that depends on the age of the infant, its handedness, and the location of the barrier. The barrier is more likely to disrupt coordinated bimanual reaching for younger (7–9 months) infants that have a hand-use preference than for those who do not. The younger infants react to the barrier by reaching with a time delay between the two arms. For those with a preference, the hand is more likely to hit the barrier if it is in the path of the nonpreferred hand. In contrast, older (10–12 months) infants are better able to cope with the barrier if they have a hand-use preference than if they do not.

The changing pattern of bilateral reaching and its interaction with hand-use preference points to a changing pattern of neuromotor control, from the initial stages of bilateral action to the more flexible bimanual coordination of late infancy. Similar conclusions are reached from studies of object manipulation. During role-differentiated bimanual manipulation, an object is held in one hand and manipulated with the other. A preferential use of one hand for manipulating is apparent by 10 to 11 months of age and remains stable for at least the next 5 months (Ramsay, Campos, & Fenson, 1979). Just as for neonatal head orientation, neonatal hand activity, and infantile reaching, the right side is preferred by the majority of infants.

Manual activity is constant during human infancy. The orderly succession of manual activities during the first year of life provides the developing infant with reliable, human-universal experiences. Motor behavior is a function of the state of development of the nervous system, but the experiences generated by the behavior can also contribute to further development of the nervous system. Of course, the correlational nature of human research makes it difficult to test this idea. However, ample evidence from animal research supports the theory that motor experience affects neural development (chapter 6; figure 8.5; box 8.1).

When a manual action is performed, large numbers of diverse neuroanatomical structures are brought into action. There must be precise control of movement in the joints of the arm and hand, and postural adjustment of the trunk and legs. The movements involved in reaching and grasping must be coordinated into an act of prehension that is appropriately adjusted to the environment. These movements must be coordinated with object manipulation and tactile exploration. Each of the neural mechanisms is subject to change by activity, use, and differential reinforcement (Matsuzaka, Aizawa, & Tanji, 1992; Nudo et al., 1992; Spinelli & Jensen, 1982).

Moreover, as Bushnell and Boudreau (1993) proposed, the development of specific manual skills (i.e, certain unimanual and role-differentiated

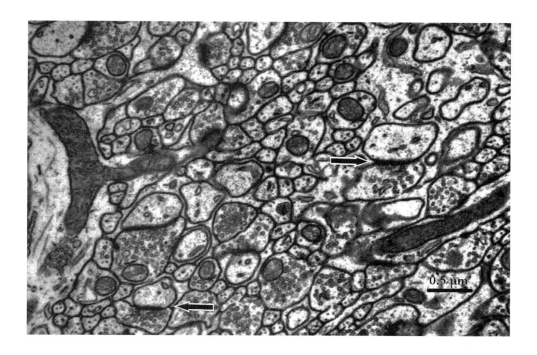

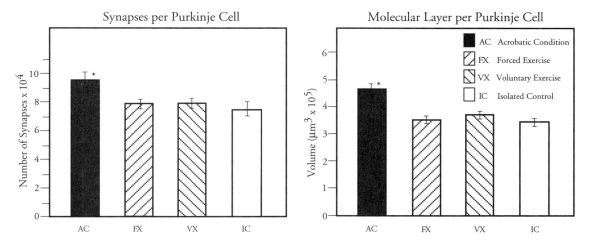

Figure 8.5 Both the volume of the molecular layer of the paramedian lobule of the cerebellar cortex, an area driven by afferents from the forelimbs and head, and number of synapses per Purkinje cell in this region increase in adult rats that acquire new motor skills through training on an acrobatic task (AC). Neither forced exercise (FX) on a treadmill nor voluntary exercise (VX) on a running wheel leads to these changes (data redrawn from Black et al., 1990. Micrograph courtesy of William T. Greenough and Jeff Kleim).

Box 8.1   Experience and Brain Structure

The experiences encountered by young organisms can affect many aspects of their neural development. But how long is this capacity retained? Many developmental events, such as determination of cell number and differentiation of neuron type, are restricted to early developmental stages. However, as Greenough (1986; Greenough & Black, 1992) showed in an intriguing series of studies, there is an enduring capacity to form new synapses. This plasticity can be observed in the growth and branching of dendrites. Rats that are weaned into an environment that offers social and physical complexity (a large cage with playmates, many varied objects) show more dendritic branching in particular brain regions such as the visual cortex than littermates weaned into individual cages. This plasticity is not restricted to adolescent rats. Indeed, it is seen even in middle-aged rats. When examined with an electron microscope, increased numbers of synapses are observed after experience in the complex environment.

The dendritic growth and synaptogenesis that occur in the complex environment are apparently the result of learning that occurs during the exploratory behavior of the animals. Similar kinds of changes have been observed with traditional learning paradigms. For a given type of experience, changes are restricted to particular brain regions. This suggests that the changes cannot be explained by some nonspecific effect, such as growth hormones or stress. Even stronger support comes from experiments with split-brain rats. By placing an opaque contact lens on one eye of such an animal before it is trained in a complex maze, only one hemisphere receives the effects of training. Dendritic changes occur in the trained, but not the untrained, hemisphere. Lateralized changes are also found when rats are trained to use one forepaw to reach for food every day, but not when reaching alternates from one forepaw to the other across days.

Not only do neurons add dendritic extent and new synapses when the animal is placed in a complex environment or given some other opportunity to learn, but the numbers of glia and capillaries also increase in regions with dendritic plasticity. These changes provide the growing, active neurons with increased oxygen, nutrients, and other support. Physical exercise with little opportunity for new learning, such as on a running wheel or treadmill, can lead to the growth of new capillaries in the cerebellum, but no new synapse formation. However, if rats are trained in an acrobatic task so that exercise is accompanied by the formation of new motor skills, increases occur in both capillaries and the number of synapses in the paramedian lobule of the cerebellar cortex.

bimanual exploratory procedures) appear to be responsible for the age-related developmental sequence of infant haptic perception. Haptic perception refers to the ability to discriminate the different properties (size, temperature, hardness, texture, weight, shape) of objects according to how they feel in the hands. Lederman and Klatzky (1987) identified specific hand movements of adults that are optimal for apprehending each of the different properties of objects. Bushnell and Boudreau (1993) note that haptic discrimination of size appears early in development between 3 and 6 months; temperature, hardness and texture discrimination at about 6 months of age; weight at about 9 months; and shape at about 12 months.

The clutching and kneading behaviors of very young infants resemble the manual exploratory procedures that Lederman and Klatzky (1987) describe as adequate for perceiving temperature, size, and hardness. The rhythmic behaviors of poking, scratching, rubbing, waving, and banging, characteristic of six- to seven-month-olds, are similar to manual actions that are adequate for perceiving the hardness, texture, and weight of objects. The role-differentiated bimanual manipulations that become apparent after nine months of age are like the manual explorations that are appropriate for perceiving the configuration of objects. Bushnell and Boudreau (1993) posit that infants are unable to discriminate objects if the differential properties require exploratory movements that are beyond their manual repertoire. Thus, manual skills are a constraint on the development of haptic perception.

The skilled use of the hands increases dramatically over the first year of life, but for the majority of infants the level of skill for right and left hands differs significantly. The patterns of ontogenetic change and of lateralization are both consistent with the idea that use of the hands contributes to the development of manual skill. As we saw in earlier chapters, the nervous system need not respect the functional categories that we impose on cognition and behavior. With this in mind, hand use may also contribute to aspects of cognition that have no obvious functional relation to manual skill. Lateralized hand use may play a constructive role in the hemispheric lateralization of language and other psychological processes.

Since manual skills involve the construction of discrete actions and the coordination of these actions in terms of both their serial order and timing, they involve processes not unlike those of cognition. Both manual skills and cognition can be described by operations and rules that affect the representation of reality in some form or another. Consequently, the study of motor control and acquisition of manual skill is not necessarily distinct from the study of cognitive processes. This is especially evident during early development. The study of infant motor processes provides insight into the infant's representations of reality, and the operations and rules by which these representations are manipulated (Olson, 1993). Thus it may be an essential link to understanding the relation between the nervous system and cognitive processes. As Piaget (1952) argued, hand use may be an early contributor to the development of intelligence.

Human prehension and manipulation differ in many aspects. They also have many similarities at both the neural and the behavioral levels with respect to manual activity and the motor behavior of other species (chapter 7). Consequently, the neural and experiential processes involved in the organization of some human manual skills can be ascertained by analogy from developmental psychobiological investigation of certain animal species. Thus, the study of manual skills is a natural link for constructing a developmental psychobiology of human cognition.

The Development of Sensorimotor Intelligence During Infancy

At the metatheoretical level, there are currently two contrasting views of intelligence during infancy (cf. Carey & Gelman, 1991). In one, infants are thought to be essentially like adults, only less complete or less able to demonstrate their intelligence because of their immaturity. Those with this orientation are likely to seek adultlike intelligence in infants, perhaps taking account of the immature sensory and motor systems by providing environmental support. They are also likely to account for the sequential emergence of new intellectual performances by postulating maturational changes in the nervous system that allow expression of existing abilities. Those who adopt the other orientation are likely to acknowledge qualitative differences in the nature of intelligence during infancy and in later stages.

Piaget is the major example of the latter orientation, as well as the major figure in the whole of cognitive development. In his theory, the **sensorimotor intelligence** of infancy is the foundation for intelligence in later stages, but fundamental transformations in the nature of intelligence occur as one stage gives way to the other. Although they do not propose an overarching theory of similar magnitude, a number of critics have offered nativistic alternatives to Piaget's account of intelligence during infancy (cf. Rosser, 1994). Generally speaking, the critics take issue with him on the grounds that abilities supposed to emerge only later in development are already present in infancy. We provide a brief account of Piaget's views and examine two of the proposed alternatives.

Piaget's Account of Sensorimotor Intelligence

Piaget (1952) proposed that infants construct their knowledge of the world from motor activity. All mental representations—ideas, plans, images, thoughts—are internalized motor activities. The basic element of knowledge is the *scheme*—the way of acting on objects. For infants, schemes are equivalent to motor skills (sucking, looking, reaching, grasping, hearing, etc.) that are used to process and acquire information from the environment. Schemes are causal systems that regulate the individual's interactions with the world; they are not a model or representation of the world (Olson, 1993). Infants manifest representational intelligence when they assign function or meaning to the various schemes that they use to interact with the events and objects in their environments.

An experience is "known" only when information is processed according to a scheme that exists within the infant's repertoire. If the scheme cannot process the information, it must be modified before the experience can be known and the infant's interaction with the experience can be regulated. Piaget proposed that schemes are modified by the "constituents and consequences" of their actions. These include sensory input from the environment, sensory and proprioceptive feedback from the actions, and information from changes in the environment. Each of these can modify a scheme by imposing constraints on the action. Schemes can combine to form new schemes, and as schemes become more complex they take on the characteristics of operations. For Piaget, manual action is both an expression of knowledge and a means of acquiring it.

The centrality of motor activity to intelligence during infancy means that, for Piaget, infants have no concepts that are independent of their activity. Their environments are defined by these activities. Indeed, when the individual's performance implies that concepts have emerged that are emancipated from attendant motor action, this is taken as evidence for a new, qualitatively distinct, developmental transformation of intelligence—the preoperational stage. This new stage represents the transformation of schemes put in place during the sensorimotor stage. Therefore, if young infants were to show evidence of intelligence that is not sensorimotor, this would provide a major challenge to his theory.

A number of researchers claimed such evidence (e.g., Mandler, 1988; Spelke, 1991). They concluded that very young infants have cognitive concepts, such as the permanent and independent existence of objects, that represent reality independent of sensorimotor abilities. Such conclusions are counter to Piaget's theoretical account of how these concepts develop. Some of their evidence also calls into question Piaget's empirical description of the development of sensorimotor intelligence in infancy.

Do Infants Have an Adult Cognitive System?

The early appearance of complex cognitive concepts has prompted views that adult commonsense knowledge and intuitive physical reasoning are constrained by innate principles that were created by natural selection to enable the individual to interact successfully with the world. Very young infants are reportedly cognizant of the physical principles of spatiotemporal continuity and the solidarity of objects. These principles are the bases of the adult's concept of object. If they are present so early, cognitive development cannot have grown out of motor activity. Rather, it is proposed, cognition emerges from innate principles that are present at the outset. What appears as cognitive development consists simply of enrichment, not change (e.g., Spelke, 1991).

The acquisition of scientific knowledge contrasts with the acquisition of commonsense knowledge because it involves radical conceptual change that is unconstrained by the innate principles that determine commonsense knowledge (Spelke, 1991). According to Spelke, scientific concepts require a distinct, "learned," thinking skill. The sophisticated scientist employs theory-building skills that depend on a special metaconceptual awareness that sets it apart from other knowledge. Thus, a dichotomy is present in cognition, with one form innate and another acquired.

A developmental psychobiologist is likely to recognize some old mistakes in this formulation (chapter 3). First is the problem of dividing cognitive concepts into those that are innately governed (commonsense concepts) and those that are not (scientific concepts). Surely the cultural skills of reading, spelling, mathematics, geography, and operating VCRs and personal computers cannot involve distinctly different developmental processes than the abilities of communicating with others, anticipating their actions, and so on. If this is a false dichotomy, it cannot be applied meaningfully to cognition. Second, an adaptationist argument is invoked to support the nativist position. Following Tinbergen's (1963a) lucid statement, ethologists and developmental psychobiologists contend that adaptation and development are completely separate questions requiring different answers: natural selection and innate principles cannot be used in mutual implication.

Third, performances that have a similar appearance in very young infants and adults are presumed to be homologous. Consequently, the only differences between them can be those of "enrichment" (a vague term that could mean anything from the decorations on a cake to the provision of essential vitamins, minerals, and other nutrients), not those of quality or substance. This assumption ignores the well-documented observation that similarity in outcomes can be achieved through very different means, including differences in environmental support that counteract very real organismic differences. It takes rather clever experimental techniques to reveal the differences underlying the similarities in infant and adult abilities. For example, although both very young infants and adults appear to possess a concept of object, initially only common movement seems to define "objectness" for infants, whereas more complex definitions of the object concept come later (Rosser, 1994). Developmental research is necessary to determine the precursors and prerequisites for how only common movement can define the initial concept of object, and how that definition can change into the richer conceptualization of children and adults.

Finally, age of appearance calls on biology (i.e., age-related conditions in the nervous system) to account for the performance of infants, with no examination of the task, organismic, and experiential factors that may have contributed to the ability. The account does not consider the contributions that functional activity makes to neural development in the infant. Instead, neural maturation is used problematically (as discussed earlier in this chapter) to provide an independent explanation of cognitive development. These are persisting problems that crop up in many contexts.

Diamond (1991a, 1991b), taking a somewhat different tack than Spelke's, arrived at similar ideas about infant cognitive development using visual fixation and habituated looking techniques. She proposed that the infant's cognitive knowledge is as rich as the adult's, and developmental differences in how that knowledge is expressed can be explained by maturational factors. Specifically, the modes of expressing the same cognitive knowledge will change with maturation of the nervous system. In particular, the child's ability to express cognitive concepts is "intimately tied to maturation of frontal cortex" (Diamond, 1991a, p. 67).

Of related interest, the development of the frontal cortex is proposed to account for much of the development of children's metacognitive abilities (Segalowitz & Rose-Krasnor, 1992) and the performance of children in Piagetian tasks (Case, 1992). The frontal lobes are a large area of the brain for which it has not been easy to assign specific functions. Damage to the frontal lobes results in deficits that are described as disruptions of organization, self-monitoring, adaptability, social responsiveness, and sensitivity to global context. These are vague descriptions, at best. Perhaps the appeal of using brain maturation to explain the development of a diverse set of complex psychological phenomena lies in the diversity and vagueness of functions assigned to the frontal lobes. Of course, these same qualities also limit the usefulness of such proposals.

Using a set of rather simple tasks (retrieval of objects from transparent boxes, of hidden objects after a short delay, or of objects from behind transparent barriers), Diamond compared the performance of infants with that of brain-damaged adults, and brain-lesioned and neurally intact adult and infant monkeys. Successful performance on each of the tasks depends on knowing certain physical principles and the ability to organize actions that are appropriate to the task. From their performance on tasks involving habituated looking, Diamond concluded that infants possess the knowledge of the relevant physical principles. Starting from this supposition, she proposed that the infant can fail to demonstrate that knowledge because of inability to organize the appropriate actions.

Diamond believes that the infant's failure is related to the immaturity of specific brain areas. She proposes that one common reason infants fail to express their knowledge is that they cannot inhibit action tendencies that interfere with the appropriate behavior. Thus, retrieval of an object from a clear box requires inhibition of the grasp and withdrawal patterns as well as integration of actions into a sequence of opposite movements. Also, infants must inhibit reaching directly for an object to retrieve it from behind a barrier.

Another common failure occurs because successful action involves relating two movements together in a sequence. When retrieving a toy from behind an obstacle, for example, an infant must change the direction of its arm and hand movements several times to meet with success. This can be studied by placing a desirable object immediately behind a transparent screen that is in front of the infant. The infant's reach must go over the barrier and beyond the object, reverse to contact and grasp the object, then change once more to clear the barrier and return toward the body.

A third common failure occurs because the task requires infants to relate information that is separated in space and time. The object is hidden in a new place in plain view of the infant, but retrieval is delayed. Consequently, the infant seeks the object in its old hiding place, rather than in a new place, even when the infant saw it hidden there only a short time ago.

According to Diamond, avoidance of each of these failures depends on abilities associated with mature functioning of the frontal cortex. "Frontal cortex and its network of neural interconnections must reach a certain level of maturity before these abilities begin to appear" (Diamond, 1991a, p. 67). Diamond maintains that relating two or more movements into a sequence is an aspect of the supplementary motor area (SMA) of the cortex. Remembering a sequence of actions, in contrast, is thought to be a consequence of the dorsolateral prefrontal cortex. Moreover, relating two different movements together simultaneously (the complementary use of the two hands) "is dependent upon maturation of the interhemispheric connections via the corpus callosum between the two SMAs on either side of the brain. Such bimanual coordination is an achievement of relational ability *and* inhibition, inasmuch as it requires not only coordinating the actions of the two hands but also inhibiting the tendency of both hands to do the same thing" (Diamond, 1991a, pp. 68–69). Diamond hypothesizes that maturational changes begin more posteriorly with the SMA, progress anteriorly to the dorsolateral prefrontal cortex, and end with interhemispheric communication. These maturational changes govern the order of behavioral development.

Diamond correctly concludes that motor skills contribute to the demonstration of cognitive concepts. Although an infant must have the appropriate motor skill to demonstrate a concept, acknowledging this dependency is very different from her assertion that the concept exists independent of the motor skill. The concept of "object" that is demonstrated by visual fixation and habituated looking may not be the same concept as that demonstrated by the use of manipulatory skills.

Fischer and Bidell (1991) argued persuasively that researchers should pay careful attention to the environmental support systems that enable young infants to demonstrate apparent cognitive sophistication. In their research they showed how the very young infant's performance depends heavily on the support provided by the adult, and the match between the task demands and the infant's spontaneous behavior. Moreover, the experimental techniques used to demonstrate very early cognitive competence in infants confuse perceptual discriminatory ability with representational knowledge and understanding (Bremner, 1993). Piaget's theory was an attempt to account for the development of understanding.

As Carey (1991) notes, both babies and adults may perceive a world as containing solid objects that exhibit spatiotemporal continuity. However, "what the baby takes as the core properties of objects are seen by the adult to be derived from more fundamental properties ... objects, for babies, are bounded, coherent, wholes and, as such, are totally distinct from liquids, gels, powder, and other nonsolid substances" (Carey, 1991, p. 289). In contrast, adults perceive all of these as substantial in the same sense that solid objects are substantial. Thus, a fundamental change in the cognitive world has occurred.

It is useful to turn once more to Piaget's proposal that the world is known by how the individual can investigate it. The physical principles known by habituated looking are different from those known by manipulation, which, in turn, are different from those known by propositions. Concepts are interrelated to other concepts differently in the conceptual systems of adults and children (Carey, 1991). Because of these differences, a major issue of developmental psychology is how adults can come to understand the concepts and propositions of infants and children. Progress will not be made if partial similarity is taken for identity.

Neural Development and Infant Intelligence

Diamond's research reminds us of the importance of considering information about the development of the nervous system when examining behavioral development. A function may not be achievable in the absence of specific neural structures. As Prechtl (1981, 1982) warned, however, analyses of the consequences of brain damage to adult behavioral expressions does not provide insight into the role that these structures play in the infant. The nervous system of the infant is an organized, adaptive structure. It is not an incomplete version of the adult's. Adult functions do not emerge as the various structures of the nervous system develop. The development of a neural structure allows it to be incorporated into the neural system, and such incorporation may contribute to the development of additional abilities. However, there is no reason to conclude that a newly appearing ability resides in the new structure. The new structure may allow older structures to engage in the new ability. There is also no reason to exclude the possibility that the new ability can be achieved without the new structure. After all, a hydrocephalic patient with virtually no cortical tissue received an honor's degree in mathematics and led a completely normal social life (Lewin, 1980).

Infants show patterns of complementary bimanual manipulation of certain objects by seven to nine months of age (Kimmerle, Mick, & Michel, 1995). If one follows Diamond's account, this occurs long before either the supplementary motor area or its interhemispheric connections are mature enough to enable such action (Michel, 1991a). By what neural mechanisms are these actions achieved, and what role does experience engendered by early complementary bimanual manipulation play in the development of the supplementary motor area and it interhemispheric connections? From a developmental psychobiological perspective these questions are more pressing and intriguing than questions designed to attach the development of a specific behavioral accomplishment to the developmental status of a particular neural structure.

Diamond's work highlights the consequences of Piaget's reliance on the use of the hands for describing the infant's cognitive abilities. Also, as Diamond noted, inhibition of inappropriate behavior is an important aspect of behavioral development that is often neglected in cognitive studies. However, inhibition is a common function of even the prenatal nervous system (chapter 7). Moreover, behavioral inhibition is not equivalent to neural inhibition. The inhibition of a movement involves both the activation and inhibition of neural networks. It would be more appropriate to propose that accomplishing certain tasks requires the orchestration of movements into actions, and that the infant (or the adult, in certain instances) has not yet worked out the "score" governing the timing of the movements.

Nothing in the modern investigation of infant cognitive development warrants either a nativistic or a maturational explanation. Nevertheless, attention must be paid to the status of the nervous system when attempting to characterize the differences between the infant's abilities and those later in development. Perhaps the kinds of solutions that developmental psychobiologists have found for analogous problems can guide the cognitive neuroscientist toward a new conception of the relation between the developing brain and developing intelligence.

Aspects of Language Development

"Possessing a language is the quintessentially human trait: all normal humans speak, no nonhuman animal does. Language is the main vehicle by which we know about other people's thought processes, and the two must be intimately related" (Pinker, 1990, p. 199). Other animals, however complex their communication systems, do not have the generative rule system that characterizes human language. The evolutionary and developmental origins of this very human trait pose challenges that have attracted many developmental psychologists.

Mastery of language is a monumental achievement of early childhood. Clearly, some relationship exists between language acquisition and other emerging cognitive skills, but what is its nature? Some adherents of Chomsky's views are persuaded that, at its core, language is a largely autonomous faculty, relatively insulated from other psychological processes. These other processes can affect some aspects of language performance, but do not enter into the fabric of its structure. Others have a different perspective and conclude that language development is woven into the development of cognitive processes, including those involved in social interaction and communication.

Some aspects of language convinced many that biological concepts are required to help explain its development. As in the study of intelligence, it is often assumed that these biological concepts must entail nativism. Nativism has taken the form of a clear dichotomy between environmental and internal sources of development, with internal equated with innate. It has also led to the characterization of neural contributions to language in terms of brain maturation.

Over the past three decades, the study of language development was dominated by Chomsky. Therefore, we begin with a brief account of his viewpoint, and then consider some alternatives that hold promise for a psychobiological integration that avoids the difficulties of nativism.

Syntactic Theory

Beginning in 1959, Chomsky theorized that no general psychological process can account for the development of language. Indeed, even if the psychological processes are adequate to the task, the environment is not. He took the position that the environment in which the child develops does not provide the information that would be required for general psychological processes to construct a language from environmental input. Chomsky proposed instead that children acquire language with a distinct, specially evolved "mental organ" (Pinker, 1990). The properties of this organ, which he called the **language-acquisition device**, are not shared with other cognitive systems. They are, instead, syntactic. Syntax applies to the rules specifying the grammatical structures (categories and relations) in which particular words are placed. Many of these are assumed to be innate.

The nativistic assumption is reached primarily from the conclusion that the presumably relevant part of the environment, the language milieu, does not provide the child with the basic grammatical structures of its language. These grammatical structures are not evident in spoken language, and adults do not provide the relevant feedback that a child could use to sort its own utterances into appropriate and inappropriate constructions. Nevertheless, all children do eventually acquire knowledge of appropriate grammatical structures. This is evidently the case because all adults demonstrate this knowledge, even if they do not articulate it. Therefore, it is stated, the child must begin language acquisition with an acquisition device that allows it to extract rules for categorizing and combining words from the spoken language that constitutes its language milieu. It is concluded that the processes comprised by the acquisition device are innate, maturing in the brain before the initiation of language acquisition. The adult language structure is encoded in the system from the outset, informing the maturation of the brain that will be used to produce the language.

The innate processes, together with the grammatical rules extracted from the milieu through their use, are the bases of language ability. An innate language-specific device is also seen as consistent with neurological reports that damage to particular areas of the left hemisphere affects specific aspects of language functioning.

Another reason for turning to innate grammatical mechanisms is the sheer speed with which language develops. Developmental studies reveal that language begins with "holophrastic" utterances consisting of single words or unitary phrases that have been memorized. Then, two-word combinations appear. These combinations represent about a dozen semantic relations, such as agent-object, object-location, action-object, possessor-object, and recurring object or event. There is no distinct three-word phase. Rather, children gradually increase their mean length of utterance based on a complex array of rule-governed combinations. It is difficult to conceive how this can be achieved without the aid of some device that is already in place to guide the combinations.

Following Chomsky's lead, Pinker (1990) proposed that the child possesses a set of innate syntactic categories. These include innate noun phrase structures, noun categories, and verb phrase structures. However, simply having the categories is not sufficient: the child must also have a means for recognizing these categories in parental speech, the major source of utterances in the language milieu. Pinker proposed that this recognition occurs through innate semantic "flags" that assign a word to one of the innate syntactic categories. For example, a word that names an object is automatically assigned to the noun class. On hearing a novel word, a child will be innately predisposed to categorize that word as a name for an object (the whole object, not its properties or parts). The innate syntactic categories and the innate semantic flags together allow a child to categorize verbal input before grammatical rules for combining words are in place. Children appear to bootstrap themselves by using these language-specific innate processes to develop a grammar for their native language (see box 8.2 for an alternative account).

Box 8.2   Development of Overregulation of English Verbs

Overregulation of the past tense in English is perhaps the aspect of language development that is most paradigmatic of the idea of an innate syntactic device. All English-speaking children pass through a phase in their language acquisition in which they produce erroneous past tense forms such as "goed" and "sitted," utterances that they are unlikely to hear in their language environment. What the children do is to apply the regular past tense rule to irregular verbs. The chronology of this stage is interesting. Children first use irregular verbs appropriately and then switch to the overregularized verb form; they subsequently go on to produce appropriately the regular past tense and the irregular exceptions.

Overregularization is described as a regression in development and is thought to be particularly revealing of endogenous processes. Specifically, the apparent regression and progression in irregular verb production has been used to support the idea of stages in language acquisition, marking endogenous periods of reorganization of the rules of language that are independent of language input.

Building on the work of Rumelhart and McClelland (1986b), Plunkett and Sinha (1992) provide examples of several neural network computer models that can account for the characteristic U-shaped, ontogenetic pattern of overregularization of the English past tense without assumptions about endogenous rules. After feeding the models language input that is reasonably characteristic of the normal milieu, the models were able to predict patterns of regression and progression. They were also able to detect subtleties of performance, such as temporally independent U-shaped curves for different types of irregular forms that had not previously been noted in children but were later verified.

Artificial neural network models are programs that simulate rather primitive properties of a nervous system. They are parallel processors, characterized by a high degree of connectivity among the individual units. Because of the connectivity, the activity of each individual unit can be affected by information arising from various sources within the system. This leads to distribution of information throughout the network, which is useful for detecting and storing invariances even in a noisy environment. What makes these models so powerful for understanding development is that they can "learn" solutions to environmental tasks in self-organizing ways. Furthermore, they do so when provided with rather minimal starting biases.

The essential ingredient required for these models to simulate the pattern of acquisition of the English past tense is exposure to the different forms of regular and irregular verbs. The different solutions that are manifested before the network arrives at the proper English rule system follow the same sequence shown by children: proper use of the irregular past, overregularization, then proper use of both verb types. These neural network models suggest that complex linguistic skills can emerge through the operation of a simple general mechanism on language input, with no requirement of an innate linguistic structure (Plunkett & Sinha, 1992).

Semantic Theory

Using "innate" as an explanatory concept is just as troublesome here as in other areas of research. Braine (1992) observed that when syntactic categories are labeled innate, this simply passes the problem to the developmental biologist without providing any indication about how the biologist could solve it. Braine proposes instead that any explanatory theory of language acquisition must include a developmental account of the primitives that are postulated, even if it is only a sketch of how the development might occur. Unfortunately, the theories of language acquisition that derive from Chomsky fail to consider how the syntactic primitives that are foundational to the rest of language development might themselves have originated (Pinker, 1984, 1990). These theories simply begin with the assertion that the foundation is innate.

It is, however, possible to create models that acquire language distinctions without assumptions of innate syntax (Braine, 1992). The semantic theorists accomplish this by refusing to accept the artificial separation between syntax and meaning (**semantics**) that Chomsky required. Instead, they assume that the child starts language acquisition by using starting materials (framework categories) that are drawn from thought processes (Braine, 1987; Schlesinger, 1988). These framework categories are the primitives that are then used to build syntactic categories.

One type of framework category that is assumed in the child is ontological categories (ability to distinguish among objects, places, time, events, propositions, and other such entities). The child is also assumed to have two other framework categories: predicate and argument. A predicate can be either concepts or relations. The argument refers to particular instances. A concept has only one argument; for example, it might be that an object has some particular property. A relation has two or more arguments, which are the specific entities that are related. The predicate-argument distinction is believed to be primitive in cognitive psychology, logic, and semantics. It is assumed that thought processes will lead children spontaneously to encode events that they see and sentences that they hear in terms of objects that have properties and that are related to other objects (Braine, 1992).

Braine's (1992) semantic theory shares with Pinker's (1990) syntactic theory two assumptions about the developmental primitives through which language is acquired. These are a learning mechanism that analyzes input from the language milieu through the use of rules that are already in place, and the semantic categories (argument, predicate, ontological categories). However, the two theories differ in their assumptions about how a child handles new words and phrases that are not classified by old rules. The syntactic theory assumes that a child will place these new words into innate syntactic categories on the basis of innate semantic flags. The semantic theory does not share this assumption. Instead, it states only that a child will have a tendency to treat new words not classified by old rules as instances of semantic categories. The interactions among the use of old rules, semantic categorization, and language input are postulated to lead to the emergence of syntactic categories. This is accomplished through progressive adjustment of the semantic categories to match the syntactic categories in the language that the child is learning (Braine, 1992).

Although there are several semantic theories of language (Maratsos & Matheny, 1994), the central difference between them and syntactic theories is that one posits innate syntactic categories and the other provides an account of how these categories can emerge during development. The semantic theorists solved the problem of explaining the initial steps of language development without appeals to devices that are special for language. This was done by moving outside the functional category of language to identify developmental primitives among more general cognitive processes.

Of course, syntactic theorists also recognized that cognitive processes that are not specific to language can contribute to language development. However, they are considered to influence only the performance aspects of language. For example, the two-word utterances that children initially form seem to be subsets of underlying patterns that contain three or more elements. Pinker (1990) interprets that to mean that children at the two-word stage can keep longer sequences of words in mind. They cannot pronounce these longer sequences, however, because their available information processing permits only two words at a time to be processed for speech.

Syntactic theorists also consider conceptual development to have an effect on the acquisition of language but, once again, it is language performance, not competence, that is affected. Certain conceptual advances may be necessary before language competence can be expressed in speech. For example, if children have not mastered a complex semantic relationship, they will not be able to master the syntax dedicated to expressing it. In addition, the order of language acquisition is related to more general aspects of cognition. This order is reflected in the fact that simpler linguistic rules are mastered before more complex rules. Thus, cognitive abilities have more of a restrictive than constructive influence on language development.

The syntactic theorists locate the innate aspects of language acquisition in particular brain circuits. They invoke maturational changes in these circuits to explain age-related changes in language development. Maturational changes in the brain are thought to account for the onset of language acquisition, individual differences in the rate and timing of language development, and the decline in language acquisition during adolescence. The last refers to the observation that the ability to learn a language and attain native proficiency is not as great in adolescents as in younger children (Newport, 1991). Pinker (1990) states that "the brain appears to have circuits, mostly in the left hemisphere, that are specific to aspects of language (though exactly how that internal wiring gives rise to rules of language is unknown). It appears that the development of these circuits may be a driving force underlying the course of language acquisition" (p. 213).

Although the semantic theorists took an important step toward explaining the origin of language by showing how syntax can emerge from beginnings outside of language, their theories do not necessarily reject nativism. In Braine's (1992) account, the semantic categories and rules from which language springs are assumed to be innate. Although the developmental problem is not confined to language, a full developmental account will also have to explain the origin of these cognitive processes and not rest content with the innate label. Some insights into how this analysis might proceed are described in earlier sections of this chapter.

Other suggestions come from a more thorough consideration of the broader developmental context in which language is embedded. As the semantic theorists pointed out, one of the dangers of compartmentalizing cognition is that we isolate language and fail to recognize commonalities in the acquisition of language and other cognitive skills. Indeed, language acquisition even shares features in common with those associated with the acquisition of motor skills in adults (Newell & van Emmerik, 1990). Furthermore, language is a communication skill, and it can also be illuminating to relate its development to the broader context of social development.

Language as a Communicative Skill

The functional compartmentalization of language has had a fundamental effect on the way it is described. Children's speech becomes so complex so quickly that it is convenient to use adult grammatical categories to describe it. No one has developed a descriptive characterization of grammatical abilities directly from the study of children's speech (Pinker, 1990). It should be remembered that linguists and psycholinguists identify grammatical rules by asking adult, native speakers whether or not a particular utterance sounds natural to them. Children cannot answer these questions with any reliability. Therefore, current linguistic methods are completely inappropriate for writing a grammar of children's speech. This absence of a descriptive base drawn from the behavior of children is an important omission, because it leads one to describe developmental steps only in terms of the finished product. For grammar, it means that children's speech is described by the ways in which their utterances conform to, or differ from, those of adults.

One theoretically important consequence of describing children's speech with adult grammatical categories is that it automatically sets the developmental problem in terms of goals rather than in terms of origins. This can lead one to overlook raw materials, or primitives, that are not captured by that adult-derived descriptive mode. It can also lead to a misleading description of the language milieu of children.

According to some developmental psycholinguists (e.g., Moerk, 1989), syntactic theorists described the language environment by using information drawn from adult speech and descriptive categories appropriate for the study of formalized grammar. This led them to characterize the language provided by adults and acquired by children as more complex and intricate than is actually the case. They then concluded that because the language milieu provides an impossible, unlearnable input, it is necessary to postulate innate sources for language acquisition. However, this postulate is not necessary, because it is based on inaccurate descriptions of both the language environment and the skill to be acquired.

Attending to the mode of description is indeed instructive. As these critics would argue, the skills that an adult has for driving an automobile could be described in a manner designed to reveal their complexity compared with those of the beginning learner. As is the case for language, the expert would not be able to articulate his or her knowledge to match the complexity in the skill or in its description. No beginning driver immediately matches the skilled performance of the expert. This is acquired. Yet, we would be unlikely to argue for a separate acquisition device for driving skills, based on the disparity between novice and expert and the inability of expert drivers to articulate the perceptual motor complexities underlying their skills.

Although in some phases the rate of language acquisition appears dramatically fast, in reality, it extends over a prolonged period. "Language mastery is ... a long-term product" (Moerk, 1989, p. 25). It is misleading to say that a child learns a language, mathematics, or a culture, because that implies a final product. The same is true even for simpler skills. We continue acquisition processes throughout the life span. As Moerk (1989) notes, "skiing, like culture, mathematics, or language, is a summary term that conceals the many fine gradations in the learning process and in the recursively improving levels of skills. In obfuscating differences and in suggesting a reified uniform product, these summary terms can easily lead to misconceptions of the tasks and of the processes involved in solving these tasks" (p. 27).

Most syntactic theorists construe the language milieu of children rather narrowly and fail to consider the dynamic character of the milieu throughout the prolonged period of development. As Bloom (1993) demonstrated, "the 'head start' with which infants begin to learn words ... includes developments in affect, cognition, and [the infant's] social connectedness to other persons" (p. 9). The milieu includes more than language, and its dynamic quality can be observed in both short-term and long-term changes in both parent and child. Language input from the mother, for example, is regulated on the basis of the immediate context provided by the child as well as on her knowledge of the child's general abilities. Developing children have rather sophisticated cognitive and social abilities during the period in which they are acquiring language, and of course these also change. For example, general information-processing abilities can be brought to bear on language input. Indeed, aspects of syntactic ability have been detected in the information processing of manual skills of preverbal children (Greenfield, 1991).

The amount of information processing that the child has to do to achieve a particular piece of language depends on the support from the social environment. Mothers provide much of the necessary supportive scaffolding, and the child's performance within that scaffolding provides much of the impetus for changing and reorganizing the structure (Bruner, 1981). Much of the information available in the language milieu is structured by the mother and can be used by the child rather directly.

As developmental psychobiologists might expect, a bidirectionality of cause-effect relations exists between the mother and child. Thus the child's level of linguistic skills influences both the kinds of models and the nature of the feedback that mothers provide; these in turn influence the child's subsequent productions. Unlike the picture created initially by Chomsky, a lot of linguistic information is present in mother-child interactions. When different forms of linguistic feedback were added together, one study estimated approximately 2000 items of maternal feedback during 20 hours of interaction, or about 2 per minute (Moerk, 1989). This input can, for example, reveal underlying linguistic structure to a child by providing a number of word-substitution sequences in rapid succession; it can provide corrective feedback by repeating the child's linguistically incorrect utterance in close but corrected form; and so forth.

Although several types of learning must be involved in language acquisition, Moerk (1989) considers perceptual learning to be especially important. Perceptual learning is a form of pattern perception that underlies procedural knowledge. Like the grammar of a language, procedural knowledge is tacit: it cannot be described by the knower and cannot be taught through instruction and prescription. It is abstracted from experience with examples and demonstrations. Also like grammar, procedural knowledge exhibits generativity of surface strings from underlying structure. Thus, pattern abstraction based on perceptual learning may be a major contributor to language acquisition.

Based on Chomsky's work, the assumption has been that the language milieu cannot provide grammatical structures to the child. However, the phenomena of perceptual learning question this assumption. Just as in Gibson's (1966) conception of perception, the structural information in language can emerge from the child's detection of the invariances in utterance patterns over many transformations (Moerk, 1989). Such invariances of syntactic patterns may provide "affordances" for the child to perceive just those syntactic structures that Chomskyans assume are never accessible to the child. Consequently, the language milieu would have the structure necessary to provide grammatical information (Moerk, 1989), but it would not be in the individual utterances themselves.

A somewhat similar model of language development proposed by Chandler (1993) uses an exemplar-based model of categorization derived from Skousen (1989, 1992). According to this model, exposure to a wide range of experiences results in the storage of many exemplars. Cognitive categories are not derived from prototypes or schemas, but emerge from experience that matches new experiences to old by way of similarity. Like connectionist models, the accumulation of these experiences forms exemplars for categorization. Chandler proposes that the child is exposed to a wide range of linguistic experiences that are stored in memory. Thus, the child accumulates "an ever larger collection of communicative experiences represented in distributed networks and available for access as a user formulates or comprehends new utterances in new communicative contexts" (Chandler, 1993, p. 604). The child and adult only behave as if they have linguistic rules. Rather they operate with an exemplar-based categorization system based on their language experience. Thus, Chandler's model also derives language acquisition from more general cognitive capabilities (in this case, exemplar-based categorization).

The Neurology of Language

The neural basis of language has been often described in terms of specific areas of the brain that are devoted to linguistic processes. Do these areas not demonstrate the presence of an innate language-acquisition device that is capable of processes not shared by other cognitive abilities? If these brain regions are specific to language acquisition and production, it would suggest that efforts to explain language acquisition in terms of such general processes as pattern extraction will meet with limited success.

The left hemisphere does appear to sustain grammatical capacity better than the right. However, modern linguistic analyses of aphasic patients challenged the conception that the manifestation of specific linguistic abilities relies exclusively on particular, devoted brain areas within the left hemisphere (Bates, 1993b; Maratsos & Matheny, 1994; Willmes & Poeck, 1993). "Whereas deficits stated over activities taken as a whole—for instance, impaired output, relatively intact comprehension—seem most often to implicate particular cortical areas, deficits stated in the abstract terms of current linguistic theory have not been shown to have this impressive lesion-localizing value" (Zurif, 1990, p. 187). Thus, there may be specificity in brain regions where damage leads to language deficits, but it may lie in mechanisms that are not unique to language.

Data from brain damaged patients may be grouped into four major **aphasia** syndromes: Broca's, Wernicke's, global, and amnesic aphasia (Willmes & Poeck, 1993). At one time, Broca's aphasia might have been described as dysfluent agrammatism and Wernicke's aphasia as fluent asemanticism because of the serious production problems associated with the

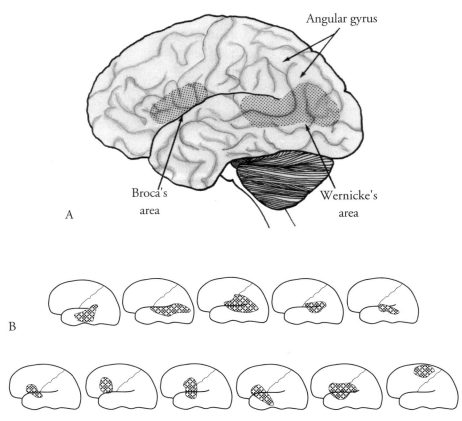

Figure 8.6   (A) The human brain, with classically defined sites of Broca's and Wernicke's aphasia indicated. (B) Acute Wernicke's aphasia (top row) and acute Broca's aphasia (bottom row) can result from varied sites of damage, as indicated by computerized tomographic scans (B redrawn from Mazzocchi & Vignolo, 1979).

former and the ready production of meaningless language associated with the latter (figure 8.6). The difficulty of classifying many instances of aphasia into these two categories prompted the recognition of global aphasia, which incorporates aspects of both Broca's and Wernicke's aphasias together with other problems, and amnesic aphasia, which is characterized by memory deficits. Furthermore, the classic categories do not accurately describe many aphasic individuals (Maratsos & Matheny, 1994). Recent evidence shows that Broca's aphasics may have difficulty comprehending and producing meaningful sentences yet show considerable skill in judging the grammaticality of sentences. Wernicke's aphasics may exhibit syntactic knowledge that is no better than the agrammatic Broca's aphasic, yet they are capable of unexpected semantic skills (e.g., substitution of semantically related words and lexical priming effects).

Careful investigation revealed that agrammatic people with Broca's aphasic are generally slower processors of representational information

(Zurif, 1990). They apparently fail to access stored word representations, but this is not really a specifically linguistic failure. Instead, their slowed processing means that word representations will not be available at the requisite time in a processing sequence. The fast-acting processing devices used in the speech domain may depend on devices in the motor system. Thus, there may be sharing of processing devices by language and motor systems.

Other attempts to characterize the differences between the dysfluent and fluent aphasias proposed differences in excitatory versus inhibitory processing functions or in temporal integration functions. This approach is prompted in part by the poor match between the pattern of language deficits associated with brain damage, and the hypothesis of separate brain modules for linguistic distinction between syntax and semantics. One important challenge to the notion of specific brain modules is provided by developmental evidence of an elastic relation between language functions and particular brain tissues revealed by age differences in response to brain damage (Maratsos & Matheny, 1994). Surgical removal of the left hemisphere during infancy has rather minimal impact on the development of language skills, but often has drastic effects in adults. Recovery of language functions after early focal lesions is also far superior to that after lesions later in life. Unlike adults, children rarely develop aphasia in response to posterior lesions and rarely exhibit the symptoms of Wernicke-like aphasia. Their symptoms are more likely to be transient and to include mutism and uncontrollable mouth movements. Finally, even in adults, prospects for recovering language functions after left hemisphere damage are quite good when the right hemisphere is completely untouched by damage. This indicates that resources in the right hemisphere are important for language functions (Smith, 1984). Taken together, these data make it unlikely that special neural tissue is necessary for the manifestation of language functions.

Elizabeth Bates (1993a, 1993b) proposed that each of the various aspects of language depends on neural mechanisms that are distributed in the nervous system. Since the processing modes of some of the mechanisms may be more conducive to achieving certain language functions than others, it creates an illusion of language-specific brain modules. In particular, damage to these mechanisms in adults can produce severe language deficits. However, even when a correspondence between the processing modes of certain neural mechanisms and the accomplishment of specific language functions is established, this does not mean that other mechanisms cannot assume these functions.

Bates (1993b) draws two interesting conclusions from her research on the neural bases of language development. Data provided by children who experienced brain damage or neurosurgery confirm that language can be accomplished by atypical neural systems. The alternative mechanisms may not be as proficient at the task, but they will nonetheless accomplish language functions. Furthermore, Bates found that language acquisition during the first three years involves quite different brain areas than those identified as specific language areas in brain-damaged adults. Thus, the regions that mediate language acquisition are not the same as those that mediate language processing in adults.

There is no denying that the brain is intimately involved in the acquisition of language and that brain damage, no matter how early in development, is not good for language (or, indeed, other cognitive functions). However, no compelling evidence points to the brain possessing a special mechanism, with innate processing characteristics, for language acquisition. The mechanisms that typically participate in the manifestation of language skills also participate in the production of other cognitive skills.

This argument should not lead one to conclude that a general mechanism regulates language and the myriad other cognitive processes. The nervous system is complex, with variations in computational power and style among its different components. Such variations can have profound effects on development and are products of development. It will require systematic developmental research founded on firm psychobiological principles to discover, for example, why the left hemisphere seems to be so involved in language functions. That discovery has been delayed by the view that the brain is innately organized according to content-specific faculties for processing language, calculation, music, faces, and so on.

The study of language development demonstrates the importance of specifying the nature of the primitive prerequisites required to develop a cognitive function. If the primitives are specified by a logical analysis of the symbolic characteristics of the mature form, however, it will of necessity require the postulation of innate symbolic cognitive functions. If, in contrast, the primitives are derived from examination of the capacities of the very young infant in relation to its milieu, then they can be seen as deriving from nonsymbolic processes that antedate and feed into cognition. A "development from" perspective provides access to developmental processes associated with the acquisition of language that are unavailable from a "development to" perspective.

Learning and Education

In much of cognitive science, the critical information for understanding knowledge is presumed to lie in the abstract structure of a symbol system. This system is thought to have an internal structure composed of abstract symbols that are interrelated by logical rules or associative connections, and that can be formalized into a mental calculus. Once the mental calculus is postulated, certain developmental requirements are set (Plunkett & Sinha, 1992). Specifically, the presence of primitive symbolic categories and micro-features must be in the system prior to physical and social interaction. In other words, some innate rules, devices, or categories must be postulated.

However, if one is committed to a developmental psychobiological perspective, it is not satisfying to use "innate" in an explanatory way. As discussed in earlier chapters, this concept merely puts an explanation on hold, avoiding the challenge of integrating biological and psychological explanations. We have attempted in this chapter to make the case for a developmental study of knowledge that starts with the antecedent conditions that can be observed and studied in the developing child and its normal milieu, and not with presumptions about these conditions drawn from an examination of the abstract, structural organization of the final product. Thus it is not necessary to endorse nativistic assumptions, and one is free to pursue an integrated developmental study.

If the goal is to achieve a developmental understanding of knowledge and its basis in neural functioning, the typical presumptions of cognitive science are unhelpful. Nevertheless, these presumptions are widely accepted in the current theory and practice of education, where they have had profound effects on concepts of education, learning, and enculturation. Moreover, as recent theories about the relation between cognition and brain function have begun to affect educational theory and practice (Friedman, Klivington, & Peterson, 1986; Iran-Nejad, Hidi, & Wittrock, 1992; Iran-Nejad, Marsh, & Clements, 1992), it is frequently those of cognition-brain relations that are dominated by the assumptions of cognitive science that have had the most impact.

The currently dominant ideas in cognition fail to consider the impact of social processes on neural processes, which in turn can affect the processes of learning (e.g., Newell, 1991). Most cognitive scientists hold a view of the nervous system that does not lend itself to asking such questions. However, recent advances in understanding how nervous systems develop and function (chapter 6) suggest a need to revise this dominant view. As Edelman (1987) noted, information processing, computational, and neural net versions of long-term storage are not consistent with the fundamentally dynamic character of brain functioning. The nervous system does not possess the precise wiring necessary to support the metaphor of static traces. Thus, the brain's generative processes are not storage-retrieval but constructional, in which social and other experiential events are essential.

Part of the problem of educational psychology can be traced to the early history of comparative psychology. At that time, learning was considered an ability that permits the individual to deal with atypical or unusual circumstances by adjustments in behavior (Boakes, 1984). Consequently, learning ability was assessed by contrived problems that were unlikely to occur in the individual's ecological setting. This was done to rule out the possibility of relying on habits, reflexes, or instincts to cope with the problems.

The standard use of arbitrary tasks reinforced the view that learning was a general-purpose ability appropriate for any environment and constrained only by gross physiological and morphological characteristics. As a result, learning took on a special character in the minds of psychologists. It was distinguished from other coping abilities that were believed to develop relatively spontaneously. The idea that learning was a separate process, which many now question, was adopted by psychology in general and educational psychology in particular.

Learning is an essential aspect of the acquisition of knowledge about an environment that has both variable and constant features. According to Johnston (1982, 1985), an evolutionary perspective on knowledge leads to the recognition that it is the consequences of knowledge in action that matter, and not knowledge itself. Knowledgeable behavior is adaptive behavior. The organism evolved in a natural environment to solve and generalize survival problems. From this broad biological perspective, it makes no sense to divorce learning as a process from learning how to cope with problems in their adaptive behavioral context. Knowledge, like all characteristics of the organism, is a product of development.

Knowledge is also a product of the functioning of the nervous system, and the specific character of the structure and functioning of the nervous system depends on experience. Thus it is possible to pose questions about the contributions of the nervous system to knowledge acquisition without separating these contributions from the processes of enculturation. For humans, the experiences that sculpt the structure and functioning of the nervous system include the enculturation processes associated with development in an extensive sociocultural milieu. Cognitive science, educational psychology, and learning theory have adopted a view of learning that does not take these facts into account. Such a view, however, is possible.

A broadly biological and developmental perspective would support the idea that "representations" in the mental calculus are created and given meaning in a socially shared perceptual space in which they are spoken, written, and drawn in the context of social activity. Knowledge is acquired through shared social activity; it "requires a community that shares practices of seeing, representing, and communicating" (Roschelle & Clancey, 1992, p. 436). There is no supportable reason to assume that perception, representation, and social interaction are three independently operating modules. Roschelle and Clancey (1992) suggest that the appropriate units for analyzing the acquisition of knowledge cross these functions and occur at three levels: mutual intelligibility, shared activity structures, and communities of practice. These are the processes of enculturation, ranging from communication to community. Through varied means that change across the life span, those who are more encultured help others to achieve the same knowledge.

Formal schooling exists to focus and accelerate this process. The growth of knowledge in school is continuous with the growth of knowledge in other social settings, but this point is sometimes lost because schools are so separated from the rest of life. Educators are engaged in various experiments to help bridge this gap, including such ideas as "whole experience schooling." This will help to reverse some of the problems associated with treating learning as a process that can develop independent of skills, abilities, and knowledge in particular adaptive contexts.

The problems of formal education at all levels in contemporary society are many and varied. It is important to bring all available resources to bear on these problems; perhaps it is the most important issue that we as a society face. Developmental psychobiology is a currently underused source of information, methods, and ideas that can relate biology to education. Its potential comes from its breadth, integrative strength, and the fresh perspective that it brings to the interrelations of biological and psychological variables.

In the domain of cognitive development, three ideas that emerge from contemporary developmental psychobiology stand out as worthy of further consideration by educators. First, development can be explained using systems approaches that avoid nativism. This can be extended to the cognitive realm: knowledge (of language, of the physical world, etc.) is constructed during interactions of the individual with its milieu, beginning with raw materials that are quite different from the elements in the adult mental calculus as described by cognitivists. Second, a bidirectional, dynamic relationship exists between the (predominantly social) milieu of an individual and its nervous system. This encourages educational psychologists to consider the role of the nervous system in learning processes without thinking that biological and psychological causations are competing alternatives. The dynamic role of the brain in behavioral function offers a different perspective than usual computer metaphors: the nervous system need not be seen as the "hardware" within which the "software" of knowledge operates. Third, development always occurs within a milieu, and this milieu has reliable features (the ontogenetic niche) that contribute importantly to the developing system. For human cognition, it is predominantly the social surround: parents, siblings, peers, teachers, and other companions. Information and methods gained through the psychobiological study of the social nexus could be called upon to augment current trends to specify educational tasks in terms that would engage learners, teachers, and community in a shared, mutually valued enculturation process.

Summary

Modern attempts to integrate brain development with cognitive development depend on certain presuppositions that grow out of the tradition of cognitive psychology. Some of these run counter to current conceptions within developmental psychobiology. The first of these is the supposition that distinct areas of the brain are innately specialized for specific cognitive functions. Cognitive functions are categorized into units similar to conventional human faculties (language, reasoning, etc.). As more is learned about the brain, it seems increasingly unlikely that its spatial organization corresponds to these conventionally accepted units. Furthermore, several philosophers recently questioned the value of these units for theories of both cognition and mind-body relations (Johnson, 1987; Lakoff, 1987; Stich, 1983). They argue that conventional categories of cognitive functioning are inaccurate and inappropriate constructs for theory construction. We expect that more sophisticated descriptions based on more meaningful units in both cognition and brain functioning will lead to progress in the developmental psychobiology of cognitive function.

The second supposition to pose difficulties is that universal sequences in cognitive development require explanation in terms of brain maturation. When developmental changes in brain structures correlate with parallel changes in the timing and order of cognitive changes, it is assumed that the neural change explains the cognitive change. However, there may be other ways to account for the sequence. In many instances of theories of cognitive development the sequences are adequately accounted for by the theory (Flavell & Wohlwill, 1969). Some sequences are logically ordered (later abilities require earlier abilities), as when prehension (reach and grasp) is a prerequisite for the acquisition of objects. Some are formally related (the form of a later ability can be described as a transformation of an earlier ability), as when deferred imitation emerges from delayed imitation. Some sequences derive from recursive effects, as when the activation of a cognitive process provides the experiences that alter the process. One of the many examples described in this chapter is drawn from lateralized hand use: the activation of a hand-use preference for reaching creates the conditions for the organization of a hand-use preference for manipulating.

When it is possible to relate brain development to cognitive development, it is important to examine both directions of causation. As experimental animal research shows, learning and other experiences lead to structural as well as functional changes in the brain, and cognitive neuroscientists would do well to incorporate this reciprocity into their theories.

Finally, the assumption that most clearly separates cognitive science from developmental psychobiology is the nativism that is endorsed in many dominant cognitive theories. A cognitive scientist is likely to start a developmental inquiry by focusing on the finished, adult product and assuming that elements from this product are present at the outset (e.g., innate language-acquisition device). A psychobiologist is more likely to begin from the other direction and focus on the individual's commerce with a sociocultural, ecological context to identify the bases for changing cognitive abilities.

The individual begins not as a tabula rasa, but as a structured system. However, that structure is not a program for instructing development. It is neither inherently cognitive nor formally similar to that of the adult. The developmental psychobiologist seeks to discover the minimum conditions of neural organization and functioning as well as the environmental conditions necessary for the progressive emergence of increasingly complex cognitive systems. The rule system and symbols for each aspect of cognition emerge from developmental processes whose only biological constraints are the general properties of neural functioning.

9 Animal Behavior, Ethology, and Human Development

The study of behavior shares with other sciences this perspective: the prospects, however remote, of eliminating mental illness, controlling aggression, improving education, understanding psychosomatic diseases, etc., seem to many people like the central justifications for the activities of behavioral scientists.... A scientist, like an engineer, is engaged in trying to understand the world, partly for the purpose of gaining control over it and being able to manipulate it, partly to make it over into the image ... of bettering the conditions for human life.

But there is another aspect of the activity and the life of a scientist, and another function for science, which is not often enough stressed. In addition to (or instead of) serving a function like that of an engineer, the scientist can also serve a function like that of an artist, of a painter or poet ... [to see] things in a way that no one has seen them before.... This function is that of widening and enriching the content of human consciousness, and of increasing the depth of the contact that human beings, scientists and nonscientists as well, can have with the world around them.
—D. S. Lehrman (1971, p. 471)

Two Orientations to Animal Behavior

As Lehrman (1971) so eloquently said, scientists can be identified by their orientation to their work as well as by the specific content of their studies. He distinguished two rather different orientations that characterize scientists who study the behavior of animals: natural history and anthropocentric orientations. He suggested that scientists who share the natural history orientation are interested in behavioral patterns that enable animals to cope with the circumstances of their natural environments. They study an animal's behavior in the setting within which it evolved, or at least they aim to relate the results of their investigations to that setting.

An implicit goal of the natural history orientation is to understand how an animal's behavior is related to evolutionary and ecological processes. Each species can be understood in relation to the particular set of ecological conditions that constitute its natural milieu. Scientists are interested in this relationship and in the contribution of the animal's behavior to the construction of its world.

We cannot stress too strongly that it is *the animal and its world* that concern natural history scientists. Such scientists express a genuine wonder and curiosity about animals and their worlds, and are sensitive to the striking diversity in these worlds (Dethier, 1969) as well as to the differences between them and the world of humans. Mindful of these differences, scientists are ever alert to possible incursions of specifically human concerns and notions into studies of animal behavior.

Scientists with an anthropocentric orientation, on the other hand, study the behavior of animals for two reasons. The first is to define and examine what are considered to be laws of behavior that apply generally to most, if not all, animals. One explicit goal of this research is to generate animal-derived general laws for application to human behavior. The general laws would be the basis of a science of behavior in which human behavior would be comprehensible. Second, the animal is studied because it is considered to be a good model of certain aspects of human functioning. Thus it can provide experimental information that, for ethical or practical reasons, cannot be acquired from human research. In this case, the scientist need not assume general laws of behavior. Rather, an animal species must be found that exhibits functions similar to those of interest in humans (box 9.1). The primary motivation for studying animals in both cases is to provide workable tools or models for investigating specifically human problems in psychology. The desire to understand the animal and its world is, if present at all, a secondary motive.

Clinical neuropsychology provides many examples of the uses and limits of the anthropocentric approach. For instance, brain damage can result in some highly selective impairments of function in humans. The selectivity of the impairments has supported the theory that the human brain functions in a modular fashion (chapter 8), with different areas of the cortex processing functionally specific information. It is assumed, therefore, that the loss of some specific function as a result of damage to a particular location will be permanent, because the remaining healthy areas cannot assume the function.

One cannot do the kinds of systematic experiments in humans that are required to investigate either the hypothesis of specific modularization of cortical function or the processes that inhibit or permit recovery of function after brain damage. The approximations to experiments that are obtained by investigating the consequences of lesions that result from disease or injury are limited. The lesions vary in size and placement, and they often damage axons passing through the area as well as resident neurons. Moreover, "virtually nothing is known about the connectional anatomy and single cell physiology of human cortex" that is so important for understanding modularization of function (Merigan, 1993, p. 226). One solution is to seek an animal model so that information about modularization of function in humans may be obtained indirectly.

Box 9.1   Animal Models of Human Neuropsychology

In a neural disorder called achromatopsia, an individual loses color perception without losing any other visual ability (Zeki, 1990). The brain damage that is associated with achromatopsia is in the visual cortex, and it is very near to the areas of visual cortex that are quite active (as determined by positron emission tomography, PET) during color-discrimination tasks.

The visual cortex of several species of macaque monkeys is well mapped connectionally, and we have a great deal of information about single neuron activity in relation to the anatomical maps. Moreover, the V4 area of the macaque visual cortex contains neurons that respond to the "contextual color" of stimuli (Zeki, 1990). That is, the neurons do not respond to the wavelength of stimuli (actual color) but to the relation of stimuli to their background. This is exactly the way humans identify color, and it is exactly this ability that is lost in achromatopsia. Thus, Zeki (1990) proposed that cortical area V4 of the macaque visual cortex corresponds to the area of the cortex that is damaged in humans with achromatopsia.

Heywood, Gadotti, and Cowey (1992) tested the color vision of three macaques before and after bilateral lesions of area V4. They performed tests of color vision like those in which deficits were found for humans with achromatopsia. However, monkeys with V4 lesions showed no deficits on color-discrimination tasks that people with achromatopsia fail. Thus, although V4 is a color-specialized area, no permanent loss of color perception occurs after it is lesioned in monkeys. The Heywood et al. study adds to a growing body of evidence that fails to support the concept of specific, modular-processing units in primate visual cortex (Merigan, 1993).

Although animal research can be an important means of comprehending human psychobiology, it frequently provides little insight into the psychobiology of the animal. For example, what is the functional significance of color perception in macaques, and how does it develop? Of course, the answers to these questions may be relevant to understanding human color perception. But even if they were not, they would still be relevant to understanding macaque color vision. Also, such knowledge is useful for discovering the differences between humans and animals. These differences are a necessary context within which to comprehend the extent and value of the similarities.

This essential research using animals as models has led to many important insights about how the human brain works. One recent result of animal research on cortical functioning was to call into question previously accepted ideas about localization and modularization of function in humans. This led researchers to reexamine information gained with image-processing techniques that can be used in humans, such as positron emission tomography (PET) scans and magnetic resonance imaging (MRI). The evidence indicates that localized, modular organization may be created in the images even if the cortex has a nonmodular and distributed representation of functions (Merigan, 1993). Furthermore, no clear or necessary relation between physical localization of damage and specificity of deficit is apparent in the human data. Sometimes very specific functional deficits may arise from very nonspecific damage as revealed in the images. Reexamination of clinical assessments resulted in the surprising conclusion that specific functional deficits appear only occasionally among the brain-damaged population (Ellis, 1987). The most frequent patterns are a general deficiency and a hodgepodge of more specific deficits.

Therefore, animal models prompted a reevaluation of both modularization and localization of functions in the human brain. There is now evidence from human cognitive development that is consistent with the animal work (Karmiloff-Smith, 1992). The practical result of such research is information that is relevant for constructing programs of therapy and rehabilitation for brain-damaged humans. What is less obvious, although at least equally as important, is that the general fund of knowledge gained through studying the extraordinary diversity in the animal kingdom can be applied in numerous and often unexpected ways to these same ends.

In light of the troubled state of human society and our concern with understanding ourselves, the anthropocentric orientation to the study of animal behavior has wide appeal on pragmatic grounds, and the natural history orientation often seems a luxury. This favored status becomes particularly apparent when expensive animal behavior research must rely on public support. Support is often contingent on the degree to which the research results are perceived to apply to human problems. Given this pressure to focus on human issues and problems, even the results of animal behavior studies that are conducted from a natural history focus may be forced into discussions that take an anthropocentric orientation. Witness the explosion of popular and "scientific" accounts of the nature of human behavior that have appeared during the past three decades, based on facile extrapolation from natural history studies of animal behavior.

The anthropocentric orientation has a long history, substantial consensual support, and considerable intrinsic merit. However, we confess greater sympathy with the natural history orientation, even for the ultimate goal of human improvement. In addition to its value for understanding animals and their worlds, this orientation, most often associated with ethology, has great value for the study of human psychological development. We believe, in fact, that it may be even more valuable than the anthropocentric orientation. This may seem whimsical in light of the explicit goal of those working from an anthropocentric orientation to acquire information that can be applied directly to the resolution of human behavioral problems. We hope to show in this chapter that it is not.

The Natural History Orientation and the Ethological Approach

Ethology

Although the roots of ethology can be traced to pre-Darwinian biologists interested in natural history (Jaynes, 1969), it was only with the writings of such self-acknowledged ethologists as Lorenz, Tinbergen, Baerends, and Kortlandt during the period 1935 to 1951 that ethology coalesced into a coherent discipline. Many of these early writings were attempts to distinguish the ideas of the new discipline from the older mechanistic and vitalistic ideas about animal behavior (e.g., Lorenz, 1971b).

Mechanism and Vitalism

Many mechanists believed that an animal's behavior consists of simple stimulus-response reflexes that may be elaborated into more complex behavior by Pavlovian conditioning, by stimulus-controlled chains of responses, or by trial-and-error learning. The observations and experiments conducted by ethologists showed, however, that an animal's behavioral repertoire consists of patterns, more complex than reflexes, that occur in the absence of Pavlovian conditioning, practice, or trial-and-error learning. In this belief, the ethologists were in agreement with the vitalists.

The vitalists, however, maintained that an animal's behavior not only is more than reflexes and conditioning, but also is organized and regulated by the goal achieved by performing the behavior. Energizing, directive, purposive forces, which the vitalists called **instincts**, were assumed to lie at the core of these complex behaviors. This conception vested the achievement of the goal or consequence of an instinctive behavior with causal efficacy for that instinct. For instance, care of the young was thought to be, simultaneously, the cause (instinctive drive) and the consequence (purposive goal) of maternal behavior in mammals. The ethologists, in contrast, sought to distinguish instinct as a cause in the vitalistic, purposive sense from instinct as a description of certain specific characteristics of the behavioral event so as to reject the former and retain the latter.

The early ethologists succeeded in this aim. They demonstrated that behaviors that could be classified as instinctive are not guided, as the vitalists proposed, by purposes or functional consequences. On the basis of several studies, including the classic case of egg rolling by greylag geese, it was concluded that the performance of an instinctive behavior is terminated by performance of the action itself and not by the achievement of its purposive goal—drawing the neck to the chest rather than retrieving the egg back into the nest. Lorenz (1937/1957) hypothesized that the performance of an instinctive act is moved by an *action-specific energy* that is released by the

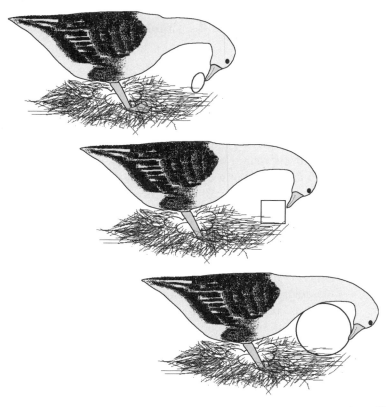

Figure 9.1 Geese retrieve eggs that have fallen from their nest by rolling them with the beak. They also retrieve cubes and oversized egg-shaped objects. Investigation of the stimuli affecting egg rolling in various ground-nesting birds provided evidence that the animals' behavior was not guided by some knowledge of the purpose of incubation (redrawn from Lorenz & Tinbergen, 1938).

appropriate environmental stimulus (*sign stimulus*) and depleted by the performance of the act (*fixed action pattern*). Thus, in response to the sight of an egg outside her nest, the goose will place its bill over the egg and draw it toward its chest in a stereotyped pattern. This may be repeated several times, but will eventually cease because the specific energy will be exhausted (figure 9.1).

Many of the constructs and explanations of the early ethological position were demonstrably wrong (Beer, 1973). For example, no good evidence supports the early theory of action-specific energies. However, it cannot be concluded that instinctive actions are organized by their ultimate functional goals. The animal's performance may instead be guided by feedback from its immediate consequences. The goose stops rolling eggs in response to tactile stimulation from large numbers of eggs in the nest (Beer, 1973). Of course, this alternative to Lorenz's explanation reinforces the major ethological point. The animal's behavior is not caused or guided by "knowledge" of purpose or functional consequences. There simply is no reason to conclude that birds are guided in any proximate sense by the ultimate goal of keeping their eggs warm enough for embryonic development. Numerous experiments have been contrived to show that this is the case for a wide variety of animal behaviors. Although debate surrounds the extent and nature of possible exceptions (e.g., Ristau, 1991), no empirical basis exists for characterizing animal behavior as purposive in this human sense. The antivitalist conclusion stands.

Natural Selection and Animal Behavior

Ethologists did more than point out the weaknesses inherent in the mechanistic and vitalistic notions. Their major contribution was to establish, as a basic feature of their discipline and as a viable foundation for the study of behavior in general, the idea that animal behavior is the product of evolution. They argued that the behavior of an animal is like its organs in the sense that both have evolutionary origins and are subject to natural selection. They concluded, therefore, that behavior can be studied by essentially the same methods that had been used so successfully in the study of organs. This, of course, was the position taken earlier by Darwin.

The inclusion of evolutionary notions in the study of behavior occurred in several ways (Tinbergen, 1951; chapter 3). The phylogenetic history of behavioral patterns was ascertained through comparisons of closely related species. Also, behavior was scrutinized for its relevance to survival in a way that previously was reserved for such anatomical characteristics as the shape of a bird's beak. The social and ecological consequences of behavior began to be evaluated. Ethologists also studied the causation and development of behavior by means of systematic experimental manipulations. Perhaps the most distinctive quality of this work was that the basis for selecting the behavioral patterns that were deemed interesting to study was evolutionary theory.

One assumption that supported all ethological research from the outset is that the understanding of any behavior can be achieved only within the context of thorough knowledge of the animal's environment and full behavioral repertoire. Thus, ethology fosters a natural history orientation to the study of animal behavior.

The Ethological Approach

As ethology took form as a discipline, it generated a number of theories and theoretical constructs designed to describe and explain why the animal behaves when and where it does. These constructs were concerned with, among other things, the specificity of stimulus cues, such as sign stimulus and its internal correlate the *innate releasing mechanism*, and the stereotypy of some behavioral patterns, such as fixed action pattern. However, these theories or constructs are not of value for the study of human development, and even in the field of ethology they have changed and will continue to change with further research (Beer, 1973, 1980; Dewsbury, 1990; Hinde, 1983). As Tinbergen (1968) observed, those interested in integrating ethology and human psychology should attend to the approach (attitudes, methods, concerns) of ethology rather than to its theories or constructs (e.g., Anderson, 1972; Wolff, 1959).

As we have indicated, the ethological approach begins with systematic descriptions of the animal's behavior in its natural, evolutionary setting. Once this has been completed, questions are posed for investigation. In the normal sequence of events, experimental questions about behavior arise directly from the initial descriptions of the particular animal behaving in a natural environment and consequently, the answers are always relevant to the animal and its world.

Although the specifics of the questions are addressed to the particular characteristics of the animal, they are always derivatives of the four types of questions we described in chapter 3: causal, functional, phylogenetic, and developmental. Thus, the behavior of an animal is considered to be as much a part of its biology as any other of its systems. When ethologists turn their attention to humans, human behavior is viewed through the same four questions.

Human Ethology

One of the basic principles of ethology is that each species must be studied as a separate entity having its own properties. This applies to humans as well. Cross-species comparisons are an integral part of ethological procedures, but knowledge gained for one species cannot be assumed automatically to apply to another. When information from some other species, be it geese, coral reef fish, or chimpanzees, illuminates humans simply by analogy, the full ethological perspective has not been taken. If the goal is to understand human behavior, insights gained from ethology complicate the search for animal models and require direct study of humans at some point in the research process.

Human ethology is a label covering a loose conglomerate of research activities that fall into two major categories: identification of human behaviors that are similar in their patterning and social consequences across all cultures, and sophisticated descriptions of behavior in typical human settings. Much research represents an attempt to describe behaviors presumed to have evolved as adaptations to selective pressures.

The field, or naturalistic-descriptive, approach is considered by many to be the definitive basis for creating a human ethology. In fact, this approach is often equated with the ethological method. The concern with behavior that occurs naturally in the field sets enormous definition problems. What is natural human behavior? It certainly cannot be defined, as it is in animals, as free from human interference. What is a field for humans? A nursery school or a street corner may be "fieldlike" in the sense that they were not designed for the purposes of studying behavior, but, like laboratories, they are human contrivances, and they do structure behavior. In sum, it is much easier to distinguish between natural and unnatural behavior and between natural and unnatural settings when another species is the subject. At least it is much easier for us to be happy with the distinctions.

The difficulty in making these distinctions for human behavior in our own society led some investigators to search for primordial human behavior and environments among hunter-gatherer cultures, cultures believed to resemble those of early humans (Bowlby, 1969; Konner, 1977). This practice raises questions of its own, but in addition, it does not really speak to the question of behavior in our society and our time. Ethologists who study human behavior or psychologists who wish to adopt naturalistic methods will have to resign themselves to the fact that there is no ready means for making a clear distinction between natural and artificial human environments.

Provided that the investigator does not become too concerned with the search for natural human conditions, careful and detailed observations of human behavior under relatively free conditions (i.e., conditions that allow the individual several options concerning what to do) can be of enormous value in suggesting useful hypotheses or avenues for further investigation (e.g., Anderson, 1972). Sophisticated observational methods, pioneered by such human ethologists such as Blurton Jones (1972, 1976) and Richards (1974), played an important and constructive role in reformulating ideas of human mother-infant relationships (Hinde, 1983).

Other human ethologists (e.g., Eibl-Eibesfeldt, 1975) turned their attention to a search for universal, or species-specific, human behavioral patterns using cross-cultural comparisons. The concern here was not so much with natural settings, but with identifying specific behavioral patterns that occur among all humans, regardless of setting. Such findings are informative and interesting, and set problems for developmental psychobiologists. They do not, as is sometimes claimed, settle developmental questions by distinguishing between learned and innate behavior. As we have explained throughout this book, the discovery that a behavioral pattern is species-universal tells nothing about how it develops, merely that the necessary conditions are present throughout the species.

It is perhaps a sign of its success that human ethology has not really caught hold as a separate subdiscipline. In recent years, the boundaries between human ethology and the social sciences have blurred, much of this attributable to the cross-disciplinary efforts of Hinde (1979, 1987; Bateson, 1991). The exchange worked both ways, greatly expanding the range of

phenomena that were studied with ethological methods, and providing etho-
logically trained scientists with concepts, methods, and information from
cultural anthropology, social psychology, and developmental psychology. At
the same time, ethologists, together with sociobiologists and others interested in animal behavior, have continued to turn their attention to humans
as part of the animal kingdom.

Contributions of the Natural History Orientation to the Study of Human Development

Some time ago, Ambrose (1968) described four contributions that were
made to the study of human psychological development by studies of animal
behavior from a natural history orientation: development of new research
techniques, clarification of concepts used in the study of human behavioral
development, identification of special features of human development, and
identification of issues in human development that require study. Ten years
after Ambrose, we (Michel & Moore, 1978) reexamined these four contributions and described how they had greatly changed developmental psychology. In this section, we demonstrate that the natural history orientation
to the study of animal behavior continues to contribute to our understanding of human psychological development.

Development of New Research Techniques

The techniques that we use to study behavior are enabling devices. They
quite literally determine what we can and do perceive. Each time we examine some event, we can perceive only a small part of what is available for
examination. Ethology has increased the diversity of techniques that are
available, with a corresponding increase in the richness of the composite
picture of human development. In 1978 we singled out two contributions
that still seem particularly useful: methods for describing and methods for
analyzing social interaction. These methods have an enduring importance in
the study of animal behavior, where they continue to be refined. Although
their application has increased within developmental psychology, they remain underemployed.

Description

Studies that examine what children do rather than what parents, children, or
others say they do owe much of their methodology to ethological studies of
animals (Blurton Jones, 1974; Richards & Bernal, 1972). That is not to say
that developmental psychologists never directly observed children before
ethological studies of animals. People have probably always observed one

another reflectively, but observation is an active process that can be accomplished in a variety of ways. What ethology provided is not merely a rejuvenation of the idea of observation as a necessary part of science, but a new way of observing behavior.

The ordinary language terms that we commonly use to describe the activities of ourselves and others are fraught with subtle biases that distort both perception and thought (Lakoff, 1987; Lakoff & Johnson, 1980). Perhaps the major example of this was pointed out by Wittgenstein. Our ordinary language leads us to expect and to perceive things even when there are no things (Brand, 1979). For example, it is quite possible for people to use highly abstract categories in describing behavior (e.g., attachment, aggression) without attending to, or even being aware of, the steps by which they have abstracted these categories. Phenomenologically, the abstracted behavioral category is "seen" directly as if it were a thing or object. Abstracted categories are derived from a series of mental manipulations that involve ordering, classifying, and predicting incoming information, but this simply escapes our attention.

Consider the word *aggressive*, a descriptive label used frequently in both scientific and lay circles. Although we readily apply it to someone, we would, if pressed, probably find it difficult to spell out all the steps we had taken to arrive at that description. We might offer a definition, such as "the person is likely to hurt someone" (also not observable), or we might relate an anecdote. Furthermore, we find that others apparently know what we are talking about and are able to use the same label in more or less the same way. Therefore, people are capable of forming complexly derived descriptive categories of behavior in an apparently immediate fashion, they can use these categories reliably, and different people can agree on the use of such abstract descriptive terms.

We encounter some problems, however. First, abstract descriptive terms may be used in more than one way: two individuals may be classified as aggressive but each for a different reason (consider a hoodlum and a corporate executive). This may or may not be fully realized by users of the term. Second, although people can agree on the use of terms of this nature, they may also disagree or, worse, only seem to agree (e.g., is the same thing meant when boys and girls are called aggressive?). What seems to be a thing and may be talked about as a thing may not have the properties of a thing.

Hinde (1983, p. 37) related how a questionnaire intended to rate types of activities apparently revealed that various forms of children's play (self, parallel, group, interactive) lie on a continuum. However, this ordering stemmed from an implicit theory of personality shared among all of the raters. The implicit theory led them to place self play in inverse relationship to interactive play. Analyses of the specific descriptions of the play patterns, using principal components analysis, revealed that self play is not on a continuum with interactive play, but rather it is orthogonal to it. Yet, the answers to questions on the questionnaire were highly related to the specific descriptions of the play.

Our common understanding of play and social interaction includes the views that all play shares common characteristics and that a continuum exists from solitary to interactive behavior. These concepts found their way into the ratings even though the children's actual play patterns did not form a continuous scale. Thus, implicit notions can bias various forms of description in ways that may not be easily identified.

A tradition of descriptive research in human psychology recognizes the problems inherent in our ordinary practice of describing one another with abstract terms. Before these terms are allowed in research, special procedures are required to ensure that they can be used reliably to describe events, and that different individuals can use them in the same way. The most widely used procedure is to have more than one observer of the same events. Before the study begins, observers typically go through a period of training during which they learn the language to be employed in the study. By correlating the data obtained by two or more independent observers, the researcher can assess the degree of interobserver reliability for each behavioral category.

Reliability training ensures that the observers perceive something in common in the behavior of their subjects. However, it does not allow, or even aim to allow, documentation of the steps taken by the observers in reaching their descriptive categories. It can be argued that, for some purposes, this doesn't matter. However, communication can break down entirely when the descriptions applied very reliably by the observers *within* a study are used by others who did not participate in the training. That is, because the understanding imparted in reliability training is primarily intuitive, it can be achieved only through shared experience: overt instruction will not work. Truly independent replication of these studies—an absolute prerequisite for establishing scientific knowledge—is therefore ruled out.

Perhaps because application of abstract descriptive terms to animals can quickly lead to anthropomorphism and confusion, ethologists are very concerned with using objective terms for their primary descriptive data. In this context, objective means capable of being transmitted without confusion to others who have not trained with the observer. What this means in practice is that specialized procedures and languages are used deliberately.

Ethologists have a number of different techniques for describing behavior (Golani, 1992; Martin & Bateson, 1986; Moran & Fentress, 1979), each of which provides a different perspective on the categories of behavioral organization. Moreover, each technique has a behavioral vocabulary that allows an alternative comprehension of the actions involved. Most often, descriptive categories are movement patterns (e.g., smiling), patterns with unambiguous immediate consequences (e.g., nest building), or patterns of orientation to some clear referent (e.g., approach). It is possible to draw, photograph, or tape-record the sort of behavioral patterns that make up these observables. It is not possible, however, to photograph aggression or other abstract descriptive categories. The motion picture of a fight documents the movements and actions of the fighters. It can be used as a representation or index of aggression only through an act of inference from the observable movements and actions. This is most noticeable when it is difficult to determine whether the scene that was filmed is actually one of aggression, play, or courtship.

Although ethologists also use abstract categories, they construct them from the observable categories in their descriptive records. The steps in the construction process must be specifiable and open to inspection and verification. A substantial portion of ethological research is devoted to the methodological issues attending this process (Colgan, 1978; Hazlett, 1977; Slater, 1973).

Descriptive behavioral data can be obtained either directly or indirectly (Hinde, 1983). Direct methods vary in their completeness. Recording on film, video, or audio tape provides records that are nearly complete and permanent. Furthermore, criteria for data sampling and behavioral categorization can be determined after the data are collected, and changed if this becomes desirable. However, these methods may generate unwieldy amounts of raw data and are often not practical. Therefore, behavior is often observed and recorded directly by researchers who have criteria to categorize and select data that are determined in advance. Indirect methods are less favored than direct methods because they produce records of impressions about behavior without archiving the behavior itself. Indirect reports can be provided by observers other than the investigator. When provided by the individuals who are the object of study, they are self-reports. Whether self-reports or reports from a third party, they are usually answers to questions about the observer's impressions of the individuals whose behavior is under study.

Indirect reports and questionnaires provide valuable information concerning our viewpoints about the behavior of ourselves and others. The information sometimes corresponds rather closely to that obtained from direct observations, but often it does not. Furthermore, indirect reports are often insensitive to important aspects of behavioral organization and fail to detect them. Therefore, direct observation is an essential initial phase in most psychological research, and was the foundation for most ethological work. This raises the questions of how to measure, sample, and record the wealth of information in a behavioral stream (Martin & Bateson, 1986).

Once a behavioral unit is measured nominally, that is, extracted from the behavioral stream, categorized, and described operationally, it can be measured quantitatively. This is typically done by measuring how much time elapses after some event of interest before the behavior occurs (*latency*), how often the behavior occurs in some unit of time (*frequency*), or how long a particular pattern of behavior lasts (*duration*). These three measures record the temporal dimension within which behavior occurs. Which one is used depends on the length of the behavior relative to the length of a recording session. Sleep, for example, is more commonly measured by its duration than by its frequency. A fourth measure, *intensity* or amplitude, is often judged without reference to time.

Because behavior is a stream of events in a changing context, often involving many participants, decisions must be made about what to sample, or how to direct one's focus of attention. Martin and Bateson (1986) refer to these decisions as *sampling rules*. Unless relatively complete records of an observational session are made using methods that retain a complete temporal record (i.e., exact information about latency, frequency, and duration) of every behavioral pattern of interest, decisions must be made about how to record samples of the behavior so that this information can be estimated. These are *recording rules* (Martin & Bateson, 1986). Sampling rules should be chosen to meet the objectives of the study, and recording rules should be chosen that will yield an accurate estimate of the complete record for the behavior.

A variety of sampling and recording rules are used to study animal behavior. Altman (1974) was the first to offer a systematic description and comparison of these observational methods. Her influential paper was followed by a number of others that continue to scrutinize and refine these methods (e.g., Martin & Bateson, 1986; Slater, 1978).

In the early stages of research, an observer may use *ad libitum sampling*, which means recording as much as possible of the most salient or most interesting events. Although it can provide information about conspicuous events and be the basis for choosing a more sophisticated sampling method, it has little quantitative usefulness because it is unsystematic. In studies of social behavior, it is often supplemented with *sociometric matrix completion*, which adds information about who is doing what to whom.

In *focal individual sampling*, an individual is selected from a group as the object of attention (e.g., the baby in a group including the mother, father, siblings, etc.). Recordings are made of this individual's behavior for the duration of an observational session. In addition to these recordings, the method can be extended to include the behavioral events directed toward that individual (e.g., from siblings or parents) and those that are elicited in others by the focal individual's actions. This method tends to inflate the impact of the focal individual on the observed situation. However, the bias is minimized if the focal individual is rotated systematically among the participants in sequential observational sessions determined in advance.

Focal individual sampling usually implies that each individual is observed for an extended period. When this period is very brief and several individuals are systematically sampled in rapid succession for set periods of time, the method is called *multiple-scan sampling*. It has the advantage of collecting information from several individuals within the same time period, but the disadvantage of restricting the repertoire to relatively few, relatively simple, or relatively conspicuous behavioral patterns. This disadvantage is even greater when all individuals in a group are rapidly scanned at the "same" instant. Known as *scan sampling*, it can provide an overview of how a group spends its time, but is easily biased by differences in visibility of individuals or conspicuousness of behavior. It is best used as an adjunct to focal individual sampling.

In *behavioral sampling*, particular behavioral patterns are the focus of attention, regardless of the performer. Thus, every occurrence of some type of behavior (e.g., a particular facial expression or vocalization) is recorded. This method tends to isolate the focal behavior from its behavioral context, and is likely to be workable only for conspicuous behavior. It is best used as an adjunct to other methods to capture rare behavioral patterns that would otherwise be missed.

In addition to deciding which individuals and what behavior to observe, one must decide when to schedule the beginning and end of a session. Observations may be made at a particular time of day, or the day may be sampled systematically in sessions of set length. Under field research conditions, systematic sampling of the day may not be possible. As an alternative to scheduling observation sessions according to time, the occurrence of particular behavioral patterns or other events (e.g., waking from a nap) may be used to start a session, and other events (e.g., start of a meal) may be used to stop a session.

It is sometimes possible to obtain a complete temporal record for the behavioral patterns that are observed using these sampling rules, however, this is not always possible or desirable. In that case, one of two recording rules is generally chosen. Each rule requires one to divide time into a series of intervals, but they differ in that one method uses the full interval and the other uses only the time point at the end of the interval. The length of the interval is set in advance, guided by preliminary information about the behavior that will be measured.

In *one-zero sampling*, the observer records whether particular behavioral events occur during each interval in a series of successive, equal intervals (e.g., every 10 or 30 seconds) during a set observational session. If several behavioral patterns are being observed, it is possible to record them in the same interval. One-zero sampling provides data on the proportion of intervals in which the behavior was recorded. It is rather well correlated with the total duration of behavior within a session; however, the correlation with frequency or bout duration of the behavior is not as good. How well the method estimates these behavioral characteristics varies with the length of the interval and the true frequency and bout duration of the behavior.

In *instantaneous sampling* the observer records only what is happening at the end of each interval during a session. The length of these intervals (e.g., every 10 seconds or every 3 minutes) is set in advance, and some signal is used to indicate points at which samples should be recorded (e.g., a quiet beep delivered through an earphone). This method is most useful for providing information about behavior that has relatively long duration (e.g., posture, orientation, sleeping, crying, general activity) and less useful for events that have short duration, particularly if those events are rare. It can provide information about the amounts of time spent in repetitive behavior (e.g., eating), even when bout duration is short. Although the method underestimates the frequencies of most behavioral patterns, this is not equally true for all behavior. Conspicuous behavior is likely to be noticed and recorded even when it occurs just before or just after the sampling time point.

Sampling and recording rules can be combined to suit the problem. The methods are best selected after becoming familiar with the behavior in its context and before starting a study. Once selected, it is important to apply the methods systematically and consistently. However sophisticated and carefully applied, sampling and recording methods will not compensate for inappropriate parsing of the behavioral stream into the behavioral events to be sampled.

Ethological methods of description are hardly the norm in developmental psychology, but they have begun to attract attention. Developmental psychologists have much to gain from their more widespread adoption. Perhaps different observers would see different things. It is possible to correct, modify, or expand the abstract categories if a quantitative record of observable behavior has been preserved. Researchers who begin with complex descriptive categories, on the other hand, have lost this opportunity and may never discover an imperfectly defined or faulty category, or, worse, their implicit assumptions. Moreover, they lose the value of comparing the effect of several different ways of describing the behavioral event for understanding its developmental causes and consequences.

From an ethological perspective, it is always important to avoid the problems of starting with abstract categorization and to start with observable units. However, it is recognized that every descriptive language influences perception and thought. There is no one "correct" way to describe behavior. Because each descriptive language sets its own pattern, it is often beneficial to apply more than one form of description to the same phenomenon (Fentress, 1988, 1991; figure 9.2; box 9.2).

Analysis of Social Behavior

Ethologists have historically had particular concern with social behaviors. Social behavior covers a wide range of phenomena, including communication, relationships, and group structure. Remarkable advances in under-

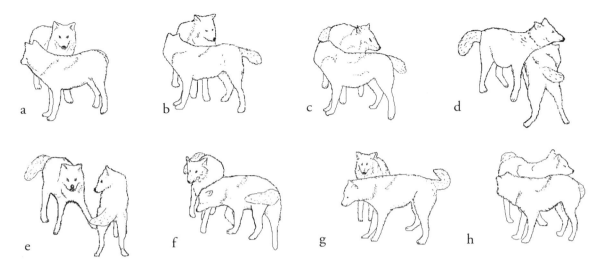

Figure 9.2 Using one technique for describing behavior, the movements of a male and female wolf represent the exchange of signals and displays. Using another technique, the movements represent the attempt of one wolf to orient its nose to the flank of the other wolf as they both remain active (redrawn from Fentress, 1981).

standing the social behavior of animals have been gained with ethological methods, and the methods have been refined in the process. We focus on only two of them, both of which offer advantages to the developmental psychologist.

Most social behaviors can be described as interactions between individuals. When they are described in observable units, one of the immediate tasks for the ethologist is to determine whether a particular unit of behavior is part of this interaction. Thus, ethologists employ sophisticated statistical procedures for analyzing streams of behavior performed by two individuals. One focus has been on what usually falls under the rubric of communication. Communication refers to the transmission of information from one individual to another. In animal behavior, it is studied by examining the effects of the sender's behavior on the behavior of the receiver (Smith, 1991).

One of the most productive procedures for analyzing animal communication is *sequence analysis*, which is concerned with the chronological order of events. When applied to social interactions, it reveals the sequential order of behavioral patterns in two individuals. Given that individual A has done one thing, what is the next thing that individual B will do? With a relatively large sample of behavioral records, it can be determined whether behavior exhibited by one individual is nonrandomly related to the next behavior performed by a second individual. If so, it can be concluded that individual B has responded to individual A and that communication has occurred. This

Box 9.2 Multiple Descriptions of the Organization of Behavior

John Fentress and his collaborators have been in the forefront of the movement to apply more than one descriptive mode when characterizing the organization of behavior. "The study of behavior rests upon a dissection of events in time and an evaluation of the various rules by which these events are combined, that is, in the study of behavioral ontogeny one must evaluate not only how these events become differentiated but also how they are integrated in the production of coherent sequences of expression" (Fentress, 1992, p. 1529). But what guides the dissection?

There are always several ways to parse the spatiotemporal stream of behavior, and no one way is best. Each parsing emphasizes certain properties of the stream and deemphasizes others. Therefore, implicit assumptions behind the taxonomies of behavioral categories are derived by each way of parsing. When the flow of behavior is parsed with methods to identify functions or consequences to action, one set of assumptions is operative. When the same flow is parsed using methods to identify dimensions of form (e.g., kinematics, trajectories, or force of individual body segments), a different set of assumptions is operative. The implicit and explicit assumptions prevent any ready translation between descriptive techniques within, much less between, these two general modes of identifying the categories of behavior.

For example, Golani and Fentress (1985) compared three ways of describing the ontogeny of facial grooming in mice. They used the Eschkol-Wachmann system of movement description that traces the pathways across the surface of imaginary spheres representing a polar coordinate system, of each body segment involved in movement or posture. They described the ontogeny of facial grooming according to the kinematics of each limb segment, the trajectories of the forepaws in space, and the contact pathways between the forepaws and the face. These three descriptions are completely independent: none can be derived from the others.

They found that infant mice performed movements that "looked like" grooming even though the forepaws seldom contacted the face. These movements occurred only when the nice were propped in a specific posture. Even then, the control of variables such as limb force was so poor that their paws often missed the face or struck it too hard. Moreover, the young mouse seems to become entrapped in facial grooming during any context in which the forepaws pass near the face. This was true even when drowning! Observations from one descriptive perspective revealed a linear pattern of development, whereas from another perspective development was nonlinear. Fentress (1992) noted "... complementary frameworks can yield complementary insights" (p. 1537).

Of course, once the flow of movement has been parsed into components or behavioral events, the rules for sequencing the components and forming them into hierarchical patterns must be identified. These rules may be different for different parsing techniques, but they may share variables that may contribute to facilitatory and inhibitory relations among functional categories of behavior that become apparent during the development and causation of behavior. As in the comparison of species, the comparison of descriptions drawn from different techniques provides the context of differences from which the similarities take their value.

information can be a valuable starting point for studies of causal factors that operate in both senders and receivers, among other things.

It seems particularly likely that sequence analysis and other statistically sophisticated methods developed to study animal communication would be useful for studying human communication when a nonverbal infant is one of the participants. The nonverbal communication of mood and emotion in infants is attracting a great deal of interest (Campos et al., 1983). These are precisely the kinds of behavioral patterns that have been approached successfully in animals by ethological methods. Applying these methods to nonverbal human communication may well yield insights into the developmental origins of human communication, as well as its transformation when linguistic and other skills become part of the child's repertoire.

Studies of animal communication start with descriptions of the units of social behavior as they can be observed in single individuals. At this level, researchers are interested in communicative patterns and the nature of the information that is transmitted. Each communicative episode is time limited; however, the sociality of an animal extends beyond these discrete encounters. An individual comes to have predictable probabilities of behaving in particular ways during social encounters, and these probabilities are different depending on the identity of the other interacting individual. In other words, many species of animals adopt roles and form relationships.

All social behavior, by definition, involves interaction between at least two individuals. Sequence analysis (e.g., Slater, 1973) can be used to study these interactions, but these techniques can be applied effectively or legitimately only to behavior that is restricted to relatively brief time periods. This restriction must be adopted because the methods require behavioral *stationarity*—maintenance of the same behavioral probabilities in the subjects throughout the measurement process. However, the nature of the relationship between the subjects often changes during prolonged interactions. To change the behavior of a partner is, indeed, the point of much social behavior. In many species, the actions of a courting male, for example, are performed to develop the female's reproductive mood. Nonstationary interactions require special analytical techniques. This may help to account for the fact that the interactive nature of much social behavior is often overlooked, with the result that higher-order terms describing interaction may be treated as properties of a behavior itself. For example, "aggressive" best describes a type of interaction, but it is often attributed to an individual as a characteristic. This is a difficult and recurrent problem with which some ethologists have begun to deal (Hinde, 1986).

It is possible to describe relationships between individuals by starting with observable units of behavior. This approach derives from the work of Hinde and colleagues who observed mother-infant dyads of rhesus monkeys (summarized in Hinde, 1974). One focus of analysis was the physical contact between a mother and her infant. Logically, a contact may be initiated by either member of a pair and may be terminated by either member. In these monkeys, early in life the behavior of the infant is more often responsible for terminating contacts than for originating them. Therefore, the primary responsibility for the physical contact between the two members of the dyad is the mother's. As development proceeds, the roles shift, and the infant gradually becomes the one primarily responsible for contact, initiating relatively more and breaking relatively fewer contacts than the mother. Simultaneously, the mother becomes more active in terminating contacts. These measures, together with several others, demonstrate clearly that the relationship is dynamic; that is, it is the product of the active contributions of both members. With thorough description in lower-order observables, the contributions of the two members can, to a certain extent, be teased apart.

This approach to the study of relationships was extended to humans (Hinde, 1979; Dunn, 1991). Dunn (1991) used methods derived from Hinde's animal work to characterize different patterns of relationships between children with other family members. She proposed that relationships provide an essential context for understanding how a child will react to major changes in the family, such as birth of a sibling. They are also the essential context used by the child to develop social cognition, as well as cognitive skills more generally. Thus, not only is it possible to describe human relationships with the methods of ethology, it is extremely helpful to do so. Descriptions of relationships can never allow firm conclusions about causes, but they are extremely powerful in clarifying problems for experimental analysis. This was demonstrated in animal research, and seems also to be true for human development.

One of the mistakes in early studies of animal social behavior was to locate properties of interactions within the individuals. A particularly striking example of this stems from efforts to characterize group structure in terms of dominance hierarchies. The tendency, quite in keeping with commonsense or folk psychological approaches to human sociality, was to treat dominance as a trait or disposition. A dominant animal was thought to impose its disposition on others in the group by threats and other aggressive acts. A *dominance hierarchy*, then, would be the composite picture yielded by a group of individuals that vary in the degree of this disposition. However, observations of baboons revealed that the hierarchy that seemed apparent was not at all imposed by those animals that seemed most dominant (Rowell, 1966, 1972). Instead, the best prediction of a dominance ranking was the number of retreats that were made to another animal's approach, whether this approach was friendly or aggressive. The animals that were judged to be least dominant were those most likely to retreat. Thus, although one "sees" a dominant baboon as somehow possessing dominance, this is an illusion.

Dominance is an emergent property of a social interaction, not of an individual. A single individual can never be characterized as dominant, but the concept of dominance may usefully describe something about the social relationships within a group, including the positions of particular individuals in those relationships.

The terms that are used to describe properties of individuals (traits, dispositions) and properties of interactions (relationships, roles) are all higher-order terms that require an act of inference. The ability to maintain clear distinctions between them depends on starting with a record of interactions described with observable units of behavior. Thus we return to perhaps the most important methodological lesson that ethology has to offer.

Clarification of Concepts

Many concepts that are used to characterize the course of human psychological development cannot be defined or evaluated adequately by research on humans. We have already shown that the usefulness of such concepts as innate and maturation associated with the nature-nurture dichotomy must be reevaluated in light of animal behavior research. These concepts are used both as descriptions and as explanations of the course of development. Applied descriptively, they can point to important features of development that must be explained, but the possibility of being misunderstood as explanations of development may make even this use inadvisable.

As was discussed in earlier chapters, these concepts suffer from a number of shortcomings that make them rather ineffective explanations of behavior. For example, "innate" may be a descriptive tag for behaviors that are relatively stable during development, but this cannot help to explain the stability. As animal research demonstrates, even if a genetic influence were identified or some experience were found to be unimportant, it would not warrant the conclusion that other individual experiences are irrelevant. Similarly, studies led to rejection of the concepts of maturation and experience as alternative explanations of behavioral development. These terms may be used, with appropriate caution, in a descriptive sense, but the processes that are described by them are irrevocably fused in development (Schneirla, 1957).

A number of similar concepts with psychobiological roots are used extensively in developmental psychology. Although not as grand as innate or maturation, they carry considerable theoretical weight. Like innate or maturation, they both describe and explain behavior. In 1978 we selected attachment, aggression, and critical period as important concepts that deserved reevaluation in the light of the natural history approach to animal research. During the interim, these concepts continued to play important roles, but underwent extensive revision.

Attachment

The concept of attachment is used to describe the social-emotional relationship of human infants to their mothers (Bretherton, 1992). It can refer to the observation that an infant comes to prefer the company and attention of particular persons during the first two years of life. It can also refer to an inferred, underlying, presumably unitary process that explains the infant's preference. Thus, it has two different meanings, one descriptive and the other explanatory (Cairns, 1972a). There is no adequate way to evaluate the explanatory meaning of attachment by studying humans. However, experiments that can be done with other mammals reveal a number of processes that are responsible for the phenomenon (chapter 7).

We agree with Cairns (1972a) that it is both artificial and misleading to extract only some of the features from this developmental nexus, lump them together as a single thing, and label them attachment. When attachment is used as a descriptive term, one is encouraged to focus attention only on certain aspects of the social experiences of the infant in relative isolation from other experiences, which deflects attention from the interactive nature of social development. The thorough examination of social development in various nonhuman mammals demonstrates that the mother-infant dyad encompasses many factors, some physiological and some behavioral (chapter 7). Furthermore, no "unattached" stage exists that must be rectified by the right social glue. Instead, the mother and infant constitute a dynamic system that originates during pregnancy and undergoes progressive changes throughout the duration of the relationship, to be replaced in humans with the mother-child and, even later, the mother-adult offspring relationships.

A method that is frequently applied to study attachment is to impose a separation between the infant and mother and examine the immediate or long-term consequences. When this separation is relatively long in duration, it is referred to as maternal deprivation. Just as the bonds of attachment do not refer to a single thing, so does maternal deprivation remove many sources of behavioral organization from the infant, often replacing them with unusual elements that have the effect of channeling development onto a different pathway (Hofer, 1978; Schneirla & Rosenblatt, 1963).

The most striking long-term effects of maternal deprivation in rhesus monkeys is the general fearfulness and incompetence of the monkeys in social contexts and novel physical environments (Harlow & Harlow, 1965). Provocative studies from Harlow's laboratory raised a number of questions that have occupied many developmental psychobiologists. One is whether the developmental effects can be reversed by providing social experience later in life. The results of several studies converged on the conclusion that some reversal is possible, but only if the older deprived monkey is placed with others, such as younger monkeys, that are tolerant of its social ineptness (Harlow, Harlow, & Soumi, 1971; Novak & Harlow, 1975).

A second question is whether the mother is solely important to the effects that are observed. Monkeys live in social groups that include several, often many, individuals other than the mother-infant dyad. When the deprivation paradigm was extended to this more natural context, it was found that other social companions could substitute for the mother, particularly when the social system allowed close interaction between the infant and an adult. Very different consequences followed when it was the mother, rather than the infant, that was removed from an otherwise intact group (Coe et al., 1985; Rosenblum & Kaufman, 1968). Furthermore, removing a mother from her infant in a bonnet macaque group led to rather mild and transient consequences in comparison with the more severe effects of removing a mother from her infant in a pigtail macaque group (Rosenblum & Kaufman, 1968). In typical social groups, maternal pigtail macaques restrict their infants from interacting with other group members, whereas maternal bonnet macaques permit or encourage such interaction. When confronted with maternal loss, the bonnet macaque infant was more likely to enter into adoptive relationships with adults in the group, and to do so rather quickly.

A third question is what it is that the mother or her substitute provides to the developmental process. This question was explored extensively and creatively by Mason and colleagues (e.g., Mason & Capitanio, 1988; Mason & Kenney, 1974). As the Harlows demonstrated, in comparison with monkeys reared with their mothers, rhesus monkeys that are reared in social isolation develop into adults with many behavioral incompetencies. Although this familiar finding underscores the critical importance of the social environment for development, it does not identify mother-infant attachment as the crucial process; nor does it, by itself, provide information about the development of social competence.

Mason found clues to this developmental process by observing differences in the behavior of previously deprived and socially reared monkeys in group situations. One major difference is that when young (6 months or 1 year) socially deprived rhesus monkeys are placed with socially reared individuals of the same age or older, they do not interact with the others. Possibly this failure to interact prevents them from building the social skills necessary for adult competency. The socially reared monkeys engaged in intense and frequent play, far beyond that exhibited by age-matched monkeys reared in deprivation, who seemed overwhelmed by the high level of activity when they were introduced to a group. Moreover, the deprived monkeys both missed the overtures of the socially reared monkeys to engage in play and often responded inappropriately to these overtures. This resulted in a downward social spiral, in which the deprived monkeys withdrew from interaction with the others, and the others either ignored or taunted the deprived monkeys. Thus, it is not surprising that the deprived monkeys could not gain social competence through interacting with peers.

Mason used a more refined version of the deprivation experiment to identify some of the conditions necessary to achieve social interaction among young monkeys. Specifically, elements of the social environment were identified and systematically replaced into the otherwise deprived rearing environment. Previously, Mason and Harlow demonstrated that a terrycloth-covered, stationary model "mother" was more important for providing the infant with a secure base from which to explore novel events than a similar model that delivered food but had no soft, clingable surface. Despite this advantage, the clingable model did little to foster the development of social skills. One difference between a real monkey mother and the model is movement. Mason therefore added movement to the model by providing it with rockers that responded when the infant climbed on it. When this had little effect, a model that moved and stopped on a random schedule around a track was added to the living environment of the isolated monkey, thus providing the infant with movement that was not contingent on its own actions. This more closely approximated the movements of real mothers (and age mates) that exhibit a certain level of capriciousness to which the young monkey must adjust. Nevertheless, social skills with age mates were only modestly improved.

Finally, Mason and Kenney, (1974) gave the monkeys live dogs to provide the monkeys with response-contingent stimulation, but not with monkey-specific social experience. An important source of experience that was missing from the inanimate maternal models was this contingency, experiences that are necessary for the development of social skills. Within a few weeks of introducing dogs, dog-monkey pairs were engaged in complex, high-intensity patterns of social interaction. These interactions had little similarity with the specific play of monkeys, but they were quite similar at the formal level of behavioral contingency. After their experience with dog companions, the deprived monkeys were better able to take advantage of interaction with age mates and build their social competencies.

In a subsequent longitudinal comparison of dog-reared monkeys and monkeys reared with fur-covered plastic horses on wheels, Mason and Capitanio (1988) found that the dogs and inanimate moving models were equivalent maternal substitutes for measures of attachment (e.g., distress after removal of model), but had very different consequences for behavioral development. The dogs, which provided response-contingent stimulation, were far superior in promoting the development of behavioral skills that could be used in problem solving, sociality with other monkeys, and various other environmental challenges.

The ability to distinguish among the various kinds of developmental contributions that originate in the social environment is essential for a clear understanding of development. This goal is not well served by blanket concepts, such as attachment. As Mason and Capitanio put it, " ... 'attachment' has come to be used as a global construct and is applied to virtually every aspect of the infant-parent relationship. The situation has reached a point where the concept has become so diluted as to compromise its descriptive and explanatory value" (1988, p. 402).

Furthermore, it is important to follow the consequences of socially derived stimulation outside the strictly social realm, a step that is not helped by incorporating all interactions between the infant and caregivers into attachment or other constructs of sociality. Although the work from Mason's laboratory identified experiences that are important for the development of social competency, it went beyond this to the more general development of behavioral and cognitive skills. One principle that emerges is that some match between the competency of the individual and the resources in the environment must be achieved before particular psychological abilities can develop. This principle, together with methods that allow one to specify the details underlying the match, was used successfully in the study of the development of human cognitive ability (e.g., Fischer & Biddell, 1991; Siegler & Jenkins, 1989). Such research provides insight into exactly how the environment must match the individual to generate the experiences that contribute to development.

Critical Period

As we indicated in chapter 1, the concept of critical period has changed extensively from its original ethological formulation and lost much of its purported explanatory value. Even its name was changed to sensitive period to reflect the overhaul necessary to incorporate all the anomalous information and caveats acquired by systematic study of the factors that initiate, terminate, and characterize the period. Nevertheless, critical period has been widely used in efforts to explain various aspects of the intellectual, social, and emotional development of humans (Bornstein, 1989). The concept is difficult to evaluate when applied to humans (Connolly, 1972), and experimental investigations showed it to be misleading when applied to behavioral development of animals.

For example, Scott (1962) used the concept to describe features of the social development of such altricial mammals as kittens and puppies. The critical period identified a time in which specific experiences were necessary that were crucial for the acquisition of sociality. In contrast, Schneirla and Rosenblatt (1963; Rosenblatt, 1976) found that no single age period could be singled out as of essential importance for social development in kittens. Rather, each phase contributes to succeeding phases in ways that are crucial. The kitten begins to adjust to the mother at birth through the behavioral systems that it has available to it. As new systems emerge in development, the kitten makes new adjustments to the mother, based on these systems and the experience gained through adjustments made during earlier phases.

By separating kittens from their mothers and littermates and keeping them on artificial brooders, Schneirla and Rosenblatt (1963) showed that the kittens have difficulty adjusting to the mother on reunion. The artificial brooder has the effect of maintaining the kitten's social behavior at the developmental level achieved at the point of separation. The mother's social behavior continues to change during the separation period, however, because of her interaction with the remaining kittens. At reunion, the separated kitten behaves toward the mother in ways appropriate to an earlier phase of their interaction, thereby producing discordant interactions between them. All separated kittens manifested difficulties in their social adjustments, no matter when during development the separation occurred.

Given this analysis, no single period during development appears to be any more crucial for social development than any other. However, the particular difficulties that are manifested after separation depend on the level of social behavior achieved by the kitten before separation. The degree of difficulty at reunion will depend on the degree of discrepancy between the kitten's level of social behavior and that of its mother. Because the process of social development is continuous, to focus attention on critical periods actually can obscure the processes involved in the transitions from one level of social skill to another.

Furthermore, the critical period as an explanatory device may cloud recognition of similar processes that occur at different ages. A clear example is provided by the study of hormonal effects on the development of neural and behavioral sex differences. Reasoning by analogy with the effects of hormones on the morphogenesis of the internal and external genitalia, it was hypothesized that gonadal hormones have organizational effects during a prenatal or early postnatal critical period, and different activational effects when the hormones are again secreted at puberty (e.g., Phoenix et al., 1959). This view was widely adopted, and it was thought that the effects of hormones during the early critical period were qualitatively different from those outside the critical period. The critical period effects were assumed to be endogenous, irreversible, and rooted in organic neural changes that prepared the system to display particular kinds of behavior at later times. In contrast, the activational effects were assumed to be transient and reversible, and could occur at any time after the close of the critical period. Activational effects turned on behavioral mechanisms organized developmentally during the critical period, but left no enduring developmental effects themselves.

However, neither the dichotomy into organizational and activational modes of hormone action nor the dichotomy into critical and noncritical periods for hormonal effects can be sustained. Studies of specific behavioral mechanisms as well as neural processes at the cellular level reveal many commonalities in the way that hormones affect the nervous system and behavior, regardless of age (Arnold & Breedlove, 1985; Moore, 1985; Williams, 1991).

As we pointed out when the concept of critical period was critically evaluated in our discussion of imprinting in an earlier chapter, the concept focuses undue attention on the age of the individual at the expense of its developmental status. It also leads one to expect that, unless some particular sort of experience has occurred before the end of some specifiable time interval, it can no longer affect development. The individual will have missed the boat, so to speak. The concept can, in other words, engender a feeling of hopelessness that can interfere with the proper work of developmentalists and have unfortunate practical consequences when applied to humans. It hardly has heuristic value; it is more likely to foreshorten developmental inquiry than to expand it. In view of these problems and of the failure of the concept to account adequately for social development of animals, the developmental psychobiologist interested in humans would be well advised to exercise skepticism when critical periods are postulated as important determinants of human developmental processes.

Aggression

Cairns (1972b) argued persuasively that the concept of aggression has had the effect of delaying recognition of the diversity of factors contributing to the development of fighting behavior. Too often aggression was used to refer to a characteristic of an individual rather than to the pattern of interaction between two individuals in a specific situation and with particular developmental histories.

For example, in mice, at least some of the observed sex differences in fighting behavior are explained by hormonally based odor differences. Androgen-dependent odors, such as are normally present in intact males, are potent stimuli for eliciting intrusive investigatory activities from a second animal and these can escalate into fighting. Females and castrated males do not typically elicit many intrusive investigations that could escalate to aggressive responses and therefore do not engage in many fights. However, when urine from intact males is used to scent females and castrated males, these odorous animals elicit more intrusive investigatory-aggressive behavior from others than they normally would (Lee & Griffo, 1973; Svare & Gandelman, 1974), and therefore they engage in more fighting.

Contextual effects on fighting behavior are commonplace. These effects may involve particular stimuli (as in the example from mice), general location (e.g., on or off home ground), familiarity with other individuals, and a host of other factors. It is important to attend to the context, because it can alter the probability or intensity of fighting in particular instances, and individuals may respond to the same context differently, depending on their condition. In addition, context can sort out different kinds of fighting. One straightforward example is the difference between offensive and defensive fighting (Blanchard & Blanchard, 1990).

Careful descriptions of the details of fighting behavior in natural social contexts identified numerous differences in the offensive and defensive fighting of rats. Furthermore, the physiological mechanisms underlying the two kinds of fighting are strikingly different. There is a tradition of investigating the physiological foundations of aggression by provoking rats with a moderate level of shock, which reliably elicits an attack response (pain-induced aggression). Of interest, the fighting behavior that results is behaviorally and physiologically identical to defensive fighting in natural social contexts and quite unlike the offensive fighting that one usually associates with aggression (Blanchard & Blanchard, 1990). Thus it is unlikely that the information generated in animal model studies will shed light on the physiology of those aspects of human aggression that prompted the studies. Research conducted with a natural history orientation, however, points the way toward more meaningful physiological studies.

The fact that two participants in a fight may be motivated and behaving quite differently—even when each is inflicting real or potential harm on the other—reminds us that aggression is inherently a social phenomenon. It is a property of the interaction; it is not equivalent to the summed properties of the interactants. Recall from Rowell's (1966, 1972) work that dominance in baboons is an interactive phenomenon, and that there is a surprisingly low correlation between aggression (threats, overt harmful behavior) and dominance. When aggression is treated as a characteristic that develops in and belongs to individuals, its emergent social character has been ignored. This can only hinder the discovery of the means whereby aggression may be regulated in humans.

Abnormal

The concepts of normal and abnormal are commonly applied in Western society, and they are prevalent in the study of human development. The lay public, both individually and through its legal, governmental, and other institutions, seeks from psychological theory and research both clarification of what constitutes normality and explanations for atypical, bizarre, socially disruptive behavior. Most clinical diagnostic techniques attribute unacceptable behavior to disorders of individual personality—abnormalities. Hence, a great deal of anthropocentrically oriented animal research has sought to identify animal models of human personality disorders (Siever & Davies, 1991). We believe that **abnormal** is another developmental concept that is significantly altered by animal research conducted in a natural history orientation.

Anthropocentrically oriented research on personality disorders requires one to identify a behavior or set of behaviors that can be elicited reliably in a convenient animal and that bears some resemblance to certain of the behaviors associated with the presumed human personality disorder. Then biochemical, neural, and other manipulations may be performed on the animal to identify the specific biological features associated with the "abnormality." Finally, pharmacological and other techniques may be employed to affect the associated biological feature to see if the animal's behavior is changed. In this way, therapeutic procedures may be tested on animals before being applied to humans.

Clearly, the design of such research makes it very unlikely that we alter our concepts of normal and abnormal. Yet, as Canguilhem (1978) stated about medicine in general, "there is no biological science of the normal. There is a science of biological situations *called* normal" (p. 138). At present, normal and abnormal or pathological are not scientific concepts (Tiles, 1993). However, Gollin et al. (1989) proposed that animal research ought to be conducted within a natural history orientation to construct the meaning of these concepts.

These investigators note that the meaning of abnormal is almost entirely derived from the meaning of **normal**. Consequently, understanding normal development is a prerequisite to understanding abnormal development. However, the various definitions of normality (e.g., socially and culturally acceptable, statistically frequent, socially and culturally typical, traditionally and authoritatively defined as healthy) depend heavily on an intuitive sense rather than on a systematic, empirical investigation of normal development.

Intuitive definitions of normality maintain certain assumptions about the individual, the environment, and the types of processes that create the individual's behavioral repertoire (including the symptoms characteristic of abnormality). These assumptions are not supported by modern animal research conducted from a natural history orientation. They have been called into question by modern advances in developmental psychobiology, as well.

One implicit assumption is that the course and outcome of development are universal and immutable. Of course, those who hold to this idea acknowledge that certain factors can alter the rate of progression or the final level achieved, but these alterations are limited and circumscribed by intrinsic conditions present at the outset. This view leads to research that is focused on observed regularities and that neglects contextual differences. Thus, normal is defined as the typical rate of progression through common universal patterns that results in a typical outcome. Factors that alter the rate or end point of progression result in deviations from the typical and are considered the causes of abnormal development. This is at variance with the understanding of development achieved from a natural history orientation, which incorporates contextual factors into the explanatory system (see Lerner, 1991).

A second implicit assumption is that the individual and the environment may be treated as separate entities. Consequently, the cause of the individual's abnormal behavioral repertoire may be assigned either to extrinsic factors of the environment or to intrinsic factors of the individual, or a simple additive combination of both types of factors. Therefore, if the environment appears to be typical but the behavior is not, then the source of any idiosyncracies in development must be attributed to the individual.

As numerous examples in the present and previous chapters attest, animal research conducted within the natural history orientation challenged these two assumptions (Miller, 1981). The assumption that normal development consists of a universal, relatively immutable, developmental sequence is challenged by the discovery of both *equifinality*, that is, the same psychological ability may arise from quite different developmental pathways and processes, and *multifinality*, a specific developmental pathway or process does not invariably result in the manifestation of one specific ability. These two phenomena, which have been identified frequently in the development of animal behavior and used recently in human development (Fischer, Knight, & van Parys, 1993), challenge intuitive concepts of abnormality and its treatment.

For example, dyslexia is considered to be a developmental disorder, an abnormality or product of a developmental process gone wrong. Two complicating generalizations emerge from research on this disorder: it can arise from a variety of etiological factors (it exhibits equifinality), but it does not necessarily arise when the same etiological factors are present (it exhibits multifinality). Clearly, it is necessary to understand the characteristics of multifinality and equifinality in the normal development of reading before it will be possible to identify the many developmental sources of dyslexia or to construct individually appropriate techniques for remediation. Despite the recognition that reading and dyslexia exhibit equifinality and multifinality in development, this is not translated into strategies for clinical intervention. Instead, dyslexia is commonly treated as if it were a unitary phenomenon and is addressed by similar remediation techniques without regard to specific developmental history. This often results in failure because of a mismatch between developmental cause and treatment. This difficulty is not restricted to reading problems, but pervades the treatment of all developmental disorders.

Moreover, it is not enough to adopt a simple eclectic approach that recognizes numerous causes and numerous treatments. This alone will not suffice to resolve the clinical difficulties because it fails to address the pattern of match or mismatch between the individual's capacities and the available resources. These resources include usable features in the tasks and problems to be undertaken or solved as well as support from the individual's social milieu. In the case of dyslexia, the successful intervention will examine the frequency and difficulty of reading tasks in relation to the individual's current capacity and the teaching skills, knowledge, commitment, and relationships of those who interact with the dyslexic individual. These and other aspects of daily life that form the context for reading are important determinants of improvement in reading skill and must be evaluated as part of diagnosis and the strategy for intervention. Thus, the likelihood of successful intervention with any abnormal behavior will increase only with adequate understanding of the various processes that can lead to the acquisition of the capacities that the individual brings to a task. Such understanding will come only from systematic investigation of the various ways in which individual capacities can develop.

Developmental analysis requires one to recognize that the individual and the environment are functionally reciprocating components of a unified system. The realization that behavior is a system property—a result of transactions between the individual and environment—follows from the natural history orientation. It challenges the assumption and common clinical practice of treating the environment and individual as independent entities. It requires new assumptions and practices that can accommodate observations such as the following.

Two individuals appear equally normal in the same context, but a similar change in context for both (e.g., loss of a loved one) results in the emergence of distinctly different behavioral adjustments, one common and the other unusual. The differences between their adjustments depend on the pattern of match between each individual's capacities and the available resources, and must be evaluated in these terms. Thus, a similar change in context need not imply a similar change in the two individual-environment systems. The concept of unusual, like that of abnormal, must not be taken merely in the statistical sense but in terms of what constitutes a perturbation for the equilibrium of the individual-environment system (Gollin et al., 1989). Furthermore, novel adjustments need not be pathological, but may represent adaptive changes in the system.

The emergence of behavioral adjustments through transactions of individual capacities with environmental resources is equally true for the so-called typical and the atypical environments. Thus, it is not possible to point either to the individual or to the environment in isolation from the other and identify normal or abnormal elements either in individual functions, capacities, or abilities, or in the range of resources or deficits in the environment. These elements have to be considered in relation to other parts of the system. It follows that no aspect of an individual's behavioral repertoire, including symptoms of abnormality, are invariant expressions of the individual's internal anatomy or physiology, or invariant reflections of some environmental event.

Development involves the active construction of a system, using capacities achieved by the individual and resources available in the social and physical environments. Systems are organized; they exhibit coherence. Perturbation of the system by alterations in any component necessitates reestablishment of coherence. When particular physiological or behavioral elements of the system are examined after such a change at the macrolevel, some changes at the microlevel may appear positive and others negative. As Goldstein (1939) argued, "symptoms" are attempts by individuals to retain coherence in the face of perturbation. Gollin et al. (1989) advocate describing and evaluating symptoms as trade-offs for achieving coherence. The significance assigned to these trade-offs necessarily derives from a perspective in which there is a socially defined and expected level of achievement. This perspective should be explicitly acknowledged and taken into account (to use what is perhaps an obvious example, dyslexia is not a problem in illiterate societies).

Symptoms are not just an outcome of development, they are also part of the continued process of development. For example, an individual with dyslexia may have acquired a reading strategy that enabled the establishment of coherence at an earlier time in development. However, that strategy later contributes to the creation of a developmental process that maintains the dyslexia.

Whether for developmental research or for deciding on clinical strategies, individuals must be examined to determine exactly what pattern of match-mismatch exists between their capacities and the characteristics of the available environment. Gollin et al. apply this approach to issues of task success and task difficulty. In tasks as diverse as performing social functions such as establishing and maintaining a career, marriage, attending school, and performing on standardized assessments of either age-related achievements or those used to obtain various jobs, the degree of success will depend on the degree to which the individual's behavior conforms with the demands imposed by the social and physical settings (e.g., home, peers, school, business). The difficulty of a task is not absolute, because it is necessarily a property of the relation between the individual's capacities and the demands of the task.

Consequently, when studying capacities, the person should be exposed to novel and demanding environmental opportunities to assess more accurately the range of capacity. Moreover, the individual should be provided every opportunity to demonstrate the highest level of functioning that he or she can achieve, so that as to reveal how the strategies match the requirements of the task. Only in this manner may the individual's personal pattern of strengths and weaknesses be identified so that appropriate rehabilitation conditions can be established to build on the former and compensate for the latter.

The natural history orientation to the issue of abnormality dovetails nicely with current evaluations of modern clinical psychology (Maddux, 1993). It is now more frequent to acknowledge that the concepts of normal and abnormal are moral, ethical, and legal rather than scientific. Their meanings are defined socioculturally and not by scientific operations. Scientific operations cannot identify *what* behaviors should be changed, but they are essential to identify *how* change may be effectively and efficiently facilitated. Scientific operations can also reveal the relative arbitrariness by which any distinction between normal and abnormal is made. Finally, scientific operations can specify how the relation of individual and situation affects the manifestation of behavior. After all, it is the behavioral effectiveness or ineffectiveness in specific circumstances that identifies whether a behavioral change is necessary. The natural history orientation provides the conceptual framework within which each of these tasks is undertaken more readily.

We conclude that the natural history orientation and studies of animal behavior conducted in this orientation can help to identify misleading and invalid concepts of behavioral development and suggest replacements that are more useful. These clarifications have important clinical and other pragmatic consequences. In addition, the natural history orientation can be applied directly to the study of human psychological development, leading to the formulation of concepts that are crucial for describing and explaining this development. In the next section we describe how this orientation also can help identify special aspects of human psychology.

Identification of Special Features of Human Development

Comparison of human psychological development with animal behavioral development, particularly primate development, can reveal specific and ubiquitous characteristics of human development. Knowledge of animal behavior can provide another, broader perspective from which to examine the phenomena of human development. In 1978 we proposed that this perspective highlights the extent to which language and symbolic reasoning skills influence and pervade the psychological development of humans. Recent work with preverbal infants suggests that the study of social and sensorimotor development, even before the appearance of symbolic language, may be aided by keeping these human features in mind (Bornstein & Lamb, 1992; Fogel, 1991).

Imitation and play are two other important features with special human characteristics (Michel & Moore, 1978). Since our earlier treatment of them, advances have been made in both human and animal studies that warrant further consideration of these features. To these we add a third: society. The acquisition of sociality is a major developmental achievement, and recent comparative studies suggest some ways in which it works in humans.

Imitation and Teaching

In striking contrast to most animals, children are able to copy environmental or social events in their actions, and they are unflagging in their determination to do so. Such copying is what we commonly mean by imitation. On inspection, however, imitation has a variety of meanings.

Imitation has been a focal issue in the history of comparative psychology since the beginning of the field, but confusion persists about what it means to assert that one animal imitates another (Galef, 1988). By the beginning of the twentieth century, comparative psychologists used the term imitation in three different ways, varying in the range of phenomena that were included. At its most inclusive, it described all instances of socially influenced changes in behavior. Thorndike (1988) offered the most rigorous definition, labeling only instances of learning to perform an act from seeing it performed, and relegating other socially influenced changes to "pseudo-imitation." Others took a middle course and suggested that imitation should be categorized as blind, instinctive, and deliberate, reflective imitation.

At the heart of these different definitions was a debate about the continuity of human and animal minds. Those who took the position that evolutionary continuity implied essential similarity in underlying processes throughout the animal kingdom placed the fullblown imitative behavior of humans on a continuum with other socially influenced changes. Those whose view of evolution embraced divergence, even qualitative divergence, from common origins thought it was important to identify distinctions among the diverse social influences on behavioral change.

The effort to sort out the distinctions among different kinds of social influences on learning led to the emergence of several new terms during the early twentieth century. The lack of consistent rules for usage in the literature added to the confusion. Galef (1988) proposed some terminological conventions to bring order to the descriptive and explanatory categories. As part of this effort, he grouped descriptive terms into three different categories: social learning, social enhancement, and social transmission.

Social learning is a generic term for any instance in which the acquisition of a behavioral pattern is influenced by social interactions. *Social enhancement* refers to the social facilitation of the expression of behaviors that are already within the individual's repertoire. Thus the distinction between the two categories lies primarily in whether new behavior is acquired. The third category offers a different kind of distinction, drawing attention to the dimension of tradition or culture. *Social transmission* occurs when social interactions result in a shared behavioral repertoire that extends beyond the period of interaction. It is often recognized by the greater homogeneity of behavior within than between local groups.

Social learning, social enhancement, or social transmission can occur for a number of different reasons apart from goal directed imitation. Galef

(1988) distinguished six different explanatory terms that do not entail purposive goal-direction: local or stimulus enhancement, social facilitation, contagious behavior, observational conditioning, matched dependent behavior, and copying.

Local or stimulus enhancement can occur because individuals approach members of their own species or aspects of the environment that they have contacted or modified. It can affect learning of behavior because it changes the probability or extent of exposure to particular stimuli, or the contextual salience of stimuli, for previously naive animals. For example, scent marks left where one animal has foraged can increase the probability that a conspecific will discover the same food item and learn what to do with it. "Enhanced exposure can lead to habituation, familiarity, perceptual learning, latent learning, increased probability of manipulation of one portion of the environment, and so forth" (Galef, 1988, p. 15).

Social facilitation and contagious behavior involve relatively simple processes and are unlikely to produce major effects on either social learning or social transmission. Social facilitation refers to an increase in the probability of behaviors elicited by nonsocial stimuli in a particular situation by the simple presence of social stimuli. For example, playing the contact calls of one species of bird (chickadees), sounds that typically indicate their presence in an area, facilitated feeding behavior of another bird species (downy woodpeckers) even when no chickadees were present (Sullivan, 1984). It is difficult to know whether this occurred because feeding was enhanced or because competing responses, such as searching for predators, were decreased. Contagious behavior accounts for the case in which performance of a common species-typical behavior initiates that action in others (e.g., yawning in humans, howling in a group of dogs, direction of movement in schools of fish, crying in human infants).

Observational conditioning accounts for the social transmission of behavior in many animal species. In certain species, individuals can learn quickly to treat a novel stimulus in a manner similar to the way conspecifics treat the stimulus, a process that allows previously neutral stimuli to become treated as food or as predators. A classic example occurred in England shortly after World War II. Certain species of birds learned to remove the paper caps from milk bottles to obtain the cream. The actions that they used to remove the caps were the same as those they used to remove bark from trees to obtain insects. Once a few birds had discovered the food under milk caps, observational conditioning enabled other birds to treat the milk bottles as trees (Hinde & Fisher, 1951).

Animals can also come to treat particular stimuli as predators as a result of observing the behavior of conspecifics. This was demonstrated in an ingenious series of experiments in which two blackbirds, teacher and learner, were arranged so that they could see and hear one another but so that each saw a different stimulus in the same central presentation box. If a teacher blackbird was exposed to an owl stimulus, it would exhibit antipredator mobbing behavior as might be expected. The learner, which did not see the owl but a different stimulus that ordinarily elicits neutral responses, would come to direct antipredator behavior to the previously neutral stimulus. This was true when the stimuli were nonpredatory birds, such as Australian honeyeaters, or even multicolored plastic bottles (Curio, 1988).

Matched dependent behavior refers to instances in which reinforcement leads individuals to match the behavior of others. Skinner (1953) observed that if several pigeons in a flock are feeding in the same field, all of them are likely to be scratching at the ground and feeding at some level. Thus, the sight of one pigeon engaged in this behavior will be temporally associated with the food uncovered by the independent, similar behavior of others in the flock, and will take on the properties of a discriminative stimulus. Eventually, the behavior of the members of the flock will be matched one to the other.

Copying is the adjustment of an individual's behavior until it resembles that of another (the model). It is commonly inferred when the term imitation is applied to instances of similarity of behavioral performance between individuals. However, two points are worth noting. As the long list of processes that can produce similarity indicates, very few instances of similarity in the acquisition or performance of animal behavior entail copying. Furthermore, copying is not always all that is meant by imitation.

An intriguing diversity in the copying behavior of animals suggests the importance of further distinctions. For example, copying is quite apparent in the developmental acquisition of song in certain bird species, and in the ability of certain parrot and other species to reproduce human vocalizations. Such acquisition depends in many instances on the nature of the social relation between the model and the imitator (West, Stroud, & King, 1983). Of interest, many differences in the details of the mechanisms lead to copying among avian species (chapter 3). The degree to which any of these overlaps with copying behavior in humans is certainly open to question. Furthermore, we have no a priori reason to assume that all copying behavior in humans is similar.

The study of imitation in humans, including the development of the ability and its role in the development of other abilities, would benefit from closer attention to the animal research. Human researchers would do well to adopt appropriate distinctions in descriptive terms, instead of describing all instances as imitation with an implicit meaning of copying.

It is important to identify the different explanations of imitative phenomena in humans and to examine their adequacy with a systematic program of research. This is especially important for understanding the role of imitation in development. To take one example, it is possible to increase the frequency of tongue protrusion in neonates by stimulating them with an adult who demonstrates tongue protrusion. But this is not prima facie evidence of copying. Animal research suggests several alternative explanations that must be investigated systematically. Moreover, it indicates that one aspect of copying appears to be relatively unique to humans. That is, in humans the model or some other external agent will reinforce behaviors according to their similarity to that of the model. This is very much a process of deliberate tuition.

The ability to imitate combines with the child's interest in being taught and with the adult's propensity to engage in tuition to generate a process of education common to all human cultures. The long period of dependency characteristic of human development makes this educational process possible, and the species has capitalized on education as a means of maximizing developmental gains. During the period of dependency, the individual not only receives a formalized education in the values and ways of his or her culture, but also is presented with a variety of social roles to occupy and master. The variety of these roles and their complicated interrelations in even the simplest of human societies are well beyond what are observed in animal social organizations. As Schneirla (1966) proposed, comparisons of human with animal behavioral development may be more instructive for the differences that are revealed than for the similarities.

Play

Consider play, which has often been used to describe certain phases of the social and sensory motor development of animals (Welker, 1971). Dolhinow and Bishop (1970) concluded that both social and solitary play of young primates are important for the development of social and sensory motor skills before adults can effectively meet the conditions of their environment and society. As important as these play patterns may be, they seem to be relatively confined to the preadult stages. It is seldom that sexually mature nonhuman primates engage in social or solitary activities having no significant immediate consequences for survival. Yet, the adult human appears to do just that. Sensory motor skills are elaborated beyond their functional necessity and are developed into art forms or formalized games. Once established as goals in themselves, they must be integrated into the social role structure. Even though patterns of play in human and nonhuman primates share some characteristics, play in humans is different because of its incorporation into other, distinctively human activities (Fisher, 1992).

In addition to formalizing sensory motor skills into art forms and games, humans create social interaction routines from functional skills and elaborate them as techniques for gaining and maintaining influence, power, fame, and control. Employment of these routines extends beyond functional necessity and appears to involve little more than a wish to "play the game." Bruner (1972) may be quite right in insisting that play is a fundamental component of human social and intellectual development. However, it is only by contrast with the play of other animals that its special, and possibly most significant, aspects become obvious.

Before play can be compared across species, it is necessary to define it. That is not easy to do. Martin and Caro (1985, p. 65), following Bekoff and Byers (1981), provided a definition that, although lengthy, captures much of what is labeled as play. They proposed that play is activity that to an observer appears to lack immediate benefits for the player. The motor patterns of the activity, although somewhat similar to those used in other functional contexts (e.g., predation, sex) are modified such that movements are exaggerated, repetitive, fragmented, and/or in the wrong sequence. Play can also be categorized by its object. Playful activities may be directed toward conspecifics (social play), or inanimate objects (object play), or living or dead prey (predatory play), or simply involve spontaneous movements (locomotor play).

Despite the apparent lack of immediate benefits, play is presumed to serve some important, delayed function. Burghardt (1988) lists six possibilities: "... benefits accruing by way of physical exercise, perfection of non-social skills, perfection of social skills (including ... social roles), cognitive [central nervous system] development, and behavioral innovation ... [and] play may inform parents about the competence of offspring" (p. 128). It is often assumed that play is energetically expensive and must therefore have important functions, or it would have been eliminated by natural selection. Its costs and benefits are difficult to measure, however, and are subject to the complications of additional variables, such as the amount and quality of available food. Careful measurements of the actual energetic costs indicate that they can be minimal (Martin, 1984). Furthermore, typical levels of play can be drastically reduced without apparent impact on its presumed advantages. For these reasons, Martin and Caro (1985) conclude that little firm evidence supports either the assumption of high energetic costs or the conclusion of delayed functional advantages of play.

Burghardt (1988) took a fresh look at the evolution of play by asking why mammals and some birds play but other vertebrates do not. Although fish, amphibians, and reptiles show some evidence of curiosity and exploration, they do not play because they are unable to sustain any vigorous activity. This is a consequence of their physiology—low maximum rates of oxygen consumption and reliance on anaerobic metabolism. Unlike other vertebrates, birds and mammals have evolved endothermy, the use of stored food to generate a stable internal temperature. This, together with increased efficiency of metabolism and improved abilities to use oxygen, provides conditions that allow them to play. The mammalian system is particularly efficient for storing energy and making it available for behavior.

The functional and phylogenetic analyses suggest that play may not have evolved as an adaptation to particular selective pressures. Having evolved, however, it may contribute importantly to the development of various abilities that do confer selective advantages and may therefore be an exaptation (chapter 4). This way of looking at the evolutionary question helps to explain the diversity of hypothesized advantages of play, the paucity of clear evidence for these advantages, and the diversity in the amount of play performed both within and among species.

Burghardt identified several testable predictions that follow from the hypothesis that play is constrained by a combination of nutritional and thermal needs and the metabolic characteristics of the animal, and he offered some comparative evidence in their support. To take a few examples from his extensive list, when needs are readily met by an environment high in resources (e.g., extensive parental care), play will be more likely; very small animals will play very little because their size sets high energy needs that require extensive time to meet; very large animals will engage in relatively little vigorous, whole-body play because it is energetically expensive, and relatively more play that involves smaller limb and head movements; animals that live in media (mud or water) that allow energy-efficient movement will play more often; and altricial species whose thermal and nutritive needs are met by parents for longer periods will play more than more precocial species within the same phyletic group.

Burghardt's novel approach and Martin and Caro's careful critical assessment of earlier ideas about the evolution of play both have interesting implications for study in humans. Perhaps a reorientation to the investigation that takes these evolutionary ideas into account is called for (Bruner, Jolly, & Sylva, 1976; Smith, Takhvar, Gore, & Vollstedt, 1985).

Society

Animals exhibit a rich diversity of social behaviors and systems. Much research for the past half-century revealed a surprising level of complexity in animal societies, and not only among primates. Kinship systems, long-term bonds, complex coordination of group activities, competition, cooperation, and leadership are just some of the phenomena observed in nonhumans. Although such achievements should not be underestimated, it is helpful to ask what, if anything, distinguishes human society from that of other species.

Rowell (1991) addressed this question thoughtfully and arrived at some interesting insights. She began her analysis with Hinde's (e.g., 1979) important distinctions among social interactions, relationships, and group structure, and his efforts to integrate these as three levels in a hierarchical system (figure 9.3). Social interactions occur at the level of individuals behaving with one another, usually in dyadic encounters. Relationships emerge out of interactions, but do not reduce to them. Unlike time-limited interactions, relationships can take the lifetime into account and can endure even when the constituent individuals are separated spatially. Hinde maintained that group structure emerges from the interactions among relationships.

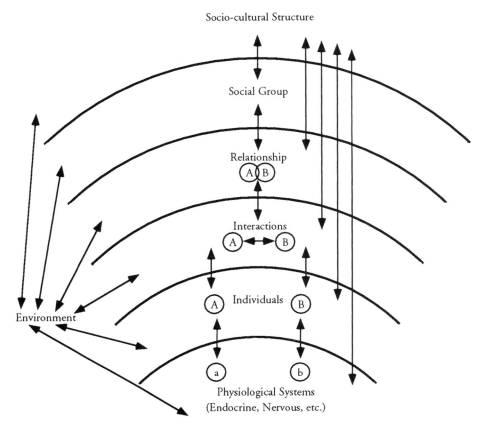

Figure 9.3 The hierarchical network of the various levels of social organization, as illustrated for two individuals, A and B (redrawn from Hinde, 1987).

According to his theory, human social systems differ from those of non-human primates primarily by the addition of institutions at a higher hierarchical level.

In Rowell's (1991) analysis, the idea of group structure proved particularly problematic. Clearly, humans and many animal species live in groups and these groups appear organized. One large question is whether a group structure, with rules, exists into which individuals must fit—an ostensive group structure (Strum & Latour, 1987). Some primatologists believe that such is the case, but others are against the reification of group structure as an entity. Although Hinde suggests that group structure emerges from interactions among relationships, it is unclear how this might happen. Even if this were to work for primates, it is unclear how well it would generalize to other animal taxa, such as ungulates and carnivores, which have sophisticated social groups.

It is interesting that the study of social groups in animals that are different from us in many ways raises a very important question: is the group the same thing for the same collection of animals doing different things? Rowell describes huddles in both rams and wolves in which each individual interacts intensively and simultaneously with each other member of the group, yet the same set of individuals can behave in a coordinated and behaviorally differentiated fashion when dealing with some external agent, such as prey or predator.

It is Strum and Latour's (1987) position that there are no ostensive societies, no structured roles established independently, as it were, into which individuals must fit. Instead, society is *performed* by its members. What emerges from this combined, shifting performance can be described at a macrolevel and given the label of society. Their focus on performance provides a way to identify what is specific to the construction of human societies. This task is helped by beginning with a clear distinction between complex and complicated.

In Strum and Latour's terminology, a social system is *complex* when the individuals in the group are involved in a large number of simultaneous social transactions. In contrast, it is complicated when the individuals are involved in a large number of simple transactions engaged in sequence. Humans have complicated social systems, whereas monkeys and wolves have complex social systems. Complicated systems are more stable and place fewer demands on the individual for a given number of transactions; thus, they permit individuals to achieve more transactions, occupy various roles, and so forth. Humans can move from complexity to complication because they can make use of particular material and symbolic resources that are unavailable to other species.

Although much has been learned about social interaction and social relationships among animals, the study of animal societies at the group level or above has far to go. Rowell (1991) suggests that continued study of group structure is likely to reveal important species differences, including specifically human characteristics. These differences raise developmental questions. Indeed, the distinction between complex and complicated social processes that grew out of comparisons of social structure in baboons and humans suggests a developmental dimension that can be profitably applied to the study of human social development.

Identification of Issues in Human Development that Need Study

Sometimes close attention to the lives of other species turns up surprisingly important effects of factors that had been overlooked or dismissed as unimportant to the lives of humans. The value of ideas gained in this way should not be underestimated, for they offer fresh insights and often open for study new domains of human development. This is very different from the value of animal research held up as a model or mirror of what we already know, even if only dimly, of humans. Earlier (Michel & Moore, 1978) we described five aspects of human psychological development that were in the early stages of having their study fostered and revitalized by research in animal behavior: the influence of prenatal conditions on postnatal development, the reciprocity of influence between parent and offspring, the role of nonadult companions in development, the continuation of developmental processes throughout the life span, and the role of self-stimulation in development.

Since the 1980s, such extensive attention has been paid to prenatal contributions and parent-offspring reciprocity that it contributed a large share to several chapters in this book. Studies of the life span and the nonadult social environment are now major subfields of human developmental psychology. Some intriguing studies of self-stimulation in human development have been published, but these are few and scattered; we believe that this is still largely an untapped but potentially fertile research domain.

Self-Stimulation

In 1957 Schneirla observed that "the individual seems to be interactive with itself throughout development" (p. 86). At each stage the organism exhibits specific behavioral abilities in interaction with its social and physical environments. The application of these abilities provides the individual with certain specific kinds of stimulation that become, in turn, experiences that influence the individual's development. These "circular relationships of self-stimulation" (p. 86) are an important source of behavioral development.

One of the difficulties with the concept of **self-generated experience** is the practical one of designing an experiment to study it. This requires ingenuity and sophisticated experimentation in any event, but can be helped by the judicious choice of a behavioral system to study. Hein and colleagues (Hein, 1980; Hein & Diamond, 1983) combined all three to trace the influence of self-generated experience on the development of visual spatial representation in cats. They demonstrated that the visual stimulation provided by kittens' own locomotion is responsible for the development of certain important visual motor perceptual abilities (Held & Hein, 1963). Eye-paw coordination, for example, develops appropriately in kittens that can simultaneously walk and look at things, but not in kittens that can only look at things while being moved passively. Subsequent studies showed that information incorporated into the development of visual space is obtained from self-produced movements. This development follows a particular sequence.

Kittens for whom there was no correlation between visual input and own body movements did not develop visually guided locomotion. Visual feedback from movements of the forelimb was essential to acquiring the ability to guide the limb to small visual targets. Only the eye that received visual feedback from the movements of a particular limb became able to guide that limb—and it guided that limb only. However, dark-reared kittens that were provided with visual feedback of a forelimb in the absence of visual feedback from locomotion failed to develop visually guided reaching. Thus, visually guided reaching depends on visual feedback from movement of the forelimb and visually guided locomotion. Visually guided locomotion, in turn, depends on visual feedback from self-produced locomotion. Thus, under normal rearing conditions, kittens provide themselves with the visual feedback to develop both visually guided locomotion and reaching.

Kittens must have information about the position of their eyes to extract information relevant to the development of visually guided behavior. Kittens that were not able to move their eyes, but were free to engage in locomotion in light, would not develop either visually guided locomotion or reaching. Thus, the visual feedback from head and body movements was not sufficient for the development of a representation of visual space necessary for these two behaviors. Of interest, immobilizing the eyes does not interfere with the visually guided behaviors for cats that have already developed these abilities. Eye movements are necessary for the development of the behaviors, but not for their expression once they have been developed (Hein, 1980).

Subsequent research revealed that it was proprioceptive input from the muscles that moves the eyes and marks their position in the orbit that allowed the development of a spatial ability that coordinated positions of things in geocentric space with the retinal location of images, the positions of the eyes, and the positions of the head, body, and limbs. Again, once proprioceptive input has helped develop the visual representation, it is no longer necessary for the expression of visually guided behavior. However, proprioceptive input was required to maintain the visual representation. Kittens denied proprioceptive input after having developed visually guided abilities would lose these abilities if they were placed in the dark for some period of time. Kittens that were not deprived of proprioceptive input while in the dark did not lose the abilities. Kittens that could not obtain proprioceptive input and subsequently lost their visually guided abilities because of dark rearing were able to reacquire their abilities after a period of time, when allowed self-produced experience in the light. Thus, proprioceptive feedback from the movement of the eyes is necessary for the initial development of visually guided abilities but not for their reacquisition once they have been lost (Hein, 1980; Hein & Diamond, 1983).

Feedback from eye and head movements is not only important for the development of visual motor coordination, but it also contributes to the development of the cortical mechanisms for vision. The neurons of the kitten's visual cortex typically exhibit orientation specificity, which means that each neuron is optimally responsive to light stimuli oriented in a particular direction relative to gravity. Sensory inputs from both eye and neck muscles, active during gaze movements, are necessary for the development of the orientation specificity of visual cortical neurons. Orientation specificity depends on self-produced congruence between visual and proprioceptive input (Buisseret, 1993). Such congruence is a ubiquitous aspect of every kitten's experience. Therefore, it is not surprising that its role in the development of orientation specificity was only recently discovered.

Just as self-produced stimulation is important for a kitten's perceptual motor development, it also appears to be important for sensorimotor development of human infants (Piaget, 1952). Infants develop coordinated sensorimotor skills and abilities as a result of feeling and seeing changes in the positions of their limbs in relation to one another, to the body, and to objects in the environment. Piaget called such self-stimulation circular reactions and considered them a major source for the intellectual development of the human infant.

Piaget's approach points the way toward a closer examination of the role of self-induced stimulation in human psychological development. The experimental work with animals, of which the study of visually guided behavior is just one particularly interesting and well-characterized example, demonstrates that such effects are crucially important and should be included in theories and studies of human psychological development.

New Directions

The 1980s and early 1990s were active and creative for developmental psychobiology, and many new suggested avenues of research were opened by animal work. We describe three of these briefly in the remainder of this chapter.

One of the recurrent themes of this book is that *phenomenological and functional criteria for identifying the boundaries of behavioral units should be discarded* when searching for the developmental causes of behavior. This point was made very forcefully and effectively by Tinbergen, Lehrman, Hinde, and others who helped the field of animal behavior to find a way to study both development and function while avoiding the perils of nativistic instinct theory (chapters 1–3). Although functional categories (and the related pull of nativism) are still the norm in studies of cognition, interesting stirrings are occurring among some developmentalists who have abandoned the functionally defined boundaries of faculties in their search for the developmental primitives of thought and language (chapter 8). The approach of the connectionist neural network theorists holds particular promise for linking these developmental fields to psychobiology.

Although the importance of experience, milieu, or context has been recognized for a fairly long time, it has often not been translated into experimentation. But, within natural history-oriented animal research, a concerted effort has been made to include *contextual factors in analytic studies of development* (chapter 7). This is part and parcel of the growing influence of systems approaches to development. A fundamental and widely accepted credo of systems theorists is that behavior is a joint product of the organism and its environment. Reasoning from this idea, we raised the possibility that some precocial appearances of adult functions in infants can be traced to contextual supports that permit superficially similar behavior, even when the underlying behavioral organization is quite different in the infant and the adult (chapter 7). The implications of the general idea go beyond this methodological caution, however.

Rovee-Collier and colleagues (Hill, Borovsky, & Rovee-Collier, 1988; Rovee-Collier & Hayne, 1987) showed that it is possible to analyze the way in which human infants use context in learning and memory, and to trace the developmental changes in this process. In their experiments, mobiles are hung above young infants who lie in their crib. When a ribbon is tied to connect the infant's leg to the mobile, the infant learns to move the mobile by kicking, an association that is evident from the increased rate of kicking. Using this technique, two- to three-month old infants remember the association after delays of several days, even responding preferentially to a visually distinct mobile that was previously reinforced. Their memory is improved by reminders such as brief exposure to the moving mobile some days after initial training. However, the memory of young infants, including their ability to respond to reminders, seems to require a stable context. Thus, memory can be demonstrated when all steps in the procedure occur in a familiar, distinctive context, such as that provided by a brightly patterned crib liner. A change in this context (e.g., removing or changing the crib liner to an entirely different pattern) can disrupt memory. Thus, one of the characteristics of the development of memory processes involves their resistance to certain sorts of contextual changes.

It is likely that contextual factors will emerge as important developmental determinants for other psychological processes as well. Furthermore, as animal research reminds us, many aspects of early developmental context are ubiquitous within a species. We inherit our environments as well as our genes. Inherited environments may be shared by all humans or by particular groups of humans, large or small (cultures, families, twins, etc.). The study of nongenetic inheritance, although difficult, has begun to reap results in animal work (chapter 5), and it is likely that an extension of some of the methods and ideas to the human case will also be productive.

Recent experiments in developmental psychobiology have drawn attention to a surprising array of *behaviorally relevant physiological events that go well beyond the traditional interest of psychologists in the nervous system* (Blass, 1986, 1988). These include not only the familiar hormones (and their not so familiar effects on muscles, glands, and other nonneural tissue), but also immune factors that are linked to behavior in so many ways, particularly during early developmental stages. Furthermore, constituents of milk, oxygen use, metabolic rate, thermogenesis, and a host of other general physiological considerations have to be taken into account to explain the developmental psychobiology of animal behavior. It is likely that the study of behavioral development in humans will benefit greatly by including a broadened range of physiology.

Summary

In this chapter we present the view that the natural history orientation to the study of animal behavior can provide an enriching outlook on human psychological development. The orientation offers the investigator with a vantage point from which to discover the species-typical characteristics. Animal behavior studies can suggest and encourage studies of human psychological development that do not fit the current mold of research efforts. Yet, although the ideas, issues, techniques, and approaches that accompany the study of behavioral development of animals may be applicable to studies of human development, the data, theories, and explanatory constructs of animal behavior studies may not. These are empirical matters because there are species differences as well as similarities.

Finally, we propose that much is to be gained from the integration of biology and psychology and from approaching human development with the tools and attitudes of developmental psychobiology. This approach is yet another perspective from which to view the psychological development of that most perplexing animal facing us in our mirrors every morning.

10   Developmental Psychobiology and the Unification of Behavioral Biology

The essence of the probabalistic conception of epigenesis is the bidirectionality of structure-function relationships.... It is important to note that this hierarchical, reciprocal, coactive definition of epigenesis holds for anatomy and physiology ..., as well as for behavior and psychological functioning. The traffic is bidirectional, neither exclusively bottom-up or top-down.
—G. Gottlieb (1992, p. 161)

The individual organism is a system that is structurally organized at many different levels. There can be no living organism apart from its immediate environmental context. This fact has two important implications: at whatever level of consideration, living organisms are necessarily *open systems*, exchanging both matter and energy with the physical surround (Bertalanffy, 1968); and at the level of whole-organism functioning (i.e., behavior), the organism and its surround constitute the system.

Although the organism can be divided into progressively more micro-levels, these levels are not independent of one another. They are partially coupled so that changes in one, say, the organ level, can have an impact on the others, say, the cellular level. Indeed, coupling can produce recursive loops, where a change in one level can promote changes in other levels that eventually feed back to promote a change in the original, initiating level. This is the bidirectionality that characterizes the work of so many developmental psychobiologists and that Gottlieb (1992) refers to in the quotation that starts this chapter.

Due to the characteristics of systems, there is no inevitability to effects in any direction. This is true for two reason. First, levels are only partly coupled and, second, the state of the system may be such (for various, perhaps entirely unrelated reasons) that changes at one level can be damped or even prevented from ramifying to other levels. These are straightforward implications of adopting a systems approach, and the previous chapters of this book offered numerous details from genetics, embryology, physiology, and behavior to give meaning to these abstractions. As we maintained in all these contexts, it is not possible to explain the functioning of an organism by relying on linear causality and directional determinism.

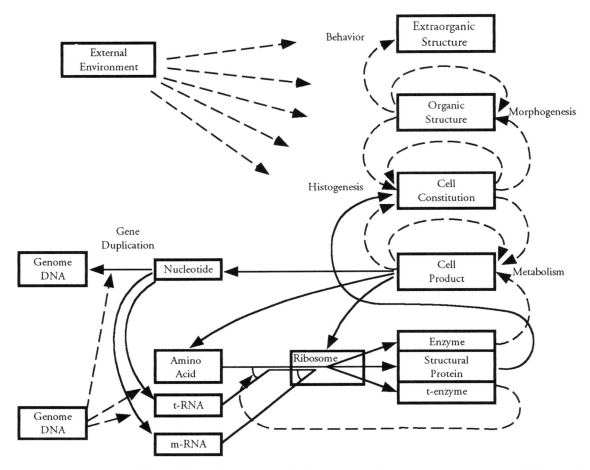

Figure 10.1 Consistent with his much earlier theoretical work, in 1968 Sewall Wright provided a more modern illustration of the complex relation between the various levels of organization of the organism from genome to behavior (redrawn from Wright, 1968).

Systems ideas, though recent, are not brand new. Gottlieb (1992) notes that in biology the embryologists Bertalanffy (1952, 1968) and Weiss (1939) and the geneticist Wright (1968) proposed similar perspectives for developmental genetics and developmental biology (figure 10.1). In psychology, Gottlieb identified this systems perspective in those developmental "approaches and theories that have been called ecological (Bronfenbrenner, 1979), transactional (Dewey & Bentley, 1949; Sameroff, 1983), contextual (Lerner & Kaufman, 1985), interactive (Johnston, 1987; Magnusson, 1988), probabilistic epigenetic (Gottlieb, 1970), individual-socioecological (Valsiner, 1987), structural-behavioral (Horowitz, 1987), and most globally speaking, interdisciplinary developmental science (Cairns, 1979)" (Gottlieb, 1992, p. 161).

Thus the perspective from which we have presented developmental psychobiology is consistent with those of several theorists in developmental biology and developmental psychology. Indeed, an underlying purpose in writing this book was to demonstrate how developmental psychobiology could serve as the framework for uniting the domains of psychology and biology.

This union requires one to place the individual organism in central focus, a suggestion entirely at variance with Wilson's (1975) forecast. He proposed that the field of biology was in a state of transition into two separate fields: cellular biology, heavily dominated by molecular biochemistry, and population biology, dominated by computational modeling techniques. Furthermore, he predicted that the integration of the behavioral sciences with biology would necessarily result in a similar division. "Although behavioral biology is traditionally spoken of as if it were a unified subject, it is now emerging as two distinct disciplines centered on neurophysiology and on sociobiology, respectively" (Wilson, 1975, p. 6). Indeed, he went on to predict that ethology and comparative psychology were "destined to be cannibalized by neurophysiology and sensory physiology from one end and sociobiology and behavioral ecology from the other" (p. 6) (figure 10.2).

To a large extent, Wilson's warnings have been confirmed. Sociobiology bloomed during the 15 years after the publication of his *Sociobiology* and came to dominate the study of animal behavior. Moreover, sociobiological ideas were frequently incorporated into the discussion and interpretation of phenomena within the social sciences (Caporeal & Brewer, 1991; Crawford, Smith, & Krebs, 1987; Gregory, Silvers, & Sutch, 1978; White, 1981), replacing psychoanalysis as a favored framework for interpreting human behavior and social phenomena. Perhaps cellular and molecular biology have loomed even larger, with behavioral scientists immigrating to these microlevels in large numbers.

But reports of the death of organismic biology have been greatly exaggerated. In his (to us) gloomy outlook, Wilson did not reckon on the complexity that would be revealed as neurophysiology dealt with the behavior of organisms. Molecular and cellular biologists made enormous advances in every area of their study—sensory physiology, mechanisms of learning, and so on. It is undeniable that these molecular achievements are essential for complete understanding of sensory phenomena, learning, or other behavioral processes. However, the more advances that are made, the more it becomes clear that an adequate account of the mechanisms underlying sensation, learning, or any behavioral phenomenon must incorporate information from levels higher in the system. Vision cannot be understood even when one completely understands all the cells involved, from rods and cones to neurons in the visual cortex. At some point, it becomes necessary to consider the system, and some biologists—including molecular geneticists

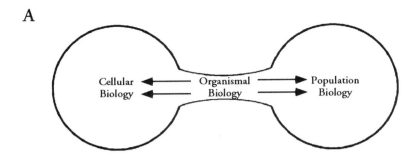

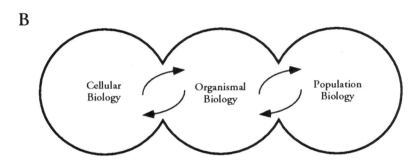

Figure 10.2 (A) E. O. Wilson's prediction of the progressive cannibalization of whole-organism psychobiology by a divided biology (after Wilson, 1975). (B) Our prediction is that organismic psychobiology will grow because of its essential linkage between populational and cellular investigations.

and developmental biologists from outside the field of behavior—are making this point and being heard (chapters 5 and 6).

If one's objective is to understand vision or sexual behavior or any other behavioral phenomenon, it is no help to go directly from the inner workings of cells to concepts derived from population biology. The split biology and cannibalized behavioral sciences that were predicted by Wilson cannot hope fully to explain behavior or any other organismic property. A necessary third level to the field, the middle level of the individual organism, has its own dynamic properties and is just as essential as molecular or population biology. Of course, eventually it may be possible to account, in principle, for all of the properties of the individual organism from molecular dynamics (just as it may be possible, in principle, to account similarly for all of the properties of populations). After all, nothing intrinsically prevents such reduction (cf. Churchland & Churchland, 1990; chapter 2). However, such reduction would be too cumbersome to be of any value for either case. Therefore, we should pursue understanding at all three levels of biological analysis.

A number of interesting consequences follow from a focus on the individual organism. One has already been described, but bears repeating: an individual is an organized, multilevel system. A second is that individuals have ancestors and, in turn, reproduce. Therefore, a connection exists between what an individual is and its evolutionary past, as well as between what an individual does and the future evolutionary consequences. Finally, an individual has a life, a continuous thread that extends from fertilization to death. Lives have their own histories, such that no two individuals are faced with exactly the same set of circumstances in exactly the same sequence— lives have contingencies.

A systems approach, with its up-down, bidirectional, nonlinear causal pathways, leads one to include the level of individual organisms in both the study of molecular biology and the study of population biology. However, neither of these two fields focuses on the individual. We suggest that the organismic level is the primary focus of the developmental sciences. The systems requirement ensures that developmentalists routinely move up to population levels and down to molecular levels. Parallel statements can be made for behavioral scientists. Thus, the developmental sciences and most particularly, developmental psychobiology are not the dispensible middle, but an indispensible cornerstone for a united biology.

In this brief chapter, we consider two scientific perspectives fostered by developmental psychobiology: unification across subdivisions of the life sciences, and historical and experimental styles of science.

Developmental Psychobiology and the Unification of Behavioral Biology

Respiratory systems respire, immune systems fight disease, muscles move limbs, but whole organisms behave. No lower level within the organism can be characterized in behavioral terms. Behavior is an emergent property of the current state of organization of the organism as a whole. Kennedy (1992) summed this up by stating that behavior may be construed as the physiology of the organism. If physiology is considered in levels, at its most microlevel it is found in single cells and at its most macrolevel in the integrated character of the whole organism's behavioral repertoire. "The integration of the whole animal's various behaviours ... is nothing more or less than the top level of that physiological hierarchy, as Tinbergen insisted" (Kennedy, 1992, p. 129). This way of looking at the issue gives us two interesting images: the study of behavior is more than the study of the nervous system, and physiology can be approached from the whole-organism level.

Despite their essential importance to behavior, not even nervous systems have the properties of behavior. This statement bring us to the structure-function puzzle that has occupied so many behavioral scientists. The systems solution can be described briefly in terms of three characteristics: systems consist of interconnected but heterogeneous elements, these elements are integrated in a hierarchically organized fashion, and bidirectional cross-talk occurs across levels. Thus, when organisms behave, they integrate activity from the nervous system, other internal elements, and elements from the milieu. The behavior is thus a property that belongs to the whole organism (in its immediate milieu), and not to lower levels. And, through the down-stroke of the bidirectional interaction across levels, a nervous system is changed by the behavior of the organism that contains it.

The physiology of the organism, in Kennedy's sense, is its behavior, something more than the physiology of its constituent organs. This is a departure from the convention in which physiology is thought of as "something that can be studied only by breaking the skin to look at the workings of the individual parts inside the animal, not by analysing the integration of the whole animal's behavior" (Kennedy, 1992, p. 128). Of course, such integration does arise from lower levels. In the language of dynamic systems, knowledge of the microstates is necessary for full comprehension of macrostates (behavior). Integration of the organism's behavior as it adjusts to, reacts to, alters, and constructs its physical and social environments depends on the status of the nervous, endocrine, and other organ systems (microstates). Nevertheless, integration of behavior constrains the variability permitted at the nervous system (microstate) level. Alteration or disruption of macrostates can have consequences for the microstates. Conversely, changes in microstates can have consequences for the status of macrostates. Thus, the integration that is behavior is not simply derived from lower levels, and it cannot be studied only by analyzing events at the lower levels. A physiology of organisms cannot be subsumed by molecular biology.

And what about the other end of Wilson's barbell? The characteristics of populations can be described in terms of adjustments to or alterations of their physical (climatological, etc.) and biotic (other populations of plants and animals) circumstances. Populations are groups of behaving organisms that are distinguished from other groups because of greater homogeneity within than between groups. The characteristics of a population can constrain the variability of the behavior of individual organisms that make up the population. Yet, population characteristics are also dependent on their constituent organisms. In systems terms, behaving organisms constitute microstates of populations, and knowledge of microstates is necessary before a macrostate can be fully understood. For example, is affiliation based on kinship, site attachment, or something else? Can metabolism and feeding pattern converge to permit fat storage and therefore hibernation or migration? The list of possible examples is long. Indeed, variation at the level of organisms (behavior, or whole-organism physiology) can have profound effects on the characteristics of the population. Considered from this side, too, organismic biology cannot be subsumed by population biology.

In short, organismic biology is not completely digestible by either of Wilson's cannibalistic giants. Those parts that have been swallowed are strong links to join the whole of biology. What remains is capable of vigorous, independent growth.

Organismic biology is now pretty much synonymous with behavioral biology (or psychobiology, biopsychology, biobehavioral studies, animal behavior, ethology). Developmental psychobiology, as a specialized part of these behavioral fields, shares focused attention on the organism as the primary unit of study. It thus has a significant role to play in the unification of biology. Not only are developmental psychobiologists well placed for this role: they are actively interested. This is well documented in several recent edited volumes (Bateson, 1991; Blass, 1986, 1988; Greenough & Juraska, 1986; Shair, Barr, & Hofer, 1991), and much of what we have summarized in this book records that interest. Specifically, developmental psychobiologists join other behavioral biologists in moving both downstream to explore the relation between cellular characteristics and behavior, and upstream to explore the relation between population characteristics and behavior.

Even a united biology is a sprawling field, encompassing a staggering range of phenomena, concepts, techniques, and methodologies. Of this diversity, perhaps none poses more difficulties than one that goes to the very heart of how we do science—the difference between experimental and historical methods for testing ideas. The developmental sciences (developmental biology, developmental psychology, developmental psychobiology) occupy an interesting position with respect to this methodological furcation, being able, as it were, to swing both ways.

The Experimental-Predictive and Historical Styles of Science

Scientists use many different specific methods to describe nature and test their explanations of what is observed, but a good many can be subsumed under the familiar, general rubric of experimentation. That is, a prediction is made, a few selected variables are manipulated while others are controlled under specified conditions, and observations are recorded. Repeatable results are then used to confirm as probably true or reject as unlikely the idea that led to the prediction. Quantification, replicability, and the identification of a relatively few explanatory causes are hallmarks of experimentation. It is a powerful method, yet not all things we want to explain can be approached in this manner.

In his account of the extraordinary information uncovered by recent descriptions of the Burgess shale fossils, Stephen J. Gould (1989b) not only narrates a revised history of life, but provides a lucid description of the historical method in the process. He points out that experimentation requires

repeatability, which means that it is a method suitable only for those domains of nature where time is symmetrical or nondirectional. When time is
directional, as in cosmology, evolution, or individual development, the tools
of historical inquiry must be used.

In domains such as these, one cannot go back to repeat the experiment
under identical conditions. One can, however, describe the conditions and
events in great narrative detail, test for consistent patterns from convergent
sources as a basis for accepting or rejecting explanations, and run the
thought experiment that Gould calls "replaying the tape." The adequacy of
historical research is judged by many of the same criteria as used for experimentation: degree of accuracy, validity of the evidence, standard rules
of reasoning, internal consistency, consistency with other valid evidence,
and ability to account for all of the apparently relevant information. But
there are important differences in the nature of the data that are gathered,
the way in which explanations are tested, and the nature of the explanations
that are sought by historical and experimental scientists.

Unlike experimental science in which the objective is to reduce observations to a sharply defined few variables, the data for historical study must be
both broad in scope and sufficiently detailed to include those unpredicted,
unique details that may hold the explanatory key. The objective is to organize the data into the form of a narrative pattern, wherein past events are
reconstructed with attention to chronology so as to identify contingencies
among events.

Both experimentation and historical science insist on testability "to determine whether our hypotheses are definitely wrong or probably correct"
(Gould, 1989b, p. 282). Neither prediction and experiment nor verification
by replication is an option for historical scientists, but there are means to
test the adequacy of a narrative as well as the relative value of competing
narratives.

Over and above evaluation for general scientific adequacy, historical
accounts are provisionally accepted as likely to be true when they have a
greater scope and more support from convergent sources than competing
accounts. Thus, narratives can be examined for the number and type of
contingent patterns that fit within it, the scope of consistent connections
with apparently disparate phenomena, and the scope of consistency with
patterns in related phenomena. As Gould (1989b) puts it, a historical interpretation is accepted only when the narrative evidence is "so abundant
and so diverse that no other coordinating interpretation could stand, even
though any item, taken separately, would not provide conclusive proof"
(p. 282). As in science generally, accepted explanations can be overturned
either when a more complete explanation is offered or when new evidence
comes to light that is inconsistent with the earlier explanation.

These methodological differences are important, but perhaps the greatest
difference between the two styles of science lies in the kinds of explanations

that are acceptable. This is not to say that the fundamental laws of causation are different: they are not. However, historical explanations are often found in chance happenings; quirky events; specific, improbable sequences or concatenations of events, what Gould calls "contingent detail." These are precisely the kinds of events that are filtered out by a well-run experiment, either through control procedures or as error variance. Historical events are by their nature unique. They cannot be repeated because they occur in directional time and because the laws of probability ensure that the same combination or sequence of events will not recur.

"A historical explanation does not rest on direct deductions from laws of nature, but on an unpredictable sequence of antecedent states, where any major change in any step of the sequence would have altered the final result. This final result is therefore dependent, or contingent, upon everything that came before—the unerasable and determining signature of history" (Gould, 1989b, p. 283).

The Burgess shale is a limestone quarry in the Canadian Rockies. In contains a mid-Cambrian deposit of soft-bodied fauna, with fossils that represent arthropods with over 20 different anatomical designs. Yet, only four of these designs have survived to modern times. Furthermore, that one quarry contains fossils of over 15 organisms that are so anatomically different that they cannot be fit into any modern phyla, and so different from one another that they probably represent several different phyla, all now extinct. We have every reason to believe that the particular anatomical forms that survived the decimation did so because of a heavy dose of randomness, contingent events that might have been otherwise. Thus, an accurate historical account of why so few basic anatomical forms remain, with great qualitative differences between them, must include those specific events that did in fact happen. If one could go back to the beginning and "play the tape again," the chance of exactly the same set of circumstances occurring in exactly the same sequence is infinitesimally small. Therefore, almost surely a different set of organisms with different anatomical plans would have escaped extinction. Perhaps this different set would not include *Pikaia*, an early chordate (figure 10.3); if so, the raw material for vertebrate evolution would have been lost. Thus, a historical explanation of human evolution is a story of contingencies—happenstance and circumstance throughout our long past (Gould, 1989b).

Evolution occurs on a grand time scale whereas development occurs within the short span of individual lives. Yet the ways the two processes are studied have a formal similarity. They share the directionality of time, and development, like evolution, involves the patterned, joint action of many variables, some inside and some outside the organism. Developmental psychobiologists have made excellent use of the methods of natural history: the study of behavior in its natural context and the inclusion of contextual detail as data. The narrative record of contingent detail that Gould

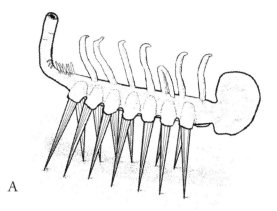

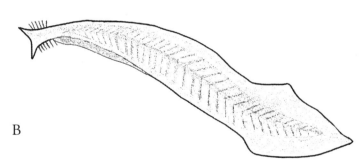

Figure 10.3 Two Burgess shale organisms from the Cambrian period. *Hallucigenia* had a body plan that is now lost due to extinction. *Pikaia* had the chordate body plan, ancestral to the vertebrates, including ourselves (redrawn from Morris, 1977, and Gould, 1989b).

describes for evolutionary history has much in common with the developmental nexus, which played such a key role in the thinking of developmental psychobiologists.

Nevertheless, important differences stem from the fact that lives are short. In evolution, the tape can be replayed only in thought; in development, it can be done in fact. Furthermore, particular events can be imposed or withheld, or manipulated to occur in a different temporal or contextual pattern; contingencies can be staged. The study of development, particularly in nonhuman species, is amenable to prediction, experimentation, verification by replication, and the formulation of general laws.

When the same developmental contingencies are restaged, similarity of developmental outcome is predicted. This restaging occurs in each new generation of each species. And there are indeed many commonalities across members of a species—universals—in both the pattern of developmental progression and outcome. Experimental intervention can also shift both progression and outcome in predictable ways. Thus the developmental sciences add empirical confirmation and refutation to the evaluation of narrative explanations.

However, similarity is not identity. No individual can develop in the same way as any other individual, because each is subject to its own set of contingencies. Nor can the same individual develop the same way twice. If it were possible to start again, nothing would have to be done differently to ensure a different outcome. The large number of internal and external factors, timing, and context provide a rich playing field for randomness. Contingencies in these developmental details are sufficient to ensure that we would develop differently if given a second opportunity (Baltes, 1983; Gould, 1989b).

However different the historical and experimental methods are for the scientist, there is no meaningful difference for the developing organism between causal factors that are ubiquitous to the species and those that are individual. The *nature of causation* for the developing organism does not differ in kind in the two instances. One is not normal and the other abnormal; one is not biological and the other cultural.

Developmental phenomena are historical in that development takes place in time and its phenomena are subject to the principle of contingency. The contingent character of developmental phenomena has fostered the incorporation of the temporal processes of dynamic systems into universal principles. As a result, theories of nonlinear causality, self-organization, and emergent properties are included in the principles used to explain development.

The distinction between historical and experimental styles of science undoubtedly contributes to the perceived qualitative difference between the evolutionary and the molecular poles of biology. Developmental scientists represent an intersection of the two and challenge their easy separation. Psychobiologists are particularly likely to move between the poles when formulating explanations of behavioral development, explanations that must include both universal laws and contingent details. Developmental psychobiologists necessarily bring together diverse phenomena, methods, and explanatory styles. Thus they have a broadly integrative role in the biological and behavioral sciences.

Summary

In this book we attempted to characterize developmental psychobiology and demonstrate how it can guide unification of psychology and biology. We

believe that such unification will have important consequences in the pragmatic realms of human life as well as in the more rarefied academic realm.
The information and ideas we chose to emphasize are those of basic science.
But history provides many demonstrations of changes in public policy and
changes in general modes of thinking among the populace that were
prompted by the ideas and information provided by basic science (Hart &
Honore, 1985). Although we did not dwell on social issues, we were mindful
of them as we wrote this book.

Developmental psychobiology is a young field. It has already provided an
impressive array of new ideas and information, and laid the foundation for a
constructive unification of the biological and behavioral sciences. And it
holds rich promise of more to come. It is too soon to predict with assurance
what specific societal consequences will follow from its accomplishments,
but already interesting glimmerings are to be seen in medicine, mental
health, and education that allow some predictions. We expect that current
theories of disease and psychosomatic illness will be greatly altered in consequence of developmental psychobiological research and theory. Within
the domain of mental health, the concepts of abnormality and adjustment
will be greatly affected. Concepts of learning and development will be
altered by theoretical and empirical advances, and result in major changes in
educational programs and systems. Medicine, mental health, and education
are basic institutions of society. Thus, changes in them will ramify throughout the society more generally.

Perhaps more important, developmental psychobiology holds promise for
widening the scope and enriching the content of human consciousness, and
for increasing the depth of respect and understanding that we human beings
have for the diversity of life around us. The consequences of such changes
for human society would be profound indeed.

References

Abercrombie, M. (1980). The crawling movement of metazoan cells. *Proceedings of the Royal Society of London [B]*, *207*, 129–147.

Adels, L. E., & Leon, M. (1986). Thermal control of mother-young contact in Norway rats: Factors mediating the chronic elevation of maternal temperature. *Physiology and Behavior*, *36*, 183–196.

Alberch, P. (1980). Ontogenesis and morphological diversification. *American Zoologist*, *20*, 653–667.

Alberch, P., & Gale, E. A. (1985). A developmental analysis of an evolutionary trend: Digital reduction in amphibians. *Evolution*, *39*, 8–23.

Alberts, J. R. (1978). Huddling by rat pups: Group behavioral mechanisms of temperature regulation and energy conservation. *Journal of Comparative and Physiological Psychology*, *92*, 231–245.

Alberts, J. R. (1984). Sensory-perceptual development in the Norway rat: A view toward comparative studies. In R. Kail & N. Spear (Eds.), *Comparative perspectives on memory development* (pp. 65–101). New York: Plenum Press.

Alberts, J. R., & Brunjes, P. C. (1978). Ontogeny of thermal and olfactory determinants of huddling in the rat. *Journal of Comparative and Physiological Psychology*, *92*, 897–906.

Alberts, J. R., & Cramer, C. P. (1988). Ecology and experience: Sources of means and meaning of developmental change. In E. M. Blass (Ed.), *Handbook of behavioral neurobiology. Vol. 9. Developmental psychobiology and behavioral ecology* (pp. 1–67). New York: Plenum Press.

Alberts, J. R., & Gubernick, D. J. (1983). Reciprocity and resource exchange: A symbiotic model of parent-offspring relations. In L. A. Rosenblum & H. Moltz (Eds.), *Symbiosis in parent-offspring interactions* (pp. 7–44). New York: Plenum Press.

Alberts, J. R., & May, B. (1984). Non-nutritive, thermotactile induction of filial huddling in rat pups. *Developmental Psychobiology*, *17*, 161–181.

Albrecht-Buehler, G. (1978). The tracks of moving cells. *Scientific American*, *238*(4), 68–76.

Alexander, R. D. (1979). *Darwinism and human affairs*. Seattle: University of Washington Press.

Alexander, R. D. (1987). *The biology of moral systems*. New York: Aldine de Gruyter.

Allen, L. S., Hines, M., Shryne, J. E., & Gorski, R. A. (1989). Two sexually dimorphic cell groups in the human brain. *Journal of Neuroscience*, *9*, 497–506.

Alper, J. S., & Natowicz, M. R. (1992). The allure of genetic explanations. *British Medical Journal*, *305*, 665–668.

Altman, J. (1974). Observational study of behaviour: Sampling method. *Behaviour*, *49*, 227–267.

Altman, S. A., & Altman, J. (1979). Demographic constraints on behavior and social organization. In E. O. Smith & I. S. Bernstein (Eds.), *Ecological influences on social organization* (pp. 1–26). New York: Garland Press.

Ambrose, J. A. (1968). The comparative approach to early child development: The data of ethology. In E. Miller (Ed.), *Foundations of child psychiatry*. Oxford: Pergamon Press.

Anderson, D. J. (1992). Molecular control of neural development. In Z. W. Hall (Ed.), *An introduction to molecular neurobiology* (pp. 355–387). Sunderland, MA: Sinauer.

Anderson, J. E. (1957). Dynamics of development: Systems in process. In D. B. Harris (Ed.), *The concept of development* (pp. 25–48). Minneapolis: University of Minnesota Press.

Anderson, J. W. (1972). Attachment behaviour out of doors. In N. Blurton Jones (Ed.), *Ethological studies of child behaviour* (pp. 199–215). London: Cambridge University Press.

Anderson, P. W. (1972). More is different. *Science, 177,* 393–396.

Annett, M. (1964). A model of the inheritance of handedness and cerebral dominance. *Nature, 204,* 59–60.

Annett, M. (1978). Genetic and nongenetic influences on handedness. *Behavior Genetics, 8,* 227–249.

Aries, P. (1962). *Centuries of childhood.* New York: Knopf.

Arnold, A. P. (1992). Developmental plasticity in neural circuits controlling birdsong: Sexual differentiation and the neural basis of learning. *Journal of Neurobiology, 23,* 1506–1528.

Arnold, A. P., & Breedlove, S. M. (1985). Organizational and activational effects of sex steroids on brain and behavior: A reanalysis. *Hormones and Behavior, 19,* 469–498.

Arnold, S. J. (1987). Genetic correlation and the evolution of physiology. In M. E. Feder, A. F. Bennett, W. W. Burggren, & R. B. Huey (Eds.), *New directions in ecological physiology* (pp. 189–215). Cambridge: Cambridge University Press.

Aslin, R. N. (1993). Commentary—The strange attractiveness of dynamic systems to development. In L. B. Smith & E. Thelen (Eds.) *Dynamic systems approach to development* (pp. 385–399). Cambridge: MIT Press.

Atchley, W. R., & Hall, B. K. (1991). A model for development and evolution of complex morphological structures. *Biological Reviews, 66,* 101–157.

Atchley, W. R., & Newman, S. (1989). A quantitative-genetics perspective on mammalian development. *American Naturalist, 134,* 486–512.

Atkinson, J. W. (1992). Conceptual issues in the reunion of development and evolution. *Synthese, 91,* 93–110.

Atz, J. W. (1970). The application of the idea of homology to behavior. In L. R. Aronson, E. Tobach, D. S. Lehrman, & J. S. Rosenblatt (Eds.), *Development and evolution of behavior* (pp. 53–74). San Francisco: Freeman.

Augros, R., & Stansiu, G. (1988). *The new biology.* Boston: Shambhala.

Ausubel, D. (1957). *Theory and problems of child development.* New York: Grune & Stratton.

Ayala, F. J. (1974). Introduction. In F. J. Ayala & T. Dobzhansky (Eds.), *Studies in the philosophy of biology* (pp. vii–xiv). New York: Macmillan.

Ayala, F. J. (1985). Reduction in biology: A recent challenge. In D. J. DePew & B. H. Weber (Eds.), *Evolution at a crossroads: The new biology and the new philosophy of science* (pp. 65–80). Cambridge: MIT Press.

Ayala, F. J., & Dobzhansky, T. (Eds.). (1974). *Studies in the philosophy of biology: Reduction and related problems.* Berkeley: University of California Press.

Baker, L. A., & Daniels, D. (1990). Nonshared environmental influences and personality differences in adult twins. *Journal of Personality and Social Psychology, 58,* 103–110.

Baldwin, J. M. (1895). *Mental development in the child and race.* New York: Macmillan.

Ballard, D. H. (1993). Sub-symbolic modeling of hand-eye coordination. In D. Broadbent (Ed.), *Simulation of human intelligence* (pp. 71–102). London: Blackwell.

Baltes, P. B. (1983). Life-span developmental psychology: Observations on history and theory revisited. In R. M. Lerner (Ed.), *Developmental psychology: Historical and philosophical perspectives* (pp. 121–180). Hillsdale, NJ: Erlbaum.

Barfield, R. J. (1971). Gonadotrophic hormone secretion in the female ring dove in response to visual and auditory stimulation by the male. *Journal of Endocrinology, 49,* 305–310.

Barfield, R. J., & Thomas, D. A. (1986). The role of ultrasonic vocalizations in the regulation of reproduction in rats. *Annals of the New York Academy of Sciences, 474,* 33–43.

Barinaga, M. (1994). From fruit flies, rats, mice: Evidence of genetic influence. *Science, 264,* 1690–1693.

Barker, G. (1993). Models of biological change: Implications of three studies of "Lamarckian" change. In P. P. G. Bateson, P. H. Klopfer, & N. S. Thompson (Eds.), *Perspectives in ethology. Vol. 10. Behavior and evolution* (pp. 229–248). New York: Plenum Press.

Bass, A., & Andersen, K. (1991). Inter- and intrasexual dimorphisms in the vocal control system of a teleost fish: Motor axon number and size. *Brain, Behavior and Evolution, 37*, 204–214.

Bates, E. (1993a). Comprehension and production in early language development. *Monographs of the Society for Research in Child Development, 58*(3–4), *222–242.*

Bates, E. (1993b). *Plasticity in language and brain development.* Presented in the invited symposium on Development of Brain and Language Functions, at the fifth annual convention of the American Psychological Society, Chicago, June 26.

Bateson, P. P. G. (1966). The characteristics and context of imprinting. *Biological Reviews, 41*, 177–220.

Bateson, P. P. G. (1973). The imprinting of birds. In S. A. Barnett (Ed.), *Ethology and development* (pp. 1–15). Philadelphia: Lippincott.

Bateson, P. P. G. (1979). How do sensitive periods arise and what are they for? *Animal Behaviour, 27*, 470–486.

Bateson, P. P. G. (1981). Control of sensitivity to the environment during development. In K. Immelmann, G. W. Barlow, L. Petrinovich, & M. Main (Eds.), *Behavioral development* (pp. 432–453). Cambridge: Cambridge University Press.

Bateson, P. (1987a). Biological approaches to the study of behavioural development. *International Journal of Behavioural Development, 10*, 1–22.

Bateson, P. (1987b). Imprinting as a process of competitive exclusion. In J. P. Rauschecker & P. Marler (Eds.), *Imprinting and cortical plasticity: Comparative aspects of sensitive periods* (pp. 151–168). New York: Wiley.

Bateson, P. (Ed.). (1991). *The development and integration of behaviour.* Cambridge: Cambridge University Press.

Baum, M. J. (1979). Differentiation of coital behavior in mammals: A comparative analysis. *Neuroscience and Biobehavioral Reviews, 3*, 265–284.

Beach, F. A. (1948). *Hormones and behavior.* New York: Harper & Row.

Beach, F. A. (1971). Hormonal factors controlling the differentiation, development, and display of copulatory behavior in the ramstergig and related species. In E. Tobach, L. R. Aronson, & E. Shaw (Eds.), *The biopsychology of development* (pp. 249–296). New York: Academic Press.

Becker, J. B., Breedlove, S. M., & Crews, D. (Eds.). (1992). *Behavioral endocrinology.* Cambridge: MIT Press.

Beer, C. G. (1973). Species-typical behavior and ethology. In D. A. Dewsbury & D. A. Rethlingshafer (Eds.), *Comparative psychology: A modern survey* (pp. 21–77). New York: McGraw-Hill.

Beer, C. G. (1980). Perspectives on animal behavior comparisons. In M. H. Bornstein (Ed.), *Comparative methods in psychology* (pp. 17–64). Hillsdale, NJ: Erlbaum.

Beer, C. G. (1991). From folk psychology to cognitive ethology. In C. A. Ristau (Ed.), *Cognitive ethology: The minds of other animals* (pp. 19–33). Hillsdale, NJ: Erlbaum.

Bekoff, A. (1981a). Embryonic development of chick motor behaviour. *Trends in Neurosciences, 4,* 181–183.

Bekoff, A. (1981b). Embryonic development of the neural circuitry underlying motor coordination. In W. M. Cowan (Ed.), *Topics in developmental neurobiology: Essays in honor of Viktor Hamburger* (pp. 134–170). New York: Oxford University Press.

Bekoff, A. (1988). Embryonic motor output and movement patterns: Relationship to postnatal behavior. In W. P. Smotherman & S. R. Robinson (Eds.), *Behavior of the fetus* (pp. 191–206). Caldwell, NJ: Telford Press.

Bekoff, A. (1992). Neuroethological approaches to the study of motor development in chicks: Achievements and challenges. *Journal of Neurobiology, 23*, 1486–1505.

Bekoff, A., & Kauer, J. A. (1982). Neural control of hatching: Role of neck position in turning on hatching leg movements in post-hatching chicks. *Journal of Comparative Physiology, 145,* 497–504.   .

Bekoff, A., Nusbaum, M. P., Sabichi, A. L., & Clifford, M. (1987). Neural control of limb coordination. I. Comparison of hatching and walking motor output patterns in normal and deafferented chicks. *Journal of Neuroscience, 7,* 2320–2330.

Bekoff, M., & Byers, J. A. (1981). A critical reanalysis of the ontogeny and phylogeny of mammalian social and locomotor play: An ethological hornet's nest. In K. Immelmann,

G. W. Barlow, L. Petrinovich, & M. Main (Eds.), *Behavioral development* (pp. 296–337). Cambridge: Cambridge University Press.

Bell, R. Q. (1968). A reinterpretation of the direction of effects in studies of socialization. *Psychological Review, 75*, 81–85.

Bell, R. Q. (1974). Contributions of human infants to caregiving and social interaction. In M. Lewis & L. A. Rosenbaum (Eds.), *The effect of the infant on its caregiver* (pp. 1–19). New York: Wiley.

Bell, R. W., & Smotherman, W. P. (Eds.). (1980). *Maternal influences and early behavior.* Jamaica, NY: Spectrum.

Benson, M. J. (1992). Beyond the reaction range concept: A developmental, contextual, and situational model of the heredity-environment interplay. *Human Relations, 45*, 937–956.

Berbel, P., & Innocenti, G. M. (1988). The development of the corpus callosum in cats: A light- and electron-microscopic study. *Journal of Comparative Neurology, 276*, 132–156.

Bernal, J. F., & Richards, M. P. M. (1973). What can zoologists tell us about human development? In S. A. Barnett (Ed.), *Ethology and development* (pp. 88–103). Philadelphia: Lippincott.

Bertram, B. C. R. (1976). Kin selection in lions and in evolution. In P. P. G. Bateson & R. A. Hinde (Eds.), *Growing points in ethology* (pp. 281–301). Cambridge: Cambridge University Press.

Bijou, S. W., & Baer, D. M. (1961). *Child development: A systematic and empirical theory* (Vol. 1). New York: Appleton-Century-Crofts.

Billings, P. R., Beckwith, J., & Alper, J. S. (1992). The genetic analysis of human behavior: A new era? *Social Science and Medicine, 35*, 227–238.

Birch, H. G. (1971). Levels, categories, and methodological assumptions in the study of behavioral development. In E. Tobach, L. R. Aronson, & E. Shaw (Eds.), *The biopsychology of development* (pp. 503–513). New York: Academic Press.

Birch, H. G. (1972). Malnutrition, learning, and intelligence. *American Journal of Public Health, 67*, 773–784.

Birnholz, J. C. (1988). On observing the human fetus. In W. P. Smotherman & S. R. Robinson (Eds.), *Behavior of the fetus* (pp. 47–60). Caldwell, NJ: Telford Press.

Bizzi, E., & Mussa-Ivaldi, F. A. (1990). Muscle properties and the control of arm movements. In D. N. Osherson, S. M. Kosslyn, & J. M. Hollerbach (Eds.), *Visual cognition and action* (pp. 213–242). Cambridge: MIT Press.

Black, I. (1982). Stages of neurotransmitter development in autonomic neurons. *Science, 215*, 1198–1204.

Black, J. E., Isaacs, K. R., Anderson, B. J., Alcantara, A. A., & Greenough, W. T. (1990). Learning causes synaptogenesis, while motor activity causes angiogenesis, in cerebellar cortex of adult rats. *Proceedings of the National Academy of Sciences U.S.A., 87*, 5568–5572.

Blakemore, C. (1974). Development of the mammalian visual system. *British Medical Bulletin, 30*, 152–157.

Blakemore, C., & Cooper, C. F. (1970). Development of the brain depends on the visual environment. *Nature, 228*, 477–478.

Blanchard, D. C., & Blanchard, R. J. (1990). The colony model of aggression and defense. In D. A. Dewsbury (Ed.), *Contemporary issues in comparative psychology* (pp. 410–430). Sunderland, MA: Sinauer.

Blass, E. M. (Ed.). (1986). *Handbook of behavioral neurobiology. Vol. 8. Developmental psychobiology and developmental neurobiology.* New York: Plenum Press.

Blass, E. M. (Ed.). (1988). *Handbook of behavioral neurobiology. Vol. 9. Developmental psychobiology and behavioral ecology.* New York: Plenum Press.

Blass, E. M., Fillion, T. J., Rochat, P., Hoffmeyer, L. B., & Metzger, M. A. (1989). Sensorimotor and motivational determinants of hand-mouth coordination in 1–3-day-old human infants. *Developmental Psychology, 25*, 963–975.

Bleier, R., Houston, L., & Byne, W. (1986). Can the corpus callosum predict gender, age, handedness, or cognitive differences? *Trends in Neurosciences, 9*, 391–394.

Bloom, L. (1993). Word learning. *SRCD Newsletter, Winter, 1–13.*

Blumberg, M. S., & Alberts, J. R. (1990). Ultrasonic vocalizations by rat pups in the cold: An acoustic by-product of laryngeal braking? *Behavioral Neuroscience, 104*, 808–817.

Blumberg, M. S., Efimova, I. V., & Alberts, J. R. (1992). Thermogenesis during ultrasonic vocalization by rat pups isolated in a warm environment: A thermographic analysis. *Developmental Psychobiology, 25*, 497–510.

Blurton Jones, N. G. (1972). Comparative aspects of mother-child contact. In N. G. Blurton Jones (Ed.), *Ethological studies of child behaviour* (pp. 305–328). London: Cambridge University Press.

Blurton Jones, N. (1974). Ethology and early socialisation. In M. P. M. Richards (Ed.), *The integration of a child into a social world* (pp. 263–293). London: Cambridge University Press.

Blurton Jones, N. G. (1976). Growing points in human ethology: Another link between ethology and the social sciences? In P. P. G. Bateson & R. A. Hinde (Eds.), *Growing points in ethology* (pp. 427–450). Cambridge: Cambridge University Press.

Blurton Jones, N., & Leach, G. M. (1972). Behaviour of children and their mothers at separation and greeting. In N. Blurton Jones (Ed.), *Ethological studies of child behaviour* (pp. 217–247). London: Cambridge University Press.

Boakes, R. (1984). *From Darwin to behaviorism: Psychology and the minds of animals.* New York: Cambridge University Press.

Bodmer, W. F., & Cavalli-Sforza, L. L. (1970). Intelligence and race. *Scientific American, 223*, 19–29.

Bolhuis, J. J. (1991). Mechanisms of avian imprinting: A review. *Biological Review, 66*, 303–345.

Bornstein, M. H. (1989). Sensitive periods in development: Structural characteristics and causal interpretations. *Psychological Bulletin, 105*, 179–197.

Bornstein, M. H., & Lamb, M. E. (1992). *Development in infancy: An introduction* (3rd ed.). New York: McGraw-Hill.

Bottjer, S. W., & Arnold, A. P. (1986). The ontogeny of vocal learning in songbirds. In E. M. Blass (Ed.), *Handbook of behavioral neurobiology. Vol. 8. Developmental psychobiology and developmental neurobiology* (pp. 129–161). New York: Plenum Press.

Bottjer, S. W., & Johnson, F. (1992). Matters of life and death in the songbird forebrain. *Journal of Neurobiology, 23*, 1172–1191.

Bouchard, T. J. (1983). Do environmental similarities explain the similarity in intelligence of identical twins reared apart? *Intelligence, 7*, 175–184.

Bouchard, T. J. (1984). Twins reared together and apart: What they tell us about human diversity. In S. S. Fox (Ed.), *The chemical and biological basis of individuality* (pp. 237–284). New York: Plenum Press.

Bouchard, T. J., Jr. (1994). Genes, environment, and personality. *Science, 264*, 1700–1701.

Bouchard, T. J., & McCue, M. (1981). Familial studies of intelligence: A review. *Science, 212*, 1055–1059.

Bower, T. G. R. (1974). *Development in infancy.* San Francisco: Freeman.

Bowlby, J. (1969). *Attachment and loss. (Vol. 1). Attachment.* New York: Basic Books.

Bowlby, J. (1988). *A secure base: Parent-child attachment and healthy human development.* New York: Basic Books.

Braine, M. D. S. (1987). What is learned in acquiring word classes: A step toward an acquisition theory. In B. MacWhinney (Ed.), *Mechanisms of language acquisition* (pp. 65–87). Hillsdale, NJ: Erlbaum.

Braine, M. D. S. (1992). What sort of innate structure is needed to "bootstrap" into syntax? *Cognition, 45*, 77–100.

Brake, S. C., Shair, H., & Hofer, M. A. (1988). Exploiting the nursing niche: The infant's sucking and feeding in the context of the mother-infant interaction. In E. M. Blass, (Ed.), *Handbook of behavioral neurobiology. Vol. 9. Developmental psychobiology and behavioral ecology* (pp. 347–388). New York: Plenum Press.

Brand, G. (1979). *The essential Wittgenstein* (R. E. Innis, Trans.). New York: Basic Books.

Brazelton, T. B., Koslowski, B., & Main, M. (1974). The origins of reciprocity: The early mother-infant interaction. In M. Lewis & R. A. Rosenblum (Eds.), *The effect of the infant on its caregiver* (pp. 49–76). New York: Wiley.

Breedlove, S. M. (1992). Sexual dimorphism in the vertebrate nervous system. *Journal of Neuroscience, 12*, 4133–4142.

Breedlove, S. M., & Arnold, A. P. (1983). Hormonal control of a developing neuromuscular system. II. Sensitive periods for the androgen-induced masculinization of the rat spinal nucleus of the bulbocavernosus. *Journal of Neuroscience, 3*, 424–432.

Bremner, J. G. (1993). Motor abilities as causal agents in infant cognitive development. In G. J. P. Savelsbergh (Ed.), *The development of coordination in infancy* (pp. 47–77). New York: Elsevier.

Bretherton, I. (1992). The origins of attachment theory: John Bowlby and Mary Ainsworth. *Developmental Psychology, 28*, 759–773.

Bronfenbrenner, U. (1972). Is 80% of intelligence genetically determined? In U. Bronfenbrenner (Ed.), *Influences on human development* (pp. 118–119). Hinsdale, IL: Dryden.

Bronfenbrenner, U. (1979). *The ecology of human development: Experiments by nature and design.* Cambridge: Harvard University Press.

Bronfenbrenner, U. (1986). Ecology of the family as a context for human development: Research perspectives. *Developmental Psychology, 22*, 723–742.

Bronowski, J. (1973). *The ascent of man.* Boston: Little, Brown.

Brown, R. E. (1994). *An introduction to neuroendocrinology.* Cambridge: Cambridge University Press.

Brown, S. D., & Bottjer, S. W. (1993). Testosterone-induced changes in adult canary brain are reversible. *Journal of Neurobiology, 24*, 627–640.

Bruner, J. S. (1969). Eye, hand and mind. In D. Elkind & J. H. Flavell (Eds.), *Studies in cognitive development* (pp. 223–236). New York: Oxford University Press.

Bruner, J. S. (1972). Nature and uses of immaturity. *American Psychologist, 27*, 687–708.

Bruner, J. S. (1981). Intention and the structure of action and interaction. In L. P. Lipsitt & C. K. Rovee-Collier (Eds.), *Advances in infancy research* (Vol. 1, pp 41–56). Norwood, NJ: Ablex.

Bruner, J. S., Jolly, A., & Sylva, K. (1976). *Play: Its role in development and evolution.* New York: Basic Books.

Brunjes, P. C., & Frazier, L. L. (1986). Maturation and plasticity in the olfactory system. *Brain Research Reviews, 11*, 1–45.

Brusca, R. C., & Brusca, G. J. (1990). *Invertebrates.* Sunderland, MA: Sinauer.

Bryant, P. (1990). Empirical evidence for causes in development. In G. Butterworth & P. Bryant (Eds.), *Causes of development* (pp. 33–48). Hillsdale, NJ: Erlbaum.

Buisseret, P. (1993). The development of visual cortical properties depends on visuo-proprioceptive congruence. In T. P. Hicks, S. Molotchnikoff, & T. Ono (Eds.), *Progress in brain research* (Vol. 95, pp. 251–256). New York: Elsevier.

Bull, J. J. (1983). *Evolution of sex determining mechanisms.* Menlo Park, CA: Benjamin/Cummings.

Burek, M. J., Nordeen, K. W., & Nordeen, E. J. (1994). Ontogeny of sex differences among newly generated neurons of the juvenile avian brain. *Developmental Brain Research, 78*, 57–64.

Burghardt, G. M. (1988). Precocity, play, and the ectotherm-endotherm transition: Profound reorganization or superficial adaptation? In E. M. Blass, (Ed.), *Handbook of behavioral neurobiology. Vol. 9. Developmental psychobiology and behavioral ecology* (pp. 107–148). New York: Plenum Press.

Burian, R. M. (1992). How the choice of experimental organism matters: Biological practices and discipline boundaries. *Synthese, 92*, 151–166.

Bushnell, E. W. (1985). The decline of visually guided reaching during infancy. *Infant Behavior and Development, 8*, 101–109.

Bushnell, E. W., & Boudreau, J. P. (1993). Motor development and the mind: The potential role of motor abilities as a determinant of aspects of perceptual development. *Child Development, 64*, 1005–1021.

Buss, D. M. (1987). Sex differences in human mate selection criteria: An evolutionary perspective. In C. Crawford, M. Smith, & D. Krebs (Eds.), *Sociobiology and psychology: Ideas, issues and applications* (pp. 335–352). Hillsdale, NJ: Erlbaum.

Buss, D. M. (1989a). Conflict between the sexes: Strategic interference and the evocation of anger and upset. *Journal of Personality and Social Psychology, 56*, 735–747.

Buss, D. M. (1989b). Sex differences in human mate preferences: Evolutionary hypotheses tested in 37 cultures. *Behavioral and Brain Sciences, 12*, 1–49.

Buss, D. M. (1991). Evolutionary personality psychology. *Annual Review of Psychology, 42*, 459–491.

Butterworth, G. (1986). Some problems in explaining the origins of movement control. In M. G. Wade & H. T. A. Whiting (Eds.), *Motor development in children: Problems of coordination and control* (pp. 23–32). Dordrecht: Martinus Nijhoff.

Butterworth, G., & Hopkins, B. (1988). Hand-mouth coordination in the new-born baby. *British Journal of Developmental Psychology, 6,* 303–314.

Byne, W., & Parsons, B. (1993). Human sexual orientation: The biologic theories reappraised. *Archives of General Psychiatry, 50,* 228–239.

Cacioppo, J. T., & Berntson, G. G. (1992). Social psychological contributions to the decade of the brain: The doctrine of multilevel analysis. *American Psychologist, 47,* 1019–1028.

Cairns, R. B. (1972a). Attachment and dependency: A psychobiological and social-learning synthesis. In J. L. Gewirtz (Ed.), *Attachment and dependency* (pp. 29–80). New York: Wiley.

Cairns, R. B. (1972b). Ontogenetic contributions to aggressive behavior. In F. J. Mönks, W. W. Hartup, & J. deWit (Eds.), *Determinants of behavioral development* (pp. 395–400). New York: Academic Press.

Cairns, R. B. (1979). *Social development: The origins and plasticity of interchanges.* San Francisco: Freeman.

Camp, L. L., & Rudy, J. W. (1988). Changes in the categorization of appetitive and aversive events during postnatal development of the rat. *Developmental Psychobiology, 21,* 25–42.

Campbell, B. (1966). *Human evolution: An introduction to man's adaptations.* Chicago: Aldine.

Campos, J. J., Barrett, K. C., Lamb, M. E., Goldsmith, H. H., & Stenberg, C. (1983). Socio-emotional development. In M. M. Haith & J. J. Campos (Eds.), *Handbook of child psychology. Vol. 2. Infancy and developmental psychobiology* (4th ed., pp. 783–915). New York: Wiley.

Canguilhem, G. (1978). *On the normal and the pathological* (C. R. Fawcett, Trans.). Dordrecht, The Netherlands: Reidel.

Capecchi, M. R. (1994). Targeted gene replacement. *Scientific American, 270,* 52–59.

Caporeal, L. R., & Brewer, M. B. (1991). The quest for human nature: Social and scientific issues in evolutionary psychology. *Journal of Social Issues, 47,* 1–9.

Capute, A. J., Accardo, P. J., Vining, E. P. G., Rubenstein, J. E., & Harryman, S. (1978). *Primitive reflex profile.* Baltimore: University Park Press.

Carey, S. (1991). Knowledge acquisition: Enrichment or conceptual change? In S. Carey & R. Gelman (Eds.), *The epigenesis of mind: Essays on biology and cognition* (pp. 257–292). Hillsdale, NJ: Erlbaum.

Carey, S., & Gelman, R. (Eds.). (1991). *The epigenesis of mind. Essays on biology and cognition.* Hillsdale, NJ: Erlbaum.

Carlier, M., Roubertoux, P. L., & Pastoret, C. (1991). The Y chromosome effect on intermale aggression in mice depends on the maternal environment. *Genetics, 129,* 231–236.

Carlson, E. A. (1966). *The gene: A critical history.* Philadelphia: Saunders.

Carmichael, L. (1970). The onset and early development of behavior. In P. H. Mussen (Ed.), *Carmichael's manual of child psychology* (Vol. 1, pp. 447–563). New York: Wiley.

Carroll, J. B. (1992). Cognitive abilities: The state of the art. *Psychological Science, 3,* 266–270.

Casaer, P. (1979). *Postural behaviour in newborn infants.* Philadelphia: Lippincott.

Casaer, P. (1992). Old and new facts about prenatal brain development. *Journal of Child Psychology and Psychiatry, 34,* 101–109.

Case, R. (1992). The role of the frontal lobes in the regulation of cognitive development. *Brain and Cognition, 20,* 51–73.

Casti, J. L. (1990). *Searching for certainty.* New York: Morrow.

Cavalli-Sforza, L. L., & Bodmer, W. F. (1971). *The genetics of human populations.* San Francisco: Freeman.

Chalmers, N. R. (1987). Developmental pathways in behaviour. *Animal Behaviour, 35,* 659–674.

Chandler, S. (1993). Are rules and modules really necessary for explaining language? *Journal of Psycholinguistic Research, 22,* 593–606.

Changeux, J.-P. (1985). *Neuronal man: The biology of mind.* New York: Oxford University Press.

Cheng, M.-F. (1979). Progress and prospect in ring dove research: A personal view. In J. S. Rosenblatt, R. A. Hinde, C. G. Beer, & M.-C. Busnel (Eds.), *Advances in the study of behavior* (Vol. 9, pp. 97–129). New York: Academic Press.

Cheng, M.-F., Klint, T., & Johnson, A. (1986). Breeding experience modulates androgen dependent courtship behavior in male ring doves (*Steptopelia risoria*). *Physiology and Behavior, 36,* 625–630.

Cheverud, J. M. (1984). Quantitative genetics and developmental constraints on evolution by selection. *Journal of Theoretical Biology, 110,* 155–171.

Chomsky, N. (1959). Review of B. F. Skinner's *Verbal behavior. Language, 35,* 16–58.

Chomsky, N. A. (1965). *Aspects of the theory of syntax.* Cambridge: MIT Press.

Chorover, S. L. (1979). *From genesis to genocide: The meaning of human nature and the power of behavioral control.* Cambridge: MIT Press.

Churchland, P. S. (1986). *Neurophilosophy: Toward a unified science of the mind-brain.* Cambridge: MIT Press.

Churchland, P. M., & Churchland, P. S. (1990). Intertheoretic reduction: A neuroscientist's field guide. *Seminars in the Neurosciences, 2,* 249–256.

Clarke, S., Kraftsik, R., van der Loos, H., & Innocenti, G. M. (1989). Forms and measures of adult and developing human corpus callosum: Is there sexual dimorphism? *Journal of Comparative Neurology, 280,* 213–230.

Clopton, B. M. (1986). Neural correlates of development and plasticity in the auditory, somatosensory, and olfactory systems. In W. T. Greenough & J. M. Juraska (Eds.), *Developmental neuropsychobiology* (pp. 363–386). Orlando: Academic Press.

Cloues, R., Ramos, C., & Silver, R. (1990). Vasoactive intestinal polypeptide-like immunoreactivity during reproduction in doves: Influence of experience and number of offspring. *Hormones and Behavior, 24,* 215–231.

Clutton-Brock, T. H., & Harvey, P. H. (1977). Primate ecology and social organisation. *Journal of Zoology (London), 183,* 1–39.

Coe, C. L., Wiener, S. G., Rosenberg, L. T., & Levine, S. (1985). Endocrine and immune responses to separation and maternal loss in nonhuman primates. In M. Reite & T. Field (Eds.), *The psychobiology of attachment and separation* (pp. 163–199). Orlando: Academic Press.

Coghill, G. E. (1929). *Anatomy and the problem of behavior.* Cambridge: Cambridge University Press.

Cohen, J. M. (1970). A comparison of invertebrate and vertebrate central neurons. In F. O. Schmitt (Ed.), *The neurosciences: Second study program* (pp. 798–812). New York: Rockefeller University Press.

Colbert, E. H. (1980). *Evolution of the vertebrates* (3rd ed.). New York: Wiley.

Colgan, P. W. (Ed.). (1978). *Quantitative ethology.* New York: Wiley.

Collins, W. A. (Ed.). (1982). *The concept of development: The Minnesota symposia on child psychology* (Vol. 15). Hillsdale, NJ: Erlbaum.

Connolly, K. (1972). Learning and the concept of critical periods in infancy. *Developmental Medicine and Child Neurology, 14,* 705–714.

Connolly, K. (1973). Factors influencing the learning of manual skills by young children. In R. A. Hinde & J. Stevenson-Hinde (Eds.), *Constraints on learning* (pp. 337–365). New York: Academic Press.

Connolly, K. J. (1981). Maturation and the ontogeny of motor skills. In K. J. Connolly & H. F. R. Prechtl (Eds.), *Maturation and development: Biological and psychological perspectives* (pp. 216–230). Philadelphia: Lippincott.

Connolly, K. J. (1986). A perspective on motor development. In M. G. Wade & H. T. A. Whiting (Eds.), *Motor development in children: Aspects of coordination and control* (pp. 3–21). Boston: Martinus Nijhoff.

Connolly, K. J., & Elliott, J. M. (1972). Evolution and ontogeny of hand function. In N. Blurton-Jones (Ed.), *Ethological studies of child behaviour* (pp. 329–383). London: Cambridge University Press.

Cooper, H. M., Herbin, M., & Nevo, E. (1993). Visual system of a naturally microphthalmic mammal: The blind mole rat, *Spalax ehrenbergi. Journal of Comparative Neurology, 328,* 313–350.

Coopersmith, R., & Leon, M. (1988). The neurobiology of early olfactory learning. In E. M. Blass, (Ed.), *Handbook of behavioral neurobiology. Vol. 9. Developmental psychobiology and behavioral ecology* (pp. 283–308). New York: Plenum Press.

Crabbe, J. C., Belknap, J. K., & Buck, K. J. (1994). Genetic animal models of alcohol and drug abuse. *Science, 264*, 1715–1723.

Cracraft, J. (1989). Speciation and its ontology: The empirical consequences of alternative species concepts for understanding patterns and processes of differentiation. In D. Otte & J. A. Endler (Eds.), *Speciation and its consequences* (pp. 28–59). Sunderland, MA: Sinauer.

Cramer, C. P., & Blass, E. M. (1983). Mechanisms of control of milk intake in suckling rats. *American Journal of Physiology, 245*, R154–R159.

Crawford, C. B. (1989). The theory of evolution: Of what value to comparative psychology? *Journal of Comparative Psychology, 103*, 4–22.

Crawford, C., Smith, M., & Krebs, D. (1987). *Sociobiology and psychology: Ideas, issues and applications*. Hillsdale, NJ: Erlbaum.

Crick, F. (1966). *Molecules and men*. Seattle: University of Washington Press.

Crook, J. H. (1965). The adaptive significance of avian social organisation. *Symposium of the Zoological Society of London, 14*, 181–218.

Crook, J. H. (Ed.). (1970a). *Social behavior in birds and mammals*. New York: Academic Press.

Crook, J. H. (1970b). The socio-ecology of primates. In J. H. Crook (Ed.), *Social behavior in birds and mammals* (pp. 103–166). New York: Academic Press.

Crook, J. H., & Gartlan, J. S. (1966). Evolution of primate societies. *Nature (London), 210*, 1200–1203.

Curio, E. (1988). Cultural transmission of enemy recognition by birds. In T. R. Zentall & B. G. Galef, Jr. (Eds.), *Social learning* (pp. 75–97). Hillsdale, NJ: Erlbaum.

Curtin, R., & Dolhinow, P. (1978). Primate social behavior in a changing world. *American Scientist, 66*, 468–475.

Daly, M., & Wilson, M. (1978). *Sex, evolution, and behavior*. North Scituate, MA: Duxbury.

Daly, M., & Wilson, M. (1988). *Homicide*. New York: Aldine de Gruyter.

Darwin, C. (1859). *On the origin of species by means of natural selection, or the preservation of favored races in the struggle for life*. London: John Murray.

Darwin, C. (1871). *Descent of man, and selection in relation to sex*. London: John Murray.

Darwin, C. (1872). *The expression of the emotions in man and animals*. London: John Murray.

Dawkins, R. (1976). *The selfish gene*. New York: Oxford University Press.

de Beer, G. R. (1958). *Embryos and ancestors* (3rd ed.). London: Oxford University Press.

DeFries, J. C., Thomas, E. A., Hegmann, J. P., & Weir, M. W. (1967). Open-field behaviour in mice: Analysis of maternal effects by means of ovarian transplantation. *Psychonomic Science, 8*, 207–208.

DeFries, J. C., Weir, M. W., & Hegmann, J. P. (1967). Differential effects of prenatal maternal stress on offspring behavior in mice as a function of genotype and stress. *Journal of Comparative and Physiological Psychology, 63*, 332–334.

de Lacoste-Utamsing, C., & Holloway, R. L. (1982). Sexual dimorphism in the human corpus callosum. *Science, 216*, 1431–1432.

Demski, L. S. (1987). Diversity in reproductive patterns and behavior in teleost fishes. In D. Crews (Ed.), *Psychobiology of reproductive behavior: An evolutionary perspective* (pp. 1–27). Englewood Cliffs, NJ: Prentice-Hall.

Denenberg, V. H., & Rosenberg, K. M. (1967). Nongenetic transmission of information. *Nature, 216*, 549–550.

Denenberg, V. H., Sherman, G. F., Morrison, L., Schrott, L. M., Waters, N. S., Rosen, G. D., Behan, P. O., & Galaburda, A. M. (1992). Behavior, ectopias and immunity in BD/DB reciprocal crosses. *Brain Research, 571*, 323–329.

Denenberg, V. H., & Whimbey, A. E. (1963). Behavior of adult rats is modified by the experiences their mothers had as infants. *Science, 142*, 1192–1193.

Dennis, M. J., & Harris, A. J. (1979). Elimination of inappropriate nerve-muscle connections during development of rat embryos. *Progress in Brain Research, 49*, 359–364.

Desmond, A. J., & Moore, J. R. (1992). *Darwin*. New York: Warner Books.

Dethier, V. G. (1969). Whose real world? *American Zoologist, 9*, 241–249.

DeVoogd, T. J., Krebs, J. R., Healy, S. D., & Purvis, A. (1993). Relations between repertoire size and the volume of brain nuclei related to song: Comparative evolutionary analyses amongst oscine birds. *Proceedings of the Royal Society of London [B], 254*, 75–82.

DeVore, I. (1965). Male dominance and mating behavior in baboons. In F. A. Beach (Ed.), *Sex and behavior* (pp. 266–289). New York: Wiley.

de Vries, J. I. P., Visser, G. H. A., & Prechtl, H. F. R. (1984). Fetal motility in the first half of pregnancy. In H. R. F. Prechtl (Ed.), *Continuity of neural functions from prenatal to postnatal life* (pp. 46–64). Oxford: Blackwell.

Dewey, J., & Bentley, A. F. (1949). *Knowing and the known*. Boston: Beacon Press.

Dewsbury, D. A. (1990). Comparative psychology: Retrospect and prospect. In D. A. Dewsbury (Ed.), *Contemporary issues in comparative psychology* (pp. 431–448). Sunderland, MA: Sinauer.

Diamond, A. (1985). The development of the ability to use recall to guide action, as indicated by infants' performance on A͟B. *Child Development, 56*, 868–883.

Diamond, A. (1991a). Neuropsychological insights into the meaning of object concept development. In S. Carey & R. Gelman (Eds.), *The epigenesis of mind: Essays on biology and cognition* (pp. 67–110). Hillsdale, NJ: Erlbaum.

Diamond, A. (1991b). Frontal lobe involvement in cognitive changes during the first year of life. In K. R. Gibson & A. C. Peterson (Eds.), *Brain maturation and cognitive development* (pp. 127–180). New York: Aldine de Gruyter.

Diamond, A., & Goldman-Rakic, P. S. (1989). Comparison of human infants and rhesus monkeys on Piaget's A͞B task: Evidence for dependence on dorsolateral prefrontal cortex. *Experimental Brain Research, 74*, 24–40.

Dobzhansky, T. (1951). *Genetics and the origin of species* (3rd ed.). New York: Columbia University Press.

Dobzhansky, T. (1955). *Evolution, genetics, and man*. New York: Wiley.

Dobzhansky, T. (1967). Of flies and men. *American Psychologist, 22*, 41–48.

Dolhinow, P. J., & Bishop, N. (1970). The development of motor skills and social relationships among primates through play. In J. P. Hill (Ed.), *Minnesota symposia in child psychology* (Vol. 4, pp. 141–201). Minneapolis: University of Minnesota Press.

Drachman, D. B., & Sokoloff, L. (1966). The role of movement in embryonic joint development. *Developmental Biology, 14*, 401–420.

Driesch, H. (1908/1929). *The science and philosophy of the organism*. London: A. &. C. Black.

Driesch, H. (1914). *The problem of individuality*. London: Macmillan.

Dunn, J. (1988). *The beginnings of social understanding*. Cambridge: Harvard University Press.

Dunn, J. (1991). Relationships and behaviour: The significance of Robert Hinde's work for developmental psychology. In P. Bateson (Ed.), *The development and integration of behaviour: Essays in honour of Robert Hinde* (pp. 375–387). Cambridge: Cambridge University Press.

Dunn, J., & Plomin, R. (1985). Differential experiences of siblings in the same family. *Developmental Psychology, 21*, 747–760.

Dunn, J., & Plomin, R. (1990). *Separate lives: Why siblings are so different*. New York: Basic Books.

Dunn, J., & Plomin, R. (1991). Why are siblings so different? The significance of differences in sibling experiences within the family. *Family Process, 30*, 271–283.

Duyme, M., & Capron, C. (1992). Socioeconomic status and I. Q.: What is the meaning of the French adoption studies? *European Bulletin of Cognitive Psychology, 12*, 585–604.

Eales, L. A. (1985). Song learning in zebra finches: Some effects of song model availability on what is learned and when. *Animal Behaviour, 33*, 1293–1300.

Edelman, G. M. (1987). *Neural Darwinism: The theory for neuronal group selection*. New York: Basic Books.

Edelman, G. M. (1988). *Topobiology: An introduction to molecular embryology*. New York: Basic Books.

Edelman, G. M. (1989). Topobiology. *Scientific American, 260*(5), 76–88.

Edelman, G. M. (1992). *Bright air, brilliant fire*. New York: Basic Books.

Egeland, J. A., Gerhard, D. S., Pauks, D. L., Sussex, J. N., Kidd, K. K., Allen, C. R., Hostetter, A. M., & Housman, D. E. (1987). Bipolar affective disorders linked to DNA markers on chromosome 11. *Nature, 325*, 783–787.

Eibl-Eibesfeldt, I. (1975). *Ethology* (2nd ed.). New York: Holt, Rinehart & Winston.

Eldredge, N. (1985). *Unfinished synthesis: Biological hierarchies and modern evolutionary thought.* New York: Oxford University Press.

Eldredge, N. (1989). *Macroevolutionary dynamics: Species, niches, and adaptive peaks.* New York: McGraw-Hill.

Eldredge, N., & Gould, S. J. (1972). Punctuated equilibria: An alternative to phyletic gradualism. In T. J. M. Schopf (Ed.), *Models in paleobiology* (pp. 82–115). San Francisco: Freeman.

Ellis, A. W. (1987). Intimations of the modularity of mind: Doing cognitive neuropsychology without syndromes. In M. Coltheart, G. Sartori, & R. Job (Eds.), *The cognitive neuropsychology of language,* (pp. 397–408). Hillsdale, NJ: Erlbaum.

Emeson, R. B., Yeakley, J. M., Hedjran, F., Merillat, N., Lenz, H. J., & Rosenfeld, M. G. (1992). Posttranscriptional regulation of calcitonin/CGRP gene expression. *Annals of the New York Academy of Sciences, 657,* 18–35.

Emlen, S. T. (1976). An alternative case for sociobiology. *Science, 192,* 736.

Evoniuk, G. E., Kuhn, C. M., & Schanberg, S. M. (1979). The effect of tactile stimulation on serum growth hormone and tissue ornithine decarboxylase activity during maternal deprivation in rat pups. *Communications in Psychopharmacology, 3,* 363–370.

Fabré, J. H. (1956). *The insect world of J. Henri Fabré.* New York: Fawcett World Library.

Fedigan, L. M. (1982). *Primate paradigms: Sex roles and social bonds.* Montreal: Eden Press.

Fentress, J. C. (1981). Order in ontogeny: Relational dynamics. In K. Immelmann, G. W. Barlow, L. Petrinovich, & M. Main (Eds.), *Behavioral development* (pp. 338–371). Cambridge: Cambridge University Press.

Fentress, J. C. (1988). Expressive contexts, fine structure, and central mediation of rodent grooming. *Annals of the New York Academy of Sciences, 525,* 18–26.

Fentress, J. C. (1991). Analytic ethology and synthetic neuroscience. In P. Bateson (Ed.), *The development and integration of behaviour: Essays in honour of Robert Hinde* (pp. 77–120). Cambridge: Cambridge University Press.

Fentress, J. C. (1992). Emergence of pattern in the development of mammalian movement sequences. *Journal of Neurobiology, 23,* 1529–1556.

Fentress, J. C., & McLeod, P. J. (1986). Motor patterns in development. In E. M. Blass (Ed.), *Handbook of behavioral neurobiology. Vol. 8. Developmental psychobiology and developmental neurobiology* (pp. 35–97). New York: Plenum Press.

Fentress, J. C., & McLeod, P. J. (1988). Pattern construction in behavior. In W. P. Smotherman & S. R. Robinson (Eds.), *Behavior of the fetus* (pp. 63–76). Caldwell, NJ: Telford Press.

Fifer, W. P., & Moon, C. (1988). Auditory experience in the fetus. In W. P. Smotherman & S. R. Robinson (Eds.), *Behavior of the fetus* (pp. 175–188). Caldwell, NJ: Telford Press.

Fine, M. L. (1989). Embryonic, larval and adult development of the sonic neuromuscular system in the oyster toadfish. *Brain, Behavior and Evolution, 34,* 13–24.

Fischer, K. W., & Bidell, T. (1991). Constraining nativist inferences about cognitive capacities. In S. Carey & R. Gelman (Eds.), *The epigenesis of mind: Essays on biology and cognition* (pp. 199–236). Hillsdale, NJ: Erlbaum.

Fischer, K. W., & Bidell, T. R. (1992). Ever younger ages: Constructive use of nativist findings about early development. *SRCD Newsletter, Winter,* 1–14.

Fischer, K. W., Knight, C. C., & Van Parys, M. (1993). Analyzing diversity in developmental pathways: Methods and concepts. *Contributions to Human Development, 23,* 33–56.

Fisher, E. P. (1992). The impact of play on development: A meta-analysis. *Play and Culture, 5,* 159–181.

Fisher, R. A. (1930). *The genetical theory of natural selection.* Oxford: Clarendon Press.

Flavell, J. H., & Wohlwill, J. F. (1969). Formal and functional aspects of cognitive development. In D. Elkind & J. H. Flavell (Eds.), *Studies in cognitive growth* (pp. 67–120). New York: Oxford University Press.

Fodor, J. (1983). *The modularity of mind.* Cambridge: MIT Press.

Fodor, J. A., & Pylyshyn, Z. W. (1988). Connectionism and cognitive architecture: A critical analysis. *Cognition, 28,* 3–71.

Fogel, A. (1991). *Infancy: Infant, family and society* (2nd ed.). New York: West.

Forssberg, H., Eliasson, A. C., Kinoshita, H., Johansson, R. S., & Westling, G. (1991). Development of human precision grip. I. Basic coordination of force. *Experimental Brain Research, 85,* 451–457.

Forssberg, H., Kinoshita, H., Eliasson, A. C., Johansson, R. S., Westling, G., & Gordon, A. M. (1992). Development of human precision grip. II. Anticipatory control of isometric forces targeted for object's weight. *Experimental Brain Research, 90,* 393–398.

Friedman, S. L., Klivington, K. A., & Peterson, R. W. (Eds.), (1986). *The brain, cognition, and education.* New York: Academic Press.

Futuyma, D. J. (1986). *Evolutionary biology* (2nd ed.). Sunderland, MA: Sinauer.

Futuyma, D. J. (1987). On the role of species in anagenesis. *American Naturalist, 130,* 465–473.

Galef, B. G., Jr. (1981). The ecology of weaning: Parasitism and the achievement of independence by altricial mammals. In D. J. Gubernick & P. H. Klopfer (Eds.), *Parental care in mammals* (pp. 211–241). New York: Plenum Press.

Galef, B. G., Jr. (1988). Imitation in animals: History, definition, and interpretation of data from the psychological laboratory. In T. R. Zentall & B. G. Galef, Jr. (Eds.), *Social learning* (pp. 3–28). Hillsdale, NJ: Erlbaum.

Geist, V. (1978). *Life strategies, human evolution, environmental design.* New York: Springer-Verlag.

Gelman, R. (1990). First principles organize attention to and learning about relevant data: Number and animate-inanimate distinction as examples. *Cognitive Science, 14,* 79–106.

Gerall, A. A. (1963). An exploratory study of the effect of social isolation variables on the sexual behaviour of male guinea pigs. *Animal Behaviour, 11,* 274–282.

Gesell, A. (1946). The ontogenesis of infant behavior. In L. Carmichael (Ed.), *Manual of child psychology* (pp. 295–331). New York: Wiley.

Gesell, A. L., & Amatruda, C. S. (1945). *The embryology of behavior: The beginnings of the human mind.* New York: Harper & Brothers.

Gesell, A., & Amatruda, C. S. (1947). *Developmental diagnosis: Normal and abnormal child development* (2nd ed.). New York: Harper & Brothers.

Gibson, J. J. (1966). *The senses considered as perceptual systems.* Boston: Houghton Mifflin.

Gibson, K. R., & Peterson, A. C. (1991). Introduction. In K. R. Gibson & A. C. Peterson (Eds.), *Brain maturation and cognitive development* (pp. 3–12). New York: Aldine de Gruyter.

Gilbert, S. F. (1991). *Developmental biology.* Sunderland, MA: Sinauer.

Gilbert, S. F. (1992a). Cells in search of community: Critiques of Weismannism and selectable units in ontogeny. *Biology and Philosophy, 7,* 473–487.

Gilbert, S. F. (1992b). Synthesizing embryology and human genetics: Paradigms regained. *American Journal of Human Genetics, 51,* 211–215.

Goertzel, B. (1992). Self-organizing evolution. *Journal of Social and Evolutionary Systems, 15,* 7–54.

Golani, I. (1992). A mobility gradient in the organization of vertebrate movement: The perception of movement through symbolic language. *Behavioral and Brain Sciences, 15,* 249–266.

Golani, I., & Fentress, J. C. (1985). Early ontogeny of face grooming in mice. *Developmental Psychobiology, 18,* 529–544.

Goldberg, S. (1991). Recent developments in attachment theory and research. *Canadian Journal of Psychiatry, 36,* 393–400.

Goldfield, E. C., & Michel, G. F. (1986a). Spatio-temporal linkage in infant interlimb coordination. *Developmental Psychobiology, 19,* 259–364.

Goldfield, E. C., & Michel, G. F. (1986b). The ontogeny of infant bimanual reaching during the first year. *Infant Behavior and Development, 9,* 87–95.

Goldstein, K. (1939). *The organism.* New York: American Book Co.

Gollin, E. S., Stahl, G., & Morgan, E. (1989). On the uses of the concept of normality in developmental biology and psychology. *Advances in Child Development and Behavior, 21,* 49–71.

Goodwin, B. C. (1984). Changing from an evolutionary to a generative paradigm in biology. In J. W. Pollard (Ed.), *Evolutionary theory: Paths into the future* (pp. 99–120). New York: Wiley.

Goodwin, B. (1990). The causes of biological form. In G. Butterworth & P. Bryant (Eds.), *Causes of development: Interdisciplinary perspectives* (pp. 49–63). Hillsdale, NJ: Erlbaum.

Gordon, A. M., Forssberg, H., Johansson, R. S., Eliasson, A. C., & Westling, G. (1992). Development of human precision grip. III. Integration of visual size cues during the programming of isometric forces. *Experimental Brain Research, 90,* 399–403.

Gordon, N. (1976). *Paediatric neurology for the clinician.* Philadelphia: Lippincott.

Gorski, R. A. (1979). Long-term hormonal modulation of neuronal structure and function. In F. O. Schmitt & F. G. Worden (Eds.), *The neurosciences: Fourth study program* (pp. 969–982). Cambridge: MIT Press.

Gorski, R. A. (1984). Critical role for the medial preoptic area in the sexual differentiation of the brain. *Progress in Brain Research, 61,* 129–146.

Gorski, R. A., Gordon, J. H., Shryne, J. E., & Southam, A. M. (1978). Evidence for a morphological sex difference within the medial preoptic area of the rat brain. *Brain Research, 48,* 333–346.

Gottesman, I. I. (1963). Genetic aspects of intelligent behavior. In N. Ellis (Ed.), *The handbook of mental deficiency* (pp. 253–296). New York: McGraw-Hill.

Gottlieb, G. (1970). Conceptions of prenatal behavior. In L. R. Aronson, E. Tobach, D. S. Lehrman, & J. S. Rosenblatt (Eds.), *Development and evolution of behavior* (pp. 111–137). San Francisco: Freeman.

Gottlieb, G. (1971). *Development of species identification in birds.* Chicago: University of Chicago Press.

Gottlieb, G. (1973). Introduction to behavioral embryology. In G. Gottlieb (Ed.), *Studies on the development of behavior and the nervous system. Vol. 1. Behavioral embryology* (pp. 3–45). New York: Academic Press.

Gottlieb, G. (1976). The roles of experience in the development of behavior and the nervous system. In G. Gottlieb (Ed.), *Studies on the development of behavior and the nervous system. Vol. 3. Neural and behavioral specificity* (pp. 25–54). New York: Academic Press.

Gottlieb, G. (1991a). Epigenetic systems view of human development. *Developmental Psychology, 27,* 33–34.

Gottlieb, G. (1991b). Experiential canalization of behavioral development: Results. *Developmental Psychology, 27,* 35–39.

Gottlieb, G. (1991c). Experiential canalization of behavioral development: Theory. *Developmental Psychology, 27,* 4–13.

Gottlieb, G. (1992). *Individual development and evolution: The genesis of novel behavior.* New York: Oxford University Press.

Gould, J. (1975). Honey bee recruitment: the dance language controversy. *Science, 189,* 685–693.

Gould, J. L. (1982). *Ethology: The mechanisms and evolution of behavior.* New York: W. W. Norton.

Gould, J. L., & Towne, W. F. (1987). Evolution of the dance language. *American Naturalist, 130,* 317–338.

Gould, S. J. (1977). *Ontogeny and phylogeny.* Cambridge: Harvard University Press.

Gould, S. J. (1981). *The mismeasure of man.* New York: Norton.

Gould, S. J. (1989a). The wheel of fortune and the wedge of progress. *Natural History, March,* 14–21.

Gould, S. J. (1989b). *Wonderful life.* New York: Norton.

Gould, S. J. (1991). Exaptation: A crucial tool for an evolutionary psychology. *Journal of Social Issues, 47,* 43–65.

Gould, S. J. (1992). A humongous fungus among us. *Natural History, July,* 10–18.

Gould, S. J., & Eldredge, N. (1993). Punctuated equilibrium comes of age. *Nature, 366,* 223–227.

Gould, S. J., & Lewontin, R. C. (1979). The spandrels of San Marco and the Panglossian paradigm: A critique of the adaptationist programme. *Proceedings of the Royal Society of London [B], 205,* 581–598.

Gould, S. J., & Vrba, E. S. (1982). Exaptation: A missing term in the science of form. *Paleobiology, 8,* 4–15.

Grant, P. R., & Grant, B. R. (1992). Hybridization of bird species. *Science, 256,* 193–197.

Greenfield, P. M. (1991). Language, tools, and brain. *Behavioral and Brain Sciences, 14,* 531–595.

Greenough, W. T. (1986). What's special about development? Thoughts on the bases of experience-sensitive synaptic plasticity. In W. T. Greenough & J. M. Juraska (Eds.), *Developmental neuropsychobiology* (pp. 387–407). Orlando: Academic Press.

Greenough, W. T., & Black, J. E. (1992). Induction of brain structure by experience: Substrates for cognitive development. In M. Gunnar & C. A. Nelson (Eds.), *Behavioral developmental neuroscience. Vol. 24. Minnesota symposia on child psychology* (pp. 35–52). Hillsdale, NJ: Erlbaum.

Greenough, W. T., Carter, C. S., Steerman, C., & DeVoogd, T. J. (1977). Sex differences in dendritic patterns in hamster preoptic area. *Brain Research, 126,* 63–72.

Greenough, W. T., & Juraska, J. M. (1979). Experience-induced changes in brain fine structure: Their behavioral implications. In M. E. Hahn, C. Jensen, & B. C. Dudek (Eds.), *Development and evolution of brain size: Behavioral implications* (pp. 295–320). New York: Academic Press.

Greenough, W. T., & Juraska, J. M. (Eds.). (1986). *Developmental neuropsychobiology* . Orlando: Academic Press.

Gregory, M. S., Silvers, A., & Sutch, D. (1978). *Sociobiology and human nature.* San Francisco: Jossey-Bass.

Griffin, D. R. (1958). *Listening in the dark.* New Haven, CT: Yale University Press.

Griffin, D. R. (1984). *Animal thinking.* Cambridge: Harvard University Press.

Grisham, W., Mathews, G. A., & Arnold, A. P. (1994). Local intracerebral implants of estrogen masculinize some aspects of the zebra finch song system. *Journal of Neurobiology, 25,* 185–196.

Grosvenor, C. E., Maiweg, H., & Mena, F. (1970). A study of factors involved in the development of the exteroceptive release of prolactin in the lactating rat. *Hormones and Behavior, 1,* 111–120.

Gruber, H. E. (1966). Factors controlling the rate of conceptual change: A study of Charles Darwin's thinking. In *Concept formation and mental activity.* Symposium presented at 18th International Congress of Psychology, Moscow, August.

Gruber, H. E. (1981) *Darwin on man: A psychological study of scientific creativity.* Chicago: University of Chicago Press.

Gruber, H. E., & Barrett, P. H. (1974). *Darwin on man: A psychological study of scientific creativity.* New York: Dutton.

Gruter, M. (1986). Ostracism on trial: The limits of individual rights. *Ethology and Sociobiology, 7,* 271–279.

Gubernick, D. J., & Alberts, J. R. (1983). Maternal licking of young: Resource exchange and proximate controls. *Physiology and Behavior, 31,* 593–601.

Gundersen, H. J. G., Bendtsen, T. F., Korbo, L., Marcussen, N., Moller, A., Nielsen, K., Nyengaard, J. R., Pakkenberg, B., Sorensen, F. B., Vesterby, A., & West, J. J. (1988). Some new, simple and efficient stereological methods and their use in pathological research and diagnosis. *APMIS, 96,* 379–394.

Haeckel, E. (1879). *The evolution of man: A popular exposition of the principal points of human ontogeny and phylogeny.* New York: Appleton.

Hailman, J. P. (1982). Evolution and behavior: An iconoclastic view. In H. C. Plotkin (Ed.), *Learning, development, and culture* (pp. 205–254). New York: Wiley.

Haldane, J. B. S. (1932). *The causes of evolution.* New York: Harper.

Hall, W. G. (1990). The ontogeny of ingestive behavior: Changing control of components in the feeding sequence. In E. M. Stricker (Ed.), *Handbook of behavioral neurobiology. Vol. 10. Neurobiology of food and fluid intake* (pp. 77–123). New York: Plenum Press.

Hall, W. G., & Oppenheim, R. W. (1987). Developmental psychobiology: Prenatal, perinatal, and early postnatal aspects of behavioral development. *Annual Review of Psychology, 38,* 91–128.

Hall, W. G., & Rosenblatt, J. S. (1977). Suckling behavior and intake control in the developing rat. *Journal of Comparative and Physiological Psychology, 91,* 1141–1155.

Hall, W. G., & Williams, C. L. (1983). Suckling isn't feeding, or is it? A search for developmental continuities. *Advances in the Study of Behavior, 13,* 219–253.

Halverson, H. M. (1931). An experimental study of prehension in infants by means of systematic cinema records. *Genetic Psychology Monographs, 10,* 107–283.

Halverson, H. M. (1932). A further study of grasping. *Journal of Genetic Psychology, 7,* 34–63.

Halverson, H. M. (1937). Studies of grasping responses of early infancy. I, II, and III. *Journal of Genetic Psychology, 51,* 371–449.

Hambley, J. (1972). Diversity: A developmental perspective. In K. Richardson & D. Spears (Eds.), *Race and intelligence* (pp. 114–127). Baltimore: Penguin Books.

Hamburger, V. (1970). Embryonic motility in vertebrates. In F. O. Schmitt (Ed.), *The neurosciences: Second study program* (pp. 141–151). New York: Rockefeller University Press.

Hamburger, V. (1973). Anatomical and physiological basis of embryonic motility in birds and mammals. In G. Gottlieb (Ed.), *Studies on the development of behavior and the nervous system. Vol. 3. Neural and behavioral specificity* (pp. 51–76). New York: Academic Press.

Hamburger, V., & Oppenheim, R. W., (1967). Prehatching motility and hatching behavior in the chick. *Journal of Experimental Zoology, 166,* 171–204.

Hamburger, V., & Oppenheim, R. W., (1982). Naturally occurring cell death in vertebrates. *Neuroscience Comment, 1,* 39–55.

Hamburger, V., Wenger, E., & Oppenheim, R. (1966). Motility in the chick embryo in the absence of sensory input. *Journal of Experimental Zoology, 162,* 133–160.

Hamilton, W. D. (1964). The genetical evolution of social behaviour. I and II. *Journal of Theoretical Biology, 7,* 1–52.

Hammer, R. P., & Jacobson, C. D. (1984). Sex difference in dendritic development of the sexually dimorphic nucleus of the preoptic area in the rat. *International Journal of Developmental Neuroscience, 2,* 77–85.

Hampson, J. L., & Hampson, J. G. (1961). The ontogenesis of sexual behavior in man. In W. C. Young (Ed.), *Sex and internal secretions* (Vol. 2, 3rd ed., pp. 1401–1432). Baltimore: Williams & Wilkins.

Handler, P. (1970). *Biology and the future of man.* New York: Oxford University Press.

Hardcastle, V. G. (1992). Reduction, explanatory extension, and the mind/brain sciences. *Philosophy of Science, 59,* 408–428.

Harlow, H. F., & Harlow, M. K. (1965). The affectional systems. In A. M. Schrier, H. F. Harlow, & F. Stollnitz (Eds.), *Behavior of nonhuman primates* (Vol. 2, pp. 287–334). New York and London: Academic Press.

Harlow, H. F., Harlow, M. K., & Soumi, S. (1971). From thought to therapy: Lessons from a primate labortory. *American Scientist, 59,* 538–549.

Harris, D. B. (Ed.). (1957). *The concept of development.* Minneapolis: University of Minnesota Press.

Harris, G. W. (1955). *Neural control of the pituitary gland.* London: Arnold.

Hart, H. L. A., & Honore, T. (1985). *Causation in the law.* New York: Oxford University Press.

Hazlett, B. A. (Ed.). (1977). *Quantitative methods in the study of animal behavior.* New York: Academic Press.

Hebb, D. O. (1949). *The organization of behavior.* New York: Wiley.

Hein, A. (1980). The development of visually guided behavior. In C. S. Harris (Ed.), *Visual coding and adaptability* (pp. 51–67). Hillsdale, NJ: Erlbaum.

Hein, A., & Diamond, R. M. (1983). Contribution of eye movement to the representation of space. In A. Hein & M. Jeannerod (Eds.), *Spatially oriented behavior* (pp. 119–133). New York: Springer-Verlag.

Held, R., & Hein, A. (1963). Movement-produced stimulation in the development of visually guided behavior. *Journal of Comparative and Physiological Psychology, 56,* 872–876.

Hepper, P. G., Shahidullah, S., & White, R. (1991). Handedness in the human fetus. *Neuropsychologia, 29,* 1107–1111.

Heywood, C. A., Gadotti, A., & Cowey, A. (1992). Cortical area V4 and its role in the perception of color. *Journal of Neuroscience, 12,* 4056–4065.

Hill, W. L., Borovsky, D., & Rovee-Collier, C. (1988). Continuities in infant memory development. *Developmental Psychobiology, 21,* 43–62.

Hinde, R. A. (1968). Dichotomies in the study of development. In J. M. Thoday & A. S. Parkes (Eds.), *Genetic and environmental influences on behaviour* (pp. 3–14). Edinburgh: Oliver & Boyd.

Hinde, R. A. (1974). *Biological bases of human social behaviour.* New York: McGraw-Hill

Hinde, R. A. (1979). *Towards understanding relationships.* London: Academic Press.

Hinde, R. A. (1982). *Ethology: Its nature and relations with other sciences.* Oxford: Oxford University Press.

Hinde, R. A. (1983). Ethology and child development. In M. M. Haith & J. J. Campos (Eds.), *Handbook of Child Psychology. Vol. 2. Infancy and developmental psychobiology* (4th ed., pp. 27–94). New York: Wiley.

Hinde, R. A. (1986). Some implications of evolutionary theory and comparative data for the study of human prosocial and aggressive behavior. In D. Owens, J. Block, & M. Radke-Yarrow (Eds.), *Development of antisocial and prosocial behavior* (pp. 13–32). New York: Academic Press.

Hinde, R. A. (1987). *Individuals, relationships and culture: Links between ethology and the social sciences.* Cambridge: Cambridge University Press.

Hinde, R. A. (1992). Commentary. *Human Development, 35,* 34–39.

Hinde, R. A., & Fisher, J. (1951). Further observations on the opening of milk bottles by birds. *British Birds, 44,* 393–396.

Hinde, R. A., & Spencer-Booth, Y. (1967). The effect of social companions on mother-infant relations in rhesus monkeys. In D. Morris (Ed.), *Primate ethology* (pp. 343–364). New York: Anchor.

Hinde, R. A., & Stevenson-Hinde, J. (Eds.). (1973). *Constraints on learning.* New York: Academic Press.

Hirsch, H. V. B. (1986). The tunable seer: Activity dependent development of vision. In E. M. Blass (Ed.), *Handbook of behavioral neurobiology. Vol. 8: Developmental psychobiology and developmental neurobiology,* (pp. 41–62). New York: Plenum Press.

Hirsch, H. V. B., & Spinelli, D. N. (1970). Visual experience modifies distribution of horizontally and vertically oriented receptive fields in cats. *Science, 168,* 869–871.

Hirsch, J. (1970). Behavior-genetic analysis and its biosocial consequences. *Seminars in Psychiatry, 2,* 89–105.

Hirsch, J. (1976). Jensenism: The bankruptcy of "science" without scholarship. *U.S. Congressional Record, 122*(73), E2671–2672.

Hirsch, J. (1990). Correlation, causation, and careerism. *European Bulletin of Cognitive Psychology, 10,* 647–652.

Ho, M. W., & Saunders, P. T. (1979). Beyond neo-Darwinism—An epigenetic approach to evolution. *Journal of Theoretical Biology, 78,* 573–591.

Ho, M., & Saunders, P. T. (Eds.). (1984). *Beyond neo-Darwinism: An introduction to the new evolutionary paradigm.* London: Academic Press.

Hodos, W. (1970). Evolutionary interpretation of neural and behavioral studies of living vertebates. In F. O. Schmitt (Ed.), *The neurosciences: Second study program* (pp. 26–39). New York: Rockefeller University Press.

Hodos, W., & Campbell, C. B. G. (1969). *Scala naturae:* Why there is no theory in comparative psychology. *Psychological Review, 76,* 337–350.

Hofer, M. A. (1978). Hidden regulatory processes in early social relationships. In P. P. G. Bateson & P. H. Klopfer (Eds.), *Perspectives in ethology* (Vol. 3, pp. 135–163). New York: Plenum Press.

Hofer, M. A. (1983). The mother-infant interaction as a regulator of infant physiology and behavior. In L. A. Rosenblum & H. Moltz (Eds.), *Symbiosis in parent-offspring interactions* (pp. 61–75). New York: Plenum Press.

Hofer, M. A., & Shair, H. N. (1992). Ultrasonic vocalization by rat pups during recovery from deep hypothermia. *Developmental Psychobiology, 25,* 511–528.

Hofman, M. A., & Swaab, D. F. (1989). The sexually dimorphic nucleus of the preoptic area in the human brain: A comparative morphometric study. *Journal of Anatomy, 164,* 55–72.

Holden, C. (1994). A cautionary tale: The sobering story of D2. *Science, 264,* 1696–1697.

Hollyday, M., & Hamburger, V. (1976). Reduction of the naturally occurring motor neuron loss by enlargement of the periphery. *Journal of Comparative Neurology, 170,* 311–320.

Hooker, D. (1952). *The prenatal origin of behavior.* Lawrence, KS: University of Kansas Press.

Hopkins, B., & Butterworth, G. (1990). Concepts of causality in explanations of development. In G. Butterworth & P. Bryant (Eds.), *Causes of development* (pp. 3–32). Hillsdale, NJ: Erlbaum.

Hopkins, B., Lems, W., Janssen, B., & Butterworth, G. (1987). Postural and motor asymmetries in newlyborns. *Human Neurobiology, 6*, 153–156.

Horowitz, F. D. (1987). *Exploring developmental theories: Toward a structural/behavioral model of development*. Hillsdale, NJ: Erlbaum.

Hrdy, S. B. (1977). Infanticide as a primate reproductive strategy. *American Scientist, 65*, 40–49.

Hubel, D. H., & Wiesel, T. N. (1962). Receptive fields, binocular interaction and functional architecture in the cat's visual cortex. *Journal of Physiology, 160*, 106–154.

Hull, D. L. (1972). Reduction in genetics—Biology or philosophy? *Philosophy of Science, 39*, 491–499.

Humphrey, T. (1964). Some correlations between the appearance of human fetal reflexes and the development of the nervous system. *Progress in Brain Research, 4*, 93–135.

Humphrey, T. (1969). Postnatal repetition of human prenatal activity sequences with some suggestions of their neuroanatomical basis. In R. J. Robinson (Ed.), *Brain and early behaviour* (pp. 43–84). New York: Academic Press.

Hutt, C. (1972). *Males and females*. Middlesex, England: Penguin Books.

Immelmann, K. (1969). Song development in the zebra finch and other estrildid finches. In R. A. Hinde (Ed.), *Bird vocalizations* (pp. 61–74). New York: Oxford University Press.

Impekoven, M., & Gold, P. S. (1973). Prenatal origins of parent-young interactions in birds: A naturalistic approach. In G. Gottlieb (Ed.), *Behavioral embryology. Vol. 1. Studies on the development of behavior and the nervous system* (pp. 325–356). New York: Academic Press.

Iran-Nejad, A., Hidi, S., & Wittrock, M. C. (1992). Reconceptualizing relevance in education from a biological perspective. *Educational Psychologist, 27*, 407–414.

Iran-Nejad, A., Marsh, G. E. II, & Clements, A. C. (1992). The figure and the ground of constructive brain functioning: Beyond explicit memory processes. *Educational Psychologist, 27*, 473–492.

Irvine, W. (1956). *Apes, angels and Victorians*. London: Readers Union.

Jacobson, A. G., Odell, G. M., & Oster, G. F. (1985). The cortical tractor model for epithelial folding: Application to the neural plate. In G. Edelman (Ed.), *Molecular determinants of animal form* (pp. 143–166). New York: Liss.

Jacobson, M. (1991). *Developmental neurobiology* (3rd ed.). New York: Plenum Press.

Jamieson, I. G. (1986). The functional approach to behavior: Is it useful? *American Naturalist, 127*, 195–208.

Jamieson, I. G. (1989). Behavioral heterochrony and the evolution of birds' helping at the nest: An unselected consequence of communal breeding? *American Naturalist, 133*, 394–406.

Jarvis, J. U. M. (1981). Eusociality in a mammal: Cooperative breeding in naked mole-rat colonies. *Science, 212*, 571–573.

Jaynes, J. (1956). Imprinting: The interaction of learned and innate behavior. I. Development and generalization. *Journal of Comparative and Physiological Psychology, 49*, 200–206.

Jaynes, J. (1969). The historical origins of "ethology" and "comparative psychology." *Animal Behaviour, 17*, 601–606.

Jeannerod, M. (1988). *The neural and behavioral organization of goal-directed movements*. New York: Oxford University Press.

Jenkins, W. M., Merzenich, M. M., Ochs, M. T., Allard, T., & Guic-Robles, E. (1990). Functional reorganization of primary somatosensory cortex in adult owl monkeys after behaviorally controlled tactile stimulation. *Journal of Neurophysiology, 63*, 82–104.

Jensen, A. R. (1969). How much can we boost IQ and scholastic achievement? *Harvard Educational Review, 39*, 1–123.

Johanson, I. B., & Terry, L. M. (1988). Learning in infancy. In E. M. Blass, (Ed.), *Handbook of behavioral neurobiology. Vol. 9. Developmental psychobiology and behavioral ecology* (pp. 245–281). New York: Plenum Press.

Johansson, R. S., & Edin, B. B. (1992). Mechanisms for grasp control. In A. Pedotti & M. Ferrarin (Eds.), *Restoration of walking for paraplegics: Recent advancements and trends* (pp. 57–63). Amsterdam: IOS Press.

Johnson, F., & Bottjer, S. W. (1994). Afferent influences on cell death and birth during development of a cortical nucleus necessary for learned vocal behavior in zebra finches. *Development, 120*, 13–24.

Johnson, M. (1987). *The body in the mind: The bodily basis of reason and imagination*. Chicago: University of Chicago Press.

Johnson, M. H., & Karmiloff-Smith, A. (1992). Can neural selectionism be applied to cognitive development and its disorders? *New Ideas in Psychology, 10*, 35–46.

Johnson, M. H., & Morton, J. (1991). *Biology and cognitive development*. Oxford: Blackwell.

Johnston, T. D. (1982). Learning and the evolution of developmental systems. In H. C. Plotkin (Ed.), *Learning, development, and culture*: *Essays in evolutionary epistemology* (pp. 411–442). New York: Wiley.

Johnston, T. D. (1985). Introduction: Conceptual issues in the ecological study of learning. In T. D. Johnston & A. T. Pietrewicz (Eds.), *Issues in the ecological study of learning* (pp. 1–24). Hillsdale, NJ: Erlbaum.

Johnston, T. D. (1987). The persistence of dichotomies in the study of behavioral development. *Developmental Review, 7*, 149–182.

Johnston, T. D., & Gottlieb, G. (1981). Development of visual species identification in ducklings: What is the role of imprinting? *Animal Behaviour, 29*, 1082–1099.

Johnston, T. D., & Gottlieb, G. (1985). Effects of social experience on visually imprinted maternal preferences in Peking ducklings. *Developmental Psychobiology, 18*, 261–271.

Juraska, J. M. (1986). Sex differences in developmental plasticity of behavior and the brain. In W. T. Greenough & J. M. Juraska (Eds.), *Developmental neuropsychobiology* (pp. 409–422). Orlando: Academic Press.

Juraska, J. M. (1990). The structure of the rat cerebral cortex: Effects of gender and the environment. In B. Kolb & R. C. Tees (Eds.), *The cerebral cortex of the rat* (pp. 483–505). Cambridge: MIT Press.

Juraska, J. M., & Kopcik, J. R. (1988). Sex and environmental influences on the size and ultrastructure of the rat corpus callosum. *Brain Research, 450*, 1–8.

Kaas, J. H. (1991). Plasticity of sensory and motor maps in adult animals. *Annual Review of Neuroscience, 14*, 137–167.

Kak, C. S. (1991). The honey bee dance language controversy. *Mankind Quarterly, 31*, 357–365.

Kamin, L. J. (1974). *The science and politics of IQ*. Potomac, MD: Erlbaum.

Kan, Y. W., & Dozy, A. M. (1978). Polymorphism of DNA sequence adjacent to human β-globin structural gene: Relationship to sickle mutation. *Proceedings of the National Academy of Sciences U.S.A., 75*, 5631–5635.

Kaplan, A. (1964). *The conduct of inquiry*. San Francisco: Chandler.

Kaplan, E. (1991). A process approach to neuropsychological assessment. In T. Boll & B. K. Bryant (Eds.), *Clinical neuropsychology and brain function: Research, measurement, and practice* (pp. 81–108). Washington, DC: American Psychological Association.

Kaplan, M. S., & Hinds, J. W. (1977). Neurogenesis in the adult rat: Electron microscopic analysis of light radioautographs. *Science, 197*, 1092–1094.

Karmiloff-Smith, A. (1992). *Beyond modularity: A developmental perspective on cognitive science*. Cambridge: MIT Press.

Katz, L. C. (1994). Somatosensory development: A new level of refinement. *Current Biology, 4*, 831–834.

Kauffman, S. A. (1987). Problems and paradigms: Developmental logic and its evolution. *Bioessays, 6*, 82–87.

Kauffman, S. A. (1993). *The origins of order: Self-organization and natural selection in evolution*. New York: Oxford University Press.

Kaufman, I. C. (1974). Mother/infant relations in monkeys and humans: A reply to Professor Hinde. In N. F. White (Ed.), *Ethology and psychiatry* (pp. 47–68). Toronto: University of Toronto Press.

Kelso, J. A., Putnam, C. A., & Goodman, D. (1983). On the space-time structure of human interlimb co-ordination. *Quarterly Journal of Experimental Psychology, 35A*, 347–375.

Kennedy, J. S. (1992). *The new anthropomorphism*. Cambridge: Cambridge University Press.

Kennedy, S., Glaser, R., & Kiecolt-Glaser, J. (1990). Psychoneuroimmunology. In J. T. Cacioppo & L. G. Tassinary (Eds.), *Principles of psychophysiology: Physical, social, and inferential elements* (pp. 177–190). New York: Cambridge University Press.

Kenny, P. A., & Turkewitz, G. (1986). Effects of unusually early visual stimulation on the development of homing behavior in the rat pup. *Developmental Psychobiology, 19*, 57–66.

Kent, R. D. (1984). The psychobiology of speech development: Consequence of language and a movement system. *American Journal of Physiology, 246,* R888–R894.

Kettlewell, H. B. D. (1956). A resume of investigations on the evolution of melanism in the Lepidoptera. *Proceedings of the Royal Society B,* 145, 297–303.

Kettlewell, H. B. D. (1961). The phenomenon of industrial melanism in the Lepidoptera. *Annual Review of Entomology, 6,* 245–262.

Ketterson, E. D., Nolan, V., Jr., Wolf, L., & Ziegenfus, C. (1992). Testosterone and avian life histories: Effects of experimentally elevated testosterone on behavior and correlates of fitness in the dark-eyed junco (*Junco hyemalis*). American Naturalist, *140,* 980–999.

Keverne, E. B., & Kendrick, K. M. (1992). Oxytocin facilitation of maternal behavior in sheep. *Annals of the New York Academy of Sciences, 652,* 83–101.

Kidd, K. K. (1991). Trials and tribulations in the search for genes causing neuropsychiatric disorders. *Social Biology, 38,* 163–178.

Kimmerle, M., Mick, L. A., & Michel, G. F. (1995). Bimanual role-differentiated toy play during infancy. *Infant Behavior and Development,* in press.

Kirkpatrick, M., & Lande, R. (1989). The evolution of maternal characters. *Evolution, 43,* 485–503.

Kitcher, P. (1984). 1953 and all that: A tale of two sciences. *Philosophical Review, 93,* 335–373.

Kitcher, P. (1985). *Vaulting ambition: Sociobiology and the quest for human nature.* Cambridge: MIT Press.

Klaus, M. H., & Kennell, J. H. (1970). Mothers separated from their newborn infants. *Pediatric Clinics of North America, 17,* 1015–1037.

Klein, D. B. (1970). *A history of scientific psychology.* New York: Basic Books.

Klopfer, P. H. (1973). Evolution and behavior. In G. Bermant (Ed.), *Perspectives on animal behavior* (pp. 48–71). Glenview, IL: Scott Foresman.

Kolb, B., & Whishaw, I. Q. (1989). Plasticity in the neocortex: Mechanisms underlying recovery from early brain damage. *Progress in Neurobiology, 32,* 235–276.

Kon, S. K., & Cowie, A. T. (Eds.). (1961). *Milk: The mammary gland and its secretion.* New York: Academic Press.

Konner, M. (1977). Infancy among the Kalahani desert san. In P. H. Leiderman, S. R. Tulkin, & A. Rosenfeld (Eds.), *Culture and infancy* (pp. 69–109). New York: Academic Press.

Konner, M. (1982). *The tangled wing.* New York: Holt, Rinehart & Winston.

Konner, M., & Worthman, C. (1980). Nursing frequency, gonadal function and birth spacing among !Kung hunter-gatherers. *Science, 207,* 788–791.

Korner, A. F. (1980). Maternal deprivation: Compensatory stimulation for the prematurely born infant. In R. W. Bell & W. P. Smotherman (Eds.), *Maternal influences and early behavior* (pp. 337–352). Jamaica, NY: Spectrum.

Koshland, D. E., Jr. (1990). The rational approach to the irrational. *Science, 250,* 189.

Krebs, J. B., & Davies, N. B. (1981). *An introduction to behavioral ecology.* Sunderland, MA: Sinauer.

Kruuk, H. (1972). *The spotted hyena.* Chicago: University of Chicago Press.

Kugler, P. N. (1986). A morphological perspective on the origin and evolution of movement patterns. In M. G. Wade & H. T. A. Whiting (Eds.), *Motor development in children: Aspects of coordinaton and control.* Boston: Martinus Nijhoff.

Kugler, P. N., Kelso, J. A. S., & Turvey, M. T. (1980). On the concept of coordinative structures as dissipative structures. 1. Theoretical lines of convergence. In G. E. Stelmach & J. Reguin (Eds.), *Tutorial in motor behavior* (pp. 3–47). Amsterdam: North-Holland.

Kuhn, C. M., Butler, S. R., & Schanberg, S. M. (1978). Selective depression of serum growth hormone during maternal deprivation in rat pups. *Science, 201,* 1034–1036.

Kummer, H. (1971). *Primate societies.* New York: Aldine.

Kuo, Z.-Y. (1967). *The dynamics of behavior development: An epigenetic view.* New York: Random House.

Kuypers, H. G. J. M. (1982). A new look at the organization of the motor system. In H. G. J. M. Kuypers & G. F. Martin (Eds.), *Progress in brain research. Vol. 57. Anatomy of descending pathways to the spinal cord* (pp. 381–404). New York: Elsevier.

Lack, D. (1947). *Darwin's finches.* London: Cambridge University Press.

Lakoff, G. (1987). *Women, fire, and dangerous things: What categories reveal about the mind.* Chicago: University of Chicago Press.

Lakoff, G., & Johnson, M. (1980). *Metaphors we live by.* Chicago: University of Chicago Press.

Lande, R., & Arnold, S. J. (1983). The measurement of selection on correlated characters. *Evolution, 37,* 1210–1226.

Lander, E. S., & Botstein, D. (1986). Strategies for studying heterogeneous genetic traits in humans by using a linkage map of restriction fragment length polymorphisms. *Proceedings of the National Academy of Sciences U.S.A., 83,* 735–737.

Landman, O. E. (1991). The inheritance of acquired characteristics. *Annual Review of Genetics, 25,* 1–20.

Larson, A., Prager, E. M., & Wilson, A. C. (1984). Chromosomal evolution, speciation and morphological change in vertebrates: The role of social behavior. *Chromosomes Today, 8,* 215–228.

Lautrey, J. (1993). Structure and variability: A plea for a pluralistic approach to cognitive development. In R. Case & W. Edelstein (Eds.), *The new structuralism in cognitive development* (pp. 101–114). Basel: Karger.

Lawrence, D. G., & Hopkins, D. A. (1976). The development of motor control in the rhesus monkey: Evidence concerning the role of corticomotoneuronal connections. *Brain, 99,* 235–254.

Lawrence, D. G., & Kuypers, H. G. J. M. (1968). The functional organization of the motor system in the monkey. I. The effects of bilateral pyramidal lesions. *Brain, 91,* 1–14.

Lederman, S. J., & Klatzky, R. L. (1987). Hand movements: A window into haptic object recognition. *Cognitive Psychology, 19,* 342–368.

Lee, C. T., & Griffo, W. (1973). Early androgenization and aggression pheromone in inbred mice. *Hormones and Behavior, 4,* 181–189.

Lee, M. H. S., & Williams, D. I. (1974). Changes in licking behaviour of rat mother following handling of young. *Animal Behaviour, 22,* 679–681.

Lehrman, D. S. (1953). A critique of Konrad Lorenz's theory of instinctive behavior. *Quarterly Review of Biology, 28,* 337–363.

Lehrman, D. S. (1962). Interaction of hormonal and experiential influences on development of behavior. In E. L. Bliss (Ed.), *Roots of behavior* (pp. 142–156). New York: Harper.

Lehrman, D. S. (1964). The reproductive behavior of ring doves. *Scientific American, 211,* 48–54.

Lehrman, D. S. (1965). Interaction between internal and external environments in the regulation of the reproductive cycle of the ring dove. In F. A. Beach (Ed.), *Sex and behavior* (pp. 355–380). New York: Wiley.

Lehrman, D. S. (1970). Semantic and conceptual issues in the nature-nurture problem. In L. R. Aronson, E. Tobach, D. S. Lehrman, & J. S. Rosenblatt (Eds.), *Development and evolution of behavior* (pp. 17–52). San Francisco: Freeman.

Lehrman, D. S. (1971). Behavioral science, engineering, and poetry. In E. Tobach, L. R. Aronson, & E. Shaw (Eds.), *The biopsychology of development* (pp. 459–471). New York: Academic Press.

Lehrman, D. S. (1974). Can psychiatrists use ethology? In N. F. White (Ed.), *Ethology and psychiatry* (pp. 187–196). Toronto: University of Toronto Press.

Lehrman, D. S., Wortis, R. P., & Brody, P. (1961). Gonadotrophin secretion in response to external stimuli of varying duration in the ring dove (*Streptopelia risoria*). *Proceedings of the Society for Experimental Biology and Medicine, 106,* 298–300.

Lemke, G., (1992). Gene regulation in the nervous system. In Z. W. Hall (Ed.), *An introduction to molecular neurobiology* (pp. 313–354). Sunderland, MA: Sinauer.

Lenneberg, E. H. (1967). *The biological foundations of language.* New York: Wiley.

Leon, M., Crosskerry, P. G., & Smith, G. K. (1978). Thermal control of mother young contact in rats. *Physiology and Behavior, 21,* 793–811.

Leon, M., & Moltz, H. (1971). Maternal pheromone: Discrimination of pre-weanling albino rats. *Physiology and Behavior, 7,* 265–267.

Lerner, R. M. (1976). *Concepts and theories of human development.* Reading, MA: Addison-Wesley.

Lerner, R. M. (1983). The history of philosophy and the philosophy of history in developmental psychology: A view of the issues. In R. M. Lerner (Ed.), *Developmental psychology: Historical and philosophical perspectives* (pp. 3–26). Hillsdale, NJ: Erlbaum.

Lerner, R. M. (1991). Changing organism-context relations as basic process of development: A developmental contextual perspective. *Developmental Psychology, 27,* 27–32.

Lerner, R. M., & Kaufman, M. B. (1985). The concept of development in contextualism. *Developmental Review, 5,* 309–333.

Lester, B. M., & Boukydis, C. F. Z. (1991). No language but a cry. In H. Papousek, U. Jurgens, & M. Papousek (Eds.) *Nonverbal vocal communication: Comparative and developmental approaches* (pp. 201–233). Cambridge: Cambridge University Press.

LeVay, S. (1991). A difference in hypothalamic structure between heterosexual and homosexual men. *Science, 253,* 1034–1037.

Levi-Montalcini, R. (1975). NGF: An uncharted route. In F. G. Worden, J. P. Swazey, & G. Adelman (Eds.), *The neurosciences: Paths of discovery. I* (pp. 244–265). Cambridge: MIT Press.

Levine, S. (1969). Infantile stimulation: A perspective. In A. Ambrose (Ed.), *Stimulation in early infancy* (pp. 3–19). New York: Academic Press.

Lewin, R. (1980). Is your brain really necessary? *Science, 210,* 1232–1234.

Lewontin, R. C. (1982). Organism and environment. In H. C. Plotkin (Ed.), *Learning, development, and culture: Essays in evolutionary epistemology* (pp. 151–172). New York: Wiley.

Lewontin, R. C. (1983). Gene, organism and environment. In D. S. Bendall (Ed.), *Evolution from molecules to men* (pp. 273–285). New York: Cambridge University Press.

Lewontin, R. C., Rose, S., & Kamin, L. J. (1984). *Not in our genes.* New York: Random House.

Li, Y., Erzurumlu, R. S., Chen, C., Jhaveri, S., & Tonegawa, S. (1994). Whisker-related neuronal patterns fail to develop in the trigeminal brainstem nuclei of NMDAR1 knockout mice. *Cell, 76,* 427–437.

Lickliter, R. (1990). Premature visual experience accelerates intersensory functioning in bobwhite quail neonates. *Developmental Psychobiology, 23,* 15–27.

Lickliter, R. (1993). Timing and the development of perinatal perceptual organization. In G. Turkewitz & D. A. Devenny (Eds.), *Developmental time and timing* (pp. 105–123). Hillsdale, NJ: Erlbaum.

Lickliter, R., Dyer, A. B., & McBride, T. (1993). Perceptual consequences of early social experience in precocial birds. *Behavioural Processes, 30,* 185–200.

Lickliter, R., & Gottlieb, G. (1987). Retroactive excitation: Posttraining social experience with siblings consolidates maternal imprinting in ducklings. *Journal of Comparative Psychology, 101,* 40–46.

Lickliter, R., & Gottlieb, G. (1988). Social specificity: Interaction with own species is necessary to foster species-specific maternal preference in ducklings. *Developmental Psychobiology, 21,* 311–321.

Lieberman, P. (1984). *The biology and evolution of language.* Cambridge: Harvard University Press.

Lima de Faria, A. (1988). *Evolution without selection.* New York: Elsevier.

Lincoln, D. W. (1983). Physiological mechanisms governing the transfer of milk from mother to young. In L. A. Rosenblum & H. Moltz (Eds.), *Symbiosis in parent-offspring interactions* (pp. 77–112). New York: Plenum Press.

Lintern, G., & Kugler, P. N. (1991). Self-organization in connectionist models: Associative memory, dissipative structures, and thermodynamic law. *Human Movement Science, 10,* 447–483.

Lloyd, R. (1987). *Explorations in psychoneuroimmunology.* Orlando: Grune & Stratton.

Lockman, J. J., & Thelen, E. (1993). Developmental biodynamics: Brain, body, behavior connections. *Child Development, 64,* 953–959.

Lorenz, K. (1937/1957). The conception of instinctive behavior. In C. H. Schiller (Ed. and Trans.), *Instinctive behavior* (pp. 129–175). New York: International Universities Press. (Original work published 1937)

Lorenz, K. (1965). *Evolution and modification of behaviour.* Chicago: University of Chicago Press.

Lorenz, K. (1966). *On aggression*. New York: Harcourt Brace Jovanovich.

Lorenz, K. (1971a). Comparative studies of the motor patterns of Anatinea (R. Martin, Trans.). In K. Lorenz, *Studies in animal and human behavior* (Vol. 2, pp. 14–114). Cambridge: Harvard University Press. (Original work published 1941)

Lorenz, K. (1971b). *Studies in animal and human behavior* (Vol. 2). Cambridge: Harvard University Press.

Lorenz, K., & Tinbergen, N. (1938). Taxis und Instinkthandlung in der Eirollbewegung der Graugans. *Zeitschrift für Tierpsychologie, 2*, 1–29.

Lott, D. F. (1984). Intraspecific variation in the social systems of wild vertebrates. *Behaviour, 88*, 266–325.

Lou, H. C. (1982). *Developmental neurology*. New York: Raven Press.

Lovejoy, A. O. (1936). *The great chain of being: A study of the history of an idea*. Cambridge: Harvard University Press. (Reprinted 1960, Harper)

Løvtrup, S. (1987). *Darwinism: Refutation of a myth*. Beckenham, England: Croon Helm.

Low, B. S. (1989). Cross-cultural patterns in the training of children: An evolutionary perspective. *Journal of Comparative Psychology, 103*, 311–319.

Lumsden, C. J., & Wilson, E. O. (1981). *Genes, mind and culture*. Cambridge: Harvard University Press.

Lund, R. D. (1978). *Development and plasticity of the brain*. New York: Oxford University Press.

Lyell, C. (1830–1833). *Principles of geology*. London: John Murray.

Mackie, J. L. (1974). *The cement of the universe*. New York: Oxford University Press.

Maddux, J. E. (1993). The mythology of psychopathology: A social cognitive view of deviance, difference, and disorder. *General Psychologist, 29*, 34–45.

Magnusson, D. (1988). *Individual development from an interactional perspective: A longitudinal study*. Hillsdale, NJ: Erlbaum.

Maier, N. R. F., & Schneirla, T. C. (1935). *Principles of animal psychology*. New York: McGraw-Hill.

Mandler, J. M. (1988). How to build a baby: On the development of an accessible representational system. *Cognitive Development, 3*, 113–136.

Manji, H. K. (1992). G proteins: Implications for psychiatry. *American Journal of Psychiatry, 149*, 746–760.

Mann, C. C. (1994). Behavioral genetics in transition. *Science, 264*, 1686–1689.

Maratsos, M., & Matheny, L. (1994). Language specificity and elasticity: Brain and clinical syndrome studies. *Annual Review of Psychology, 45*, 487–516.

Marler, P. (1991). Song-learning behavior: The interface with neuroethology. *Trends in Neurosciences, 14*, 199–205.

Marshall, E. (1994). Highs and lows on the research roller coaster. *Science, 264*, 1693–1695.

Marshall, F. H. A. (1936). Sexual periodicity and the causes which determine it. *Philosophical Transactions, 226B*, 423–456.

Martin, M. B., Owen, C. M., & Morisha, J. M. (1987). An overview of neurotansmitters and neuroreceptors. In R. E. Hales & S. C. Yudofsky (Eds.), *Textbook of neuropsychiatry* (pp. 55–88). Washington, DC: American Psychiatric Press.

Martin, P. (1984). The time and energy costs of play behaviour in the cat. *Zeitschrift für Tierpsychologie, 64*, 298–312.

Martin, P., & Bateson, P. (1986). *Measuring behaviour: An introductory guide*. Cambridge: Cambridge University Press.

Martin, P., & Caro, T. M. (1985). On the functions of play and its role in behavioral development. *Advances in the Study of Behavior, 15*, 59–103.

Mason, W. A., & Capitanio, J. P. (1988). Formation and expression of filial attachment in rhesus monkeys raised with living and inanimate mother substitutes. *Developmental Psychobiology, 21*, 401–430.

Mason, W. A., & Kenny, W. D. (1974). Redirection of filial attachments in rhesus monkeys: Dogs as mother surrogates. *Science, 183*, 1209–1211.

Matsuzaka, Y., Aizawa, H., & Tanji, J. (1992). A motor area rostral to the supplementary motor area (presupplementary motor area) in the monkey: Neuronal activity during a learned motor task. *Journal of Neurophysiology, 68*, 653–662.

Maynard Smith, J. (1964). Group selection and kin selection. *Nature, 210*, 1145–1147.

Maynard Smith, J. (1977). Parental investment: A prospective analysis. *Animal Behaviour, 29*, 1–9.

Maynard Smith, J. (1982). *Evolution and the theory of games.* Cambridge: Cambridge University Press.

Mayr, E. (1963). *Animal species and evolution.* Cambridge: Harvard University Press.

Mayr, E. (1964). *Systematics and the origin of species from the viewpoint of a zoologist.* New York: Dover. (original work published 1942)

Mayr, E. (1969). Footnotes on the philosophy of biology. *Philosophy of Science, 36*, 197–202.

Mayr, E. (1970). *Populations, species, and evolution.* Cambridge: Harvard University Press.

Mayr, E. (1982). *The growth of biological thought: Diversity, evolution, and inheritance.* Cambridge: Harvard University Press.

Mayr, E. (1984). Typological versus population thinking. In E. Sober (Ed.), *Conceptual issues in evolutionary biology* (pp. 14–17). Cambridge: MIT Press.

Mayr, E., & Provine, W. B. (Eds.). (1980). *The evolutionary synthesis: Perspectives on the unification of biology.* Cambridge: Harvard University Press.

Mazzocchi, D., & Vignolo, L. A. (1979). Localisation of lesions in aphasia: Clinical-CT correlations in stroke patients. *Cortex, 15*, 627–654.

McConnell, S. K. (1991). The generation of neuronal diversity in the central nervous system. *Annual Review of Neuroscience, 14*, 269–300.

McDonnell, P. M. (1979). Patterns of eye hand coordination in the first year of life. *Canadian Journal of Psychology, 33*, 253–267.

McDougall, W. (1973). *An introduction to social psychology.* Kennebunkport, ME: Milford House. (Original work published 1926)

McGinnis, W., & Kuziora, M. (1994). The molecular architects of body design. *Scientific American, 270*, 58–64.

McGraw, M. B. (1946). Maturation of behavior. In L. Carmichael (Ed.) *Manual of child psychology* (pp. 332–369). New York: Wiley.

Mead, M. (1928). *Coming of age in Somoa.* New York: William Morrow.

Meisami, E. (1976). Effects of olfactory deprivation on postnatal growth of the rat olfactory bulb utilizing a new method for production of neonatal unilateral anosmia. *Brain Research, 107*, 437–444.

Merigan, W. H. (1993). Human V4? *Current Biology, 3*, 226–229.

Merzenich, M. M., Nelson, R. J., Stryker, M. P., Cynder, M. S., Shoppmann, A., & Zook, J. M. (1984). Somatosensory cortical map changes following digit amputation in adult monkeys. *Journal of Comparative Neurology, 224*, 591–605.

Merzenich, M. M., Recanzone, G. H., Jenkins, W. M., & Nudo, R. J. (1990). How the brain functionally rewires itself. In M. Arbib & J. Robinson (Eds.), *Natural and artificial parallel computations* (pp. 177–210). Cambridge: MIT Press.

Michel, G. F. (1981). Right-handedness: A consequence of infant supine head orientation preference? *Science, 212*, 685–687.

Michel, G. F. (1983). Development of hand-use preference during infancy. In G. Young, S. Segalowitz, C. Corter, & S. Trehub (Eds.), *Manual specialization and the developing brain* (pp. 33–70). New York: Academic Press.

Michel, G. F. (1986). Experiential influences on hormonally dependent ring dove parental care. *Annals of the New York Academy of Sciences, 474*, 158–169.

Michel, G. F. (1987). Self-generated experience and the development of lateralized neurobehavioral organization in infants. *Advances in the Study of Behavior, 17*, 61–83.

Michel, G. F. (1991a). Development of infant manual skills: Motor programs, schemata, or dynamic systems? In J. Fagard & P. H. Wolff (Eds.), *The development of timing control and temporal organization in coordinated action* (pp. 175–199). New York: Elsevier.

Michel, G. F. (1991b). Human psychology and the minds of other animals. In C. A. Ristau (Ed.), *Cognitive ethology: The minds of other animals* (pp. 253–272). Hillsdale, NJ: Erlbaum.

Michel, G. F. (1994). *Infant manual skills: A developmental psychobiological perspective.* Keynote lecture for XIIIth Biennial Meeting of the International Society for the Study of Behavioral Development, June 28–July 2, Amsterdam, The Netherlands.

Michel, G. F., & Goodwin, R. (1979). Intrauterine birth position predicts newborn supine head position preference. *Infant Behavior and Development, 2,* 29–38.

Michel, G. F., & Moore, C. L. (1978). *Biological perspectives in developmental psychology.* Monterey, CA: Brooks/Cole.

Michelsen, A. (1993). The transfer of information in the dance language of honeybees: Progress and problems. *Journal of Comparative Physiology A, 173,* 135–141.

Milkman, R. (1982). Toward a unified selection theory. In R. Milkman (Ed.), *Perspectives on evolution* (pp. 105–118). Sunderland, MA: Sinauer.

Mill, J. S. (1843/1973). *A system of logic.* Toronto: University of Toronto Press.

Miller, D. B. (1981). Conceptual strategies in behavioral development: Normal development and plasticity. In K. Immelmann, G. W. Barlow, L. Petrinovich, & M. Main (Eds.), *Behavioral development* (pp. 58–82). Cambridge: Cambridge University Press.

Miller, J. G., & Miller, J. L. (1992). Cybernetics, general systems theory, and living systems theory. In R. L. Levin & H. E. Fitzgerald (Eds.), *Analysis of dynamic psychological systems. Vol. 1. Basic approach to general systems, dynamic systems, and cybernetics* (pp. 9–34). New York: Plenum Press.

Millikan, R. G. (1984). *Language, thought, and other biological categories.* Cambridge: MIT Press.

Milne, L. J., & Milne, M. (1976). The social behavior of burying beetles. *Scientific American, 232,* 84–89.

Mitchell, S. D. (1992). On pluralism and competition in evolutionary explanations. *American Zoologist, 32,* 135–144.

Miyadi, D. (1964). Social life of Japanese monkeys. *Science, 143,* 783–786.

Moerk, E. L. (1989). The LAD was a lady and the tasks were ill-defined. *Developmental Review, 9,* 21–57.

Moltz, H. (1965). Contemporary instinct theory and the fixed action pattern. *Psychology Review, 72,* 27–47.

Moltz, H., & Stettner, L. J. (1961). The influence of patterned light deprivation on the critical period of imprinting. *Journal of Comparative and Physiological Psychology, 54,* 279–283.

Money, J., & Ehrhardt, A. A. (1972). *Man and woman, boy and girl.* Baltimore: Johns Hopkins University Press.

Moore, C. L. (1984). Maternal contributions to the development of masculine sexual behavior in laboratory rats. *Developmental Psychobiology, 17,* 346–356.

Moore, C. L. (1985). Another psychobiological view of sexual differentiation. *Developmental Review, 5,* 18–55.

Moore, C. L. (1990). Comparative development of vertebrate sexual behavior: Levels, cascades, and webs. In D. A. Dewsbury (Ed.), *Contemporary issues in comparative psychology* (pp. 278–299). Sunderland, MA: Sinauer.

Moore, C. L. (1992). The role of maternal stimulation in the development of sexual behavior and its neural basis. *Annals of the New York Academy of Sciences, 662,* 160–177.

Moore, C. L., & Chadwick-Dias, A.-M. (1986). Behavioral responses of infant rats to maternal licking: Variations with age and sex. *Developmental Psychobiology, 19,* 427–438.

Moore, C. L., Dou, H., & Juraska, J. M. (1992). Maternal stimulation affects the number of motor neurons in a sexually dimorphic nucleus of the lumbar spinal cord. *Brain Research, 572,* 52–56.

Moore, D. J., & Shiek, D. A. (1971). Toward a theory of early infantile autism. *Psychological Review, 78,* 451–456.

Moran, G. A., & Fentress, J. C. (1979). A search for order in wolf social behavior. In E. Klinghammer (Ed.), *The behavior and ecology of wolves* (pp. 245–283). New York: Garland Press.

Morgan, J. I., & Curran, T. (1991). Stimulus-transcription coupling in the nervous system: Involvement of the inducible protooncogenes *fos* and *jun. Annual Review of Neuroscience, 14,* 421–451.

Morris, S. C. (1977). A new metazoan from the Cambrian Burgess shale, British Columbia. *Palaeontology, 20,* 623–640.

Murakami, F., Song, W.-J., & Katsumaru, H. (1992). Plasticity of neuronal connections in developing brains of mammals. *Neuroscience Research, 15,* 235–253.

Myers, M. M. (1991). Identifying relationships between early life experiences and adult traits. In H. N. Shair, G. A. Barr, & M. A. Hofer (Eds.), *Developmental psychobiology: New methods and changing concepts* (pp. 5–18). New York: Oxford University Press.

Myers, M. M., Brunelli, S. A., Squire, J. M., Shindledecker, R. D., & Hofer, M. A. (1989). Maternal behavior of SHR rats and its relationship to offspring blood pressures. *Developmental Psychobiology, 22*, 29–53.

Napier, J. R. (1956). The prehensile movements of the human hand. *Journal of Bone and Joint Surgery, 38b*, 902–913.

Napier, J. R. (1976). *The human hand.* Carolina Biological Readers, No. 61. Burlington, NC: Carolina Biological Supply Co.

Narayanan, C. H., & Malloy, R. B. (1974). Deafferentation studies on motor activity in the chick. I. Activity patterns of hindlimbs. *Journal of Experimental Zoology, 189*, 163–176.

Nash, J. (1978). *Developmental psychology: A psychobiological approach* (2nd ed.). Englewood Cliffs, N. J.: Prentice-Hall.

Nelson, G. J. (1970). Outline of a theory of comparative biology. *Systematic Zoology, 19*, 373–384.

Nestler, E. J., & Duman, R. S. (1994). G proteins and cyclic nucleotides in the nervous system. In G. J. Siegel, B. W. Agranoff, R. W. Albers, & P. B. Molinoff (Eds.), *Basic neurochemistry: Molecular, cellular, and medical aspects* (5th ed., pp. 429–448). New York: Raven Press.

Nestler, E. J., & Greengard, P. (1994). Protein phosphorylation and the regulation of neuronal function. In G. J. Siegel, B. W. Agranoff, R. W. Albers, & P. B. Molinoff (Eds.), *Basic neurochemistry: Molecular, cellular, and medical aspects* (5th ed., pp. 449–474). New York: Raven Press.

Newell, K. M. (1991). Motor skill acquisition. *Annual Review of Psychology, 42*, 213–237.

Newell, K. M., Scully, D. M., McDonald, P. V., & Baillargeon, R. (1989). Task constraints and infant grip configurations. *Developmental Psychobiology, 22*, 817–832.

Newell, K. M., & van Emmerik, R. E. A. (1990). Are Gesell's developmental principles general principles for the acquisition of coordination? In J. E. Clark & J. H. Humphrey (Eds.), *Advances in motor development research.* (Vol. 3, pp. 143–164). New York: AMS Press.

Newport, E. L. (1991). Contrasting concepts of the critical period for language. In S. Carey & R. Gelman (Eds.), *The epigenesis of mind*: Essays on biology and cognition (pp. 111–131). Hillsdale, NJ: Erlbaum.

Newton, B. W., & Hamill, R. W. (1989). Target regulation of the serotonin and substance P innervation of the sexually dimorphic cremaster nucleus. *Brain Research, 485*, 149–156.

Nijhout, H. F. (1990). Metaphors and the role of genes in development. *BioEssays, 12*, 441–446.

Noirot, E. (1972). Ultrasounds and maternal behaviour in small rodents. *Developmental Psychobiology, 5*, 371–387.

Nottebohm, F. (1981). A brain for all seasons: Cyclical anatomical changes in song-control nuclei of the canary brain. *Science, 214*, 1368–1370.

Nottebohm, F. (1991). Reassessing the mechanisms and origins of vocal learning in birds. *Trends in Neuroscience, 14*, 206–210.

Novak, M. A., & Harlow, H. F. (1975). Social recovery of monkeys isolated for the first year of life. 1. Rehabilitation and therapy. *Developmental Psychology, 11*, 453–465.

Nowicki, S., Westneat, M., & Hoese, W. (1992). Birdsong: Motor function and the evolution of communication. *Neurosciences, 4*, 385–390.

Nudo, R. J., Jenkins, W. M., Merzenich, M. M., Prejean, T., & Grenda, R. (1992). Neurophysiological correlates of hand preference in primary motor cortex of adult squirrel monkeys. *Journal of Neuroscience, 12*, 2918–2947.

Odling-Smee, F. J. (1988). Niche-constructing phenotypes. In H. C. Plotkin (Ed.), *The role of behavior in evolution* (pp. 73–132). Cambridge: MIT Press.

Okado, N., & Oppenheim, R. W. (1984). Cell death of motoneurons in the chick embryo spinal cord. IX. The loss of motoneurons following removal of afferent inputs. *Journal of Neuroscience, 4*, 1639–1652.

O'Leary, D. D. M. (1989). Do cortical areas emerge from a protocortex? *Trends in Neuroscience, 12*, 400–406.

Oller, D. K. & Eilers, R. E. (1988). The role of audition in infant babbling. *Child Development, 59*, 441–449.

Olson, D. R. (1993). The development of representations: The origins of mental life. *Canadian Journal of Psychology, 34,* 293–306.

Oppenheim, R. W. (1970). Some aspects of embryonic behaviour in the duck (*Anas platyrhynchos*). *Animal Behaviour, 18,* 335–352.

Oppenheim, R. W. (1972). Experimental studies on hatching behavior in the chick. III. The role of the midbrain and forebrain. *Journal of Comparative Neurology, 146,* 479–505.

Oppenheim, R. W. (1973). Prehatching and hatching behavior: A comparative and physiological consideration. In G. Gottlieb (Ed.), *Behavioral embryology: Studies on the development of behavior and the nervous system* (Vol. 1, pp. 163–244). New York: Academic Press.

Oppenheim, R. W. (1975). The role of supraspinal input in embryonic motility: A re-examination in the chick. *Journal of Comparative Neurology, 160,* 37–50.

Oppenheim, R. W. (1981a). Neuronal cell death and some related regressive phenomena during neurogenesis: A selective historical review and progress report. In W. M. Cowan (Ed.), *Studies in developmental neurobiology: Essays in honor of Viktor Hamburger* (pp. 74–133). New York: Oxford University Press.

Oppenheim, R. W. (1981b). Ontogenetic adaptations and retrogressive processes in the development of the nervous system and behaviour: A neuroembryological perspective. In K. J. Connolly & H. F. R. Prechtl (Eds.), *Maturation and development: Biological and psychological perspectives* (pp. 73–109). Philadelphia: Lippincott.

Oppenheim, R. W. (1982a). Preformation and epigenesis in the origins of the nervous system and behavior: Issues, concepts, and their history. In P. P. G. Bateson & P. Klopfer (Eds.), *Perspectives in ethology* (Vol. 5, pp. 1–100). New York: Plenum Press.

Oppenheim, R. W. (1982b). The neuroembryological study of behavior: Progress, problems, prospectives. *Current Topics in Developmental Biology, 17,* 257–309.

Oppenheim, R. W. (1984). Ontogenetic adaptations in neural and behavioural development: Toward a more "ecological" developmental psychobiology. In H. F. R. Prechtl (Ed.), *Continuity of neural functions from prenatal to postnatal life* (pp. 16–29). Philadelphia: Lippincott.

Oppenheim, R. W. (1991). Cell death during development of the nervous system. *Annual Review of Neuroscience, 14,* 453–501.

Oppenheim, R. W., & Haverkamp, L. (1986). In E. M. Blass (Ed.), *Handbook of behavioral neurobiology. Vol. 8. Developmental psychobiology and developmental neurobiology* (pp. 1–33). New York: Plenum Press.

Oppenheim, R. W., & Nunez, R. (1982). Electrical stimulation of hindlimb increases neuronal cell death in chick embryo. *Nature, 295,* 57–59.

Oppenheim, R. W., Pittman, R., Gray, M., & Maderdrut, H. K. (1978). Embryonic behavior, hatching and neuromuscular development in the chick following a transient reduction of spontaneous motility and sensory input by neuromuscular blocking agent. *Journal of Comparative Neurology, 179,* 619–640.

Orions, G. H. (1969). On the evolution of mating systems in birds and mammals. *American Naturalist, 103,* 589–603.

Osherson, D. N., & Lasnik, H. (1990). The study of cognition. In D. N. Osherson & H. Lasnik (Eds.), *An invitation to cognitive science. Vol. 1. Language* (pp. xi–xix). Cambridge: MIT Press.

Oyama, S. (1985). *The ontogeny of information: Developmental systems and evolution.* Cambridge: Cambridge University Press.

Oyama, S. (1989). Innate selfishness, innate sociality. *Behavioral and Brain Sciences, 12,* 717–718.

Oyama, S. (1991). Bodies and minds: Dualism in evolutionary theory. *Journal of Social Issues, 47,* 27–42.

Page, R. E., Jr., & Mitchell, S. D. (1991). Self-organization and adaptation in insect societies. In A. Fine, M. Forbes, & L. Wessels (Eds.), *PSA 1900* (Vol. 2, pp. 289–298). New York: Philosophy of Science Association.

Palka, J. (1982). Genetic manipulation of sensory pathways in *Drosophila*. In N. C. Spitzer (Ed.), *Neuronal development* (pp. 121–170). New York: Plenum Press.

Paterson, H. E. H. (1985). The recognition concept of species. In E. S. Vrba (Ed.), *Species and speciation. Transvaal Museum Monographs, 4,* 21–29.

Patten, B. C. (1982). Environs: Relativistic elementary particles for ecology. *American Naturalist, 119*, 179–219.

Patten, B. C., & Auble, G. T. (1981). System theory of the ecological niche. *American Naturalist, 117*, 893–922.

Patterson, P. H. (1978). Environmental determination of autonomic neurotransmitter functions. *Annual Review of Neuroscience, 1*, 1–17.

Patterson, P. H. (1992). Process outgrowth and the specificity of connections. In Z. W. Hall (Ed.), *An introduction to molecular neurobiology* (pp. 388–427). Sunderland, MA: Sinauer.

Pedersen, P. E., & Blass, E. M. (1981). Olfactory control over suckling in albino rats. In R. N. Aslin, J. R. Alberts, & M. R. Petersen (Eds.), *Development of perception. Vol. 1. Audition, somatic perception, and the chemical senses* (pp. 359–381). New York: Academic Press.

Pedersen, P. E., Williams, C. L., & Blass, E. M. (1982). Activation and odor conditioning of suckling behavior in 3-day-old albino rats. *Journal of Experimental Psychology: Animal Behavior Processes, 8*, 329–341.

Peiper, A. (1963). *Cerebral function in infancy and childhood.* New York: The International Behavioral Sciences Series.

Petrinovich, L. (1988). The role of social factors in white-crowned sparrow song development. In T. R. Zentall & B. G. Galef, Jr. (Eds.), *Social learning* (pp. 255–278). Hillsdale, NJ: Erlbaum.

Pfister, J. F., Cramer, C. P., & Blass, E. M. (1986). Suckling in rats extended by continuous living with dams and the preweanling litters. *Animal Behaviour, 34*, 415–420.

Phifer, C. B., Ladd, M. D., & W. G. Hall (1991). Effects of hydrational state on ingestion in infant rats: Is dehydration the only ingestive stimulus? *Physiology and Behavior, 49*, 695–699.

Phoenix, C. H., Goy, R. W., Gerall, A. A., & Young, W. C. (1959). Organizing action of prenatally administered testosterone propionate on the tissues mediating mating behavior in the female guinea pig. *Endocrinology, 65*, 369–382.

Piaget, J. (1952). *The origins of intelligence in children.* New York: International Universities Press.

Piaget, J. (1978). *Behavior and evolution.* New York: Pantheon Books.

Pinker, S. (1984). *Language learnability and language development.* Cambridge: Harvard University Press.

Pinker, S. (1990). Language acquisition. In D. N. Osherson & H. Lasnik (Eds.), *Language: An invitation to cognitive science* (pp. 199–242). Cambridge: MIT Press.

Pittendrigh, C. S. (1958). Adaptation, natural selection, and behavior. In A. Roe & G. G. Simpson (Eds.), *Behavior and evolution* (pp. 390–416). New Haven, CT: Yale University Press.

Pittman, R., & Oppenheim, R. W. (1978). Neuromuscular blockade increases motoneuron survival during normal cell death in the chick embryo. *Nature, 271*, 364–366.

Pittman, R., & Oppenheim, R. W. (1979). Cell death of motoneurons in chick embryo spinal cord. IV. Evidence that a functional neuromuscular interaction is involved in the regulation of naturally occurring cell death and the stabilization of synapses. *Journal of Comparative Neurology, 187*, 425–446.

Platt, S. A., & Sanislow, C. A. III. (1988). Norm-of-reaction: Definition and misinterpretation of animal research. *Journal of Comparative Psychology, 102*, 254–261.

Plomin, R. (1990). The role of inheritance in behavior. *Science, 248*, 183–188.

Plomin, R., & Daniels, D. (1987). Why are children in the same family so different from one another? *Behavioral and Brain Sciences, 10*, 1–60.

Plomin, R., DeFries, J. C., & Fulker, D. W. (1988). *Nature and nurture during infancy and early childhood.* New York: Cambridge University Press.

Plomin, R., DeFries, J. C., & McClearn, G. E. (1990). *Behavioral genetics: A primer* (2nd ed.). New York: Freeman.

Plomin, R., Owen, M. J., & McGuffin, P. (1994). The genetic basis of complex human behaviors. *Science, 264*, 1733–1739.

Plotnikoff, N. P. (1987). Psychoneuroimmunology, new approaches to neurobehavioral testing. *Neurotoxicology and Teratology, 9*, 465–471.

Plunkett, K., & Sinha, C. (1992). Connectionism and developmental theory. *British Journal of Developmental Psychology, 10,* 209–254.

Potter, D. D., Landis, S. C., & Furshpan, E. J. (1980). Dual function during development of rat sympathetic neurones in culture. *Journal of Experimental Biology, 89,* 57–71.

Prechtl, H. F. R. (1965). Problems of behavioral studies in the newborn infant. In D. S. Lehrman, R. A. Hinde, & E. Shaw (Eds.), *Advances in the study of behavior* (Vol. 1, pp. 75–98). New York: Academic Press.

Prechtl, H. F. R. (1981). The study of neural development as a perspective on clinical problems. In K. J. Connolly & H. F. R. Prechtl (Eds.), *Maturation and development: Biological and psychological perspectives* (pp. 198–215). Philadelphia: Lippincott.

Prechtl, H. F. R. (1982). Regressions and transformations during neurological development. In T. G. Bever (Ed.), *Regressions in mental development* (pp. 103–118). Hillsdale, NJ: Erlbaum.

Prechtl, H. F. R. (1983). Assessment methods for the newborn infant: A critical evaluation. In P. Stratton (Ed.), *Psychology of the human newborn* (pp. 21–52). New York: Wiley.

Prechtl, H. F. R. (1984). Motor behaviour of preterm infants. In H. F. R. Prechtl (Ed.), *Continuity of neural functions from prenatal to postnatal life* (pp. 79–93). Philadelphia: Lippincott.

Prechtl, H. F. R. (1986). Prenatal motor development. In M. G. Wade & H. T. A. Whiting (Eds.), *Motor development in children: Aspects of coordination and control* (pp. 53–64). Dordrecht, The Netherlands: Martinus Nijhoff.

Prechtl, H. F. R., & Nolte, R. (1984). Motor behavior of preterm infants. In H. F. R. Prechtl (Ed.), *Continuity of neural functions from prenatal to postnatal life* (pp. 79–92). Philadelphia: Lippincott.

Previc, F. H. (1991). A general theory concerning the prenatal origins of cerebral lateralization in humans. *Psychological Review, 98,* 299–334.

Priestnall, R. (1973). Effects of handling on maternal behaviour in the mouse (*Mus musculus*): An observational study. *Animal Behaviour, 21,* 383–386.

Prigogine, I., & Stengers, I. (1984). *Order out of chaos: Man's new dialogue with nature.* New York: Bantam Books.

Provine, R. R. (1986). Behavioral neuroembryology: Motor perspectives. In W. T. Greenough & J. M. Juraska (Eds.), *Developmental neuropsychobiology* (pp. 213–239). Orlando: Academic Press.

Provine, R. R. (1988). On the uniqueness of embryos and the difference it makes. In W. P. Smotherman & S. C. Robinson (Eds.), *Behavior of the fetus* (pp. 35–46). Caldwell, NJ: Telford Press.

Purves, D. (1988). *Body and brain: A trophic theory of neural connections.* Cambridge: Harvard University Press.

Purves, D., & Lichtman, J. W. (1985). *Principles of neural development.* Sunderland, MA: Sinauer.

Purves, D., Riddle, D. R., & LaMantia, A. S. (1992). Iterated patterns of brain circuitry (or how the cortex gets its spots). *Trends in Neurosciences, 15,* 362–367.

Purves, D., Riddle, D., & LaMantia, A. (1993). Reply. *Trends in Neuroscience, 16,* 180–181.

Quinn, K., & Geffen, G. (1986). The development of tactile transfer of information. *Neuropsychologia, 24,* 793–804.

Raff, R. A., & Kaufman, T. C. (1983). *Embryos, genes, and evolution: The developmental-genetic basis of evolutionary change.* New York: Macmillan.

Raff, R. A., & Raff, E. C. (Eds). (1987). *Development as an evolutionary process.* New York: Liss.

Rakic, P. (1971). Guidance of neurons migrating to the fetal monkey neocortex. *Brain Research, 33,* 471–476.

Rakic, P. (1978). Neuronal migration and contact guidance in the primate telencephalon. *Postgraduate Medical Journal, 54,* 23–37.

Rakic, P. (1981). Neuronal-glial interaction during brain development. *Trends in Neuroscience, 4,* 184–187.

Ramón y Cajal, S. (1894/1990). *New ideas on the stucture of the nervous system in man and vertebrates* (N. Swanson & L. W. Swanson, Trans.). Cambridge: MIT Press.

Ramsay, D. S., Campos, J. J., & Fenson, L. (1979). Onset of bimanual handedness in infants. *Infant Behavior and Development, 2,* 69–76.

Rand, M. N., & Breedlove, S. M. (1988). Progress report on a hormonally sensitive neuromuscular system. *Psychobiology, 16,* 398–405.

Rauschecker, J. P., & Marler, P., Eds. (1987). *Imprinting and cortical plasticity.* New York: Wiley.

Read, A. F., & Weary, D. M. (1992). The evolution of birdsong: Comparative analyses. *Philosophical Transactions of the Royal Society of London [B], 338,* 165–187.

Reid, R. G. B. (1985). *Evolutionary theory: The unfinished synthesis.* Ithaca, NY: Cornell University Press.

Rennie, J. (1993). DNA's new twists. *Scientific American, 266,* 122–132.

Ressler, R. H. (1962). Parental handling in two strains of mice reared by foster parents. *Science, 137,* 129–130.

Ressler, R. H. (1963). Genotype-correlated parental influences in two strains of mice. *Journal of Comparative and Physiological Psychology, 56,* 882–886.

Ressler, R. H. (1966). Inherited environmental influences on the operant behavior of mice. *Journal of Comparative and Physiological Psychology, 61,* 264–267.

Richards, M. P. M. (1974). First steps in becoming social. In M. P. M. Richards (Ed.), *The integration of a child into a social world.* London: Cambridge University Press.

Richards, M. P. M., & Bernal, J. F. (1972). An observational study of mother-infant interaction. In N. Blurton Jones (Ed.), *Ethological studies of child behaviour* (pp. 175–197). London: Cambridge University Press.

Richter, J. D. (1993). Translational control in development: A perspective. *Developmental Genetics, 14,* 407–411.

Ringler, N. M., Kennell, J. H., Jarvella, R., Navojosky, B. J., & Klaus, M. H. (1974). Mother-to-child speech at two years—Effects of early postnatal contact. *Journal of Pediatrics, 86,* 141–144.

Ristau, C. A. (1991). Cognitive ethology: An overview. In C. A. Ristau (Ed.), *Cognitive ethology: The minds of other animals* (pp. 291–312). Hillsdale, NJ: Erlbaum.

Robinson, S. R., & Smotherman, W. P. (1992). Fundamental motor patterns of the mammalian fetus. *Journal of Neurobiology, 23,* 1574–1600.

Roschelle, J., & Clancey, W. J. (1992). Learning as social and neural. *Educational Psychologist, 27,* 435–454.

Rosen, K. M., McCormack, M. A., Villa-Komaroff, L., & Mower, G. D. (1992). Brief visual experience induces immediate early gene expression in the cat visual cortex. *Proceedings of the National Academy of Sciences U.S.A., 89,* 5437–5441.

Rosenblatt, J. S. (1970). Views on the onset and maintenance of maternal behavior in the rat. In L. R. Aronson, E. Tobach, D. S. Lehrman, & J. S. Rosenblatt (Eds.), *Development and evolution of behavior* (pp. 489–515). San Francisco: Freeman.

Rosenblatt, J. S. (1976). Stages in the early behavioral development of altricial young of selected species of non-primate mammals. In P. P. G. Bateson & R. A. Hinde (Eds.), *Growing points in ethology* (pp. 345–383). Cambridge: Cambridge University Press.

Rosenblatt, J. S., & Siegel, H. I. (1981). Factors governing the onset and maintenance of maternal behavior among nonprimate mammals: The role of hormonal and nonhormonal factors. In D. J. Gubernick & P. H. Klopfer (Eds.), *Parental care in mammals* (pp. 13–76). New York: Plenum Press.

Rosenblum, L. A., & Kaufman, I. C. (1968). Variations in infant development and response to maternal loss in monkeys. *American Journal of Orthopsychiatry, 38,* 418–426.

Rosenblum, L. A., & Moltz, H. (Eds.). (1983). *Symbiosis in parent-offspring interactions.* New York: Plenum Press.

Ross, E. M. (1992). G proteins and receptors in neuronal signaling. In Z. W. Hall (Ed.), *An introduction to molecular neurobiology* (pp. 181–206). Sunderland, MA: Sinauer.

Rosser, R. (1994). *Cognitive development: Psychological and biological perspectives.* Needham Heights, MA: Allyn & Bacon.

Rovee-Collier, C., & Hayne, H. (1987). Reactivation of infant memory: Implications for cognitive development. *Advances in Child Development and Behavior, 20,* 185–238.

Rowan, W. (1931). *The riddle of migration.* Baltimore: Williams & Wilkins.

Rowell, T. E. (1966). Hierarchy in the organization of a captive baboon group. *Animal Behaviour, 14*, 430–443.

Rowell, T. E. (1972). *Social behaviour of monkeys*: Middlesex, England: Penguin Books.

Rowell, T. E. (1991). What can we say about social structure? In P. Bateson (Ed.), *The development and integration of behaviour: Essays in honour of Robert Hinde* (pp. 255–270). Cambridge: Cambridge University Press.

Ruff, H. A., & Halton, A. (1978). Is there directed reaching in the human neonate? *Developmental Psychology, 14*, 425–426.

Ruit, K. G., & Snider, W. D. (1991). Administration or deprivation of nerve growth factor during development permanently alters neuronal geometry. *Journal of Comparative Neurology, 314*, 106–113.

Rumelhart, D. E., & McClelland, J. L. (Eds.). (1986a). *Parallel distributed processing: Explorations in the microstructure of cognition* (Vols. 1 and 2). Cambridge: MIT Press.

Rumelhart, D. E., & McClelland, J. L. (1986b). P.D.P. models and general issues in cognitive science. In D. E. Rumelhart & J. L. McClelland (Eds.), *Parallel distributed processing: Explorations in the microstructure of cognition. (Vol. 1). Foundations* (pp. 110–145). Cambridge: MIT Press.

Ryan, J. (1972). IQ—The illusion of objectivity. In K. Richardson & D. Spears (Eds.), *Race and intelligence* (pp. 36–55). Baltimore: Penguin Books.

Sachs, B. D. (1982). Role of the rat's striated penile muscles in penile reflexes, copulation and induction of pregnancy. *Journal of Reproduction and Fertility, 66*, 433–443.

Salamy, A. (1978). Commissural transmission: Maturational changes in humans. *Science, 200*, 1409–1411.

Salk, L. (1962). Mother's heart beat as an imprinting stimulus. *Transactions of the New York Academy of Sciences, 24*, 753–763.

Salk, L. (1973). The role of the heart beat in the relations between mother and infant. *Scientific American, 228*, 24–29.

Sameroff, A. J. (1983). Developmental systems: Contexts and evolution. In W. Kessen (Ed.), *Handbook of child psychology. Vol. 1. History, theory, and methods* (pp. 237–294). New York: Wiley.

Sander, L. W. (1970). Regulation and organization in the early infant-caretaker system. In R. J. Robinson (Ed.), *Brain and early behavior* (pp. 311–333). New York: Academic Press.

Saunders, S. R. (1985). The inheritance of acquired characters: A concept that will not die. In L. R. Godfrey (Ed.), *What Darwin began* (pp. 148–161). Boston: Allyn & Bacon.

Scarr, S. & Kidd, K. K. (1983). Developmental behavior genetics. In M. M. Haith & J. J. Campos (Eds.) *Handbook of child psychology Vol. 2. Infancy and developmental psychobiology* (4th ed., pp. 345–434). New York: Wiley.

Scarr-Salapatek, S. (1976). Genetic determinants of infant development: An overstated case. In L. Lipsitt (Ed.), *Developmental psychobiology: The significance of infancy* (pp. 59–79). Hillsdale, NJ: Erlbaum.

Schanberg, S. M., & Field, T. M. (1987). Sensory deprivation, stress and supplemental stimulation in the rat pup and preterm human neonate. *Child Development, 58*, 1431–1447.

Schiff, M., & Lewontin, R. (1986). *Education and class*. Oxford: Clarendon Press.

Schiller, C. H. (Ed.). (1957). *Instinctive behavior: The development of a modern concept*. New York: International Universities Press.

Schilling, K., Curran, T., & Morgan, J. I. (1991). Fosvergnügen: The excitement of immediate-early genes. *Annals of the New York Academy of Sciences, 627*, 115–123.

Schlesinger, I. M. (1988). The origin of relational categories. In Y. Levy, I. M. Schlesinger, & M. D. S. Braine (Eds.), *Categories and processes in language acquisition* (pp. 15–51). Hillsdale, NJ: Erlbaum.

Schmidt-Nielsen, K. (1990). *Animal physiology: Adaptation and environment* (4th ed.). Cambridge: Cambridge University Press.

Schneirla, T. C. (1949). Levels in the psychological capacities of animals. In R. W. Sellars, V. J. McGill, & M. Farber (Eds.), *Philosophy for the future* (pp. 243–286). New York: Macmillan.

Schneirla, T. C. (1957). The concept of development in comparative psychology. In D. B. Harris (Ed.), *The concept of development* (pp. 78–108). Minneapolis: University of Minnesota Press.

Schneirla, T. C. (1962). Psychological comparison of insect and mammal. *Psychologische Beitrage, 6,* 509–520.

Schneirla, T. C. (1966). Behavioral development and comparative psychology. *Quarterly Review of Biology, 41,* 283–302.

Schneirla, T. C. (1971). *Army ants: A study in social organization.* H. R. Topoff (Ed.). San Francisco: Freeman.

Schneirla, T. C., & Rosenblatt, J. S. (1963). "Critical periods" in the development of behavior. *Science, 139,* 1110–1115.

Schulte, F. J. (1974). Neurological development of the neonate. In J. A. Davis & J. Dobbing (Eds.), *Scientific foundations of paediatrics* (pp. 587–614). Philadelphia: Saunders.

Schwagmeyer, P. L. (1990). Ground squirrel reproductive behavior and mating competition: A comparative perspective. In D. A. Dewsbury (Ed.), *Contemporary issues in comparative psychology* (pp. 175–196). Sunderland, MA: Sinauer.

Schwartz, C., & Michel, G. (1992). Posture and head orientation direction affect patterns of manual coordination in 11–25 hour old human neonates. *Infant Behavior and Development, 15,* 686.

Scott, J. P. (1962). Critical periods in behavioral development. *Science, 138,* 949–958.

Searle, J. B. (1992). When is a species not a species? *Current Biology, 2,* 407–409.

Seeback, B. S., Intrator, N., Lieberman, P., & Cooper, L. N. (1994). A model of prenatal acquisition of speech parameters. *Proceedings of the National Academy of Sciences, 91,* 7473–7476.

Segalowitz, S. J., & Rose-Krasnor, L. (1992). The construct of brain maturation in theories of child development. *Brain and Cognition, 20,* 1–7.

Seligman, M. E. P. (1970). On the generality of the laws of learning. *Psychological Review, 77,* 406–418.

Shair, H. N., Barr, G. A., & Hofer, M. A. (Eds.). (1991). *Developmental psychobiology: New methods and changing concepts.* New York: Oxford University Press.

Shair, H. N., Brake, S. C., Hofer, M. A., & Myers, M. M. (1986). Blood pressure responses to milk ejection in the young rat. *Physiology and Behavior, 37,* 171–176.

Shapiro, D. Y. (1983). Distinguishing behavioral interactions from visual cues as causes of adult sex change in a coral reef fish. *Hormones and Behavior, 17,* 424–432.

Shatz, M. (1981). On mechanisms of language acquisition: Can features of the communication environment account for development? In L. Gleitman & E. Wanner (Eds.) *Language acquisition: The state of the art* (pp. 102–130). Cambridge: Cambridge University Press.

Shaw, E. (1970). Schooling in fishes: Critique and review. In In L. R. Aronson, E. Tobach, D. S. Lehrman, & J. S. Rosenblatt (Eds.), *Development and evolution of behavior* (pp. 452–480). San Francisco: Freeman.

Shirley, M. M. (1933). *The first two years: A study of twenty-five babies. Vol. 2. Intellectual development.* Minneapolis: University of Minnesota Press.

Siegler, R. S., & Jenkins, E. (1989). *How children discover new strategies.* Hillsdale, NJ: Erlbaum.

Siegler, R. S., & Munakata, Y. (1993). Beyond the immaculate transition: Advances in the understanding of change. *SRCD Newsletter, Winter,* 3–13.

Siever, L. J., & Davies, K. L. (1991). A psychobiological perspective on the personality disorder. *American Journal of Psychiatry, 148,* 1647–1658.

Simpson, D. C. (1976). The functioning hand, the human advantage. *Journal of the Royal College of Surgeons of Edinburgh, 21,* 329–340.

Simpson, G. G. (1953). *The major features of evolution.* New York: Columbia University Press.

Simpson, G. G. (1958). The study of evolution: Methods and present status of theory. In A. Roe & G. G. Simpson (Eds.), *Behavior and evolution* (pp. 7–26). New Haven, CT: Yale University Press.

Singer, M., & Berg, P. (1991). *Genes and genomes: A changing perspective.* Mill Valley, CA: University Science Books.

Skinner, B. F. (1953). *Science and human behavior.* New York: Macmillan.

Skinner, B. F. (1966). The phylogeny and ontogeny of behavior. *Science, 153,* 1205–1213.

Skousen, R. (1989). *Analogical modeling of language.* Dordrecht, The Netherlands: Kluwer Academic.

Skousen, R. (1992). *Analogy and structure*. Dordrecht, The Netherlands: Kluwer Academic.

Slater, P. J. B. (1973). Describing sequences of behavior. In P. P. G. Bateson & P. H. Klopfer (Eds.), *Perspectives in ethology* (Vol. 1, pp. 131–153). New York: Plenum Press.

Slater, P. J. B. (1978). Data collection. In P. W. Colgan (Ed.), *Quantitative ethology* (pp. 7–24). New York: Wiley.

Smith, A. (1984). Early and long-term recovery from brain damage in children and adults: Evolution of concepts of localization, plasticity, and recovery. In C. R. Almi & S. Finger (Eds.), *Early brain damage. Vol. 1. Research orientations and clinical observations* (pp. 102–189). New York: Academic Press.

Smith, M. S. (1987). Evolution and developmental psychology: Toward a sociobiology of human development. In C. Crawford, M. Smith, & D. Krebs (Eds.), *Sociobiology and psychology* (pp. 224–252). Hillsdale, NJ: Erlbaum.

Smith, N. W. (1992). The distant past and its relation to current psychology: A tour of psychophysical dualism and non-dualism. *Mankind Quarterly, 32,* 261–273.

Smith, P. K., Takhvar, M., Gore, N., & Vollstedt, R. (1985). Play in young children: Problems of definition, categorization and measurement. *Early Child Development and Care, 19,* 25–41.

Smith, W. J. (1991). Animal communication and the study of cognition. In C. A. Ristau (Ed.), *Cognitive ethology: The minds of other animals* (pp. 209–230). Hillsdale, NJ: Erlbaum.

Smotherman, W. P., & Bell, R. W. (1980). Maternal mediation of early experience. In R. W. Bell & W. P. Smotherman (Eds.), *Maternal influences and early behavior* (pp. 201–210). Jamaica, NY: Spectrum.

Smotherman, W. P., & Robinson, S. R. (1988). The uterus as environment: The ecology of fetal behavior. In E. M. Blass (Ed.), *Handbook of behavioral neurobiology. Vol. 9. Developmental psychobiology and behavioral ecology* (pp. 149–196). New York: Plenum Press.

Smotherman, W. P., & Robinson, S. B. (1990). The prenatal origins of behavioral organization. *Psychological Science, 1,* 97–106.

Smotherman, W. P., & Robinson, S. R. (1991). Accessibility of the rat fetus for psychobiological investigation. In H. N. Shair, G. A. Barr, & M. A. Hofer (Eds.), *Developmental psychobiology: New methods and changing concepts* (pp. 148–163). New York: Oxford University Press.

Snow, C. E. (1987). Sensitive periods in language development. In M. H. Bornstein (Ed.), *Sensitive periods in development: Interdisciplinary perspectives* (pp. 269–288). Hillsdale, NJ: Erlbaum.

Snowdon, C. T. (1990). Mechanisms maintaining monogamy in monkeys. In D. A. Dewsbury (Ed.), *Contemporary issues in comparative psychology* (pp. 225–251). Sunderland, MA: Sinauer.

Sober, E. (1984). *The nature of selection*. Cambridge: MIT Press.

Southwick, C. H. (1972). *Aggression among nonhuman primates*. New York: Academic Press.

Spelke, E. S. (1988). Where perceiving ends and thinking begins: The apprehension of objects in infancy. In A. Yonas (Ed.), *Perceptual development in infancy: Minnesota symposium on child development* (Vol. 20, pp. 197–234). Hillsdale, NJ: Erlbaum.

Spelke, E. S. (1991). Physical knowledge in infancy: Reflections on Piaget's theory. In S. Carey & R. Gelman (Eds.), *The epigenesis of mind: Essays on biology and cognition* (pp. 133–170). Hillsdale, NJ: Erlbaum.

Spemann, H. (1938/1967). *Embryonic development and induction*. New York: Hafner. (Original work published 1938).

Spencer-Booth, Y., & Hinde, R. A. (1967). The effects of separating rhesus monkey infants from their mothers for six days. *Journal of Child Psychology and Psychiatry, 7,* 179–197.

Sperry, R. W. (1965). Mind, brain, and humanist values. In J. R. Platt (Ed.), *New views of the nature of man* (pp. 71–92). Chicago: University of Chicago Press.

Spiegel, A. M. (1989). Receptor-effector coupling by G-proteins. Implications for endocrinology. *Trends in Endocrinology and Metabolism, 2,* 72–76.

Spinelli, D. N., & Jensen, F. E. (1982). Plasticity, experience and resource allocation in motor cortex and hypothalamus. In C. D. Woody (Ed.), *Conditioning* (pp. 161–169). New York: Plenum Press.

Stanfield, B. B. (1992). The development of the corticospinal projection. *Progress in Neurobiology, 38,* 169–202.

Stehouwer, D. J. (1986). Behavior of larval and juvenile bullfrogs (*Rana catesbeiana*) following chronic spinal transection. *Behavioral and Neural Biology, 45*, 12–134.

Stehouwer, D. J. (1991). Amphibian metamorphosis: A model of vertebrate motor development. In H. N. Shair, G. A. Barr, & M. A. Hofer (Eds.), *Developmental psychobiology: New methods and changing concepts* (pp. 128–147). New York: Oxford University Press.

Stelzner, D. J. (1986). Ontogeny of the encephalization process. In W. T. Greenough & J. M. Juraska (Eds.), *Developmental neuropsychobiology* (pp. 241–270). Orlando: Academic Press.

Stent, G. S. (1981). Strength and weakness of the genetic approach to the development of the nervous system. *Annual Review of Neuroscience, 4,* 163–194.

Stern, J. M. (1986). Licking, touching, and suckling: Contact stimulation and maternal psychobiology in rats and women. *Annals of the New York Academy of Sciences, 474*, 95–107.

Stern, J. M. (1989). Maternal behavior: Sensory, hormonal, and neural determinants. In F. R. Brush & S. Levine (Eds.), *Psychoendocrinology* (pp. 105–226). New York: Academic Press.

Stern, J. M. (1990). Multisensory regulation of maternal behavior and masculine sexual behavior: A revised view. *Neuroscience and Biobehavioral Reviews, 14*, 183–200.

Stich, S. (1983). *From folk psychology to cognitive science.* Cambridge: MIT Press.

Strohman, R. C. (1994). Epigenesis: The missing beat in biotechnology? *Bio/Technology, 12*, 112–164.

Strum, S. B., & Latour, B. (1987). Redefining the social link: From baboons to humans. *Social Science Information, 26*, 783–802.

Sturtevant, A. H. (1915). The behavior of the chromosomes as studied through linkage. *Zeitschrift für Induktive Abstammungs und Verersbungslehre, 13*, 234–287. Cited in Carlson, 1966, p. 69.

Sullivan, K. A. (1984). Information exploitation by downy woodpeckers in mixed-species flocks. *Behaviour, 91*, 294–311.

Sulloway, F. J. (1984). Darwin and the Galapagos. *Biological Journal of the Linnean Society, 21,* 29–59. (Volume reprinted as Berry, R. J. (Ed.). (1984). *Evolution in the Galapagos Islands.* London: Academic Press.)

Super, C. M. (1976). Environmental effects on motor development: The case of "African infant precocity." *Developmental Medicine and Child Neurology, 18*, 561–567.

Sutherland, J. D. (1963). The concepts of imprinting and critical period from a psychoanalytic viewpoint. In B. M. Foss (Ed.), *Determinants of infant behaviour* (Vol. 2, pp. 235–239). New York: Wiley.

Suzuki, D., & Knudston, P. (1989). *Genethics: The ethics of engineering life.* London: Unwin & Hyman.

Svare, B., & Gandelman, R. (1974). Stimulus control of aggressive behavior in androgenized female mice. *Behavioral Biology, 10*, 447–459.

Swaab, D. F., & Fliers, E. (1985). A sexually dimorphic nucleus in the human brain. *Science, 228*, 1112–1115.

Swaab, D. F., & Hofman, M. A. (1988). Sexual differentiation of the human hypothalamus: Ontogeny of the sexually dimorphic nucleus of the preoptic area. *Developmental Brain Research, 44*, 314–318.

Swaab, D. F., & Hofman, M. A. (1990). An enlarged suprachiasmatic nucleus in homosexual men. *Brain Research, 537,* 141–148.

Symons, D. (1990). Adaptiveness and adaptation. *Ethology and Sociobiology, 11*, 427–444.

Tallamy, D. W. (1984). Insect parental care. *Bioscience, 34*, 20–24.

Taub, E. (1976). Motor behavior following deafferentation in the developing and motorically mature monkey. In R. M. Herman, S. Grillner, P. S. G. Stein, & D. G. Stuart (Eds.), *Neural control of locomotion* (pp. 675–705). New York: Plenum Press.

Templeton, A. R. (1989). The meaning of species and speciation: A genetic perspective. In D. Otte & J. A. Endler (Eds.), *Speciation and its consequences* (pp. 3–27). Sunderland, MA: Sinauer.

ten Cate, C. (1989). Behavioral development: Toward understanding processes. In P. P. G. Bateson & P. Klopfer (Eds.), *Perspectives in ethology* (Vol. 8, pp. 243–269). New York: Plenum Press.

Thelen, E. (1981). Rhythmical behavior in infancy: An ethological perspective. *Developmental Psychology, 17*, 237–257.

Thelen, E. (1992). Development of locomotion from a dynamic systems approach. In H. Forssberg & H. Hirschfield (Eds.) *Movement disorders in children* (pp. 169–173). Basel: Karger.

Thelen, E. (1993). Timing and developmental dynamics in the acquisition of early motor skills. In G. Turkewitz & D. A. Devenny (Eds.) *Developmental time and timing* (pp. 85–104). Hillsdale, NJ: Erlbaum.

Thelen, E., & Cooke, D. W. (1987). The relation between newborn stepping and later locomotion: A new interpretation. *Developmental Medicine and Child Neurology, 29*, 380–393.

Thelen, E., & Fisher, D. M. (1982). Newborn stepping: An explanation for the "disappearing reflex." *Developmental Psychology, 18*, 760–775.

Thelen, E., & Fogel, A. (1989). Toward an action-based theory of infant development. In J. Lockman & N. Hazen (Eds.), *Action in social context: Perspectives on early development* (pp. 23–63). New York: Plenum Press.

Thompson, W. D. (1961). *On growth and form.* Cambridge: Cambridge University Press. (Original work published 1917)

Thomson, K. S. (1988). *Morphogenesis and evolution.* New York: Oxford University Press.

Thorndike, E. L. (1898). Animal intelligence: An experimental study of the associative process in animals. *Psychological Review Monographs, 2*, No. 8.

Thorndike, E. L. (1932). *The fundamentals of learning.* New York: Columbia University Press.

Thornhill, R., & Thornhill, N. W. (1987). Human rape: The strengths of the evolutionary perspective. In C. Crawford, M. Smith, & D. Krebs (Eds.), *Sociobiology and psychology: Ideas, issues and applications* (pp. 269–292). Hillsdale, NJ: Erlbaum.

Thornhill, R., & Thornhill, N. W. (1992). The evolutionary psychology of men's coercive sexuality. *Behavioral and Brain Sciences, 15*, 363–376.

Tieman, S. B., & Hirsch, H. V. B. (1982). Exposure to lines of only one orientation modifies dendritic morphology of cells in the visual cortex of the cat. *Journal of Comparative Neurology, 211*, 353–362.

Tiles, M. (1993). The normal and pathological: The concept of a scientific medicine. *British Journal of the Philosophy of Science, 44*, 729–742.

Tinbergen, N. (1951). *The study of instinct.* Oxford: Oxford University Press.

Tinbergen, N. (1963a). On aims and methods of ethology. *Zeitschrift für Tierpsychologie, 20*, 410–433.

Tinbergen, N. (1963b). The shell menace. *Natural History, 72*, 28–35.

Tinbergen, N. (1965). Behavior and natural selection. In J. A. Moore (Ed.), *Ideas in modern biology* (Vol. 6, pp. 521–542). Washington, DC: Proceedings of the 16th International Zoological Congress.

Tinbergen, N. (1968). On war and peace in animals and man. *Science, 160*, 1411–1418.

Tinbergen, N., Broekhuysen, G. J., Feekes, F., Houghton, J. C. W., Kruuk, H., & Szulc, E. (1962). Egg shell removal by the black-headed gull, *Larus ridibundus L.*, a behavioural component of camouflage. *Behaviour, 19*, 74–117.

Tobet, S. A., & Fox, T. O. (1989). Sex- and hormone-dependent antigen immunoreactivity in developing rat hypothalamus. *Proceedings of the National Academy of Sciences U.S.A., 86*, 382–386.

Tobet, S. A., & Fox, T. O. (1992). Sex differences in neuronal morphology influenced hormonally throughout life. In A. A. Gerall, H. Moltz, & I. L. Ward (Eds.), *Handbook of behavioral neurobiology. Vol. 11. Sexual differentiation* (pp. 41–83). New York: Plenum Press.

Toran-Allerand, C. D. (1976). Sex steroids and the development of the neworn mouse hypothalamus and preoptic area in vitro: Implications for sexual differentiation. *Brain Research, 106*, 407–412.

Torrey, E. F. (1992). Are we overestimating the genetic contribution to schizophrenia? *Schizophrenia Bulletin, 18*, 159–170.

Travis, C. B., & Yeager, C. P. (1991). Sexual selection, parental investment, and sexism. *Journal of Social Issues, 47*, 117–129.

Trivers, R. L. (1971). The evolution of reciprocal altruism. *Quarterly Review of Biology, 46*, 35–57.

Trivers, R. L. (1972). Parental investment and sexual selection. In B. Campbell (Ed.), *Sexual selection and the descent of man, 1871–1971* (pp. 136–179). Chicago: Aldine.

Tronick, E. A., Winn, S., & Morelli, G. A. (1985). Multiple caretaking in the context of human evolution: Why don't the Efé know the western prescription for child care? In M. Reite & T. Field (Eds.), *The psychobiology of attachment and separation* (pp. 293–322). Orlando: Academic Press.

Turing, A. M. (1952). The chemical basis of morphogenesis. *Philosophical Transactions of the Royal Society of London [B]*, *237*, 37–72.

Turkewitz, G. (1977). The development of lateral differences in the human infant. In S. Harnad, R. W. Doty, L. Goldstein, J. Jaynes, & G. Krauthamer (Eds.), *Lateralization in the nervous system* (pp. 251–259). New York: Academic Press.

Turkewitz, G., & Kenny, P. A. (1982). Limitation on input as a basis for neural organization and perceptual development: A preliminary theoretical statement. *Developmental Psychobiology*, *15*, 357–368.

Turkheimer, E., & Gottesman, I. I. (1991). Individual differences and the canalization of human behavior. *Developmental Psychology*, *27*, 18–22.

Vale, R. D., Banker, G., & Hall, Z. W. (1992). The neuronal cytoskeleton. In Z. W. Hall (Ed.), *An introduction to molecular neurobiology* (pp. 247–280). Sunderland, MA: Sinauer.

Valenstein, E. S., Riss, W., & Young W. C. (1955). Experiential and genetic factors in the organization of sexual behavior in male guinea pigs. *Journal of Comparative and Physiological Psychology*, *48*, 397–403.

Valsiner, J. (1987). *Culture and the development of children's action*. Chichester, England: Wiley.

Vandel, D. L. (1979a). A macroanalysis of toddlers' social interaction with mothers and fathers. *Journal of Genetic Psychology*, *134*, 299–312.

Vandel, D. L. (1979b). The effect of a playgroup experience on mother-son and father-son interaction. *Developmental Psychology*, *15*, 379–385.

Van der Kloot, W. G., & William, C. M. (1953a). Cocoon construction by the cecropia silkworm. I. The role of the external environment. *Behaviour*, *5*, 141–156.

Van der Kloot, W. G., & William, C. M. (1953b). Cocoon construction by the cecropia silkworm. II. The role of the internal environment. *Behaviour*, *5*, 157–174.

Van der Loos, H., Welker, E., Dörfl, J., & Rumo, G. (1986). Selective breeding for variations in patterns of mystacial vibrissae of mice. *Journal of Heredity*, *77,* 66–82.

van der Maas, H. L. J., & Molenaar, P. C. M. (1992). Stagewise cognitive development: An application of catastrophe theory. *Psychological Review*, *99*, 395–417.

van der Weel, C. (1993). Explaining embryological development: Should integration be the goal? *Biology and Philosophy*, *8*, 385–397.

van Geert, P. (1991). Theoretical problems in developmental psychology. In P. van Geert & L. P. Mass (Eds.), *Annals of Theoretical Psychology* (*Vol. 7*, pp. 1–54). New York: Plenum Press.

Vedeler, D. (1991). Infant intentionality as object directedness: An alternative for representationalism. *Journal for the Theory of Social Behaviour*, *21*, 431–448.

Vihman, M. M. (1991). Early syllables and the construction of phonology. In C. A. Ferguson, L. Menn, C. Stoel-Gammon (Eds.), *Phonological development: Models, research, implications* (pp. 69–84). Hillsdale, NJ: Erlbaum.

Vince, M. A. (1974). Some environmental effects on the activity and development of the avian embryo. In G. Gottlieb (Ed.), *Behavioral embryology. Vol. 1. Studies on the development of behavior and the nervous system* (pp. 285–323). New York: Academic Press.

Vomachka, A. J., & Lisk, R. D. (1986). Androgen and estradiol levels in plasma and amniotic fluid of late gestational male and female hamsters: Uterine position effects. *Hormones and Behavior*, *20*, 181–193.

von Bertalanffy, L. (1952). *Problems of life: An evaluation of modern biological and scientific thought*. New York: Harper & Brothers.

von Bertalanffy, L. (1968). *General system theory*. New York: Braziller.

von Frisch, K. (1964). *Bees: Their vision, chemical senses, and language*. Ithaca, NY: Cornell University Press.

von Hofsten, C. (1982). Eye-hand coordination in newborns. *Developmental Psychology, 18,* 450–461.

von Hofsten, C. (1990). A perception-action perspective on the development of manual movements. In M. Jeannerod (Ed.), *Attention and performance. Vol. 13. Motor representation and control* (pp. 739–762). Hillsdale, NJ: Erlbaum.

von Uexküll, J. (1957). A stroll through the world of animals and men. In C. H. Schiller (Ed.), *Instinctive behavior* (pp. 5–80). New York: International Universities Press.

Vowles, D. M. (1961). Neural mechanisms in insect behaviour. In W. H. Thorpe & O. L. Zangwill (Eds.), *Current problems in animal behaviour* (pp. 1–29). London: Cambridge University Press.

Waddington, C. H. (1956). Genetic assimilation of the *Bithorax* phenotype. *Evolution, 10,* 1–13.

Waddington, C. H. (1966). *The nature of life.* New York: Harper & Row.

Waddington, C. H. (1975). *The evolution of an evolutionist.* Ithaca, NY: Cornell University Press.

Wahlsten, D. (1990). Insensitivity of the analysis of variance to heredity-environment interactions. *Behavioral and Brain Sciences, 13,* 109–161.

Wall, J. T., Huerta, M. F., & Kaas, J. H. (1992). Changes in the cortical map of the hand following postnatal median nerve injury in monkeys: Modification of somatotopic aggregates. *Journal of Neuroscience, 12,* 3445–3455.

Wallach, S. J. R., & Hart, B. L. (1983). The role of the striated penile muscles of the male rat in seminal plug dislodgement and deposition. *Physiology and Behavior, 31,* 815–821.

Walsh, C., & Cepko, C. L. (1992). Widespread dispersion of neuronal clones across functional regions of the cerebral cortex. *Science, 235,* 434–255.

Wapner, S., & Werner, H. (1957). *Perceptual development.* Worcester, MA: Clark University Press.

Ward, I. L. (1992). Sexual behavior: The product of perinatal hormonal and prepubertal social factors. In A. A. Gerall, H. Moltz, & I. L. Ward (Eds.), *Handbook of behavioral neurobiology. Vol. 11. Sexual differentiation* (pp. 157–180). New York: Plenum Press.

Watson, J. B. (1924). *Behaviorism.* Chicago: University of Chicago Press.

Watson, J. D., & Crick, F. H. (1953). Molecular structure of nucleic acids: A structure for deoxyribose nucleic acid. *Nature, 171,* 964–967.

Watson, S. J., & Bekoff, A. (1990). A kinematic analysis of hindlimb motility in 9- and 10-day-old chick embryos. *Journal of Neurobiology, 21,* 651–660.

Weismann, A. (1894). *The effect of external influences upon development.* London: Frowde.

Weiss, P. A. (1939) *Principles of development.* Chicago: University of Chicago Press.

Welker, W. I. (1971). Ontogeny of play and exploratory behaviors: A definition of problems and a search for new conceptual solutions. In H. Moltz (Ed.), *The ontogeny of vertebrate behavior* (pp. 171–228). New York: Academic Press.

Wells, P. H., & Wenner, A. M. (1973). Do bees have a language? *Nature, 241,* 171–174.

Wenner, A. M. (1967). Honey bees: Do they use the distance information contained in their dance maneuver? *Science, 155,* 847–849.

Wenner, A. M., & Wells, P. H. (1990). *Anatomy of a controversy: The question of a "language" among bees.* New York: Columbia University Press.

Werner, H. (1948). *Comparative psychology of mental development.* New York: International Universities Press.

Werner, H. (1957). The concept of development from a comparative and organismic point of view. In D. B. Harris (Ed.), *The concept of development* (pp. 125–148) Minneapolis: University of Minnesota Press.

Werner, H., & Kaplan, B. (1963). *Symbol formation.* New York: Wiley.

West, M. J., & King, A. P. (1987). Settling nature and nurture into an ontogenetic niche. *Developmental Psychobiology, 20,* 549–562.

West, M. J., & King, A. P. (1988). Female visual displays affect the development of male song in the cowbird. *Nature, 334,* 244–246.

West, M. J., King, A. P., & Arberg, A. A. (1988). The inheritance of niches: The role of ecological legacies in ontogeny. In E. M. Blass (Ed.), *Handbook of behavioral neurobiology. Vol. 9. Developmental psychobiology and behavioral ecology* (pp. 41–62). New York: Plenum Press.

West, M. J., Stroud, A. N., & King, A. P. (1983). Mimicry of the human voice by Eurasian starlings (*Sturnus vulgaris*): The role of social interaction. *Wilson Bulletin, 95,* 635–640.

Wexler, N., Rose, E. A., & Housman, D. E. (1991). Molecular approaches to hereditary diseases of the nervous system: Huntington's disease as a paradigm. *Annual Review of Neuroscience, 14,* 503–529.

White, B. L., Castle, P., & Held, R. (1964). Observations on the development of visually directed reaching. *Child Development, 35,* 349–364.

White, E. (1981). *Sociobiology and human politics.* Lexington, MA: Heath.

White, G. (1981). *The illustrated natural history of Selborne.* New York: St. Martin's Press. (Original work published 1789)

Whitman, C. O. (1894). Evolution and epigenesis. *Woods Hole Biological Lectures, 10,* 203–224.

Wiesner, B. F., & Sheard, N. M. (1933). *Maternal behaviour in the rat.* Edinburgh: Oliver & Boyd.

Wilcock, J. (1969). Gene action and behavior: An evaluation of major gene pleiotropism. *Psychological Bulletin, 72,* 1–29.

Williams, C. L. (1991). Development of a sexually dimorphic behavior: Hormonal and neural controls. In H. N. Shair, G. A. Barr, & M. A. Hofer (Eds.), *Developmental psychobiology: New methods and changing concepts* (pp. 206–222). New York: Oxford University Press.

Williams, G. C. (1966). *Adaptation and natural selection.* Princeton, NJ: Princeton University Press.

Willmes, K., & Poeck, K. (1993). To what extent can aphasic syndromes be localized? *Brain, 116,* 1527–1540.

Wilson, E. O. (1975). *Sociobiology.* Cambridge: Harvard University Press.

Wilson, E. O. (1978). *On human nature.* Cambridge: Harvard University Press.

Windle, W. F. (1940). *Physiology of the fetus: Origin and extent of function in prenatal life.* Philadelphia: Saunders.

Witt, P. N., Reed, C. F., & Peakall, D. B. (1969). *A spider's web: Problems in regulatory biology.* New York: Springer-Verlag.

Wohlwill, J. F. (1970). The age variable in psychological research. *Psychological Review, 77,* 49–64.

Wolf, L., Ketterson, E. D., & Nolan, V., Jr. (1988). Paternal influence on growth and survival of dark-eyed junco young: Do parental males benefit? *Animal Behaviour, 36,* 1601–1618.

Wolff, P. H. (1959). Observations on newborn infants. *Psychosomatic Medicine, 21,* 110–118.

Wolff, P. H. (1960). The developmental psychologies of Jean Piaget and psychoanalysis. *Psychological Issues Monograph Series* (Vol. 2, No. 1). New York: International Universities Press.

Wolff, P. H. (1987). *The development of behavioral states and the expression of emotions in early infancy.* Chicago: University of Chicago Press.

Wolff, P. H. (1992). How do genetic abnormalities influence developmental pathways? Keynote lecture, 2nd International Symposium From Genes to Behaviour, Society for the Study of Behavioural Phenotypes, Welshpool, U.K., November 19–21.

Wolpert, L. (1992a). Gastrulation and the evolution of development. *Development (Suppl), 116,* 7–13.

Wolpert, L. (1992b). *The triumph of the embryo.* New York: Oxford University Press.

Woodruff, D. S. (1978). Brain electrical actifity and behavior relationships over the lifespan. In P. B. Baltes (Ed.), *Life-span development and behavior* (Vol. 1, pp. 111–179). New York: Academic Press.

Woolsey, T. A., Durham, D., Harris, R. M., Simons, D. J., & Valentino, K. L. (1981). Somatosensory development. In R. N. Aslin, J. R. Alberts, & M. R. Petersen (Eds.), *Development of perception. Vol. 1. Audition, somatic perception, and the chemical senses* (pp. 259–292). New York: Academic Press.

Wright, S. (1932). The roles of mutation, inbreeding, cross-breeding, and selection in evolution. *Proceedings of the 6th International Congress of Genetics, 1,* 356–366.

Wright, S. (1968). *Evolution and the genetics of populations. Vol. 1. Genetic and biometric foundations.* Chicago: University of Chicago Press.

Wright, S. (1980). Genic and organismic selection. *Evolution, 34,* 825–843.

Xerri, C., Stern, J. M., & Merzenich, M. M. (1994). Alterations of the cortical representation of the rat ventrum induced by nursing behavior. *Journal of Neuroscience, 14,* 1710–1721.

Yahr, P. (1988). Sexual differentiation of behavior in the context of developmental psychobiology. In E. M. Blass (Ed.), *Handbook of behavioral neurobiology. Vol. 9. Developmental psychobiology and behavioral ecology* (pp. 197–243). New York: Plenum Press.

Yates, E. F. (1987). *Self-organizing systems: The emergence of order.* New York: Plenum Press.

Zeki, S. (1990). A century of cerebral achromatopsia. *Brain, 113,* 1721–1777.

Zelazo, P. R. (1983). The development of walking: New findings and old assumptions. *Journal of Motor Behavior, 15,* 99–137.

Zurif, E. B. (1990). Language and the brain. In D. N. Osherson & H. Lasnik (Eds.), *Language: An invitation to cognitive science* (pp. 177–198). Cambridge: MIT Press.

Glossary

abnormal   Significant departure from the norm or average for a population. The term causes difficulties when it implies violation of biological imperatives.

adaptation   Close functional fit between a character and aspects of the environment. According to the synthetic theory of evolution, this fit is achieved gradually by a process of natural selection, but there are alternative explanations (see *exaptation*).

adaptive radiation   Extensive evolutionary diversification from a parental taxon into several new taxa having different adaptations (e.g., several new species from one originating population, as in Darwin's finches).

adhesion molecules   Molecules, produced by cells, having selective binding properties that allow cells to adhere to one another (cell adhesion molecules) or to the substrate (substrate adhesion molecules). Selective adhesion contributes to cellular movement and morphogenesis during early development.

allele   An alternative form of a gene, identified as such by the alternative phenotype that is expressed.

allometric growth   Changes in the relative size of two features of an organism with growth; usually refers to changes that are not isometric, achieved by different rates of growth.

altricial   Relatively immature at birth or hatching, requiring substantial parental care for survival.

altruistic behavior   Behavior contributing to the reproductive success of another that is achieved at some cost to the reproductive success of the individual behaving animal.

analogy   Similar characters in two different species, where the similarity is achieved through convergent evolution (i.e., similar adaptation) rather than through descent from a common ancestral form (compare *homology*).

anecdotalists   An early group of natural historians who relied on anecdotes for behavioral data.

anterior pituitary   A lobe of the pituitary gland having a vascular connection to the hypothalamic region of the brain, from which it receives regulatory hormones. Hormones produced by the anterior pituitary, in turn, regulate many other glands in the body.

anthropomorphism   Ascribing human thoughts and feelings to animals to explain their behavior.

aphasia   A disorder involving problems with production, meaning, or memory of language.

asexual reproduction   Reproduction from a single parent achieved, for example, by budding, cloning, or developing an unfertilized egg.

attachment   The bond between mammalian infant and caregiver, or the process though which the bond is formed. The word encompasses several regulatory processes embedded in the mother-infant relationship, some physiological and some behavioral.

attractor (attractor state)   In dynamic systems theory, a preferred, relatively stable state of the system, always relative to particular conditions; when conditions change, so may the attractor.

autonomic nervous system   The portion of the peripheral nervous system of vertebrates that innervates smooth muscles and glands.

axon   A process, extending from the body or primary dendrite of a neuron that carries action potentials to targets.

Baldwin effect   An idea originating with James Mark Baldwin to the effect that individuals vary in the adaptive plasticity of some feature with respect to a specific environmental challenge; that variation in this plasticity is heritable; and that selection can operate on the heritable plasticity in the feature to improve adaptation over generations (see *genetic assimilation*).

bauplan (*pl*, bauplâne)   The general body plan of an organism and its constituent organs, including both structural and functional considerations. The German word is used because it has a richer meaning than any single English word.

behavior   Movements or adjustments of a whole organism with respect to its environment.

behavioral ecology   The study of the evolutionary functions of behavior.

behavioral embryology   The study of behavior in very young organisms. A strict definition would restrict this specialty to embryos, but species vary in maturity at birth or hatching, which argues for flexible application of the label to include the early postnatal period in some species.

bimanual coordination   The coordinated use of the two hands, including complementary motor patterns; a distinctive and important human trait that develops during infancy.

biological function   The relatively immediate consequence or end accomplished by an individual's behavior or other characteristic. (Compare *fitness*.)

biological imperative   The misguided idea that to identify a biological cause is to identify a necessary human condition.

blastula   An early developmental stage, after several divisions of the zygote but before gastrulation, in which the organism has the shape of a hollow ball.

blueprint   Used metaphorically to capture the predeterministic idea that genes encode detailed plans of developmental outcomes.

cascade   A metaphor useful for describing the concatenation and multiplication of (proximate) causal events that can originate from one change in internal or external conditions.

caudal   Toward the tail; posterior.

causation   Unless further modified, used here to mean proximate causation, one of Tinbergen's four questions; underlying mechanism.

character   A measurable feature of an organism; a trait; a phenotype.

chimera   An organism that develops as a mosaic from the tissues of two different species.

cleavage   In embryology, rapid cell division in the earliest stage to form a ball of cells from the zygote.

closed system   A system that is isolated from the matter in its environment. Although energy can be exchanged, matter cannot (as in a closed pot of water over heat).

coevolution   Evolution of two or more entities (species; variants within a species; organism and habitat/environment) that are joined as a system.

cognition   A loosely defined term used to refer to human intelligence, perception, thinking, knowing, and knowledge acquisition.

connectionist modeling   An approach to the study of cognition that uses computer programs to simulate the way in which symbolic representations of input can be achieved without the need for a priori specification of symbols.

constraint   Applied to both development and evolution, a factor or set of factors that either restricts particular changes from happening or makes them more likely.

conspecific   Member of the same species.

control parameter   In dynamic systems theory, a parameter to which the system is particularly sensitive.

corpus callosum   A large fiber tract that connects the two cerebral hemispheres.

cross-foster   The experimental procedure of fostering the young of one strain (or species) onto a mother from a second strain (or species).

culture-biology dualism   A variant of nature-nurture dualism in which it is assumed that a strict division can be maintained between two sources of behavioral development, a position as problem filled as other forms of dualism.

dendrite   A process extending from the cell body of a neuron that is a major site of synapses with the axon terminals of other neurons. Dendrites are highly variable in size and shape, often branching into dendritic arbors.

deprivation study   An experimental procedure in which an organism is removed from a normal environmental input so as to measure the importance of the input to development.

descending pathway   A neural pathway from relatively more rostral to more caudal regions; pathway from brain to spinal cord.

differentiation   The progression of cells from a generalized beginning at cell division to more specialized form as development proceeds.

dimorphism   Two variants of a character found in a population, most often used with respect to sexual dimorphism.

DNA   Deoxyribonucleic acid, a molecule that is capable of self-replication during cell division as well as the regulated replication (transcription) of small portions of itself onto RNA as a step in protein synthesis.

dominant   In Mendelian genetics, the allele that is expressed in the heterozygous condition.

dualism   The position that causes fall into two exclusive categories, those of nature and those of nurture.

dynamic systems theory   Modern systems theory that has incorporated relatively recent advances in mathematics that are useful for describing both qualitative changes in systems and nonlinear causation.

ectotherm   An organism that regulates its temperature from environmental sources (e.g., by gaining heat through conduction).

egg   A gamete. With sexually dimorphic gametes, the egg is the larger one, defining its producer as female.

emergent   A property of one level in a system that arose from interactions of elements at a lower level but that cannot be identified in those elements, taken either singly or collectively.

environmentalism   A theory that the outcome of development is impressed by the environment on a highly plastic organism.

epigenesis   The conception of development as qualitative change, not reducible to genes or programs in genes, involving interactions within and among many levels of the organism and its external milieu.

epithelia   Sheets of cells having distinct basilar and apical surfaces, joined to one another laterally through the actions of cell adhesion molecules.

exaptation   A character having a currently adaptive function, but that did not arise as a result of natural selection acting on that function.

extracellular matrix   The matrix of molecules found in the spaces between cells, including substrate adhesion molecules that guide cellular movements during morphogenesis.

facilitative experience   Experience that affects development in a quantitative fashion by altering the rate, timing, or extent of some developmental process.

faculty   One discrete compartment of cognition (language, reason) in one questionable conception of human cognition.

fate   Used metaphorically to capture the point that at some stage before it is apparent by outward appearance, the final form, function, or location of a cell has been determined.

fauna   Animal life present in a particular time or place.

fertilization   Joining of egg and sperm to create a zygote having the chromosome number characteristic of somatic cells in the species.

fitness   A measure of response to natural selection in an individual, stated in terms of probable contribution to future gene pools.

flora   Plant life present in a particular time or place.

folding   In embryology, one of the fundamental processes underlying morphogenesis, where growth and proliferation of cells that adhere to one another in sheets lead to characteristic buckling.

forward reference   The development of organismic features before their mature function is required.

gamete   A cell specialized for reproduction, capable of fusing with another cell at fertilization; egg or sperm.

gastrulation   An early embryonic stage marking the beginning of morphogenesis, when the embryo consists of three germ layers.

gene   A construct used to explain heredity, variously defined as a unit of inheritance identified by an associated phenotype; a location on a chromosome; and as a transcribable sequence of nucleotides within a DNA molecule.

genealogy   The lineage of a taxon.

gene pool   The sum of all genes and the relative frequencies of their alleles available to a population.

genetic drift   Random changes in the frequencies of alleles within a population; sampling error applied to genotypes.

genome   The complete set of genes possessed by an individual.

genotype   Often used to refer to the known or inferred allele(s) of a gene or genes correlated with a particular phenotype; also used to refer to the complete set of genes possessed by an individual.

glia   Nonneural cells associated with neurons, providing a variety of support functions.

growth cone   Leading edge of a developing axon or dendrite, specialized to travel and to add length to these processes.

habitat   The effective environment of an animal described in terms of resources and challenges that affect survival and reproduction.

handedness   Asymmetrical use of the two hands. Although the extent and direction of preference varies with the task both within and across individuals, most humans prefer to use the right hand for the majority of tasks.

heredity   Transmitted from generation to generation.

heterochrony   A difference between species (or intraspecific variants) in the relative timing of developmental processes (e.g., eye opening before or after birth). Heterochrony is a major developmental source of diversity.

holism   A conception of behavioral development that considers behavior to be a property of the whole organism rather than of its constituent parts.

homeotherm   An organism that regulates its temperature through endogenous mechanisms (e.g., by generating heat through increased metabolism).

homeotic mutations   Mutations that permit the development in one body segment of structures that normally develop in a different segment (e.g., legs in the head region in place of antennae).

homology   Two structures (or behavioral patterns) that have descended from a common ancestral structure or pattern, owing any similarity to that fact.

imprinting   Restriction of social responses to particular objects as a result of familiarity.

inclusive fitness   The fitness of an individual combined with the fitness of its relatives, weighted by the extent of genetic sharing between the individual and its relatives.

inductive experience   An experience that leads to qualitative developmental changes.

inheritance   The passing of traits from generation to generation through genetic or nongenetic means.

innate   Most neutrally, present at birth or hatching; but most frequently, genetically predetermined. This is a problem word; see *instinct*.

intentionality   Performance of an action guided by knowledge of its end.

interdisciplinary   The integration rather that the simple juxtaposition of disciplines with the goal of better understanding some phenomenon.

instinct   A complex, vague, notorious term. Its most neutral meaning is species-typical behavior, but this usage is rare. As generally used, it means (variously) unlearned, genetically programmed, developed without experience, predetermined, and other synonyms of the equally complex, vague, notorious term *innate*.

isolated system   A system that is isolated from both matter and energy in its environment.

kin selection   A conception within the synthetic theory of evolution whereby natural selection favors traits that improve the reproductive success of relatives, mediated by shared genes.

language-acquisition device   Chomsky's nativisitic conception of a structure in the brain that is equipped with innate rules of grammar.

level   The hierarchical organization of a system. Any given pattern of organization is a component of a higher-level pattern and, simultaneously, has constituent components that occupy a lower level; for example, the brain contributes to the organism as a whole and it contains neurons, glia, and so on.

linear causation   The conception that causes have effects in a direct, linear fashion, usually with the assumption of correspondence between the size of the causal agent and its effect.

linkage disequilibrium   In population genetics, nonrandom linkage between alleles at two different locations.

macro (macrolevel)   With respect to a hierarchically ordered system, a relative term designating the higher of two levels that are under discussion.

macroevolution   Evolution above the species level.

maintenance experience   Experience that affects development by sustaining features that have already developed.

markers   In genetics, morphologically distinctive parts of a chromosome used to locate genes of interest that are linked by contiguity to the marker.

materialism   The philosophical position that explanations of behavior can be found in material terms.

mating system   Patterns of association between reproducing males and females, described using labels from human systems (e.g., monogamy, polygyny).

maturation   Development considered in terms of organismic structure. Although it is frequently assumed that structural changes precede and cause functional changes, this assumption is not necessary and has been increasingly contradicted by fact.

mechanists   Scientists who, in contrast to vitalists, sought explanations in materialist terms.

meiosis   Special cell division that results in gametes having half the number of chromosomes of the original cell.

mesenchyme   Cells that are not bound into sheets, such that each cell can move independently in the surrounding extracellular matrix.

micro (microlevel)   With respect to a hierarchically ordered system, a relative term that designates the lower of two levels that are under discussion.

microevolution   Evolution within populations by gradual processes.

migration   In development, the movement of cells from one location to another, a phenomenon that plays a central role in morphogenesis.

milieu interieur   The internal, physiologically defined environment of an organism.

mitosis   Cell division resulting in exact duplication of the genome.

molecules   The smallest constituents of organisms, formed of atoms linked together to make a great variety of stable structures.

morphogenesis   The development of animal form.

mutation   A change in a gene or genome.

myelination   The process of glia or Schwann cells wrapping around axons, forming myelin, and having the effect of speeding conduction of neural action potentials.

nativism   The theoretical position that behavioral patterns are preformed or, in a more modern form, that genetic blueprints for behavior are innate, guiding development without significant input from the environment.

natural selection   Darwin's explanation of evolution.

naturalistic fallacy   The erroneous belief that the familiar is natural whereas the new and different is unnatural.

necessary condition   An explanatory concept in which a condition that must be present before a phenomenon will occur has been identified.

neoteny   A particular type of heterochrony in which the juvenile form of some character is retained in adulthood.

nerve growth factor   The first trophic factor to be identified in the nervous system.

neurons   Nerve cells.

neurite   A process, dendrite or axon, extending from a neuron. The generic term is particularly applicable in early, undifferentiated stages.

neurogenesis   Growth of new neurons by mitosis, or cell division.

neuronal death   The disintegration and elimination of neurons from the nervous system occurring extensively as part of a normal early developmental process.

nonlinear causation   Causation having multidirectional, looping, often unexpected, and nonobvious pathways and effects that may be disproportionate in size.

normal   Within the norm or average for a population. (Compare *abnormal*.)

novelty   In evolution, the emergence of new features.

object permanence   A stage in Piagetian development wherein an infant comes to recognize that an object continues to exist although it is not available to perception.

ontogeny   A synonym for development; one of Tinbergen's four questions.

open system   A system that can exchange both matter and energy with its environment.

organicists   Theorists who thought that the structure of organisms reflected Plato's eternal laws of form.

organogenesis   The formation of organs from cells in the three embryonic germ layers.

phenotype   An observable, measurable feature of an organism that identifies its correlated genotype; a trait; a character.

phylogeny   The genealogy of a species (or other taxon) or of a trait; evolutionary history; one of Tinbergen's four questions.

polymorphism   The existence of more than one qualitatively distinct variant of a trait in a population.

precocial   Relatively mature at birth or hatching. (Compare *altricial*.)

predeterminism   A theory that the final outcome of development is specified in an inherited blueprint.

preformationism   An old theory that development entails only growth, with no qualitative change.

prehension   Reach and grasp.

primitive   The raw material for some developmental process, often used in discussions of cognitive development.

radial glia   A developmentally transient form of glia having processes that form roadways along which neurons migrate.

recessive   In Mendelian genetics, the allele that is expressed only in the homozygous condition.

reciprocal altruism   A sociobiological explanation of altruistic behavior observed among unrelated individuals (see kin selection) whereby the reproductive costs of an altruistic act are counterbalanced by reproductive benefits from similar behavior on the part of conspecifics at a different time.

reductionism   An explanatory mode that seeks to explain phenomena at one level of a system in terms of events and components at lower levels. This term encompasses several theoretical stances that vary in their compatibility with a systems approach to the explanation of behavior or with the complete integration of biology and psychology.

regulatory elements   Components of chromosomes that bind to transcription factors, thereby regulating transcription of adjacent genes.

reification   A fallacy in scientific thought wherein the naming of a concept has the effect of making it seem like a concrete thing.

remodeling   In developmental neuroscience, the retraction of axon branches and elimination of synapses that occurs after the early exuberant growth of axons, often accompanied by growth of new branches and synapses at different locations.

rostral   Toward the head; anterior.

self-generated experience   Experience generated by an individual's own behavior that can affect further development.

semantics   The meanings of words.

sensorimotor intelligence   A Piagetian stage in which intelligence is characterized by actions on the environment.

social organization   Structure of a local group of conspecifics, defined demographically, spatially, by the nature of social interactions, or by the totality of relationships; society.

social structure   Another name for social organization or animal society.

sociobiology   Most generally, the study of the evolution of social behavior. More specifically, it has come to designate a theoretical approach that uses the synthetic theory of evolution to explain social behavior, with an explicit goal of explaining human behavior and culture.

software   As used here, part of the hardware-software distinction used metaphorically to separate the functions of the nervous system from its structure.

speciation   Splitting of one species into two.

species   The most generally accepted definition is a population of organisms that can in principle reproduce with one another but that are reproductively isolated from those in other populations. This definition does not cover all populations that one would on other grounds want to designate as species.

sperm   A gamete. With sexually dimorphic gametes, the sperm is the smaller, defining its producer as male.

sufficient condition   A type of causal explanation that has identified antecedent conditions that always initiate some phenomenon.

syntax   The rules of grammar.

taxonomy   The study of the classification of plants and animals resulting in the hierarchical phylogenetic tree, and in which species, genus, family, and so on are the taxa.

teleological   Explanation in terms of final causes or purposes. This form of reasoning is fallacious when the antecedent (proximate, developmental, phylogenetic) causes of biological phenomena are located in their functions, confusing consequence with cause.

territory   A physical location defended by an individual animal (or small group— pair, family, etc.) against conspecifics.

trait   A measurable feature of an organism; a character; a phenotype.

transcription   The transfer of a nucleotide sequence from DNA to RNA for transport outside the nucleus as a step in protein synthesis.

transcription factor   Any factor that alters the probability, timing, or rate of transcription in a given cell.

translation   Nucleotide sequences on messenger RNA that regulate the sequence of amino acid synthesis at ribosomes.

trophic factor   A substance produced in one cell that can support the growth, functioning, or survival of another cell.

Umwelt   The perceptual-reactive world of an animal, it underscores the fact that different species are differentially selective in how they perceive and respond to energies in the environment.

unfolding   A nativistic metaphor where innate characteristics simply unfold rather that emerge or change during development.

value-based argument   As used here, a pseudobiological argument that begins with a personal value about human nature and seeks support by finding in some other species something that is similar to the desired human social policy or arrangement. This is fallacious because natural diversity among animals is sufficient to yield an example for virtually any position about human nature.

variation   Individual differences among members of a population.

vitalists   A school of thought that used mystical, nonmaterial causes to explain biological development.

zygote   A fertilized egg.

Name Index

Subject Index